# Unveiling Social Dynamics and Community Interaction in the Metaverse

Brij Gupta
*Asia University, Taichung City, Taiwan*

IGI Global
Scientific Publishing
Publishing Tomorrow's Research Today

| | |
|---|---|
| Vice President of Editorial | Melissa Wagner |
| Managing Editor of Acquisitions | Mikaela Felty |
| Managing Editor of Book Development | Jocelynn Hessler |
| Production Manager | Mike Brehm |
| Cover Design | Phillip Shickler |

Published in the United States of America by
IGI Global Scientific Publishing
701 East Chocolate Avenue
Hershey, PA, 17033, USA
Tel: 717-533-8845
Fax: 717-533-7115
Website: https://www.igi-global.com E-mail: cust@igi-global.com



Library of Congress Cataloging-in-Publication Data

Names: Gupta, Brij B., 1982- editor
Title: Unveiling social dynamics and community interaction in the metaverse / [edited by] Brij Gupta.
Description: Hershey, PA : IGI Global, [2025] | Includes bibliographical references and index. | Summary: "This publication is set to have a substantial impact on the research community. As one of the first comprehensive resources on metaverse security, it will establish a pioneering knowledge base in this emerging field. The book is expected to stimulate interdisciplinary research, fostering collaborations among experts in cybersecurity, virtual reality, legal studies, and ethics. It will be instrumental in advancing security measures within virtual environments by highlighting current vulnerabilities and anticipating future threats"-- Provided by publisher.
Identifiers: LCCN 2024049773 (print) | LCCN 2024049774 (ebook) | ISBN 9798369386286 hardcover | ISBN 9798369386293 paperback | ISBN 9798369386309 ebook
Subjects: LCSH: Metaverse--Social aspects | Virtual reality--Social aspects
Classification: LCC TK5105.8864 .U58 2025 (print) | LCC TK5105.8864 (ebook)
LC record available at https://lccn.loc.gov/2024049773
LC ebook record available at https://lccn.loc.gov/2024049774

British Cataloguing in Publication Data
A Cataloguing in Publication record for this book is available from the British Library.

This book is dedicated with profound appreciation and affection to our families, whose unwavering support and encouragement have been a constant source of strength throughout this journey.

Brij B. Gupta

# Table of Contents

# Detailed Table of Contents

seen in real life. Instead of physical monitoring, virtual platforms can use behavior tracking and user feedback to enforce norms. Clear rules, virtual rewards for adherence, and penalties for violations can be integrated through gamification. This approach allows communities to self-regulate and maintain positive behaviors, ensuring a more structured and engaged virtual environment, much like in physical spaces.



The chapter "Communication Modalities and Tools" in the book "Unveiling Social Dynamics and Community Interaction in the Metaverse" explores the diverse range of communication technologies and methods that enable social interaction in the metaverse. This digital realm, combining virtual reality (VR), augmented reality (AR), and mixed reality (MR), offers new and immersive ways for users to connect and build communities. The chapter traces the evolution of communication tools from traditional text and video-based methods to advanced VR and AR systems, emphasizing the role of avatars, virtual environments, and sensory feedback in enhancing social presence. It examines the technological infrastructure supporting these communication tools, including network requirements, platform interoperability, and data privacy. Key challenges such as scalability, user accessibility, and ethical considerations are discussed. Through current research and case studies, the chapter provides insights into the future trajectory of communication in the metaverse and offers practical recommendations for developers, policymakers, and researchers to create inclusive, engaging, and sustainable virtual communities.



This study explores user behavior and interaction patterns across digital platforms to understand engagement and responses in online environments. By analyzing data from social media, e-commerce sites, and mobile apps, the research identifies key factors affecting user decisions, such as content relevance, interface design, and social influence. It examines behavioral habits like browsing patterns, click-through rates, and time spent on activities to uncover trends and preferences. Interaction dynamics, including user-to-user communication, feedback mechanisms, and engagement with interactive elements, are evaluated for their impact on user experience. Findings reveal that user behavior is greatly influenced by navigation ease, personalized content, and community features, impacting retention and satisfaction. This research offers valuable insights for UX design, guiding the development of user-centered digital products and services. Understanding these behavior patterns is essential for enhancing user engagement and creating more effective and engaging digital experiences.

The metaverse, a growing digital universe, presents new ways for individuals to express themselves and shape their online identities. This chapter explores the complex relationship between virtual identity and self-expression in this immersive environment. It discusses how users craft and shape their digital personas, the factors influencing these choices, and the impact of virtual identities on real-life interactions. The idea of "digital doppelgängers," virtual representations that may differ from our true selves, is examined. The chapter also investigates the blending of real and virtual identities, including the role of social media and targeted advertising in shaping self-presentation. It highlights the metaverse as a space for creativity and identity exploration while addressing ethical concerns like privacy, addiction, and social isolation. Additionally, the metaverse is seen as a potential tool for social change, providing platforms for marginalized voices. This analysis reveals the opportunities and challenges of virtual identity in this evolving digital world.



This chapter examines the essential components of virtual economies in the metaverse and their transformative effects on user interactions, community development, and economic engagements. It explores various virtual economies, from MMOs like *World of Warcraft* to platforms like *Second Life* and blockchain-based systems such as *Axie Infinity*. Key elements analyzed include digital assets, currencies, trading venues, labor, supply and demand, and governance frameworks. The chapter discusses how traditional economic theories are applied in virtual spaces, fostering ecosystems that reflect and enhance real-world economies. Social structures, such as guilds, digital social capital, and cooperative economies, are highlighted for their role in community building. The governance of these

# Foreword

The Metaverse, once a concept relegated to the realm of science fiction, is now rapidly becoming a significant part of our everyday digital lives. With advancements in virtual reality (VR), augmented reality (AR), artificial intelligence (AI), and blockchain technologies, we are witnessing the formation of a new virtual space that blends physical reality with immersive, interactive environments. These virtual worlds are transforming how we connect, work, socialize, and even redefine our identities. As this transformation continues, one of the most pressing questions we face is how human social interaction and community dynamics will evolve within these digital spaces. This book, Unveiling Social Dynamics and Community Interaction in the Metaverse, provides a deep exploration into this critical question, offering a comprehensive analysis of the social, ethical, and technological aspects of the Metaverse.

In this book, we aim to bridge the gap between theory and practice, investigating how communities are created, maintained, and transformed in these virtual environments. The convergence of multiple disciplines—social sciences, technology, law, ethics, and business—has opened up new avenues for understanding the dynamics of the Metaverse. It has become clear that as the Metaverse continues to grow, it will shape our social landscapes in profound ways, and our ability to understand these shifts will determine how well we can manage the opportunities and challenges that come with it.

The Metaverse offers an unprecedented level of interconnectedness. It allows individuals from all over the world to come together in ways that were previously unimaginable, enabling the creation of global virtual communities. But these communities are not without their complexities. They are shaped by diverse social dynamics, including user behavior, identity construction, and the influence of technological forces like AI, blockchain, and deep learning. The book covers all of these aspects in depth, providing an insightful look at how social interactions manifest in the Metaverse, how virtual identities are formed, and how community members engage with each other.

The chapters in this book explore multiple facets of social dynamics and community interaction within the Metaverse. For instance, Exploring the Metaverse: Foundations of Social Interaction and Community Building lays the groundwork for understanding the essential elements of virtual communities. Communication Modalities and Tools explores how people communicate in these digital spaces and the technologies that facilitate these interactions. User Behavior and Interaction Patterns takes a closer look at how users behave within virtual environments, shedding light on the psychological and social factors that drive interaction.

One of the most compelling aspects of this book is its attention to the intersection of technology and human behavior. From Virtual Identity and Self-Expression in the Metaverse to The Influence of AI on Social Interactions and Community Dynamics, the book delves into how emerging technologies shape the way individuals express themselves and interact with others. Chapters such as Enhancing Community Detection with Hybrid Quantum-Inspired Evolutionary Algorithms highlight the cutting-edge tools and technologies that are being developed to address the complexities of community building and maintenance in virtual spaces.

Additionally, Theoretical Frameworks for Analyzing Social Dynamics and Legal Personality in the Metaverse: A Jurisprudential Examination provide crucial academic perspectives that help contextualize the broader implications of virtual communities. These chapters offer valuable insights into how the Metaverse challenges our traditional concepts of identity, privacy, and governance, while also highlighting the ethical dilemmas and legal questions that arise in these virtual spaces. The inclusion of Ethical Considerations and Privacy in the Metaverse ensures that we approach the Metaverse with a responsible, user-centered mindset, addressing the potential harms and risks posed by these virtual environments.

What sets this book apart is its practical approach to these complex issues. Chapters like Creating and Sustaining Virtual Communities in the Metaverse: Concept and Case Study provide readers with actionable insights into how to build thriving, inclusive communities that respect both users and their digital assets. Real-world case studies help illuminate the principles discussed in theory and showcase how these ideas can be applied in practice.

Finally, the book does not shy away from the darker side of the Metaverse. A Review of Understanding Social Engineering in the Context of Cybersecurity and Unmasking Virtual Crimes: Investigating and Proving Evidence in the Metaverse tackle the critical issues of security and trust in virtual spaces. These chapters discuss how malicious actors exploit vulnerabilities within these digital ecosystems and the steps that can be taken to safeguard users and their digital assets from phishing, fraud, and other cyber threats.

The Metaverse is still in its infancy, and its future is both exciting and uncertain. As we continue to explore and develop this virtual space, understanding the intricate web of social, technological, ethical, and legal dynamics that underpin it will be essential. This book serves as a valuable resource for anyone interested in the future of the Metaverse, from scholars and researchers to developers, policymakers, and enthusiasts. It provides the knowledge necessary to navigate this new frontier and to build virtual communities that are not only innovative and engaging but also ethical, secure, and sustainable.

In conclusion, Unveiling Social Dynamics and Community Interaction in the Metaverse offers a rich, interdisciplinary exploration of the forces shaping our digital future. It will serve as an indispensable guide for those looking to understand the complexities of virtual communities and the societal impacts of the Metaverse. As we stand on the threshold of this new digital era, it is our responsibility to shape it in ways that benefit all. This book is a step in that direction, providing essential insights into how we can build and sustain virtual communities that are secure, inclusive, and prosperous.

**Priyanka Chaurasia**
*University of Ulster, UK*

# Preface

The rapid emergence of the Metaverse as a new digital frontier is reshaping the ways in which individuals, organizations, and societies interact. As virtual spaces expand, they offer unprecedented opportunities for social engagement, community building, and the creation of entirely new economies. However, with this expansive virtual realm comes a range of complex challenges that require thoughtful exploration and strategic intervention. "Unveiling Social Dynamics and Community Interaction in the Metaverse" seeks to shed light on these issues, offering comprehensive insights into the intricacies of social interaction and community formation in the Metaverse.

This book is a collective endeavor that brings together experts from diverse fields to analyze, discuss, and propose solutions for the evolving dynamics of virtual societies. Through the 18 chapters of this book, readers are introduced to the foundational concepts of the Metaverse, the core components of social interaction in these spaces, and the role of emerging technologies in shaping user experiences. From exploring virtual identities and self-expression to understanding the ethical implications of privacy and legal frameworks, each chapter delves into key themes that are vital for navigating the complexities of the Metaverse.

The first few chapters provide a deep dive into the Metaverse's foundations, including its evolution, the mechanics of building virtual communities, and the tools and communication modalities that facilitate social interaction. As we progress through the book, we examine how human behavior manifests in virtual environments and how the presence of AI and emerging algorithms can enhance or disrupt community dynamics. Furthermore, the impact of virtual economies, cybersecurity challenges, and the regulation of digital spaces are explored in depth, providing readers with a comprehensive understanding of how virtual worlds function at both a micro and macro level.

A particularly exciting aspect of this book is its focus on practical applications and real-world case studies. Chapters like "Creating and Sustaining Virtual Communities in the Metaverse" and "Exploring Ethical and Cultural Considerations in Metaverse-based Digital Marketing" bridge theoretical frameworks with actionable insights. The book culminates in an examination of critical issues such as social engineering in cybersecurity and the investigation of virtual crimes—topics that are crucial for securing digital assets and ensuring the safety of users in the Metaverse.

The goal of this book is not only to inform but to inspire further research, innovation, and collaboration in the realm of Metaverse studies. As we continue to shape this virtual landscape, understanding the nuances of social dynamics and community interaction will be essential in building sustainable, ethical, and vibrant digital ecosystems.

We hope that this work serves as a valuable resource for researchers, practitioners, policymakers, and enthusiasts alike, providing them with the knowledge and tools necessary to navigate the evolving Metaverse.

Through the contributions of all those involved in the creation of this book, we aim to offer a comprehensive and interdisciplinary approach to understanding the social complexities of virtual spaces, encouraging a future where digital communities can thrive, innovate, and connect in meaningful ways.

Editor

Brij B. Gupta

# Acknowledgement

I would like to express my sincere gratitude to everyone who has contributed to the completion of this book, Unveiling Social Dynamics and Community Interaction in the Metaverse. This endeavor would not have been possible without the invaluable support, guidance, and dedication of many individuals.

First and foremost, I extend my heartfelt appreciation to the authors and reviewers of each chapter. Their expertise, insightful feedback, and unwavering commitment have played a crucial role in shaping the depth and quality of this book. Their contributions have been instrumental in ensuring that this volume serves as a comprehensive resource in the field.

I am also profoundly grateful to the team at IGI Global Publishing for their continuous support, technical expertise, and encouragement throughout this journey. Their professional guidance and commitment have been invaluable in bringing this project to fruition.

A special note of thanks goes to my family, whose unwavering love, patience, and encouragement have been a constant source of strength. Their support has sustained me through the challenges of this endeavor and has been instrumental in its successful completion.

Lastly, I am deeply thankful to the Almighty for granting me the strength, resilience, and determination to navigate this journey and see this work through to completion.

To all those who have contributed in various ways, I extend my deepest gratitude. Your support and efforts are truly appreciated.

January 27, 2025

Brij B. Gupta

# Chapter 1
# Exploring the Metaverse: Foundations of Social Interaction and Community Building

**Nizirwan Anwar**
https://orcid.org/0000-0003-1189-9093
*Universitas Esa Unggul, Indonesia*

**Hendry Gunawan**
*Universitas Esa Unggul, Indonesia*

**Binastya Anggara Sekti**
https://orcid.org/0000-0001-5489-4888
*Universitas Esa Unggul, Indonesia*

**Arief Ichwani**
*Universitas Esa Unggul, Indonesia*

**Nixon Erzed**
*Universitas Esa Unggul, Indonesia*

**Ryan Putra Laksana**
*Universitas Esa Unggul, Indonesia*

**Hasanudin Hasanudin**
*Medika Suherman University, Indonesia*

**Yuhefizar Yuhefizar**
https://orcid.org/0000-0001-9861-7962
*Politeknik Negeri Padang, Indonesia*

## ABSTRACT

*The Metaverse represents a transformative digital ecosystem integrating augmented reality (AR), virtual reality (VR), and blockchain to create immersive, interactive environments where users engage in social, educational, and economic activities. This study examines its evolution, emphasizing its potential in fostering inclusivity, creativity, and collaborative learning while addressing challenges like privacy, accessibility, and ethical concerns. By leveraging decentralized technologies and user-generated content, the Metaverse encourages active participation and social cohesion. However, issues such as data protection, equitable access, and psychological impacts necessitate robust governance and ethical frameworks. The implications of the Metaverse extend across sectors, including education, urban planning, and commerce, highlighting its role in reshaping interaction, community building, and professional collaboration. Future research should address technological and sociocultural dynamics to ensure the equitable and sustainable growth of the Metaverse.*

DOI: 10.4018/979-8-3693-8628-6.ch001

## 1.1 INTRODUCTION

The Metaverse represents a transformative digital landscape that integrates augmented reality (AR), virtual reality (VR), and the internet, creating a shared virtual space where users can interact, socialize, and engage in various activities. This immersive environment is characterized by its ability to facilitate real-time communication and dynamic interactions among users, often represented as avatars, which fosters a sense of presence and community (M. Cruz, 2024b) (Mystakidis, 2022) (Wang et al., 2023). As the Metaverse evolves, it is reshaping social dynamics, commerce, and entertainment, offering unprecedented opportunities for user engagement and interaction (M. Cruz, 2024a) (M. Cruz et al., 2023). One of the critical aspects of the Metaverse is its reliance on user-generated content, which significantly enhances community interaction and engagement. The creation and sharing of content by users not only promote a sense of ownership but also encourage sustained participation in virtual communities (Hussain et al., 2023) (Song et al., 2023). This participatory culture leads to the formation of long-lasting relationships as users engage in social interactions that mirror real-world dynamics, thereby enriching the virtual experience (Hussain et al., 2023). Furthermore, the Metaverse serves as a platform for diverse social interactions, accommodating various user preferences and fostering inclusivity, particularly for individuals who may find traditional social environments challenging (Hutson, 2022). The educational implications of the Metaverse are also noteworthy, as it provides innovative avenues for learning and collaboration. The integration of immersive technologies allows for enhanced educational experiences, where students can engage in interactive learning environments that transcend geographical limitations (Mistretta, 2022; Tural, 2023; Zheng, 2023). This shift towards virtual education not only addresses the challenges posed by conventional teaching methods but also promotes creativity and socialization among learners (Tural, 2023; Zheng, 2023). As educational institutions increasingly adopt Metaverse technologies they are likely to witness a transformation in pedagogical approaches, emphasizing collaboration and engagement in virtual settings (Mistretta, 2022). Moreover, the Metaverse's potential extends beyond education and social interaction; it is also poised to impact various sectors, including tourism and urban development. By creating immersive experiences that blend the physical and digital realms, the Metaverse can enhance public engagement in cultural heritage and historical tourism (Maier, 2024; Santosa et al., 2023). This integration of virtual environments into urban planning and community engagement strategies highlights the Metaverse's role in fostering sustainable development and enhancing the quality of life in urban settings (Allam et al., 2022; Maier, 2024).

## 1.2 WHAT IS THE METAVERSE?

The Metaverse is a multifaceted digital ecosystem that integrates various technologies, including VR, AR and Blockchain, to create immersive, interactive environments where users can engage in social, economic, and creative activities. It represents a convergence of the physical and digital worlds, allowing users to interact with each other and digital objects in real-time, thereby fostering a sense of presence and community (Ritterbusch & Teichmann, 2023; M. M. De Cruz et al., 2022). The Metaverse is often described as a persistent, shared virtual space that is accessible via the internet, where users can create, explore, and interact in a 3D environment (M. M. De Cruz et al., 2022; Akin, 2024). One of the defining characteristics of the Metaverse is its emphasis on user-generated content and decentralized structures. As the Metaverse evolves, it is expected to be built on Web 3.0 principles, which prioritize decentralization and user ownership facilitated by blockchain technologies (Elsadig, 2024; Ritterbusch & Teichmann, 2023). This decentralization allows for a more democratic and participatory environment, where users can create and monetize their content without the constraints imposed by traditional centralized platforms (Huang et al., 2023; Elsadig, 2024). Furthermore, the integration of blockchain technology enhances security and transparency, enabling users to own and trade digital assets in a verifiable manner (Q. Yang et al., 2022; Elsadig, 2024). The Metaverse also serves as a platform for various applications across multiple domains, including gaming, education, social networking, and commerce. In gaming, for instance, the Metaverse provides immersive experiences that allow players to interact with each other and the game world in unprecedented ways (Oliveira & Cruz, 2023; Ii. Li & Kim, 2023). In education, it offers innovative learning environments that promote collaboration and engagement among students and educators (Murala, 2024; Wang et al., 2022). Additionally, the Metaverse is reshaping consumer behavior by providing new avenues for marketing and brand engagement, as businesses explore virtual storefronts and interactive advertising (Hadi et al., 2023; Zhong, 2023). Moreover, the Metaverse is characterized by its potential for social interaction and community building. Users can create avatars that represent them in the virtual space, allowing for self-expression and identity exploration (M. M. De Cruz et al., 2022; Song et al., 2023). This aspect of the Metaverse is particularly significant for younger generations, who often navigate complex social dynamics in both virtual and real-world contexts (Song et al., 2023; R. Yang et al., 2023). The ability to connect with others in immersive environments fosters a sense of belonging and community, which is crucial in an increasingly digital world (R. Yang et al., 2023; Liang, 2023). Despite its promising potential, the Metaverse also faces challenges, including issues related to security, privacy, and ethical considerations. As users engage in these virtual spaces, concerns about data protection and the implications of surveillance become increasingly relevant (Huang et al., 2023; Wang et al., 2022). Moreover, the rapid evolution of the Metaverse raises questions about accessibility and inclusivity, as not all users may have equal access to the necessary technologies (S. Yang, 2024; R. Yang et al., 2023; Liang, 2023).

## 1.3 SOCIAL NETWORKS IN THE METAVERSE

The emergence of the Metaverse has significantly transformed the landscape of social networks, creating new paradigms for interaction, collaboration, and community building. The Metaverse is characterized by its immersive, interactive environments where users, represented as avatars, can engage with each other and digital entities in real-time, thereby mirroring real-life social interactions (Elizondo-García, 2023; U.-K. Lee & Kim, 2022). This convergence of virtual and physical realities allows for a unique social experience that transcends traditional social media platforms, fostering deeper connections among users (Schöbel & Leimeister, 2023). One of the defining features of social networks within the Metaverse is the ability to facilitate synchronous interactions across vast distances. Users can collaborate, socialize, and participate in shared experiences regardless of their physical location, enhancing the sense of community and belonging (U.-K. Lee & Kim, 2022). However, it is important to note that the nature of these interactions can differ from those in the physical world. For instance, while the Metaverse allows for rich, immersive experiences, some studies suggest that the strength of social connections formed in these virtual environments may be weaker compared to face-to-face interactions (H. Kim & Kim, 2023; M. Kim, 2023). This highlights the need for ongoing research to explore the nuances of social dynamics in the Metaverse and their implications for user engagement and community building (M.

Kim, 2023). Moreover, the Metaverse presents unique opportunities for self-expression and identity construction. Users often curate their avatars and virtual environments to reflect their personalities, interests, and social affiliations, which can influence their interactions within these digital spaces (Nugrahawati et al., 2019; Y. Park et al., 2023). This aspect of self-presentation is particularly relevant for younger users, who may navigate complex social dynamics related to gender, sexuality, and identity in both virtual and real-world contexts (Nugrahawati et al., 2019). As such, the Metaverse serves as a platform for exploring and negotiating social identities, which can have profound implications for personal development and social relationships. In addition to fostering social connections, the Metaverse also supports collaborative learning and knowledge sharing. Educational applications within the Metaverse leverage its immersive capabilities to create engaging learning environments that promote interaction among students and educators (X. Zhang et al., 2022; Reis & Escudeiro, 2012). These virtual spaces facilitate informal communication and chance encounters, which can enhance social awareness and community engagement among learners (Prasolova-Førland & Divitini, 2003). As educational institutions increasingly adopt Metaverse technologies, they are likely to witness a transformation in pedagogical approaches that emphasize collaboration and active participation (X. Zhang et al., 2022). Furthermore, the interoperability of various Metaverse platforms plays a crucial role in shaping social dynamics. The ability for users to seamlessly transition between different virtual environments enhances their overall experience and fosters a sense of continuity in their social interactions (Al-kfairy, 2024).

## 1.4 KEY CHARACTERISTICS OF SOCIAL DYNAMICS IN THE METAVERSE

The Metaverse is a complex and evolving digital ecosystem characterized by several key social dynamics that shape user interactions and community engagement. Understanding these dynamics is crucial for grasping how individuals navigate this immersive environment and the implications for social behavior, identity, and community building. One of the primary characteristics of social dynamics in the Metaverse is immersion. The Metaverse provides users with a highly immersive experience that allows them to interact with others and digital entities in real-time, creating a sense of presence that is often lacking in traditional online platforms (Mystakidis, 2022). This immersion is facilitated by advanced technologies such as VR and augmented reality (AR), which enhance the user experience by enabling multisensory interactions (Mystakidis, 2022; Wang et al., 2023). As users engage in these environments, they often report heightened emotional connections and a stronger sense of community compared to conventional social media (Hussain et al., 2023). Another significant aspect of social dynamics in the Metaverse is the role of user-generated content. The ability for users to create, share, and monetize their content fosters a sense of ownership and agency within the community (Hussain et al., 2023). This participatory culture not only encourages engagement but also leads to the formation of long-lasting relationships among users. The collaborative nature of content creation in the Metaverse enhances social interactions and contributes to a vibrant community atmosphere (Hussain et al., 2023). Furthermore, the decentralized nature of the Metaverse allows for diverse expressions of identity and creativity, enabling users to curate their avatars and virtual spaces to reflect their personalities (Othman, 2024). Socialization is another critical characteristic of the Metaverse. The platform facilitates various forms of social interaction, from casual chats to organized events, allowing users to connect with others who share similar interests (Ng & Kit Ng, 2022; Othman, 2024). This socialization is particularly important for marginalized groups, as the Metaverse can provide a safe space for individuals to express themselves and build connections without the constraints of physical world biases (Allam et al., 2022). The ability to engage in shared experiences, such as virtual concerts or gaming sessions, further strengthens community bonds and fosters a sense of belonging among users (Hussain et al., 2023). Moreover, the Metaverse is characterized by a mature economic system that supports virtual economies. Users can engage in commerce through the buying and selling of digital assets, such as virtual real estate, clothing for avatars, and non-fungible tokens (NFTs) (Bhattacharya et al., 2023). This economic dimension not only incentivizes participation but also creates opportunities for entrepreneurship within the Metaverse, allowing users to establish businesses and generate income through their virtual activities (Bhattacharya et al., 2023; Jauhiainen et al., 2022). The integration of economic activities into social interactions adds another layer of complexity to the dynamics of community engagement in the Metaverse. Finally, the interoperability of different Metaverse platforms plays a crucial role in shaping social dynamics. The ability for users to seamlessly transition between various virtual environments enhances their overall experience and fosters continuity in their social interactions (Al-kfairy, 2024).

## 1.5 THE RISE OF VIRTUAL WORLDS AND IMMERSIVE EXPERIENCES

The rise of virtual worlds and immersive experiences, particularly within the context of the Metaverse, has transformed how individuals interact, learn, and engage with digital content. This evolution is characterized by several key factors that highlight the potential of virtual environments to enhance social dynamics, educational practices, and user experiences. One of the most significant aspects of this rise is the enhanced interactivity and immersion provided by advanced technologies such as VR, AR and mixed reality (MR). These technologies create rich, interactive environments where users can engage with one another and digital entities in real-time, fostering a sense of presence that is often absent in traditional online interactions (Mystakidis, 2022; Y.-J. Li et al., 2022). The immersive nature of these experiences allows for more meaningful social interactions, as users can communicate through avatars, utilize body language, and express emotions in ways that mirror real-life interactions (Mystakidis, 2022; Elizondo-García, 2023).This capability not only enhances social engagement but also democratizes access to experiences, enabling individuals from diverse geographical backgrounds to participate equally (Mystakidis, 2022). Moreover, the collaborative potential of virtual worlds is noteworthy. These environments facilitate group interactions and collaborative learning, allowing geographically dispersed individuals to work together on common tasks in a shared virtual space (Ii. Li & Kim, 2023; X. Zhang et al., 2022). This collaborative aspect is particularly beneficial in educational settings, where the Metaverse can support active pedagogies and foster deeper learning experiences (X. Zhang et al., 2022). By providing platforms for collaborative projects, discussions, and simulations, virtual worlds can enhance the educational landscape, making learning more engaging and effective (Ii. Li & Kim, 2023; X. Zhang et al., 2022). The social dynamics within these virtual environments also reflect a shift in how individuals construct their identities and relationships. Users often curate their avatars and virtual spaces to express their personalities and interests, which can lead to new forms of self-expression and community building (Damayanti, 2023; McKenna & Chughtai, 2020). The ability to interact in immersive environments allows for complex social engagements that are influenced by users' identities, orientations, and social views (McKenna & Chughtai, 2020). This aspect of virtual worlds can empower marginalized groups by providing safe spaces for expression and connection, thus fostering inclusivity. Furthermore, the rise of virtual economies within the Metaverse has introduced new dimensions to user engagement. Users can create, buy, and sell digital assets, such as virtual real estate and non-fungible tokens (NFT's), which not only incentivizes participation but also encourages innovation and entrepreneurship (Hussain et al., 2023; Joy et al., 2022). The integration of economic activities into social interactions adds complexity to community dynamics, as users navigate both social relationships and economic transactions within these virtual spaces (Hussain et al., 2023; Joy et al., 2022). However, the rise of virtual worlds also presents challenges, particularly concerning addiction and mental health. The immersive nature of these environments can lead to excessive engagement, potentially resulting in negative psychological outcomes (Z. W. Y. Lee et al., 2020; Xun et al., 2023). Understanding the balance between beneficial engagement and potential addiction is crucial for fostering healthy interactions within the Metaverse.

## 1.6 IDENTITY AND REPRESENTATION IN THE METAVERSE

Identity and representation in the Metaverse are critical aspects that shape user experiences and interactions within these immersive digital environments. As users navigate the Metaverse, they often engage in complex processes of self-representation, which can significantly influence their social interactions, community building, and personal identity formation. One of the key features of identity construction in the Metaverse is the customization of avatars. Users have the freedom to create and modify their avatars to reflect their desired identities, which can include aspects such as gender, ethnicity, and personal style (XU, 2023; J. Park & Kim, 2022). This level of customization allows individuals to explore different facets of their identity and express themselves in ways that may not be possible in the physical world. For marginalized groups, this can provide an opportunity to challenge societal norms and stereotypes, fostering a sense of empowerment and belonging (J. Park & Kim, 2022). The ability to curate one's digital representation can lead to a more inclusive environment where users can connect with others who share similar experiences or interests. Moreover, the social dynamics within the Metaverse play a crucial role in shaping identity. The interactions that occur in these virtual spaces can reinforce or challenge existing social identities. For instance, users may find that their experiences in the Metaverse differ based on their avatar's appearance or the communities they engage with (R. Yang et al., 2023; S. Yang, 2024)(Yang, 2024). This phenomenon highlights the importance of social context in identity formation, as users navigate various social norms and expectations that govern behavior within these digital environments. The Metaverse can serve as a platform for users to negotiate their identities through interactions with others, leading to a dynamic and evolving sense of self (S. Yang, 2024). The concept of self-expansion is also relevant in the context of identity in the Metaverse. Users often seek to broaden their sense of self through immersive experiences, which can enhance their self-esteem and overall life satisfaction. This desire for self-expansion can drive individuals to explore new identities and engage with diverse communities, further enriching their experiences within the Metaverse (R. Yang et al., 2023). However, it is essential to recognize that the pursuit of self-expansion can also lead to challenges, such as identity confusion or the pressure to conform to certain social standards. Furthermore, the impact of cultural immersion on identity transformation cannot be overlooked. Engaging with different cultural narratives and experiences within the Metaverse can shape users' perspectives and contribute to their identity development (Onosu, 2021; Wu et al., 2019). For example, cultural immersion experiences, such as participating in virtual events or exploring diverse cultural representations, can foster a deeper understanding of one's own identity and the identities of others.

## 1.7 INTERPERSONAL INTERACTIONS AND RELATIONSHIPS

Interpersonal interactions and relationships in the context of immersive experiences, particularly within online gaming and the Metaverse, are shaped by various social dynamics that influence how individuals connect, communicate, and form communities. These dynamics are crucial for understanding the impact of virtual environments on social behavior and mental health. One of the primary factors influencing interpersonal interactions in immersive environments is the social capital that emerges from in-game relationships. Research indicates that social interactions within online games can lead to the development of community bonds and prosocial attitudes (Molyneux et al., 2015). Players often form friendships and support networks that extend beyond the gaming experience, contributing to their social capital and enhancing their real-world social skills (Molyneux et al., 2015; Khan et al., 2021). This phenomenon is particularly significant in massively multiplayer online role-playing games (MMORPGs), where players collaborate to achieve common goals, fostering a sense of belonging and community (Khan et al., 2021). Moreover, the nature of online interactions can significantly affect players' mental health. Studies have shown that positive social interactions in gaming environments can provide emotional support and reduce feelings of loneliness and social anxiety (Khan et al., 2021; W. Zhang, 2020). For instance, players who engage in supportive interactions within MMORPGs report improved mental health outcomes, suggesting that these virtual communities can serve as valuable social support systems. Conversely, negative interactions, such as cyberbullying or toxic behavior, can lead to adverse effects on players' well-being (Kwak et al., 2015). This duality highlights the importance of fostering positive social dynamics within gaming communities to promote healthy interpersonal relationships. The role of family dynamics also plays a crucial part in shaping gaming behaviors and social interactions. Research has indicated that family cohesion is associated with healthier gaming habits, while problematic gaming is often linked to family conflict and poor relationships (Sugaya et al., 2019). This suggests that the social environment in which individuals engage with gaming can significantly influence their online interactions and relationships. Encouraging family involvement and communication can help mitigate potential negative impacts of gaming on social relationships. Additionally, the impact of anonymity in online gaming environments can affect how players interact with one another. While anonymity can provide a sense of freedom for self-expression, it can also lead to disinhibition and negative behaviors, such as aggression and toxic interactions (Wang et al., 2023; Wang et al., 2022). Studies suggest that reducing anonymity and encouraging players to adopt recognizable names can help bridge the gap between online and real-world identities, enhancing social skills and relationships. This highlights the need for game designers to consider the implications of anonymity on social interactions and community dynamics. Furthermore, the use of virtual reality (VR) technologies in gaming has been shown to influence interpersonal communication significantly. VR environments can enhance the feeling of social presence, making interactions feel more authentic and engaging (Falah, 2023; Oh et al., 2018).

## 1.8 SOCIAL HIERARCHIES AND POWER DYNAMICS

The social dynamics of identity in immersive experiences, particularly within the Metaverse, represent a complex interplay of self-representation, social interaction, and community formation. As users engage in these virtual environments, they navigate various dimensions of identity that are influenced by the unique characteristics of immersive technologies. One of the fundamental aspects of identity in the Metaverse is avatar customization, which allows users to create digital representations that reflect their desired identities. This customization can encompass various attributes, including gender, ethnicity, and personal style, enabling individuals to explore different facets of their identity (Kurt, 2023; Yılmaz & Peña, 2012). The freedom to curate one's avatar can empower users, particularly those from marginalized backgrounds, to express themselves in ways that may not be possible in the physical world (Wadley et al., 2014). However, this freedom also raises questions about authenticity and the potential for users to adopt identities that differ significantly from their real-life selves, leading to discussions about the congruence between virtual and real identities (Köles & Nagy, 2012). The social dynamics within immersive environments further complicate identity formation. Research indicates that social categories and interpersonal behaviors significantly influence how users interact and form subgroups within virtual teams (Yılmaz & Peña, 2012). These dynamics are often shaped by social identity theory, which posits that individuals categorize themselves and others based on shared characteristics, leading to ingroup and outgroup distinctions (Gabbiadini et al., 2014). In the context of the Metaverse, users may gravitate towards others who share similar social identities, which can enhance feelings of belonging but may also reinforce social divisions (Gabbiadini et al., 2014). Moreover, the use of voice communication in virtual worlds adds another layer to identity dynamics. Voice chat can alter the social opacity of these environments, making identity construction more complex (Wadley et al., 2014). Users must navigate how their vocal presence interacts with their visual representation, which can influence social perceptions and interactions. This interplay between voice and avatar can affect how individuals are perceived and how they perceive themselves within these digital spaces (Wadley et al., 2014). The concept of virtual safe spaces is also relevant in discussions of identity in immersive experiences. Some users find comfort in virtual environments where they can explore their identities without the constraints of societal norms (Szita, 2022). These spaces can facilitate discussions around sensitive topics, allowing individuals to connect with others who share similar experiences or challenges. However, the effectiveness of these safe spaces depends on the design of the virtual environment and the presence of supportive community dynamics (Szita, 2022). Furthermore, the impact of cultural immersion in the Metaverse can significantly shape identity development. Engaging with diverse cultural narratives and experiences can foster a deeper understanding of one's own identity and the identities of others (Onosu, 2021; Wu et al., 2019). This cultural engagement can be particularly beneficial for individuals from minority backgrounds, as it allows them to gain cultural knowledge and develop a sense of pride in their heritage.

## 1.9 COMMUNICATION AND LANGUAGE IN THE METAVERSE

Communication and language in the Metaverse are pivotal elements that shape user interactions and experiences within these immersive environments. As users engage in virtual worlds, the dynamics of communication evolve, influenced by the unique characteristics of the Metaverse, including avatar representation, immersive technologies, and the social context of interactions. One of the primary features of communication in the Metaverse is the use of avatars as a means of self-representation. Avatars allow users to express their identities visually, which can significantly influence how they communicate with others (Mystakidis, 2022). The fidelity of avatar body language and facial expressions enhances the realism of interactions, making virtual communication feel more authentic and engaging (Mystakidis, 2022). This immersive aspect of communication can foster deeper connections among users, as they can convey emotions and social cues that are often lost in traditional text-based online interactions (Mystakidis,

2022). Moreover, the social dynamics of the Metaverse play a crucial role in shaping communication patterns. Users often form communities based on shared interests or identities, which can influence the language and communication styles adopted within those groups (Tural, 2023). For instance, specific jargon or slang may emerge within particular communities, reflecting their unique culture and experiences (Tural, 2023). This phenomenon highlights the importance of understanding the social context in which communication occurs, as it can affect both the content and style of interactions. The impact of immersive technologies on communication is also significant. Virtual reality (VR) and augmented reality (AR) enable users to interact in ways that mimic face-to-face communication, enhancing the overall experience (Mystakidis, 2022). These technologies allow for multimodal interactions, where users can combine verbal communication with gestures, body language, and spatial awareness (Amalia, 2023). Such interactions can lead to richer and more nuanced conversations, fostering a sense of presence and connection among participants (Amalia, 2023). However, the Metaverse also presents challenges related to language barriers and communication accessibility. As users from diverse linguistic backgrounds come together in virtual spaces, the potential for misunderstandings and miscommunications increases (Sahin, 2023). To address these challenges, the integration of natural language processing (NLP) technologies can facilitate real-time translation and improve communication among users who speak different languages (Sumon, 2024). This technological support can enhance inclusivity and ensure that all users can participate meaningfully in conversations. Furthermore, the educational implications of communication in the Metaverse are noteworthy. The immersive nature of these environments can provide unique opportunities for language learning and practice (Rahman, 2023). For instance, language instructors can create virtual classrooms where students engage in interactive language exercises, enhancing their communication skills in a supportive environment (Rahman, 2023). The use of avatars and immersive scenarios can also help learners practice real-life conversations, thereby improving their language proficiency and confidence (Celik, 2023).

## 1.10 EMERGENT NORMS AND SOCIAL CUSTOMS

Emergent norms and social customs in the Metaverse are shaping the way individuals interact, communicate, and form relationships within these immersive digital environments. As users navigate virtual worlds, they encounter unique social dynamics that influence their behaviors and expectations, leading to the development of new norms and customs that differ from those in the physical world. One of the key factors contributing to the emergence of social norms in the Metaverse is the concept of telepresence. Telepresence refers to the feeling of being present in a virtual environment, which can significantly enhance user engagement and interaction (Muhammad Sohail Jafar et al., 2024). When users experience a high level of telepresence, they are more likely to adhere to social norms that promote positive interactions, such as politeness and cooperation. This phenomenon suggests that the immersive nature of the Metaverse can foster a sense of social responsibility among users, encouraging them to behave in ways that align with established social customs (Muhammad Sohail Jafar et al., 2024). Additionally, interpersonal distance plays a crucial role in shaping social interactions within virtual environments. Research indicates that social crowding can influence the required interpersonal distance between avatars, affecting how users position themselves in relation to others (Han et al., 2022). As users become accustomed to the norms of personal space in virtual settings, they may develop new customs regarding proximity and interaction, which can differ from their real-world experiences. This adaptation to virtual social norms can lead to changes in how users perceive and engage with one another, potentially impacting their overall experience in the Metaverse (Han et al., 2022). The impact of virtual touch on social interactions is another area of interest. Studies have shown that simulated interpersonal touch can affect perceived closeness and social affiliation between avatars (Saini, 2024). While virtual touch may not replicate the nuances of physical contact, it can still influence users' perceptions of social connection and intimacy. As users experiment with these new forms of interaction, they may develop emergent norms around the appropriateness and significance of virtual touch in their relationships (Saini, 2024). Moreover, the effects of immersion and real-world distractions on virtual social interactions highlight the importance of context in shaping social customs. Research suggests that immersion can enhance interpersonal closeness, leading to more meaningful interactions between users (Oh et al., 2018). However, distractions from the real world can disrupt this immersion, potentially leading to misunderstandings or conflicts in virtual communication. As users navigate these challenges, they may establish new norms for managing distractions and maintaining engagement in their virtual interactions (Oh et al., 2018). The emergence of gender norms in interactions with avatars also warrants attention. Studies have indicated that users may exhibit different behaviors based on the gender of their avatars, influencing their interpersonal dynamics and the social customs that develop within virtual environments (Menshikova et al., 2018). This highlights the role of identity and representation in shaping social interactions, as users adapt their behaviors to align with the expectations associated with their avatars' appearances (Menshikova et al., 2018). Furthermore, the ethical considerations surrounding realism in virtual interactions can impact the development of social norms. As users engage with highly realistic avatars and environments, they may grapple with the moral implications of their actions and interactions (Slater et al., 2020). This ethical dimension can lead to the establishment of norms that prioritize respect and empathy in virtual communication, reflecting users' desires to treat others as they would expect to be treated in real life (Slater et al., 2020).

## 1.11 COMMUNITY BUILDING AND SOCIAL COHESION

Community building and social cohesion in the Metaverse are essential components that influence user interactions, relationships, and the overall experience within these immersive environments. As users engage in virtual spaces, they create and navigate social norms, customs, and networks that foster a sense of belonging and collective identity. One of the primary factors contributing to community building in the Metaverse is the role of social networks. Online platforms facilitate connections among users, allowing them to form communities based on shared interests, goals, or identities (Robaeyst et al., 2022). These networks can enhance social cohesion by providing users with opportunities to engage in collaborative activities, share resources, and support one another. For instance, studies have shown that online neighborhood networks can strengthen social ties and improve perceived social support, which is crucial for community well-being (Robaeyst et al., 2022). This highlights the importance of communication practices in fostering social cohesion within virtual neighborhoods. Moreover, trust is a critical element in building social cohesion in the Metaverse. Research indicates that trust among community members is essential for effective collaboration and problem-solving (Nesterova et al., 2020). In virtual environments, where anonymity can sometimes hinder trust-building, fostering transparent communication and encouraging positive interactions can enhance users' sense of security and belonging. This trust can lead to stronger community bonds and a greater willingness to engage in collective actions, such as participating in community events or supporting fellow members during challenges. The impact of shared experiences on community cohesion cannot be overlooked. Engaging in collective activities, such as virtual events, games, or collaborative projects, can strengthen social ties and foster a sense of unity among users (Welton-Mitchell et al., 2018). For example, community-led initiatives, such as health interventions or disaster preparedness programs, have been shown to enhance social cohesion by encouraging collaboration and mutual support among participants (Welton-Mitchell et al., 2018; Fan et al., 2020). These shared experiences create a sense of collective identity, reinforcing the bonds that hold communities together. Furthermore, the cultural context of virtual communities plays a significant role in shaping social cohesion. Different cultural backgrounds and values can influence how users interact and form relationships within the Metaverse (Lippman et al., 2018). Understanding these cultural dynamics is crucial for fostering inclusive communities that respect diversity and promote collaboration. For instance, language-based initiatives can enhance social cohesion by recognizing and valuing the linguistic diversity of community members (Tamang, 2024). By creating spaces that celebrate cultural differences, the Metaverse can facilitate stronger connections among users and promote a sense of belonging. Additionally, emergent norms and customs within the Metaverse contribute to community building. As users interact and form relationships, they establish social norms that guide behavior and expectations within the community (Qin et al., 2022).

## 1.12 CHALLENGES AND ETHICAL CONSIDERATIONS

The Metaverse presents a unique set of challenges and ethical considerations that must be addressed to ensure a safe, inclusive, and equitable environment for all users. As this digital landscape evolves, it is essential to examine the implications of user interactions, data privacy, and governance structures within these immersive spaces. One of the primary challenges in the Metaverse is user safety and harassment. The immersive nature of virtual environments can amplify experiences of cyberbullying and harassment, as users may feel more vulnerable when interacting through avatars (Jim, 2023). Establishing effective moderation strategies is crucial to mitigate these risks. This includes implementing community guidelines that clearly define unacceptable behaviors and providing users with tools to report harassment (Said & El Said, 2023). Additionally, fostering a culture of respect and empathy within virtual communities can help reduce instances of toxic behavior (Jim, 2023). Data privacy is another significant ethical concern in the Metaverse. As users engage in these environments, they generate vast amounts of personal data, including behavioral patterns, preferences, and biometric information (Sánchez-Adame, 2023). Protecting this data is essential to maintain user trust and ensure compliance with privacy regulations. Organizations must implement robust data protection measures, such as encryption and anonymization, to safeguard user information from unauthorized access (Sánchez-Adame, 2023). Furthermore, transparent data usage policies should be established to inform users about how their data will be collected, stored, and utilized (Sánchez-Adame, 2023). The digital divide is also a critical consideration in the development of the Metaverse. Access to immersive technologies, such as virtual reality headsets and high-speed internet, is not uniform across different demographics and regions (Parker et al., 2023). This disparity can exacerbate existing inequalities, limiting participation for marginalized groups. To promote inclusivity, it is essential to develop strategies that enhance accessibility, such as creating low-cost alternatives for accessing the Metaverse and ensuring that content is designed with diverse user needs in mind (Parker et al., 2023). Moreover, the governance structures within the Metaverse must be carefully considered. As various platforms emerge, the potential for fragmented governance increases, leading to inconsistent policies and user experiences (Parker et al., 2023). Establishing a cohesive governance framework that incorporates user input and promotes accountability is vital for fostering trust within virtual communities (Jim, 2023). Decentralized governance models, enabled by blockchain technology, can empower users to participate in decision-making processes and contribute to the development of community standards (Truong et al., 2023). Ethical considerations surrounding representation and identity in the Metaverse are also paramount. Users may choose to create avatars that reflect different aspects of their identity, which can lead to both positive and negative experiences (Wang et al., 2022; Wang et al., 2023). While avatar customization can empower self-expression, it may also result in the reinforcement of stereotypes or the perpetuation of harmful behaviors (Wang et al., 2022). It is essential to promote awareness of these issues and encourage users to engage in respectful and inclusive interactions (Mystakidis, 2022). Finally, the psychological impacts of immersive experiences in the Metaverse warrant attention. Prolonged engagement in virtual environments can lead to addiction, social isolation, and negative mental health outcomes (Xu et al., 2022).

## 1.13 IMPLICATIONS FOR EDUCATION AND WORK

The implications of the Metaverse for education and work are profound, as this emerging digital landscape offers innovative opportunities for learning, collaboration, and professional development. The integration of immersive technologies within educational frameworks and workplace environments has the potential to transform traditional practices, enhancing engagement and accessibility for diverse populations. One of the most significant advantages of the Metaverse in education is its accessibility. The Metaverse transcends geographical barriers, allowing students from remote or underserved regions to participate in immersive learning experiences (Saphira, 2024). This democratization of education can lead to increased engagement and motivation, as students can visualize complex concepts and interact with content in dynamic ways (Saphira, 2024). For instance, platforms within the Metaverse can facilitate hands-on experiences in STEM education, bringing abstract scientific phenomena to life and fostering a deeper understanding of the subject matter (Saphira, 2024). Moreover, the Metaverse supports personalized learning experiences. By leveraging technologies such as artificial intelligence and data analytics, educators can tailor educational content to meet individual student needs, preferences, and learning styles (Agarwal, 2023). This adaptability can enhance student engagement and improve learning outcomes, as students are more likely to thrive in environments that cater to their unique requirements. Additionally, the immersive nature of the Metaverse allows for experiential learning opportunities, where students can engage in simulations and role-playing scenarios that mirror real-world situations (Alhakimi, 2023). In the context of work, the Metaverse presents opportunities for collaborative and remote work environments. Virtual offices and meeting spaces can facilitate seamless communication and collaboration among team members, regardless of their physical locations (Díaz et al., 2020). This shift towards remote work in the Metaverse can lead to increased flexibility and productivity, as employees can engage in immersive meetings and brainstorming sessions that enhance creativity and innovation (Díaz et al., 2020). Furthermore, the Metaverse can serve as a platform for professional development, offering training programs and workshops that utilize immersive technologies to enhance skill acquisition (Nguyen, 2024). However, the integration of the Metaverse into education and work also presents challenges that must be addressed. Digital literacy is a critical concern, as both educators and students may require training to effectively navigate and utilize Metaverse technologies (Chen et al., 2023). Ensuring that all users have the necessary skills to engage with these platforms is essential for maximizing their potential benefits. Additionally, issues related to data privacy and security must be prioritized, as the collection and management of user data in the Metaverse raise ethical concerns (Kalınkara, 2023). Organizations must implement robust data protection measures and transparent policies to safeguard user information and maintain trust. Furthermore, the digital divide remains a significant barrier to the widespread adoption of the Metaverse in education and work. Access to the necessary technologies, such as high-speed internet and immersive devices, is not uniform across different demographics and regions (Çalışkan, 2024). To promote inclusivity, it is essential to develop strategies that enhance accessibility, ensuring that all individuals can benefit from the opportunities presented by the Metaverse.

## 1.14 THE FUTURE OF SOCIAL INTERACTION IN THE METAVERSE

The future of social interaction in the Metaverse is poised to transform how individuals communicate, collaborate, and build relationships in both personal and professional contexts. As this immersive digital landscape evolves, several key trends and implications are emerging that will shape social interactions in the Metaverse. One of the most significant aspects of social interaction in the Metaverse is the enhanced telepresence that immersive technologies provide. Users can engage with one another in real-time through avatars, allowing for a more authentic and engaging communication experience (Mystakidis, 2022). The fidelity of avatar body language and facial expressions can enhance social interactions, making virtual participation feel more akin to face-to-face communication (Mystakidis, 2022). This increased sense of presence can foster deeper connections among users, as they can convey emotions and social cues that are often lost in traditional online interactions. The social dynamics within the Metaverse are also evolving, with the potential for new forms of community building and social cohesion. By dismantling entrenched social platforms and siloed applications, the Metaverse allows for massive and intensive social interactions among user-controlled avatars (Wang et al., 2022). This shift can lead to the creation of long-lasting social spaces where users can engage in collaborative activities, share resources, and support one another (Wang et al., 2023). As anticipated by industry experts, over 2 billion people are expected to spend at least one hour a day engaging in social activities in the Metaverse by 2026, highlighting the growing significance of these virtual interactions (Wang et al., 2023). Moreover, the impact of user-generated content on social interactions cannot be overlooked. The Metaverse encourages users to create and share their own content, which can enhance engagement and foster a sense of ownership within communities (Hussain et al., 2023). This participatory culture not only promotes social interaction but also drives innovation and economic participation in virtual economies (Hussain et al., 2023). As users contribute to the creation of shared spaces and experiences, they are likely to develop stronger connections with one another, reinforcing community bonds. However, the rise of the Metaverse also presents challenges related to inequities and ethical considerations. As the Metaverse reshapes social equality laws, it is crucial to address the potential for exacerbating existing disparities in access to technology and resources (Kaddoura & Husseiny, 2023). Ensuring that all users can participate meaningfully in the Metaverse requires a commitment to inclusivity and accessibility, particularly for marginalized groups (Kaddoura & Husseiny, 2023). Developers and community leaders must prioritize creating environments that respect diversity and promote equitable participation. The integration of blockchain technology and decentralized governance models in the Metaverse can further enhance social interactions by fostering transparency and accountability. Users can have a say in decision-making processes regarding community standards and rules, which can promote a sense of ownership and responsibility. This participatory approach can lead to more inclusive and respectful virtual communities, as users work together to uphold shared values and norms. Finally, the psychological impacts of social interactions in the Metaverse warrant attention. While immersive experiences can enhance engagement and connection, they may also lead to challenges such as addiction, social isolation, and negative mental health outcomes (Farooq, 2023). It is essential for developers and community leaders to promote healthy usage patterns and provide resources for users who may be struggling with their engagement in the Metaverse.

## REFERENCES


Adel, M. (2023). The Role of Metaverse to Create an Interactive Experience for Tourists. *Journal of Association of Arab Universities for Tourism and Hospitality*, 24(1), 242–269. DOI: 10.21608/ja-auth.2023.216690.1473

Agarwal, A., & Alathur, S. (2023). Metaverse Revolution and the Digital Transformation: Intersectional Analysis of Industry 5.0. *Transforming Government*, 17(4), 688–707. DOI: 10.1108/TG-03-2023-0036

Akin, I., & Akın, M. (2024). Valuation, Accounting Principles, and Classification of Assets in the Metaverse. *Journal of Metaverse*, 4(1), 43–53. DOI: 10.57019/jmv.1412352

Al-kfairy, M. (2024). *Unveiling the Metaverse: A Survey of User Experience, Social Dynamics, and Technological Interoperability*. DOI: 10.20944/preprints202402.0785.v1

Alhakimi, H. (2023). Development of the Metaverse and Learning. *Ijolii*, 1(01), 17–21. DOI: 10.20961/ijolii.v1i01.918

Allam, Z., Sharifi, A., Bibri, S. E., Jones, D., & Krogstie, J. (2022). The Metaverse as a Virtual Form of Smart Cities: Opportunities and Challenges for Environmental, Economic, and Social Sustainability in Urban Futures. *Smart Cities*, 5(3), 771–801. DOI: 10.3390/smartcities5030040

Amalia, R. F. (2023). *Legal Protection for Virtual Land Trading Investment Transactions in the Metaverse*. 488–496. DOI: 10.3390/smartcities5030040

Bhattacharya, P., Saraswat, D., Savaliya, D., Sanghavi, S., Verma, A., Sakariya, V., Tanwar, S., Sharma, R., Răboaca, M. S., & Manea, D. L. (2023). Towards Future Internet: The Metaverse Perspective for Diverse Industrial Applications. *Mathematics*, 11(4), 941. DOI: 10.3390/math11040941

Blackwell, L., Ellison, N. B., Elliott-Deflo, N., & Schwartz, R. (2019). Harassment in Social Virtual Reality. *Proceedings of the Acm on Human-Computer Interaction, 3*(CSCW), 1–25. DOI: 10.1145/3359202

Çalışkan, G., & Maya, İ. (2024). Opinions and Expectations of Instructors on Metaverse Applications in Higher Education. *Journal of Educational Technology and Online Learning*, 7(2), 273–285. DOI: 10.31681/jetol.1439812

Celik, F. (2023). *The Effect of Metaverse on L2 Vocabulary Learning, Retention, Student Engagement, Presence, and Community Feeling*. DOI: 10.21203/rs.3.rs-3763892/v1

Chen, W., Zhang, J., & Yu, Z. (2023). A Bibliometric Analysis of the Use of the Metaverse in Education Over Three Decades. *International Journal of Information and Communication Technology Education*, 19(1), 1–16. DOI: 10.4018/IJICTE.322101

Cruz, M., & Oliveira, A. (2024a). Unravelling Virtual Realities—Gamers' Perceptions of the Metaverse. *Electronics (Basel)*, 13(13), 2491. DOI: 10.3390/electronics13132491

Cruz, M., & Oliveira, A. (2024b). Where Are We Now?—Exploring the Metaverse Representations to Find Digital Twins. *Electronics (Basel)*, 13(10), 1984. DOI: 10.3390/electronics13101984

Cruz, M., Oliveira, A., & Pinheiro, A. (2023). Meeting Ourselves or Other Sides of Us?—Meta-Analysis of the Metaverse. *Informatics (MDPI)*, 10(2), 47. DOI: 10.3390/informatics10020047

Damayanti, A., Hidayat, R., & Afdhal, A. (2023). Building Sociological Imagination Through Social Media. *The Journal of Society & Media*, 7(2), 425–445. DOI: 10.26740/jsm.v7n2.p425-445

De Cruz, M. M., Oliveira, A., Pinheiro, A., La Cruz, M. M. D., Oliveira, A., & Pinheiro, A. (2022). Flowing Through Virtual Animated Worlds – Perceptions of the Metaverse. *Euro-Asia Conference on Frontiers of Computer Science and Information Technology (FCSIT)*, 241–245. DOI: 10.1109/FCSIT57414.2022.00057

Díaz, J. E. M., Saldaña, C. A. D., Ávila, C. A. R., Márquez Díaz, J. E., Domínguez Saldaña, C. A., & Rodríguez Ávila, C. A. (2020). Virtual World as a Resource for Hybrid Education. *International Journal of Emerging Technologies in Learning*, 15(15), 94–109. DOI: 10.3991/ijet.v15i15.13025

Elizondo-García, M. E. (2023). *Breaking Boundaries*. Ascilite Publications., DOI: 10.14742/apubs.2023.526

Elsadig, M., Alohali, M. A., Ibrahim, A. O., & Abulfaraj, A. W. (2024). Roles of Blockchain in the Metaverse: Concepts, Taxonomy, Recent Advances, Enabling Technologies, and Open Research Issues. *IEEE Access : Practical Innovations, Open Solutions*, 12, 38410–38435. DOI: 10.1109/ACCESS.2024.3367014

Falah, Z. (2023). Exploring the Influence of Virtual Reality on Interpersonal Communication: A Novel Study in Communication Science. *Journal of Social Science (Joss)*, 2(8), 654–660. DOI: 10.57185/joss.v2i8.99

Fan, C., Jiang, Y., & Mostafavi, A. (2020). Emergent Social Cohesion for Coping With Community Disruptions in Disasters. *Journal of the Royal Society, Interface*, 17(164), 20190778. DOI: 10.1098/rsif.2019.0778 PMID: 32126194

Farooq, M. S., Ishaq, K., Shoaib, M., Khelifi, A., & Atal, Z. (2023). The Potential of Metaverse Fundamentals, Technologies, and Applications: A Systematic Literature Review. *IEEE Access : Practical Innovations, Open Solutions*, 11, 138472–138487. DOI: 10.1109/ACCESS.2023.3338627

Gabbiadini, A., Mari, S., Volpato, C., & Monaci, M. G. (2014). Identification Processes in Online Groups. *Journal of Media Psychology*, 26(3), 141–152. DOI: 10.1027/1864-1105/a000119

Gupta, A., Khan, H. U., Nazir, S., Shafiq, M., & Shabaz, M. (2023). Metaverse Security: Issues, Challenges and a Viable ZTA Model. *Electronics (Basel)*, 12(2), 391. DOI: 10.3390/electronics12020391

Hadi, R., Melumad, S., & Park, E. S. (2023). The Metaverse: A New Digital Frontier for Consumer Behavior. *Journal of Consumer Psychology*, 34(1), 142–166. DOI: 10.1002/jcpy.1356

Han, M., Wang, X.-M., & Kuai, S.-G. (2022). Social Rather Than Physical Crowding Reduces the Required Interpersonal Distance in Virtual Environments. *PsyCh Journal*, 12(1), 34–43. DOI: 10.1002/pchj.595 PMID: 36129003

Huang, Y., Li, Y. J., & Cai, Z. (2023). Security and Privacy in Metaverse: A Comprehensive Survey. *Big Data Mining and Analytics*, 6(2), 234–247. DOI: 10.26599/BDMA.2022.9020047

Hussain, Z., Khan, A., & Ali, A. (2023). The Impact of User-Generated Content, Social Interactions and virtual Economies on Metaverse Environments. *Journal of Sustainable Economics*, 1(2), 34–44. DOI: 10.32734/jse.v1i2.13798

Hutson, J. H. (2022). Social Virtual Reality: Neurodivergence and Inclusivity in the Metaverse. *Societies (Basel, Switzerland)*, 12(4), 102. DOI: 10.3390/soc12040102

Jauhiainen, J. S., Krohn, C., & Junnila, J. (2022). Metaverse and Sustainability: Systematic Review of Scientific Publications Until 2022 and Beyond. *Sustainability (Basel)*, 15(1), 346. DOI: 10.3390/su15010346

Jim, J. R., Hosain, M. T., Mridha, M. F., Kabir, M. M., & Shin, J. (2023). Toward Trustworthy Metaverse: Advancements and Challenges. *IEEE Access : Practical Innovations, Open Solutions*, 11, 118318–118347. DOI: 10.1109/ACCESS.2023.3326258

Joy, A., Zhu, Y., Peña, C., & Brouard, M. (2022). Digital Future of Luxury Brands: Metaverse, Digital Fashion, and Non-fungible Tokens. *Strategic Change*, 31(3), 337–343. DOI: 10.1002/jsc.2502

Kaddoura, S., & Al Husseiny, F. (2023). The Rising Trend of Metaverse in Education: Challenges, Opportunities, and Ethical Considerations. *PeerJ. Computer Science*, 9, e1252. DOI: 10.7717/peerj-cs.1252 PMID: 37346578

Kalınkara, Y., & Özdemir, O. (2023). Anatomy in the Metaverse: Exploring Student Technology Acceptance Through the UTAUT2 Model. *Anatomical Sciences Education*, 17(2), 319–336. DOI: 10.1002/ase.2353 PMID: 37942914

Khan, I., Flores, A. F., & Subhani, A. (2021). It's Just a Game: A Quantitative Study on the Effects of Social Interactions Inside MMORPGs and Its Impact on Loneliness, Depression, and Social Anxiety. *Journal of Administrative and Business Studies*, 7(3). Advance online publication. DOI: 10.20474/jabs-7.3.4

Kim, H., & Kim, M. (2023). Presence and Effectiveness of Online Learning Using a Metaverse Platform: Gather.town. *International Journal of Information and Education Technology (IJIET)*, 13(4), 690–695. DOI: 10.18178/ijiet.2023.13.4.1854

Kim, M., Oh, J., Son, S., Park, Y., Kim, J., & Park, Y. (2023). Secure and Privacy-Preserving Authentication Scheme Using Decentralized Identifier in Metaverse Environment. *Electronics (Basel)*, 12(19), 4073. DOI: 10.3390/electronics12194073

Köles, B., & Nagy, P. (2012). Who Is Portrayed in Second Life: Dr. Jekyll or Mr. Hyde? The Extent of Congruence Between Real Life and Virtual Identity. *Journal of Virtual Worlds Research*, 5(1). Advance online publication. DOI: 10.4101/jvwr.v5i1.2150

Kurt, İ. (2023). Agents of Socialization Keep in Touch With Socio-Virtualization. *London Journal of Social Sciences*, 5(5), 1–9. DOI: 10.31039/ljss.2023.5.90

Kwak, H., Blackburn, J., & Han, S. (2015). *Exploring Cyberbullying and Other Toxic Behavior in Team Competition Online Games*. 3739–3748. DOI: 10.1145/2702123.2702529

Lee, J.-E. R., & Park, S. G. (2011). "Whose Second Life Is This?" How Avatar-Based Racial Cues Shape Ethno-Racial Minorities' Perception of Virtual Worlds. *Cyberpsychology, Behavior, and Social Networking*, 14(11), 637–642. DOI: 10.1089/cyber.2010.0501 PMID: 21486164

Lee, U.-K., & Kim, H.-K. (2022). UTAUT in Metaverse: An "Ifland" Case. *Journal of Theoretical and Applied Electronic Commerce Research*, 17(2), 613–635. DOI: 10.3390/jtaer17020032

Lee, Z. W. Y., Cheung, C. M. K., Chan, T. K. H., & Lee, Y. (2020). Understanding Massively Multiplayer Online Role-playing Game Addiction: A Hedonic Management Perspective. *Information Systems Journal*, 31(1), 33–61. DOI: 10.1111/isj.12292

Li, I., & Kim, J. (2023). How Russian Teenagers Are Engaged in the Metaverse Games. *Journal of Digital Art Engineering and Multimedia*, 10(1), 71–79. DOI: 10.29056/jdaem.2023.03.07

Li, Y.-J., Cheung, M. K., Shen, X.-L., & Lee, M. K. O. (2022). Promoting Collaborative Learning in Virtual Worlds: The Power of "We.". *Information Technology & People*, 36(6), 2563–2586. DOI: 10.1108/ITP-11-2021-0870

Liang, G., Xin, J., Wang, Q., Ni, X., Guo, X., & Chen, P. (2023). Research on Metaverse Security and Forensics. *Computers, Materials & Continua*, 77(1), 799–825. DOI: 10.32604/cmc.2023.038403

Lippman, S. A., Leslie, H. H., Neilands, T. B., Twine, R., Grignon, J., MacPhail, C., Morris, J., Rebombo, D., Sesane, M., El Ayadi, A. M., Pettifor, A., Kahn, K., Ayadi, A. M. E., Pettifor, A., & Kahn, K. (2018). Context Matters: Community Social Cohesion and Health Behaviors in Two South African Areas. *Health & Place*, 50, 98–104. DOI: 10.1016/j.healthplace.2017.12.009 PMID: 29414427

Maier, F., & Weinberger, M. (2024). Metaverse Meets Smart Cities—Applications, Benefits, and Challenges. *Future Internet*, 16(4), 126. DOI: 10.3390/fi16040126

McKenna, B., & Chughtai, H. (2020). Resistance and Sexuality in Virtual Worlds: An LGBT Perspective. *Computers in Human Behavior*, 105, 106199. DOI: 10.1016/j.chb.2019.106199

Menshikova, G., Tikhomandritskaya, O. A., Savel'eva, O. A., & Popova, T. V. (2018). Gender Differences in Interactions With Avatars of Diverse Ethnic Appearances. *Psychology in Russia : State of the Art*, 11(4), 211–222. DOI: 10.11621/pir.2018.0414

Mistretta, S. (2022). The Metaverse—An Alternative Education Space. *Ai Computer Science and Robotics Technology*, 2022, 1–23. DOI: 10.5772/acrt.05

Molyneux, L., Vasudevan, K., de Zúñiga, H. G., & Zúñiga, H. G. (2015). Gaming Social Capital: Exploring Civic Value in Multiplayer Video Games. *Journal of Computer-Mediated Communication*, 20(4), 381–399. DOI: 10.1111/jcc4.12123

Muhammad Sohail Jafar, R., Ahmad, W., & Chen, Y. (2024). Metaverse in Human Behavior: The Role of Telepresence and Flow Experience on Consumers' Shopping Behavior in the Metaverse. *SAGE Open*, 14(2), 21582440241261256. DOI: 10.1177/21582440241261256

Murala, D. K. (2024). METAEDUCATION: State-of-the-Art Methodology for Empowering Feature Education. *IEEE Access : Practical Innovations, Open Solutions*, 12, 57992–58020. DOI: 10.1109/ACCESS.2024.3391903

Mystakidis, S. (2022). Metaverse. *Encyclopedia*, 2(1), 486–497. DOI: 10.3390/encyclopedia2010031

Nesterova, M., Dielini, M., Shynkaruk, L., & Yatsenko, O. (2020). Trust as a Cognitive Base of Social Cohesion in the University Communities. *International Journal of Cognitive Research in Science Engineering and Education*, 8(1), 15–23. DOI: 10.5937/IJCRSEE2001015N

Ng, D. T. K., & Kit Ng, D. T. (2022). What Is the Metaverse? Definitions, Technologies and the Community of Inquiry. *Australasian Journal of Educational Technology*, 38(4), 190–205. DOI: 10.14742/ajet.7945

Nguyen, B.-H. T., Dang, T.-Q., Nguyen, L.-T., & Tran, T.-T. T. (2024). Are We Ready for Education in Metaverse? PLS-SEM Analysis. *Edelweiss Applied Science and Technology*, 8(2), 73–83. DOI: 10.55214/25768484.v8i2.693

Nugrahawati, E. N., Dwarawati, D., Rizal, A. R. S., & Syamsoul Rizal, A. R. (2019). *Muru'ah and Self-Presentation Through Virtual Display of Affection in UNISBA Female Students*. DOI: 10.2991/sores-18.2019.65

Oh, C. S., Bailenson, J. N., & Welch, G. (2018). A Systematic Review of Social Presence: Definition, Antecedents, and Implications. *Frontiers in Robotics and AI*, 5, 114. Advance online publication. DOI: 10.3389/frobt.2018.00114 PMID: 33500993

Oliveira, A., & Cruz, M. (2023). Virtually Connected in a Multiverse of Madness?—Perceptions of Gaming, Animation, and Metaverse. *Applied Sciences (Basel, Switzerland)*, 13(15), 8573. DOI: 10.3390/app13158573

Onosu, O. G. (2021). The Impact of Cultural Immersion Experience on Identity Transformation Process. *International Journal of Environmental Research and Public Health*, 18(5), 2680. DOI: 10.3390/ijerph18052680 PMID: 33799969

Othman, A. (2024). Accessible Metaverse: A Theoretical Framework for Accessibility and Inclusion in the Metaverse. *Multimodal Technologies and Interaction*, 8(3), 21. DOI: 10.3390/mti8030021

Park, J., & Kim, S.-C. (2022). How Do People With Physical Disabilities Want to Construct Virtual Identities With Avatars? *Frontiers in Psychology*, 13, 994786. Advance online publication. DOI: 10.3389/fpsyg.2022.994786 PMID: 36176810

Park, Y., Ko, E., & Do, B. (2023). The Perceived Value of Digital Fashion Product and Purchase Intention: The Mediating Role of the Flow Experience In metaverse Platforms. *Asia Pacific Journal of Marketing and Logistics*, 35(11), 2645–2665. DOI: 10.1108/APJML-11-2022-0945

Parker, C., Yoo, S., Lee, Y., Fredericks, J., Dey, A., Cho, Y., & Billinghurst, M. (2023). *Towards an Inclusive and Accessible Metaverse*. DOI: 10.1145/3544549.3573811

Prasolova-Førland, E., & Divitini, M. (2003). *Collaborative Virtual Environments for Supporting Learning Communities*. DOI: 10.1145/958160.958170

Qin, C., Li, Q., Du, M., Yan, W., Tao, L., Wang, Y., Liu, M., & Liu, J. (2022). Neighborhood Social Cohesion Is Associated With the Willingness Toward the Booster Dose of COVID-19 Vaccines Among the Chinese Older Population. *Human Vaccines & Immunotherapeutics*, 18(6), 2140530. Advance online publication. DOI: 10.1080/21645515.2022.2140530 PMID: 36375815

Rahman, M., Attaufiq, M. M., & Setiyowati, E. (2023). Impact of Metaverse in Educational Environment. *Jurnal Obsesi Jurnal Pendidikan Anak Usia Dini*, 7(6), 7715–7720. DOI: 10.31004/obsesi.v7i6.5820

Reis, R., Escudeiro, N., & Escudeiro, N. (2012). Comparing Social Virtual Worlds for Educational Purposes. *Education*, 1(1), 21–26. DOI: 10.5923/j.edu.20110101.04

Ritterbusch, G. D., & Teichmann, M. (2023). Defining the Metaverse: A Systematic Literature Review. *IEEE Access : Practical Innovations, Open Solutions*, 11, 12368–12377. DOI: 10.1109/ACCESS.2023.3241809

Robaeyst, B., Baccarne, B., De Meulenaere, J., & Mechant, P. (2022). Online Neighborhood Networks: The Relationship Between Online Communication Practices and Neighborhood Dynamics. *Media and Communication*, 10(2), 108–118. DOI: 10.17645/mac.v10i2.5129

Sahin, D. (2023). *Understanding English Language Teachers' Digital Literacies and Their Willingness to Change*. Focus on Elt Journal., DOI: 10.14744/felt.2023.5.2.3

Said, G. R. E., & El Said, G. R. (2023). Metaverse-Based Learning Opportunities and Challenges: A Phenomenological Metaverse Human–Computer Interaction Study. *Electronics (Basel)*, 12(6), 1379. DOI: 10.3390/electronics12061379

Saini, G., Zain, M., Noronha, M., Bonin, R. P., & Lomanowska, A. M. (2024). Virtually Simulated Interpersonal Touch Negatively Affects Perceived Closeness and Social Affiliation to an Avatar Partner. *Scientific Reports*, 14(1), 1347. Advance online publication. DOI: 10.1038/s41598-024-51773-6 PMID: 38228629

Sánchez-Adame, L. M., Monroy-Rodríguez, G., Mendoza, S., Decouchant, D., & Mateos-Papis, A. P. (2023). Framework for Ethically Designed Microtransactions in the Metaverse. *IEEE Access : Practical Innovations, Open Solutions*, 11, 140687–140700. DOI: 10.1109/ACCESS.2023.3341057

Santosa, H. P., Yudono, A., Sutikno, F. R., Adhitama, M. S., Tolle, H., & Zuliana, E. (2023). *Development of a Public Engagement Scenario in Metaverse Toward Maintaining the Sustainability of Valuable Historic Buildings in the Kayutangan Area.*, DOI: 10.2991/978-94-6463-140-1_26

Saphira, H. V. (2024). Metaverse: A Paradigm Shift in STEM Education for Science Learning Beyond the Review. *E3s Web of Conferences, 482*, 4004. DOI: 10.1051/e3sconf/202448204004

Schöbel, S., & Leimeister, J. M. (2023). Metaverse Platform Ecosystems. *Electronic Markets*, 33(1), 12. Advance online publication. DOI: 10.1007/s12525-023-00623-w

Seo, J., Ko, H., & Park, S. (2024). Space Authentication in the Metaverse: A Blockchain-Based User-Centric Approach. *IEEE Access : Practical Innovations, Open Solutions*, 12, 18703–18713. DOI: 10.1109/ACCESS.2024.3357938

Slater, M., Gonzalez-Liencres, C., Haggard, P., Vinkers, W., Gregory-Clarke, R., Jelley, S., Watson, Z., Breen, G., Schwarz, R., Steptoe, W., Szostak, D., Halan, S., Fox, D., & Silver, J. (2020). The Ethics of Realism in Virtual and Augmented Reality. *Frontiers in Virtual Reality*, 1, 1. Advance online publication. DOI: 10.3389/frvir.2020.00001

Song, C., Shin, S.-Y., & Shin, K.-S. (2023). Exploring the Key Characteristics and Theoretical Framework for Research on the Metaverse. *Applied Sciences (Basel, Switzerland)*, 13(13), 7628. DOI: 10.3390/app13137628

Sugaya, N., Shirasaka, T., Takahashi, K., & Kanda, H. (2019). Bio-Psychosocial Factors of Children and Adolescents With Internet Gaming Disorder: A Systematic Review. *BioPsychoSocial Medicine*, 13(1), 3. Advance online publication. DOI: 10.1186/s13030-019-0144-5 PMID: 30809270

Sumon, R. I., Uddin, S. M. I., Akter, S., Mozumder, M. A. I., Khan, M. O., & Kim, H.-C. (2024). Natural Language Processing Influence on Digital Socialization and Linguistic Interactions in the Integration of the Metaverse in Regular Social Life. *Electronics (Basel)*, 13(7), 1331. DOI: 10.3390/electronics13071331

Szita, K. (2022). A Virtual Safe Space? *Journal of Digital Social Research*, 4(3), 34–55. DOI: 10.33621/jdsr.v4i3.91

Tamang, D. B. (2024). Fostering Social Cohesion in Ethnolinguistic Communities Through Mother Tongue-Based Initiatives in Nepal. *Forum for Linguistic Studies*, 6(1). Advance online publication. DOI: 10.59400/fls.v6i1.2092

Truong, V. T., Le, L. B., & Niyato, D. (2023). Blockchain Meets Metaverse and Digital Asset Management: A Comprehensive Survey. *IEEE Access : Practical Innovations, Open Solutions*, 11, 26258–26288. DOI: 10.1109/ACCESS.2023.3257029

Tural, A., & Koçak, N. (2023). Awareness Levels of Social Studies Pre-Service Teachers Regarding Metaverse Use. *Advanced Education*, 11(23), 69–86. DOI: 10.20535/2410-8286.284683

Upadhyay, U., Kumar, A., Sharma, G., Gupta, B. B., Alhalabi, W., Arya, V., & Chui, K. T. (2023). Cyberbullying in the Metaverse. *Journal of Global Information Management*, 31(1), 1–25. DOI: 10.4018/JGIM.325793

Wadley, G., Carter, M., & Gibbs, M. (2014). Voice in Virtual Worlds: The Design, Use, and Influence of Voice Chat in Online Play. *Human-Computer Interaction*, 30(3–4), 336–365. DOI: 10.1080/07370024.2014.987346

Wang, Y., Su, Z., Zhang, N., Xing, R., Liu, D., Luan, T. H., Shen, X., Zhou, S., Zhang, N., Liu, D., Xing, R., Luan, T. H., Shen, X., Su, Z., Zhang, N., Xing, R., Liu, D., Luan, T. H., Shen, X., & Shen, X. (2022). A Survey on Metaverse: Fundamentals, Security, and Privacy. *IEEE Communications Surveys and Tutorials*, 25(1), 319–352. DOI: 10.1109/COMST.2022.3202047

Wang, Y., Zhou, S., & Yan, M. (2023). *Social Metaverse: Challenges and Solutions*. https://doi.org//arxiv.2301.10221DOI: 10.48550

Welton-Mitchell, C., James, L., Khanal, S. N., & James, A. S. (2018). An Integrated Approach to Mental Health and Disaster Preparedness: A Cluster Comparison With Earthquake Affected Communities in Nepal. *BMC Psychiatry*, 18(1), 296. Advance online publication. DOI: 10.1186/s12888-018-1863-z PMID: 30223822

Wu, Y., Outley, C., & Matarrita-Cascante, D. (2019). Cultural Immersion Camps and Development of Ethnic Identity in Asian American Youth. *Journal of Youth Development*, 14(2), 166–182. DOI: 10.5195/jyd.2019.708

Xu, C., Zhong, R., Li, C., & Yan, X.XU. (2023). From Fiction to Reality: Harnessing the Power of Imaginative Narratives to Shape the Future of the Metaverse. *Journal of Metaverse*, 3(2), 108–120. DOI: 10.57019/jmv.1277525

Xu, J., Papagelis, K., Dunham, J., Gonçalves, J., LaLone, N., Chamberlain, A., Lykourentzou, I., Vinella, F. L., & Schwartz, D. J. (2022). Metaverse: The Vision for the Future. *CHI Conference on Human Factors in Computing Systems*. DOI: 10.1145/3491101.3516399

Xun, Y., Zheng, X., Lee, M., & Yang, F. (2023). The Influence of Technology Affordance on Addictive Use In MMOGs: From the Perspective Of virtual-Domain Perfectionism. *Internet Research*. Advance online publication. DOI: 10.1108/INTR-08-2022-0646

Yang, Q., Zhao, Y., Huang, H., Xiong, Z., Kang, J., & Zheng, Z. (2022). Fusing Blockchain and AI With Metaverse: A Survey. *IEEE Open Journal of the Computer Society*, 3, 122–136. DOI: 10.1109/OJCS.2022.3188249

Yang, R., Li, L., Gan, W., Chen, Z., & Qi, Z. (2023). The Human-Centric Metaverse: A Survey. *ACM Web Conference 2023 - Companion of the World Wide Web Conference, WWW 2023*, 1296–1306. DOI: 10.1145/3543873.3587593

Yang, S., Kim, H., Song, M., Lee, S., & Jang, J. (2024). The Double-Edged Influence of Self-Expansion in the Metaverse: A Two-Wave Panel Assessment of Identity Perception, Self-Esteem, and Life Satisfaction. *Cyberpsychology, Behavior, and Social Networking*, 27(1), 37–46. DOI: 10.1089/cyber.2022.0400 PMID: 38197839

Yılmaz, G., & Peña, J. (2012). The Influence of Social Categories and Interpersonal Behaviors on Future Intentions and Attitudes to Form Subgroups in Virtual Teams. *Communication Research*, 41(3), 333–352. DOI: 10.1177/0093650212443696

Zhang, W. (2020). *Social Interaction Research on Mobile Games: A Case Study of Peace Elite*. DOI: 10.2991/assehr.k.200331.036

Zhang, X., Chen, Y., Hu, L., & Wang, Y. (2022). The Metaverse in Education: Definition, Framework, Features, Potential Applications, Challenges, and Future Research Topics. *Frontiers in Psychology*, 13, 1016300. Advance online publication. DOI: 10.3389/fpsyg.2022.1016300 PMID: 36304866

Zheng, Y. (2023). *The Potential of Metaverse in Speaking Skills of English Education*. DOI: 10.4108/eai.8-9-2023.2340056

Zhong, L., Xu, Z., Morrison, A. M., Li, Y., & Zhu, M. (2023). Metaverse Customer Journeys in Tourism: Building Viable Virtual Worlds. *Tourism Review*, 79(8), 1409–1426. DOI: 10.1108/TR-07-2023-0492

## APPENDIX

*Figure 1. Interconnected futures*

*Figure 2. Digital new world: Welcome to the metaverse*

*Figure 3. Blooming metropolis: Futuristic city*

*Figure 4. Digital harmony: Avatars of nature and technology*

*Figure 5. Communities collaborate in futuristic city centers*

*Figure 6. The crossroads of digital worlds: Humans and technology*

*Figure 7. Digital economy: Futuristic cities, cryptocurrencies*

*Figure 8. Digital conversation: In the world of the Metaverse (Avatar)*

# Chapter 2
# Building Communities in the Metaverse

**Nur Aini**
*Institut Teknologi dan Bisnis Ahmad Dahlan, Indonesia*

**Ratna Yulika Go**
*Universitas Esa Unggul, Indonesia*

**Riska Tezara Go**
*IPB University, Indonesia*

## ABSTRACT

*The Metaverse presents unique challenges for community building, such as user anonymity, decentralized governance, and the lack of physical boundaries. Unlike physical environments, such as the Non-Smoking Area initiative at Socio Technopreneur University, virtual spaces lack direct authority and tangible enforcement, making it harder to regulate and manage behavior. However, strategies from physical settings can be adapted to virtual communities. In the Metaverse, virtual spaces designated for specific behaviors and immersive campaign efforts can replicate the greening and community-building activities seen in real life. Instead of physical monitoring, virtual platforms can use behavior tracking and user feedback to enforce norms. Clear rules, virtual rewards for adherence, and penalties for violations can be integrated through gamification. This approach allows communities to self-regulate and maintain positive behaviors, ensuring a more structured and engaged virtual environment, much like in physical spaces.*

## I. INTRODUCTION

The study on the communal-based development of a Non-Smoking Area at Socio Technopreneur University offers valuable insights into the principles of community-building, which can be applied to both physical and virtual spaces. By examining how such initiatives are implemented and their impact on stakeholders, this research provides a framework that can be translated into strategies for creating and managing communities in the Metaverse. In physical environments, like the Muhammadiyah campus, establishing a Non-Smoking Area involves understanding and influencing the behaviors and attitudes of various stakeholders, including university leadership, lecturers, students, and staff. This process requires

DOI: 10.4018/979-8-3693-8628-6.ch002

comprehensive planning, stakeholder engagement, and continuous monitoring. The study highlights that successful implementation relies on factors such as effective campaigns, campus greening initiatives, and a system of rewards and penalties. These strategies help foster a culture that supports non-smoking, aligning with broader community goals (Muza & Debnath, 2021).

Similarly, building communities in the Metaverse requires a nuanced approach to user engagement and behavior management. The Metaverse, as a digital environment, presents unique challenges and opportunities for community development. Virtual communities, like their physical counterparts, need clear guidelines, active governance, and supportive infrastructure to thrive (Curtis et al., 2023). Just as the development of a Non-Smoking Area involves engaging university stakeholders, building communities in the Metaverse requires active involvement from users and community leaders. Engaging users in the creation and enforcement of community norms is crucial. This can be achieved through virtual forums, focus groups, and participatory design processes, ensuring that diverse perspectives are considered and integrated into community guidelines (Park & Ahn, 2023). The study identifies campaigns and educational initiatives as essential for promoting non-smoking. In the Metaverse, similar strategies can be employed to influence user behavior. For instance, virtual campaigns, educational events, and interactive experiences can be designed to promote positive behaviors and discourage harmful activities. Just as physical spaces benefit from clear signage and information, virtual environments can use visual and interactive elements to communicate community norms and values (Moghaieb, 2020).

Campus greening and the creation of smoking areas are physical manifestations of the university's commitment to a non-smoking culture. In the Metaverse, creating supportive environments involves designing virtual spaces that facilitate community interaction and support positive engagement.

This includes well-designed virtual meeting spaces, interactive areas for socialization, and environments that encourage collaboration and mutual support (Stingl & Geraldi, 2021). The study emphasizes the need for monitoring and adapting strategies to ensure the effectiveness of the Non-Smoking Area. Similarly, virtual communities require ongoing monitoring to address issues such as user misconduct or evolving community needs. This can be achieved through data analytics, user feedback, and regular assessments of community health (Ul Islam & Rahman, 2017).

Applying the principles of community-building from the Socio Technopreneur University case study to virtual environments highlights several key strategies for success. Effective governance in physical spaces, such as clear policies and structured oversight, can be mirrored in the Metaverse by establishing well-defined social norms, virtual moderators, and systems for addressing user issues. Similarly, the role of targeted campaigns and reward systems in promoting non-smoking can be adapted for virtual communities through virtual events and achievements that encourage positive behavior and recognize contributions. Cultural and environmental adaptation remains crucial in both contexts, requiring an understanding of diverse user backgrounds and the creation of inclusive, culturally sensitive virtual spaces. Integrating these principles helps translate successful physical community strategies into vibrant, cohesive, and supportive virtual communities in the Metaverse (Habiba et al., 2018).

Around 87% of Indonesia's population are Muslims, making Indonesia the largest Muslim majority country in the world. The dynamics of Muslims are often colored by differences of opinion in looking at a problem, including the status of smoking in Islamic law. Different religious organizations have diverse beliefs about the act of smoking in relationship with all the chemicals in cigarette (Bast et al., 2019).

The prohibition on smoking in charity business (*amal usaha*) environment, secretarial offices and activities within Muhammadiyah has been enforced based on PP Muhammadiyah Collective Agreement Statement Year 2011 (Lian, 2019). The agreement refers to Law Number 36 Year 2009 concerning

Health. Fatwa of Muhammadiyah PP No. 6/SM/MTT/III/2010 regarding the law of smoking contains (1) that it is not allowed for medical personnel, patients, educators, students, visitors and managers to smoke in the organization, (2) to refuse all forms of promotion, product sponsorship and sales of cigarette in the charity business environment and the organization's offices, (3) to actively enforce this agreement by posting banners, stickers and similar media regarding No-Smoking Areas in every charity business and organization's office, to supervise the implementation of the agreement and the assembly (majlis) is obliged to give a caution or warning if it is not implemented (Jufri & Awali, 2015).

The argument for the prohibition of smoking in Muhammadiyah circles include was that cigarettes contain poisonous elements. The act of smoking is included in the category of doing something that is debilitating and endangering the health of the smokers and those around who have been exposed to cigarette smoke. Therefore, spending money on cigarettes means doing redundant deeds, as stated in the Al Quran Chapter 17 Verse 26-27.

The campus environment of Socio Technopreneur University-Jakarta was established in 1968. The campus is one of the campuses where various activities take place, such as teaching and learning processes, activities related to research and lecturer service, registration and student services, as well as various student activities. All of these activities take place within the framework of Islam under the Muhammadiyah banner.

Based on the age category of the population, the Socio Technopreneur University academic community is in the age category of over 15 years. According to reports of the results of health research in Indonesia, the prevalence of cigarette consumption at that age category increased from 33% in 2016 to 34% in 2018 with the percentage of male smokers was as much as 63% and 4.8% for female smokers (Cai, 2020). The Socio Technopreneur

University academic community in the 2018-2019 academic year consisted of 600 students, 159 lecturers, 71 staff in the academic, financial, and general fields including cleaning service, security and pantry. According to observations, various stakeholders of the academic community are still frequently found consuming cigarettes in public spaces in the campus environment, even though warnings for no smoking have been announced in several strategic easy to read places.

This condition is in stark contrast to the provisions of the Law on Health Number 36 of 2009 concerning Smoking Free Areas in workplaces and places of education as well as the PP Muhammadiyah Joint Agreement Statement of 2010. Furthermore, Article 115 paragraphs (1) and (2) of the Law explains that public places can provide a designated area for smoking and the placement of a Non-smoking Area must holistically consider all aspects.

Previous research that became a reference includes the research conducted (Jufri & Awali, 2015) regarding the supervision by supervisors (*pembina*) to students (*santri*), discipline of students, sanctions given to students with the effectiveness of Non-Smoking Area at Nurul Falah Kawatuna Islamic Boarding School, Palu City.

The research suggests providing counseling and increasing the supervision carried out by the supervisors, increasing the discipline of the students and giving sanctions to students who do not heed the no smoking regulations, so that an effective Non-Smoking Area environment can be created.

The appeal for the establishment of Non-Smoking Area in the environment of all Muhammadiyah charity businesses, facilities and forums is that health development must be aimed at increasing awareness, willingness and ability of community to live healthily as an investment for human resource development. However, this was not meant to prohibit smoking or the cultivation of tobacco plants. "What Muhammadiyah expects is that smokers should smoke 'properly and correctly', and not be practiced in public facilities, public transportation, educational institutions, houses of worship and so on, as regulated by regulations.

The plan for the establishment of Non-Smoking Area will be implemented in all Muhammadiyah buildings, hospitals, schools, universities and all Muhammadiyah business charities and also, no less important, in Muhammadiyah official forums throughout Indonesia from the central leadership level to the branch leadership level.

The hazard of this tobacco product needs to be watched more closely with the increasing trend of smoking among adolescents. In 2001 the prevalence of smokers aged 15 to 19 years was 12.7 percent and continued to increase until it reached 23.1 percent in 2016.

Even in that year the prevalence of male teenage smokers reached a very high number, namely 54.8 percent or an increase of 17.5 percent compared to 2013.

Responding to the threat, Majlis Tarjih and Tajdid of the Muhammadiyah Central Leadership firmly consider that smoking was haram as smoking contains elements of plunging oneself into destruction and even is an act of suicide so that it is against the teachings of the Al Quran. In addition, the act of smoking harms oneself and others who are exposed to cigarette smoke because cigarettes are addictive and dangerous substances.

Prospective analysis is a technique for analyzing a variety of strategies that can occur in the future based on current conditions. The aim of a prospective analysis is to strategize what changes are needed in the future. This prospective approach emphasizes the long-term evolutionary process so that time is a very important factor in making the decisions. This is why this method is not a forecast but a scenario designed to achieve long-term goals (Bourgeois & Jésus, 2004).

The objectives of this study are: (1) To analyze what stakeholders are most influential regarding the implementation of Law on Health Number 36 Year 2009 concerning

No-Smoking Areas as well as the 2010 PP Muhammadiyah Joint Agreement Statement at Socio Technopreneur University, (2) Analyze needs stakeholders in implementing the development of Non-Smoking Area in the workplace and education areas at Socio Technopreneur University, and (3) Formulating the implementation of the No Smoking development in the Socio Technopreneur University environment.

The key gap in community management within the Metaverse lies in the challenges of decentralized governance, user anonymity, and difficulties in enforcing social norms in a virtual space. In the physical world, communities are managed with clear rules, supervision systems, and governing authorities, such as in the implementation of a Non-Smoking Area on a university campus. However, in the Metaverse, users tend to be more anonymous and dispersed across different time zones, making it harder to enforce consistent control or rules.

This paper addresses these gaps by proposing the adaptation of physical community strategies to virtual environments. Strategies like awareness campaigns, rewards, and penalties that are effective in the physical world can be implemented in the Metaverse through gamification features, digital incentives, and automated feedback systems. Additionally, the paper explores methods to build community engagement through technology-based interactions, such as using analytics tools to monitor user behavior and new methods to manage identity and anonymity. By offering these approaches, the paper provides solutions to overcome the challenges of building cohesive and well-regulated communities in the Metaverse.

## II. METHOD

The method used in this research was descriptive qualitative method. Descriptive research aims to make systematic, factual, and accurate descriptions of the facts and characteristics of a particular population orarea (Djamba & Neuman, 2002). The subjects of this research were the leadership elements at Socio Technopreneur University. The elements of leadership in question were the heads of units in charge of several staffs/members/students in activity units related to the development of Non-Smoking Area in the Ciputat campus environment. The leadership elements were Vice Rector II, Head of General Bureau, Head of Human Resources, Head of MUHAMMADIYAH AL-ISLAMIC STUDY CENTER, Head of Business Development Agency, Head of Finance, Head of Public Relations, Head of Security and Environment Bureau, Head of Security Unit, lecturers, and students who are part of the academic community representing several batches (Student Executive Board/BEM, Student Representative Body/BPM, Muhammadiyah Student Association/IMM, Sports Student Activity Units/UKM).

Secondary data collection was carried out by collecting data via the internet and archives, including books on opinions, theories, arguments or laws and others related to research problems (Djamba & Neuman, 2002). The primary data collection used semi-structured ethnographic techniques (Abidin & Rachma, 2018) with the link http://bit.ly/kuesionerNon-Smoking Area. The questions asked contained the name of the respondent, the unit in charge, the needs related to the development of a communal-based Non-Smoking Area in Socio Technopreneur University campus environment, and status of smoking.

Data analysis to analyze needs in the system used participatory prospective analysis which aims to design stakeholder involvement in determining future possibilities (Bourgeois & Jésus, 2004). In this analysis, Prospective Analysis software was used to calculate the direct and indirect effects between factors. Expert assessment of direct influence between factors was then processed and visualized in a diagram. The magnitude of influence and dependence between factors can be seen in the table. Visualization of the diagrams and tables was then conducted to show the most influential key factors. These key factors were then used to see the relationships of the efforts to develop a communal-based Non-Smoking Area in the Socio Technopreneur University environment.

*Figure 1. Step-by-step process of community building*

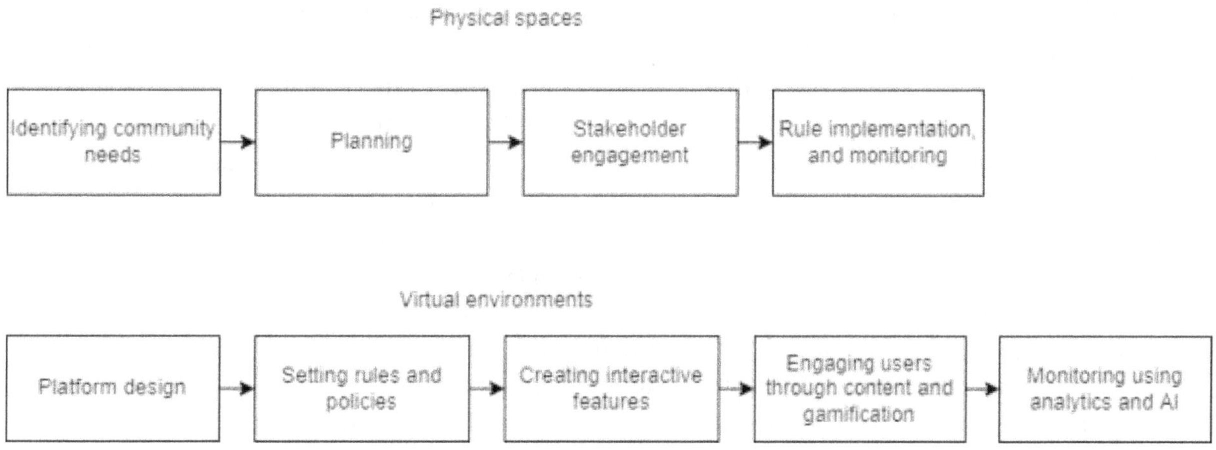

## III. RESULTS AND DISCUSSION

The results of the prospective analysis showed that five stakeholders were in the upper left quadrant (Quadrant I). The stakeholders were MUHAMMADIYAH AL-ISLAMIC STUDY CENTER (Center of Islam and Muhammadiyah Development/Pusat Pengembangan Al-Islam dan Kemuhammadiyahan), Vice Rector II, LP3M (Institution for Research,

Development, and Community Service/*Lembaga Penelitian, Pengembangan, dan Pengabdian kepada Masyarakat*), General Bureau and HR Bureau. The five stakeholders have had a high influence on the development of Non-Smoking Area at Socio Technopreneur University. The stakeholders categorized in this quadrant were the determinant stakeholders in the development of Non-Smoking Area.

The stakeholder with the highest influence was MUHAMMADIYAH AL-ISLAMIC STUDY CENTER with a score of 21. Things that were needed by this stakeholder in the development of Non-Smoking Area at Socio Technopreneur University were Non-Smoking Area campaigns, along with greening the campus with parks, as well as enforcement of reward and punishment. The second highest influence was Vice Rector II with a score of 18. This stakeholder required a policy regulation related to the development of Non-Smoking Area at Socio Technopreneur University accompanied by firm and measurable sanctions for smoking violations in the Non-Smoking Area area.

The No Smoking Area aims to reduce smoke pollution that is detrimental to health. Tobacco smoke can cause lung cancer, heart disease, asthma in children, and infant mortality (Kossova et al., 2018). The KTR discourse on campus is a health promotion activity for the academic community in the campus environment. Risk factors for being a smoker can be avoided from fostering a smoke-free campus environment (Trinidad et al., 2005).

The implementation of the rules regarding KTR is still not optimal at the ITB Ahmad Dahlan campus, because smoking behavior is still found in some elements of leadership, lecturers, students, and it can be seen from the finding of cigarette butts in several corners of the campus such as behind the student association room and behind “Toko Kita”. ITB Ahmad Dahlam campus is one of the private universities under the Muhammadiyah association which has issued a fatwa on smoking (Kementerian Pendidikan, Kebudayaan, 2018). A smoke- free environment on campus is very necessary because this is one way to reduce tobacco smoke pollution, reduce the negative impact on passive smokers, reduce the prevalence of smokers in productive age, and become a means of tobacco control (Sawyer et al., 2018).

This stakeholder also expressed the need of fund/budget and human resources to carry out the Non-Smoking Area policy at Socio Technopreneur University, and as an initial stage it was deemed necessary to provide a smoking area and its supporting equipment. The needs of this stakeholder were in line with the needs of the stakeholders LP3M, the General Bureau and the HR Bureau.

Other stakeholders in the development of Non-Smoking Area at Socio Technopreneur University were in the lower right quadrant (Quadrant III). These stakeholders had low influence and high dependence on the linkages between stakeholders, so that they were the results in the system. These result stakeholders were influenced by the determinant stakeholders in the development of Non-Smoking Area at the Socio Technopreneur University. Stakeholders in Quadrant III were Lecturers, Finance Bureau, Business Development Agency, Security Unit, and Students.

In virtual or online platforms, community building focuses on creating spaces where users can interact meaningfully. This involves designing interfaces that facilitate communication, building features like forums, groups, and avatars that reflect user identities, and developing algorithms that encourage ongoing engagement. Technologies such as chatbots and AI can help strengthen social connections and address user queries or issues automatically.

Challenges such as anonymity, decentralized governance, and technological limitations make managing communities in the Metaverse different from physical communities. Anonymity increases the risk of unethical behavior due to a lack of direct accountability. Decentralized governance complicates the enforcement of uniform rules, while existing technology may struggle to manage millions of users effectively, both in monitoring and analytics. Major challenges include obtaining accurate feedback from users who are geographically dispersed and often anonymous. Methods such as online surveys, real-time analytics tracking user behavior (e.g., time spent on the platform, click activity, and content preferences), and behavior tracking through sensors or AI algorithms can help. This data can be used to improve user experience and adjust engagement strategies.

In decentralized virtual environments, "rewards and penalties" can be implemented through gamification systems offering digital incentives, such as special items or status upgrades, for users who follow rules. Educational campaigns can be conducted through interactive content like 3D videos, educational avatars, and in-game or platform-wide advertisements. Rule enforcement can be automated, with temporary bans for offenders or based on community feedback.

## Implementation of NON-SMOKING AREA Development Policies

Based on the results of this study, the stakeholders in Quadrant I as the determinant factors for Non-Smoking Area development efforts held several positions in the institutional structure, thus providing more power in implementing the policies

(Bourgeois & Jésus, 2004). Stakeholders who were the output variables in this case consisted of several stakeholders such as the Finance Bureau, Lecturers, Business Development Bodies, Security Units and Students who implement the policies made by the driving stakeholders.

Stakeholders in Quadrant III should have a strong commitment to implement the Non- Smoking Area development in Socio Technopreneur University. Efforts suggested for the Non-Smoking Area implementation are jointly disseminating any policies related to the development of Non-Smoking Area, always conducting monitoring or supervising, as well as creating and enforcing firm sanctions so that the Non-Smoking Area campus policy can run as expected. The importance level of stakeholders influencing the development of Non-Smoking can be seen in Figure 2.

*Figure 2. Importance level of stakeholders influencing the development of Non-Smoking Area in Socio Technopreneur University*

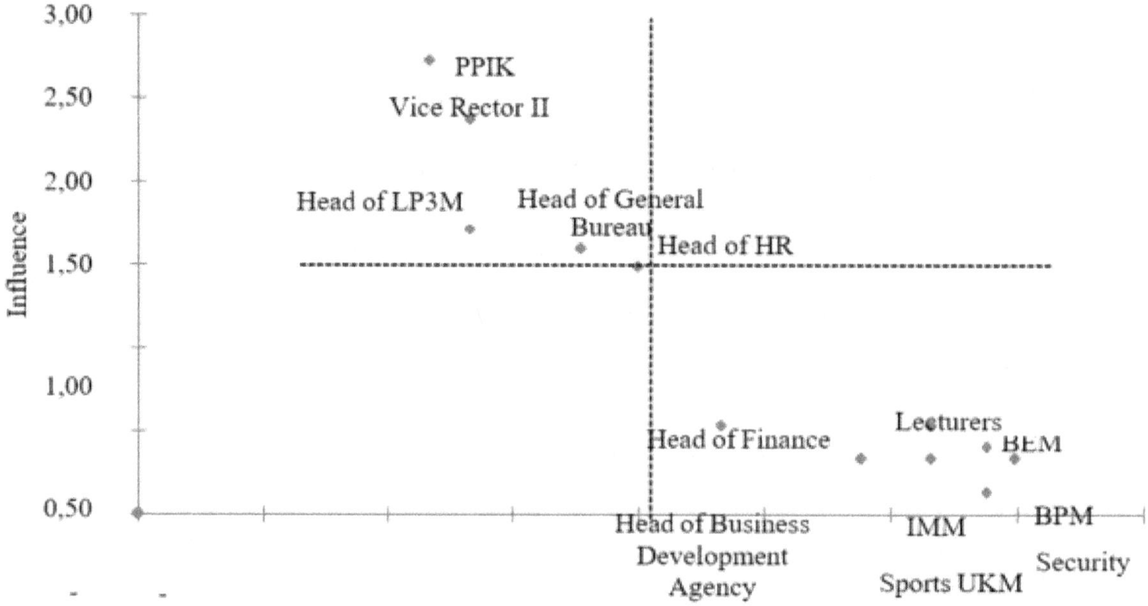


*Source: Processed survey data*

An alternative solution for Non-Smoking Area violations is to directly reprimand and give a warning to students who are caught smoking in the campus environment because the losses due to cigarette smoke does not only affect the active smokers but passive smokers can also be affected by cigarette smoke. This is in line with the mission and vision of Socio Technopreneur University to carry out *amar ma'ruf nahi munkar*. Another alternative in socializing the development of a Non-Smoking Area in Socio Technopreneur University as through seminars on the impacts and dangers of smoking. These solutions need to involve all interested parties in Socio Technopreneur University. An equally important solution is to provide smoking areas.

Environments, particularly communities, have an indirect impact on the decisions made. There are various pros and cons associated with both physical and virtual communities. Here is a comparison table between physical and virtual community strategies, showing how principles from the Non-Smoking Area (NSA) initiative can be adapted to the Metaverse.

*Table 1. Comparison between physical and virtual community strategies*

| Principle | Strategy in Physical Communities (NSA) | Adaptation to Virtual Communities in the Metaverse |
|---|---|---|
| **Awareness Campaign** | Education through posters, seminars, and awareness about smoking dangers | Virtual campaigns with interactive content such as 3D videos, educational avatars, and in-game or platform ads |
| **No-Smoking Zones** | Establishing physical smoke-free areas on campus or public buildings | Creating virtual zones free of specific activities, such as areas free of negative behavior or harmful content |
| **Rewards and Penalties** | Rewards for compliance, fines for violations | Gamification systems with virtual rewards (e.g., badges or digital items) and penalties (e.g., restricted access) |
| **Monitoring and Enforcement** | Supervision by staff or CCTV | Automated monitoring through behavior analytics and notifications, as well as direct user reporting |
| **Stakeholder Engagement** | Involvement of university, staff, and students in decision-making | Engagement of users, platform developers, and community moderators to establish virtual rules and policies |
| **Greening Campaigns** | Development of campus gardens and green spaces | Development of virtual environments that support positive social interactions, such as visually pleasing and user-friendly elements |

## IV. CONCLUSION

The most influential stakeholder regarding the implementation of Law on Health Number 36 Year 2009 concerning Non-Smoking Areas as well as Muhammadiyah Central Leadership Joint Agreement Statement year 2009 in Socio Technopreneur University was Muhammadiyah Al-Islamic Study Center. The needs of stakeholders in implementing development of Non-Smoking Area in Socio Technopreneur University were Non-Smoking Area campaigns, campus greenings with parks, and enforcement of reward and punishment. Some of the implementation of Non-Smoking Area development in Socio Technopreneu University are monitoring and the need for smoking area.

AI can play a significant role in managing virtual communities, especially in moderating user behavior, detecting suspicious activity, and providing personalized recommendations. Different Metaverse platforms may use AI to analyze engagement data, tailor content for individual users, and monitor conversations in real-time. Community-building strategies can scale by automating moderation, using algorithms to group users by interests, and leveraging cloud technology to support millions of users simultaneously.

Stakeholder engagement principles from physical communities can be adapted to virtual environments such as online games or virtual workplaces. In games, stakeholders like players, developers, and moderators can be involved in community decision-making, such as designing game rules and social features. In virtual workplaces, collaboration between management, employees, and technology providers can help create an efficient and inclusive digital workspace, with ongoing engagement facilitated through virtual discussions and feedback loops.

## REFERENCES


Abidin, A. Z., & Rachma, I. (2018). Etnografi Virtual Sebagai Teknik Pengumpulan Data Dan Metode Penelitian. *The Journal of Society & Media*, 2(2), 130–145. https://journal.unesa.ac.id/index.php/jsm/index. DOI: 10.26740/jsm.v2n2.p130-145

Bast, L. S., Andersen, A., Ersbøll, A. K., & Due, P. (2019). Implementation fidelity and adolescent smoking: The X:IT study—A school randomized smoking prevention trial. *Evaluation and Program Planning, 72*(September 2018), 24–32. DOI: 10.26740/jsm.v2n2.p130-145

Bourgeois, R., & Jésus, F. (2004, January). Participatory Prospective Analysis: Exploring and anticipating Challenges with Stakehoders. *CAPSA Monograph*, 46, 112.

Cai, H. (2020). Sex difference and smoking predisposition in patients with COVID-19. *The Lancet. Respiratory Medicine*, 8(4), e20. DOI: 10.1016/S2213-2600(20)30117-X PMID: 32171067

Curtis, S. J., Trewin, A., McCormack, L. M., Were, K., McDermott, K., & Walsh, N. (2023). Building a safety culture for infection prevention and control adherence at Howard Springs: A workplace survey. *Infection, Disease & Health*, 28(1), 47–53. DOI: 10.1016/j.idh.2022.07.004 PMID: 36127286

Djamba, Y. K., & Neuman, W. L. (2002). Social Research Methods: Qualitative and Quantitative Approaches. In *Teaching Sociology* (Vol. 30, Issue 3). DOI: 10.2307/3211488

Habiba, M., Islam, M. R., & Ali, A. B. M. S. (2018). A component based unified architecture for utility service in cloud. *Future Generation Computer Systems*, 87, 725–742. https://doi.org/https://doi.org/10.1016/j.future.2017.10.017. DOI: 10.1016/j.future.2017.10.017

Jufri, M., & Awali, N. (2015). FAKTOR-FAKTOR YANG BERHUBUNGAN DENGAN EFEKTIVITAS AREA KAWASAN TANPA ROKOK DI PONDOK PESANTREN NURUL FALAH KAWATUNA KOTA PALU Healthy Tadulako Journal (Muh. Jufri & Nazliani : 33-42) Di Indonesia daerah yang telah menerapkan kawasan tanpa rokok ini ada. *Jurnal Kesehatan Tadulako*, 1(2), 1–78.

Kossova, T., Kossova, E., & Sheluntcova, M. (2018). Anti-smoking policy in Russia: Relevant factors and program planning. *Evaluation and Program Planning, 69*(March 2017), 43–52. DOI: 10.1016/j.evalprogplan.2018.04.006

Lian, B. (2019). Tanggung Jawab Tridharma Perguruan Tinggi Menjawab Kebutuhan Masyarakat. *Jurnal Cakrawala Ilmiah*, 100–106.

Moghaieb, H. S. (2020). Estimating local administrators' participation in planning: Case of "Egypt vision 2030.". *Review of Economics and Political Science*, 4(3), 197–223. DOI: 10.1108/REPS-11-2018-0016

Muza, O., & Debnath, R. (2021). Disruptive innovation for inclusive renewable policy in sub-Saharan Africa: A social shaping of technology analysis of appliance uptake in Rwanda. *Renewable Energy*, 168, 896–912. https://doi.org/https://doi.org/10.1016/j.renene.2020.12.091. DOI: 10.1016/j.renene.2020.12.091 PMID: 33942003

Park, J. H., & Ahn, H. K. (2023). Development of the Capital City of Taebong Kingdom Metaverse and King Gungye Artifical Intelligence Digital Human. In Jung, T., tom Dieck, M. C., & Correia Loureiro, S. M. (Eds.), *Extended Reality and Metaverse* (pp. 217–227). Springer International Publishing. DOI: 10.1007/978-3-031-25390-4_19

Pendidikan, K. Kebudayaan, R. dan T. (2018). *Data Pokok Pendidikan Direktorat Jenderal Pendidikan Anak Usia Dini, Pendidikan Dasar dan Pendidikan Menengah*. Kementerian Pendidikan, Kebudayaan, Riset Dan Teknologi. https://dapo.kemdikbud.go.id/pd

Sawyer, S. M., Azzopardi, P. S., Wickremarathne, D., & Patton, G. C. (2018). The age of adolescence. *The Lancet. Child & Adolescent Health*, 2(3), 223–228. DOI: 10.1016/S2352-4642(18)30022-1 PMID: 30169257

Stingl, V., & Geraldi, J. (2021). A research agenda for studying project decision-behaviour through the lenses of simple heuristics. *Technological Forecasting and Social Change*, 162, 120367. https://doi.org/https://doi.org/10.1016/j.techfore.2020.120367. DOI: 10.1016/j.techfore.2020.120367

Trinidad, D. R., Gilpin, E. A., & Pierce, J. P. (2005). Compliance and support for smoke-free school policies. *Health Education Research*, 20(4), 466–475. DOI: 10.1093/her/cyg143 PMID: 15572436

Ul Islam, J., & Rahman, Z. (2017). The impact of online brand community characteristics on customer engagement: An application of Stimulus-Organism-Response paradigm. *Telematics and Informatics*, 34(4), 96–109. https://doi.org/https://doi.org/10.1016/j.tele.2017.01.004. DOI: 10.1016/j.tele.2017.01.004

# Chapter 3
# Communication Modalities and Tools

**Mosiur Rahaman**
https://orcid.org/0000-0003-0521-2080
*International Center for AI and Cyber Security Research and Innovations, Taiwan*

**Princy Pappachan**
https://orcid.org/0000-0001-6728-0228
*College of Education, National Chengchi University, Taiwan*

**Ifat Batul**
*Vidyasagar University, India*

**Agung Mulyuo Widodo**
https://orcid.org/0000-0002-9792-7114
*Universitas Esa Unggul, Indonesia*

**Brij B. Gupta**
https://orcid.org/0000-0003-4929-4698
*Asia University, Taiwan*

## ABSTRACT

*The chapter "Communication Modalities and Tools" in the book "Unveiling Social Dynamics and Community Interaction in the Metaverse" explores the diverse range of communication technologies and methods that enable social interaction in the metaverse. This digital realm, combining virtual reality (VR), augmented reality (AR), and mixed reality (MR), offers new and immersive ways for users to connect and build communities. The chapter traces the evolution of communication tools from traditional text and video-based methods to advanced VR and AR systems, emphasizing the role of avatars, virtual environments, and sensory feedback in enhancing social presence. It examines the technological infrastructure supporting these communication tools, including network requirements, platform interoperability, and data privacy. Key challenges such as scalability, user accessibility, and ethical considerations are discussed. Through current research and case studies, the chapter provides insights into the future trajectory of communication in the metaverse and offers practical recommendations for developers, policymakers, and researchers to create inclusive, engaging, and sustainable virtual communities.*

DOI: 10.4018/979-8-3693-8628-6.ch003

## INTRODUCTION

The metaverse represents a revolutionary shift in the way humans interact, communicate, and build communities (Dwivedi et al., 2022). As an evolving digital ecosystem that blends the physical and virtual worlds, the metaverse offers limitless possibilities for social interaction, education, entertainment, and commerce (Mitra, 2023). Central to this dynamic environment are the communication modalities and tools that enable users to connect, collaborate, and engage in meaningful ways.

In the early stages of digital communication, text-based chat and video conferencing were the primary means of interaction. However, the advent of VR, AR, and MR technologies has transformed these rudimentary tools into sophisticated platforms that offer immersive and interactive experiences (Bonfert et al., 2023). Avatars, virtual environments, and haptic feedback have become integral components of communication, allowing users to express themselves more authentically and establish deeper connections with others (Praetorius & Görlich, 2020).

This chapter aims to explore the diverse range of communication modalities and tools available in the metaverse, their impact on social dynamics, and the technological infrastructure that supports them. We begin by tracing the evolution of communication technologies, highlighting the shift from 2D interfaces to 3D immersive experiences. This historical perspective sets the stage for a deeper examination of the current state of communication in the metaverse.

We then delve into the role of avatars and virtual environments in enhancing social presence. Avatars, as digital representations of users, play a crucial role in identity formation and self-expression. Virtual environments, on the other hand, provide the context within which interactions occur, influencing social norms and behaviours. The interplay between these elements shapes the overall experience of users and their sense of community.

The chapter also addresses the technological requirements for effective communication in the metaverse. This includes discussions on network capabilities, platform interoperability, and data privacy. As the metaverse continues to grow, ensuring robust and secure communication infrastructure becomes paramount. We explore the challenges associated with scalability, user accessibility, and ethical considerations, providing insights into how these issues can be addressed.

In addition to examining current technologies, this chapter looks ahead to the future of communication in the metaverse. Through a review of emerging trends and innovations, we identify potential developments that could further enhance user interaction and engagement. Practical recommendations for developers, policymakers, and researchers are provided, aimed at fostering inclusive, engaging, and sustainable virtual communities.

In conclusion, communication modalities and tools are the lifeblood of the metaverse, shaping the way users interact and build relationships. By understanding the complexities and potential of these technologies, we can better navigate the evolving digital landscape and harness its potential for positive social impact.

# 1. INTRODUCTION

## 1.1 Overview of the Metaverse

The metaverse is a new area of technology that is developing quickly. It removes the lines between the real and virtual worlds, giving people new ways to connect, create, and explore. The metaverse is thought of as a shared virtual place for everyone. It is made up of both virtually improved real life and physically persistent virtual areas (Tukur et al., 2023). Virtual reality (VR), augmented reality (AR), and mixed reality (MR) are some of the new technologies that have made this merging easier. These technologies make it possible to create immersive, dynamic spaces where people can work, learn, connect, and have fun in ways that were not possible before.

When powerful computers and fast internet became available, the idea of the metaverse became very popular in both pop culture and science. This is because they made it possible for such complex virtual worlds to exist. A lot of money has been spent by big tech companies and developers on building platforms and ecosystems that make it easy for people to connect with each other in these virtual places (Dwivedi et al., 2022). These investments have led to improvements in both technology and software, which has made the metaverse easier for more people to reach and more fun for them to play in.

## 1.2 Importance of Communication in Virtual Environments

Communication, which is integral to encouraging social contact and community building, is at the heart of the metaverse. In the metaverse, communication tools and methods are necessary to build the social web that connects people. As opposed to regular digital communication, which mostly uses text and video, conversation in the metaverse uses a wider range of methods, which makes exchanges more complex and richer (Hennig-Thurau et al., 2023). The use of avatars, virtual settings, and sensory input systems enhances the feeling of presence and immersion, rendering virtual encounters more real and emotionally impactful.

Numerous reasons make being able to speak clearly in the metaverse essential. When people use it, they can create online groups where they can share experiences, work together on projects, and help each other. Users' mental health depends on this communal part because it makes them feel like they belong and are linked (Vaingankar et al., 2022). Second, virtual settings can't really work without good communication tools. From simple socializing to working together professionally, learning, and doing business, they make it easier for everyone. People are clearly wanting more safe, reliable, and easy-to-use contact tools as they do these things (Thornhill-Miller et al., 2023).

## 1.3 Objectives and Scope of the Chapter

The chapter “Communication Modalities and Tools” seeks to offer a thorough investigation of the several technologies and tools allowing metaverse communication. It follows the development of these technologies from their crude origins in text and video-based platforms to the advanced VR and AR systems defining the contemporary scene. Through an analysis of the technology developments driving these transformations, the chapter emphasizes the essential elements supporting successful virtual environment communication.

This chapter's main goal is to clarify how virtual environments, avatars, and sensory input could improve social presence. Acting as the user's digital persona, avatars enable interaction and self-expression inside the virtual environment. Virtual environments give the background against which these exchanges take place, therefore establishing location and context. Haptic and auditory signals among other sensory inputs help users to be more fully immersed in the experience, therefore enhancing the palpable and interesting interactions. The chapter also explores the technology needed to enable these sophisticated communication instruments. This covers the network needs for real-time data flow, platform interoperability to guarantee flawless user experiences across many platforms, and data privacy issues to guard user information in these large virtual environments (Jain et al., 2023).

The chapter also covers important issues confronting metaverse communication like scalability, user accessibility, and ethical questions. Scalability in communication technologies is their capacity to sustain increasing user and interaction count without compromising performance. Making these technologies accessible and useable for people of various backgrounds and ability is known as user accessibility. Ethical concerns cover things like user permission, data security, and the possibility of communication technology abuse. By means of a survey of existing studies and actual case studies, the chapter offers understanding of the future direction of communication inside the metaverse. Targeting inclusive, interesting, and sustainable virtual communities, it provides pragmatic advice for developers, legislators, and academics. Understanding the complexity and possibilities of communication tools in the metaverse helps stakeholders to better negotiate the opportunities and difficulties this expanding digital terrain presents.

## 2. EVOLUTION OF COMMUNICATION TOOLS

### 2.1 Early Digital Communication Methods

In the digital age, communication tools started out as simple text-based ones. In the early days of the internet, email was the main way people talked to each other online. Users could send notes to each other at any time, which changed the way information was shared. Instant message (IM) services like ICQ and AOL Instant Messenger (AIM) came after email and let people text each other in real time (Dwivedi et al., 2021). These sites gave people a faster way to talk to each other, which led to faster exchanges and more active contacts. Bulletin board systems (BBS) and the first online groups were also very important in the growth of digital communication. Users could send messages and have conversations about a wide range of issues on these sites, which led to the creation of the first online communities (Shinder & Cross, 2008). Usenet boards were another early form of communication. They let people read and post messages in an open network, which brought people with similar interests together.

As internet technology improved, voice over IP (VoIP) services like Skype made it possible to talk on the internet. VoIP let people call each other over the internet, which was a more personal and quick way to talk than texting. Soon, video calling came out, letting people talk to each other online while seeing each other. People could see and hear each other in real time through services like Skype and later Zoom, which made them important for both personal and business contact. Social media sites like Facebook, Twitter, and LinkedIn have changed the way people communicate online even more by letting them share text, photos, and videos with their networks. These platforms made communication more social and engaging by giving users new ways to interact with information and connect with others.

## 2.2 Transition to 3D Immersive Communication

The change from standard digital methods of communication to 3D interactive communication was a big change in how people talk to each other online. Virtual reality (VR), augmented reality (AR), and mixed reality (MR) technologies have come a long way, opening up new ways to have realistic, interactive experiences (Rauschnabel et al., 2022). Users can interact with a computer-generated world as if they were really there thanks to VR technology, which makes fully immersive digital settings. The Oculus Rift and other early VR systems let users interact with virtual worlds using head-mounted screens and motion controllers. These systems showed what immersive communication could be like. Users had a stronger sense of presence and immersion with these tools, which made exchanges feel more real and interesting.

Augmented reality (AR) technology, which adds digital information to the real world, made seamless contact even more possible. AR apps like Pokémon Go and Microsoft HoloLens let people connect with digital content in the real world, making the experience more like a mix of reality and digital content. Through this technology, people can share and connect with digital information in new ways, even when they're not online.MR technology, which is a mix of VR and AR, makes worlds where real and virtual things live together and interact in real time. Users can interact with both the real and digital worlds at the same time with this technology, which makes seamless conversation even more advanced. In mixed reality settings, MR apps like Magic Leap make it possible for people to communicate and work together in complex ways.

## 2.3 Case Studies of Communication Evolution in Virtual Worlds

A number of well-known case studies show how communication tools in virtual worlds have changed over time, from simple digital tools for talking to each other to advanced 3D realistic technologies.

**Third Life (2003):** Second Life, which was created by Linden Lab and opened in 2003, is one of the first and most popular virtual worlds. Users can make characters and connect with each other in a huge world that they have created. There are many ways to communicate in Second Life, such as text chat, live chat, and group messaging, which let users meet new people, work together, and make content together. The tool has been used for many different things, from educational and virtual meetings to social events and shows. In the middle of the 2000s, IBM used Second Life for virtual meetings and training events, showing how useful it is for business contact.

**(2004):** World of Warcraft (WoW), an MMORPG (massively multiplayer online role-playing game), has been a big part of the development of virtual contact. It was made by Blizzard Entertainment and came out in 2004. WoW has text and voice chat features that let players talk to each other in real time. Guilds, which are player-run groups in the game, use these tools a lot to communicate and work together. Strong contact tools in the game have helped players form strong friendships and work together on plans.

**(2000):** Sulake Corporation's Habbo Hotel was one of the first virtual social platforms. Teenagers can use Habbo Hotel to make images, arrange virtual rooms, and talk to other users. Text-based conversation and customizing avatars were big parts of the platform, which paved the way for later virtual worlds.

**(2014):** VRChat, which came out in 2014, is a big step forward in 3D virtual conversation. Users can connect with imaginary worlds on the app using VR headsets and motion controls, making the experience very immersive. VRChat lets you talk to each other in a number of ways, such as through voice chat, text chat, and characters that make expressive movements. A large and active group of people from all walks of life use the platform to connect with each other, play games, and share their creativity. VR chat app VRChat shows how VR technology can be used to make social events more interesting and realistic. People use the platform to host events like live shows and virtual reality dance parties, which show how flexible it is.

**AltspaceVR (2015):** A VR social platform that was released in 2015 and later bought by Microsoft in 2017. It lets users go to virtual events, hang out with friends, and work together in realistic settings. AltspaceVR lets you talk to people through voice chat, text chat, and activities with avatars, making conversation dynamic and interesting. There were virtual meetings and conferences, live shows, and training classes on the site. The VR Church, a completely digital congregation, holds its meetings in AltspaceVR, which shows that the platform can help people connect in important ways.

**Rec Room (2016):** Against Gravity released Rec Room in 2016, which is a social VR app that focuses on games and socializing. There are many things that users can do, such as playing games, going to events, and making their own material. Rec Room lets you talk and use your body to talk, so you can have lively conversations. Users can post their own material and events on the platform, which makes it a popular choice for VR gathering and teamwork.

**Horizon (2020):** Facebook Horizon is a social VR app that was released in test in 2020. It was made by Facebook (now Meta). Horizon lets users make and explore virtual places, chat with other users, and do activities. Voice chat, interactions based on avatars, and collaborative tools are all built into the platform, making it a complete space for both personal and business contact. Horizon has become an important part of Meta's idea for the metaverse, with a focus on how it can be used for virtual socializing and working together.

**Firefox Hubs (2018):** Firefox Hubs is an open-source platform that lets people make and share virtual places that can be accessed through web browsers and VR gear. It was released in 2018. Hubs allows live chat, text chat, and 3D avatars, which makes it easier to talk and work together in real time. It has been used for virtual meetings, workshops, and social events, which shows how flexible and easy to use it is. As an example, the 2020 IEEEVR meeting took place in Mozilla Hubs, which let people talk to each other and make connections in a virtual space.

**Microsoft Mesh (2021):** Microsoft Mesh is a mixed reality tool that, when released in 2021, lets people work together to communicate in hybrid settings. Using AR and MR devices like HoloLens, Mesh lets users communicate with both real and virtual things in real time. The platform allows realistic characters, spatial sounds, and haptic feedback, making the experience very engaging and collaborative. Microsoft Mesh is meant to help professionals work together by giving them a shared virtual area to do their work. The platform shows that MR technology has the ability to change how people in many fields communicate and work together.

**Gather.Town (2020):** Introduced in 2020, Gather.Town is a web-based service that mixes live chat with a 2D virtual world. People can move around in the virtual world using avatars, and they can talk to each other through proximity-based voice and video chat. Gather. Town is a unique mix of video chat and online contact that has been used for virtual workshops, social events, and team meetings. The platform's ease of use and popularity make it a good choice for many types of online meetings.

*Figure 1. Evolution of virtual worlds and social VR platforms*

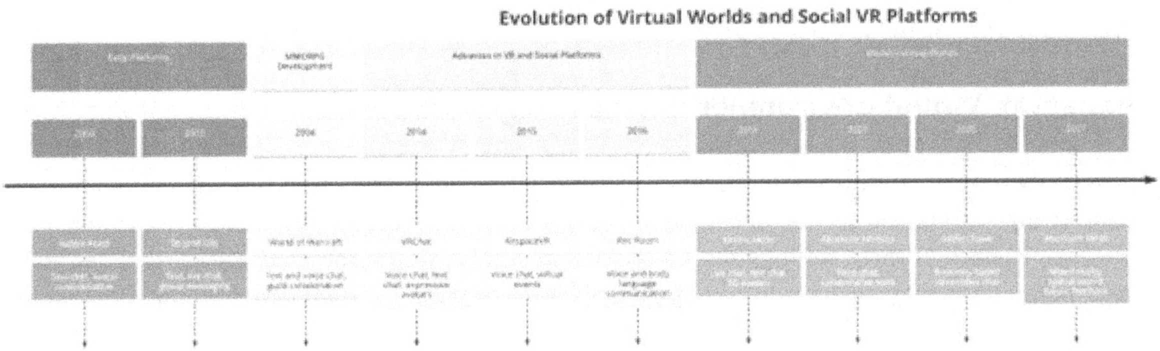


As depicted in Figure 1, from the first digital methods to advanced 3D interactive technologies, these case studies show how quickly communication tools have changed. They show how VR, AR, and MR technologies can change the way people communicate and work together by making new and interesting ways to meet and cooperate. Every platform has helped make communication tools that are more immersive, dynamic, and flexible. This paves the way for how people will connect with each other in the metaverse in the future.

## 3. AVATARS AND VIRTUAL ENVIRONMENTS

### 3.1 Role of Avatars in Identity Formation

Identity development is much aided by avatars, computerized representations of individuals in virtual worlds. Through which users express themselves, communicate with others, and negotiate virtual environments, they operate as the visual and interactive proxies. Avatars let users portray different facets of their identity, whether they mirror their actual self or whole new identities by means of customizing and personalizing them. Extensive customizing of avatars affects users' view of themselves and how others view them. Platforms like Second Life and VRChat, for example, provide great customizing choices so users may change the look, clothes, and accessories of their avatars. From realistic depictions to fanciful or abstract shapes, this flexibility lets one express themselves across a great spectrum. Users may play with several personas, investigating facets of themselves they might not feel comfortable presenting in the actual world.

Studies on avatars' influence on users' behaviour and self-perception a phenomenon sometimes referred to as the Proteus effect have shown Studies have revealed that users often adopt attitudes and actions fit for their avatars. A user with a handsome or authoritative avatar, for instance, could show greater confidence and aggressiveness in their contacts. This effect emphasizes the psychological influence avatars may have on users' social and cognitive experiences, therefore beyond simple visual depiction. Within virtual communities, avatars also significantly contribute to social identity. They can indicate group affiliation, social level, and personal personality features. Avatars in multiplayer online games such as World of

Warcraft, for instance, frequently include objects or symbols signifying a player's achievements, talents, or connections, therefore strengthening a feeling of community and belonging. In professional virtual environments such as Microsoft Mesh, avatars may also mirror professional positions and knowledge, therefore supporting networking and teamwork.

## 3.2 Impact of Virtual Environments on Social Interactions

Virtual environments greatly affect users' communication and connection with one another as they offer the setting and context for social contacts. From accurate replicas of physical areas to creative and fanciful realms, each of these settings shapes the nature and quality of interactions. Virtual worlds' design and architecture may either help or impede social interactions. Virtual offices, conference rooms, or cafes— environments that replicate real-world situations—offer familiar surroundings that let users feel comfortable and naturally negotiate conversations. From informal chats to official meetings, these environments may enable a range of social events, essentially reproducing the dynamics of real venues in a digital form.

On the other hand, fanciful or abstract virtual worlds can spark imagination and discovery, therefore motivating users to participate in fresh approaches. Platforms like VRChat and AltspaceVR let users converse in locations that hover in mid-air, underwater, or in outer space, therefore transcending actual limitations. These environments may inspire surprise and excitement, therefore improving the social experience by offering special and unforgettable surroundings for interaction. Virtual worlds' degree of involvement and immersion influences social relationships as well. Highly interactive environments—where users may explore dynamic surroundings, control objects, or engage in activities—tend to foster more interesting and cooperative relationships. Users of Rec Room, for example, can participate in different games and activities together, therefore strengthening social bonds and collaboration.

Using VR and AR technology, immersive environments improve the sensation of presence and realism, hence enhancing the authenticity and immediateness of interactions. For VR settings, for instance, the spatial audio lets users perceive noises from certain directions, therefore producing a more realistic and immersive auditory experience. Because users can sense closeness and orientation, akin to in-person encounters, this spatial awareness might help talks seem more realistic.

## 3.3 Enhancing Social Presence through Sensory Feedback

Improving social presence in virtual settings depends critically on sensory feedback—visual, aural, and haptic signals as well as others. A key component of meaningful and interesting interactions, social presence is the sense of being "with" people in a shared environment.

In virtual worlds, the most instantaneous kind of sensory input is visual feedback via avatars and surroundings. Detailed settings, lifelike avatar motions, and excellent visuals help to create immersion and presence. Advanced motion capture technology allows avatars that can replicate users' facial emotions and body language in real-time, therefore offering rich nonverbal communication signals that improve social contacts. Sophisticated avatar systems used by platforms like Facebook Horizon and Microsoft Mesh collect and show users' gestures and facial motions, hence enhancing the expressive and complex nature of interactions. Especially spatial audio, auditory feedback—which creates a realistic soundscape—much improves social presence. Spatial audio lets users in VR and AR settings hear sounds as though they were coming from certain points of view related to their position. Users using this function may find people by sound, sense distance, and enjoy a more natural conversation flow. AltspaceVR, for instance, lets users hear other people's voices emanating from the direction of their avatars, therefore simulating a genuine aural experience akin to actual encounters.

By letting users "feel" the virtual environment, haptic feedback—which comprises tactile sensations adds even another level of immersion. Gloves and vests among other haptic devices give physical input in response to virtual world interactions. In a virtual world, for example, haptic feedback allows one to feel a handshake or a tap on the shoulder, therefore enhancing the real and tactile aspect of the contact. This sensory information improves the sensation of presence and could increase the effect of social contacts. These sensory feedback systems taken together produce a more complete and immersive experience, which gives virtual interactions more realistic and interesting. Virtual worlds may emulate the intricacies of real-world communication by using visual, aural, and haptic input, therefore strengthening bonds, and increasing more significant social interactions.

Finally, the development of identity, social contacts, and the general sensation of presence in virtual worlds is much shaped by avatars and virtual surroundings. Customizing and expressive powers help avatars let users discover and project their personalities in several ways. While sensory feedback systems improve the realism and immersion of interactions, virtual worlds with their design and interactivity offer the setting for social involvement. These components taken together produce rich and dynamic virtual experiences that change user connection and communication in the digital sphere.

## 4. TECHNOLOGICAL INFRASTRUCTURE

### 4.1 Network Requirements for the Metaverse

To support its intense and complex experiences, the metaverse, a huge digital world that combines virtual reality (VR), augmented reality (AR), and mixed reality (MR), needs a strong and advanced network infrastructure. For real-time exchanges to work smoothly in these virtual worlds, you need a fast internet connection with low delay as illustrated in Figure 2.

*Figure 2. Network requirements for the Metaverse*

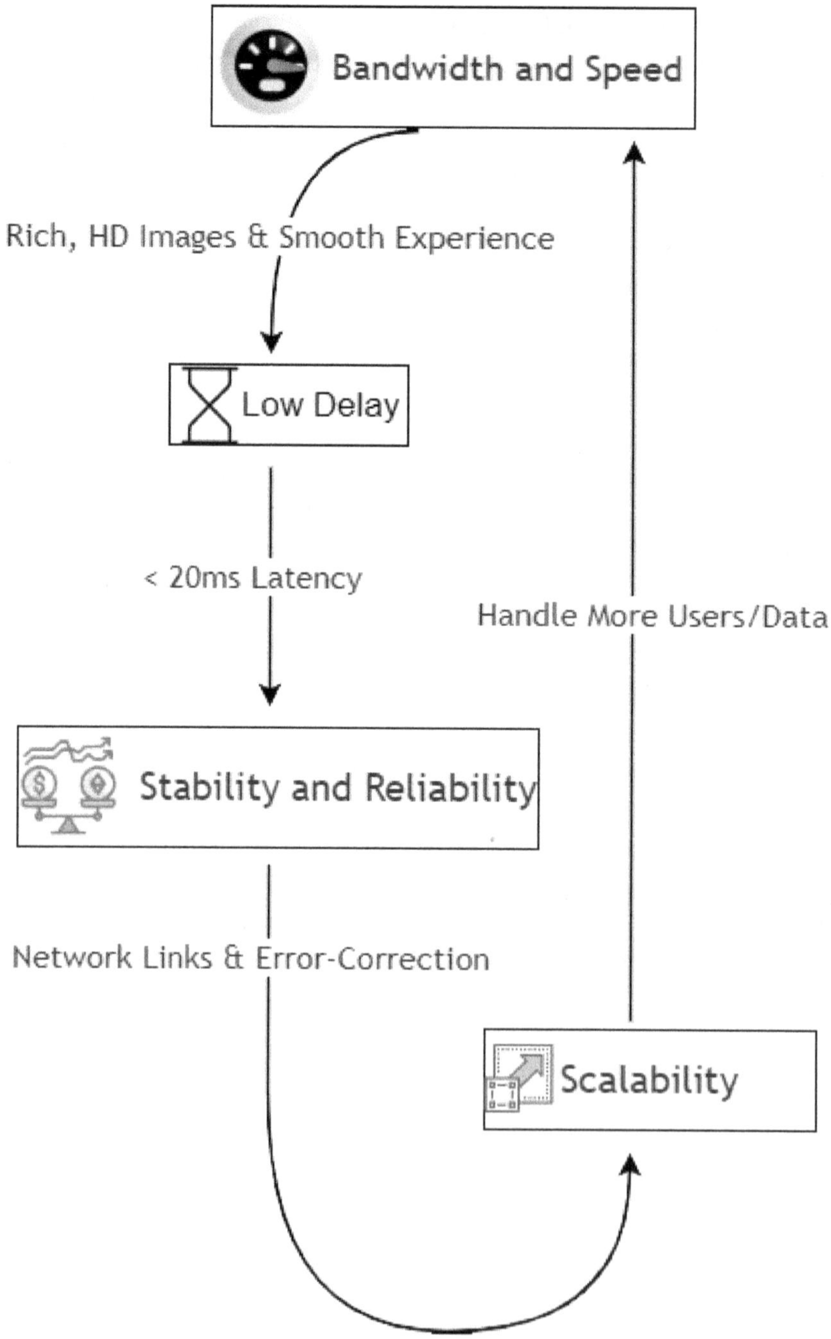


**Bandwidth and Speed:** A lot of bandwidth is needed to provide the rich, high-definition images and smooth exchanges that people expect in the metaverse. When it comes to data transfer rates, VR and AR apps need a lot more than regular web apps. For example, a normal VR experience might need a connection speed of at least 50 Mbps per person to keep the graphics and movements smooth. The demand for bandwidth goes up in direct measure to the amount of data that users are doing. Examples of this include multi-user settings and interactive games.

**Delay:** The metaverse needs low delay so that users can have an engaging and responsive experience. The time it takes for the system to respond to a user's move is called latency. When using VR and AR apps, too much delay can make you feel sick and break the experience. The delay must be less than 20 milliseconds (ms) for a smooth experience. This requirement is very hard for current network technologies to handle, especially for people who are far from data centers. Latency problems can be fixed by bringing processing closer to the user and shortening the distance that data has to travel. Edge computing and 5G networks are two new technologies that can do this.

**Stability and Reliability:** The metaverse also needs network links that are very stable and reliable. Breaks in the engagement or changes in the network's speed can make the user experience worse. Network stability is especially important for real-time teamwork apps like virtual meetings and multiplayer games. Metaverse systems must have strong error-correction methods and multiple network paths to make sure they always work well.

**Scalability:** Scalability becomes a big issue as the metaverse grows and more people join it. The network system needs to be able to handle more users and data flow at the same time without slowing down. By spreading data and processing power across many servers and places, content delivery networks (CDNs) and distributed computing tools can help handle this load.

## 4.2 Platform Interoperability

When different virtual worlds, gadgets, and apps in the metaverse can talk to each other and work together without any problems, this is called platform cooperation as shown in Figure 3. Getting connectivity is important for making the metaverse experience feel unified and whole.

**Standardization and Procedures:** Interoperability is based on setting up shared standards and procedures. These standards, which include data formats, communication methods, and application programming interfaces (APIs), are being made by organizations and business groups. The Khronos Group's OpenXR standard, for instance, wants to build a unified framework for VR and AR apps, which will let developers make content that works on many devices and platforms. The WebXR API also lets you make VR and AR experiences that run on the web and on different browsers and devices.

**Cross-Platform Compatibility:** Making sure that users can access and connect with the metaverse no matter what gear or software they use is another part of interoperability. This means that it works with a variety of VR gear, AR devices, smartphones, and regular computers. For example, someone wearing an Oculus Rift headset should be able to easily talk to someone using an HTC Vive or an augmented reality app on their phone. For this level of compatibility to be reached, device makers, software writers, and platform providers need to work together.

**Data and Asset Portability:** The ability to move data and digital assets between different systems and virtual settings is another important part of interoperability. It should be possible for users to move their avatars, virtual items, and digital material between different metaverse systems without losing quality or usefulness. Standardized data forms and powerful converting tools are needed for this to work. Using the GLTF (GL Transmission Format) for 3D models, for instance, makes it easy to move files between apps and devices.

**Integration of Services:** It's possible that the metaverse will have a lot of services and apps that work together, from social networks and game platforms to business solutions and educational tools. It's important for a smooth user experience that these services can work together and connect without any problems. Different services can share data and functions with each other thanks to APIs and software solutions that make interaction easier. A project management tool might be able to connect with a virtual meeting platform, letting users work together on papers and tasks in the same virtual area.

*Figure 3. Platform interoperability*

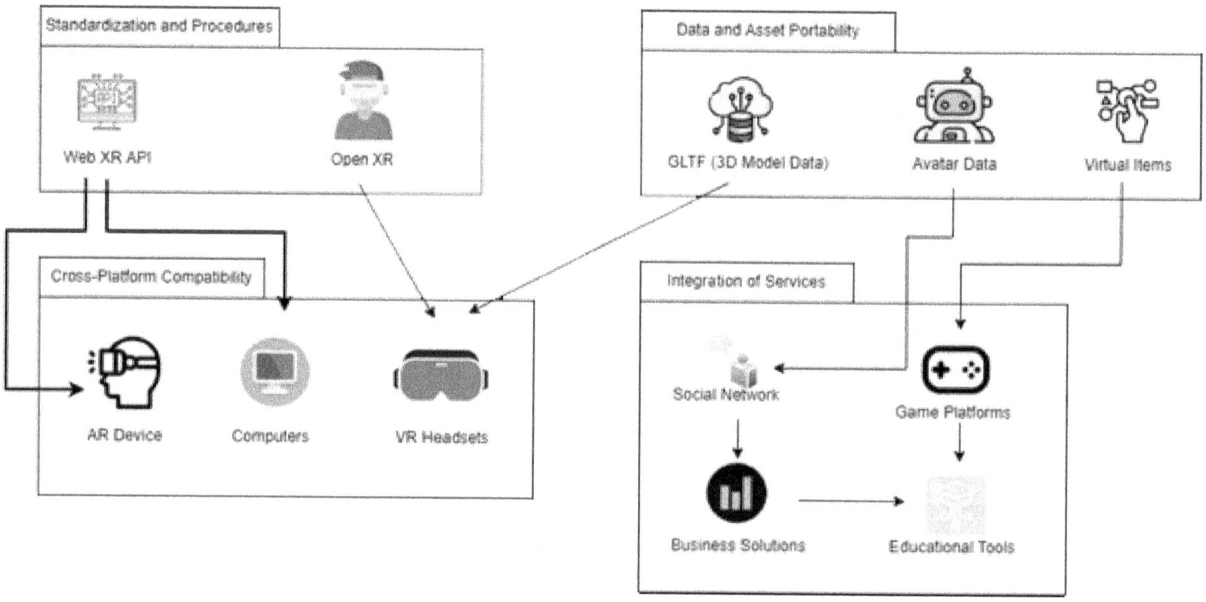


## 4.3 Data Privacy and Security Concerns

In the metaverse, where a lot of personal data and digital assets are saved and traded, data protection and security are important. Protecting user data and keeping trust are critical issues that need to be dealt with so that the metaverse can be used by many people.

**Personal Data Protection:** The metaverse records a lot of your confidential data, such as biometric data (like watching your eyes and facial expressions), behavioural data (like how you move and interact with others), and standard personal data (like your name and contact information). It is important to keep this info safe from people who should not be able to see or use it. Strong encryption methods, like end-to-end encryption, can keep data safe while it's being sent and stored. Metaverse systems must follow rules for data safety and privacy set by regulatory frameworks, such as the General Data safety Regulation (GDPR) in Europe.

**Identity for Users and Permission:** For privacy in the metaverse, it is important to keep users' identity and get their informed permission. Users should be able to choose who they share information with and what information they share. Privacy options and ways for users to give permission should be clear and simple to use. Users should be able to pick which apps or services can see their location or personal information, for example. There should also be clear information on platforms about how data will be kept and used.

**Security Threats and How to Reduce Them:** Hacking, data breaches, and identity theft are just some of the security threats that can happen in the metaverse. Strong cybersecurity means, like multi-factor authentication (MFA), intrusion detection systems (IDS), and regular security checks, are needed to keep the metaverse safe. Platforms should also teach users about possible dangers and how to stay safe, like how to spot scam attempts and keep personal devices safe (Zhang et al., 2024).

**Blockchain and Decentralization:** Blockchain technology and decentralized networks look like good ways to make the metaverse safer and more private. Blockchain can keep records of deals and assets that are clear and can't be changed. This lowers the risk of fraud and data manipulation. Multiple nodes can store and handle data on decentralized platforms. This lowers the risk of centralized data leaks and improves data sovereignty. For instance, blockchain-based virtual worlds like Decentral and use autonomous networks to handle who owns what and how interactions happen in virtual land and goods.

**Regulatory Compliance:** As the metaverse grows, regulatory compliance will become more and more important for keeping data safe and private. It's possible that governments and regulatory groups will make new laws and rules that apply only to virtual environments. Metaverse platforms need to keep up with these changes and make sure they follow the rules to protect users and stay out of trouble with the law. For ongoing compliance, it is necessary to work with legal professionals and keep an eye on the rules and regulations.

**Ethical Considerations:** The creation and use of the metaverse must be guided by more than just technical and legal issues. It is very important to make sure that data policies are clear, fair, and protect user rights. Ethical models should talk about things like who owns the data, how users give permission, and how personal data could be misused. Getting involved with users, developers, and lawmakers can help create moral standards that safeguard user interests and boost trust in the metaverse.

*Figure 4. Data privacy and security concerns*

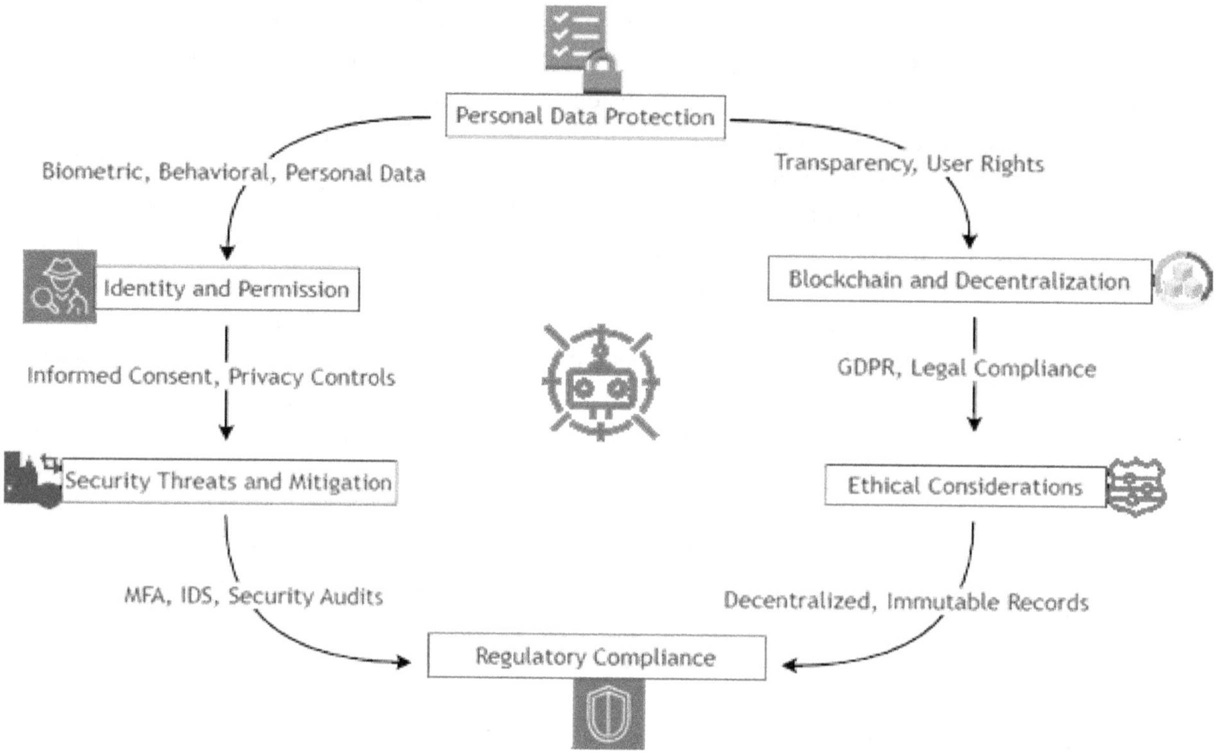


The meta universe's technological framework includes many important parts, such as the need for networks and platforms that can work together, as well as worries about data privacy and security. For the metaverse to reach its full potential as a changing digital place, it needs infrastructure that is strong, scalable, and safe. The metaverse can become a safe, welcoming, and ever-changing place for people all over the world by tackling these problems with new technologies, following the rules, and thinking about what is right and wrong as shown in Figure 4.

## 5. CHALLENGES AND OPPORTUNITIES

### 5.1 Scalability Issues

The metaverse's ability to serve an increasing number of users, interactions, and sophisticated virtual environments without diminishing performance depends critically on scalability—that is, its capacity as depicted in Figure 5. Solving scalability problems is crucial to provide a flawless and interesting user experience while the metaverse keeps growing.

**Infrastructure Demands:** The metaverse calls for a strong and wide-ranging infrastructure able to manage low latency needs, massive data volume, and real-time interactions. This means large expenditures on servers, data centers, and network capacity. Platforms for cloud computing include Microsoft Azure and Amazon Web Services (AWS) provide scalable resources that may be dynamically distributed depending on need. It is difficult to properly manage these resources, nevertheless, to accommodate peak demand while yet keeping cost-effectiveness (Ramadan et al., 2024).

**Network Bandwidth and Latency:** Demand for bandwidth rises dramatically as more people enter the metaverse and participate in data-intensive activities. Maintaining seamless and continuous experiences depends on fast internet connections. Furthermore, especially in VR and AR contexts, latency must be reduced if real-time interactions are to be maintained. Emerging as possible answers to these problems are 5G networks and edge computing technologies, which process data closer to the consumer thereby lowering latency and increasing speeds.

**Server Load Balancing:** Good load balancing is necessary to disperse the computational demand among several servers and stop any one server from turning into a bottleneck. Often used are horizontal scaling—where extra servers are added to distribute the load—and vertical scaling—where the capacity of current servers is raised. By dynamically allocating resources depending on real-time consumption patterns, innovative algorithms help to improve scalability and further maximize server performance.

**Data Synchronization:** Maintaining a coherent virtual environment depends on reliable and synced data across many devices and users. Real-time data replication methods and distributed databases help to accomplish this by guaranteeing that changes made by one user are promptly reflected for all other users. Technical difficulties in a distributed system, however, arise from controlling data consistency and resolving disputes.

**Content Delivery Networks (CDNs):** Material Distribution Networks (CDNs) are essential for effectively providing material to consumers by means of data cache and server data delivery from sites nearer to end users. This lowers latency and enhances the content delivery speed. Large files such as 3D models and high-definition videos—common in the metaverse—are especially easy for CDNs to handle. By distributing traffic from central servers and thereby lightening the stress on the core network, leveraging CDNs can improve scalability.

**User-Generated Content**: The metaverse mostly depends on user-generated material, which has special scaling difficulties. Platforms must be able to manage user dynamic content generation, modification, and sharing. Key are putting strong content management systems into use and guaranteeing effective storage and retrieval methods. Platforms also must handle problems with intellectual property rights, content moderation, and guaranteeing the quality and security of user-generated material.

**Cross-Platform Compatibility:** Scalability depends on guaranteeing cross-platform compatibility as the metaverse comprises several platforms and devices. Whether they utilize hardware or software, users should be able to easily access and engage with the metaverse. Achieving this may be done by means of developing standardized protocols and APIs enabling interoperability across many systems. True cross-platform compatibility, however, calls cooperation among developers, platform providers, and hardware producers.

*Figure 5. Scalability issues*

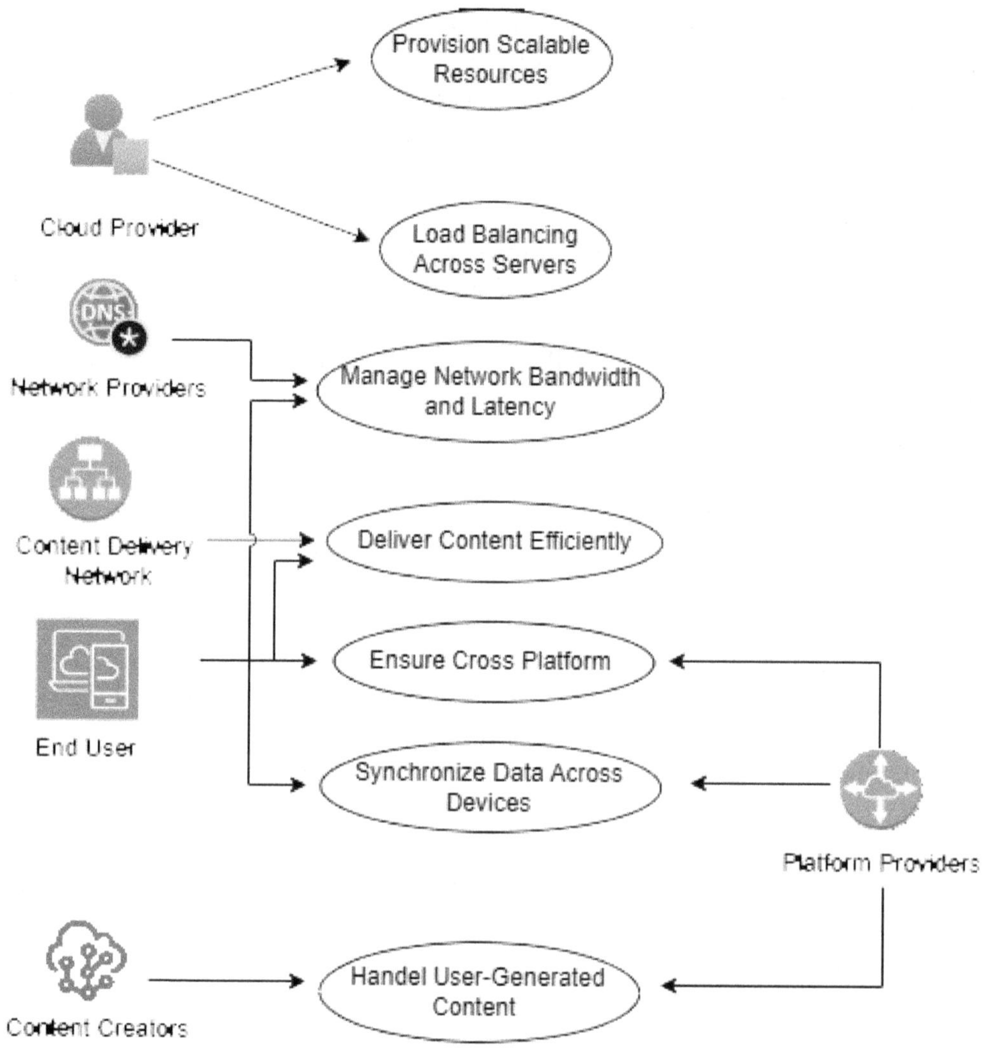


## 5.2 User Accessibility and Inclusivity

Success and longevity of the metaverse depend on its accessibility and inclusion for all users. This addresses social, cognitive, financial, and physical hurdles that can keep people from completely engaging in virtual settings.

**Physical Accessibility:** Many users of the metaverse have physical limitations that would make interaction difficult. Ensuring accessibility is building hardware and software that can meet certain physical requirements. For those with restricted movement or dexterity, VR headgear and controllers should be useable, for instance. Furthermore, improving accessibility for those with physical disabilities is using alternate input techniques like eye-tracking and voice control. To guarantee that interfaces are accessible and usable by persons with disabilities, platforms should also follow accessibility standards such the Web Content Accessibility Guidelines (WCAG).

**Cognitive Accessibility:** Users with cognitive disabilities might find it difficult to negotiate and comprehend intricate virtual worlds. Clear instructions, simple interfaces, and clever design let these users access the metaverse. Furthermore, improving accessibility is offering configurable user interfaces that let people change settings based on their requirements and preferences. Giving consumers in-world guidance and training will also help them to understand how to engage with virtual worlds.

**Economic Accessibility:** Many consumers might find great difficulty paying for the technology and software needed to enter the metaverse. Extremely costly are VR headsets, high-performance PCs, and consistent internet connections. Platforms can investigate means to make their products more reasonably priced, like creating less expensive equipment, giving financing choices, or granting subsidized access to low-income consumers. Using cloud-based solutions can also help consumers to enjoy premium experiences without requiring costly hardware.

**Cultural and Social Inclusivity**: The metaverse must be inclusive of several civilizations, languages, and social backgrounds. Developing an inclusive virtual environment depends on guaranteeing cultural representation and avoiding prejudices. To let users from all linguistic backgrounds engage naturally, platforms should include language support and translating tools. Furthermore, helping to stop harassment and discrimination is encouraging a polite and welcome society by means of moderation, reporting systems, and community norms.

**Education and Digital Literacy:** Improving digital literacy is crucial to make sure every user may completely engage in the metaverse. Giving people instruction on how to utilize VR and AR technology, negotiate virtual worlds, and produce content will enable them and lower entrance obstacles. Providing these tools and assistance may be much aided by educational institutions and community groups.

**User-Centered Design:** Creating inclusive and accessible virtual environments requires including users in the design and development process, so user-centered design is very vital. Accessibility challenges may be found and addressed using user-centered design techniques like usability testing and participatory design. To guarantee that their demands are satisfied, platforms should get comments from several user groups including those with impairments.

**Regulatory and Policy Support:** Governments and regulatory agencies may greatly help to encourage inclusiveness and accessibility in the metaverse. Policies requiring accessibility criteria and offering rewards for inclusive design will help platforms give these concerns top priority. Funding and support for research and development in accessibility technologies can also spur creativity and increase metaverse access overall.

## 5.3 Ethical Considerations in Virtual Communication

As the metaverse becomes more reliant on virtual communication, it is imperative to address ethical concerns in order to guarantee a digital environment that is safe, respectful, and equitable. These factors incorporate concerns regarding privacy, consent, behavior, and the societal consequences of virtual interactions.

**Privacy and Data Protection:** The metaverse necessitates the collection and processing of substantial quantities of personal data, such as biometric information, behavioral data, and social interactions. The security and privacy of this data are of the utmost importance. User information must be protected by platforms that implement robust data protection measures, including encryption, access controls, and regular security audits. Additionally, it is imperative that users comprehend and regulate the utilization of their data through the implementation of user consent mechanisms and transparent privacy policies.

**Autonomy and Consent:** In virtual communication, informed consent is a fundamental ethical principle. Users should have the ability to make informed judgments about their interactions and data sharing with the autonomy to do so. Platforms should furnish thorough and transparent details regarding their data collection, utilization, and storage procedures. In addition, users should be able to effortlessly monitor their privacy settings and revoke consent at any given moment. Consent mechanisms that are user-friendly and straightforward are essential for the preservation of user autonomy (Sun et al., 2023).

**Behaviour and Conduct:** The presence of a secure and respectful environment in the metaverse necessitates the resolution of issues related to behaviour and conduct. User well-being can be significantly impacted by hate speech, intimidation, and harassment. Platforms must establish comprehensive moderation and complaint systems to identify and rectify inappropriate conduct. The consistent enforcement and explicit communication of community guidelines and regulations of conduct are essential. Support resources are also crucial for cultivating a secure virtual environment for users who have been subjected to harassment or abuse (Chen, 2023).

**Digital Identity and Representation:** The manner in which users interact and convey themselves in the metaverse is dramatically influenced by avatars and virtual identities. To ensure that users have control over their digital identities and that these identities are respected by others, ethical considerations must be given consideration (Rahaman et al., 2024). Furthermore, it is imperative that platforms address concerns regarding identity theft and impersonation by instituting appropriate measures to safeguard and verify user identities. Ensuring that avatars and virtual representations are inclusive and do not perpetuate detrimental stereotypes is also a component of ethical design.

The metaverse's user experiences are significantly influenced by algorithms, which are responsible for content recommendations and moderation decisions. This is known as algorithmic bias and fairness. Promoting equity necessitates guaranteeing that these algorithms are impartial and equitable. It is imperative that platforms implement consistent audits to detect and rectify biases within their algorithms. In addition, user trust can be fostered by transparency regarding algorithms' operations and the criteria they employ. Also, it is crucial to engage with a variety of user groups in order to comprehend the effects of algorithms on various communities in order to advance equity.

In terms of mental health and well-being, the metaverse's immersive nature can have both positive and detrimental effects on users. Virtual environments can offer opportunities for social connection and support; however, they can also exacerbate problems such as tension, isolation, and addiction. It is imperative that platforms encourage the development of healthy utilization habits and offer users the necessary resources to effectively manage their mental health. Negative consequences may be alleviated by incorporating features that promote physical activity, social interaction, and occasional breaks.

The creation and sharing of digital content in the metaverse raise significant ethical concerns regarding intellectual property and content proprietorship. Creators must be guaranteed equitable compensation and the ability to maintain control over their work. Platforms should establish policies that are transparent and equitable in terms of content ownership, licensing, and monetization. Furthermore, Creators' rights must be safeguarded by addressing concerns regarding plagiarism and unauthorized content use.

**Implications for the Environment:** The metaverse's infrastructure necessitates substantial environmental impacts, such as electronic waste and energy consumption. One ethical consideration is the promotion of sustainability in the development and operation of virtual environments. Platforms may capitalize on renewable energy sources, implement energy-efficient technologies, and encourage the responsible disposal of electronic devices and recycling. Additionally, increasing awareness of the environmental consequences of digital technologies can motivate users to adopt more sustainable lifestyles.

**Influence on Social and Cultural Dynamics:** The metaverse has the capacity to significantly impact social and cultural dynamics. Virtual environments must facilitate positive cultural exchange and social interactions, among other ethical considerations. The cultural implications of their designs and practices should be considered by platforms, which should strive to avoid cultural appropriation and promote cultural sensitivity. Engaging with a variety of stakeholders and communities can contribute to the development of virtual spaces that are culturally respectful and inclusive.

The metaverse presents a multitude of opportunities and challenges. For the development of a sustainable and equitable metaverse, it is imperative to address scalability issues, ensure user accessibility and inclusivity, and navigate ethical considerations. By utilizing ethical frameworks, regulatory support, and technological innovation, stakeholders can collaborate to establish a digital future that is inclusive, secure, and advantageous for all users.

## 6. FUTURE TRENDS AND INNOVATIONS

### 6.1 Emerging Communication Technologies

The communication technologies landscape is undergoing a rapid evolution, with a plethora of innovations that are poised to revolutionize and improve our interactions within the metaverse. These emerging technologies have the potential to enhance the immersion, intuitiveness, and naturalness of virtual interactions.

**5G and Beyond:** The metaverse's communication is poised to undergo a revolution with the introduction of 5G networks, which will offer ultra-fast, low-latency connections. This advancement is essential for the support of high-quality VR and AR experiences, as it allows for real-time interactions without latency. In addition to 5G, research into 6G technology is being conducted to attain even greater bandwidth and connectivity, which could potentially support more complex and data-intensive virtual environments.

**Haptic Feedback:** The technology of haptics, which offers tactile feedback to consumers, is experiencing a surge in sophistication. Advanced haptic gloves and devices that simulate the sensation of contact are being developed by companies such as HaptX and Ultraleap. This technology enables users to experience textures, shapes, and forces in the virtual world. This technology has the potential to considerably improve the realism and immersion of virtual interactions, thereby increasing the level of engagement in activities such as virtual sculpting, gaming, and social contact.

**Brain-Computer Interfaces (BCIs):** BCIs are a new frontier in communication technology, allowing for direct interaction between the brain and digital devices. Implantable devices that can receive and interpret brain signals are being developed by companies such as Neuralink. In the metaverse, BCIs could enable users to interact with virtual environments and control avatars through thought alone, circumventing conventional input methods. This technology has the potential to revolutionize accessibility by enabling individuals with physical disabilities to completely participate in virtual environments.

**AI-Driven Avatars and Virtual Assistants:** Virtual communication is predicted to be significantly improved by artificial intelligence (AI). More personalized and responsive experiences can be achieved through AI-driven avatars that are capable of learning and adapting in response to user interactions. Virtual assistants, such as those that are equipped with natural language processing (NLP) technologies, can enhance communication by comprehending and responding to spoken or written commands in real time. These assistants are capable of facilitating the seamless interaction between users, managing duties, and navigating virtual environments.

**Volumetric Video:** This technology captures and renders three-dimensional video, enabling users to record and view holographic, realistic representations of objects and people. This technology is being advanced by companies such as Microsoft, which have established Mixed Reality Capture Studios. In the metaverse, volumetric video can be employed for virtual meetings, performances, and educational experiences, offering a level of realism and presence that transcends that of conventional video.

**Spatial Audio:** The integration of spatial audio technology, which generates a three-dimensional sound experience, is becoming increasingly prevalent in VR and AR systems. This technology enhances the authenticity and immersion of virtual environments by enabling users to perceive the direction and distance of sounds. Spatial audio is already being implemented by platforms such as AltspaceVR and VRChat to enhance communication, thereby facilitating more intuitive and natural conversations in virtual environments.

## 6.2 Potential Developments in VR and AR

The metaverse is fundamentally composed of virtual reality (VR) and augmented reality (AR) technologies, and their ongoing advancements are expected to expand the capabilities and experiences of virtual environments.

**Increased Visual Fidelity:** The visual fidelity of VR and AR experiences is expected to be significantly improved by advancements in display technology. High-resolution displays that offer a wider colour gamut, higher refresh rates, and a higher pixel density can mitigate the screen door effect and deliver more realistic visuals. Company's such as Varjo are creating VR devices with human-eye resolution, which can generate highly detailed and realistic virtual environments.

**Ergonomic and Lightweight Headsets:** The bulkiness and discomfort of headsets have been a challenge to the widespread adoption of VR. Future developments are intended to generate designs that are more ergonomic and lightweight. Innovations in optics and materials science, including micro-OLED displays and pancake lenses, can decrease the size and weight of headsets, thereby enhancing their comfort during extended use. It has been reported that Facebook (Meta) and Apple are developing next-generation headsets that prioritize wearability and comfort.

A continuation of the trend toward wireless and standalone VR and AR devices is probable. The appeal of untethered VR experiences has been evidenced by devices such as the Oculus Quest 2, which provide the freedom of movement necessary for VR without the need for a connected PC or console. It is probable that future iterations will emphasize enhanced connectivity, battery life, and computational capacity, thereby rendering them even more adaptable and accessible.

**Integration of Mixed Reality:** Mixed reality (MR), which integrates aspects of virtual reality (VR) and augmented reality (AR), is primed for substantial expansion. Users can engage with digital content that is superimposed on the physical world using MR headgear, such as the Microsoft HoloLens and the Magic Leap. The integration of virtual and physical spaces will be made more seamless through the implementation of more sophisticated spatial mapping, gesture recognition, and environmental interaction in future developments in MR technology.

**Facial Recognition and Eye-Tracking:** The ability to monitor a user's gaze through eye-tracking technology can substantially improve the quality of VR and AR experiences. Foveated rendering is enabled by this technology, which minimizes the graphical burden by rendering only the portion of the scene that the user is currently viewing. Companies such as Tobii are incorporating eye-tracking technology into VR headsets to facilitate more natural interactions and enhanced performance. By capturing and replicating users' facial expressions on their avatars, facial recognition technology can improve social interactions by offering more realistic and expressive representations.

**Tactile and Sensory Feedback:** Alongside haptic feedback, VR and AR may incorporate sophisticated sensory feedback technologies in the future. This may involve the use of devices that replicate temperature, pressure, or even scents, thereby delivering a more immersive and multi-sensory experience. Various methods are being investigated by researchers to incorporate these sensory inputs, with the potential to create virtual environments that engage all of the senses.

AR wearables, including smart spectacles and contact lenses, are anticipated to have a greater prevalence. Companies such as Apple, Google, and North (which was acquired by Google) are in the process of creating AR spectacles that add digital information to the physical world. By integrating the digital and physical realms in innovative and practical ways, these devices can offer hands-free access to information, navigation, and communication.

## 6.3 Forecasting the Future of Social Interaction in the Metaverse

In the metaverse, the potential for social interaction to revolutionize the way we communicate, collaborate, and connect is immense. The evolution of virtual interactions is expected to be influenced by a variety of trends and innovations, which will enhance their immersive Ness, engagement, and significance.

**Persistence of Virtual Worlds:** The concept of persistent virtual worlds, which are characterized by the existence and evolution of environments even when users are not signed in, will gain more prominence. These environments are capable of hosting continuous social activities, events, and experiences that users may participate in at any given moment. This persistence promotes a sense of community and continuity, as users can revisit familiar locations and engage in ongoing interactions.

**Social Hybrid Experiences:** The integration of virtual and physical social experiences will become more seamless. In the future, hybrid events will become increasingly prevalent, in which some participants are literally present while others participate virtually. The integration of technologies such as volumetric video and MR will facilitate these blended experiences, enabling users to interact in a natural manner, irrespective of their physical location. For instance, virtual concerts or conferences may involve attendees from various countries in addition to those stationed on-site.

**Decentralized Social Platforms:** The future of social interaction in the metaverse will be significantly influenced by blockchain technology and decentralized networks. Decentralized social platforms can facilitate peer-to-peer interactions, facilitate greater control over personal data, and reduce dependence on centralized authorities (Kakade et al., 2024). Crypto voxels and Decentral and are among the platforms that are currently investigating these concepts, which allow users to establish decentralized communities and own virtual real estate.

**Advanced Social AI:** Social interactions will be improved by AI-driven avatars and virtual companions, which will offer more personalized and responsive experiences. Advanced Social AI. These AI entities have the capacity to facilitate interactions between users, offer companionship, and assist with duties. With the ability to comprehend context, emotions, and social signals, advanced AI can facilitate more intuitive and natural virtual interactions. In virtual storefronts, for example, customer service agents that are powered by AI can offer personalized recommendations and assistance.

**Cultural and Linguistic Inclusivity:** Ensuring cultural and linguistic inclusivity will be essential as the metaverse expands globally. Users from diverse linguistic origins can engage in seamless communication using real-time translation services that are propelled by AI. Platforms will be required to consider cultural differences and sensitivities when creating virtual environments and interactions, thereby promoting a metaverse that is truly global and inclusive.

**Virtual Economies and Social Commerce:** The metaverse will be significantly impacted by virtual economies, which allow users to earn, spend, and trade virtual currencies and assets. In the future, social commerce will flourish, enabling users to purchase, trade, and exhibit virtual products. The trend of robust virtual economies is anticipated to continue, as evidenced by platforms such as Fortnite and Roblox. Users can partake in virtual marketplaces, monetize their creations, and engage in economic activities that are reminiscent of real-world commerce.

**Security and Privacy Improvements:** As the metaverse's social interactions become increasingly complex, it will be essential to prioritize security and privacy. Secure communication protocols, decentralized identity verification, and encryption advancements will safeguard users' interactions and data. The necessity for immersive social experiences must be balanced with the implementation of robust security measures by platforms to preserve trust and safety.

**Digital Wellness:** As consumers spend an increasing amount of time in virtual environments, it will be imperative to prioritize their digital wellness. To encourage healthy utilization patterns, platforms must incorporate features such as mental health resources, pauses, and time management tools. For the cultivation of a healthy virtual community, it will be imperative to promote positive social interactions and help users who are subjected to harassment or abuse.

**Interoperable Social Networks:** In the metaverse, future social networks will prioritize interoperability, enabling users to transition seamlessly between various virtual environments and platforms. Throughout a variety of environments, this interoperability will allow users to preserve their digital identities and social networking connections. Driven by collaborative endeavours to establish common standards and protocols, this trend will guarantee a metaverse that is both interconnected and cohesive.

## 7. CONCLUSION

In virtual settings, the metaverse marks a transforming change in our communication, interaction, and building of communities. Important issues covered include the technological developments and infrastructure required to enable the metaverse—that is, high-speed networks, platform compatibility, and strong data protection policies. Emphasizing their influence on the development of identity and social relationships, the functions of avatars and virtual worlds were underlined While ethical issues underlined the need of preserving user confidence and safety, scalability, user accessibility, and inclusiveness became clear as major difficulties. Emerging communication technologies, VR and AR breakthroughs, and the possibility for more social connections point to a dynamic and changing terrain that promises to significantly alter our digital experiences.

Looking ahead, the metaverse will probably become a necessary component of our everyday life providing until unheard-of chances for immersive communication, teamwork, and community formation. The lines separating actual and virtual worlds will dissolve as technology developments keep ahead, allowing more natural and logical interactions. This development affects sectors like education, healthcare, and business, therefore beyond entertainment and socializing. Stakeholders have to solve scalability, accessibility, and ethical issues while creating an inclusive and safe environment if they are to fully utilize the metaverse. Exciting opportunities for communication in the metaverse promise to revolutionize our digital age connection and interaction.

## REFERENCES


Bonfert, M., Reinschluessel, A. V., Putze, S., Lai, Y., Alexandrovsky, D., Malaka, R., & Döring, T. (2023). Seeing the faces is so important—Experiences from online team meetings on commercial virtual reality platforms. *Frontiers in Virtual Reality*, 3, 945791. Advance online publication. DOI: 10.3389/frvir.2022.945791

Chen, Y. (2023). MEC Network Resource Allocation Strategy Based on Improved PSO in 5G Communication Network. [IJSWIS]. *International Journal on Semantic Web and Information Systems*, 19(1), 1–17. DOI: 10.4018/IJSWIS.328526

Dwivedi, Y. K., Hughes, L., Baabdullah, A. M., Ribeiro-Navarrete, S., Giannakis, M., Al-Debei, M. M., Dennehy, D., Metri, B., Buhalis, D., Cheung, C. M. K., Conboy, K., Doyle, R., Dubey, R., Dutot, V., Felix, R., Goyal, D. P., Gustafsson, A., Hinsch, C., Jebabli, I., & Wamba, S. F. (2022). Metaverse beyond the hype: Multidisciplinary perspectives on emerging challenges, opportunities, and agenda for research, practice and policy. *International Journal of Information Management*, 66, 102542. DOI: 10.1016/j.ijinfomgt.2022.102542

Dwivedi, Y. K., Ismagilova, E., Hughes, D. L., Carlson, J., Filieri, R., Jacobson, J., Jain, V., Karjaluoto, H., Kefi, H., Krishen, A. S., Kumar, V., Rahman, M. M., Raman, R., Rauschnabel, P. A., Rowley, J., Salo, J., Tran, G. A., & Wang, Y. (2021). Setting the future of digital and social media marketing research: Perspectives and research propositions. *International Journal of Information Management*, 59, 102168. DOI: 10.1016/j.ijinfomgt.2020.102168

Hennig-Thurau, T., Aliman, D. N., Herting, A. M., Cziehso, G. P., Linder, M., & Kübler, R. V. (2023). Social interactions in the metaverse: Framework, initial evidence, and research roadmap. *Journal of the Academy of Marketing Science*, 51(4), 889–913. DOI: 10.1007/s11747-022-00908-0

Jain, D. K., Eyre, Y. G.-M., Akshi, K., Gupta, B. B., & Ketan, K. (2023). *Knowledge-based Data Processing for Multilingual Natural Language Analysis.* ACM Transactions on Asian and Low-Resource Language Information Processing., DOI: 10.1145/3583686

Kakade, M. S., Anupama, K. R., Nayak, S., & Garang, S. (2024). Custom Network Protocol Stack for Communication Between Nodes in a Cloudlet System. [IJCAC]. *International Journal of Cloud Applications and Computing*, 14(1), 1–24. DOI: 10.4018/IJCAC.339891

Mitra, S. (2023). Metaverse: A Potential Virtual-Physical Ecosystem for Innovative Blended Education and Training. *Journal of Metaverse*, 3(1), 1. Advance online publication. DOI: 10.57019/jmv.1168056

Praetorius, A. S., & Görlich, D. (2020). How Avatars Influence User Behavior: A Review on the Proteus Effect in Virtual Environments and Video Games. *Proceedings of the 15th International Conference on the Foundations of Digital Games*, 1–9. DOI: 10.1145/3402942.3403019

Rahaman, M., Lin, C.-Y., Pappachan, P., Gupta, B. B., & Hsu, C.-H. (2024). Privacy-Centric AI and IoT Solutions for Smart Rural Farm Monitoring and Control. *Sensors (Basel)*, 24(13), 13. Advance online publication. DOI: 10.3390/s24134157 PMID: 39000936

Ramadan, O. R. S., Afifi, M. Y. I., & Yahya, A. (2024). A Distributed Cloud Architecture Based on General De Bruijn Overlay Network. *International Journal of Cloud Applications and Computing*, 14(1), 1–19. DOI: 10.4018/IJCAC.339892

Rauschnabel, P. A., Felix, R., Hinsch, C., Shahab, H., & Alt, F. (2022). What is XR? Towards a Framework for Augmented and Virtual Reality. *Computers in Human Behavior*, 133, 107289. DOI: 10.1016/j.chb.2022.107289

Shinder, L., & Cross, M. (2008). The Evolution of Cybercrime. In Shinder, L., & Cross, M. (Eds.), *Scene of the Cybercrime* (2nd ed., pp. 41–75). Syngress., DOI: 10.1016/B978-1-59749-276-8.00002-9

Sun, L., Wang, P., Liu, P., & Nie, Z. (2023). Image Processing Method of a Visual Communication System Based on Convolutional Neural Network. [IJSWIS]. *International Journal on Semantic Web and Information Systems*, 19(1), 1–19. DOI: 10.4018/IJSWIS.333063

Thornhill-Miller, B., Camarda, A., Mercier, M., Burkhardt, J.-M., Morisseau, T., Bourgeois-Bougrine, S., Vinchon, F., El Hayek, S., Augereau-Landais, M., Mourey, F., Feybesse, C., Sundquist, D., & Lubart, T. (2023). Creativity, Critical Thinking, Communication, and Collaboration: Assessment, Certification, and Promotion of 21st Century Skills for the Future of Work and Education. *Journal of Intelligence*, 11(3), 54. DOI: 10.3390/jintelligence11030054 PMID: 36976147

Tukur, M., Schneider, J., Househ, M., Dokoro, A. H., Ismail, U. I., Dawaki, M., & Agus, M. (2023). The metaverse digital environments: A scoping review of the challenges, privacy and security issues. *Frontiers in Big Data*, 6, 1301812. DOI: 10.3389/fdata.2023.1301812 PMID: 38074486

Vaingankar, J. A., van Dam, R. M., Samari, E., Chang, S., Seow, E., Chua, Y. C., Luo, N., Verma, S., & Subramaniam, M. (2022). Social Media–Driven Routes to Positive Mental Health Among Youth: Qualitative Enquiry and Concept Mapping Study. *JMIR Pediatrics and Parenting*, 5(1), e32758. DOI: 10.2196/32758 PMID: 35254285

Zhang, T., Shen, J., Yang, H., Vijayakumar, P., Gupta, B. B., & Arya, V. (2024). Sustainable Authentication and Key Agreement Protocol Using Chaotic Maps for Industry 5.0. *IEEE Transactions on Consumer Electronics*, 70(1), 1580–1589. DOI: 10.1109/TCE.2023.3339818

# Chapter 4
# User Behavior and Interaction Patterns

**Ratna Yulika Go**
*Department of Informatic Engineering, Faculty of Computer Science, Universitas Esa Unggul, Jakarta, Indonesia*

## ABSTRACT

*This study explores user behavior and interaction patterns across digital platforms to understand engagement and responses in online environments. By analyzing data from social media, e-commerce sites, and mobile apps, the research identifies key factors affecting user decisions, such as content relevance, interface design, and social influence. It examines behavioral habits like browsing patterns, click-through rates, and time spent on activities to uncover trends and preferences. Interaction dynamics, including user-to-user communication, feedback mechanisms, and engagement with interactive elements, are evaluated for their impact on user experience. Findings reveal that user behavior is greatly influenced by navigation ease, personalized content, and community features, impacting retention and satisfaction. This research offers valuable insights for UX design, guiding the development of user-centered digital products and services. Understanding these behavior patterns is essential for enhancing user engagement and creating more effective and engaging digital experiences.*

## INTRODUCTION

### Overview of User Behavior and Interaction Patterns

In the digital landscape, understanding user behavior and interaction patterns has become increasingly vital for the development and optimization of online platforms, applications, and services. User behavior refers to the actions and decisions made by individuals when interacting with digital interfaces, such as websites, social media platforms, and mobile apps. These behaviors encompass a wide range of activities, including browsing, searching, clicking, sharing, purchasing, and more. Interaction patterns, on the other hand, describe the recurring sequences of actions users follow while engaging with digital

DOI: 10.4018/979-8-3693-8628-6.ch004

environments, including how they navigate through content, respond to interactive elements, and communicate with other users or the system itself (Cerezo et al., 2016).

The study of user behavior and interaction patterns offers valuable insights into how individuals engage with digital products and services, revealing their preferences, motivations, and pain points. By analyzing these patterns, designers, marketers, and developers can create more user-centric experiences that align with the needs and expectations of their target audiences. This analysis not only improves the usability and appeal of digital platforms but also enhances user satisfaction, loyalty, and overall engagement. In today's highly competitive digital market, the ability to attract and retain users is crucial for the success of any online platform (Sbeyti, 2016). User behavior and interaction patterns play a central role in determining whether a platform can achieve these goals. A deep understanding of how users interact with digital environments allows businesses to design interfaces that are intuitive, engaging, and tailored to the specific needs of their users. This understanding is particularly important as users are often faced with an overwhelming array of choices online, making it essential for platforms to stand out by offering superior user experiences (Yuan & Hsu, 2017).

Moreover, the importance of user behavior analysis extends beyond just improving the user interface (UI) or user experience (UX) design. It also informs strategic decision-making in areas such as content creation, marketing, and customer support. By recognizing how users behave and interact, companies can tailor their content strategies to deliver relevant and personalized information, optimize marketing campaigns to reach the right audiences, and enhance customer service by anticipating user needs and addressing potential issues before they arise (Dharmarajan & Dorairangaswamy, 2017). In addition, as digital environments continue to evolve with the integration of new technologies like artificial intelligence (AI), machine learning, and predictive analytics, understanding user behavior and interaction patterns becomes even more critical. These technologies rely on accurate behavioral data to deliver personalized experiences, predict future actions, and adapt to changing user preferences in real-time. Therefore, businesses that invest in understanding these patterns are better positioned to leverage emerging technologies and stay ahead in the digital economy (Fu et al., 2023).

## Objectives of the Chapter

The primary objective of this chapter is to provide a comprehensive analysis of user behavior and interaction patterns within digital environments (Ehatisham-ul-Haq et al., 2018). This analysis will be approached from both theoretical and practical perspectives, offering readers a deep understanding of the factors that influence user behavior and the implications of these behaviors for digital platform design and strategy.

Specifically, the chapter aims to:

- **Define and contextualize user behavior and interaction patterns:** By exploring the key concepts, theories, and principles that underpin user behavior in digital environments, the chapter will establish a foundational understanding necessary for more advanced analysis.
- **Identify and analyze the factors influencing user behavior:** The chapter will examine the various factors that shape user decisions and actions, including content relevance, interface design, social influence, and psychological drivers. These factors will be discussed in relation to their impact on user engagement and satisfaction.

- **Explore behavioral and interaction patterns across different digital platforms:** By analyzing how users interact with various digital interfaces, such as websites, social media platforms, and mobile apps, the chapter will highlight common patterns and trends that can inform the design and development of user-centric digital experiences.

By the end of this chapter, readers should have a well-rounded understanding of the complexities of user behavior and interaction patterns, as well as practical knowledge that can be applied to enhance the design and strategy of digital platforms (Patwardhan, 2017).

## THEORETICAL FOUNDATIONS

### Definitions and Key Concepts

To effectively analyze user behavior and interaction patterns, it is crucial to define several foundational terms and concepts. These include user behavior, interaction patterns, user experience (UX), user interface (UI), cognitive load, and user journey (Li et al., 2019).

### User Behavior

User behavior encompasses the spectrum of actions, decisions, and responses exhibited by individuals as they interact with digital environments. This includes activities such as navigating through websites, clicking links, making purchases, and engaging with content or other users. Understanding these behaviors is pivotal for developing digital products that align with user needs and expectations. Insights into user behavior enable designers and developers to tailor functionalities and design elements to enhance user satisfaction and engagement (Han et al., 2024).

### Interaction Patterns

Interaction patterns refer to the recurring sequences of actions that users perform while interacting with digital interfaces. These patterns often reflect users' navigational habits, responses to interactive elements, and task completion processes. Identifying and analyzing these patterns allows designers to create more intuitive and user-friendly interfaces by anticipating user needs and streamlining interactions. For example, recognizing that users frequently access certain features through specific navigation paths can inform the design of more efficient and accessible menu structures (Nie, 2022).

### User Experience (UX)

User Experience (UX) encompasses the overall experience a user has when interacting with a digital product. It includes all aspects of the interaction, such as emotional, psychological, and functional dimensions. A positive UX is characterized by ease of use, satisfaction, and high engagement levels, while a negative UX may lead to user frustration, confusion, and abandonment. Ensuring a positive UX involves creating interfaces that are not only functional but also enjoyable and aligned with users' expectations and needs (Alamsyah et al., 2018).

## User Interface (UI)

User Interface (UI) pertains to the visual and interactive elements that users engage with, including buttons, menus, icons, and layouts. The design of the UI significantly impacts how users interact with a digital product, affecting the efficiency and ease of navigation. A well-designed UI facilitates user interactions by providing clear, intuitive, and aesthetically pleasing elements, which directly influences the overall UX (Gokulapriya & Ganesh Kumar, 2019).

## Cognitive Load

Cognitive load refers to the mental effort required to process and understand information presented in a digital interface. High cognitive load can overwhelm users, leading to errors and dissatisfaction, while low cognitive load promotes a smoother and more enjoyable experience. Effective UX and UI design aim to minimize cognitive load by presenting information clearly and avoiding unnecessary complexity, thereby enhancing user efficiency and satisfaction (Mohamed & Saunier, 2015).

## User Journey

The user journey describes the path a user takes from their initial interaction with a digital product to the completion of their intended task. This journey typically involves multiple touchpoints and interactions. Understanding the user journey is essential for optimizing the overall UX, ensuring that the product meets user needs effectively at every stage, and identifying potential pain points or opportunities for improvement (Juhaňák et al., 2019).

These definitions and concepts provide a foundational understanding of the key elements involved in analyzing and designing user interactions. By grasping these fundamentals, designers and researchers can better address user needs, create intuitive interfaces, and enhance overall user satisfaction.

## Theories of User Behavior

Several theoretical frameworks have been developed to explain and predict user behavior in digital environments. These theories draw from disciplines such as psychology, sociology, and cognitive science, and provide valuable insights into the factors that influence how users interact with digital products (Du et al., 2020).

### 1. The Technology Acceptance Model (TAM)

The Technology Acceptance Model, developed by Davis in 1989, is one of the most widely used frameworks for understanding user behavior in digital environments. TAM posits that the likelihood of a user accepting and using a new technology is determined by two key factors: perceived usefulness (the degree to which a user believes that the technology will enhance their performance) and perceived ease of use (the degree to which a user believes that the technology will be easy to use). TAM has been extensively applied in studies of user behavior, particularly in the context of new software, apps, and online services (Du et al., 2020). The framework can be seen in Figure 1.

*Figure 1. The Technology Acceptance Model (TAM) framework*

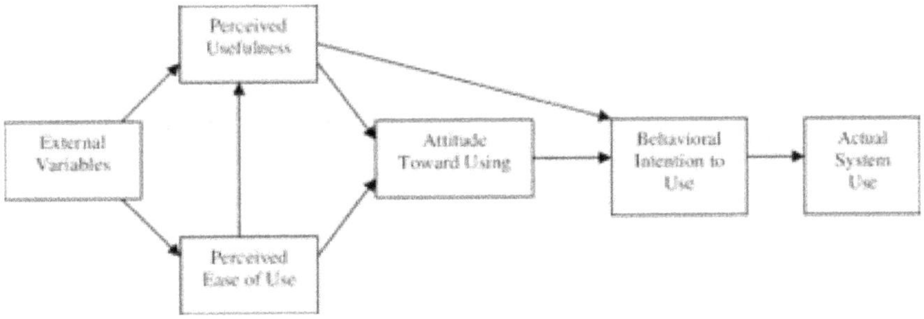


Here is an example case of adopting an ERP System in a Company. In this case, a large company aims to implement an Enterprise Resource Planning (ERP) system to unify various business functions like finance, HR, and logistics into a single platform. Using the Technology Acceptance Model (TAM), the company evaluates how the ERP system's perceived usefulness (PU) could enhance work efficiency and productivity by providing accurate and timely reports. Additionally, the perceived ease of use (PEOU) is assessed through training programs to ensure that employees find the new system intuitive and user-friendly. Surveys conducted before and after the ERP system's implementation help gauge employees' perceptions of its usefulness and ease of use. The company then uses this feedback to make necessary adjustments, improving the user experience and easing the transition to the new system.

## 2. The Theory of Planned Behavior (TPB)

The Theory of Planned Behavior, developed by Ajzen in 1991, extends the earlier Theory of Reasoned Action by adding the concept of perceived behavioral control. According to TPB, user behavior is influenced by three factors: attitudes toward the behavior (beliefs about the likely outcomes of the behavior), subjective norms (beliefs about the expectations of others), and perceived behavioral control (the perceived ease or difficulty of performing the behavior). TPB is particularly useful for understanding behaviors that are influenced by social factors, such as the decision to engage in online communities or participate in social media activities (Koreng & Krömker, 2021). The framework can be seen in Figure 2.

*Figure 2. Theory of Planned Behavior (TPB) framework*

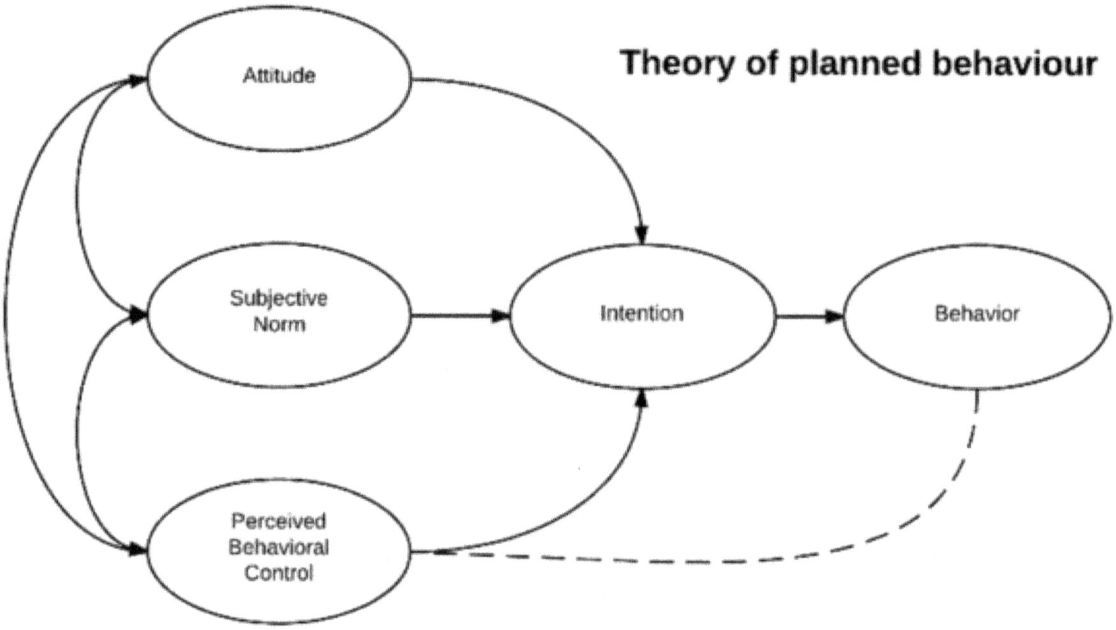


Here is an example case of Anti-Smoking Campaign. A public health organization launches a campaign aimed at reducing smoking rates among teenagers. The campaign employs the Theory of Planned Behavior (TPB) to influence behavior by addressing three key factors. First, it changes teenagers' attitudes towards smoking through targeted advertisements and educational content that highlight the health risks and negative consequences. Second, it shapes subjective norms by involving community leaders and celebrities who convey that smoking is socially unacceptable within their circles. Third, it enhances perceived behavioral control by offering resources such as counseling and smoking cessation programs to assist those who wish to quit. The effectiveness of the campaign is evaluated through surveys that measure changes in smoking intentions and actual smoking behavior, assessing the impact on attitudes, social norms, and perceived control.

## 3. The Fogg Behavior Model (FBM)

The Fogg Behavior Model, developed by B.J. Fogg, posits that three elements must converge simultaneously for a behavior to occur: motivation, ability, and triggers. Motivation refers to the user's desire to perform the behavior, ability refers to the user's capability to perform the behavior, and triggers are cues that prompt the behavior. The FBM is often used in the context of persuasive design, where the goal is to encourage users to adopt certain behaviors, such as signing up for a service or making a purchase (Kuflik et al., 2012). The framework can be seen in Figure 3.

*Figure 3. The Fogg Behavior Model (FBM) framework*

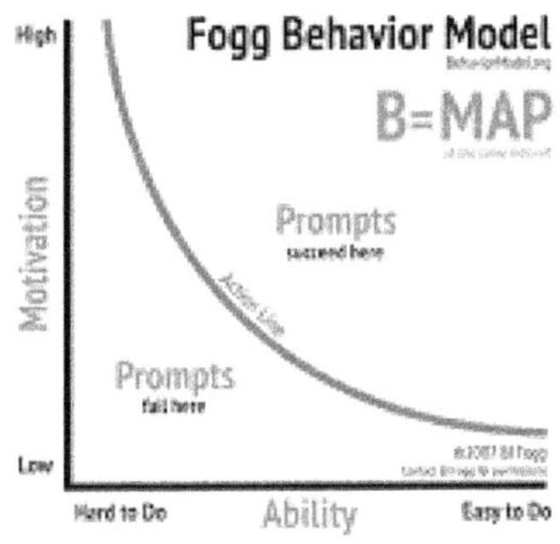


Here is an example case of Health App Design. A company develops a health app designed to help users establish and maintain healthy exercise habits. Applying the Fogg Behavior Model, the app focuses on three key elements to drive user behavior. Motivation is addressed through features like rewards, challenges, and gamification to engage users and encourage regular use. Ability is enhanced by providing easy-to-follow exercise guides and personalized plans tailored to individual fitness levels, making workouts more accessible and manageable. Triggers are incorporated in the form of reminders and notifications to prompt users to stay committed to their exercise routines. Analysis of user data reveals that these strategies effectively increase exercise frequency and duration, contributing to the development of healthier habits among users.

## 4. The Uses and Gratifications Theory (UGT)

The Uses and Gratifications Theory, originally developed in the context of mass media, has been adapted to study digital media usage. UGT suggests that users actively seek out media to satisfy specific needs and desires, such as entertainment, information, social interaction, or personal identity. In digital environments, this theory helps explain why users choose certain platforms or content and how they interact with them to fulfill their needs (Ku et al., 2019). The framework can be seen in Figure 4.

*Figure 4. The Uses and Gratifications Theory (UGT) framework*

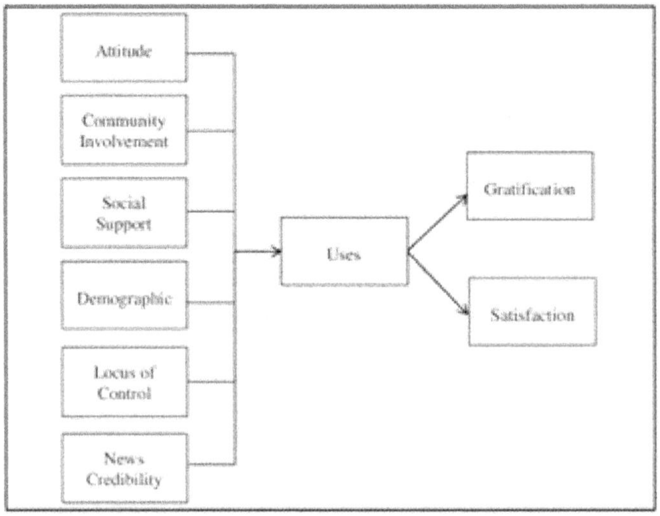


## 5. Cognitive Load Theory

Cognitive Load Theory, developed by Sweller, focuses on the mental effort required to learn new information or perform tasks. In the context of digital environments, this theory is applied to understand how the design of a user interface affects the cognitive load on users. By minimizing unnecessary complexity and presenting information in a clear, organized manner, designers can reduce cognitive load and improve the user experience (Khan et al., 2023). The framework can be seen in Figure 5.

*Figure 5. Cognitive Load Theory framework*

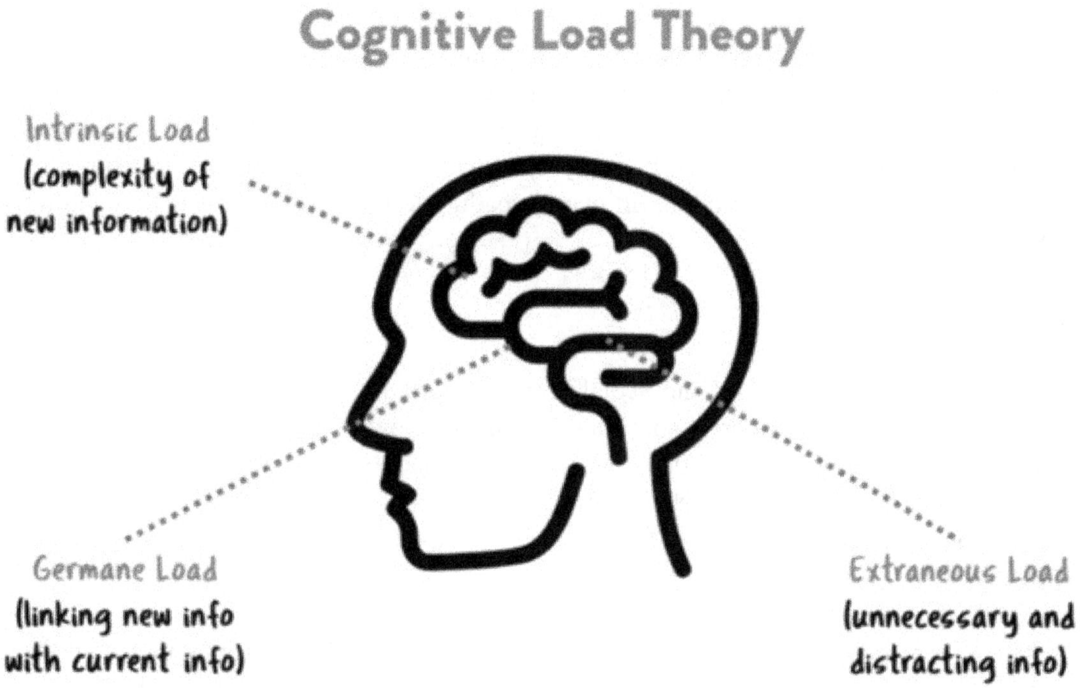


Here is a table summarizing the differences and main applications of the theory.

*Table 1. The differences and main applications of the theory*

| Aspect | Technology Acceptance Model (TAM) | Theory of Planned Behavior (TPB) | Fogg Behavior Model |
|---|---|---|---|
| **Primary Goal** | Understanding technology acceptance by users | Predicting an individual's intention to perform a behavior | Influencing behavior through three main elements |
| **Key Components** | - Perceived Usefulness (PU)<br>- Perceived Ease of Use (PEOU) | -Attitude<br>-Subjective Norms<br>-Perceived Behavioral Control | -Motivation<br>-Ability<br>- Triggers |
| **Research Focus** | Users' attitudes and intentions towards Technology Adoption | Psychological factors influencing behavioral intentions | Behavior change triggered by specific conditions |
| **Usage Context** | Technology acceptance and usage across various environments | Various behavioral decisions, especially in social and health domains | Digital product design and direct behavior change |
| **Determinant Factors** | -Perceived benefits<br>- Ease of use | -Attitudes<br>-Social norms<br>- Behavioral control | -Motivation<br>-Ability<br>- Triggers |

This table provides an overview of each model's goals, components, research focus, usage contexts, and determinant factors, highlighting their distinct approaches to understanding and influencing behavior.

## Interaction Design Principles

Interaction design principles are essential guidelines and best practices that shape the creation of effective and user-friendly digital interfaces. These principles are based on a deep understanding of user behavior and aim to enhance usability, accessibility, and overall user experience. They encompass strategies for designing intuitive navigation, providing clear feedback, and ensuring consistency across interfaces, all of which contribute to a seamless and engaging interaction. By adhering to these principles, designers can create digital products that not only meet users' needs and expectations but also foster a more efficient and enjoyable interaction, ultimately leading to higher user satisfaction and retention (Peng & Yu, 2016).

### 1. Affordance

Affordance refers to the perceived and actual properties of an object that determine how it can be used. In digital design, affordances are visual cues that suggest how a user can interact with an element, such as buttons that look clickable or sliders that look draggable. Proper use of affordances helps users understand how to interact with the interface intuitively.

### 2. Feedback

Feedback is the response a system provides to a user's actions, helping them understand the result of their interaction. Effective feedback can be visual (e.g., a button changing color when clicked), auditory (e.g., a notification sound), or haptic (e.g., vibration in a mobile device). Providing timely and appropriate feedback is crucial for maintaining user engagement and preventing confusion (Pollmann & Ziegler, 2021).

## METHODOLOGY

To collect data for research on user behavior and interaction patterns across digital platforms, a comprehensive methodology is essential. First, conduct a literature review to understand existing theories and models related to user behavior, which will help refine research questions and identify gaps in current knowledge. Additionally, conduct interviews and focus groups to gain qualitative insights into user motivations and attitudes, providing a deeper understanding of their interactions and experiences. User analytics tools should be used to collect objective data on user behavior, such as click-through rates and time spent on activities, offering valuable metrics on engagement. A/B testing can then be employed to evaluate the impact of different design elements on user behavior, allowing for comparisons between variations. Usability testing helps assess how intuitive and user-friendly a digital platform is by observing users as they complete specific tasks and collecting their feedback. Case studies provide an in-depth analysis of particular instances of user behavior, offering detailed insights into specific trends or issues. Finally, ethnographic studies involve observing users in their natural digital environments to understand their behaviors and motivations in context. Combining these methods ensures a robust and multifaceted approach to understanding user behavior and improving digital experiences.

## RESULTS AND DISCUSSION

### Factors Influencing User Behavior

Understanding the factors that influence user behavior is crucial for designing digital environments that effectively engage users and meet their needs. User behavior is shaped by a complex interplay of various elements, including the relevance of content, the design and usability of interfaces, social influences, and emotional and psychological drivers. Each of these factors contributes to how users interact with digital products and the overall experience they have (Wentzlaff & Specker, 2006).

### 1. Content Relevance

Content relevance is one of the most significant factors influencing user behavior. In the digital age, users are inundated with vast amounts of information, making it crucial for content to be highly relevant to their needs, interests, and contexts. Relevant content captures users' attention, encourages engagement, and drives them to take desired actions, such as clicking on links, sharing information, or making purchases. Personalization plays a key role in content relevance. By tailoring content to individual users based on their preferences, past behavior, and demographic information, digital platforms can provide a more engaging and satisfying experience (Ao et al., 2019). For instance, a restaurant recommendation app might prioritize nearby dining options during meal times, or a news app might highlight breaking news stories that are relevant to the user's location. Content that aligns with the user's immediate context is more likely to be perceived as valuable and useful (Liu et al., 2017).

### 2. Interface Design and Usability

Interface design and usability are critical components that directly impact how users interact with digital products. A well-designed interface not only facilitates ease of use but also significantly influences user satisfaction, engagement, and retention. Simplicity in design helps reduce cognitive load, allowing users to focus on their tasks without unnecessary distractions. Clear layouts, straightforward navigation, and unambiguous calls to action (CTAs) are essential for creating a user-friendly interface. When users can easily understand and interact with an interface, they are more likely to have a positive experience and complete their desired tasks efficiently. With the proliferation of devices such as smartphones, tablets, and desktops, responsive design has become a necessity. A responsive design ensures that a digital interface adapts seamlessly to different screen sizes and orientations, providing a consistent user experience across all devices. This adaptability is crucial for maintaining usability, as users increasingly switch between devices throughout their interactions with digital platforms (Märtin et al., 2016).

### 3. Social Influence and Peer Interactions

Social influence and peer interactions play a significant role in shaping user behavior in digital environments. Users are often influenced by the opinions, behaviors, and actions of others, whether through direct communication or observing trends and behaviors within their social networks. Social proof is a psychological phenomenon where people conform to the actions of others under the assumption that those actions reflect correct behavior (Tingting, 2020). In digital environments, social proof can take the form of user reviews, ratings, testimonials, and social media shares. For example, a product with numerous positive reviews on an e-commerce site is more likely to be perceived as trustworthy and desirable, influencing other users to make a purchase (Gupta et al., 2023).

### 4. Emotional and Psychological Drivers

Emotional and psychological drivers are fundamental aspects of user behavior, influencing how individuals interact with digital products on a deeper, often subconscious level. These drivers include emotions, motivations, cognitive biases, and psychological needs. Emotions play a powerful role in decision-making and user behavior. Positive emotions such as joy, excitement, and satisfaction can enhance user engagement and loyalty, while negative emotions like frustration, anxiety, or boredom can lead to abandonment. Designers often use emotional triggers strategically to create engaging experiences—such as incorporating gamification elements that evoke a sense of achievement or designing visually appealing interfaces that elicit pleasure (Rossi et al., 2017). Cognitive biases are systematic patterns of deviation from rationality in judgment, which can significantly influence user behavior. For example, the scarcity effect—where users perceive something as more valuable when it is limited—can drive urgency and prompt immediate action, such as making a purchase during a limited-time sale (Faison, 1998).

Digital environments often tap into fundamental psychological needs, such as the need for autonomy (control over one's actions), competence (a sense of achievement), and relatedness (connection with others). Platforms that fulfill these needs are more likely to engage users on a deeper level. For example, social media platforms fulfill the need for relatedness by enabling users to connect with friends and share personal experiences, while gamified systems fulfill the need for competence by offering challenges and rewards. User expectations are shaped by past experiences, cultural norms, and social influences, and they play a crucial role in determining how users interact with digital products. If a digital product meets or exceeds these expectations, users are likely to have a positive experience and continue using the product. Conversely, if expectations are not met, users may experience frustration and disengage. Understanding and managing user expectations is therefore essential for creating satisfying and effective digital experiences (Tang et al., 2024).

## Behavioral Patterns in Digital Environments

In digital environments, user behavior is not random but follows certain patterns that can be observed and analyzed to improve design, functionality, and user experience. Understanding these behavioral patterns helps in creating digital products that align with users' needs and expectations. Key patterns include browsing habits, decision-making processes, engagement dynamics, and multi-platform behavior (Askarizad & Safari, 2020).

### 1. Browsing Habits and Navigation

Browsing habits refer to the way users explore digital content, moving from one piece of information to another, often without a predetermined goal. Navigation involves how users find their way through a digital product, such as a website or an app, to locate the information or tools they need (Vellingiri et al., 2015).

- **Scanning vs. Reading:** Users often scan digital content rather than reading it word for word. They look for keywords, headings, and other visual cues that stand out. This scanning behavior means that content needs to be well-organized with clear headings, bullet points, and concise paragraphs to capture attention quickly. Designers must ensure that key information is easily accessible at a glance.
- **F-pattern and Z-pattern:** Eye-tracking studies have revealed common patterns in how users scan web pages. The F-pattern is typical for text-heavy content, where users first scan the top horizontal line (the headline), then move down slightly and scan another horizontal line (subheadings), and finally, scan down the left side of the content. The Z-pattern is common on pages with less text and more images, where users follow a Z-shaped path starting from the top left, moving horizontally to the top right, then diagonally down to the bottom left, and finally horizontally to the bottom right. Understanding these patterns can help designers place important elements where users are most likely to see them.
- **Navigation Menus and Links:** Effective navigation is crucial for a positive user experience. Users tend to favor simple, intuitive navigation menus that are easy to understand and use. Drop-down menus, breadcrumb trails, and consistent placement of navigation elements across pages help users find their way without confusion. Clear, descriptive labels and logically organized links reduce cognitive load and prevent users from getting lost.

## 2. Decision-Making Processes

The decision-making process in digital environments involves how users make choices, such as selecting a product, subscribing to a service, or interacting with content. This process is influenced by various factors including the design of the interface, the information provided, and the user's goals (Xi Liu Chaogui Kang & Liu, 2016). Digital environments often present users with a vast array of choices, leading to information overload. When overwhelmed, users may struggle to make decisions or may resort to simplifying strategies, such as choosing the first option or relying on recommendations. Designers can help mitigate information overload by organizing content logically, using filters and categories, and providing clear comparisons (Godon et al., 2011).

A/B testing involves presenting users with two different versions of a webpage or app interface to see which one performs better. This testing method is often used to optimize decision-making processes by determining which design elements, such as button colors, text, or layouts, lead to higher conversion rates. Continuous testing and refinement based on user data help improve decision-making experiences. Trust is a critical factor in decision-making, especially when it involves transactions, sharing personal information, or committing to a service. Users are more likely to make a decision if they perceive the platform as trustworthy. Elements that build trust include secure payment systems, clear privacy policies, user testimonials, and professional design. Establishing credibility through these means can significantly influence user decisions (Wang et al., 2016).

## 3. Engagement and Interaction Dynamics

Engagement refers to the depth of user involvement with digital content or platforms, while interaction dynamics describe how users interact with digital products, including the frequency, duration, and nature of these interactions. Users can be actively engaged, such as when they participate in a discussion, share content, or customize a product, or passively engaged, such as when they consume content without interaction. Active engagement is generally more desirable as it indicates a higher level of user investment and can lead to greater retention and loyalty. Encouraging active participation through interactive features, challenges, or incentives can enhance user engagement (Jeong, 2005). Gamification involves applying game-like elements to non-gaming environments to increase user engagement. This can include points, badges, leaderboards, and challenges that motivate users to interact more frequently and intensively with the platform. Gamification taps into users' desire for achievement and competition, driving deeper engagement and longer interaction times. Social features, such as comments, likes, shares, and user-generated content, foster a sense of community and encourage ongoing interaction. Users are more likely to engage with content that others have interacted with, creating a feedback loop of increasing engagement. Integrating social dynamics into digital environments can significantly enhance user interaction and retention. The frequency and recency of user interactions are key indicators of engagement (Fatahi et al., 2018). High-frequency interactions, such as daily logins or regular content consumption, suggest strong user engagement (Johann Füller Katja Hutter & Matzler, 2014).

## 4. Interaction Patterns

Interaction patterns are the ways in which users engage with digital products and systems, reflecting how they communicate and interact with both other users and the system itself. These patterns include user-to-user interactions, user-system interactions, feedback loops, and the impact of personalization. Analyzing these patterns provides valuable insights into enhancing user experience and engagement (Gui & MacGill, 2018). User-to-user interactions involve the ways users communicate, collaborate, and influence each other within digital environments. These interactions are central to many social, collaborative, and community-driven platforms. Social networking platforms like Facebook, Twitter, and LinkedIn facilitate various forms of user-to-user interaction, including posts, comments, likes, and shares. These interactions help users connect with others, share information, and engage in discussions. Effective design of social features, such as notifications, tagging, and messaging, enhances these interactions and fosters a sense of community (Jorritsma et al., 2016). Collaborative tools such as Slack, Microsoft Teams, and Google Workspace enable users to work together on projects, share files, and communicate in real time. Features like group chats, file sharing, and collaborative editing support seamless teamwork. Designing these tools to facilitate easy communication and efficient collaboration is crucial for maintaining productivity and user satisfaction. Community forums and discussion boards, such as Reddit or specialized industry forums, provide spaces for users to exchange knowledge, seek advice, and discuss topics of interest. The design of these forums, including thread organization, search functionality, and moderation tools, impacts the quality and efficiency of user-to-user interactions. Ensuring clear and intuitive navigation and fostering a positive environment are key to successful community engagement (Yang, 2022).

User-system interactions focus on how users interact with the digital system itself, including how they input information, navigate through interfaces, and receive feedback from the system. The UI design determines how users interact with the system, including how they input data, navigate menus, and access features. Effective UI design involves clear labeling, intuitive controls, and responsive elements that make interactions smooth and efficient. Designing for ease of use, accessibility, and visual appeal is crucial for enhancing user satisfaction. Feedback mechanisms, such as visual cues, sounds, and haptic responses, inform users about the system's response to their actions. For example, a button might change color when clicked, or a form might display a success message upon submission. Providing timely and clear feedback helps users understand the consequences of their actions and prevents errors. How a system handles errors and provides error messages is an essential aspect of user-system interactions. Clear, constructive error messages that guide users on how to correct issues can improve user experience and reduce frustration. Designing robust error handling and support systems helps users navigate problems effectively and maintain confidence in the system (W. Zhang et al., 2019).

Users often expect systems to adapt to their preferences and needs. Customization options, such as adjustable settings, themes, and personalized content, enhance user satisfaction by allowing individuals to tailor their experience. Personalization algorithms that recommend content or features based on user behavior and preferences further improve interaction by providing relevant and engaging experiences. Adaptive systems use data and analytics to adjust their behavior based on user interactions. For example, a recommendation engine might suggest products based on previous searches and purchases. Designing adaptive systems that respond dynamically to user needs can enhance engagement and create a more personalized experience. Feedback loops involve the continuous exchange of information between users and the system, which influences future interactions and engagement. Effective feedback loops are essential for maintaining user interest and improving user experience (Yu et al., 2019). Providing mechanisms for users to offer feedback, such as surveys, ratings, and comments, allows them to share their experiences and suggestions. Collecting and analyzing user feedback helps identify areas for improvement and informs design decisions. Ensuring that feedback mechanisms are easy to access and use encourages more users to participate. How a system or platform responds to user feedback is crucial for maintaining engagement. Acknowledging and acting on feedback demonstrates that user input is valued and can lead to positive changes.

Personalization enhances user engagement and satisfaction by making interactions more relevant and meaningful. Personalization algorithms that recommend content based on user preferences, past behavior, and contextual factors can increase user engagement (Shen et al., 2020). For example, streaming services like Netflix use personalization to suggest movies and shows that align with users' viewing history, enhancing their experience and encouraging continued use. Personalized marketing campaigns, such as targeted ads and promotions, reach users with relevant offers and messages. By analyzing user data and behavior, marketers can deliver customized promotions that are more likely to resonate with individual users, leading to higher conversion rates and improved customer satisfaction. Personalization can extend to the design of interfaces, allowing users to customize layouts, themes, and settings according to their preferences. Adaptive interfaces that adjust based on user behavior and interactions create a more comfortable and intuitive experience, increasing user satisfaction and engagement. Leveraging data from user interactions to gain insights into preferences, habits, and needs allows for more effective personalization. By analyzing patterns in user behavior, systems can deliver tailored experiences that address individual preferences, leading to more relevant and engaging interactions (David Codish & Ravid, 2019).

While personalization enhances user experience, it also raises concerns about privacy and data security. Ensuring that users have control over their data, understand how it is used, and can opt in or out of personalization features is essential for building trust and maintaining user confidence. Analyzing real-world case studies provides valuable insights into the successful implementation of interaction patterns and personalization strategies. Examining how leading platforms have leveraged these concepts can offer practical applications and lessons for improving user experience. Platforms such as Amazon, Facebook, and Spotify offer successful examples of integrating interaction patterns and personalization. Amazon's recommendation engine, Facebook's social interactions and algorithms, and Spotify's personalized playlists demonstrate how understanding user behavior and preferences can drive engagement and satisfaction. UX design principles informed by behavioral insights can lead to more effective and engaging digital products. Case studies of companies like Airbnb and Dropbox show how applying behavioral research to design decisions can enhance user experience, increase conversion rates, and improve overall satisfaction (Z. Zhang et al., 2019). Strategies such as gamification, personalized recommendations, and seamless multi-platform experiences have proven effective in enhancing user engagement. Examining how companies like Duolingo and Slack have implemented these strategies provides practical examples of how to create engaging and user-centered digital environments. The iterative design process, informed by user feedback and behavioral data, is crucial for continuous improvement. Case studies of platforms that have successfully implemented iterative design, such as Google and LinkedIn, highlight the importance of ongoing optimization and responsiveness to user needs. Balancing personalization with privacy considerations is essential for maintaining user trust. Case studies of companies that have navigated this balance, such as Apple and Microsoft, offer insights into how to implement effective personalization while respecting user privacy and data security.

## Challenges and Considerations

In the real of user behavior and interaction patterns, several critical challenges and considerations must be addressed to ensure ethical and effective design and analysis. This section explores these challenges, focusing on ethical considerations, privacy concerns, and the need to address diverse user needs (Nie, 2022).

### 1. Ethical Considerations in User Behavior Analysis

- **Informed Consent:** Users must be adequately informed about how their data will be collected, used, and analyzed. This involves providing clear, transparent information about data practices and obtaining explicit consent before gathering data. Informed consent ensures that users understand and agree to how their information will be used, fostering trust and compliance with ethical standards.
- **Data Integrity and Accuracy:** Maintaining the integrity and accuracy of collected data is crucial for valid analysis and decision-making. Ethical considerations involve using reliable methods for data collection and ensuring that the data is accurately represented. Misrepresenting or manipulating data can lead to incorrect conclusions and potentially harm users.
- **Avoiding Manipulation:** Analysis of user behavior should not lead to manipulative practices. This includes avoiding the exploitation of psychological biases or vulnerabilities to drive engagement or revenue. Ethical design focuses on creating positive user experiences without resorting to manipulative tactics.
- **Transparency and Accountability:** Organizations must be transparent about their data collection and analysis practices and hold themselves accountable for their actions. This includes providing users with access to their data, offering options to modify or delete their information, and clearly communicating how data is used to inform system decisions.
- **Bias and Fairness:** Ensuring that data analysis and algorithmic decisions do not reinforce biases or result in unfair treatment is essential. Ethical practices involve using diverse datasets, continuously evaluating algorithms for bias, and striving for fairness in decision-making processes.

## 2. Privacy Concerns

Protecting user data from unauthorized access and breaches is a fundamental privacy concern. Implementing robust security measures, such as encryption, secure storage, and access controls, helps safeguard sensitive information and prevent data breaches. Adhering to the principle of data minimization involves collecting only the data necessary for specific purposes and avoiding excessive data collection (Sbeyti, 2016). This approach reduces the risk of data misuse and enhances user privacy by limiting the scope of data collection. Techniques such as anonymization and de-identification help protect user privacy by removing or obscuring personal identifiers in the data. These methods allow for useful analysis while minimizing the risk of re-identifying individuals. Providing users with control over their data is essential for respecting privacy. This includes offering options for users to access, modify, or delete their information, and allowing them to opt-in or opt-out of data collection and personalization features (Fu et al., 2023). Compliance with data protection regulations, such as the General Data Protection Regulation (GDPR) and the California Consumer Privacy Act (CCPA), is crucial for maintaining privacy standards. Adhering to these regulations ensures that privacy practices align with legal requirements and industry standards (Cerezo et al., 2016).

## 3. Addressing Diverse User Needs

Designing digital products that are accessible to users with disabilities is a key consideration. This includes adhering to accessibility standards, such as the Web Content Accessibility Guidelines (WCAG), and incorporating features like screen readers, alternative text for images, and keyboard navigation to ensure an inclusive experience for all users. Understanding and accommodating cultural differences in user behavior, preferences, and expectations is essential for creating effective digital experiences. This involves localizing content, supporting multiple languages, and designing with cultural relevance in mind. Users have varying preferences for personalization. Offering customizable options allows users to tailor their experiences according to their needs and preferences (Dharmarajan & Dorairangaswamy, 2017). This can include adjustable settings, personalized content, and user-driven interface modifications. Considering the context in which users interact with digital products is important for creating relevant experiences. Factors such as location, device type, and usage scenario influence user behavior and should be incorporated into the design to enhance usability and engagement. Regularly collecting feedback from diverse user groups and iterating based on their needs helps ensure that digital products remain effective and responsive (Ehatisham-ul-Haq et al., 2018). Engaging with a wide range of users during the design process and continuously refining based on their input supports the development of inclusive and user-centered experiences.

Addressing these challenges and considerations ensures that user behavior analysis and interaction design are ethical, respectful of privacy, and inclusive of diverse needs. By focusing on these aspects, designers and researchers can create digital experiences that are both effective and responsible, fostering positive user interactions and outcomes (Li et al., 2019).

## Future Trends in User Behavior and Interaction Patterns

As digital environments evolve, several emerging trends are set to shape user behavior and interaction patterns. Understanding these trends is crucial for designers and researchers to create relevant and forward-thinking experiences. This section explores key future trends, including the impact of AI and predictive analytics, the role of emerging technologies, and the anticipation of changes in user behavior (Koreng & Krömker, 2021). Artificial Intelligence (AI) and predictive analytics are revolutionizing how user behavior is understood and anticipated. These technologies offer powerful tools for enhancing user experiences and optimizing interactions. AI algorithms can analyze vast amounts of data to deliver highly personalized experiences. Predictive analytics enables systems to anticipate user needs and preferences based on past behavior, leading to more tailored content, recommendations, and interactions. For example, streaming services like Netflix and Spotify use AI to recommend content based on users' viewing or listening history. Predictive models can forecast user behavior, such as purchasing patterns or content engagement, allowing businesses to make data-driven decisions (Ku et al., 2019). These insights can inform marketing strategies, product development, and user experience design, ensuring that offerings align with user expectations and trends. AI can automate routine tasks, such as customer support through chatbots or virtual assistants, improving efficiency and user satisfaction. These systems can handle common queries and provide instant responses, freeing up human resources for more complex interactions. Advanced analytics tools powered by AI can uncover deep insights into user behavior, identifying patterns and trends that might not be immediately apparent. This information helps in understanding user motivations, optimizing interfaces, and enhancing overall user experience (Liu et al., 2017). As AI becomes more integrated into user interactions, ethical considerations regarding data use, transparency, and algorithmic fairness are increasingly important. Ensuring that AI systems are used responsibly and ethically will be crucial for maintaining user trust.

Emerging technologies are reshaping how users interact with digital environments, introducing new possibilities and challenges. AR overlays digital information onto the physical world, creating immersive and interactive experiences. Applications in gaming, retail, and education demonstrate AR's potential to enhance user engagement and provide contextually relevant information. VR creates fully immersive digital environments, offering new ways for users to interact with content and each other. From virtual meetings and training simulations to entertainment and social experiences, VR is expanding the boundaries of user interaction. IoT connects everyday devices to the internet, enabling seamless interaction between the physical and digital worlds (Pollmann & Ziegler, 2021). Smart home devices, wearables, and connected vehicles are examples of how IoT is enhancing user convenience and creating new interaction opportunities. The rollout of 5G technology promises significantly faster internet speeds and lower latency, enhancing real-time interactions and supporting more complex applications. 5G will facilitate advancements in AR, VR, and IoT by providing the necessary bandwidth and responsiveness. Blockchain technology offers new approaches to data security and transparency, with potential applications in user identity management and transaction verification. Decentralized systems can empower users with greater control over their data and interactions (El-Ansary, 2002).

By staying attuned to these future trends, designers and researchers can anticipate changes in user behavior, leverage emerging technologies, and harness the power of AI and predictive analytics to create engaging and relevant digital experiences. Embracing these trends will ensure that digital products remain at the forefront of innovation and meet evolving user expectations (Liu et al., 2017).

## CONCLUSION

In examining user behavior and interaction patterns, this chapter provides a comprehensive overview of the factors influencing how users engage with digital environments. The insights gained underscore the importance of understanding these patterns for designing effective and engaging digital experiences.

### Summary of Key Insights

- **Diverse Interaction Patterns:** User behavior encompasses a range of interaction patterns, including browsing habits, decision-making processes, and engagement dynamics. Understanding these patterns helps in designing interfaces that align with user expectations and improve usability.
- **Influence of Design and Personalization:** Effective interface design and personalization significantly impact user interaction. Clear, intuitive designs and personalized experiences enhance user satisfaction, engagement, and loyalty. Personalization must be balanced with privacy considerations to maintain trust.
- **Challenges and Ethical Considerations:** Ethical considerations, including informed consent, data privacy, and avoidance of manipulation, are critical in user behavior analysis. Designers must navigate these challenges to ensure responsible and user-centric practices.
- **Future Trends and Technologies:** Emerging technologies such as AI, AR, VR, and IoT are shaping the future of user interactions. Anticipating changes in user behavior and adapting to technological advancements are essential for staying relevant and competitive.

### Implications for Designers and Marketers

Understanding the trends and challenges in user behavior and interaction patterns carries significant implications for designers and marketers. By adopting user-centered design principles, practicing ethical data handling, leveraging emerging technologies, and embracing continuous improvement, professionals can create effective and engaging digital experiences.

### User-Centered Design

Adopting a user-centered approach is crucial for designing interfaces and experiences that genuinely meet user needs and preferences. Key aspects include:

- **Accessibility:** Designing for accessibility ensures that digital products are usable by people with diverse abilities. This involves adhering to accessibility standards, such as the Web Content Accessibility Guidelines (WCAG), and incorporating features like keyboard navigation, screen readers, and alternative text for images. Accessible design not only complies with legal requirements but also expands the reach of digital products to a broader audience.
- **Personalization:** Personalization enhances user engagement by tailoring content and interactions based on individual preferences and behaviors. By leveraging data insights, designers can create customized experiences that resonate with users. This can include personalized recommendations, adaptive content, and user-specific settings that cater to individual needs and enhance satisfaction.

- **Seamless Multi-Platform Experiences:** Users interact with digital products across various devices and platforms, including smartphones, tablets, desktops, and wearables. Designing for a seamless multi-platform experience ensures consistency and continuity across different touchpoints. This involves creating responsive designs that adapt to different screen sizes and maintaining a cohesive user experience across platforms.
- **Empathy and Usability Testing:** Understanding user needs through empathy and conducting usability testing are essential for refining designs. Engaging with users through surveys, interviews, and testing sessions provides valuable feedback and insights, allowing designers to make informed decisions and create more intuitive and user-friendly interfaces.

## Ethical Practices

Implementing ethical practices in data collection, analysis, and personalization is essential for building trust and fostering positive user experiences. Key considerations include:

- **Transparency:** Being transparent about data collection practices, usage, and storage helps build trust with users. Clear communication about how data is used and providing users with access to their information are crucial for maintaining transparency.
- **User Control:** Empowering users with control over their data is fundamental to ethical design. This includes offering options to opt-in or opt-out of data collection, allowing users to modify or delete their information, and providing clear privacy settings. User control enhances trust and ensures that users have agency over their personal data.
- **Fairness and Non-Manipulation:** Avoiding manipulative practices that exploit psychological biases or vulnerabilities is crucial. Designing with fairness in mind involves ensuring that algorithms and personalization efforts do not lead to discrimination or unfair treatment. Ethical practices focus on creating positive user experiences without compromising user rights or well-being.
- **Compliance with Regulations:** Adhering to data protection regulations, such as GDPR and CCPA, is necessary for ensuring compliance and protecting user privacy. Designers and marketers should stay informed about legal requirements and integrate them into their practices to avoid legal issues and maintain ethical standards.

## Leveraging Emerging Technologies

Leveraging emerging technologies can enhance user engagement and provide innovative experiences. Key considerations include:

- **AI and Predictive Analytics:** Utilizing AI and predictive analytics allows for advanced personalization and insights into user behavior. Designers and marketers can use these technologies to create more relevant content, anticipate user needs, and optimize interactions based on data-driven insights.
- **AR and VR:** Augmented Reality (AR) and Virtual Reality (VR) offer immersive and interactive experiences that can significantly enhance user engagement. Integrating AR and VR into digital products can provide new ways for users to interact with content, explore virtual environments, and participate in novel experiences.

- **IoT Integration:** The Internet of Things (IoT) connects devices and enables seamless interactions between physical and digital worlds. Designers should consider how IoT can be integrated into their products to enhance convenience and create cohesive experiences that span multiple devices and contexts.
- **5G Technology:** The advent of 5G technology offers faster speeds and lower latency, enabling more responsive and real-time interactions. Designers and marketers should explore how 5G can enhance user experiences, particularly for applications that require high performance and instant feedback.
- **Continuous Improvement:** Continuous improvement involves regularly collecting and analyzing user feedback, monitoring engagement metrics, and iterating based on insights. This iterative approach ensures that digital products remain effective and responsive to user needs:
- **User Feedback Collection:** Gathering feedback through surveys, user testing, and analytics provides valuable insights into user experiences and areas for improvement. Regularly engaging with users and listening to their feedback helps identify pain points and opportunities for enhancement.
- **Monitoring Metrics:** Tracking key engagement metrics, such as user activity, conversion rates, and retention, helps assess the effectiveness of design and marketing strategies. Analyzing these metrics provides insights into user behavior and the impact of design changes.

By focusing on user-centered design, ethical practices, leveraging emerging technologies, and embracing continuous improvement, designers and marketers can create digital experiences that meet user needs, respect privacy, and adapt to evolving trends. This holistic approach ensures that digital products remain engaging, effective, and aligned with user expectations.

## Future Directions for Research

Analyzing user behavior in complex digital environments presents several specific challenges. Firstly, the variability in user behavior, influenced by context, devices, and environments, can make it difficult to identify consistent patterns. To address this, researchers can employ a range of data collection methods, such as surveys, interviews, and user analytics, and segment users to uncover patterns within specific contexts. Secondly, integrating data from multiple sources, such as various devices and platforms, can be challenging. Using data integration tools and centralized analytics platforms can simplify this process, while standardizing data ensures consistency and accuracy. Thirdly, privacy and security concerns arise when handling personal user data. Adhering to data protection regulations and implementing strong security practices, such as anonymization and encryption, is crucial. Furthermore, the influence of environmental factors on user behavior, such as physical surroundings and personal habits, can complicate analysis. Ethnographic research and contextual measurement scales can provide deeper insights into these influences.

- **Impact of Emerging Technologies:** Further research is needed to explore how emerging technologies like AI, AR, VR, and IoT will influence user behavior and interaction patterns. Investigating how these technologies can be integrated into user experiences while addressing potential challenges will be valuable.
- **Ethical Implications of AI and Personalization:** Studying the ethical implications of AI-driven personalization and data practices will provide insights into how to balance innovation with user

rights and privacy. Research should focus on developing guidelines and best practices for ethical AI use.

- **Diverse User Needs:** Research should continue to explore how diverse user needs and preferences can be addressed in digital design. Understanding cultural, demographic, and contextual variations will support the development of inclusive and accessible digital experiences.
- **Behavioral Analytics and Predictive Models:** Advancing behavioral analytics and predictive models will enhance the ability to anticipate and respond to user needs. Research in this area should focus on improving the accuracy and reliability of predictive analytics to create more personalized and engaging experiences.
- **Human-Centered Design Evolution:** Investigating the evolution of human-centered design principles and practices will provide insights into creating more empathetic and effective user experiences. Research should explore how to integrate emotional and psychological considerations into design strategies.

To study user behavior patterns in complex digital environments, such as multi-device ecosystems or smart environments, a comprehensive approach is essential. Behavioral tracking tools should be employed to observe real-time user activities across devices and smart technologies, providing valuable data on user behavior transitions. User journey mapping helps visualize the complete experience across different touchpoints, revealing how users move between devices and environments. Usability testing in these complex settings involves creating scenarios that simulate real-life interactions, allowing for the observation of user navigation and feedback on usability issues.

## REFERENCES


Alamsyah, A., Bratawisnu, M. K., & Sanjani, P. H. (2018). Finding Pattern in Dynamic Network Analysis. *2018 6th International Conference on Information and Communication Technology (ICoICT)*, 141–146. DOI: 10.1109/ICoICT.2018.8528779

Ao, M., Dong, M., Chu, B., Zeng, X., & Li, C. (2019). Revealing the User Behavior Pattern Using HN-CORS RTK Location Big Data. *IEEE Access : Practical Innovations, Open Solutions*, 7, 30302–30312. DOI: 10.1109/ACCESS.2019.2902577

Askarizad, R., & Safari, H. (2020). The influence of social interactions on the behavioral patterns of the people in urban spaces (case study: The pedestrian zone of Rasht Municipality Square, Iran). *Cities (London, England)*, 101, 102687. https://doi.org/https://doi.org/10.1016/j.cities.2020.102687. DOI: 10.1016/j.cities.2020.102687

Cerezo, R., Sánchez-Santillán, M., Paule-Ruiz, M. P., & Núñez, J. C. (2016). Students' LMS interaction patterns and their relationship with achievement: A case study in higher education. *Computers & Education*, 96, 42–54. https://doi.org/https://doi.org/10.1016/j.compedu.2016.02.006. DOI: 10.1016/j.compedu.2016.02.006

David Codish, E. R., & Ravid, G. (2019). User behavior pattern detection in unstructured processes – a learning management system case study. *Interactive Learning Environments*, 27(5–6), 699–725. DOI: 10.1080/10494820.2019.1610456

Dharmarajan, K., & Dorairangaswamy, M. (2017). Web User Navigation Pattern Behavior Prediction Using Nearest Neighbor Interchange from Weblog Data. *International Journal of Pure and Applied Mathematics*, 116(21), 761–775.

Du, Y., Yin, H., Wang, C., & Li, C. (2020). Visual analysis of customer switching behavior pattern mining for takeout service. *Journal of Computer Languages*, 57, 100946. https://doi.org/https://doi.org/10.1016/j.cola.2020.100946. DOI: 10.1016/j.cola.2020.100946

Ehatisham-ul-Haq. M., Awais Azam, M., Naeem, U., Amin, Y., & Loo, J. (2018). Continuous authentication of smartphone users based on activity pattern recognition using passive mobile sensing. *Journal of Network and Computer Applications, 109*, 24–35. https://doi.org/https://doi.org/10.1016/j.jnca.2018.02.020

El-Ansary, A. (2002). Behavioral Pattern Analysis: towards a new representation of systems requirements based on actions and events. *Proceedings of the 2002 ACM Symposium on Applied Computing*, 984–991. DOI: 10.1145/508791.508983

Faison, T. (1998). *Interaction Patterns for Communicating Processes 1 Abstract 2 Introduction 3 Interaction Dynamics and the Patterns Movement*. 1–35.

Fatahi, S., Shabanali-Fami, F., & Moradi, H. (2018). An empirical study of using sequential behavior pattern mining approach to predict learning styles. *Education and Information Technologies*, 23(4), 1427–1445. DOI: 10.1007/s10639-017-9667-1

Fu, C., Zheng, G., Huang, C., Yu, Y., & Dong, J. (2023). Multiplex Heterogeneous Graph Neural Network with Behavior Pattern Modeling. *Proceedings of the 29th ACM SIGKDD Conference on Knowledge Discovery and Data Mining*, 482–494. DOI: 10.1145/3580305.3599441

Godon, M., Feki, M. A., Roelands, M., & Trappeniers, L. (2011). The First Interaction Design Pattern Library for Internet of Things User Created Applications. In Jacko, J. A. (Ed.), *Human-Computer Interaction. Design and Development Approaches* (pp. 229–237). Springer Berlin Heidelberg. DOI: 10.1007/978-3-642-21602-2_26

Gokulapriya, R., & Ganesh Kumar, R. (2019). Research aligned analysis on web access behavioral pattern mining for user identification. *International Journal of Engineering and Advanced Technology*, 8(6), 5062–5067. DOI: 10.35940/ijeat.F9552.088619

González-Briones, A., Prieto, J., De La Prieta, F., Demazeau, Y., & Corchado, J. M. (2021). Virtual agent organizations for user behaviour pattern extraction in energy optimization processes: A new perspective. *Neurocomputing*, 452, 374–385. https://doi.org/https://doi.org/10.1016/j.neucom.2020.05.117. DOI: 10.1016/j.neucom.2020.05.117

Greenberg, S., Boring, S., Vermeulen, J., & Dostal, J. (2014). Dark patterns in proxemic interactions: a critical perspective. *Proceedings of the 2014 Conference on Designing Interactive Systems*, 523–532. DOI: 10.1145/2598510.2598541

Gui, E. M., & MacGill, I. (2018). Typology of future clean energy communities: An exploratory structure, opportunities, and challenges. *Energy Research & Social Science*, 35, 94–107. https://doi.org/https://doi.org/10.1016/j.erss.2017.10.019. DOI: 10.1016/j.erss.2017.10.019

Gupta, S., Maple, C., Crispo, B., Raja, K., Yautsiukhin, A., & Martinelli, F. (2023). A survey of human-computer interaction (HCI) & natural habits-based behavioural biometric modalities for user recognition schemes. *Pattern Recognition*, 139, 109453. https://doi.org/https://doi.org/10.1016/j.patcog.2023.109453. DOI: 10.1016/j.patcog.2023.109453

Han, D., Huang, Y., Liu, J., Liao, K., & Lin, K. (2024). LSAB: User Behavioral Pattern Modeling in Sequential Recommendation by Learning Self-Attention Bias. *ACM Transactions on Knowledge Discovery from Data*, 18(3), 1–20. Advance online publication. DOI: 10.1145/3632625

Huang, L., & Xia, Z. (2009). User Character and Communication Pattern Detecting on Social Network Site. *2009 International Conference on Engineering Computation*, 261–264. DOI: 10.1109/ICEC.2009.70

Jeong, A. (2005). A Guide to Analyzing Message–Response Sequences and Group Interaction Patterns in Computer-mediated Communication. *Distance Education*, 26(3), 367–383. DOI: 10.1080/01587910500291470

Johann Füller Katja Hutter, J. H., & Matzler, K. (2014). User Roles and Contributions in Innovation-Contest Communities. *Journal of Management Information Systems*, 31(1), 273–308. DOI: 10.2753/MIS0742-1222310111

Jorritsma, W., Cnossen, F., Dierckx, R. A., Oudkerk, M., & van Ooijen, P. M. A. (2016). Pattern mining of user interaction logs for a post-deployment usability evaluation of a radiology PACS client. *International Journal of Medical Informatics*, 85(1), 36–42. https://doi.org/https://doi.org/10.1016/j.ijmedinf.2015.10.007. DOI: 10.1016/j.ijmedinf.2015.10.007 PMID: 26574241

Juhaňák, L., Zounek, J., & Rohlíková, L. (2019). Using process mining to analyze students' quiz-taking behavior patterns in a learning management system. *Computers in Human Behavior*, 92, 496–506. https://doi.org/https://doi.org/10.1016/j.chb.2017.12.015. DOI: 10.1016/j.chb.2017.12.015

Khan, M. F., Lu, L., Afzal, H., & Nasir, J. A. (2023). PredictionMiner: Mining the latest individual behavioral rules for personalized contextual pattern predictions. *Soft Computing*. Advance online publication. DOI: 10.1007/s00500-023-08572-4

Koreng, R., & Krömker, H. (2021). User Interface Pattern for AR in Industrial Applications. *Information (Basel)*, 12(6), 251. Advance online publication. DOI: 10.3390/info12060251

Ku, Y., Park, L. H., Shin, S., & Kwon, T. (2019). Draw It As Shown: Behavioral Pattern Lock for Mobile User Authentication. *IEEE Access : Practical Innovations, Open Solutions*, 7, 69363–69378. DOI: 10.1109/ACCESS.2019.2918647

Kuflik, T., Boger, Z., & Zancanaro, M. (2012). Analysis and Prediction of Museum Visitors' Behavioral Pattern Types. In A. Krüger & T. Kuflik (Eds.), *Ubiquitous Display Environments* (pp. 161–176). Springer Berlin Heidelberg. DOI: 10.1007/978-3-642-27663-7_10

Li, X., Han, D., He, J., Liao, L., & Wang, M. (2019). Next and Next New POI Recommendation via Latent Behavior Pattern Inference. *ACM Transactions on Information Systems*, 37(4), 1–28. Advance online publication. DOI: 10.1145/3354187

Liu, Z., Wang, Y., Dontcheva, M., Hoffman, M., Walker, S., & Wilson, A. (2017). Patterns and Sequences: Interactive Exploration of Clickstreams to Understand Common Visitor Paths. *IEEE Transactions on Visualization and Computer Graphics*, 23(1), 321–330. DOI: 10.1109/TVCG.2016.2598797 PMID: 27875148

Ma, W., Sartipi, K., & Bender, D. (2016). Knowledge-Driven User Behavior Pattern Discovery for System Security Enhancement. *International Journal of Software Engineering and Knowledge Engineering*, 26(03), 379–404. DOI: 10.1142/S0218194016500169

Mao, Q., Wang, W., You, F., Zhao, R., & Li, Z. (2022). User behavior pattern mining and reuse across similar Android apps. *Journal of Systems and Software*, 183, 111085. https://doi.org/https://doi.org/10.1016/j.jss.2021.111085. DOI: 10.1016/j.jss.2021.111085

Märtin, C., Herdin, C., Engel, J., & Kampfer, F. (2019). A Structured Approach for Designing Adaptive Interactive Systems by Unifying Situation-Analytics with Model- and Pattern-Based User Interface Development. In Holzinger, A., Silva, H. P., & Helfert, M. (Eds.), *Computer-Human Interaction Research and Applications* (pp. 45–65). Springer International Publishing. DOI: 10.1007/978-3-030-32965-5_3

Märtin, C., Rashid, S., & Herdin, C. (2016). Designing Responsive Interactive Applications by Emotion-Tracking and Pattern-Based Dynamic User Interface Adaptation. In Kurosu, M. (Ed.), *Human-Computer Interaction. Novel User Experiences* (pp. 28–36). Springer International Publishing. DOI: 10.1007/978-3-319-39513-5_3

Mohamed, M. G., & Saunier, N. (2015). Behavior Analysis Using a Multilevel Motion Pattern Learning Framework. *Transportation Research Record: Journal of the Transportation Research Board*, 2528(1), 116–127. DOI: 10.3141/2528-13

Nie, B. (2022). Pattern Mining of Smart Home User Behavior in The Context of The Internet of Things: based on Sensor Networks. *2022 3rd International Conference on Smart Electronics and Communication (ICOSEC)*, 398–401. DOI: 10.1109/ICOSEC54921.2022.9952128

Patwardhan, A. (2017). Three-Dimensional, Kinematic, Human Behavioral Pattern-Based Features for Multimodal Emotion Recognition. *Multimodal Technologies and Interaction*, 1(3), 19. Advance online publication. DOI: 10.3390/mti1030019

Peng, Y., & Yu, K. (2016). User behavior analysis of automobile websites based on distributed computing and sequential pattern mining. *2016 IEEE International Conference on Network Infrastructure and Digital Content (IC-NIDC)*, 84–88. DOI: 10.1109/ICNIDC.2016.7974540

Pollmann, K., & Ziegler, D. (2021). A Pattern Approach to Comprehensible and Pleasant Human–Robot Interaction. *Multimodal Technologies and Interaction*, 5(9), 49. Advance online publication. DOI: 10.3390/mti5090049

Rossi, S., Ferland, F., & Tapus, A. (2017). User profiling and behavioral adaptation for HRI: A survey. *Pattern Recognition Letters*, 99, 3–12. https://doi.org/https://doi.org/10.1016/j.patrec.2017.06.002. DOI: 10.1016/j.patrec.2017.06.002

Sbeyti, H. (2016). [MOUBE]. *Mobile User Authentication Based On User Behavioral Pattern*, 10, 120–139.

Shen, C., Chen, Y., Guan, X., & Maxion, R. A. (2020). Pattern-Growth Based Mining Mouse-Interaction Behavior for an Active User Authentication System. *IEEE Transactions on Dependable and Secure Computing*, 17(2), 335–349. DOI: 10.1109/TDSC.2017.2771295

Tang, B., Wang, N., Li, J., & Shen, Z. (2024). A Multi-task Learning Framework with Features Based on Behavioral Pattern Conversation. In Zaslavsky, A., Ning, Z., Kalogeraki, V., Georgakopoulos, D., & Chrysanthis, P. K. (Eds.), *Mobile and Ubiquitous Systems: Computing, Networking and Services* (pp. 256–267). Springer Nature Switzerland. DOI: 10.1007/978-3-031-63992-0_17

Tingting, W. (2020).. . *Research on User Access Pattern Mining Based on Web Log.*, 6(8), 135–148.

Vellingiri, J., Kaliraj, S., Satheeshkumar, S., & Parthiban, T. (2015). A novel approach for user navigation pattern discovery and analysis for web usage mining. *Journal of Computational Science*, 11(2), 372–382. DOI: 10.3844/jcssp.2015.372.382

Wang, N., Zhang, Q., Yang, L., & Chen, M. (2016). *A Novel E-Commerce Recommendation System Model based on the Pattern Recognition and User Behavior Preference Analysis. 138*(Isi), 105–110. DOI: 10.14257/astl.2016.138.23

Wentzlaff, I., & Specker, M. (2006). Pattern-based development of user-friendly web applications. *Workshop Proceedings of the Sixth International Conference on Web Engineering*, 2–es. DOI: 10.1145/1149993.1149996

Xi Liu Chaogui Kang, L. G., & Liu, Y. (2016). Incorporating spatial interaction patterns in classifying and understanding urban land use. *International Journal of Geographical Information Science*, 30(2), 334–350. DOI: 10.1080/13658816.2015.1086923

Yang, Z. (2022). FCM Clustering on Interaction Pattern Analysis of Chinese Language Learner Behavior. *Computational Intelligence and Neuroscience*, 2022, 1–8. Advance online publication. DOI: 10.1155/2022/8256646 PMID: 35720927

Yu, K., He, L., Yu, P. S., Zhang, W., & Liu, Y. (2019). Coupled Tensor Decomposition for User Clustering in Mobile Internet Traffic Interaction Pattern. *IEEE Access : Practical Innovations, Open Solutions*, 7, 18113–18124. DOI: 10.1109/ACCESS.2019.2894267

Yuan, S.-T. D., & Hsu, S.-T. (2017). Enhancing service system design: An entity interaction pattern approach. *Information Systems Frontiers*, 19(3), 481–507. DOI: 10.1007/s10796-015-9604-z

Zhang, W., Zhou, W., & Luo, J. (2019). Mining And Application of User Behavior Pattern Based on Operation And Maintenance Data. *2019 IFIP/IEEE Symposium on Integrated Network and Service Management (IM)*, 614–618.

Zhang, Z., Sun, R., Wang, X., & Zhao, C. (2019). A Situational Analytic Method for User Behavior Pattern in Multimedia Social Networks. *IEEE Transactions on Big Data*, 5(4), 520–528. DOI: 10.1109/TBDATA.2017.2657623

# Chapter 5
# Virtual Identity and Self-Expression in the Metaverse

**Aditi Sharma**
https://orcid.org/0009-0003-8996-6097
*Chandigarh College of Engineering and Technology, Panjab University, Chandigarh, India*

**Sudhakar Kumar**
https://orcid.org/0000-0001-7928-4234
*Chandigarh College of Engineering and Technology, Panjab University, Chandigarh, India*

**Sunil K. Singh**
https://orcid.org/0000-0003-4876-7190
*Chandigarh College of Engineering and Technology, Panjab University, Chandigarh, India*

**Shashi Jawla**
https://orcid.org/0000-0002-7363-4966
*SVIET, Mohali, India*

**Varsha Arya**
*Hong Kong Metropolitan University, Hong Kong*

**Kwok Tai Chui**
*Hong Kong Metropolitan University, Hong Kong*

## ABSTRACT

*The metaverse, a growing digital universe, presents new ways for individuals to express themselves and shape their online identities. This chapter explores the complex relationship between virtual identity and self-expression in this immersive environment. It discusses how users craft and shape their digital personas, the factors influencing these choices, and the impact of virtual identities on real-life interactions. The idea of "digital doppelgängers," virtual representations that may differ from our true selves, is examined. The chapter also investigates the blending of real and virtual identities, including the role of social media and targeted advertising in shaping self-presentation. It highlights the metaverse as a space for creativity and identity exploration while addressing ethical concerns like privacy, addiction, and social isolation. Additionally, the metaverse is seen as a potential tool for social change, providing platforms for marginalized voices. This analysis reveals the opportunities and challenges of virtual identity in this evolving digital world.*

DOI: 10.4018/979-8-3693-8628-6.ch005

## 1. INTRODUCTION

The concept of the metaverse has emerged as a transformative paradigm, redefining how individuals interact, create, and express themselves in digital spaces. This interconnected virtual universe integrates augmented reality (AR), virtual reality (VR), and traditional digital environments, offering a dynamic platform where users can engage in real-time social activities, gaming, artistic creation, and business transactions. Unlike conventional online platforms that limit interaction, the metaverse fosters immersive experiences, raising profound questions about identity, self-expression, and the influence of virtual lives on real-world existence. At the core of the metaverse lies the concept of virtual identity, defined as the persona users craft in these digital environments. This identity is embodied by customizable avatars, which serve as proxies facilitating user interactions and experiences. Beyond superficial design, avatar customization holds significant meaning, enabling individuals to experiment with how they present themselves, communicate, and engage with others. By modifying appearance, behavior, and even backstory, users can explore facets of their identity often constrained by societal norms in the physical world. The metaverse serves as a unique platform for self-expression, enabling users to challenge societal conventions and embrace alternative identities. Freed from the limitations of physical reality, individuals can experiment with diverse personas, fostering creativity and empowerment. This capability holds particular significance for marginalized communities, offering a safe space to explore and express identities away from societal judgments. The metaverse's potential as a haven for self-discovery highlights its role in promoting inclusivity and representation in digital spaces.

However, the exploration of virtual identity and self-expression in the metaverse is not without its challenges. Ethical concerns such as data privacy loom large, as platforms collect vast amounts of personal information, preferences, and behavioral patterns. This data, often monetized for targeted advertising and personalized experiences, raises questions about the commodification of virtual identities. Additionally, the blending of virtual and real-world personas may lead to psychological challenges, particularly when users become overly attached to their avatars or rely on the escapism the metaverse offers. Issues of addiction, mental health, and emotional well-being emerge as critical areas of concern. Authenticity versus performance presents another challenge in the metaverse. While users may feel liberated to express their identities more freely, the pressure to conform to ideals perpetuated by social media and marketing is significant. The commercialization of identity, driven by virtual goods like avatar clothing and accessories, can blur the line between genuine self-expression and curated performance. Users may find themselves navigating a landscape where identity becomes a currency for social validation, complicating motivations for engagement.

Despite these challenges, the metaverse also holds immense potential for social change. It provides a platform for diverse voices to advocate for causes, fostering connections and collaboration among individuals from various backgrounds. Virtual rallies, art exhibitions, and educational initiatives demonstrate how the metaverse can raise awareness about critical social issues and create a shared sense of purpose. This ability to amplify marginalized voices and drive activism underscores the transformative potential of virtual spaces.

This chapter delves into the complexities of virtual identity and self-expression in the metaverse, examining the factors that shape digital personas, the concept of "digital doppelgängers," and the influence of social media and advertising. It explores the ethical implications of virtual identity, including risks of addiction and isolation, while highlighting the metaverse's potential to foster empowerment and social change. By addressing these themes, this chapter seeks to answer pressing questions about identity in the digital age: How are virtual personas constructed, and what influences these choices? What are the implications of self-expression in a space that merges reality and fantasy? As we navigate this emerging digital frontier, understanding the interplay between the metaverse, identity, and self-expression becomes critical to shaping meaningful connections in both virtual and real-world contexts.

## 2. WHAT IS VIRTUAL IDENTITY?

Virtual identity refers to the online persona that individuals create and project within the digital realms of the metaverse, offering a unique space where users can redefine themselves in contrast to the fixed traits that define their physical self, such as race, gender, and age (Cheng, 2023). Unlike these immutable characteristics, virtual identity is inherently flexible, allowing for a profound level of customization and self-representation. As individuals navigate the metaverse, they do so through avatars—digital stand-ins or representations of themselves in virtual spaces. These avatars can mirror real-world identities or represent entirely different constructs, facilitating a vast range of self-expression and exploration of alternate aspects of selfhood.

**Figure 1** illustrates the typical steps users take when creating and customizing avatars in the metaverse, including selecting physical features, attire, and accessories to reflect their desired persona. These steps emphasize the extensive personalization options that allow users to experiment and express diverse aspects of their identity across digital platforms.

*Figure 1. Common steps for avatar customization across platforms*

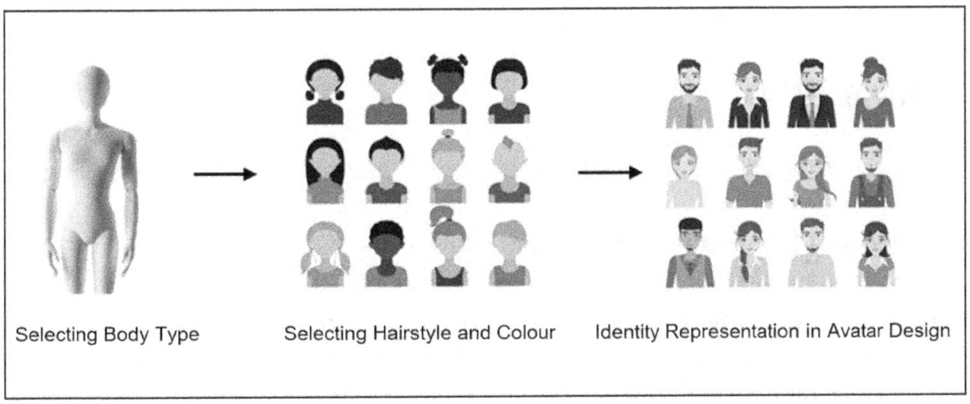


The avatars users choose to embody are not simply vessels for interaction; they are extensions of identity, often acting as primary conduits for engagement in virtual spaces. These avatars allow users to communicate, form relationships, and navigate social dynamics that mirror those in the real world, but with greater freedom to customize and transform. The process of identity construction within the metaverse offers a compelling lens through which to examine the evolving nature of selfhood in digital environments, where users can simultaneously embody multiple identities or personas that differ from their physical, offline selves. This capacity for self-representation in the metaverse opens up opportunities for a deeper exploration of one's identity, offering spaces for experimentation with gender, appearance, and behaviour that might not be possible in offline life. Some users opt for avatars that closely reflect their true selves, emphasizing authenticity in virtual spaces(Kiaer, 2024). However, others prefer to craft entirely new personas, deviating from their real-world characteristics in order to explore alternative identities. This divergence raises complex questions about the nature of authenticity, representation, and psychological well-being. For instance, individuals engaging in the creation of virtual identities may experience a disconnect between their real-world self and the avatar they present, leading to a complex dynamic in which the digital self becomes both an extension of the real self and an independent construct. This phenomenon can be seen in the quantified self-movement, where individuals use digital tools to track and measure their behaviours, thus creating a "digital doppelgänger" that may reflect an idealized or altered version of themselves. In the context of avatars, this process is even more pronounced, as users have the ability to completely transform their appearance and behaviours in ways that would not be feasible in offline settings.

The duality of virtual identity—where one can be both the same and different from one's real-world persona—raises questions about the psychological effects of managing multiple identities. For some users, this flexibility is liberating, offering them a chance to explore facets of selfhood that were previously constrained by societal expectations and norms. However, for others, the boundary between real-world identity and virtual identity can become blurred, leading to potential psychological challenges. The increasing complexity of virtual identities also introduces concerns about the security and privacy of personal data, as these digital representations of selfhood may be subject to manipulation or theft. As the rise of sophisticated digital technologies and forensic tools in virtual environments raises the stakes for ensuring the authenticity and security of digital representations, particularly in the context of online interactions that increasingly shape social and professional dynamic. The future of virtual identity will likely continue to evolve, challenging traditional understandings of selfhood and offering new insights into the role of technology in shaping our sense of who we are.

## Factors Shaping Virtual Identity

The construction of virtual identity is shaped by several interrelated factors, including:

a) **Customization and Personalization:** Avatars allow users to express individuality through diverse customization options, ranging from hairstyles and clothing to altering physical attributes such as height and body type. While some platforms offer hyper-realistic avatar designs, others provide stylized, cartoon-like representations. The availability and depth of customization significantly affect how users perceive their virtual selves and engage with others. Customization serves as more than a superficial activity—it is a creative outlet. Experimenting with different designs, colors, and styles fosters a sense of ownership and empowerment, enabling users to align their virtual identity with their values and aspirations.
b) **Social Influence and Group Identity:** Social dynamics within the metaverse heavily influence identity construction. Users often draw inspiration from their communities and peers when designing their avatars. Group identity is reflected in shared aesthetics, behaviors, and social practices (Dwivedi et al., 2023). For instance, within gaming communities, users might adopt specific styles or features that signify their allegiance to a faction or ideology. Similar to real-world trends, metaverse fashions can shape user behavior. Popular styles, themes, or iconic characters may inspire users to modify their avatars, reflecting a desire for social acceptance or belonging within their virtual communities.

c) **Platform and Technological Limitations:** The choice of metaverse platform profoundly impacts virtual identity. Each platform comes with unique tools, capabilities, and design philosophies that determine the scope of customization available. Advanced platforms may enable intricate designs, while simpler ones might limit personalization options. Technological disparities also highlight issues of access and inclusivity. Users with limited technological proficiency or resources may find it challenging to engage fully with avatar customization, underscoring the need for platforms to consider accessibility. Addressing these limitations is critical for ensuring equitable participation in virtual spaces(Setia et al., 2024).

d) **Cultural and Personal Preferences:** Real-world backgrounds, cultures, and personal experiences significantly shape virtual identities. Cultural expression often influences avatar design, as users incorporate elements of their heritage, traditions, and values into their virtual personas. This allows for the celebration and preservation of identity in a global digital space. Moreover, the metaverse offers a safe and accepting environment for users to explore aspects of their identity that may be stigmatized or constrained in the physical world. For instance, individuals can experiment with gender identities, sexual orientations, or other facets of their personalities, fostering empowerment and self-discovery. Virtual identity in the metaverse represents a convergence of creativity, cultural expression, and technological innovation(Sarin et al., 2023). As users navigate these digital spaces, the interplay of personalization, social influences, platform capabilities, and cultural preferences shapes how they construct and engage with their virtual personas. Understanding these dynamics is crucial for appreciating the opportunities and challenges inherent in this new frontier of self-expression.

## 3. THE FLUID NATURE OF VIRTUAL IDENTITY

The fluid nature of virtual identity is one of the defining features of the metaverse. Unlike the fixed attributes that define physical identity, users can change their avatars at any time, allowing them to adapt their virtual selves to suit different contexts or social situations. This fluidity fosters a sense of experimentation and exploration, enabling users to test new identities without the constraints of real-world consequences.

For instance, someone might choose to present themselves as a bold, adventurous character in a gaming environment while opting for a more reserved or professional persona in a work-related virtual meeting. This versatility opens doors to creativity and self-expression, as individuals can explore various aspects of their personality and identity. Additionally, federated learning techniques in metaverse platforms ensure personalized interactions while maintaining user privacy, enabling secure and adaptable identity management. The implications of this fluidity are profound, offering transformative opportunities for self-awareness and growth. By experimenting with different identities, users can embark on a journey of self-discovery that fosters greater self-awareness and confidence (Bode & Kristensen, 2016). Virtual personas provide a safe space for individuals to explore aspects of themselves they may not have previously acknowledged or felt comfortable expressing in their physical lives. This fluidity also encourages creative freedom, as users can redefine their sense of self by reflecting on real-world experiences while simultaneously enriching their understanding of identity. Furthermore, the integration of advanced techniques like chaotic watermarking plays a crucial role in safeguarding the authenticity and integrity of creative, self-expressive content, ensuring that users' contributions in virtual environments remain protected against tampering or misuse.

This fluidity brings with it notable challenges. One significant issue is the question of authenticity. With the ability to adopt multiple identities, users may find it difficult to determine which persona truly represents their "real" self. This tension between genuine self-expression and role-playing to gain social acceptance can foster feelings of disconnection or even confusion. Additionally, the psychological effects of maintaining and balancing virtual and real-world identities can be complex. Cognitive dissonance may arise as users struggle to reconcile their curated virtual personas with their physical identities, and an over-reliance on these avatars may lead to feelings of alienation or detachment from their real-world selves. These challenges highlight the need for users to navigate this fluidity carefully to ensure a harmonious integration of their virtual and physical identities.

### Balancing Opportunities and Challenges

While the fluid nature of virtual identity offers exciting possibilities for exploration and creativity, it necessitates a thoughtful examination of authenticity and self-integration. By mindfully engaging with these dynamics, users can foster both personal growth and meaningful virtual interactions (Nelson, Leema & Kumar, Sudhakar, 2023). Through this unique characteristic, the metaverse becomes a powerful platform for identity exploration, but its potential must be navigated with care to ensure a positive impact on one's sense of self and belonging in both virtual and physical realms.

## 4. SELF-EXPRESSION IN THE METAVERSE

Self-expression in the metaverse is not limited to avatar customization. It includes how users express themselves through interactions, creativity, and connections. This provides unique opportunities for individuals to express parts of their identity that might not be possible in the physical world.

**Creative Freedom in the Metaverse:** In the metaverse, users can enjoy creative freedom that is often unavailable in real life. Avatars can be customized in unique ways, from fashion to appearance, allowing individuals to express their personal style and identity. Virtual fashion, in particular, has become a thriving sector, with users experimenting with diverse styles that reflect their cultural influences, aesthetics, or even fantasy themes. The lack of physical limitations like affordability or societal judgment allows users to create bold fashion statements and explore trends in an entirely new way.Beyond fashion, users can design their own virtual spaces, whether it's a social hangout or a creative studio. These personalized environments give users the ability to express their personalities through interior design and interactive elements. Inviting others into these virtual spaces fosters social interaction and builds communities centered around shared interests (K. Aggarwal et al., 2022).

**User Interactions and Social Engagement:** In the metaverse, social interactions go beyond text and voice chat. Users communicate through avatars and non-verbal cues like gestures and actions. Table 1 highlights several key interaction types in the metaverse, detailing their descriptions and the impact they have on self-expression and social engagement(Sarin et al., 2024a).

*Table 1. Types of interaction in the metaverse*

| Interaction Type | Description | Effect on Self-Expression |
|---|---|---|
| **Avatar Gestures** | Non-verbal communication through actions (e.g., waving, dancing). | Adds emotional depth to conversations, conveys personality, and enhances social engagement. |
| **Social Groups** | Join virtual communities or networks based on shared interests. | Fosters collaboration, belonging, and shared experiences, shaping group identity. |
| **Virtual Events** | Participate in events like meetups, concerts, or exhibitions. | Provides new ways for people to connect through shared activities, encouraging creativity. |
| **Voice Communication** | Real-time voice chat during interactions. | Adds a personal, emotional layer to communication, making connections feel more genuine. |
| **Text-based Communication** | Conversations via chat or messaging within the metaverse. | Reflects personality through writing style and tone, creating an immediate, accessible form of expression. |
| **Avatar Customization** | Modify avatars to reflect personality, mood, or identity. | Offers a visual form of self-expression, allowing individuals to experiment with appearance and identity. |
| **Collaborative Projects** | Work with others on creative endeavors (art, gaming, etc.). | Encourages shared creativity, teamwork, and expression through collective effort. |

### Authenticity vs. Performance

As users express themselves in the metaverse, they face the challenge of balancing authenticity with performance, a tension that significantly influences both identity construction and social interactions. Authenticity becomes a central question, as users must navigate whether they are presenting their true selves or a carefully curated version designed to fit specific contexts or expectations. This balancing act is further complicated by the performative nature of the metaverse, where users may feel compelled to modify their avatars or behaviours to gain social approval, align with group norms, or project an idealized image(Chhabra et al., 2024).In this virtual space, where avatar customization and social pressures are prominent, the boundary between genuine self-expression and performative adaptation often blurs. Users must grapple with questions about the extent to which their virtual personas reflect their real identities or simply act as tools for navigating social landscapes. This complexity underscores the importance of fostering an environment in the metaverse that supports both creative exploration and meaningful self-expression, without imposing excessive pressure to conform or perform for acceptance.

## 5. TECHNOLOGICAL FRAMEWORKS BEHIND VIRTUAL IDENTITY CREATION

The construction and management of virtual identities in the metaverse rely on advanced technologies and frameworks that enable seamless customization and interaction. Among these, Linux plays a vital role as an open-source operating system that powers many backend infrastructures and servers in virtual environments. Its robust architecture, scalability, and security make it an ideal choice for handling the complex computational needs of the metaverse(Sunil et al., 2021). Linux supports efficient resource management and high performance, ensuring seamless avatar creation, interaction dynamics, and data integration in immersive virtual environments.

Key components include:

1. **3D Modeling and Rendering Technologies:** Avatars are designed using sophisticated 3D modeling software, such as Blender, Autodesk Maya, or proprietary tools developed by metaverse platforms (Badwa, E., et al., 2024). These tools allow for intricate customization of body types, facial features, and clothing. Rendering engines like Unreal Engine and Unity power real-time graphics, enabling visually realistic or stylized avatars that align with user preferences.
2. **Artificial Intelligence (AI) and Machine Learning (ML):** AI-driven systems enable features like real-time emotion detection and adaptive behavior modeling. For instance: Emotion Detection Algorithms use facial recognition and voice analysis to reflect users' emotional states in avatar expressions. Recommendation Systems to suggest customization options based on user preferences and social trends.AI also personalizes user interactions by adapting avatars to different scenarios or communities (Kumar, 2024; Mengi, G., et al., 2023).
3. **Blockchain and Non-Fungible Tokens (NFTs):** Blockchain technology ensures ownership and authenticity of digital assets like avatar accessories, clothing, and even identity data. NFTs provide users with unique, tradable virtual items, promoting exclusivity and personalization (T. Aggarwal et al., 2024).
4. **Augmented Reality (AR) and Virtual Reality (VR):** AR and VR devices, such as Meta Quest and HTC Vive, allow users to interact with their avatars in immersive environments, blending real-world and virtual elements. These devices use sensors and haptic feedback to enhance the sense of presence and realism.
5. **Data Management Frameworks:** Cloud computing plays a pivotal role in the metaverse by storing and processing the massive datasets necessary for avatar interactions and the dynamic creation of virtual environments. The vast amount of data generated by user interactions, including movements, communications, and customization choices, requires robust infrastructure to ensure seamless performance (Goyal et al., 2024). Cloud computing allows for the real-time processing and storage of this data, ensuring that virtual worlds remain responsive and interactive without being hindered by local device limitations. By distributing this data across a network of servers, cloud technology enables users from around the world to access the metaverse simultaneously, promoting a global, interconnected experience. Alongside cloud computing, privacy-preserving protocols are essential for safeguarding user data within the metaverse. Frameworks like differential privacy and encryption are implemented to protect sensitive information, ensuring that user data is not exposed to unauthorized access or misuse. Differential privacy, for example, allows for the analysis and sharing of aggregated data without compromising the privacy of individual users, while encryption ensures that communications and personal data are securely transmitted across the platform. These privacy-preserving measures enable users to customize their avatars and engage in virtual environments with confidence, knowing that their personal information is protected. As the metaverse continues to evolve, maintaining these privacy standards will be crucial to fostering trust and ensuring that users can navigate virtual spaces safely and securely.

The diagram below represents the process of virtual identity creation, highlighting the integration of technologies and user-driven customization.

*Figure 2. Process of virtual identity creation*

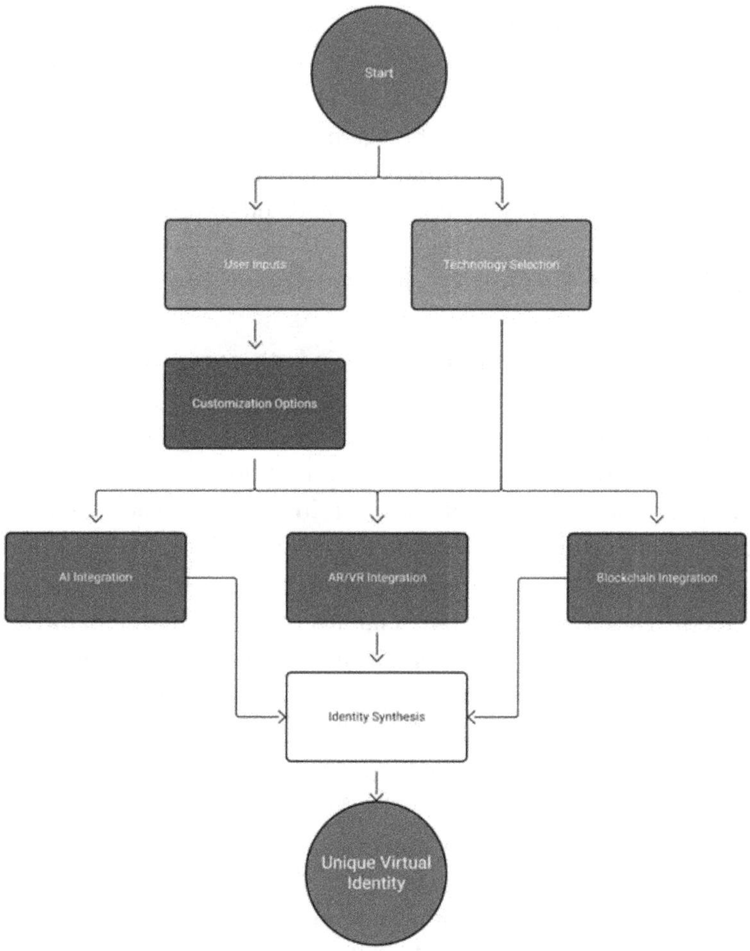


**Figure 2** illustrates the ***process of virtual identity creation*** and the integration of user inputs, technologies, and outcomes. It demonstrates how various technologies such as AI, AR/VR, and blockchain interact with user-driven customization to result in unique virtual identities. Let me know if additional details or refinements are needed.

## 6. DIGITAL DOPPELGÄNGER: THE VIRTUAL MIRROR OF OURSELVES

The concept of the digital doppelgänger is crucial to understanding virtual identity, as it represents the avatar users create in the metaverse. This avatar can either mirror their real-world selves or embody an entirely different persona (Kumar et al., 2024; Singh et al., 2024). For some individuals, their avatar acts as a digital replica, reflecting their appearance, style, and even emotional states. For others, it serves as a space for experimentation, allowing them to explore idealized versions of themselves or roles that are unattainable in the physical world.

## Exploring Identity Through the Digital Doppelgänger

The digital doppelgänger provides a platform for users to experiment with and explore identity in ways that transcend the limitations of the physical world. It allows individuals to express themselves freely, unbound by real-world social norms. Whether the avatar closely mirrors their real selves or embodies a completely fantastical persona, it serves as a bridge between an individual's real-world identity and their virtual presence in the metaverse. This dynamic creates opportunities for users to test and redefine aspects of who they are, in a way that fosters creativity and self-expression.

## The Relationship Between Real and Virtual Identities

The interaction between real and virtual identities is both complex and multifaceted. Many users create avatars that closely reflect their physical selves, drawing on their real-world appearance and personality. However, the metaverse also provides an avenue for individuals to explore entirely different identities. This duality creates a space where self-expression, creativity, and experimentation can flourish. For example, some users design **idealized versions of themselves**, enhancing physical traits, projecting confidence, or adding unique features to their avatars. This approach allows users to transcend real-world limitations and embody aspirations, such as designing an avatar that exudes confidence to overcome low self-esteem. This process not only enables richer social interactions in the virtual world but can also lead to personal growth and greater self-awareness in the real world. Others embrace the metaverse to explore **alternative personalities**, expressing aspects of themselves that may be hidden or suppressed in their daily lives(Vats, T., et al., 2024). This might involve experimenting with different gender identities, cultural backgrounds, or even fantastical roles like mythical creatures. The ability to explore these alternative identities without fear of judgment offers a sense of liberation, empowering users to discover and develop new dimensions of their personality.

The decision-making process for avatar creation, as shown in Figure 3, highlights the diversity of user intentions. It reflects the choice to design avatars that range from realistic depictions to idealized versions or entirely alternative identities, each shaped by the individual's goals for self-expression and exploration in the metaverse.

*Figure 3. Decision-making path for avatar customization*

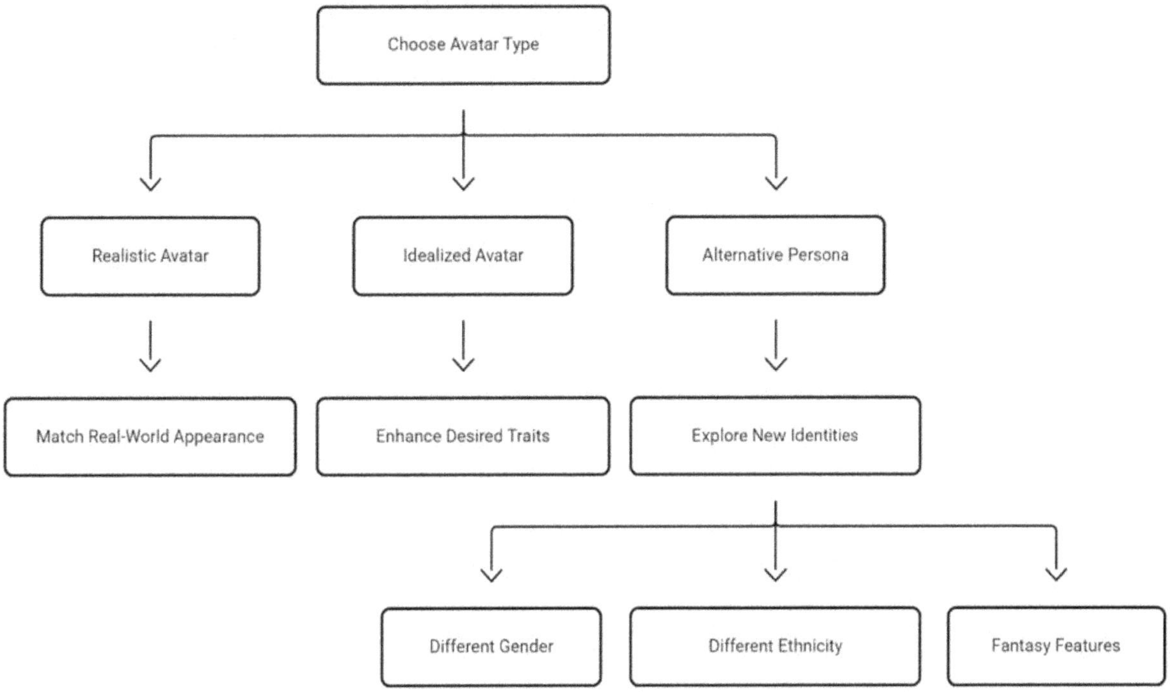


## 7. THE PSYCHOLOGICAL EFFECTS OF DIGITAL DOPPELGÄNGERS

The relationship between a user's real-world identity and their virtual doppelgänger can have profound psychological implications. Research has shown that the avatars people choose can affect their behavior, emotions, and social interactions.

1) **Impact on Self-Esteem:** Users with avatars that align with their self-image may experience increased self-esteem and confidence, while those with avatars that starkly contrast with their real-world selves may struggle with feelings of disconnection or inauthenticity. This psychological duality raises questions about the extent to which users internalize their digital identities and the emotional consequences of their virtual interactions.

A visual chart (**Figure 4**) shows these potential outcomes and their contributing factors.

2) **Identity Dissociation:** The phenomenon of identity dissociation may also arise when users become overly immersed in their virtual personas. In extreme cases, individuals may experience difficulty distinguishing between their real-world selves and their avatars, leading to challenges in maintaining a coherent sense of identity(Sharma et al., 2024). This dissociation can have negative consequences for mental health, potentially resulting in anxiety, depression, or feelings of isolation.

*Figure 4. Psychological effects of digital doppelgängers*

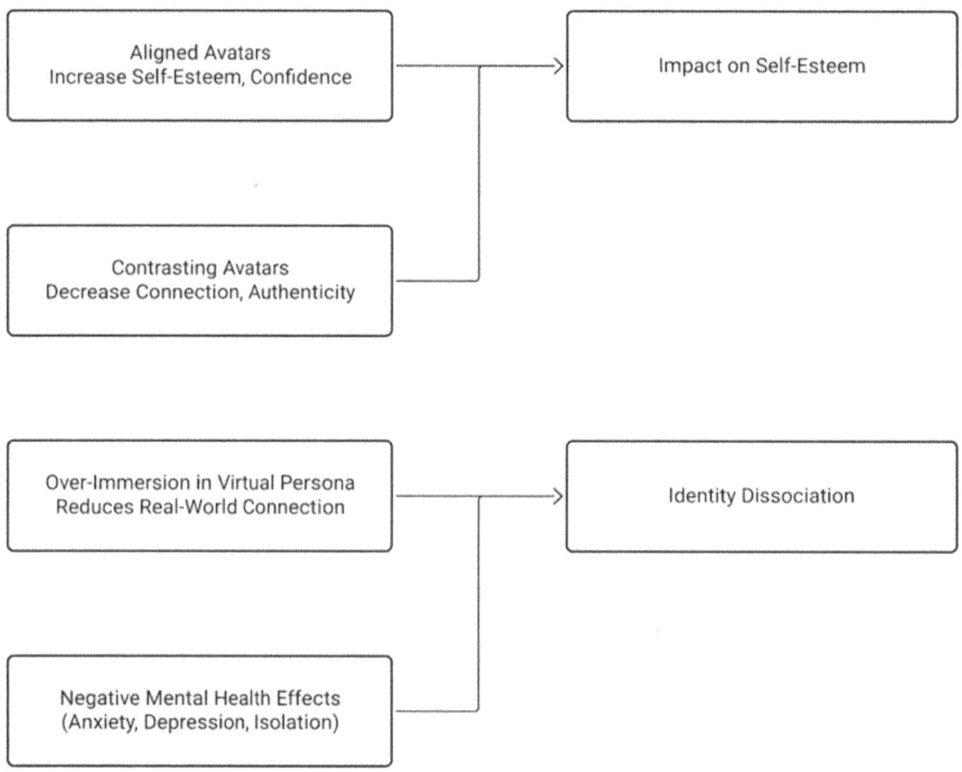


## 8. THE ROLE OF SOCIAL MEDIA AND ADVERTISING IN SHAPING VIRTUAL IDENTITIES

Social media and advertising heavily influence how users curate their virtual identities, setting trends and creating pressures in the metaverse. Social Media Influences Social media platforms shape how users present themselves online by propagating trends and idealized standards. Influencers and celebrities often set these trends, which are quickly adopted in the metaverse. A 2024 study by Metaverse Trends reported that 70% of users adjusted their avatars to match popular online styles. Additionally, the concept of curated realities—where only the best versions of life are displayed online—affects virtual identity. Users feel pressure to design flawless avatars, often prioritizing approval over authenticity. For instance, 40% of respondents in a 2022 survey by Social Impact Analytics admitted to modifying their avatars to gain social validation. Advertising and Commercialization Brands leverage the metaverse to promote virtual goods, such as digital clothing or accessories, enabling users to express themselves creatively. However, this commercialization can lead to authenticity concerns. Users may feel compelled to buy virtual items to conform to social norms or signal status.

The ethical implications are significant. Advertising algorithms collect vast user data to personalize experiences, raising concerns about privacy and consent. A 2024 Consumer Rights Report found that 55% of metaverse users were unaware of how their data was being used for targeted ads (Vats et al., 2024). Simplified diagrams showing data flows in metaverse platforms can help clarify these issues.

## 9. ETHICAL IMPLICATIONS OF VIRTUAL IDENTITY

Exploring virtual identities in the metaverse involves several ethical challenges that affect user well-being. Privacy concerns in the metaverse have become a significant issue, particularly regarding the collection and use of personal data. Companies often gather extensive information on user preferences and interactions to fuel targeted advertising, frequently without obtaining clear and informed consent. A 2023 study conducted by Digital Privacy Advocates revealed that 60% of metaverse users expressed a desire for stricter regulations on data collection practices. This underscores the importance of ensuring transparency and providing users with greater control over their data to safeguard their privacy in virtual environments. The impact of the metaverse on mental health and well-being is another critical area of concern. Virtual identities and immersive experiences can sometimes lead to addiction and escapism. For instance, a survey by TechWellness found that 25% of users spend over 20 hours per week in virtual worlds as a way to escape real-life stress. While this provides temporary relief, such behavior can lead to the neglect of real-world responsibilities and increased isolation from reality, ultimately posing risks to users' mental health and overall well-being. Social comparison in the metaverse, similar to that on social media, can harm self-esteem. Idealized avatars and glamorous virtual lifestyles create unrealistic benchmarks (Sarin et al., 2024b). A 2022 Mental Health Foundation study found that 45% of users felt inadequate after comparing their avatars to others. Reducing these pressures requires promoting diverse and authentic self-representations.

### The Potential for Social Change in the Metaverse

The metaverse, despite its challenges, holds immense promise for driving social change by creating unique opportunities for activism, advocacy, and community-building. As a digital platform, it provides marginalized groups with the ability to amplify their voices and advocate for social justice, human rights, and environmental causes. Unlike traditional activism, which is often restricted by geographic, logistical, or political barriers, the metaverse connects people worldwide, enabling them to organize virtual rallies, workshops, and discussions. These virtual spaces foster a sense of solidarity and community, allowing individuals to feel supported in their efforts while gaining the visibility necessary to challenge stereotypes and share their stories. By collaborating with organizations and like-minded individuals, marginalized communities can mobilize resources, engage with a broader audience, and push for meaningful societal transformation. One of the metaverse's greatest strengths lies in its capacity to host large-scale virtual events, such as rallies and awareness campaigns, that transcend physical boundaries. These events can attract a global audience, uniting participants in their shared goals and fostering collective action. For example, discussions about climate change or human rights within the metaverse enable users to connect, share their concerns, and brainstorm solutions in real time. Such virtual activism not only raises awareness but also inspires others to join the cause, thereby expanding the movement and driving tangible real-world changes. Metaverse promotes representation and visibility by offering a space where people from diverse backgrounds can share their cultures, perspectives, and experiences. By showcasing a wide range of voices, it fosters understanding and empathy, encouraging individuals to question their biases and develop a deeper appreciation for the struggles of others. This inclusivity is crucial for advancing social change, as empathy often serves as the foundation for meaningful action. It also facilitates collaboration and connection on a global scale, breaking down geographic and cultural barriers to unite people from all walks of life. In this shared digital space, users can work together on creative projects, social initiatives, and solutions to global challenges such as education or climate change. Powered by cloud computing, the metaverse ensures seamless interaction and real-time collaboration, enabling users to share ideas, resources, and expertise with ease. This interconnectedness drives innovation and collective action, leading to impactful solutions that have the potential to bring about real change in the physical world.

For instance, recent initiatives within the metaverse have demonstrated its capacity to enhance global collaboration and activism. Virtual climate summits and forums have brought together scientists, activists, and policymakers from across the globe to discuss sustainable solutions and share best practices. These immersive and inclusive events highlight how the metaverse can act as a catalyst for global cooperation, empowering individuals and organizations to work together and address the most pressing challenges facing society. By fostering empathy, representation, and collaboration, the metaverse emerges as a powerful platform for creating a more inclusive and equitable world.

## Case Study: The Global Collaboration Village

The Global Collaboration Village, created by Accenture in partnership with the World Economic Forum (WEF) and Microsoft, is a cutting-edge metaverse platform designed to facilitate global collaboration and activism (Kumar, 2024). This virtual space brings together leaders, changemakers, and activists worldwide, enabling them to address pressing global issues such as climate change, poverty, and inequality. By harnessing the power of the metaverse, the platform transcends traditional geographic barriers, offering immersive, real-time collaboration through avatars and 3D tools. These tools allow users to model, simulate, and visualize potential solutions, speeding up decision-making and accelerating real-world impact.

## Key Features and Benefits

The platform serves as a digital meeting ground for leaders from various sectors, including government, corporate entities, NGOs, and activists, enabling collaboration on global issues without the constraints of physical distance. Utilizing 3D tools and immersive virtual environments, it allows participants to visualize complex data, simulate solutions, and refine initiatives like sustainable infrastructure or environmental policies before real-world implementation. By fostering empathy through immersive experiences, the platform helps participants understand diverse challenges, promoting awareness and solidarity. Its focus on multi-stakeholder engagement ensures that activists, officials, and organizations contribute to holistic problem-solving. Breaking geographic barriers, the platform enables real-time interaction across time zones, accelerating cross-border cooperation and driving innovative, effective responses to global challenges.

## REFERENCES


Aggarwal, K., Singh, S. K., Chopra, M., Kumar, S., & Colace, F. (2022). Deep Learning in Robotics for Strengthening Industry 4.0.: Opportunities, Challenges and Future Directions. In Nedjah, N., Abd El-Latif, A. A., Gupta, B. B., & Mourelle, L. M. (Eds.), *Robotics and AI for Cybersecurity and Critical Infrastructure in Smart Cities* (pp. 1–19). Springer International Publishing., DOI: 10.1007/978-3-030-96737-6_1

Aggarwal, T., Kumar, S., Singh, S. K., Gupta, B. B., Nedjah, N., & Castiglione, A. (2024). Zero Knowledge Proofs and Their Applications in Cryptography: Advancements, Challenges, and Future Aspects. In *Innovations in Modern Cryptography* (pp. 55–74). IGI Global Scientific Publishing. DOI: 10.4018/979-8-3693-5330-1.ch003

Badwa, E., et al. (2024). *Deep learning model for digital forensics face sketch synthesis*. DOI: 10.4018/979-8-3693-5330-1.ch003

Bode, M., & Kristensen, D. B. (2016). The digital doppelgänger within: A study on self-tracking and the quantified self movement. In Canniford, R., & Bajde, D. (Eds.), *Assembling Consumption* (pp. 119–135). Routledge.

Cheng, S. (2023). Metaverse. In Cheng, S. (Ed.), *Metaverse: Concept, Content and Context* (pp. 1–23). Springer Nature Switzerland., DOI: 10.1007/978-3-031-24359-2_1

Chhabra, A., Singh, S. K., Sharma, A., Kumar, S., Gupta, B. B., Arya, V., & Chui, K. T. (2024). Sustainable and intelligent time-series models for epidemic disease forecasting and analysis. *Sustainable Technology and Entrepreneurship*, 3(2), 100064. Advance online publication. DOI: 10.1016/j.stae.2023.100064

Dwivedi, Y. K., Kshetri, N., Hughes, L., Rana, N. P., Baabdullah, A. M., Kar, A. K., Koohang, A., Ribeiro-Navarrete, S., Belei, N., Balakrishnan, J., Basu, S., Behl, A., Davies, G. H., Dutot, V., Dwivedi, R., Evans, L., Felix, R., Foster-Fletcher, R., Giannakis, M., & Yan, M. (2023). Exploring the Darkverse: A Multi-Perspective Analysis of the Negative Societal Impacts of the Metaverse. *Information Systems Frontiers*, 25(5), 2071–2114. DOI: 10.1007/s10796-023-10400-x PMID: 37361890

Goyal, S., Singh, S. K., Kumar, S., Sarin, S., Gupta, B. B., Arya, V., & Chui, K. T. (2024). Hyperdimensional Consumer Pattern Analysis with Quantum Neural Architectures using Non-Hermitian Operators. *Proceedings of the 5th International Conference on Information Management & Machine Intelligence*, 1–5. DOI: 10.1145/3647444.3652458

Kiaer, J. (2024). *Conversing in the Metaverse: The Embodied Future of Online Communication*. Bloomsbury Academic. DOI: 10.5040/9781350338548

Kumar, S., Singh, S. K., Gupta, B. B., Psannis, K., & Wu, J. (2024). Homomorphic Encryption in Smart City Applications for Balancing Privacy and Utility. In *Innovations in Modern Cryptography* (pp. 245–274). IGI Global Scientific Publishing., DOI: 10.4018/979-8-3693-5330-1.ch010

Mengi, G., Singh, S.K., Kumar, S., Mahto, D., & Sharma, A. (2023). Automated Machine Learning (AutoML): The Future of Computational Intelligence. In International Conference on Cyber Security, Privacy and Networking (ICSPN 2022). ICSPN 2021. Lecture Notes in Networks and Systems (vol. 599). Springer. https://doi.org/10.1007/978-3-031-22018-0_28

Nelson, Leema & Kumar, Sudhakar. (2023). *Enhancing Haemorrhage Detection in Head CT Scans Using Deep Learning. 1-6.*.DOI: 10.1109/SMARTGENCON60755.2023.10442342

Sarin, S., Singh, S. K., Kumar, S., Goyal, S., Gupta, B. B., Arya, V., & Chui, K. T. (2023). Forging Faces: 13th IEEE International Conference on Consumer Electronics - Berlin, ICCE-Berlin 2023. *IEEE International Conference on Consumer Electronics - Berlin, ICCE-Berlin*. DOI: 10.1109/ICCE-Berlin58801.2023.10649659

Sarin, S., Singh, S. K., Kumar, S., Goyal, S., Gupta, B. B., Arya, V., & Chui, K. T. (2024a). SEIR-driven semantic integration framework: Internet of Things-enhanced epidemiological surveillance in COVID-19 outbreaks using recurrent neural networks. *IET Cyber-Physical Systems*, 9(2), 135–149. DOI: 10.1049/cps2.12091

Sarin, S., Singh, S. K., Kumar, S., Goyal, S., Gupta, B. B., Arya, V., & Chui, K. T. (2024b). SEIR-driven semantic integration framework: Internet of Things-enhanced epidemiological surveillance in COVID-19 outbreaks using recurrent neural networks. *IET Cyber-Physical Systems*, 9(2), 135–149. DOI: 10.1049/cps2.12091

Setia, H., Chhabra, A., Singh, S. K., Kumar, S., Sharma, S., Arya, V., Gupta, B. B., & Wu, J. (2024). Securing the road ahead: Machine learning-driven DDoS attack detection in VANET cloud environments. *Cyber Security and Applications*, 2, 100037. DOI: 10.1016/j.csa.2024.100037

Sharma, A., Singh, S. K., Kumar, S., Preet, M., Gupta, B. B., Arya, V., & Chui, K. T. (2024). Revolutionizing Healthcare Systems: Synergistic Multimodal Ensemble Learning & Knowledge Transfer for Lung Cancer Delineation & Taxonomy. *2024 IEEE International Conference on Consumer Electronics (ICCE)*, 1–6. DOI: 10.1109/ICCE59016.2024.10444476

Singh, N., Singh, S. K., Kumar, S., Rawat, Y., Arya, V., Bansal, R., & Chui, K. T. (2024). Next Gen Security With Quantum-Safe Cryptography. In *Innovations in Modern Cryptography* (pp. 133–166). IGI Global Scientific Publishing., DOI: 10.4018/979-8-3693-5330-1.ch006

Sunil, S. K. (2021). *Linux Yourself: Concept and Programming*. Routledge & CRC Press. https://www.routledge.com/Linux-Yourself-Concept-and-Programming/KSingh/p/book/9781032037073

Vats, T. (2024). OPTUNA—Driven Soft Computing Approach for Early Diagnosis of Diabetes Mellitus Using ANN. In *Proceedings of the 12th International Conference on Soft Computing for Problem Solving. SocProS 2023. Lecture Notes in Networks and Systems* (vol. 995). Springer. https://doi.org/10.1007/978-981-97-3292-0_25

Vats, T., Kumar, S., Singh, S. K., Madan, U., Preet, M., Arya, V., Bansal, R., & Almomani, A. (2024). Navigating the landscape: Safeguarding privacy and security in the era of ambient intelligence within healthcare settings. *Cyber Security and Applications*, 2, 100046. DOI: 10.1016/j.csa.2024.100046

# Chapter 6
# Virtual Economies and Social Structures in the Metaverse

**Jaiveer Singh**
*Chandigarh College of Engineering and Technology, Panjab University, Chandigarh, India*

**Sudhakar Kumar**
https://orcid.org/0000-0001-7928-4234
*Chandigarh College of Engineering and Technology, Panjab University, Chandigarh, India*

**Sunil K. Singh**
https://orcid.org/0000-0003-4876-7190
*Chandigarh College of Engineering and Technology, Panjab University, Chandigarh, India*

**Deependra Singh**
*Chandigarh College of Engineering and Technology, Panjab University, Chandigarh, India*

**Animesh Singh**
*Chandigarh College of Engineering and Technology, Panjab University, Chandigarh, India*

**Varsha Arya**
*Hong Kong Metropolitan University, Hong Kong*

**Abhay Ratnaparkhi**
*IBM, Austin, USA*

## ABSTRACT

*This chapter examines the essential components of virtual economies in the metaverse and their transformative effects on user interactions, community development, and economic engagements. It explores various virtual economies, from MMOs like *World of Warcraft* to platforms like *Second Life* and blockchain-based systems such as *Axie Infinity*. Key elements analyzed include digital assets, currencies, trading venues, labor, supply and demand, and governance frameworks. The chapter discusses how traditional economic theories are applied in virtual spaces, fostering ecosystems that reflect and enhance real-world economies. Social structures, such as guilds, digital social capital, and cooperative economies, are highlighted for their role in community building. The governance of these economies, from centralized platforms to DAOs, is evaluated for its impact on economic stability and user engagement. The chapter also explores real-world consequences, including job creation, innovation, and ethical concerns, providing valuable insights for developers, policymakers, and researchers.*

DOI: 10.4018/979-8-3693-8628-6.ch006

# 1. INTRODUCTION

## 1.1 Background

The metaverse is swiftly becoming a transformative digital frontier, fundamentally changing how individuals interact, form communities, and participate in economic activities. At the heart of this expansive virtual realm are virtual economies (Evison, 2016), which encompass the production, distribution, and consumption of goods and services within digital spaces such as online games, virtual worlds, and blockchain-based platforms. Unlike traditional economies, virtual economies operate under unique platform-specific rules, blending economic principles with social interactions that both mirror and enhance real-world systems.

Massively multiplayer online games (MMOs) like World of Warcraft and EVE Online prominently feature virtual economies where players trade virtual goods, currencies, and services. These environments replicate real-world economic activities—such as supply and demand, labor, and capital—allowing users to engage with and influence economic systems in controlled digital settings. Similarly, virtual worlds like Second Life (Boellstorff, 2015) enable users to create, buy, and sell digital assets, further blurring the lines between virtual and real-world economies.

The advent of blockchain technology has introduced a new dimension to virtual economies, enabling decentralized platforms where cryptocurrencies (Nakamoto, n.d.) and non-fungible tokens (NFTs) facilitate innovative economic models(Swan, 2015). Games like Axie Infinity leverage blockchain to allow players to earn real-world value through in-game activities, demonstrating the tangible impact of virtual economies beyond their digital confines. These advancements raise critical questions about the functionality, core components, and broader implications of virtual economies, underscoring their significance in the evolving landscape of the metaverse.

*Table 1. Table depicting differences between real and virtual economies*

| S.No. | Aspect | Real Economy | Virtual Economy |
|---|---|---|---|
| 1 | Currency | Tangible fiat currency (e.g., USD, EUR) backed by governments. | Digital currencies (e.g., in-game currency, cryptocurrencies) created by platforms. |
| 2 | Labor | Labor involves physical work or intellectual tasks paid with real money. | Labor involves playing games, creating digital content, or managing virtual assets. |
| 3 | Supply and Demand | Determined by natural resources, manufacturing capacity, and consumer demand. | Controlled by platform mechanics (e.g., item drop rates, resource generation). |
| 4 | Marketplaces | Physical marketplaces (stores, stock exchanges) where goods are bought/sold. | In-game markets, auction houses, or decentralized exchanges for trading virtual items. |
| 5 | Regulation | Regulated by governments and international bodies, subject to taxation, and labor laws. | Regulated by platform rules or decentralized protocols (limited external regulation). |
| 6 | Ownership | Clear ownership, backed by legal frameworks (e.g., property rights). | Ownership often determined by platform rules or smart contracts (e.g., NFTs). |
| 7 | Scarcity | Limited by natural resources, technology, or time. | Scarcity controlled artificially by the platform (e.g., limited-edition items). |

continued on following page

*Table 1. Continued*

| S.No. | Aspect | Real Economy | Virtual Economy |
|---|---|---|---|
| 8 | Value Fluctuation | Fluctuates based on economic conditions (e.g., inflation, interest rates). | Subject to platform changes, player demand, and external market forces (e.g., cryptocurrency value). |
| 9 | Monetary Exchange | Real money is earned, spent, and transferred through traditional banking systems. | Virtual currencies can sometimes be exchanged for real money (e.g., NFTs, cryptocurrencies). |

## 1.2 Purpose

In Unveiling Social Dynamics and Community Interaction in the Metaverse, this chapter examines the foundational elements of virtual economies across various digital platforms, including online games, virtual worlds, and blockchain-based environments. It explores how economic principles are adapted in virtual contexts, creating ecosystems that both mirror and enhance real-world economic and social systems. The chapter delves into the interplay between economic activities and social structures, illustrating how virtual economies shape community formation, social hierarchies, and collaborative efforts within the metaverse.

## 1.3 Scope

Understanding virtual economies is essential as they significantly influence user experiences and the functionality of the metaverse. This chapter covers the different types of virtual economies—gaming economies, virtual worlds, and blockchain-based economies—and their core components such as virtual goods, currencies, marketplaces, labor, supply and demand dynamics, and governance structures. It highlights how these economic mechanisms affect social interactions and community building, addressing issues like social stratification, social capital accumulation, and collaborative economies. Additionally, the chapter explores the real-world implications of virtual economic activities, including legal challenges, regulatory considerations, and their potential impact on global economic and social systems.

## 1.4 Objectives

*Table 2. Table depicting objectives*

| Objective | Description |
|---|---|
| Comprehensive Exploration of Virtual Economies | Explore the types, core components, and operational mechanisms of virtual economies within the metaverse. This includes examining gaming economies, virtual worlds, and blockchain-based platforms to elucidate how economic principles are applied and adapted in virtual settings, enabling value creation, digital asset ownership, and participation in complex markets. |
| Analysis of Social Structures | Analyze the social structures emerging from virtual economic activities, such as guilds and clans, virtual social capital, and collaborative economies. Assess their influence on community building and the formation of social hierarchies within the metaverse. |
| Investigation of Governance and Regulation | Investigate governance and regulation within virtual economies, focusing on platform governance and decentralized models like Decentralized Autonomous Organizations (DAOs). Examine their impact on economic stability and user participation, highlighting how different governance structures affect the sustainability and fairness of virtual economies. |
| Assessment of Real-World Impacts | Assess the real-world impacts of virtual economies, including employment opportunities, innovation, and ethical considerations. Explore how virtual economic activities intersect with real-world systems, influencing global economic and social landscapes. Identify research gaps and suggest areas for future study to deepen the understanding of the complexities of virtual economies. |

## 1.5 Significance

This chapter bridges theoretical concepts with practical applications, offering a nuanced perspective on how virtual economies shape social dynamics and community interactions within the metaverse. By exploring the relationships between economic activities and social structures, it provides valuable insights for game developers, policymakers, businesses, and researchers. Understanding virtual economies is crucial for fostering fair and sustainable economic practices, encouraging meaningful social interactions, and supporting the growth and stability of the metaverse. Moreover, the chapter contributes to the broader discourse on digital economies, emphasizing the potential of virtual systems to transform real-world economic and social landscapes.

## 2. LITERATURE REVIEW

The study of virtual economies has become an increasingly significant area of research as digital platforms and online interactions have grown exponentially. Scholars from various disciplines have explored the multifaceted aspects of virtual economies, focusing on user motivations, ethical considerations, psychological impacts, legal issues, and methodological approaches. This literature review synthesizes key academic contributions relevant to understanding the complexities of virtual economies and social structures within the metaverse, without delving into the specific topics covered in subsequent sections of this chapter.

## 2.1 User Motivations and Behavioral Economics

Understanding why individuals participate in virtual economies is crucial for comprehending their growth and sustainability. Researchers have examined the psychological drivers behind the purchase of virtual goods (Guo & Barnes, 2009), identifying factors such as self-expression, social influence, and the desire for functional advantages within virtual environments. Studies have explored player motivations in online games, categorizing them into achievement, social, and immersion components, which directly impact economic behaviors within virtual worlds (Yee, 2006).

## 2.2 Ethical Considerations and Virtual Labor

The rise of virtual economies has introduced complex ethical issues, particularly concerning virtual labor and exploitation (Lessig, 2009). The phenomenon of "gold farming," where individuals perform repetitive in-game tasks to acquire virtual currency or goods that are then sold for real money, raises questions about labor rights, fair compensation, and the exploitation of vulnerable populations. Scholars argue about the need to address these ethical concerns to ensure equitable practices within virtual economies.

## 2.3 Psychological and Sociocultural Impacts

Participation in virtual economies can have significant psychological effects on users (Yee, 2006). Research has investigated the potential for online gaming addiction, emphasizing how economic incentives and reward systems in games can contribute to compulsive behavior. The concept of "playbour," where play and labor intersect, blurs the lines between leisure and work. This intersection affects how users perceive their activities within virtual environments, potentially impacting their real-life behaviors and social interactions.

## 2.4 Legal Issues and Intellectual Property Rights

The legal landscape surrounding virtual economies is complex and continually evolving. There are challenges in applying traditional legal frameworks to virtual goods and currencies. Issues such as ownership rights, intellectual property, and contract enforcement in virtual environments pose significant challenges for lawmakers and regulators (Fairfield, 2005). Some argue for recognizing virtual property rights to protect users' investments and promote fairness within virtual economies. These legal considerations are critical for the sustainable development of virtual economies and the protection of participants' rights.

## 2.5 Methodological Approaches in Virtual Economy Research

Researchers have employed various methodologies to study virtual economies, ranging from quantitative analyses to qualitative ethnographic studies. Some have pioneered economic modeling within virtual worlds, applying traditional economic theories to virtual marketplaces to analyze supply, demand, and pricing mechanisms (Evison, 2016). Others have adopted ethnographic methods to immerse themselves in virtual communities, providing rich, detailed accounts of user behaviors, cultural norms, and social interactions. These diverse methodological approaches have enriched the understanding of virtual economies from multiple perspectives.

## 2.6 Technological Innovations and Their Influence

Technological advancements have significantly influenced the evolution of virtual economies. The integration of virtual reality (VR) and augmented reality (AR) technologies has enhanced user immersion, offering new possibilities for economic interactions within virtual spaces. Artificial intelligence (AI) and machine learning algorithms (Sharma et al., 2023) are being utilized to create more dynamic and responsive virtual environments, influencing economic activities and user experiences. These innovations present both opportunities and challenges for the development and regulation of virtual economies.

## 2.7 Environmental and Sustainability Concerns

As virtual economies expand, concerns about their environmental impact have emerged (M. Singh et al., 2023). Energy consumption associated with maintaining virtual environments and processing transactions, particularly in blockchain-based economies, has significant environmental implications. Researchers are calling for more sustainable approaches to technology development and virtual economic management to mitigate negative environmental effects.

## 2.8 Gaps in the Literature and Future Research Needs

While substantial research has been conducted on various aspects of virtual economies, gaps remain that warrant further investigation. There is a need for longitudinal studies examining the long-term psychological and social effects of participation in virtual economies. Additionally, interdisciplinary research combining insights from economics, psychology, sociology, and environmental studies could provide a more holistic understanding of virtual economies. The ethical implications of emerging technologies within virtual economies also require deeper exploration to inform policy and regulation.

## 3. TYPES AND COMPONENTS OF VIRTUAL ECONOMIES

*Figure 1. Illustration of the various types and components of virtual economies*

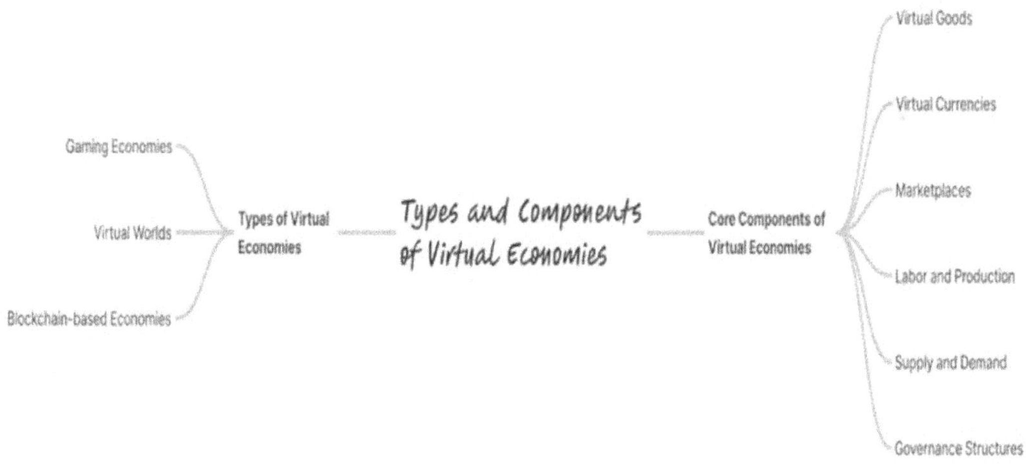


Virtual economies have become integral to the metaverse, manifesting in various digital environments with distinct characteristics and underlying components that facilitate their operation. Understanding the different types of virtual economies and their core components (refer to Figure 1) is essential to grasp how these digital ecosystems function and thrive.

### 3.1 Types of Virtual Economies

Virtual economies can be broadly categorized into three main types: gaming economies, virtual worlds, and blockchain-based economies.

*Figure 2. Illustration depicting different virtual economies*

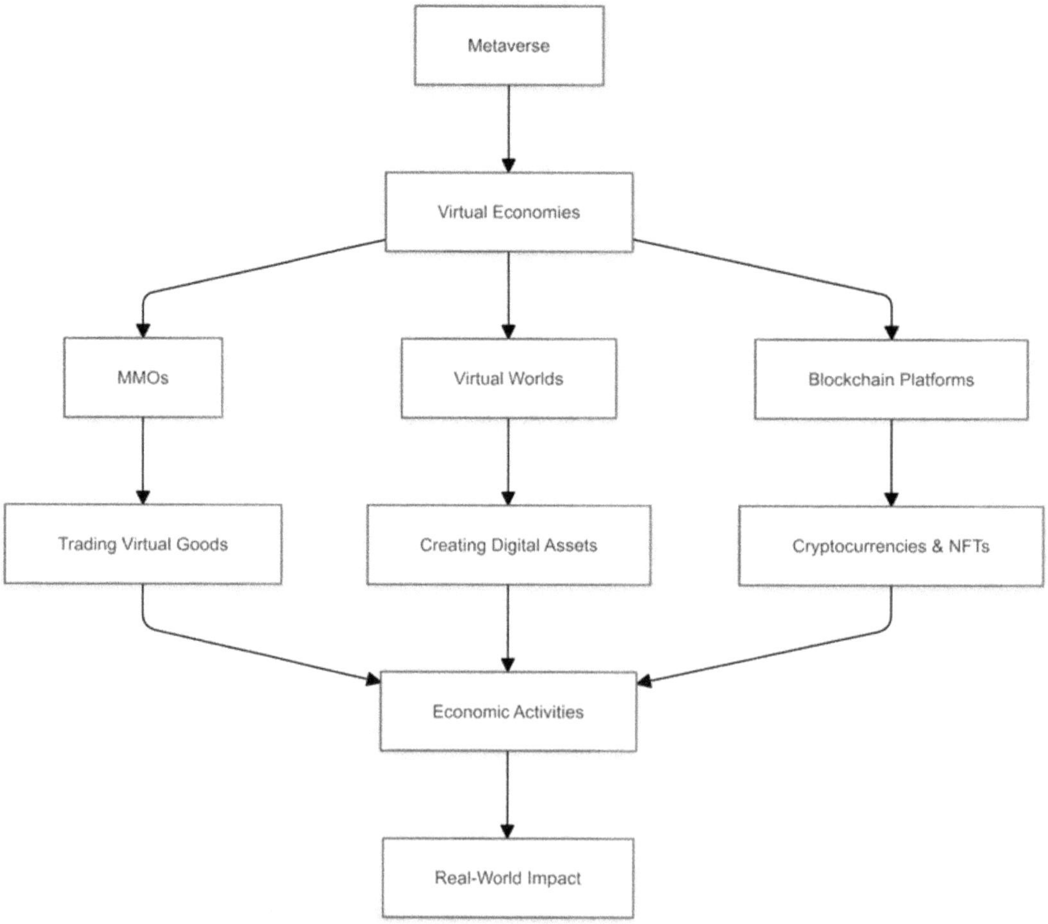


### 3.1.1. Gaming Economies

Gaming economies are prevalent in massively multiplayer online games (MMOs) (Castronova, 2006) such as World of Warcraft and EVE Online. In these environments, players engage in economic activities that mirror real-world systems. Virtual goods like weapons, armor, and resources are essential for gameplay and serve as primary drivers of player engagement and progression. Players earn or purchase virtual currencies to acquire these goods, pay for services, or trade with others. Marketplaces within these games, such as auction houses or trading systems, enable the buying and selling of virtual goods using virtual currency, creating an active and dynamic economy. The game developers establish governance structures by setting rules and mechanics that oversee the economy, including item drop rates, currency inflation, and trade regulations.

### 3.1.2. Virtual Worlds

Virtual worlds like Second Life (Boellstorff, 2015) offer user-driven economies where participants can create, buy, and sell digital assets, including clothing, property, and services. In these platforms, users act as both creators and consumers, investing time to design and produce virtual goods and services. Virtual currencies, such as Linden Dollars, facilitate transactions and can often be exchanged for real money, blurring the lines between virtual and real-world economies. Marketplaces allow users to trade these goods, contributing to a vibrant economic environment. Governance structures in virtual worlds are established through platform policies that govern intellectual property rights, trade rules, and dispute resolution, ensuring a fair and functional economy.

### 3.1.3. Blockchain-Based Economies

Blockchain-based economies represent a transformative approach to virtual economies, leveraging decentralized technologies to redefine asset ownership, trading mechanisms, and governance. Blockchain, a distributed ledger technology, ensures that all transactions are recorded chronologically and immutably across a network of nodes, eliminating the need for centralized oversight while guaranteeing transparency and security (Swan, 2015). Cryptocurrencies, such as Bitcoin (Nakamoto, 2008) and Ethereum, serve as the lifeblood of these economies, acting as both a medium of exchange and a store of value. Unlike traditional currencies, cryptocurrencies operate on blockchain networks, enabling peer-to-peer transactions that are verified and secured through consensus algorithms such as proof of work (PoW) or proof of stake (PoS) (Tasca & Tessone, 2017).

A cornerstone of blockchain-based economies is the use of Non-Fungible Tokens (NFTs) (Figure 3 shows the NFT trade volume of the past 23 months). NFTs are unique digital assets represented on blockchain networks, offering verifiable ownership and scarcity for virtual goods like land parcels in Decentraland or collectible creatures in Axie Infinity. These tokens utilize standards like ERC-721 or ERC-1155 on Ethereum to ensure interoperability across decentralized platforms. This tokenization fosters the creation of marketplaces where users can trade NFTs securely without intermediaries, leveraging smart contracts—self-executing contracts coded to enforce terms autonomously. These smart contracts underpin trustless transactions, eliminating reliance on central authorities and minimizing the risk of fraud.

*Figure 3. (Monthly NFT Trade Volume (USD), Dune)*

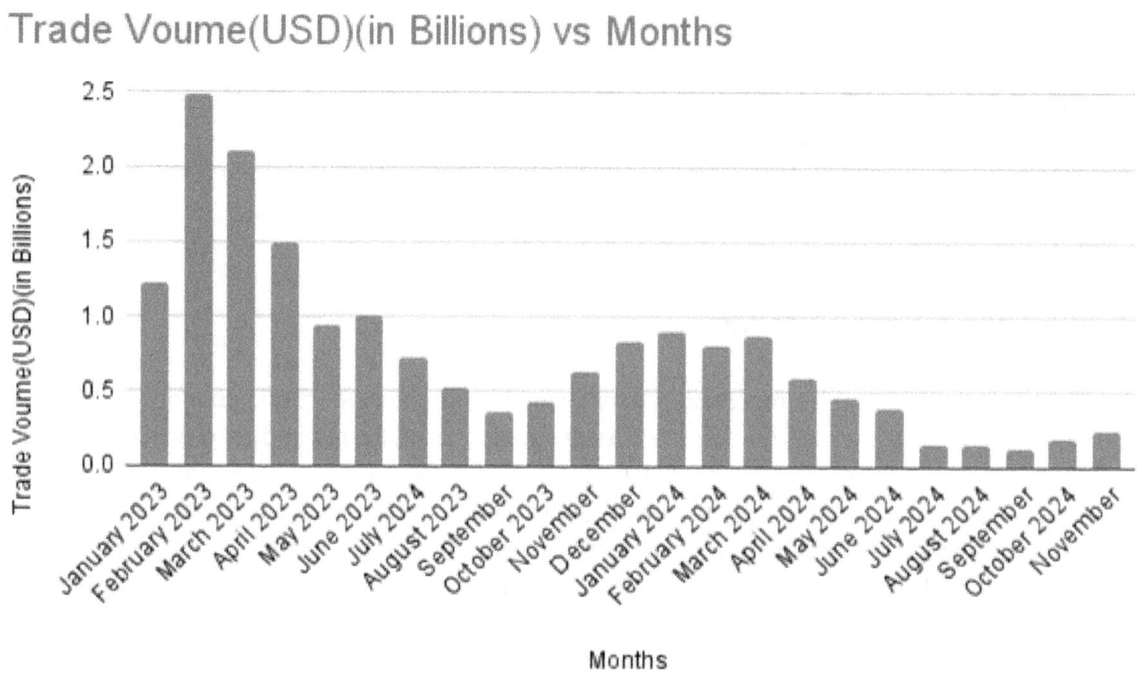


Blockchain also introduces innovative mechanisms for labor representation and reward within virtual economies. Participants earn tokens through activities such as gameplay, content creation, or staking assets. These tokens can often be exchanged for real-world currency, bridging virtual and physical economic systems. For instance, Axie Infinity's "play-to-earn" model enables players to generate real income by breeding, battling, and trading Axies, providing alternative revenue streams in regions with limited economic opportunities.

Moreover, blockchain facilitates decentralized governance through Decentralized Autonomous Organizations (DAOs). DAOs empower users by distributing decision-making authority among stakeholders, who vote on platform policies, economic changes, or community initiatives. These systems exemplify democratic governance structures, ensuring that platform development aligns with user interests. The transparency and immutability of blockchain bolster user trust, while decentralized governance enhances community participation and accountability.

## 3.2 Core Components of Virtual Economies

Despite their differences, these virtual economies share core components(Evison, 2016) fundamental to their operation:

### 3.2.1. Virtual Goods

Virtual goods are digital items that users can own, trade, or consume within the virtual environment (Guo & Barnes, 2009). These range from functional items like weapons and tools in games to aesthetic items like clothing and decorations in virtual worlds. The value of virtual goods is determined by their utility, rarity, and demand within the platform.

### 3.2.2. Virtual Currencies

Virtual currencies facilitate transactions within the virtual economy, serving as a medium of exchange and a store of value. In gaming economies, virtual currencies are often earned through gameplay achievements. In virtual worlds and blockchain-based economies, they can be purchased with real money or earned by contributing to the ecosystem.

### 3.2.3. Marketplaces

Marketplaces are platforms where users buy, sell, and trade virtual goods and services. They are essential for economic interaction, allowing users to engage in commerce within the virtual environment. Marketplaces can be regulated by the platform or operate in a decentralized manner, especially in blockchain-based economies.

### 3.2.4. Labor and Production

Users contribute labor by creating content, completing tasks, or engaging in activities that generate value within the virtual economy. In gaming economies, this may involve completing quests or crafting items. In virtual worlds, users design virtual goods or offer services to others. Labor and production drive the supply side of the economy, influencing the availability of virtual goods and services.

### 3.2.5. Supply and Demand Dynamics

Supply and demand dynamics determine the pricing and availability of virtual goods and services. The scarcity of items, user preferences, and overall economic health affect market conditions. In-game events, updates, or changes in user behavior can shift supply and demand, leading to fluctuations in the virtual economy.

## 4. REAL-WORLD IMPACT OF VIRTUAL ECONOMIES

Virtual economies, once confined to the boundaries of online games and digital platforms, are now exerting substantial influence on real-world economies and societies. One of the most prominent impacts is the creation of new income streams and employment opportunities. Individuals around the globe are earning real money by engaging in activities such as trading virtual goods, providing in-game services, and creating digital content. For example, in countries like the Philippines, players of blockchain-based games like Axie Infinity have generated incomes that surpass local averages, highlighting the potential of virtual economies to affect livelihoods and economic conditions (Kshetri, 2017).

The practice of Real Money Trading (RMT) bridges virtual economies with real-world financial systems. Virtual assets and currencies acquire tangible value, leading to secondary markets where they are bought and sold for actual money (Castronova, 2006). This convergence introduces complex legal and regulatory challenges, including taxation, intellectual property rights, and concerns over fraud and money laundering. Governments and regulatory bodies are increasingly attentive to these issues, striving to develop frameworks that can effectively monitor and manage virtual economic activities while protecting consumers.

Innovation in business models is another significant real-world impact. Companies are leveraging virtual platforms for marketing, customer engagement, and even hosting virtual events and conferences. The rise of virtual real estate investment in platforms like Decentraland demonstrates new avenues for investment and asset ownership. Brands are exploring opportunities in virtual advertising, creating immersive experiences that connect with consumers in novel ways.

Social implications are equally profound. Virtual economies facilitate global interaction and collaboration, allowing individuals from diverse backgrounds to connect, cooperate, and transact in shared digital spaces. However, they also raise ethical considerations regarding digital labor (Kuo Siong Tan, 2024). Issues such as unfair compensation, exploitation of vulnerable populations, and unhealthy work practices in virtual environments mirror real-world labor concerns and necessitate attention.

The integration of blockchain technology and cryptocurrencies within virtual economies has spurred broader interest and adoption of decentralized finance (DeFi). This development promotes financial inclusion by providing access to financial services for unbanked or underbanked populations through virtual platforms. Moreover, it encourages the democratization of financial systems by reducing reliance on traditional intermediaries.

Psychological and behavioral impacts on individuals are noteworthy. Engagement in virtual economies can influence user behavior and social dynamics, sometimes leading to addiction, excessive spending, or escapism. The allure of virtual success and wealth may affect real-world responsibilities and relationships, highlighting the need for balance and potential regulatory measures.

Educationally, virtual economies serve as valuable tools for studying economic theories, market behaviors, and social interactions in controlled environments. Economists and researchers can observe the effects of policy changes, supply and demand fluctuations, and user behaviors without the risks associated with real-world experimentation. Insights gained from these studies can inform both virtual and real-world economic policies and practices.

## 5. SOCIAL STRUCTURES IN VIRTUAL ECONOMIES

The evolution of virtual economies within the metaverse has fostered intricate social structures that shape user interactions in these digital environments. These structures often mirror real-world societal organizations, reflecting human tendencies to form communities, establish hierarchies, and create systems of cooperation and competition. Key aspects include guilds and clans, virtual social capital, collaborative economies, and social stratification based on wealth and resource access.

## 5.1 Guilds and Clans

Guilds and clans are formal groups that unite users to achieve common goals, such as completing quests, engaging in battles, or pooling resources for economic gain (Yee, 2006). Typically hierarchical, these organizations have leaders who coordinate activities and enforce rules, facilitating efficient communication and task delegation similar to real-world institutions. Membership provides users with a sense of belonging, social support, and access to exclusive resources, thereby enhancing their experiences and promoting community cohesion within the metaverse.

## 5.2 Virtual Social Capital

Virtual social capital refers to the influence and prestige users gain through their achievements, assets, and social networks. Similar to real-world social capital, it allows individuals to receive preferential treatment in trades, invitations to elite groups, and leadership roles. Accumulating social capital fosters trust and cooperation, encouraging deeper engagement and contributing to the sustainability and vibrancy of virtual economies.

## 5.3 Collaborative Economies

Collaborative economies are essential to virtual economies, where users specialize in roles like crafting, resource gathering, or combat and trade goods and services to meet mutual needs. This interdependence promotes partnerships, trade networks, and joint projects, enhancing economic efficiency and fostering innovation. Collaboration strengthens social bonds, leading to a more engaged and cohesive community, and supports a dynamic and resilient economic environment.

## 5.4 Social Stratification

Social stratification arises from disparities in wealth, resource access, and social connections. Users who accumulate significant virtual assets gain higher status and influence, creating social classes with advantages like superior equipment and market influence(Guo & Barnes, 2009). Conversely, less affluent users may struggle to compete, leading to community divides. This concentration of power can result in monopolistic behaviors and economic imbalances, raising concerns about fairness and accessibility and prompting discussions on platform design and regulation to ensure a more equitable virtual environment.

# 6. GOVERNANCE AND REGULATION OF VIRTUAL ECONOMIES

Governance and regulation within the metaverse critically shape user experiences, social dynamics, and the sustainability of virtual economies, aligning with the themes of Unveiling Social Dynamics and Community Interaction in the Metaverse. Governance structures range from centralized platform control to decentralized models enabled by blockchain technology. Additionally, the integration of virtual economies with real-world legal systems introduces significant policy implications regarding government intervention, taxation, and regulation.

## 6.1 Platform Governance

In traditional virtual worlds and online games, companies manage governance by establishing rules for the creation and distribution of virtual goods, operating marketplaces, and enforcing trade policies. Developers control item scarcity and adjust drop rates, directly influencing supply and demand dynamics. They also set terms of service that regulate player behavior (Lessig, 2009), trade restrictions, and dispute resolution mechanisms. While centralized governance allows for coordinated management, it can lead to tensions if users perceive decisions as unfair, impacting trust and community cohesion within the metaverse.

## 6.2 Decentralized Governance

Blockchain-based virtual economies leverage decentralized governance models that shift control from centralized entities to the user community. At the core of this paradigm are Decentralized Autonomous Organizations (DAOs), which represent a transformative approach to governance by employing blockchain technology and smart contracts. DAOs are organizations governed by rules encoded in smart contracts—self-executing programs that run on decentralized networks like Ethereum. These contracts automate decision-making processes, enforce rules transparently, and reduce reliance on intermediaries or centralized authorities. Participants in a DAO typically hold governance tokens, which grant them voting rights proportional to their stake, enabling them to propose, deliberate, and vote on key changes or policies.

The mechanics of a DAO enable a wide range of applications in virtual economies. For example, token holders in platforms like Decentraland can vote on modifications to transaction fees, the introduction of new assets, or the allocation of funds from a communal treasury. This participatory model ensures that the direction of the economy reflects the collective will of its stakeholders, fostering inclusivity and community engagement. Furthermore, the immutable nature of blockchain transactions ensures transparency, with all decisions and financial movements recorded on a public ledger accessible to all participants.

However, implementing and managing DAOs in virtual economies is not without challenges. One major concern is achieving effective coordination among a diverse and geographically dispersed user base, which can slow decision-making processes. The potential for governance capture, where a few large stakeholders dominate decisions, is another significant risk that may undermine the democratic ethos of a DAO. Additionally, the irreversibility of blockchain transactions complicates the resolution of disputes or the correction of errors, requiring meticulous planning and robust smart contract design.

To address these challenges, innovations such as quadratic voting—where users' voting power diminishes with repeated voting on the same proposal—and reputation-based systems are being explored. These methods aim to enhance fairness and prevent power concentration. DAOs exemplify the decentralization and democratization aspirations of virtual economies, offering unparalleled transparency, community-driven decision-making, and resilience against centralized control. As virtual economies continue to mature, refining and advancing DAO structures will be critical in ensuring equitable governance, economic stability, and long-term sustainability.

## 6.3 Policy Implications

The convergence of virtual economies with real-world financial systems has drawn significant attention from governments and regulatory bodies, raising several policy implications. Governments may seek to regulate virtual economies to prevent illegal activities such as money laundering, fraud, and tax evasion. The anonymity and global reach of virtual transactions complicate enforcement efforts, leading to regulatory measures (Lessig, 2009) like requiring Know Your Customer (KYC) protocols and complying with Anti-Money Laundering (AML) regulations. Additionally, the conversion of virtual assets into real-world money presents taxation challenges, as governments consider how to tax income derived from virtual economies through capital gains taxes, income taxes, or sales taxes. The borderless nature of virtual transactions and the difficulty in tracking and valuing virtual assets further complicate tax regulation.

As virtual economies expand in scale and complexity, they may significantly impact real-world economies, necessitating the development of legal frameworks that address market manipulation (Kumar et al., 2024), monopolistic practices, consumer protection, and intellectual property rights within virtual platforms. Recognizing and enforcing ownership rights of virtual assets is essential to protect creators and foster innovation. Policymakers must balance the promotion of innovation within virtual economies with the need to protect users and maintain economic stability. Overregulation can stifle creativity and limit the benefits of virtual economies, while under regulation may lead to abuses and systemic risks. Collaborative efforts between governments, platform operators, and users are essential to develop regulatory approaches that support healthy virtual economies and vibrant social structures within the metaverse.

## 6.4 Impact on Social Dynamics

Governance and regulation directly influence social dynamics and community interactions within virtual economies. Effective governance models and regulatory frameworks promote trust, cooperation, and fairness, enhancing social cohesion. Transparent and inclusive governance can encourage community engagement and collective action, while opaque or autocratic governance may lead to alienation and fragmented communities. Addressing governance and regulatory challenges is vital for fostering equitable and sustainable virtual economies that support positive social interactions and community development in the metaverse.

### Case Study: Decentralized Governance in "Axie Infinity"

Axie Infinity (Figure 4 shows Axie Infinity player-count), a blockchain-based game, employs decentralized governance where players stake the native token AXS to influence game development and economic parameters. This model fosters community ownership and engagement, enhancing social cohesion within the metaverse. However, it also presents challenges in coordinating a large user base and preventing power concentration among wealthy stakeholders, which can impact community dynamics and equity.

*Figure 4. (Axie Infinity Monthly Players, Axie Infinity)*

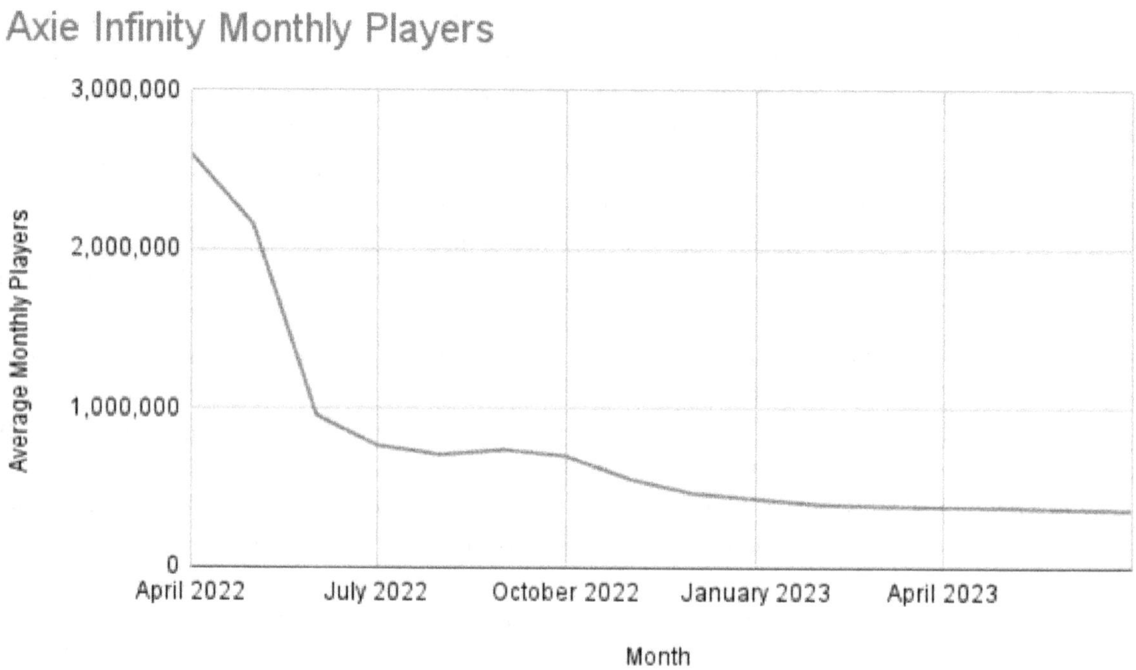


## 7. CHALLENGES AND LIMITATIONS

The proliferation of virtual economies within the metaverse presents a myriad of challenges and limitations that affect their functionality, sustainability, and impact on users and societies. These challenges span technological, regulatory, ethical, economic, and social domains, necessitating comprehensive strategies to address them.

*Table 3. Table depicting challenges in virtual economics(in brief)*

| Category | Challenges | Example |
|---|---|---|
| Technological | Scalability, lack of interoperability | CryptoKitties causing Ethereum transaction delays |
| Regulatory/Legal | Jurisdiction issues, taxation, intellectual property | NFT ownership and authenticity issues |
| Ethical/Social | Privacy risks, addiction, and mental health concerns | WHO's recognition of gaming disorder |
| Economic | Volatility, wealth inequality | Bitcoin price fluctuations affecting markets |
| Environmental | High energy consumption from blockchain activities | Bitcoin mining criticized for energy use |
| Governance | Centralized control vs. decentralized governance | Coordination issues in decentralized platforms |

## 7.1 Technological Challenges

One of the primary technological challenges is scalability. As virtual economies grow and user participation increases, platforms may struggle to maintain performance and stability(Kumar et al., 2024). High user traffic can lead to server overloads, latency issues, and degraded user experiences. For example, the blockchain-based game CryptoKitties experienced significant slowdowns and transaction backlogs on the Ethereum network due to high demand, highlighting scalability limitations inherent in current blockchain technologies.

Interoperability between different virtual platforms is another significant limitation. Users often cannot transfer assets or currencies between platforms, restricting the fluidity of virtual economies and limiting user autonomy. Technical barriers to interoperability hinder the development of a unified metaverse where virtual economies can seamlessly interact.

## 7.2 Regulatory and Legal Challenges

Virtual economies operate across global networks, leading to complex regulatory and legal challenges. Jurisdictional issues arise because virtual economic activities transcend national boundaries, complicating the enforcement of laws and regulations. Taxation of virtual income and assets remains a contentious issue, with governments grappling to define and implement appropriate tax policies.

Intellectual property rights within virtual economies pose significant challenges. Users who create digital content may face difficulties in protecting their creations due to ambiguous legal privacy frameworks. Additionally, the rise of non-fungible tokens (NFTs) has raised questions about ownership and authenticity of digital assets.

## 7.3 Ethical and Social Concerns

Privacy and data security (Vats et al., 2024) remain critical issues in virtual economies, where users frequently share sensitive personal information and engage in transactions that necessitate a high level of trust in platform security. Data breaches not only expose users to financial losses but also compromise their digital identities, significantly eroding user confidence in these ecosystems. The risk of cyberattacks, such as JavaScript code injection vulnerabilities (S. Gupta & Gupta, 2018) on Online Social Networks, further exacerbates these concerns. To address these challenges, platforms must prioritize robust cybersecurity measures, including the use of multi-factor authentication, end-to-end encryption, and advanced intrusion detection systems powered by machine learning. Additionally, adopting privacy-preserving technologies like Zero-Knowledge Proofs (Aggarwal et al., 2024) can enhance user trust by enabling secure transactions without disclosing sensitive data.

Addiction and mental health impacts present another pressing ethical issue. The immersive and often competitive nature of virtual economies can lead to excessive engagement, potentially disrupting users' real-world responsibilities and well-being. The World Health Organization's recognition of "gaming disorder" underscores the urgency of addressing this problem. Platforms should implement strategies to mitigate these risks, such as introducing gameplay limits, promoting healthy engagement through reminders or time-tracking features, and providing access to mental health resources for users exhibiting signs of problematic behavior. Furthermore, incorporating ethical design principles, such as ensuring transparency in reward mechanisms and minimizing exploitative features like predatory monetization models, can foster a healthier virtual ecosystem.

Exploitation within virtual economies, particularly in play-to-earn models, also raises significant ethical concerns. Users in economically disadvantaged regions are often drawn to these platforms as alternative income sources, but they may face unfair compensation and exploitative working conditions. To mitigate these issues, developers should establish fair labor policies, enforce transparency in revenue-sharing models, and ensure that all participants have equitable opportunities to succeed. International regulations and standards can further protect users from exploitation, ensuring that virtual labor markets remain fair and inclusive.

## 7.4 Economic Challenges

Economic instability within virtual economies can manifest through inflation of virtual currencies, market manipulation, and speculative bubbles (Sarin et al., 2024). The volatility of cryptocurrency values can affect virtual economies that rely on them, leading to unpredictability in asset values and user earnings. An illustrative case is the rapid fluctuation of Bitcoin prices, which can impact virtual marketplaces that accept it as a form of payment.

Inequality and wealth disparity are also prevalent challenges. As some users accumulate vast virtual wealth, social stratification can deepen, leading to monopolistic behaviors and reduced accessibility for new or less affluent users. This concentration of wealth can stifle competition and innovation within the virtual economy.

## 7.5 Environmental Sustainability

The environmental impact of virtual economies, particularly those based on blockchain technologies, is a growing concern. The energy consumption required for mining cryptocurrencies and maintaining blockchain networks contributes to carbon emissions and environmental degradation (Kumar et al., 2023). For example, Bitcoin mining has been criticized for its substantial energy usage, prompting discussions about the sustainability of proof-of-work consensus mechanisms.

Researchers are calling for more sustainable approaches to technology development and virtual economy management to mitigate negative environmental effects (Kumar et al., 2023).

## 7.6 Governance Challenges

Balancing centralized control with decentralized governance presents significant challenges. Centralized governance can lead to unilateral decisions that may not reflect user interests, while decentralized models can suffer from coordination difficulties and governance capture by a few influential stakeholders. Ensuring fairness, transparency, and accountability within governance structures is essential to maintain user trust and economic stability.

To enhance the security of decentralized governance frameworks, the implementation of quantum-safe cryptographic techniques (N. Singh et al., 2024) and the implementation of Zero Knowledge Proofs (ZKPs)(Aggarwal et al., 2024) can be crucial. These techniques protect the integrity of voting systems, transaction records, and decision-making processes from potential quantum-based attacks, thereby ensuring that governance mechanisms remain secure and trustworthy. By integrating quantum-safe cryptography, virtual economies can safeguard their governance structures against emerging threats, fostering a more resilient and equitable metaverse.

### Case Study: The Collapse of the Virtual Economy in "Diablo III"

An illustrative example of challenges in virtual economies is the initial launch of the Real Money Auction House in Blizzard Entertainment's Diablo III (El-Shagi & Von Schweinitz, 2016). The platform allowed players to buy and sell in-game items for real currency. However, it led to significant economic imbalance, rampant inflation of in-game currency, and a decline in player satisfaction. The system was exploited by a few players who manipulated the market, creating disparities and undermining the game's integrity. Eventually, Blizzard decided to shut down the Real Money Auction House to restore balance and refocus the game on gameplay rather than economic transactions. This case highlights the complexities and risks associated with integrating real-world monetary systems into virtual economies without adequate safeguards.

The landscape of virtual economies is poised for significant evolution, driven by technological advancements, regulatory developments, and shifting social paradigms. Anticipating these future directions (Nedjah et al., 2022) and trends is crucial for stakeholders seeking to harness the potential of virtual economies within the metaverse.

## 8. ADVANCEMENTS IN TECHNOLOGY

Technological innovations are set to revolutionize the functionality and user experience of virtual economies, making them more immersive, efficient, and secure. Developments in virtual reality (VR) and augmented reality (AR) technologies are projected to redefine user engagement by 2030, offering hyper-realistic, interactive environments. Companies like Meta and Apple are investing heavily in hardware, such as advanced VR headsets and AR glasses, that aim to bridge the gap between virtual and physical worlds, creating seamless experiences that blend both realities.

The blockchain landscape is also undergoing significant transformations, with the development of more scalable and energy-efficient technologies (Aldweesh et al., 2023). Emerging blockchain frameworks like Ethereum 2.0 and Solana are addressing current scalability and sustainability challenges, with transaction speeds projected to increase exponentially while reducing energy consumption by up to 90%. These advancements are expected to be fully operational within the next five years, aligning with global sustainability goals.

*Figure 5. Advancements in technology*

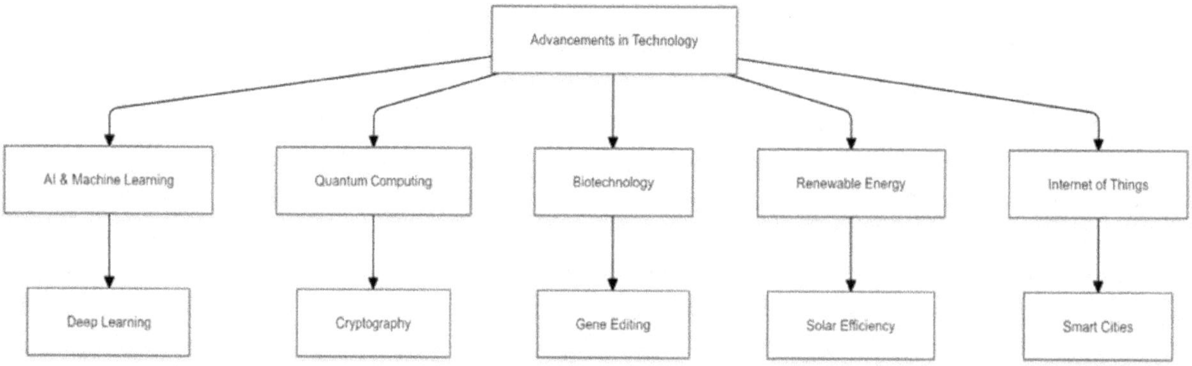


Artificial intelligence (AI) and machine learning (Mengi et al., 2023) will play increasingly significant roles in personalizing user experiences, optimizing economic interactions, and enhancing security measures. For instance, AI-driven algorithms could facilitate dynamic pricing models, match users for trade opportunities, or detect fraudulent activities in real-time.

## 8.1 Integration With Real-World Economies

The convergence of virtual and real-world economies is poised to accelerate, driven by the growing acceptance of virtual currencies and digital assets in mainstream financial systems. Virtual earnings, such as those from gaming platforms or blockchain-based economies, are increasingly being converted into real-world value, creating a seamless link between digital and physical marketplaces. This progression has captured the attention of central banks and financial institutions, which are actively exploring the implementation of central bank digital currencies (CBDCs). Unlike decentralized cryptocurrencies, CBDCs are state-issued digital currencies backed by sovereign governments, offering a stable and trusted medium of exchange. They hold the potential to standardize transactions across virtual and traditional economies, facilitating secure and regulated trade.

The introduction of CBDCs into virtual economies could address challenges related to trust, volatility, and compliance. For instance, transactions involving virtual assets like non-fungible tokens (NFTs) or in-game currencies could be seamlessly converted into CBDCs, bypassing the instability often associated with cryptocurrencies like Bitcoin or Ethereum. Furthermore, CBDCs could enhance financial inclusion by providing secure and accessible payment systems to users who may not have access to traditional banking infrastructure, particularly in regions where virtual platforms serve as primary sources of income. This integration, however, necessitates robust regulatory frameworks to mitigate risks, including anti-money laundering (AML) violations, tax evasion, and consumer fraud. Governments would need to establish clear policies for cross-border transactions, ownership rights of virtual assets, and the taxation of virtual earnings to ensure equitable and transparent operations.

In parallel, technological advancements in high-performance computing, such as automatic parallelization algorithms, play a crucial role in optimizing the backend processes that power virtual platforms. These algorithms (Kumar et al., 2021) can significantly reduce computational overheads, allowing platforms to process vast amounts of data and transactions more efficiently. By enhancing scalability and responsiveness, such technologies ensure that virtual economies can manage the increasing complexity and transaction volumes inherent in metaverse ecosystems. This optimization is vital for maintaining seamless user experiences, reducing latency, and fostering robust economic interactions.

The concept of the "metaverse economy" highlights the potential of virtual economies to become major contributors to global economic activity. Emerging sectors, including virtual real estate (Hutson et al., 2023), digital fashion, and virtual services, represent lucrative opportunities for investment and entrepreneurship. For example, virtual real estate platforms like Decentraland have already facilitated multimillion-dollar transactions for digital property. Similarly, digital fashion brands are leveraging the metaverse to redefine consumer engagement through virtual try-on experiences and avatar personalization. As these markets expand, the adoption of CBDCs and the development of comprehensive regulatory frameworks will be instrumental in ensuring their sustainable integration into the global financial system.

Regulatory frameworks must balance innovation with oversight, enabling virtual economies to flourish while safeguarding stakeholders. Policymakers will need to address key challenges, such as intellectual property rights for digital assets, taxation of income generated in virtual environments, and standardization of cross-platform transactions. By creating a harmonized ecosystem where virtual economies and traditional financial systems coexist, stakeholders can unlock the full potential of the metaverse economy while ensuring ethical, transparent, and sustainable practices. Soth korea

## 8.2 Evolution of Governance Models

Governance structures within virtual economies are expected to evolve towards more sophisticated models that balance user participation with effective management. Hybrid governance models that combine decentralized decision-making with centralized oversight could emerge, leveraging the strengths of both approaches. The implementation of advanced machine learning algorithms, such as those used for optimizing computational processes (I. Singh et al., 2022), can enhance the efficiency and responsiveness of governance systems, ensuring more accurate predictions of economic trends and better resource allocation within the metaverse. Additionally, the role of Decentralized Autonomous Organizations (DAOs) (Sims, 2019) may expand, enabling users to have greater influence over platform policies and economic parameters. Innovations in governance mechanisms, such as quadratic voting or reputation-based systems, could enhance fairness and prevent governance capture.

## 8.3 Regulatory Developments

Governments and international bodies are anticipated to develop more comprehensive regulatory frameworks for virtual economies. Regulations may focus on consumer protection, anti-money laundering (AML), know-your-customer (KYC) requirements, and taxation policies.

International cooperation may be necessary to address the global nature of virtual economic activities. Standardization of regulations could facilitate smoother operations for platforms and users, while promoting legal compliance and economic stability.

## 8.4 Social and Cultural Impact

Virtual economies are poised to exert significant social and cultural influence, reshaping user interactions, community structures, and societal norms within the metaverse. These digital ecosystems foster global connectivity, enabling individuals from diverse backgrounds to collaborate and participate in shared economic and social activities. However, cultural and regional differences play a critical role in shaping the adoption and functioning of these virtual economies. For instance, the acceptance of blockchain-based platforms and virtual currencies varies widely due to differing regulatory environments, technological infrastructure, and societal attitudes toward digital innovation. In countries like Japan and South Korea, where technology adoption is high, virtual economies have rapidly gained traction, while in regions with limited digital literacy or stringent financial regulations, adoption remains slower.

Ensuring the authenticity and reliability of information is vital for maintaining trust and cohesion within these global virtual communities. Advanced neural network models (Girdhar et al., 2023) are instrumental in combating fake news and misinformation, which can fragment communities and undermine social harmony.

Work practices within virtual economies are also influenced by regional disparities in access and opportunity. The "virtual gig economy" offers flexible employment opportunities, particularly in regions with limited formal job markets. For example, blockchain-based games like Axie Infinity have provided income streams for individuals in the Philippines, demonstrating the potential of virtual economies to alleviate financial instability in developing nations. However, these opportunities also raise concerns about job security, fair compensation, and the exploitation of labor, particularly in regions with weak labor protections.

### Case Study: The Rise of Virtual Fashion

An emerging trend illustrating these future directions is the rise of virtual fashion (Bardzell et al., 2010) within the metaverse. Brands like Gucci and Balenciaga have ventured into virtual spaces, offering digital clothing and accessories for avatars. Users purchase these virtual goods, often at significant prices, for self-expression and status within virtual communities. For example, in 2021, a virtual Gucci bag was sold for over $4,000 on the Roblox platform, exceeding the price of its real-world counterpart.

This trend reflects the integration of virtual economies with real-world industries, blurring the lines between digital and physical markets. It also raises questions about intellectual property rights, ownership of digital goods, and the environmental impact of producing and maintaining virtual assets.

*Figure 6. (Digital Fashion Purchase Interest in the U.S. 2021, Statista)*

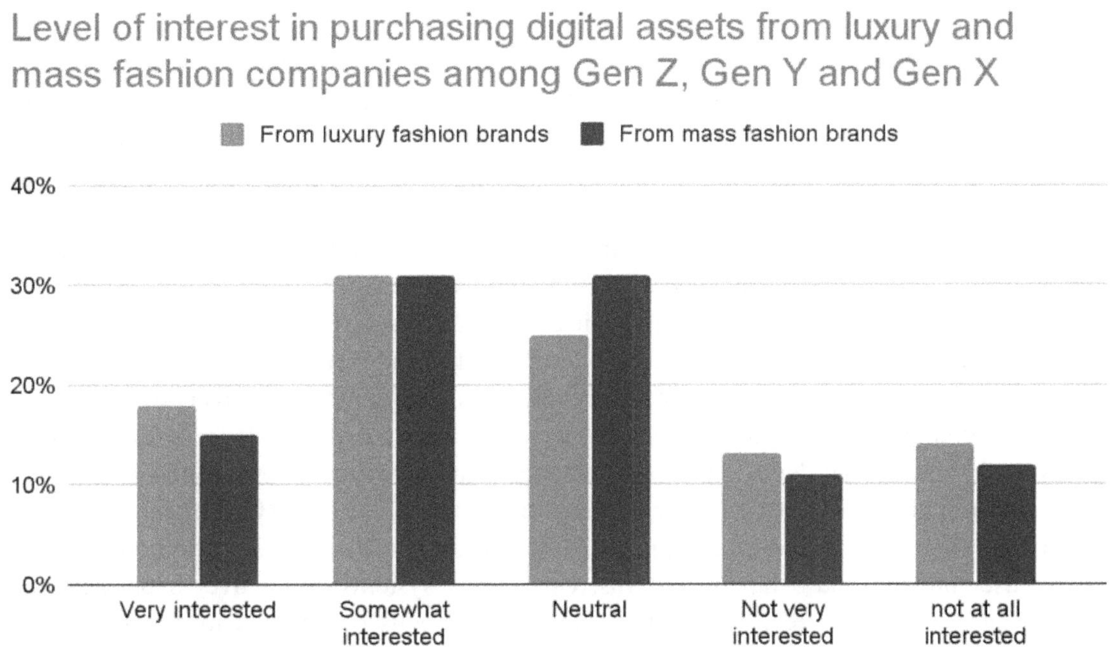


## 8.5 The Emergence of Play-to-Earn Models

Another significant trend is the emergence of "play-to-earn" models (Duguleană et al., 2024), where users earn real-world value through in-game activities. Axie Infinity is a notable example, where players can earn cryptocurrency by breeding, trading, and battling virtual creatures called Axies. This model has gained popularity in regions with limited economic opportunities, providing alternative income sources. However, the integrity and security of play-to-earn systems are crucial for their sustainability. Advanced security measures, such as CNN-based intrusion detection systems, play a vital role in protecting these platforms from cyber threats and unauthorized access. The evolution of CNN-based intrusion detection in network security (Abd El-Latif et al., 2025), showcases how these systems can safeguard virtual marketplaces from malicious activities, ensuring that economic interactions remain secure and trustworthy. Implementing such security frameworks is essential for maintaining user trust and the long-term viability of play-to-earn models.

The success of play-to-earn games highlights the potential for virtual economies to impact real-world livelihoods and suggests a shift towards more economically integrated gaming experiences.

## 8.6 Advanced Machine Learning Applications

The evolution of virtual economies has necessitated the integration of advanced machine learning (ML) techniques to optimize economic processes, enhance personalization, and bolster security. These technologies are pivotal in ensuring the scalability and sustainability of virtual marketplaces.

Hybrid models, such as neuro-fuzzy systems (Sarin, Singh, Kumar, Chauhan, et al., 2024), combine the reasoning capabilities of fuzzy logic with the learning adaptability of neural networks. In virtual marketplaces, these systems can adapt to fluctuating market dynamics by analyzing historical transaction data and user behavior to forecast trends, recommend pricing strategies, and optimize resource allocation. For example, a neuro-fuzzy model could analyze seasonal variations in demand for virtual goods, enabling platforms to adjust supply chains or pricing models dynamically.

Generative Adversarial Networks (GANs) (Sarin et al., 2023) play a crucial role in producing synthetic data that can simulate user interactions and test economic models under various conditions. GANs consist of two neural networks—a generator and a discriminator—that work in tandem to create highly realistic data. In virtual economies, this technology could generate synthetic trading data for testing marketplace algorithms or simulating user demand patterns, enhancing the robustness of economic systems.

The Unet model (Gaurav et al., 2024) is a convolutional neural network (CNN) architecture widely used for image segmentation but increasingly adapted for personalization in virtual economies. By segmenting user profiles and behavior patterns, Unet-based systems can deliver hyper-personalized experiences, such as tailored recommendations for virtual goods or targeted marketing campaigns. This level of personalization drives user engagement and increases transaction rates, contributing to the overall vibrancy of the economy.

Advanced ML techniques also address the critical need for security in virtual economies. Chaotic watermarking (Kaur et al., 2024) ensures the protection of digital assets against tampering and unauthorized modifications by embedding robust, encrypted identifiers into virtual items. These watermarks, generated using chaotic systems, are resilient against cyberattacks and preserve the integrity of ownership records, which is essential for maintaining user trust in virtual marketplaces.

Securing platforms from cyber threats like DDoS attacks is paramount. A machine learning-driven DDoS detection framework tailored for VANET cloud environments (Setia et al., 2024) demonstrates the efficacy of ML algorithms in identifying malicious traffic patterns in real time. Applying similar frameworks to virtual economies ensures that platforms remain resilient against cyber threats, maintaining transaction integrity and platform availability. These systems leverage supervised and unsupervised ML techniques to detect anomalies, enabling proactive threat mitigation without disrupting economic activities.

## 9. CONCLUSION

Virtual economies are fundamental to the metaverse, profoundly shaping how users interact, build communities, and engage in economic activities. This chapter has examined various types of virtual economies—gaming, virtual worlds, and blockchain-based platforms—and their essential components, including virtual goods, currencies, marketplaces, and governance structures. It concludes that decentralized governance models can increase transparency and community engagement, while FT-driven marketplaces expand opportunities for creators and investors, and labor within these economies introduces both new income avenues and global workforce challenges. Recommendations include adopting equitable policies to mitigate wealth inequality, implementing robust security frameworks to sustain user trust, and exploring balanced governance structures that combine efficiency with transparency. By analyzing the social structures that emerge from these economies, such as guilds, virtual social capital, and collaborative efforts, we understand their significant impact on community building and social hierarchies. Additionally, the chapter highlighted the real-world implications of virtual economies, including new employment opportunities, innovation, and ethical challenges, while addressing the complexities of regulation and sustainability. As the metaverse continues to evolve, fostering fair and sustainable virtual economies will require ongoing research and collaborative efforts among developers, policymakers, and users to ensure positive social interactions and the overall growth and stability of these digital ecosystems.

## REFERENCES


Abd El-Latif, A. A., Tawalbeh, L., Mohanty, M., Gupta, B., & Psannis, K. E. (Eds.). (2025). *Digital forensics and cyber crime investigation: Recent advances and future directions* (1st ed.). CRC Press.

Aggarwal, T., Kumar, S., Singh, S. K., Gupta, B. B., Nedjah, N., & Castiglione, A. (2024). Zero Knowledge Proofs and Their Applications in Cryptography: Advancements, Challenges, and Future Aspects. In Gupta, B. B., Kalra, D., & Almomani, A. (Eds.), (pp. 55–74). Advances in Information Security, Privacy, and Ethics. IGI Global., DOI: 10.4018/979-8-3693-5330-1.ch003

*Axie Infinity Monthly players*. [Dataset]. https://prioridata.com/data/axie-infinity-users/#:~:text=Axie%20Infinity%20Key%20Stats,Axies%20to%20play%20and%20earn

Bardzell, J., Pace, T., & Terrell, J. (2010). Virtual fashion and avatar design: A survey of consumers and designers. *Proceedings of the 6th Nordic Conference on Human-Computer Interaction: Extending Boundaries*, 599–602. DOI: 10.1145/1868914.1868983

Boellstorff, T. (2015). *Coming of Age in Second Life: An Anthropologist Explores the Virtually Human*. Princeton University Press., DOI: 10.1515/9781400874101

Castronova, E. (2006). On the Research Value of Large Games: Natural Experiments in Norrath and Camelot. *Games and Culture*, 1(2), 163–186. DOI: 10.1177/1555412006286686

*Digital fashion purchase interest in the U.S.2021*. Statista. Retrieved October 18, 2024, from https://www.statista.com/statistics/1311669/digital-fashion-asset-buying-interest/

Duguleană, A. R., Tănăsescu, C. R., & Duguleană, M. (2024). Emerging Trends in Play-to-Earn (P2E) Games. *Journal of Theoretical and Applied Electronic Commerce Research*, 19(1), 486–506. DOI: 10.3390/jtaer19010026

El-Shagi, M., & Von Schweinitz, G. (2016). The Diablo 3 Economy: An Agent Based Approach. *Computational Economics*, 47(2), 193–217. DOI: 10.1007/s10614-014-9480-5

Evison, L. (2016). Virtual Economics: Design and Analysis, written by Vili Lehdonvirta and Edward Castronova. *Asiascape: Digital Asia*, 3(1–2), 103–105. DOI: 10.1163/22142312-12340052

Fairfield, J. A. T. (2005). Virtual Property. *Boston University Law Review. Boston University. School of Law*, 85, 1047.

Guo, Y., & Barnes, S. (2009). Virtual item purchase behavior in virtual worlds: An exploratory investigation. *Electronic Commerce Research*, 9(1–2), 77–96. DOI: 10.1007/s10660-009-9032-6

Kshetri, N. (2017). Will blockchain emerge as a tool to break the poverty chain in the Global South? *Third World Quarterly*, 38(8), 1710–1732. DOI: 10.1080/01436597.2017.1298438

Kumar, S., Singh, S. K., & Aggarwal, N. (2023). Sustainable Data Dependency Resolution Architectural Framework to Achieve Energy Efficiency Using Speculative Parallelization. *2023 3rd International Conference on Innovative Sustainable Computational Technologies (CISCT)*, 1–6. DOI: 10.1109/CISCT57197.2023.10351343

Kumar, S., Singh, S. K., Ayushi, , Chilkoti, V., Arya, V., Chui, K. T., & Gupta, B. B. (2024). Metaversal 6G: Deciphering Complex Requirements and Multivariate KPIs in High-Performance Computing. *Procedia Computer Science*, 238, 914–919. DOI: 10.1016/j.procs.2024.06.112

Kuo Siong Tan, G. (2024). Playing for keeps: Digital labor and blockchain precarity in play-to-earn gaming. *Geoforum*, 151, 104009. DOI: 10.1016/j.geoforum.2024.104009

Lessig, L. (2009). *Code: And Other Laws of Cyberspace*. ReadHowYouWant.com.

Mengi, G., Singh, S. K., Kumar, S., Mahto, D., & Sharma, A. (2023). Automated Machine Learning (AutoML): The Future of Computational Intelligence. In Nedjah, N., Martínez Pérez, G., & Gupta, B. B. (Eds.), *International Conference on Cyber Security, Privacy and Networking (ICSPN 2022)* (Vol. 599, pp. 309–317). Springer International Publishing. DOI: 10.1007/978-3-031-22018-0_28

*Monthly NFT Trade Volume (USD)*. [Dataset]. https://dune.com/queries/2344153/3838186

Nakamoto, S. *A Peer-to-Peer Electronic Cash System*.

Nedjah, N., Abd El-Latif, A. A., Gupta, B. B., & Mourelle, L. M. (Eds.). (2022). *Robotics and AI for Cybersecurity and Critical Infrastructure in Smart Cities* (Vol. 1030). Springer International Publishing., DOI: 10.1007/978-3-030-96737-6

Sarin, S., Singh, S. K., Kumar, S., Goyal, S., Gupta, B. B., Alhalabi, W., & Arya, V. (2024). Unleashing the Power of Multi-Agent Reinforcement Learning for Algorithmic Trading in the Digital Financial Frontier and Enterprise Information Systems. *Computers, Materials & Continua*, 80(2), 3123–3138. DOI: 10.32604/cmc.2024.051599

Sharma, A., Singh, S. K., Chhabra, A., Kumar, S., Arya, V., & Moslehpour, M. (2023). A Novel Deep Federated Learning-Based Model to Enhance Privacy in Critical Infrastructure Systems. *International Journal of Software Science and Computational Intelligence*, 15(1), 1–23. DOI: 10.4018/IJSSCI.334711

Sims, A. (2019). Blockchain and Decentralised Autonomous Organisations (DAOs): The Evolution of Companies? SSRN *Electronic Journal*. DOI: 10.2139/ssrn.3524674

Singh, I., Singh, S. K., Singh, R., & Kumar, S. (2022). Efficient Loop Unrolling Factor Prediction Algorithm using Machine Learning Models. *2022 3rd International Conference for Emerging Technology (INCET)*, 1–8. DOI: 10.1109/INCET54531.2022.9825092

Singh, M., Singh, S. K., Kumar, S., Madan, U., & Maan, T. (2023). Sustainable Framework for Metaverse Security and Privacy: Opportunities and Challenges. In Nedjah, N., Martínez Pérez, G., & Gupta, B. B. (Eds.), *International Conference on Cyber Security, Privacy and Networking (ICSPN 2022)* (Vol. 599, pp. 329–340). Springer International Publishing. DOI: 10.1007/978-3-031-22018-0_30

Singh, N., Singh, S. K., Kumar, S., Rawat, Y., Arya, V., Bansal, R., & Chui, K. T. (2024). Next Gen Security With Quantum-Safe Cryptography. In Gupta, B. B., Kalra, D., & Almomani, A. (Eds.), (pp. 131–164). Advances in Information Security, Privacy, and Ethics. IGI Global., DOI: 10.4018/979-8-3693-5330-1.ch006

Swan, M. (2015). *Blockchain: Blueprint for a New Economy*. O'Reilly Media, Inc.

Yee, N. (2006). Motivations for Play in Online Games. *Cyberpsychology & Behavior*, 9(6), 772–775. DOI: 10.1089/cpb.2006.9.772 PMID: 17201605

# Chapter 7
# Theoretical Frameworks for Analyzing Social Dynamics

**Princy Pappachan**
https://orcid.org/0000-0001-6728-0228
*College of Education, National Chengchi University, Taiwan*

**Prakash Purshewar**
*Anuvadini Foundation, AICTE Ministry of Education, New Delhi, India*

**Mosiur Rahaman**
https://orcid.org/0000-0003-0521-2080
*International Center for AI and Cyber Security Research and Innovations, Asia University, Taiwan*

## ABSTRACT

*The Metaverse, a fully immersive digital realm that merges physical and virtual realities, has fundamentally transformed social interactions, creating new forms of social dynamics. While traditional studies focused on face-to-face interactions within geographic boundaries, the Metaverse enables global, identity-flexible, and boundary-less interactions through avatars in interconnected virtual worlds. This chapter explores key theoretical frameworks, including Social Identity Theory, Network Theory, Actor-Network Theory, and Social Capital Theory, to analyze the unique social interactions in the Metaverse. The chapter concludes by reflecting on the future of social dynamics in the Metaverse, considering the impact of emerging technologies like AI, brain-computer interfaces, and quantum computing, offering practical recommendations for designing and managing virtual communities that are inclusive, engaging, and supportive of positive social interactions.*

## 1. INTRODUCTION

The concept of social dynamics refers to the patterns, processes, and changes that occur in a society or community when individuals and groups interact. In the past, social dynamics were only studied in real-life, face-to-face situations, where relationships, behavior, and conversation developed over time. However, the rapid evolution of digital technologies has resulted in new forms of interaction, particularly within virtual worlds like the Metaverse that merges physical and digital reality (Kraus et al., 2021).

DOI: 10.4018/979-8-3693-8628-6.ch007

Unlike traditional digital platforms, Metaverse provides users with a fully immersive experience, allowing users to interact through avatars that can navigate complex digital landscapes, engage in economic transactions, participate in governance, and build relationships (Tukur et al., 2023). Considering how the Metaverse is a network of interconnected virtual worlds, there will be a significant shift in how we perceive and engage in social interactions when using multiple personas and interacting in ways that might be difficult or impracticable in the real world. Examples of new kinds of social interaction that have emerged due to this are virtual gatherings, online communities, and digital economies, influencing real-world behavior and societal structures.

Understanding social dynamics in the Metaverse necessitates a multidisciplinary approach by drawing insights from sociology, psychology, communication studies, economics, and computer science to frame a theoretical framework that will help analyze, interpret, and uncover the underlying patterns and principles (Song et al., 2023). Figure 1 illustrates the various reasons why theoretical frameworks are essential to understanding social dynamics.

*Figure 1. Reasons why theoretical frameworks are essential to understanding social dynamics in the Metaverse*

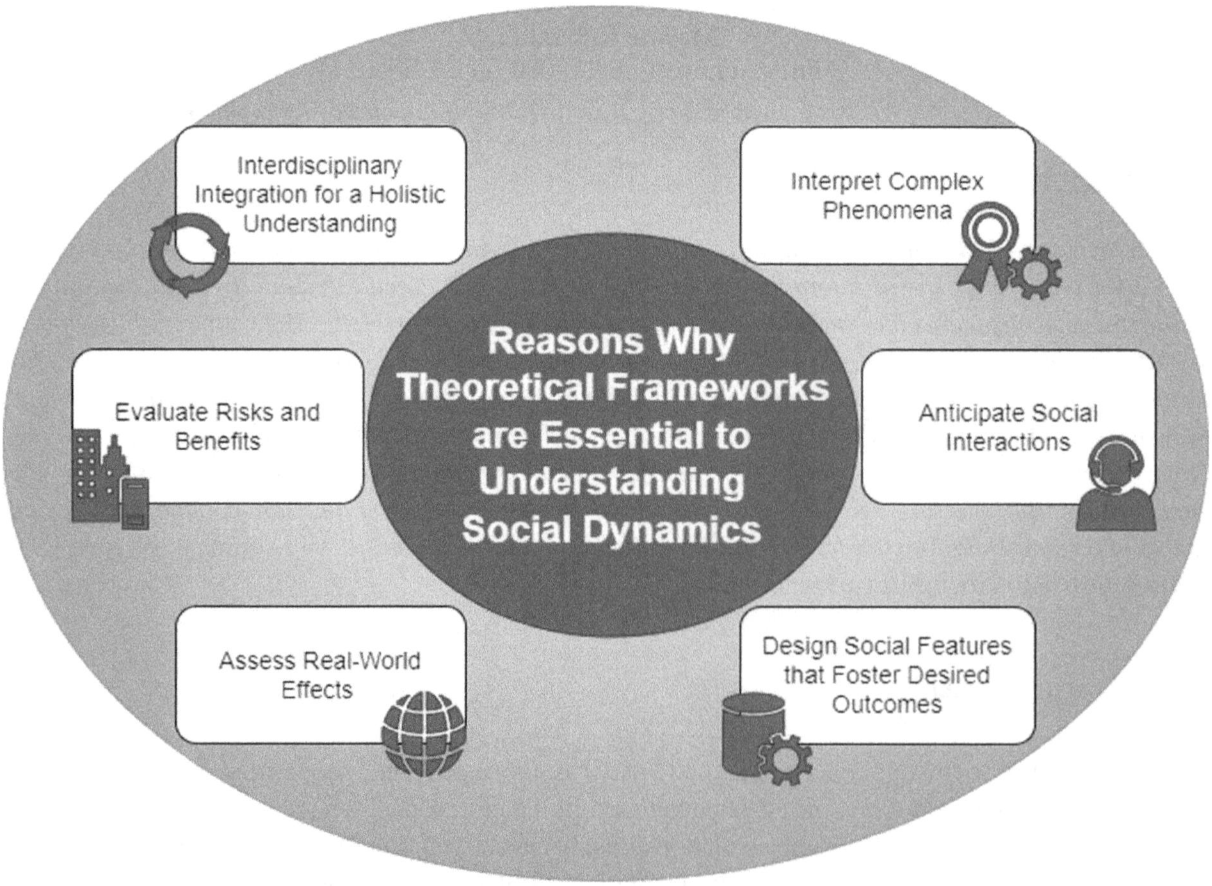

In addition to identifying patterns in social behavior, theoretical frameworks can enable researchers and designers to anticipate social interactions and predict the emergence of social hierarchies within the virtual space (Park & Kim, 2022). This predictive capability will help in designing social features that foster inclusivity, cooperation, and positive community building within the Metaverse. Furthermore, these frameworks will allow researchers to assess the real-world effects of virtual interactions, evaluating both the risks and benefits, which will help ensure that the Metaverse is developed in a way that supports positive social outcomes and mitigates potential negative consequences. Thus, by integrating knowledge across disciplines, researchers can create a more comprehensive view of how virtual interactions influence individual behavior and societal trends, contributing to creating richer and more meaningful virtual communities (Naeem et al., 2023; Blascovich et al., 2002).

The following section will discuss the different theories and concepts that have guided the concept of social dynamics, with the subsequent section examining the unique characteristics of social interactions within virtual spaces by focusing on the emergence of virtual communities and the role of digital identity. The chapter will conclude by examining how these theoretical frameworks can be applied to the Metaverse and reflecting on the future of social dynamics in the Metaverse.

## 2. THEORETICAL FOUNDATIONS OF SOCIAL DYNAMICS

In traditional settings, social dynamics are observed through behaviors, communication, and relationship-building patterns among individuals and groups in face-to-face settings, as everything centers on geographic proximity. However, in modern digital environments such as the Metaverse, social dynamics take on new dimensions due to the virtual nature of interactions that allows for greater flexibility in identity and the formation of communities based on shared interests rather than geographic proximity.

As a result, there are several unique factors one must consider when defining social dynamics within the context of Metaverse. Firstly, the concept of identity as in the Metaverse, a user can adopt multiple personas or avatars, each representing different aspects of their identity, granting users the flexibility to engage in new forms of social interaction that may otherwise be constrained or stigmatized in the physical world. Secondly, the lack of physical boundaries in the Metaverse facilitates the formation of global communities where individuals from diverse cultural backgrounds can interact and collaborate, leading to the emergence of new cultural norms and practices that are specific to virtual spaces. Finally, the Metaverse blurs the lines between reality and virtuality as interactions in virtual environments can have real-world consequences, influencing behavior, relationships, and even social status (Dwivedi et al., 2022). For instance, when real money is involved in the Metaverse, it can have direct implication in the physical world.

Thus social dynamics in the Metaverse involve a complex interplay between identity, space, and community. However to understand this, one must explore existing theoretical frameworks of social dynamics theories.

## 2.1. Defining Social Dynamics

At its core, social dynamics refers to the study of how individuals and groups interact within a society, how these interactions shape social structures, and how these structures, in turn, influence behavior and societal outcomes. It is concerned with the movement and evolution of social entities, which can range from individual relationships to large-scale social institutions.

Considering how human behavior and societal structures are inherently dynamic and complex, often defying simple explanations, there is no single theory—whether social, anthropological, psychological, political, or scientific—that can fully encompass the intricacies of human nature and society as a whole. Society is thus more than just a collection of individuals, it is a complex network of relationships, interactions, and shared cultural practices that bind people together within a specific geographic or virtual space (Zakaria et al., 2004).

Prominent scholars have offered various definitions of society that highlight its complexity and organization. For instance, Giddens et al. (2009) describe society as "a complex network of relationships and interactions among individuals who share a common culture, institutions, and collective activities within a specific geographic area or community." Similarly, Ember et al. (2015) define society as "an organized group of individuals who live together in a more or less ordered community, bound by shared norms, values, customs, and laws that regulate their interactions and relationships."

However, despite the diversity of customs, traditions, and individual behaviors within a society, there exists a shared platform for interaction, idea exchange, and collective interest. To understand this dynamic nature of society or specific communities within it, theoretical frameworks are essential. These frameworks provide the tools needed to analyze the intricate and evolving patterns of social dynamics, offering insights that help decode the complexity of human interactions.

The most fundamental underlying assumption in social dynamics is that society is not static, as social relationships, norms, and institutions are continuously changing, responding, and adapting to internal and external pressures, such as technological advancements, changes in political systems, economic shifts, and cultural evolution. Social dynamics thus involves understanding stability and change, where the former manifests itself in the preservation of social order and persistence of cultural norms while the latter manifests in the shifts in social norms, the emergence of new social institutions, and the transformation of existing social structures. Figure 2 effectively illustrates how social dynamics is a balance between stability and change, where the inner circle highlights the persistence of social order and cultural norms, and the outer circle depicts the transformation of social structures, new institutions, and shifting new norms, symbolizing change. This visualization highlights the coexistence and interaction of enduring and evolving social forces that define social dynamics.

*Figure 2. Visualization of social dynamics, highlighting the dual forces of stability and change*

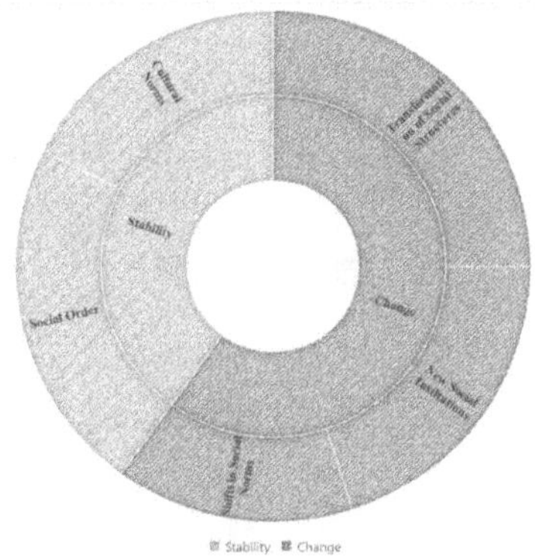


## 2.2. Historical Perspectives on Social Dynamics

The study of social dynamics has a rich intellectual history, with its roots in classical sociology and extending through various theoretical backgrounds in the 20th and 21st centuries. The origins of social dynamics can be traced to the work of early sociologists such as Karl Marx, Max Weber, and Émile Durkheim.

Figure 3 presents a historical outline of how the concept of social dynamics evolved to the present contemporary approaches discussed in the next section.

*Figure 3. Timeline of key sociological theories and thinkers*

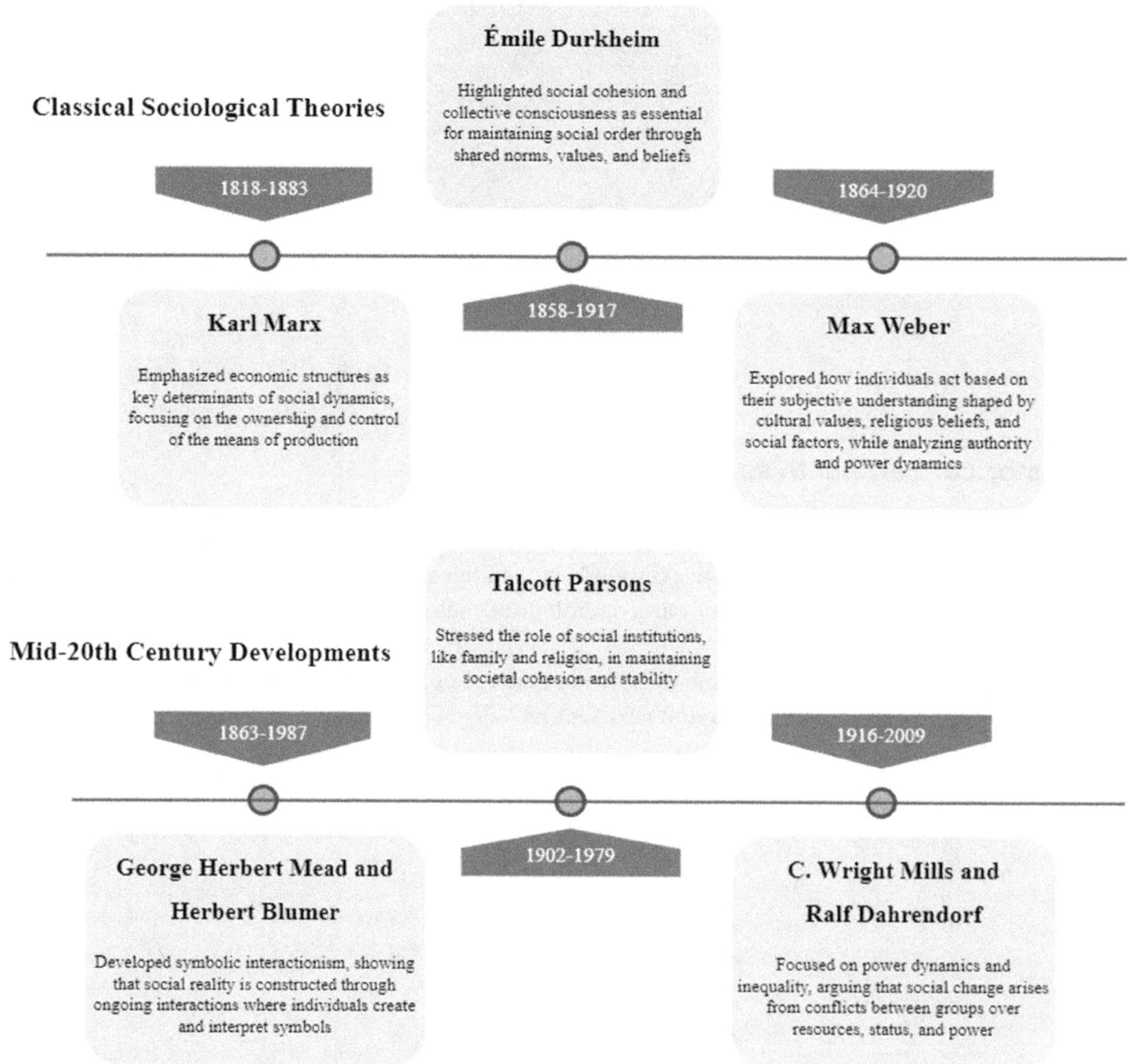


Early classical sociological thought focused on the importance of economic forces, social cohesion, and the role of cultural values in shaping human behavior (Ritzer & Stepnisky, 2020). These foundational theories emphasized how economic and power dynamics drive societal transformation and how social order is maintained through shared beliefs. Moving forward to the mid-20th century, there was a shift towards understanding the complexities of modern society, where the focus expanded to include symbolic meanings created through everyday interactions and the crucial role of social institutions like family and religion in maintaining stability. Subsequently, the study of social dynamics has addressed the complexities of modern society to explore how social relationships are structured through networks of connections, providing insights into the flow of information, influence, and resources within social groups.

The study of social dynamics has thus continuously evolved over the years by incorporating new frameworks and perspectives allowing for a more comprehensive analysis of contemporary social issues, enabling better responses to challenges such as globalization, technological change, and social inequality.

## 3. CONTEMPORARY THEORETICAL APPROACHES

Social dynamic theories are inherently multidisciplinary, examining the patterns and behaviors of society from various perspectives, including political, social, economic, and individual levels. These theories also place significant emphasis on the style and patterns of communication, as well as the interactions between individuals, communities, and groups across physical and virtual platforms. Each of the theories discussed in this section offers unique perspectives and analytical tools for understanding how individuals and groups interact, form communities, and influence one another in modern social contexts, including virtual spaces like the Metaverse.

### 3.1. Social Identity Theory

The Social identity theory developed by Henri Tajfel (1978) and John Turner (Tajfel 1978) explores how individuals define themselves based on their membership in social groups and how this group identity influences their behavior, attitudes, and perceptions. According to them, "social identity theory explores the phenomenon of the 'in-group' and 'out-group" (Tajfel & Turner, 1979). This psychological framework emerged as a fundamental theory in the field of group dynamics, intergroup relations, and social behavior as it is mainly based on how a community, group, or individuals frame themselves to particular groups based on their choice, comfortability, interest, and status.

The creation of group identities involves social categorization, where individuals identify themselves and others into social groups based on shared characteristics, such as ethnicity, gender, nationality, or interests. This leads to the creation of in-groups (the groups to which individuals belong) and out-groups (the groups to which the individuals do not belong) (Turner, 1999).

Social Identity theory has become important and relevant in exposing the different aspects of the social structure, the motivation behind self-identity, and group identity following the internalization of values, norms, and behaviors associated with the groups. This also leads to social comparison, wherein individuals compare their in-group with relevant out-groups, leading to a positive or negative evaluation of one's own group relative to others and influencing intergroup relations and social behavior. Figure 4 illustrates the different concepts of this theory. Positive comparisons that emerge as a result of this can enhance self-esteem and group cohesion, while negative comparisons can lead to prejudice, discrimination and intergroup conflict.

*Figure 4. The process of social identity formation and its impact on self-esteem*

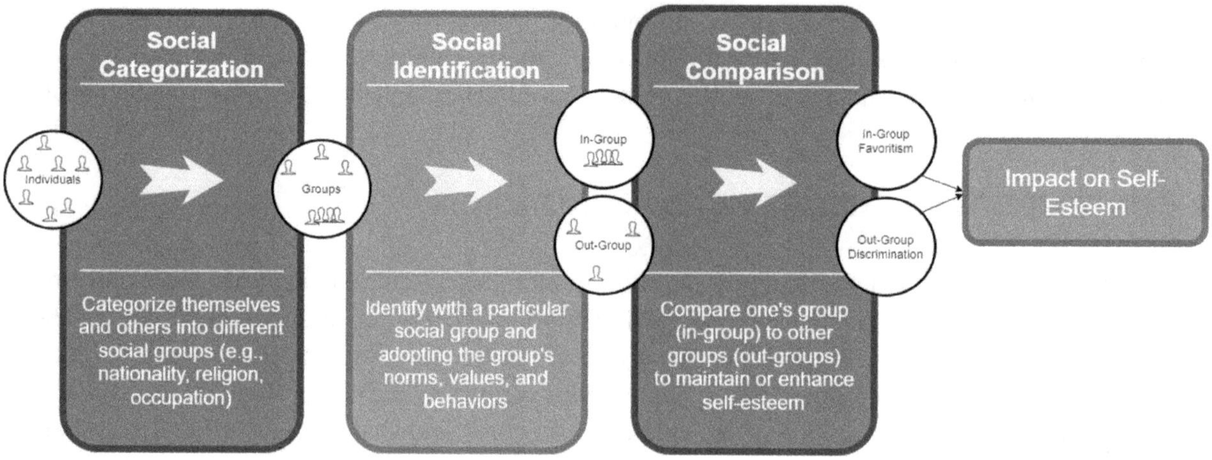


The theory also explains how a particular group of individuals can threaten each other in the context of political power for resources. A number of studies and experiments have been conducted to test these, such as "Negative out-group characterizations can result from perceptions of out-groups as competing for resources" (Cooper & Fazio, 1986). Considering the selective and dynamic nature of a group or community, the choice of an individual can fluctuate between groups, making social identity theory useful in psychological studies.

## 3.2. Social Presence Theory

The social presence theory is mainly developed in the context of virtual communication and the interaction of people on online platforms, influenced by the advancements in telecommunication, the emergence of digital platforms, and the interaction between human-computer. This theory mainly examines how a particular environment or platforms, such as online and social media, play an important role in the pattern of communication and interactions. The theory originally developed by Short, Williams, and Christie (1976) suggests that different media vary in their ability to convey social presence, affecting the quality and effectiveness of communication. It, therefore, mainly argues that the different electrical mediums of communication, such as media with high richness like face-to-face communication, video calls, and text messages with multimedia, have a higher level of social presence than lesser interactive leaner media like text-based communication.

Short et al. (1976) defined "social presence as the degree of salience (i.e., quality or state of being there) between two communicators using a communication medium". (Short et al., 1976). Many researchers have subsequently examined and applied the 'social presence' theory (Garrison et al., 2000; Gunawardena, 1995; Gunawardena & Zittle, 1997; Swan, 2003b; Walther, 1996). The level of social presence in a communication medium affects various aspects of interaction, including immediacy, intimacy, and emotional connection. High social presence is associated with more engaging and personal communication, leading to stronger relationships and more effective collaboration.

### 3.3. Network Theory and Social Networks

Network Theory examines the patterns of connections between entities- such as individuals, groups, or organizations- and how these patterns influence the flow of information, resources, and influence within a social system (Cross & Prusak, 2002). The theory is centered on the concept of a social network, which is a collection of nodes (representing individuals or entities) connected by ties (representing relationships or interactions). The structure of a such a social context can vary significantly depending on the nature of the relationship and the context in which they occur (Camacho et al., 2020). Figure 5 illustrates common network structures- Ego Networks, Dyadic Networks, Triadic Networks, and Whole Networks as it occur in a friendship network.

*Figure 5. Representation of network structures in a friendship network*

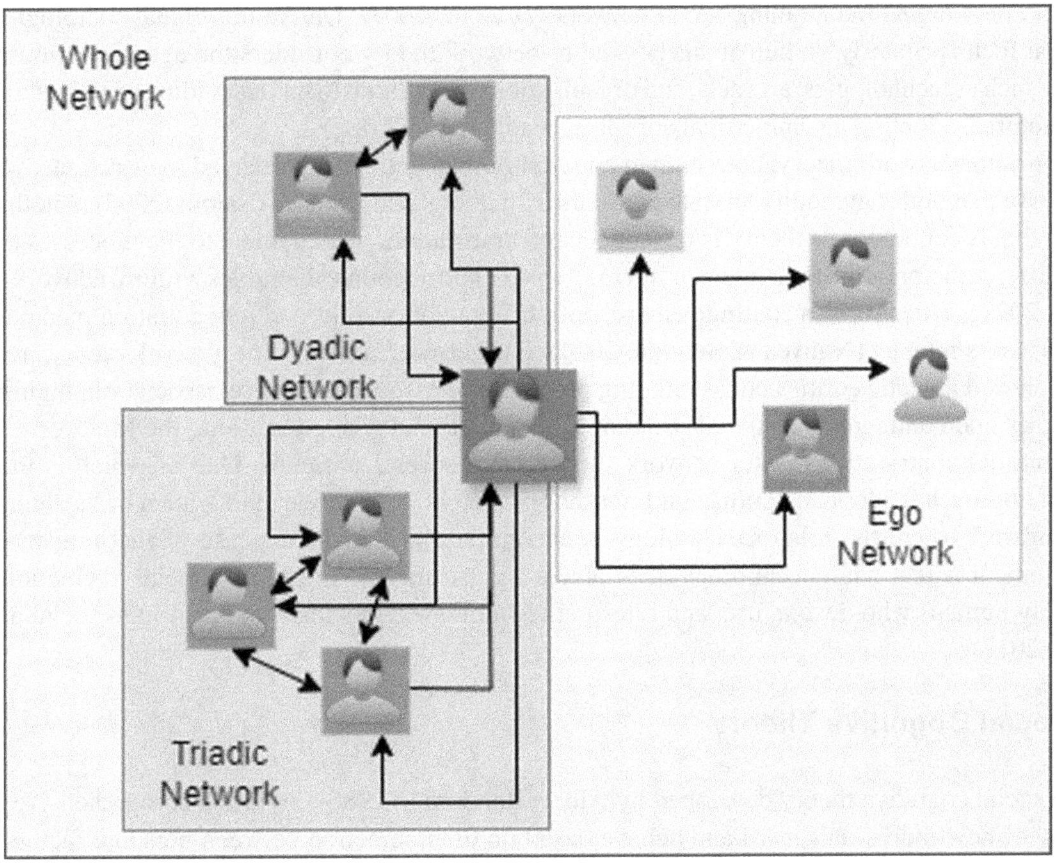


As depicted in Figure 5, centrality, density, and clustering are some key concepts in understanding and analyzing social networks. Centrality measures the importance or influence of a node within a network, which includes degree centrality (the number of direct connections a node has), betweenness centrality (the extent to which a node lies on the shortest path between other nodes), and closeness centrality (how quickly a node can reach all other nodes in the network). Typically, in social networks, the highly central nodes often play crucial roles in information dissemination, decision-making, and resource allocation

(Jiang & Jiang, 2014). On the other hand, density refers to the proportion of possible connections in a network, while clustering measures the degree to which nodes in a network tend to form tightly knit groups to indicate the presence of subgroups or communities where trust and collaboration will be stronger.

An additional important concept in social network theory is Homophily, which is the tendency for individuals to form connections with others who are similar to themselves in terms of characteristics such as age, gender, ethnicity, and interests (McPherson et al., 2001). Considering how the digital landscape has been transformed with high connectivity, the scale and scope of social interactions with individuals from across the globe have expanded, and this can be explored using social network theory.

## 3.4. Actor-Network Theory

The actor-network theory introduced by sociologists Bruno Latour, Michel Callon, and John Law offers a unique perspective on social dynamics by emphasizing the role of both human and non-human actors in creating and maintaining social networks (Latour, 2007). Unlike traditional sociological theories that focus primarily on human agency, actor-network theory considers the agency of non-human entities- such as technologies, artifacts, and organizations- as integral to understanding social interactions and structures, adopting a symmetrical approach (Fadliansyah, 2022).

In the actor-network theory, both human and non-human entities are referred to as actants, with the perspective that both can modify "a state of affairs by making a difference" (Latour, 2005). Another core concept that is central to the theory is the concept of 'translation,' which refers to the processes through which different actors align their interests, form alliances, and negotiate their roles within a network (Jeong & Kim, 2023). This involves continuously reconfiguring relationships and renegotiating meanings and goals as actors interact (Nguyen & Beijnon, 2024). Furthermore, in the actor-network theory, networks are not viewed as static entities but as ongoing processes of association and re-association, highlighting the fluidity and contingency of social structures that are crucial when discussing the Metaverse.

Despite its contributions, actor-network theory faces several critiques. One of which is the symmetrical approach it adopts on human and non-human actors, as it can lead to a form of "technological determinism," where the role of technology is overemphasized at the expense of the human agency. The argument is that while technology does play a significant role in shaping social interactions, it is ultimately humans who design, use, and interpret technologies, making them central to social analysis (Hauer, 2017).

## 3.5. Social Cognitive Theory

The social cognitive theory developed by Albert Bandura in 1986 provides a comprehensive understanding of how individuals learn and behave based on the interaction between personal factors, environmental influences, and behaviors (Chiu et al., 2006). This theory emerged from the Social Learning Theory proposed in the 1960s, which considered an individual's past experience to influence their behavioral action (Bandura, 1986).

The central tenets of the social cognitive theory are 'reciprocal determinism,' 'observational learning,' 'self-efficacy,' 'behavioral factors,' 'outcome expectation,' and 'reinforcement.' Reciprocal determinism posits that behavior, personal, and environmental factors interact and influence one another, denoting that individuals are not passive recipients of environmental stimuli as they shape their behavior and decisions. On the other hand, observational learning refers to the process by which individuals learn new behaviors by observing others in physical and digital spaces.

While behavioral capability refers to the knowledge and skills required to perform a behavior, self-efficacy is the belief in one's ability to perform a specific behavior. Self-efficacy thus plays a crucial role as it determines whether an individual will engage in a particular behavior, how much effort they will put into it, and how persistent they will be in the face of challenges.

The last two tenets focus on the result of the behavior. Outcome expectations refer to one's belief in the consequences of their action, which can be either positive or negative expectations influencing their behavior. In contrast, reinforcement involves using rewards or punishments to increase or decrease the likelihood of the behavior.

## 3.6. Social Capital Theory

Building on the theoretical framework of social cognitive theory, social capital theory extends to examine the value of social networks in providing individuals with access to resources, information, and support. Initially defined by Bourdieu in 1985, this concept is influential in understanding the dynamics of social cohesion, collective action, and economic development by examining core components of trust, reciprocity, and social norms. Considering how the digital age has transformed how social capital is generated, maintained, and utilized, it presents challenges related to trust, reciprocity, and social norms.

In social capital theory, trust facilitates cooperation, allowing individuals to rely on others for support, information, and resources, enhancing the efficiency and effectiveness of social change while reducing the need for formal enforcement mechanisms in social interactions. Conversely, reciprocity is the mutual exchange of benefits and favors, which creates a sense of obligation and interdependence, fostering social cohesion and collective action. Social norms are the shared expectations and rules that guide behavior within the social network, which help to maintain stability and proper functioning of the network as individuals adhere to agreed-upon standards of behavior.

Based on how these concepts are addressed, social capital can be categorized into two types: bonding social capital and bridging social capital (Shiu et al., 2024). While the former refers to the strong ties within close-knit groups, such as families or close-knit communities, the latter refers to the weaker ties that connect individuals across different social groups or communities. This distinction is blurry in virtual environments as the digital space offers unique opportunities for building bonding and bridging social capital, as users can form close-knit communities based on shared interests while connecting with individuals across different virtual worlds.

# 4. APPLYING THEORETICAL FRAMEWORKS TO THE METAVERSE

The concept of virtual communities has evolved alongside advancements in digital technology. In the early days of the Internet, virtual communities were mostly text-based, with members communicating via bulletin boards, email lists, and chat rooms. These early communities were frequently niche and restricted in scope, drawing users with specific interests or requirements. However, with the introduction of social media platforms, virtual communities expanded in terms of accessibility and diversity. So platforms such as Facebook, Twitter, Reddit, and Discord facilitated the formation of large, global communities where users could connect with others who shared their interests, regardless of geographic location (Kiene,

2020). These platforms also introduced new ways of interacting, such as real-time messaging, multimedia sharing, and algorithm-driven content discovery, enhancing the sense of community and engagement.

The latest evolution in virtual communities, which is the rise of immersive virtual environments as found in the Metaverse, allows users to interact through avatars in a fully digitalized world, participating in activities ranging from socializing and gaming to shopping and attending virtual events, allowing users to create and inhabit shared virtual spaces that can mimic, extend, or completely reimagine the physical world. Due to this immersive, interactive digital environment, the dynamics of social interaction in the Metaverse are shaped by the interplay between real-world identities, virtual identities such as the role of avatars and identity, and new forms of social interaction.

## 4.1. The Role of Avatars and Identity in the Metaverse

Avatars are digital representations of users as they embody the user's identity, allowing them to navigate virtual spaces and communicate with others (Zimmermann et al., 2023). In this identity formation, customization plays a vital role as the Metaverse offers a wide range of options for avatars, from basic choices like gender and appearance to more complex features like personality traits, abilities, and behaviors. Taking advantage of this some users may create avatars that closely resemble their physical appearance or reflect their real-world personality and values, while others can select avatars that represent a completely different identity or persona. This option of discontinuity can often be a deliberate choice, allowing users to explore their new virtual identity without the constraints and societal expectations present in the physical world, allowing them to explore and affirm their sense of skill (Gilbert & Forney, 2013). Figure 6 illustrates this possibility of customization and identity formation.

*Figure 6. Continuity and discontinuity in identity representation between users and avatars in the Metaverse*

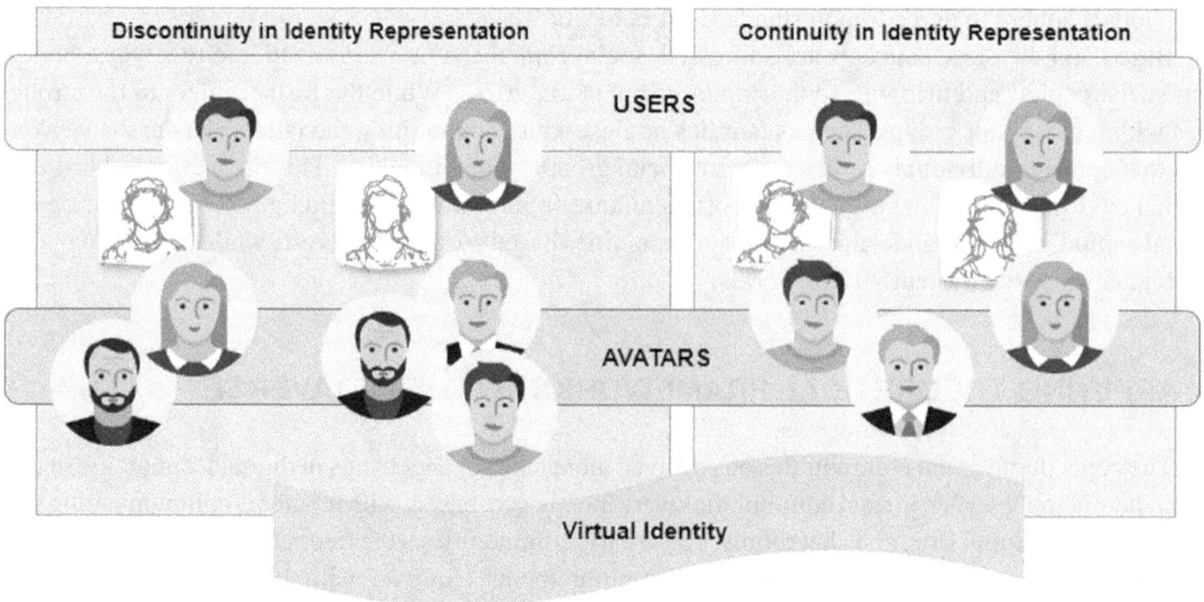

This customization of avatars can directly impact social interaction in the Metaverse since the choices they make in designing their avatars influence how others perceive them, how they are treated, and how they engage with the virtual community, impacting self-concept. For instance, the confidence gained from successfully leading a virtual community or achieving success in a virtual endeavor will have real-world implications, translating into increased self-efficacy and leadership skills. The converse can also happen when a user presents a more confident and outgoing persona in the Metaverse while maintaining a more reserved identity in the physical world. This experimentation can lead to new insights and understandings about the self as users discover new aspects of their identity that they may not have been aware of in the physical world.

## 4.2. Unique Social Characteristics of the Metaverse

The Metaverse presents distinct social characteristics that differentiate it from traditional online platforms and social networks, which redefines how individuals interact and present challenges to existing paradigms of identity, space, and social capital. Table 1 lists the different social characteristics and their descriptions.

*Table 1. Key social characteristics of the Metaverse*

| Social Characteristics | Description |
|---|---|
| Fluidity of Identity | Allows users to create multiple avatars, enabling identity exploration and challenging traditional authenticity. |
| Spatial and Temporal Flexibility | Enables global interactions beyond physical and time constraints, fostering diverse communities and customizable virtual spaces. |
| New Forms of Social Capital | Accumulated through virtual interactions, with novel elements like reputation systems, virtual currencies, and digital assets. |
| Collective and Emergent Behavior | Encourages spontaneous collaboration and community formation, adapting to new technologies and evolving social norms. |

The Metaverse, often described as a collective virtual shared space, is a persistent, real-time environment where users, represented by avatars, can interact with each other and the virtual world around them. What makes this particularly different from traditional digital platforms is that the Metaverse is not a single platform or application but a network of interconnected virtual worlds, each with its own rules, culture, and economy, transforming the interpretation of real-world social dynamics.

## 4.3. Analyzing Social Interactions in the Metaverse

As a collective virtual shared space that merges physical and digital realities, the Metaverse offers a new frontier for social interaction, where traditional boundaries are blurred, and new social dynamics emerge. This section will discuss different aspects of the Metaverse and explore how social dynamic theories can be applied.

**Identity and Group Dynamics in the Metaverse:** In the Metaverse, identity is fluid and flexible as users can create and adopt multiple avatars, each representing different aspects of their personality or entirely new personas. This flexibility allows individuals to align themselves with various virtual communities based on shared interests, activities, and values and even express affiliations with specific groups and communities they may not be part of in real life. In such cases, the digital extensions of themselves, that is, their avatars, are discontinued representations of their self-identity, which can be positive as the Metaverse helps them to experience a strong sense of belonging that would be lacking in real life.

Furthermore, social identity theory can be used to understand the dynamics of in-group favoritism and out-group bias/discrimination in the Metaverse, as users may form strong in-group affiliations leading to positive evaluations of their own group and negative perceptions of out-groups, reflecting real-world social phenomena of group cohesion and intergroup rivalry.

**Communication and Presence:** Social presence theory is crucial for understanding the effectiveness of immersive experiences critical to communications in the Metaverse. According to the theory, the degree of presence, or the feeling of "being there," varies depending on the richness of the communication medium. So, in the Metaverse, high-immersion environments like virtual reality can offer a strong sense of social presence, allowing users to feel as though they are interacting face-to-face, even when they are miles apart, leading to deeper, more emotionally resonant interactions, be it a virtual business meeting, a social gathering, or a collaborative creative session. On the other hand, less immersive, text-based communication might result in a weaker sense of connection, affecting the quality and depth of social interactions. So, the social presence theory will help facilitate effective communication and strong social bonds in virtual environments.

**Social Networks and Connectivity:** In the Metaverse, users form social networks based on their interactions, shared activities, and common interests. For instance, in a virtual world like Roblox, users might be connected through various games and collaborative projects, forming networks that range from small, tightly-knit groups to large, diffuse communities (Du et al., 2021; Han et al., 2021). In this scenario, network theory can explore how these social networks are structured—identifying key nodes (users with many connections) who act as influencers or leaders within the community. Additionally, concepts like centrality and clustering can be applied to analyze how closely users are connected and how these connections influence the overall dynamics of the Metaverse.

Moreover, the Metaverse introduces new dimensions to network analysis, such as the role of avatars as proxies for identity, the impact of virtual economies on social relationships, and the influence of digital artifacts (e.g., virtual goods, spaces, and tools) on network structures. Understanding all these different dynamics requires adapting traditional network analysis techniques for fostering community engagement, facilitating collaboration, and managing the spread of information within the Metaverse.

**The Role of Human and Non-Human Actors:** Considering how Metaverse is only possible with human users and non-human entities, such as avatars, algorithms, and digital infrastructures, the actor-network theory can be adopted to understand the significant role of the non-human actors in creating and maintaining the Metaverse. For example, in designing virtual platforms that influence how users interact, algorithms that govern virtual economies that affect the distribution of resources, and the customization options for avatars that impact how identity is constructed and perceived.

Another significant contribution of actor-network theory is its concept of translation, which is the process through which different actors, both human and non-human, align their interests, negotiate roles, and form networks. For instance, when a group of users comes together to form a virtual guild or community around a shared interest, such as gaming, social activism, or professional networking, the virtual platform must support the necessary interactions (e.g., communication tools, event spaces), the algorithms must facilitate engagement (e.g., by promoting group activities), and the avatars must adequately represent the users' identities and roles within the group.

Actor-network theory also introduces the concept of black-boxing, which allows users to interact with these technologies without needing to understand or question their inner workings. For instance, a virtual currency system within the Metaverse may become widely accepted and trusted despite users being unaware of the complex blockchain technology that underpins it (Jim et al., 2023). However, actor-network theory also emphasizes the importance of "opening the black box" to examine the underlying technologies and systems contributing to Metavere's stability, allowing researchers to scrutinize the algorithms governing content moderation to uncover biases or inequalities affecting user experiences. Similarly, examining the technical foundations of virtual platforms can reveal how certain design choices impact social interactions and community formation.

Furthermore, as new technologies are introduced into the Metaverse, such as advanced AI, immersive virtual reality experiences, and decentralized governance, the actor-network theory can help map out how these innovations are integrated into existing networks and how they reconfigure relationships and power dynamics within the virtual world.

**Learning and Behavioral Dynamics:** Behavioral patterns in the Metaverse are influenced by both individual learning processes and the surrounding environment, as new users often learn how to navigate virtual space, engage in social interactions, and participate in community activities by observing the behavior of more experienced users. Social cognitive theory can be particularly useful for examining this dynamic, as one of the core components of this theory is observational learning. So, an evaluation of how this works in the Metaverse using social cognitive theory can help design virtual environments that facilitate learning by showcasing best practices, offering role models, and providing opportunities for users to learn from each other.

Additionally, social cognitive theory can help in the development of self-efficacy by incorporating features such as guided tutorials, supportive communities, and incremental challenges that allow users to build their skills progressively and gain self-confidence. Another factor that plays a great role in shaping user behavior is reinforcements, such as positive outcomes, such as rewards, recognition, or social approval, which will encourage users to repeat certain actions, while negative outcomes discourage them. Through social cognitive theory, developers can apply the principles of reinforcement to design virtual environments that promote positive behavior and discourage negative actions by creating systems that reward collaboration, creativity, and helpfulness while also implementing measures to discourage toxic behavior, such as harassment or cheating.

Accordingly, by applying the principles of social cognitive theory, developers can create virtual environments that enhance learning, build confidence, and encourage positive social interactions.

**Building and Utilizing Social Capital:** In the Metaverse, there are numerous opportunities for users to build social capital through interactions that foster trust, reciprocity, and shared norms, enhancing users' ability to thrive in digital spaces. This social capital can be in the form of bonding capital (strong ties within close-knit groups) and bridging capital (weaker ties that connect different groups). For example, in a virtual world like World of Warcraft (Bainbridge, 2012), players often form guilds that provide emotional support, collaboration opportunities, and a sense of belonging (bonding capital) while also interacting with members of other guilds or participating in cross-guild activities (bridging capital) that grants them access to a broader range of resources and information. Social capital theory helps explore how these network relationships contribute to users' overall experience and success in the Metaverse through the importance of trust, reciprocity, and shared norms in maintaining healthy virtual communities.

However, maintaining social capital in the interconnected Metaverse is challenging as there will need to be mechanisms that allow users to maintain and transfer their social capital across different platforms by developing universal reputation systems or blockchain-based identity verification that ensures a user's social capital is recognized and valued across multiple virtual worlds (Ud Din et al., 2023).

Figure 7 illustrates how the above-discussed theoretical frameworks can be adapted better to understand the unique social dynamics of the Metaverse.

*Figure 7. Application of theoretical frameworks to social dynamics in the Metaverse*

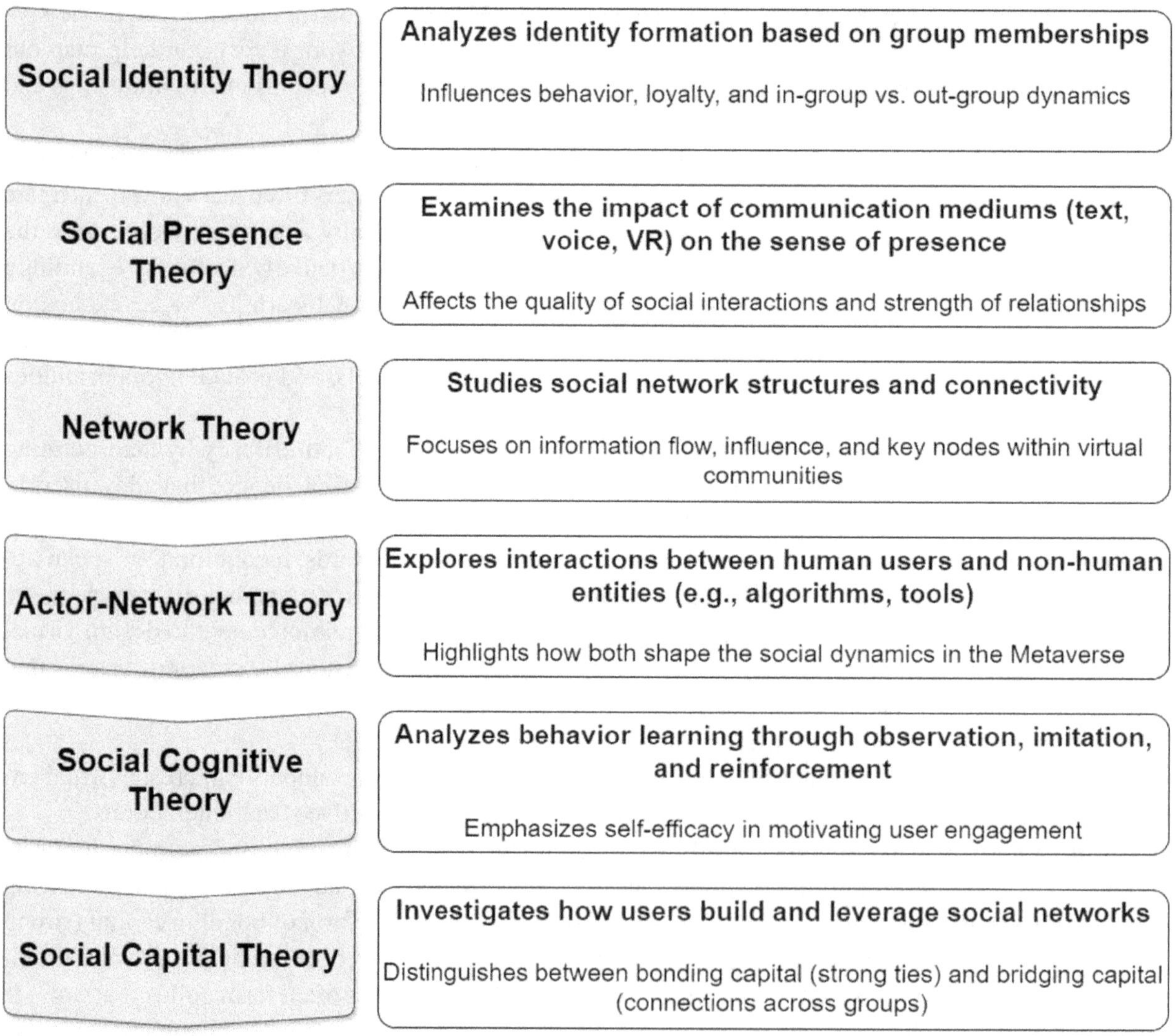

## 4.4. The Future of Technology and Social Dynamics in the Metaverse

Emerging technologies, such as brain-computer interfaces, quantum computing, and advanced AI, have the potential to transform the social environment of the Metaverse further, creating new possibilities for interaction, expression, and community. Brain-computer interfaces, which enable direct connection between the brain and digital devices, could allow users to control avatars, manage virtual items, and interact with others only via their thoughts, resulting in a more seamless and intuitive experience (Banaeian & Imani Rad, 2024).

However, incorporating these interfaces into the Metaverse poses ethical and societal concerns about privacy, autonomy, and the nature of human identity (Widodo et al., 2024). Similarly, although using AI-powered avatars, personalized virtual environments, and predictive social algorithms could enhance user experience, it raises concerns about agency, control, and the potential for algorithmic bias. Furthermore, quantum computing could create even more realistic and immersive virtual worlds where the boundaries between the physical and digital will become increasingly indistinguishable (Tuli et al., 2024; Kwon et al., 2022). Additionally, the threat to personal privacy and protection becomes even more pronounced as the lines between the physical and virtual worlds blur, especially when virtual platforms are not equipped with adequate privacy and protection laws (Rahaman et al., 2024).

Thus, while the Metaverse operates on the advanced capabilities of AI, minimizing the need for direct human intervention, it brings forth significant concerns related to content moderation, privacy, data protection, and the balance between freedom and personal safety (Zhuk, 2024). Considering how these factors pose challenges, the Metaverse must adhere to ethical and moral principles to safeguard individual privacy and ensure the responsible use of AI technologies.

# 5. CONCLUSION AND THE FUTURE OF SOCIAL DYNAMICS IN THE METAVERSE

The study of social dynamics in the Metaverse highlights the importance of applying and adapting theoretical approaches from sociology, psychology, communication studies, and other disciplines, as it provides the tools needed to analyze the complex interactions, identities, and communities that emerge in virtual environments and to understand how these dynamics influence both virtual and real-world behavior.

Although theoretical frameworks can account for many distinctive features of virtual environments, such as the use of avatars, the spatial and temporal flexibility of the Metaverse, and the impact of immersive technologies on social presence, existing frameworks must be expanded to include new variables, such as the influence of AI, the role of decentralized governance (Goldberg & Schär, 2023), or the impact of virtual economies on social behavior.

Looking forward, the Metaverse presents an unprecedented opportunity to explore and redefine social interactions. However, this potential is accompanied by significant challenges, particularly concerns about privacy, security, and the ethical use of advanced AI technologies. Thus, by expanding and refining the theoretical frameworks, researchers, developers, and policymakers can work together to ensure that the Metaverse evolves into a space that enriches social connection while addressing these concerns to foster an innovative, immersive, inclusive, secure, and ethically sound digital environment.

## REFERENCES

Bainbridge, W. S. (2012). *The Warcraft civilization: Social science in a virtual world.* MIT Press.

Banaeian Far, S., & Imani Rad, A. (2024). All Things will be Dominated/Controlled by Humans' Imaginations in the Next Generation of Internet of Brains. *Wireless Personal Communications*, 137(2), 795–811. DOI: 10.1007/s11277-024-11053-y

Bandura, A. (1986). Social foundations of thought and action. *Englewood Cliffs, NJ, 1986*(23-28), 2.

Blascovich, J., Loomis, J., Beall, A. C., Swinth, K. R., Hoyt, C. L., & Bailenson, J. N. (2002). Immersive virtual environment technology as a methodological tool for social psychology. *Psychological Inquiry*, 13(2), 103–124. DOI: 10.1207/S15327965PLI1302_01

Camacho, D., Panizo-LLedot, A., Bello-Orgaz, G., Gonzalez-Pardo, A., & Cambria, E. (2020). The four dimensions of social network analysis: An overview of research methods, applications, and software tools. *Information Fusion*, 63, 88–120. DOI: 10.1016/j.inffus.2020.05.009

Chiu, C. M., Hsu, M. H., & Wang, E. T. (2006). Understanding knowledge sharing in virtual communities: An integration of social capital and social cognitive theories. *Decision Support Systems*, 42(3), 1872–1888. DOI: 10.1016/j.dss.2006.04.001

Cooper, J., & Fazio, R. H. (1986). The formation and persistence of attitudes that support intergroup conflict. In Worchel, S., & Austin, W. (Eds.), *Psychology of intergroup relations* (pp. 183–195). Nelson-Hall.

Cross, R., & Prusak, L. (2002). The people who make organizations go–or stop. *Networks in the Knowledge Economy*, 80(6), 248–260. PMID: 12048992

Du, Y., Grace, T. D., Jagannath, K., & Salen-Tekinbas, K. (2021). Connected play in virtual worlds: Communication and control mechanisms in virtual worlds for children and adolescents. *Multimodal Technologies and Interaction*, 5(5), 27. DOI: 10.3390/mti5050027

Dwivedi, Y. K., Hughes, L., Baabdullah, A. M., Ribeiro-Navarrete, S., Giannakis, M., Al-Debei, M. M., Dennehy, D., Metri, B., Buhalis, D., Cheung, C. M. K., Conboy, K., Doyle, R., Dubey, R., Dutot, V., Felix, R., Goyal, D. P., Gustafsson, A., Hinsch, C., Jebabli, I., & Wamba, S. F. (2022). Metaverse beyond the hype: Multidisciplinary perspectives on emerging challenges, opportunities, and agenda for research, practice and policy. *International Journal of Information Management*, 66, 102542. DOI: 10.1016/j.ijinfomgt.2022.102542

Fadliansyah, H. D. (2022). *Imagining the Metaverse Worlds: The Perspectives of Meta and Indonesians.* Lub.lu.se. https://lup.lub.lu.se/student-papers/search/publication/9079505

Giddens, A., Duneier, M., Appelbaum, R., & Carr, B. (2009). *Introduction to sociology.* WW Norton & Company.

Gilbert, R., & Forney, A. (2013). The distributed self: Virtual worlds and the future of human identity. In *The immersive internet: Reflections on the entangling of the virtual with society, politics and the economy* (pp. 23–36). Palgrave Macmillan UK. DOI: 10.1057/9781137283023_3

Goldberg, M., & Schär, F. (2023). Metaverse governance: An empirical analysis of voting within Decentralized Autonomous Organizations. *Journal of Business Research*, 160, 113764. DOI: 10.1016/j.jbusres.2023.113764

Han, J., Heo, J., & You, E. (2021, October). Analysis of metaverse platform as a new play culture: Focusing on roblox and zepeto. In *Proceedings of the 2nd International Conference on Human-centered Artificial Intelligence (Computing4Human 2021). CEUR Workshop Proceedings, Da Nang, Vietnam (Oct 2021).*

Hauer, T. (2017). Technological determinism and new media. *International Journal of English Literature and Social Sciences*, 2(2), 239174.

Jeong, M., & Kim, S. (2023). What makes' aespa', the first metaverse girl group in the K-pop universe, succeed in the global entertainment industry? Jiang, Y., & Jiang, J. C. (2014). Diffusion in social networks: A multiagent perspective. *IEEE Transactions on Systems, Man, and Cybernetics. Systems*, 45(2), 198–213.

Jim, J. R., Hosain, M. T., Mridha, M. F., Kabir, M. M., & Shin, J. (2023). Towards trustworthy Metaverse: Advancements and challenges. *IEEE Access : Practical Innovations, Open Solutions*, 11, 118318–118347. DOI: 10.1109/ACCESS.2023.3326258

Kiene, C. (2020). *Challenges and Adaptations to Technological Change in Online Communities* (Doctoral dissertation).

Kraus, S., Jones, P., Kailer, N., Weinmann, A., Chaparro-Banegas, N., & Roig-Tierno, N. (2021). Digital Transformation: An Overview of the Current State of the Art of Research. *SAGE Open*, 11(3), 21582440211047576. DOI: 10.1177/21582440211047576

Kwon, H. J., El Azzaoui, A., & Park, J. H. (2022). Metaq: A quantum approach for secure and optimized metaverse environment. *Hum.-. Cent. Comput. Inf. Sci*, 12, 42.

Latour, B. (2005). An introduction to actor-network-theory. *Reassembling the social.*

Latour, B. (2007). *Reassembling the social: An introduction to actor-network-theory*. Oup Oxford.

McPherson, M., Smith-Lovin, L., & Cook, J. M. (2001). Birds of a feather: Homophily in social networks. *Annual Review of Sociology*, 27(1), 415–444. DOI: 10.1146/annurev.soc.27.1.415

Naeem, M., Ozuem, W., Howell, K., & Ranfagni, S. (2023). A Step-by-Step Process of Thematic Analysis to Develop a Conceptual Model in Qualitative Research. *International Journal of Qualitative Methods*, 22, 16094069231205789. DOI: 10.1177/16094069231205789

Nguyen, D., & Beijnon, B. (2024). The data subject and the myth of the 'black box'data communication and critical data literacy as a resistant practice to platform exploitation. *Information Communication and Society*, 27(2), 333–349. DOI: 10.1080/1369118X.2023.2205504

Park, S. M., & Kim, Y. G. (2022). A metaverse: Taxonomy, components, applications, and open challenges. *IEEE Access : Practical Innovations, Open Solutions*, 10, 4209–4251. DOI: 10.1109/ACCESS.2021.3140175

Rahaman, M., Pappachan, P., Orozco, S. M., Bansal, S., & Arya, V. (2024). AI Safety and Security. In *Challenges in Large Language Model Development and AI Ethics* (pp. 354–383). IGI Global. DOI: 10.4018/979-8-3693-3860-5.ch011

Ritzer, G., & Stepnisky, J. (2020). *Classical sociological theory*. Sage publications.

Shiu, J. M., Dallas, M. P., & Lin, P. H. (2024). Collaboration and social capital in meta-organisations: Bonding or bridging? *Technology Analysis and Strategic Management*, •••, 1–13. DOI: 10.1080/09537325.2024.2330549

Short, J., Williams, E., & Christie, B. (1976). The social psychology of telecommunications.

Song, C., Shin, S.-Y., & Shin, K.-S. (2023). Exploring the Key Characteristics and Theoretical Framework for Research on the Metaverse. *Applied Sciences (Basel, Switzerland)*, 13(13), 13. Advance online publication. DOI: 10.3390/app13137628

Tajfel, H. (1978). *Differentiation between social groups. Studies in the social psychology of intergroup relations*. Academic Press.

Tajfel, H., & Turner, J. (1979). An integrative theory of intergroup conflict. In Williams, J. A., & Worchel, S. (Eds.), *The social psychology of intergroup relations* (pp. 33–47). Wadsworth.

Tukur, M., Schneider, J., Househ, M., Dokoro, A. H., Ismail, U. I., Dawaki, M., & Agus, M. (2023). The metaverse digital environments: A scoping review of the challenges, privacy and security issues. *Frontiers in Big Data*, 6, 1301812. DOI: 10.3389/fdata.2023.1301812 PMID: 38074486

Tuli, E. A., Lee, J. M., & Kim, D. S. (2024). Integration of Quantum Technologies into Metaverse: Applications, Potentials, and Challenges. *IEEE Access : Practical Innovations, Open Solutions*, 12, 29995–30019. DOI: 10.1109/ACCESS.2024.3366527

Turner, J. C. (1999). Some current issues in research on social identity and self-categorization theories. In Ellemers, N., Spears, R., & Dossje, B. (Eds.), *Social identity: Context, commitment, content* (pp. 6–34). Blackwell.

Ud Din, I., Awan, K. A., Almogren, A., & Rodrigues, J. J. (2023). Integration of IoT and blockchain for decentralized management and ownership in the Metaverse. *International Journal of Communication Systems*, 36(18), e5612. DOI: 10.1002/dac.5612

Widodo, A. M., Wisnujati, A., Asianto, A. M., Aryani, D. M., Rahaman, M., Arya, V., & Pappachan, P. (2024). Understanding the Metaverse. In *Metaverse Security Paradigms* (pp. 1–38). IGI Global. DOI: 10.4018/979-8-3693-3824-7.ch001

Zakaria, N., Amelinckx, A., & Wilemon, D. (2004). Working together apart? Building a knowledge-sharing culture for global virtual teams. *Creativity and Innovation Management*, 13(1), 15–29. DOI: 10.1111/j.1467-8691.2004.00290.x

Zimmermann, D., Wehler, A., & Kaspar, K. (2023). Self-representation through avatars in digital environments. *Current Psychology (New Brunswick, N.J.)*, 42(25), 21775–21789. DOI: 10.1007/s12144-022-03232-6

# Chapter 8
# Ethical Considerations and Privacy in Metaverse

**Munawar Munawar**
*Esa Unggul University, Indonesia*

## ABSTRACT

*There are several ethical and privacy issues in the metaverse, a huge and immersive virtual environment where people communicate via avatars. Problems like digital identification, data security, and user autonomy grow more important as this virtual world gets more and more integrated into everyday life. The employment of AI systems to control interactions in these areas raises ethical questions because of the possibility of bias, exploitation, and harassment. Significant data gathering and surveillance put user security and confidence at danger, putting privacy at risk as well. The decentralized, global character of the metaverse makes regulation more difficult, so developers, regulators, and users must work together to create strong ethical standards and privacy safeguards. The metaverse must balance innovation with the need to preserve individual dignity and digital rights to develop into a place that is safe, welcoming, and respectful of human rights. Overcoming these obstacles is essential to accomplishing this.*

## I. INTRODUCTION

The metaverse, a concept once confined to the realm of science fiction, is rapidly becoming a reality. Envisioned as a collective virtual shared space, the metaverse merges augmented reality (AR), virtual reality (VR), and the internet to create immersive digital environments where individuals can interact, work, play, and socialize (Haynes, 2024). As technology giants and startups alike invest heavily in developing this digital frontier, the metaverse promises to transform how we live and connect. However, this transformation is accompanied by significant ethical considerations and privacy challenges that must be addressed to ensure the metaverse develops in a manner that is both equitable and secure (Peña-Acuña & Rubio-Alcalá, 2024).

As the metaverse continues to evolve and expand, addressing the ethical considerations and privacy challenges it presents is paramount. The development of the metaverse should prioritize the protection of user rights, equitable access, and the creation of safe and respectful virtual environments (Zhuk, 2024). By navigating these challenges focusing on ethics and privacy, stakeholders can ensure that the metaverse becomes a transformative and inclusive digital frontier, benefiting all users and society. This paper aims

DOI: 10.4018/979-8-3693-8628-6.ch008

to delve deeper into these issues, offering insights and recommendations for building a metaverse that is ethical, secure, and equitable.

## II. ETHICAL CONSIDERATIONS IN THE METAVERSE

In the context of the metaverse, ethical concerns are the moral guidelines and norms that direct acts, choices, and interactions in virtual spaces. Several significant ethical dilemmas emerge as the metaverse becomes an essential component of our digital lives (Adomaitis et al., 2022; Peña-Acuña & Rubio-Alcalá, 2024):

### A. Digital Identity and Representation

In the metaverse, users create and manage digital identities through avatars. These representations raise significant ethical questions regarding identity and authenticity (Arismendy Mengual, 2024). The ability to adopt different personas can be empowering but also opens avenues for deception and identity theft. Ensuring that users can control their digital identities while maintaining authenticity is a key ethical challenge.

Monitoring how people morally create, represent, and alter their avatars and digital personas in the metaverse is crucial. This entails considering problems with integrity, deceit, and the right to free speech. It is problematic to ensure that digital identities are used properly and are not lost, stolen, or misrepresented.

There are important ramifications for identity, behavior, social interaction, and psychological health associated with avatar representation in the metaverse. Although avatars give users never-before-seen flexibility to express and discover who they are, they also present difficult moral and societal issues (Wang & Wang, 2023). It is critical to recognize and address these effects as the metaverse evolves to guarantee that it continues to be a friendly, inclusive, and courteous space for all users:

#### 1. Personality and Expression of Self

Users can explore many aspects of their identities through avatars, which provide a degree of flexibility and self-expression that may not be feasible in the actual world. Users may feel more empowered as a result, which may boost their creativity and self-esteem. It also calls into question the veracity of digital identities and the degree to which they correspond with users' offline identities.

#### 2. Communication and Social Interaction

In contrast to those who deviate, avatars who adhere to specific aesthetic or cultural standards may enjoy greater social acceptance. Partnerships, friendships, and even disputes in the real world might result from relationships forged through avatars in the metaverse. The look, actions, and perceived identities of the participating avatars have a significant impact on the nature of these partnerships.

## 3. Behavioral Consequences

Changes in user behavior might result from the anonymity or pseudonymity afforded by avatars; this phenomenon is commonly known as the 'online disinhibition effect'. In real life, users may engage in activities that they would never do. The usage of avatars in the metaverse can make ethical accountability more difficult. Potential abuses may result from the inability to hold people accountable for unethical activity while they are anonymous.

To guarantee that all users are held to the same standards of behavior, regardless of how they identify themselves, this calls for the creation of strong ethical rules and enforcement methods.

## 4. Impacts on Emotion and Psychology

Avatars are generally seen as emotional extensions of their users, who frequently form close emotional bonds with them. Because of the metaverse's immersive qualities and the capacity to build idealized avatars, users may become escapism-prone and come to prefer their virtual lives to the real ones. This may skew how they perceive the world and harm their mental health, leading to identity confusion, despair, or social disengagement.

## B. Equity and Access

To guarantee that everyone benefits from this new digital frontier, regardless of their background, skills, or economic status, equity, and access in the metaverse are vital challenges that need to be addressed. The metaverse runs the potential of turning into an elite area that widens the gap rather than closes it if intentional steps are not taken to reduce expenses, increase inclusion, improve accessibility, bridge the digital divide, and solve linguistic and cultural hurdles. To ensure that everyone can fully engage in this growing digital environment, technology developers, policymakers, educators, and communities must work together to create a metaverse that is truly egalitarian and accessible.

How we connect, collaborate, and pass our time could be completely transformed by the metaverse, which is envisioned as a vast, immersive digital environment where users can create, communicate, and engage in a wide range of activities. The creation of a fair and open metaverse, however, will need to overcome a few significant obstacles. To prevent the metaverse from widening already existing social, economic, and digital inequalities, these problems must be resolved (Zallio & Clarkson, 2022).

The difference in access to digital technology between those who do and do not is known as the 'digital divide'. Numerous factors, including geography, education, and financial level, impact this disparity. The digital divide may make it difficult for sizable segments of the world's population to engage in virtual environments inside the metaverse since they do not have access to essential technology like fast internet, VR/AR headsets, and potent computer hardware. Given that people without access to the metaverse would be deprived of the social, economic, and educational opportunities that these virtual worlds offer, the digital gap has the potential to exacerbate already-existing social and economic disparities.

For many people, the expense of entering the metaverse can be unaffordable. This covers the cost of buying powerful computers, dependable internet access, and VR/AR gear. Exorbitant prices might lead to a tier-based metaverse where users with more money can access premium experiences and those with less can only use lower-quality or less immersive settings. Social differences within the metaverse could result from this economic stratification, reflecting and exacerbating inequality in the actual world.

Creating an inclusive metaverse that reflects a range of identities, cultures, and experiences is a big challenge. In the past, heteronormative, Western, and male viewpoints have controlled a lot of virtual worlds. Users belonging to marginalized or underrepresented groups may feel invisible or unwanted in the metaverse if there is a lack of inclusivity and representation. As a result, the metaverse may become less vibrant and richer in virtual interactions, with a homogenized culture that suppresses difference rather than celebrates it.

All users, regardless of physical, sensory, or cognitive limitations, must be able to fully participate in the metaverse through design that makes it accessible to people with disabilities. If accessibility is not given priority, a sizable section of the populace may be prevented from engaging in the metaverse and may not be able to take advantage of its social, educational, and financial advantages. People with impairments would continue to be marginalized in an inaccessible metaverse, which would serve to strengthen rather than lower social boundaries.

## C. Behavior and Conduct

Users' actions and conduct are essential to ensure that the metaverse remains a secure, welcoming, and moral place. Preventive and cooperative measures are needed to address concerns about virtual economy, ethical behavior, content monitoring, harassment, anonymity, and cultural sensitivity. The metaverse can become a positive place where all users can engage and flourish if established with clear guidelines, respect, and accountability.

Cyberbullying and harassment can become more severe due to the metaverse's immersive and participatory features (Upadhyay et al., 2023). Users may experience severe psychological effects from harassment and cyberbullying, such as tension, worry, and a reluctance to engage in metaverse activities. In addition to undermining the metaverse's promise as an inclusive space, such actions make surroundings unfriendly, especially for marginalized groups. Clear anti-bullying and harassment rules that are supported by strong enforcement mechanisms must be established by platforms. Safer virtual settings can be achieved by combining mechanisms for reporting or blocking offenders with campaigns and education about polite behavior.

The metaverse presents a complex content moderation challenge due to the size of these virtual locations and the variety of content created by users (Hine, 2023). It might be difficult to strike a balance between the right to free speech and the obligation to stop destructive behavior. When content moderation is inconsistent or insufficient, abusive behavior can thrive and create conditions where hate speech, abuse, and other wrongdoings are tolerated. However, excessively stringent moderation can also restrict originality and speech, raising questions about censorship. Platforms must set up open governance mechanisms with community involvement. For the metaverse to remain orderly, there must be clear rules about what constitutes appropriate behavior and the penalties for breaking them.

There are new social situations created by the metaverse that might not adhere to the same moral standards as the real world (Haynes, 2024). Users may experiment with actions that go against established moral standards, creating moral conundrums. The absence of well-established social norms in the metaverse might cause misunderstandings regarding appropriate behavior, which can lead to harmful or unethical activities. To regulate behavior in the metaverse, it is crucial to establish a common set of moral principles and social standards. To make sure they represent a wide range of viewpoints and values, these should be produced cooperatively with the participation of many stakeholders.

Sensitive personal data is frequently collected as part of the massive data collection process in the metaverse. The possibility of data exploitation or privacy violations can make people less trusting in the metaverse. Furthermore, illicit data acquisition may be used for nefarious activities like identity theft or manipulation. Additionally, platforms must give users clear information about how their data is utilized and prioritize ethical data practices.

## D. Intellectual Property

To safeguard creators, companies, and consumers, intellectual property issues in the metaverse are intricate and multidimensional, necessitating thought and proactive steps. A vibrant, equitable, and creative digital environment will be fostered as the metaverse develops through the creation of precise legal frameworks, strong enforcement procedures, and participant education regarding their rights and responsibilities. The metaverse will continue to be an environment where innovation and creativity can thrive while upholding the rights of all participants if these intellectual property issues are resolved (Bahuguna, 2022).

Users can create, purchase, sell, and trade digital assets including avatars, virtual land, clothes, artwork, and more through the metaverse. Ownership disputes may emerge in the absence of defined norms and laws, resulting in court cases and instability in the market. It is crucial to establish distinct and enforceable intellectual property (IP) rights for digital assets in the metaverse. Creating legal structures that acknowledge ownership and offer safe means of transferring or licensing these rights is part of this.

Users may generate and share content more easily in the metaverse, which increases the risk of widespread copyright violations. It is possible for unauthorized use of virtual spaces to quickly and widely distribute copies of protected assets (such as software, music, or photos) or to alter them. The worry of easy theft or exploitation of creative works can be a deterrent to innovation, leading creators to fear copyright violation. Sites must implement strong copyright protection measures, like automated content recognition software and digital rights management. Users must also be educated about copyright laws and the value of protecting intellectual property.

Brand names, logos, and other identifiers are protected by trademarks, yet they can be abused in the metaverse. The value and prestige of companies can be damaged by trademark infringement, particularly if consumers confuse illegal or subpar goods with genuine trademarks. Additionally, it may deceive customers into thinking they are engaging with or buying from a legitimate business. Platforms should implement rules that forbid the unapproved use of trademarks to address this problem. Along with keeping an eye out for possible infractions, rights holders should take steps to safeguard their brands in the metaverse.

In the metaverse, license agreements are frequently involved in the production and marketing of virtual commodities. Under these agreements, producers let third parties use, alter, or commercialize their works. These contracts may differ greatly from conventional license structures and are often rather complicated. Contentious relationships between authors, users, and platforms can result from misunderstandings or disagreements about license terms. Therefore, to guarantee that consumers are aware of their rights and responsibilities when purchasing or accessing licensed content, creators and platforms must collaborate.

The metaverse is a network of interconnected virtual worlds and platforms rather than a single, cohesive one. It might be difficult to guarantee that intellectual property rights are upheld on various platforms, particularly when users move or utilize assets amongst them. Inconsistent enforcement of intellectual property rights can result from a lack of interoperability, as assets that are safeguarded on one platform may be exploited or unprotected on another.

Consistent intellectual property protection requires the development of standards and agreements that are compatible across platforms. Platforms ought to work together to establish a single structure that guarantees IP rights are upheld throughout the metaverse.

## E. Consent and Autonomy

To build an ethical, welcoming, and empowering metaverse for all users, consent and autonomy are essential. Platforms may create a secure and reliable environment by emphasizing informed consent, honoring users' privacy and virtual borders, and guaranteeing that users have control over their data, identities, and communications. These values will be vital in creating a digital environment that upholds people's freedoms and rights as the metaverse develops, enabling users to fully interact with and take advantage of this new frontier.

The metaverse's immersive quality makes it difficult to distinguish between real and virtual environments, thus it is important to respect individual boundaries (Chawki et al., 2024). Users could feel uncomfortable, harassed, or even traumatized if personal boundaries are not respected. It is critical to set and uphold boundaries since infractions of personal space within the metaverse can seem just as intrusive as physical incursions. Platforms ought to give users the ability to establish and uphold personal boundaries. These should include the ability to mute or block other users, regulate closeness, and demand explicit agreement for specific kinds of interactions (like virtual touch or speech).

Mass gathering and exchange of personal data, including biometric information, behavioral patterns, and social contacts, is common in the metaverse. It must be possible for users to consent to the collection, usage, and sharing of their data or to withdraw it. Users might feel pressured to share information or be uninformed of how their data is being used if they don't give their consent. Loss of control over personal data, privacy issues, and possible data misuse can result from this. It's imperative to have clear consent procedures and open data policies. The types of data being gathered, their necessity, and the intended usage should all be disclosed to users. Users ought to be able to withdraw their consent or opt out at any moment.

Users can construct and live virtual identities in the metaverse through avatars. Users ought to have complete control over how they show themselves in these settings, including the option to modify or alter their gender, appearance, and other facets of who they are. Platforms should give users complete choice over their virtual personas by providing a variety of avatar customization options and making sure that users are not coerced into unwelcome representations. This involves honoring the decisions users make regarding their gender, race, and other identity indicators.

Mutual consent is necessary for interpersonal interactions in the metaverse, including friendships, love relationships, and talks. Users must own the liberty to select the individuals they engage with and establish limits on said interactions. Users could experience unwelcome encounters, such as pressure, harassment, or stalking if they do not give their consent. It is critical to have features that let users manage who can get in touch with them, start conversations, or join groups. For users who have non-consensual encounters, platforms ought to provide reporting and support mechanisms.

## III. PRIVACY ISSUES IN THE METAVERSE

With the lines between the digital and real world becoming hazier, privacy is a major concern in the metaverse (Pietro & Cresci, 2021). Privacy concerns must be addressed to create a safe, secure, and reliable environment for all users as the metaverse develops. Platforms may safeguard user privacy and promote a dynamic and diverse virtual ecosystem by implementing rigorous security protocols, transparent data policies, and strong user controls.

### A. Data Collection and Usage

The gathering and use of data is essential to the metaverse's operation, but it also poses serious privacy issues. Building a metaverse in which people can confidently participate requires that these processes are transparent, consensual, and secure. Platforms can safeguard users' privacy while facilitating the rich, immersive experiences that the metaverse promises by tackling concerns like informed consent, data security, and cross-platform sharing.

Users' data is collected by the metaverse in an unprecedented volume, significantly more than that which is usually obtained by standard internet platforms. This encompasses comprehensive behavioral data, such as motions, gestures, and facial expressions; interaction data, such as discussions and social interactions; and even biometric data, such as heart rate and eye tracking. Users might not be completely aware of the degree of information being obtained, which can raise privacy concerns given the massive volume and granularity of data being collected. The most important thing is transparency. Users should be informed by platforms about the types of data being gathered, how they will be used, and who will have access to it. Users should be able to restrict or refuse specific forms of data gathering, giving them control over their personal information.

Users of the metaverse must accept intricate terms of service and privacy rules that control data collection and usage, making informed consent a crucial issue. These permission forms are frequently lengthy, intricate, and challenging to read, which puts consumers in circumstances where they might not completely understand what they are agreeing to. When consumers provide their consent without giving their full knowledge, they may unintentionally consent to data practices that make them uncomfortable, such as selling or exchanging their information with outside parties. Mechanisms for obtaining consent should be clear and easy to utilize. Platforms must make privacy rules simple to comprehend, simplify them, and offer succinct, understandable descriptions of their data practices. It should also be simple for users to check and adjust their consent settings at any time.

User data on many metaverse sites may be sold to advertising or data brokers to generate revenue. Without the user's express knowledge or consent, this data may be sold to other businesses or used for market research and targeted advertising. The exploitation of users' personal information in ways they did not intend or approve of might result from the monetization of user data. Unwanted profiling, invasive advertising, and an overall feeling of being commodified might arise from this. Users should be able to opt out of having their data shared for commercial purposes, and platforms should be transparent about how user data is monetized. In addition, if users' data is exploited for commercial gain, they should receive payment or other incentives.

Constant gathering of metaverse data can result in the construction of comprehensive user profiles encompassing social interactions, purchasing patterns, and even psychological characteristics. Tracking, profiling, and surveillance can all be done with this data. Users' autonomy and privacy may be violated by surveillance and profiling, which might give them the impression that they are continuously being observed or assessed. It should be possible for users to choose not to participate in surveillance and profiling. Platforms must also disclose all information on their profiling policies, including the data they use and why. Robust security measures ought to be put in place to stop this data from being misused.

## B. Surveillance and Monitoring

The metaverse functions in large part because of surveillance and monitoring, but they also pose serious problems that must be handled with caution. Platforms may solve these issues while preserving a balance between immersive experiences and user privacy by placing a high priority on transparency, informed consent, and user control. A digital environment that respects and protects its users will be shaped by constant discussion and ethical considerations as the metaverse develops.

The metaverse makes it possible to monitor users in real time, which raises privacy concerns if private conversations or actions are followed without the user's knowledge or consent. Private discussions, individual virtual world exploration, or close social encounters could all fall under this category. In addition to violating users' privacy, this damages users' trust in the site by giving them the impression that their private moments are not valued. Users should be able to decide what can be watched in real-time, and platforms should enforce strong privacy limits. When monitoring is in progress, users ought to be informed, and areas inside the metaverse marked as private should have monitoring turned off or reduced.

Advertisers, data brokers, and even governmental organizations may receive access to surveillance data gathered in the metaverse. When third parties obtain access to surveillance data, users may lose control over their personal information, and have it used for uses they did not consent to. This may also make it more likely that third parties without the user's control will misuse data or violate it. Users should have the option to opt out of any third-party data-sharing agreements, and platforms should be open and honest about any such policies. Furthermore, agreements for data sharing should only be made with organizations that follow stringent security and privacy guidelines.

In cases where platforms participate in surveillance tactics that may be lawful in some places but are morally dubious, the absence of clear legal norms can lead to ethical breaches. This may erode user confidence and give rise to legal disputes. It is recommended that platforms adopt surveillance techniques that uphold user privacy, obtain informed consent, and conduct periodic policy reviews to ensure compliance with legal and ethical standards.

## C. User Tracking and Profiling

The metaverse relies heavily on user tracking and profiling to provide targeted content and individualized experiences. To preserve user liberty, privacy, and confidence, these methods do, however, also provide serious management issues (Gita Krishna Murti et al., 2023). Platforms may mitigate the hazards of monitoring and profiling while maintaining a dynamic and inclusive digital environment by emphasizing openness, informed permission, and ethical data usage.

Building behavioral profiles that can be utilized for personalized content or targeted advertising is common use for the data gathered via metaverse surveillance. Information like shopping patterns, social interests, and even presumed psychological characteristics may be included in this profile. Platforms need to make sure users understand exactly how their data is used for targeted advertising and profiling.

Users should be able to choose not to be profiled and should be given simple, unambiguous options for controlling their data.

Significant privacy hazards are created by the vast amounts of data that are gathered for monitoring and profiling reasons. Inadequate protection of this data leaves it open to hacking, illegal access, and third-party misuse. By putting in place robust encryption, frequent security audits, and strict access limits, platforms must place a high priority on data protection. Users ought to be aware of the safeguards in place for their data as well as the steps taken to avoid breaches.

The use of profiles may result in exploitation—the targeting of susceptible users with deceptive content—or discrimination—where users are treated differently according to their data profiles. With an emphasis on justice, openness, and respect for user autonomy, ethical standards for profiling techniques in the metaverse should be developed. The use of profile data by platforms in ways that could damage or exploit users should be avoided, and they should periodically evaluate their procedures to make sure they comply with moral principles.

Users' interactions with the metaverse may change if they become aware that they are being watched and profiled, possibly because they will behave differently to meet expectations. This may limit the freedom of expression and diminish the genuineness of user interactions. The advantages of personalization should be weighed against the requirement to preserve user autonomy by platforms. Platforms may support the preservation of the autonomy and genuineness of user interactions by giving consumers obvious choices to restrict or disable tracking.

## D. Data Security

A fundamental concern for the metaverse's viability and success is data protection. As these virtual spaces become more and more integrated into our online lives, it is critical to protect user data. Metaverse platforms may safeguard their users and create a reliable and secure digital environment by putting strong security measures in place, adhering to international laws, and constantly changing to counter new threats.

Many interconnected platforms and services make up the metaverse, and they are all responsible for gathering and analyzing enormous volumes of user data. Data is exchanged and transported across numerous networks and systems, which makes this data ecosystem more complicated and raises the possibility of security flaws. Metaverse platforms must have extensive security policies covering all aspects of the data lifecycle, from collection and storage to transfer and deletion, to reduce these threats. All metaverse components must adhere to strict access rules, secure APIs, and robust encryption.

The vast amount of data gathered in the metaverse increases the attack surface and opens new avenues for cyberattacks. Advanced cybersecurity techniques including multi-factor authentication, intrusion detection systems, and ongoing activity monitoring should be used by metaverse platforms. Regular vulnerability assessments and security audits are also crucial to detect and lessen such risks.

In the metaverse, user authentication entails cross-platform and cross-device identity verification. Attackers can obtain sensitive data and user accounts without authorization by taking advantage of weak authentication procedures. To secure user accounts, platforms should incorporate robust authentication methods like biometric verification and multi-factor authentication (MFA). Apart from safeguarding user identities on various platforms, identity management solutions must provide features for restoring hacked accounts.

Attackers may use social engineering and phishing techniques to take advantage of the metaverse's immersive qualities. Users may fall victim to deception that results in the disclosure of private information or activities that jeopardize their security. In addition to putting safety precautions in place like alert systems for questionable activity and protected in-app chats, platforms must inform users about the dangers of social engineering and phishing. Furthermore, networks have to keep an eye out for these risks and act quickly to counter them.

Technology advancements, user behavior shifts, and the growing value of digital assets will all contribute to the emergence of new security concerns as the metaverse develops. A failure to future-proof data security can result in vulnerabilities that new adversaries can take advantage of, eroding user confidence and jeopardizing metaverse security. Platforms should take a proactive stance when it comes to data security, funding R&D to foresee potential risks. This entails implementing cutting-edge security innovations, such as encryption that is impervious to quantum fluctuations and regularly revising security procedures to take on new threats.

## E. Anonymity and Pseudonymity

In the metaverse, pseudonyms and anonymity are useful tools that have both potential advantages and disadvantages. They provide people more power by preserving their privacy and allowing for the freedom of speech, but they may also be abused in ways that are detrimental to both the person and the larger community. Metaverse platforms can guarantee that these features improve user experience rather than diminish it by putting in place intelligent policies, strong security mechanisms, and encouraging a culture of respect and accountability. The long-term viability of the metaverse will depend on how well anonymity and pseudonymity are balanced with the demands of safety and trust.

Users can interact in the metaverse while maintaining their anonymity and pseudonymity without disclosing who they really are. For people who want to keep their online persona separate from their real-life identity, whistleblowers, and members of marginalized groups, the option to be anonymous or use a pseudonym can be quite helpful. This can encourage innovation, liberty of speech, and engagement with many communities. Metaverse systems need to give users the means to maintain control over who can access their personal information in the real world and guarantee that their anonymity is preserved when interacting with other users.

It is critical to realize that people can participate in destructive activities, like harassment, trolling, fraud, and disseminating false information, without fear of consequences when employing anonymity and pseudonyms. Encouraging participation can be detrimental to the metaverse community, particularly for individuals who are the targets of such behavior. Therefore, to handle harmful activity while balancing the demand for anonymity, platforms must have strong moderation and reporting systems. Users who want to participate in specific activities or transactions that demand a higher level of confidence should have the option to verify their identity.

Maintaining a safe and reliable community while also preserving individual privacy through pseudonymity and anonymity is a difficulty faced by the metaverse. While too little privacy can inhibit involvement and self-expression, excessive anonymity can cause trust to break down. Platforms should provide transparent and unambiguous policies that deal with the use of pseudonyms and anonymity. These policies should include instructions on when and how user identities can be revealed. Promoting an environment of accountability and respect inside the community—where people are urged to act morally even when anonymous—can also help build trust.

## IV. REGULATORY AND LEGAL FRAMEWORK

Regarding privacy and ethics, the metaverse offers both opportunities and difficulties. The legal and regulatory structure that oversees these digital frontiers must change as they grow. To handle the issues the metaverse presents, it will be essential to make sure that this structure is resilient, adjustable, and versatile (Kalyvaki, 2023). Metaverse platforms can establish secure, equitable, and welcoming settings that uphold moral principles and innovation by working together with authorities, implementing best practices, and placing a high priority on safeguarding user rights. There are several requirements about the laws that currently exist, the changes that must be done, the worldwide issues that must be considered, and the difficulties that must arise in the future, including:

### 1. **Regulations Regarding Data Protection and Privacy**

Financial, biometric, and behavioral data are among the many types of personal information that the metaverse gathers. This gives rise to serious privacy concerns, especially in light of how this data is gathered, saved, shared, and used. User privacy in the metaverse is safeguarded by extant data protection laws, such as the General Data Protection Regulation (GDPR) in the European Union. These regulations provide users the right to view, correct, and delete their data, mandate that platforms seek users' explicit agreement before collecting personal data, and guarantee that it is handled securely.

Due to the global nature of the metaverse and the possibility of data transfer across jurisdictions with differing degrees of data protection, implementing these standards can be challenging. Furthermore, the immersive and real-time nature of the metaverse could make it more difficult to secure meaningful permission and guarantee that data protection regulations are followed.

New laws that are especially suited to the special features of the metaverse might be required, with an emphasis on matters like cross-border data transfers, biometric data protection, and real-time data processing. Platforms and regulators should collaborate closely to create and execute best practices that protect user privacy while complying with regulatory requirements.

### 2. **Content and Online Resources**

Digital assets including virtual property, artwork, and digital goods can be created and exchanged through the metaverse. In this context, it is critical to protect intellectual property (IP) rights to guarantee both users respect ownership rights and producers receive just compensation. Authors and owners of digital content are safeguarded by the application of current intellectual property laws to the metaverse. It can be difficult to enforce these rights, though, because transactions in the metaverse are decentralized and frequently anonymous.

It can be challenging to find and prosecute IP violators, particularly in cases where the infringers use pseudonyms or operate in countries with lax IP enforcement laws. A further degree of complication is introduced by the advent of non-fungible tokens (NFTs), which raise concerns about the ownership and transfer of digital assets.

To handle IP concerns unique to the metaverse, more precise regulations and legislative frameworks might be required. This might involve international collaboration to enforce IP rights internationally, uniform processes for registering digital assets, and dispute resolution procedures.

### 3. Content Moderation and Ethical Guidelines

Like other digital platforms, the metaverse can harbor unethical activity such as hate speech, harassment, and the dissemination of false information. Numerous legal frameworks regulate conduct on the internet, including prohibitions against hate speech, cyberbullying, and the dissemination of illicit material. Because interactions in the metaverse are immersive and occur in real-time, content moderation presents unique challenges (Hine, 2023). In a three-dimensional interactive environment, moderating content using conventional methods like text filtering or post-removal might not be enough to curb dangerous behavior.

It will be crucial to create new moral standards and content control techniques, especially for the metaverse. This could entail creating community norms that represent the distinctive features of the metaverse, utilizing AI-driven moderation tools, and making sure that platforms are responsible for enforcing these standards.

### 4. Issues with Jurisdiction and Cross-Border Law

The metaverse is a worldwide phenomenon, with users and platforms frequently dispersed among several nations. This presents difficult jurisdictional problems, especially in the context of transnational law and regulatory enforcement.

A foundation for cross-border legal cooperation is provided by international treaties and accords, such as those that regulate cybercrime and data protection. These agreements might not, however, adequately address the difficulties brought on by the metaverse. It can be challenging to ascertain which jurisdiction's laws are in effect in the metaverse (Kasiyanto & Kilinc, 2022), particularly when actions occur in virtual places that do not match any one physical location. This may result in difficulties enforcing regulations and legal uncertainty.

New international agreements about the metaverse may be required to address matters like data sovereignty, cross-border enforcement of court orders, and harmonizing legislation from various jurisdictions. It may also be necessary for platforms to specify explicitly which jurisdiction's laws apply to their user agreements and how they operate.

### 5. Financing and Anti-Money Laundering Regulations

Virtual economies, in which users can purchase, sell, and exchange digital assets, are supported by the metaverse. Due to the possibility of criminal exploitation of the decentralized and anonymous nature of transactions, this raises issues over money laundering, fraud, and other financial crimes (Castaldo, 2022; Kasiyanto & Kilinc, 2022).

Financial laws, such as those about anti-money laundering (AML), are applicable to transactions that take place in the metaverse. These laws mandate that platforms establish know-your-customer (KYC) protocols, keep an eye on transactions for any unusual activity, and report money laundering investigations.

It can be challenging to enforce financial laws in the metaverse, particularly when transactions take place via cryptocurrencies or other decentralized financial instruments. The worldwide reach of the metaverse and the anonymity of its users provide further challenges to adherence to regulations.

Financial regulations that are specifically designed for the metaverse might be required to handle matters like the usage of virtual currencies, user identification in virtual economies, and the tracking of cross-border transactions. To stop financial crimes, platforms might also be forced to put stronger KYC and AML policies in place.

## V. ETHICAL CASE STUDIES

It takes the initiative to address privacy concerns and ethical issues in the metaverse, as well as a dedication to respecting user rights and fostering a welcoming atmosphere. The ensuing case studies demonstrate the difficulties in traversing the metaverse's ethical terrain and emphasize the significance of openness, inclusivity, and safeguarding users. Metaverse platforms can establish policies and practices that uphold ethical standards and foster user trust by taking cues from these examples.

### Case Study 1: Cybersecurity Vulnerability in an Online Conference

The annual conference of a large technology corporation was hosted in the metaverse, with virtual attendance from people all over the world. Participants can establish avatars on the platform used for this event and participate in networking, presentations, and conversations. The participants were unaware, though, that the platform was gathering copious amounts of data about their activities, exchanges, and even private discussions that took place in virtual "rooms." Without the express approval of the user, the corporation sells this data to third-party advertising and uses it to analyze user behavior.

There are various ethical concerns in this situation:

- **Informed Consent:** Participants were not provided enough information about the nature of the data collection or its intended use. The concept of informed consent, which states that users must be informed of and give their approval for the use of their data, is broken by this lack of openness.
- **Privacy Breach:** Gathering and vending personal information without authorization from users constitutes a grave breach of their privacy. Participants expected their conversations to be private, particularly in quiet areas, however this expectation was not met.
- **Data Security:** The possibility of data misuse or abuse is brought up by the improper handling of sensitive information, particularly when consent is not obtained.

Here is one possible way to solve this issue:

- **Transparent Data Policy:** Organizations are required to give participants the option to consent to or decline data sharing by giving them easily accessible and understandable information about their data-gathering methods. To solve the issue of informed consent, robust consent procedures that allow users to make informed choices should be implemented.
- Platforms should acquire only the information required for the event to run smoothly to minimize the amount of data they collect. Without express consent, it should be illegal to sell data to third parties. Additionally, all data should be anonymized to safeguard user identification.

- A public apology, the ability for participants to have their data deleted, and restitution should be provided by the firm for the betrayal of trust. This answer will show a dedication to moral behavior and aid in regaining consumer trust.

### Case Study 2: Impersonation and Theft of Avatars

Malevolent actors impersonate the avatars of well-known content providers on major metaverse sites. False information is disseminated, donations are solicited, and participants are harassed—all fraudulent acts carried out by impersonators using identical usernames and avatar designs to trick other users. When users begin to perceive content creators as being like their copycats, content creators are aware of the issue when it arises.

In this instance, there are moral concerns that include:

- Identity theft is evident when someone impersonates a content producer, taking advantage of the trust and reputation that the original creator has established to commit fraud.
- Defamation and Harassment: Impersonator behaviors harm content authors' reputations and may lead to psychological suffering in both them and other users. The concepts of justice and respect are broken by this immoral behavior.
- Platforms must safeguard their users against this kind of nefarious action. Questions concerning the platform's efficacy in maintaining a secure and reliable environment arise when impersonation is not prevented or promptly dealt with.

These issues could be resolved by:

- Quick Reaction System: To report and handle identity theft and impersonation, platforms need to have a quick response system in place. This entails a verification procedure to separate authentic users from imposters and prompt account suspension for phony accounts.
- User education can stop these kinds of situations by teaching users how to secure their identities and avatars, such as by using two-factor authentication and strong passwords. Users should also be made aware of any hazards and the proper way to report any suspicious conduct.
- Solutions and Assistance: To salvage the creator's reputation, platforms ought to take action to eliminate any content or communications that the impersonator has produced, as well as make public announcements to elucidate the circumstances. A thorough settlement may also include providing impacted users with support services like counseling or legal support.

## VI. ADDRESSING ETHICAL AND PRIVACY CHALLENGES

A multidimensional strategy that puts user rights, inclusion, and transparency first is needed to address ethical and privacy issues in the metaverse. Metaverse platforms may establish a trustworthy and innovative environment that is fair, courteous, and safe by putting these best practices into effect. Engaging with users, regulators, and ethical experts regularly will be essential to navigating the complex difficulties that occur in this new digital frontier as the metaverse develops.

## A. Best Practices for Users

In the metaverse, users have the ability and responsibility to shape the moral environment of these virtual spaces. They can safeguard their personal information, act morally, and make the metaverse a safer and more respectful place for all. To successfully navigate the opportunities and challenges of this new frontier, users must be well-informed, exercise caution, and participate actively in the community. Users can effectively handle the ethical and privacy difficulties in the metaverse by adhering to the following best practices:

### 1. Use the Following Best Practices to Comprehend and Manage Privacy Settings

- **Examine the Privacy Statement:** Users should take the time to read and comprehend the platform's privacy policy outlining what data is collected, how it is used, and with whom it is shared before using any metaverse platform. This can assist users in choosing their participation with knowledge.
- **Customize Privacy Settings:** You may customize privacy settings on most platforms. To manage who may see their information, how it is used, and what information is shared with third parties, users should routinely check and modify these settings. If you can, select more stringent privacy settings.
- **Limit Data Sharing:** Individuals using the metaverse should use caution while disclosing personal information. Save private information like real names, addresses, or bank account information until when it is really essential to share it with reliable sources.

### 2. The Best Ways to Act Ethically and with Respect for Others

- **Respecting Other Users:** Act as though you would expect the same decency and consideration from other users and avatars in real life. Avoiding harassment, hate speech, and any other actions that can injure or discomfort other people are all part of this.
- **Having Positive Interactions:** Encourage a positive community by having courteous conversations, helping out new users, and denouncing unethical behavior when you see it. It is the responsibility of users to contribute to a secure and friendly environment by becoming good digital citizens.
- **Preventing Misrepresentation:** Users ought to refrain from taking on the identity of others or making potentially damaging or deceptive avatars. Accurately portraying oneself without taking advantage of the identity or reputation of others is a component of the ethical use of avatars.

### 3. The Best Practices for Protecting Digital Identity and Personal Information

- **Using Robust Passwords:** Use secure, one-of-a-kind passwords for several platforms to safeguard accounts. To create and safely save complicated passwords, think about utilizing a password manager.
- **Two-Factor Authentication (2FA):** To further secure your account, turn on two-factor authentication wherever it's available. This increases the difficulty of unauthorized people accessing your accounts and data.

- **Frequent Monitoring:** Keep an eye out for any indications of strange activity or unwanted access to your account. Check frequently for alerts regarding attempts to log in from strange devices or locations.

## B. Responsibilities of Developers and Providers

The metaverse's ethical and privacy environment is greatly influenced by developers and suppliers. They can design platforms that uphold user rights while being secure and welcoming. Sustaining trust and cultivating a pleasant digital environment in the metaverse will need continued dedication to these tasks. These are the principal obligations they must fulfil:

### 1. The Obligation to Design With Privacy by Default and by Design

- **Privacy by Design:** When creating metaverse platforms, developers must consider privacy principles throughout the entire architectural and design process. By taking this approach, privacy is guaranteed to be a core feature of the platform rather than an afterthought.
- **Privacy by Default:** User privacy ought to come first in default configurations. This implies that unless consumers specifically request to participate, they should automatically opt out of data collecting and sharing activities.

One way to put this into practice is to

✓ Protect user data from the moment it is obtained by using techniques like encryption and anonymization.

✓ Provides an easy-to-use interface for privacy settings that makes it simple for consumers to manage their data and change their privacy choices.

✓ Adopt data minimization strategies to make sure that the platform is only collecting the data that is required for it to function.

### 2. Accountability for Maintaining Openness and Informed Consent

- **Clear Communication:** Users must understand how developers and providers gather, use, and share their data. This entails offering a clear, accessible privacy policy that describes what information is gathered, how it will be used, and who will receive access to it.
- **Informed Consent:** Prior to the collection or use of any personal data, users must give their express consent. Users must give informed consent, which requires them to fully comprehend the terms of their agreement.

The following actions are referred to as implementation:

✓ Create a brief, easily understood privacy policy by avoiding legalese and other technical terms that could confuse users.

✓ Instead of accepting everything without question, implement comprehensive consent processes that allow users to select the kinds of data they are comfortable giving.

- ✓ Request that users review and update their privacy settings on a regular basis, particularly if there are modifications to the way data is handled.

### 3. The Obligation to Uphold the Autonomy and Control of Users

- **User Control:** Developers ought to provide users authority over their digital identities and data, enabling them to export, import, and change their data whenever they like.
- **Algorithmic Transparency:** When algorithms are used to tailor user experiences (such as matchmaking or content suggestions), developers should provide consumers the ability to modify or opt out of these algorithms as well as be open and honest about how they operate.

Application:

- ✓ Provide consumers with simple-to-use data management options, like the ability to remove outdated accounts, export data, and change privacy preferences.
- ✓ Give users the option to modify how much algorithm-driven content they are exposed to, along with transparency reports that detail the platform's algorithmic usage.

### 4. Adhering to Law and Regulation Requirements

- **Legal Compliance:** Platform developers and providers are required to make sure that their systems abide by all applicable privacy and data protection regulations, including the California Consumer Privacy Act (CCPA) and the General Data Protection Regulation (GDPR) in Europe.
- **International Standards:** Developers should aim to comply with international data protection regulations and tackle the difficulties associated with cross-border data transfers, considering the global scope of the metaverse.

Implementation:

- ✓ To guarantee adherence to national and international legal requirements, evaluate and update platform policies regularly.
- ✓ To ensure that user data is managed in compliance with the highest standards and to traverse the complexity of cross-border data protection, collaborate with legal professionals.
- ✓ Provide tools that make it simple for people to exercise their legal rights regarding data privacy, such as the right to request access to their data or the right to be forgotten.

## C. Role of Governments and Regulators

Regulators and governments have a significant influence on how the metaverse develops in the future. They can contribute to the creation of a metaverse that is secure, welcoming, and considerate of privacy by putting in place strong legislative frameworks, encouraging moral behavior, and guaranteeing the preservation of users' rights. Governments, businesses, and civil society must continue to work together as the metaverse expands to handle new issues that arise and make sure that this new digital frontier is responsibly controlled.

The following are the principal duties and functions that regulators and governments need to carry out:

## 1. Creating Unambiguous Legal and Regulatory Structures

Role:

- **Creating All-Inclusive Law:** Governments must enact rules and regulations that are tailored to the difficulties presented by the metaverse. Data protection, user privacy, intellectual property rights, digital identities, and ethical behavior are just a few of the many topics they ought to address.
- **Modifying Current Laws:** Where necessary, current laws—such as those pertaining to consumer protection, data security, and anti-discrimination—should be modified to include provisions for activities conducted within the metaverse.
- Governments and regulators play a crucial role in developing comprehensive policies that protect users' rights and promote ethical standards. This includes enforcing regulations, monitoring compliance, and fostering international cooperation.

Implementation:

✓ To safeguard users' digital rights, draft and enact laws that particularly address data collection, storage, and use in virtual environments.

✓ Make sure that rules are relevant to different types of digital and virtual environments, not just the metaverse, by making them technology-neutral.

✓ Update legal frameworks often to stay up with the quick advancement of technology and the introduction of fresh difficulties in the metaverse.

## 2. Upholding Data Protection and Privacy Laws

Role:

- **Control and Enforcement:** Regulators ought to be in charge of monitoring how privacy rules are applied in the metaverse. This involves making certain that platforms abide by local, state, federal, and international data protection laws, such as the CCPA in California and the GDPR in Europe.
- **Penalties for Non-Compliance:** Governments ought to set and implement sanctions for metaverse platforms that disregard privacy laws. This may entail penalties, limitations, or even a business end.

Execution:

✓ Create new regulatory agencies or broaden the purview of already-existing ones to cover metaverse platform and data practices supervision.

- ✓ To guarantee adherence to data protection regulations, conduct routine audits and inspections of metaverse systems.
- ✓ Establish severe fines and unambiguous penalties for violating privacy regulations to discourage unethical behavior.

### 3. Safeguarding the Rights and Digital Identity of Users

Part:

- **Protecting Digital Rights:** States must make sure that people's rights—like the freedom of speech, the right to privacy, and the ability to avoid discrimination—are respected in the metaverse. This involves identifying and safeguarding users' virtual assets and digital identities.
- **Resolving Conflicts and Complaints:** If users' rights are infringed upon in the metaverse, governments ought to set up channels for them to file complaints and seek compensation. This can entail establishing specialized tribunals for conflicts about the metaverse or digital ombudsman services.

Execution:

- ✓ Make sure that digital rights are honored in both real and virtual environments by enshrining them in national legislation.
- ✓ Provide easily available legal channels so that people can report infringements on their rights and pursue damages or other remedies.
- ✓ Collaborate with worldwide organizations to create international guidelines for digital rights in the metaverse.

### 4. Promoting International Harmonization and Collaboration

Part:

- **Cross-Border Regulation:** Because the metaverse is an international space, international cooperation is necessary for regulation to be effective. Governments ought to cooperate to handle cross-border issues, exchange best practices, and harmonize rules.
- **International Standards Development:** To create worldwide standards for the metaverse, governments can take the initiative and collaborate with organizations like the World Telecommunication Union, the United Nations, and the World Economic Forum.

Execution:

- ✓ Make sure that national interests and values are represented in international negotiations and agreements concerning the governance of virtual environments.
- ✓ Participate in the creation of international frameworks or treaties that set uniform guidelines for user rights, data protection, and moral behavior in the metaverse.

- ✓ Promote bilateral or multinational agreements that help with information sharing about metaverse governance and enforcement collaboration.

## VII. FUTURE OUTLOOK

The metaverse's future has great promise, but it also poses serious privacy and ethical issues. To overcome these obstacles as technology develops, stakeholders—including developers, governments, and users—will need to work closely together. Through proactive resolution of privacy, moral, and regulatory concerns, we can guarantee that the metaverse develops into a secure, welcoming, and individual rights-abiding environment. It will be imperative that these stakeholders continue to communicate to shape a metaverse that minimizes dangers and safeguards the most vulnerable members of society.

The metaverse's future is expected to be influenced by technological developments, changes in user behavior, and the constantly changing legal and regulatory environment. Here are some significant patterns and things to think about going forward:

### 1. Increasing Privacy Management Complexity

The metaverse's integration of more elements of everyday life will make privacy control a lot more difficult. Existing privacy protocols will be put to the test by the sheer volume and variety of data generated within the metaverse, ranging from behavioral patterns to biometric data.

Decentralized methods of data ownership, where consumers have more control over their data, may become more prevalent in the future. For instance, blockchain technology may make it possible for people to more securely and openly own and control their data.

There will be a need for sophisticated privacy solutions that let users precisely manage their data as privacy concerns increase. AI-powered privacy assistants that guide users through intricate privacy settings and support them in making well-informed decisions about sharing data are one example of this.

### 2. Changing Ethical Guidelines and Standards

As new use cases and social dynamics arise, the metaverse's ethical landscape will continue to change. Concerns like digital identity theft, cyberbullying, and the moral application of AI in the metaverse will all need to be addressed in the future. In the metaverse, moral principles must be flexible and dynamic, changing to meet the demands of the times and the expectations of the public.

Because the metaverse is decentralized, it may lead to the emergence of community-driven ethical frameworks, in which users collaborate to set standards and guidelines for conduct in particular virtual environments.

### 3. Adjustment to Law and Regulation

Governance will need to be significantly modified and innovative due to the metaverse's rapid development, which will exceed the current legal and regulatory frameworks. The necessity for international cooperation on regulatory norms will increase as the metaverse expands internationally. This could result in the creation of international treaties or accords that include digital rights, platform accountability, and cross-border data flows.

To anticipate future difficulties and create frameworks that are adaptable enough to take into account unanticipated metaverse developments, governments may choose to take more proactive methods to regulation.

### 4. Automation and Artificial Intelligence's Growth

Automation and artificial intelligence (AI) will become more and more prevalent in the metaverse, from user interaction to content generation. Though there are many advantages to these technologies, there are also moral conundrums, especially when it comes to responsibility, bias, and decision-making.

To guarantee that AI-driven interactions are impartial, transparent, and devoid of bias, ethical AI frameworks created especially for the metaverse will probably be developed in the future. It will be necessary to set up precise parameters and rules for human-AI cooperation as AI becomes more incorporated into the metaverse. This calls for resolving concerns including user permission, decision-making authority, and AI autonomy.

### 5. Tighter Supervision and Its Consequences

Because the metaverse is immersive, it makes unprecedented levels of surveillance possible, which raises worries about user privacy and possible data exploitation by platforms and third parties. Stronger defenses against surveillance, such as the usage of encryption, anonymization software, and decentralized networks that lessen the possibility of tracking and data collection, may be demanded by users and advocacy organizations.

To shield users from intrusive surveillance, platforms will come under growing pressure to provide robust accountability measures and be open about their data-gathering activities.

## VIII. CONCLUSION

With its enormous potential to change social, economic, and cultural environments, the metaverse offers both ground-breaking possibilities and serious privacy and ethical issues. Addressing the issues of user privacy, moral behavior, and the wider ramifications of virtual worlds is becoming more and more crucial as this digital frontier develops. By doing this, we may create a metaverse that genuinely embodies the ideals of our culture, providing not only the latest in technology but also a dedication to the values of justice, equity, and respect for all users.

## REFERENCES


Adomaitis, L., Grinbaum, A., & Lenzi, D. (2022). Identification and specification of potential ethical issues and impacts and analysis of ethical issues Analysis of ethical issues D2.2 Identification and specification of potential ethical issues and impacts and analysis of ethical issues. *TechEthos D2.2, 101006249*. DOI: 10.31009/InDret.2024.i2.03

Arismendy Mengual, L. (2024). A legal status for Avatars in the Metaverse from a Private Law perspective. In *InDret* (Issue 2). DOI: 10.31009/InDret.2024.i2.03

Bahuguna, A. (2022). Intellectual Property and Metaverse. [IJSR]. *International Journal of Science and Research (Raipur, India)*, 11(9), 371–374. DOI: 10.21275/SR22905165231

Castaldo, A. R. (2022). Anti-Money Laundering Strategies and The Metaverse: New Dangers and Opportunities. *Iura & Legal Systems*, IX(11), 94–97.

Chawki, M., Basu, S., & Choi, K. S. (2024). Redefining Boundaries in the Metaverse: Navigating the Challenges of Virtual Harm and User Safety. *Laws*, 13(3), 1–23. DOI: 10.3390/laws13030033

Gita Krishna Murti, K., Sri Darma, G., Putu Mahyuni, L., & Ngurah Eddy Supriyadinata Gorda, A. (2023). Immersive Experience in the Metaverse: Implications for Tourism and Business. *International Journal of Applied Business Research*, 2023(2), 187–207. DOI: 10.35313/ijabr.v5i02.329

Haynes, D. (2024). Ethics of information and the metaverse. *Communication, Technologies et Développement, 14*(December 2023), 0–6. DOI: 10.4000/ctd.9497

Hine, E. (2023). Content Moderation in the Metaverse Could Be a New Frontier to Attack Freedom of Expression. *Philosophy & Technology*, 36(3), 1–11. DOI: 10.1007/s13347-023-00645-4

Kalyvaki, M. (2023). Navigating the Metaverse Business and Legal Challenges: Intellectual Property, Privacy, and Jurisdiction. *Journal of Metaverse*, 3(1), 87–92. DOI: 10.57019/jmv.1238344

Kasiyanto, S., & Kilinc, M. R. (2022). Legal Conundrums of the Metaverse. *Journal of Central Banking Law and Institutions*, 1(2), 299–322. DOI: 10.21098/jcli.v1i2.25

Peña-Acuña, B., & Rubio-Alcalá, F. D. (2024). Ethical approach to the use of immersive technologies. Advance about digitalisation of multilingual programs in the EHEA. *Frontiers in Virtual Reality*, 5(July), 1–10. DOI: 10.3389/frvir.2024.1357595

Pietro, R., & Cresci, S. (2021). *Metaverse: Security and Privacy Issues*. DOI: 10.1109/TPSI-SA52974.2021.00032

Upadhyay, U., Kumar, A., Sharma, G., Gupta, B. B., Alhalabi, W., Arya, V., & Chui, K. T. (2023). Cyberbullying in the metaverse: A prescriptive perception on global information systems for user protection. *Journal of Global Information Management*, 31(1), 1–25. DOI: 10.4018/JGIM.325793

Wang, S., & Wang, W. (2023). A review of the application of digital identity in the Metaverse. *Security and Safety*, 2, 2023009. DOI: 10.1051/sands/2023009

Zallio, M., & Clarkson, P. J. (2022). Designing the metaverse: A study on inclusion, diversity, equity, accessibility and safety for digital immersive environments. *Telematics and Informatics*, 75(September), 101909. DOI: 10.1016/j.tele.2022.101909

Zhuk, A. (2024). Ethical implications of AI in the Metaverse. *AI and Ethics*, 0123456789. Advance online publication. DOI: 10.1007/s43681-024-00450-5

# Chapter 9
# Legal Personality in the Metaverse:
## A Jurisprudential Examination

**Karun Sanjaya**
https://orcid.org/0009-0005-1647-1549
*Symbiosis Law School, Symbiosis International University, Pune, India*

**Rushil Chandra**
https://orcid.org/0000-0002-8687-6294
*Dr. Vishwanath Karad MIT World Peace University, Pune, India & Gujarat National Law University, Gandhinagar, India*

**Anushree S. Panikkassery**
https://orcid.org/0000-0001-7355-204X
*Department of Economics, Christ University, Bangalore, India*

**Kavya Sanjaya**
*School of Economics, University of Hyderabad, Gachibowli, India*

**Soumya Srivastava**
*Symbiosis Law School, Symbiosis International University, Pune, India*

## ABSTRACT

*One of the novel legal issues we see developing in the metaverse is whether or not avatars and AI agents should be given standing as legal people? This chapter advances a jurisprudence that discusses the rights, responsibilities and autonomy of digital entities in virtual spaces and assesses elements of jurisprudence, such as corporate personhood, which may be relevant in the absence of physical presence. Through examples of both popular, widely known platforms sites like Second Life and Decentraland as well as recent blows to idealism around digital legal spheres through experimental governance projects like Estonia's e-Residency program, the chapter addresses some current junctures to discuss challenges about issues such as accountability, jurisdiction, and intellectual property. It draws attention to the necessity of creative legal mechanisms and global norms for regulating new digital frontiers, propelling the conversation on how we apply our jurisprudence to digital environments forward.*

DOI: 10.4018/979-8-3693-8628-6.ch009

## 1. INTRODUCTION

The metaverse is one of the biggest changes in the digital world and has started changing how folks engage with each other, socialize, or conduct business. The metaverse is a permanent, collective and fully immersive digital universe, consisting of interconnected virtual worlds in which people (or their avatars) interact with one another and digital objects in real-time. Although the metaverse was first conceived in fiction, (Neal Stephenson wrote about it in his book called Snow Crash back in 1992), with the accelerating advances of virtual reality (VR) and augmented reality (AR) technologies, that possibility has become a physical truth now. Now billions of dollars are being poured into metaverse platforms by major corporations like Meta (formerly Facebook) and Microsoft, as they seek to create digital worlds that mirror —and at some point will even substitute— real-life interactions (Dionisio et al., 2013).

Exciting news emerges in the metaverse, a development that inevitably raises all kinds of challenging legal questions — not least those about the concept of legal personality. Legal personality has traditionally been the recognition of an entity (natural or artificial/legal) as having rights and obligations under law, and that a legal person is any human being or organization (Salmond 1907). Historically, this idea reflected the practice of focusing on natural people and later to some extent on legal entities such as corporations that have been constructed with particular rights and responsibilities distinct from or even independent of the individuals forming them. But as virtual spaces become more complicated with avatars and digital creatures investing really social and economic capital in the metaverse, an essential question emerges: Are some avatars or entities within the metaverse afforded a type of legal personality? And if yes, then under what conditions and limitations?

This question has legal ramifications that go way beyond the ivory tower. The metaverse is a combination of assets, property rights, contract meshes and quasi-political structures between users and companies. Certain digital platforms have built in-world economies, complete with the ability to buy, sell and even rent virtual assets ranging from land to clothing to more generic digital goods. Existing platforms such as Second Life, Decentraland, and Roblox feature flourishing digital markets that emulate the economic exchange of the real-world where the line between virtual and physical is becoming less distinct (Fairfield, 2005). This convergence leads to a never-seen before combination of digital and physical legal systems, raising the question for re-examination if avatars or virtual entities are capable —or should even be capable— of holding rights.

The answer to this question is a classical jurisprudential task. Legal personality has historically been implicated in theories of the law ranging from positivism to natural law. The distinguishing characteristics of legal personality and its boundaries have sparked far-reaching debate among jurists, especially in the context of corporate personhood, environmental personhood, and more recently, AI legal status. Building on these theories, this chapter examines alternative principles of legal personality that might be applicable to the metaverse by analogy (if avatars or digital personae are treated much like corporations or other doctrinally established legal actors, for example). It also examines whether metaverse should be attributed legal personality and if granting this status to given metaverse traits ensues logical reasoning within the current legal structure or if it will require creating unique paradigms (Dwivedi, 2022).

This question is not just an academic one. The practical and ethical implications of potential recognition of metaverse entities as legal personalities arise in the context of accountability, rights and responsibilities. If an avatar can enter into contracts or have assets, who is liable for breaching those agreements? If, say, an automated character in a game gets one of my characters hurt — or worse! — does it have legal consequences? Moreover, given that many new social and economic life will take place in these virtual environments the issue of user rights — including privacy, free speech and property rights — is even more prominent (Kasiyanto & Klinic, 2022).

The chapter starts with the historical and jurisprudential roots of legal personality, how personhood is granted not just to natural people but also to corporations, states and even in some cases natural entities. It then places those principles within the metaverse, discussing how avatars and other native digital objects and entities have characterized legal lines by cross-over. This chapter aims to offer a detailed jurisprudential analysis of legal personality in the metaverse through the analysis of case studies, survey of jurisdictional variations and consideration of ethical dimensions. It aims to answer some of the essential questions concerning rights, responsibilities and accountability in virtual spaces, as part of a broader debate on the legal framework that should govern our digital spheres.

## 2. HISTORICAL AND JURISPRUDENTIAL BASIS OF LEGAL PERSONALITY

Legal personality, that is, the basis of who or what has rights and duties in law, is a key pillar of most modern legal systems. Legal personality, sometimes called legal personhood, is historically derived from the initial forms of law in which only natural people—human beings—were recognized as subjects to the law. Nevertheless, jurisprudence quickly expanded the scope of personhood to include all kinds of artificial entities, most famously corporations, so that they may participate in the legal system as if individual human beings. All Custom Content from the Plan This section traces how the concept of legal personality has evolved within legal systems, their justifications for extending it to non-natural people and whether such rationales might apply to entities in the metaverse.

Legal personality has been the subject of theoretical debates for as long as there have been legal theorists. Primitive theorisation had already been provided as well by jurists, John Salmond (1907) and H.L.A. Hart (1961). While Salmond's treatise did not define legal personality in the way that many rewrote it, both suggested that legal personality was essentially an artifice through which rights and duties are allocated within a legal system. Salmond (1907) stated that a legal person is anyone who can be recognised by the law as having certain capacities, such as the capacity to own property or enter contracts and be held liable. But this conceptual elasticity has permitted legal systems to keep up with the social and economic changes by endowing individuals that, although not human, take on such a fundamental function in society more generally.

The fact that legal personality of corporations can be extended is one example of this adaptability. Corporate personhood was born of necessity, allowing groups of people to act together and be treated as one person in economic life. This evolution was cemented in landmark decisions including Trustees of Dartmouth College v. Woodward (1819) and Santa Clara County v. Southern Pacific Railroad Co. Those decisions enabled corporations to hold property, enter into contracts, and be sued—making complicated transactions straightforward and stimulating economic growth. That legal recognition was controversial, with opponents claiming that corporate personhood allowed people to escape liability when their actions were property-based. However, corporate personhood has inevitably made its way into contemporary legal systems across the planet.

Jurisprudential theories of personhood have also explored what might be considered less traditional uses, namely granting legal personality to environmental entities and animals. In countries as diverse as Ecuador and New Zealand, advocates have successfully lobbied for legal personhood for certain rivers, forests, or ecosystems in order to enable third parties to sue on behalf of these natural entities (Viktoria

Kahui et al., 2024). However, these extensions of personality show that this conception is not limited to classical 'human being' with economic interests at stake but also any entity which the society deems fit to be endowed with legal protections or responsibilities (Stone 1972). This flexibility in assigning personhood does provide a path to include digital entities participating within the metaverse as they continue to take on greater role and significance both virtually and otherwise.

In addition, the emerging discourse around AI and machine learning contains insights useful for understanding whether legal personality should be applied to these digital bodies. Since AI systems are becoming more self-ruling and making independent decisions, a few legal theorists contend that there is an argument for at least some limited form of legal personality to be allotted in the unitary at any point or another to an AI. This belief is grounded in the understanding that just as corporations are capable of actions with legal ramifications, so too can AI systems and thus a level of responsibility must be established (Kasiyanto & Klinic, 2022). For example, if an autonomous AI in the metaverse injures someone or even enters into a contract, should he answer for his actions or should it be his human creators who pay the price? According to legal scholars such as Staszkiewicz et al. (2024), these questions could be answered by giving artificial intelligence a form of limited personhood that would allow for clearer accountability systems while also protecting human interests.

But the things you have mentioned, these historical and jurisprudential frameworks will be applied to the metaverse and that is different. Avatars and other living digital entities in virtual worlds are neither totally free nor truly human; they occupy a liminal realm of user intent (and agency), platform limits, and complex digital programming. Digital avatars are specific entities that exist in the realm of digital information so do not require a physical form, living within their particular system. They may not possess human aspects, or socialize as humans do; however, they start to become more of a reflection of us when conducting transactions and creating connections within social structures in the metaverse. Thus, this duality creates challenges for traditional legal boundaries suggesting that digital entities (whether they are controlled by humans or not), should be seen as legal people in a way that balances both their independent and dependent nature (Dionisio, Burns, & Gilbert, 2013).

Given the economic value expected to be generated inside the metaverse, there is an urgent need for a legal framework that accounts for digital business entities. Land, collectibles and currencies of every flavor exist in the metaverse, which can all have serious dollar signs attached to them. In a virtual property dispute involving an avatar, the legal system must figure out if it is the avatar that is legally liable or responsible for wrongful acts, or merely the user or even the entire service. Present laws of the personhood of corporations and environmental beings offer marginal comparators but do not capture adequately any unique characteristics that may render a metaverse entity singularly human-like. Therefore, as the metaverse continues to develop, two questions need to be considered: can traditionally views of personhood meaningfully spans the digital divides or should entirely new legal categories be developed (Fairfield 2005.)

The following analysis of legal personality, from historical and jurisprudential perspectives, prepares the ground for an examination of how to view the metaverse through a lens that deviates from its conventional framework. Through taking into account the specific characteristics of digital beings and through comparative reflections in business and environmental law, this chapter intends to evaluate if and how legal personality can be granted to the metaverse or whether avatars and other digital gravitas will require an entirely new type of jurisprudence for their rights and duties within virtual worlds.

## 3. LEGAL PERSONHOOD IN DIGITAL SPACES AND THE METAVERSE

While the metaverse continues to balloon with relevance, the subject of legal personality for individuals in virtual worlds emerges. The metaverse differs from conventional physical spaces in that it is no longer bound to the physics of our world but is defined by user interaction and its orchestration through digital shaping. But as users commit actual economic and social capital in the metaverse, interactions and transactions typically found in the real world occur in digital spaces; with this transition come a host of legal issues relating to status and recognition of avatars, other kinds of digital entities, and artificial intelligence (AI)-driven agents.

When virtual worlds first emerged (Second Life and World of Warcraft, being two early examples), academic interest around the notion of legal personhood within digital spaces began. They also offered the first examples of virtual economies, social structures, and exchange of property — thus establishing a primitive base for legal inquiry. Since then, scholars have argued that the properties and avatars within these virtual worlds are entitled to certain human rights because they cost significant amounts of real money to develop and therefore should be considered human (Lastowka & Hunter 2004). This reasoning is based on a much larger legal tradition recognizing the worth of abstract goods—like intellectual property—which, albeit incorporeal in nature, are afforded considerable defenses by law. Digital assets in the metaverse are also being recognized as an emerging industry and some academics have argued for providing avatars with a limited form of legal personality as a means of protecting investments (Fairfield 2005).

This has inspired several different lines of thought, with the most notable being looking at whether avatars should have legal rights and obligations. In the metaverse, avatars act as a proxy for users: they pleasure action on behalf of you, build relationships and mystery digital property. As intermediaries, they pose the question of whether we should imbue avatars with something like a quasi-personhood, similar to corporations. Corporate personhood permits an organization to operate independently from its individual authors by entering into legal agreements and owning property. Well, if avatars could be comparable to a person, an avatar might make contracts, hold digital property and be another legal personality (Hildebrandt & Rouvroy, 2011). On the other hand, granting legal personhood to avatars would lead to further complications in that the law would need to make a distinction between behaviours driven by a user and automated decisions made from an AI or from the platform itself.

AI does much to define digital interactions in the metaverse of the future. Other metaverse platforms leverage the use of characters powered by AI, or non-player characters (NPCs) to enhance realistic experience. These automated agents powered by AI function independently, frequently with the provision of automatic interaction with users and automation of dealing within virtual properties or generating content inside digital platforms. Some legal scholars like Staszkiewicz et al. (2024) have even contended that, depending on the circumstances, entities driven by AI in digital spaces may deserve a type of restricted legal personhood — especially if they act freely and independently. Ethical dilemmas arise from the potential for autonomous AI-driven entities to possess some sort of natural rights within digital environments, and practical ones from the question of whether AI systems can be held accountable if they act in ways that can affect the real world and real people.

A different method of endowing digital beings with legal personality is based on contract law. Others argue that platforms could create a sort of "avatar contract," where users recognize the rights and responsibilities of their avatars within the platform (Cheong, 2022). This would be a user agreements-type approach like we see with many online services but delineate the rights of avatars operating within the metaverse alongside accountability from users who consent to certain parameters. Such contracts may determine avatars' roles in transactions, outline their ownership rights to digital goods and provide dispute resolution mechanisms, enabling legal issues to be handled without granting full personhood to avatars or digital entities.

In addition, the use of blockchain technology in the metaverse has made this discussion on legal personhood even more complex. Through blockchain, Users can own things in the metaverse: digital assets like non-fungible tokens (NFTs) that users can buy/sell/trade. NFTs are unique tokens, representing everything from virtual real estate to digital art, that have a value in the real world and can be transferred outside of the platform. Therefore, such digital property rights taking place on the metaverse would be possible due to blockchain technology, as it could indeed support arguments granting avatars legal entity status with respect to being able to own and transfer digital assets. Nonetheless, there is a scholarly debate on whether avatars acquire legal personhood able to create ownership rights that can regulate how blockchain movements are recognized within virtual spaces (Gadekallu et al., 2022).

The argument for these rights also has to do with the user rights within digital spaces such as privacy and data protection. Metaverse users also invested a lot of their private information and exposed themselves to risks by doing things that they cross in the metaverse. Giving avatars a limited form of legal personhood would allow platforms to define and deliver protections for user data and privacy since they would treat avatars as legal stand-ins for users. Such a strategy would be consistent with the increasing acknowledgment of digital rights—most notably reflected in regulations like the General Data Protection Regulation (GDPR) in Europe, which provides users of digital environments with extensive data protection rights (Kasiyanto & Klinic, 2022). While avatars are subservient objects serving the user, attributing limited personhood to those avatars may enable users to protect their data and privacy in the metaverse by asserting rights through them.

Legal Personhood in the metaverse is a fundamentally multifaceted concept deeply dependent on multiple interconnections like property rights, contract law obligations or data privacy. Legal scholars can analyze avatars and digital entities in the metaverse from a jurisprudential perspective to find where conventional legal dogma is unaffected but may need recalibration or even reframing due to distinct nature of virtual spaces. Nevertheless, granting legal personality to avatars and virtual beings in the metaverse prompts fundamental issues of accountability, autonomy and the tension between users' rights and platform obligations that warrants prudence on how best to legally define digital entities.

Figure 1 below depicts the areas of similarities and dissimilarities between traditional and metaverse entities. While the major difference is with respect to the type of assets (tangible vs digital) and nature of existence (physical vs virtual), the aspects such and legal compliance and taxation will become comparatively easier as everything is digitised and automated. It is noteworthy that the same is achieved without compromising the ability to enter into and abide by the contractual obligations.

*Figure 1. A graphical representation of the traditional and metaverse entities' features*

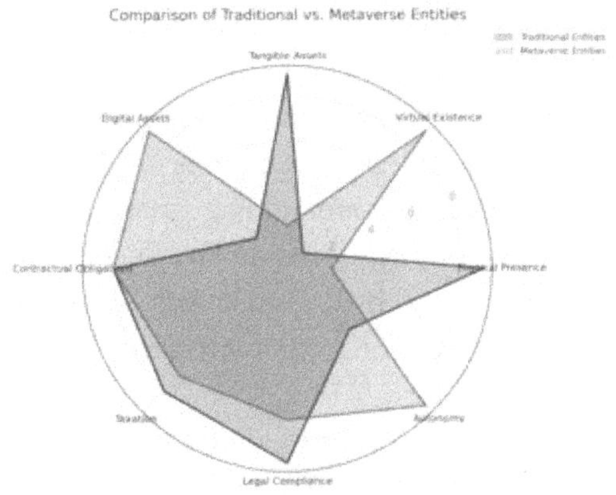


## 4. LEGAL AND REGULATORY CHALLENGES IN ASSIGNING PERSONHOOD TO METAVERSE ENTITIES

A metaverse that could have granted legal personhood to digital entities would create huge tension with existing law and regulation. They are complicated by the newness of digital environments and assets, but amplified by the conceptual difficulties in identifying rights and obligations for non-corporeal entities. Though some others have laid the jurisprudential groundwork for acknowledging particular kinds of non-human subjects as legal people, putting those ideas into practice will demand a wholesale and deep rethinking of both what it means to own rights, be held accountable or interact with other individuals in terms of the law—whether human or when applied digital.

One of the first hurdles in giving legal personhood to metaverse entities is third parties — avatars run by humans vs autonomous agents driven by AI. Avatars in a User-centric metaverse are proxies of actual users, conducting activities that reflect the will and desire of the user behind the avatar. Consequently, they can typically be more readily tied to the legal rights and obligations of the natural people who exercise control over them. Nevertheless, this association is made more complex with autonomous AI agents. Such agents can act autonomously, performing tasks without any direct human mediation or input and one implication of this is the question of whether these agents should be held responsible for their own actions within the metaverse or alternatively whether responsibility should be assigned to those (developers, platform operators or users) who created, operated and/or interacted with such agents (Koops et al., 2010).

Is it feasible for legal frameworks to conclude that the digital subjects in the metaverse maintain enough degree of autonomy to deserve limited personhood, similar to corporate sentience? For example, corporate law typically recognizes that corporations function as independent institutions and therefore need a type of legal personality to facilitate economic decision-making. In contrast, digital entities are beholden to the technical limitations and parameters of software code and platforms that govern the metaverse. So, while digital actors may demonstrate behavior that superficially resembles autonomy, they are ultimately bound by (1) procedural rules of conduct inside programmatic departments and (2) the terms of service enforced by the platforms in which these agents exist (Chesterman 2021). Due to this programmed nature, autonomy is a much more complicated concept; actions taken by digital beings are ultimately determined by algorithms and decisions made by the designers or operators of platforms.

Accountability is a much more complicated matter in the form of digital entities playing in a decentralized metaverse infrastructure. In fact, some metaverse environments — especially those based on blockchain technology and decentralized governance models — do not have any one governing entity at all. In some cases, these digital entities could operate in a system managed by many different users or stakeholders, frequently with an anonymous participant. The decentralized nature further complicates the chain of accountability for acts committed by digital actors. Without a single authority in charge of monitoring and managing these spaces, providing legal standards for personhood and responsibility is trickier (Porto & Foà, 2023).

Then we have the metaverse itself, which is cross-jurisdictional in nature. Having said that the metaverse as a digital space can be accessed from near enough anywhere on earth, it theoretically sits outside the framework of any one jurisdiction. Which jurisdiction's laws apply if a digital representation in the metaverse infringes upon the rights of an individual user living within one country while acting under the guise of another? The metaverse is naturally global and demands coordinated cross-jurisdictional legal attention. International organisations like the United Nations and European Union might also contribute towards developing harmonised legal structures or principles to mitigate the transnational problem of regulating virtual entities in the metaverse (Schmidt & Cohen, 2013) But will take some stern negotiating to see a framework that works for all as many nations will not want to give up sovereignty over their borders, let alone digital spaces.

Privacy and data protection regulations create additional challenges for assigning legal personhood to digital personas in the metaverse. Whether avatars, digital agents or whatever name is used for software characters interacting in virtual environments, they are willing to collect and process user data en masse. The European Union's GDPR is one of several laws that impose heavy burdens on data handling and privacy protection, which could be implicated against digital entities in the metaverse who touch user data. However, if avatars or other digital beings are given legal personhood status, privacy regulations might have to follow them and govern the sharing of data from users on behalf of some digital entity (Kasiyanto & Klinic, 2022). If we lack such guidance, then digital twins and other entities may be used as proxies against established privacy laws for the purpose of data collection from individuals in ways that circumvent user privacy.

The issue of regulatory compliance also extends to IP rights in the context of the metaverse. When avatars and other digital beings create and disseminate digital content, they may potentially violate IP rights or generate new products that need protection. Without clear attribution to a single creator, ownership and authorship may be difficult to establish in the metaverse–especially since digital entities might create jointly or even without human control. This could help mitigate some of these hurdles by creating a clear legal pathway for digital entities to own, license, and transact IP rights over digital assets (Gervais, 2021). However, implementing legal rights for digital beings would require adaptations in the existing IP laws to address that digital creators are not human and often cooperate fluidly in designing content across a unique interactive landscape of the metaverse.

Lastly, ethical issues present real regulatory problems. We need to ponder over what it would really mean for an AI entity, or a synthetic human with autonomy, if given legal personality? Would you be less inclined to treat non-human actors as moral agents? Ethicists have suggested that by granting legal personality to digital entities, the very meaning of personhood would be eroded away from human rights towards dehumanization (Balkin, 2017). Such ethical issue outlines a desire for caution in a step toward legal personality with digital entities in the metaverse, suggesting proper custom to weigh greater impacts on both society and law.

Long story short, the regulatory challenges of granting legal personhood to digital entities in the metaverse are extremely complex, balancing autonomy with accountability and jurisdiction with privacy as well as intellectual property and ethical considerations. Digital beings cannot be sufficiently sanctioned by the means of traditional law (for instance, criminal, civil and commercial laws always attribute liability to a 'person', be it legal or natural), and so processes for the operationalisation of these rules must conform fully to the possibilities afforded us through advances in technology without trampling on either human rights as we have always known them or high standard legal principles. You don't need a crystal ball to see the future challenges posed by metaverses, and as digital environments continue to evolve at unprecedented rates, the development of robust, flexible legal frameworks will be essential for meeting these challenges head on whilst also safeguarding that they represent a coherent and legally responsible space of operation.

## 5. CASE STUDIES IN LEGAL PERSONALITY WITHIN THE METAVERSE

Exploring case studies in which features of legal personality have been contemplated in digital and virtual environments reveals insight into the opportunities and limitations involved with adapting them to the metaverse. Throughout jurisdictions, real-world cases and pilot programs convey the complexities and details in how rights, responsibilities, and recognition are assigned to digital entities. These issues reflect how laws are being challenged and, in some instances, redefined within the digital context—especially in terms of property rights, breach of contracts and privacy protections.

### 5.1 Second Life and Virtual Property Rights

An early and much cited case about virtual worlds is Bragg v. Linden Research, Inc., where virtually property rights and the ownership of digital goods in the metaverse became legal questions. He became a user of Second Life and brings suit against Linden Lab to restore his suspended account and access to digital assets within the platform. Bragg stated going so far as to say that he had used real funds made investment in FOB, and therefore Linden Lab was seizing his virtual property without due process. Although this case did settle out of court, it does raise the interesting point that do users have property rights to digital goods they purchase in online virtual worlds (Fairfield, 2005)? It also raised discussion over whether user agreements are enforceable and how much users can be considered "owners" of digital property. If metaverse entities are to hold property apart from their user or platform, this case highlights the need for clearer rights in regard to that digital property.

### 5.2 Decentraland and Blockchain-Based Digital Assets

Coined as a blockchain-based virtual world, Decentraland provides a decentralized platform where users can create, experience, and monetize content and applications by buying, selling or developing parcels of virtual real estate represented by NFTs. Because Decentraland is based on blockchain technology for ownership and transference of assets, the rights that users have to digital property in this virtual environment are embedded into a ledger that is decentralized and not under the jurisdiction of any central organization. It now provides a framework that has allowed users to hold more power over their virtual property than ever before in regular virtual worlds. This in turn, also raises issues of regulatory scope, IP rights and taxation for digital transactions but within a decentralized framework (Atzori, 2017). A landmark in virtual property law, Decentraland highlights the potential and peril of blockchain-based assets. Whatever the case may be, these developments only reinforce the idea that the future of legal personality for digital entities will exist in a post-legal world away from centralized systems that allow for autonomy.

### 5.3 AI Agents in Virtual Platforms and Liability Concerns

Another new area of legal inquiry are those AI agents, or NPCs, who are behaving independently in the metaverse. AI agents have been trained over the past few years to communicate with users, generate content and take actions in digital spaces while also being independent of human operation. The question of whether AI agents could be held liable has been discussed in the context of tort cases starting from autonomous machines (for instance, self-driving cars) where accountability and intention are involved. AI agents are a significant expression of our time with respect to human artifice; in digital contexts, their actions and processes are underpinned by algorithms that orient the way a system works — that is, it guides its decision-making to replicate complex behaviors normally ascribed to human agency. Jurisdictions differ to a certain extent on the issues of AI liability; legal scholars have claimed limited personhood be granted to AIs as agents in order for them to be liable (Staszkiewicz et al., 2024). This would allow for greater accountability and responsibility for AI-driven actions in the metaverse, enabling digital entities to enter legal arrangements and be held liable independent of the human beings that created them.

### 5.4 Estonia's Digital Identity Program and the E-Residency Model

For example, the e-Residency program in Estonia connects citizens and non-citizens to its innovative digital identity system with individuals able to be digitally present for business and transactions in an official capacity even without being physically present in the nation. This has specific relevance to the metaverse, as it can set precedent for a legal system that recognises digital entities without physical presence. E-Residents receive a kind of digital citizenship that allows them to access banking, tax and legal services from anywhere. For example, Estonia has a digital identity initiative that serves as an approach to both identifying digital entities and awarding these limited legal rights despite the fact they do not have the classic corporeal or national one (Middlemiss, 2022). This case study is an example of state sponsored systems to ensure individuals have digital identities and rights that could be adjusted when it comes both physical, natural people/-entities and maybe also legal people from the metaverse.

## 6. CONCLUSION

As for many other business and commercial matters, the ultimate evolution of digital environments into complex social, economic and creative spaces pose questions around legal personality in the metaverse. The legal landscape of the virtual environment is changing fast from early generations such as in Second Life to more recent blockchain-powered iterations like Decentraland. These cases simplistically demonstrate different facets of ownership, liability and government regulation that make the validation of legal entities in cyberspace a complicated task. Digital property rights and user agreements already have us scratching our heads over virtual worlds; decentralized platforms, not to mention AI agents – including in social media – add layers of complexity with matters including autonomy and accountability, jurisdiction.

Because the metaverse is growing and soon digital entities will become a significant part of its infrastructure, it becomes necessary for jurisdictions to grapple with what it means to afford rights (and impose responsibilities) on actors that are not human. Disputed as the concept of digital personhood will be, such a concept could serve as a basis for delineating stronger protections and liabilities around avatars, AI agents and other metaverse entities. Building on frameworks that exist in the real world, such as corporate personhood, transformative legal personality and blockchain governance, legislators and scholars alike may consider new techniques to recognize digital entities as autonomous actors within their own digital ecosystems. But, of course, those innovations will need to account for what is right and good from an ethical, social and regulatory perspective if digital spaces are to embody user rights alongside public policy aims.

Finally, whether or not the metaverse community recognizes legal personality rests on the extent society is willing to modify traditional legal constructs for modern digital realities. The implications of this jurisprudential discussion are endless, particularly as virtuality continues to develop: digital personhood will be at the heart of future conversations around digital rights, accountability and governance. Going ahead, the promise of global uniformity and inter-discipline approach will be crucial in establishing a just and easy legally sound regime for the metaverse.

## REFERENCES


Atzori, M. (2017). Blockchain Technology and Decentralized Governance: Is The State Still Necessary? *Journal of Governance and Regulation*, 6(1), 45–62. Advance online publication. DOI: 10.22495/jgr_v6_i1_p5

Balkin, J. M. (2017, August 27). *The Three Laws of Robotics in the Age of Big Data*. Papers.*ssrn*.com. https://papers.ssrn.com/sol3/papers.cfm?abstract_id=2890965

Cheong, B. C. (2022). Avatars in the metaverse: Potential legal issues and remedies. *International Cybersecurity Law Review*, 3(2), 467–494. Advance online publication. DOI: 10.1365/s43439-022-00056-9

Chesterman, S. (2021). *We, the Robots?* Cambridge University Press., DOI: 10.1017/9781009047081

Dionisio, J. D. N., Burns, W. G.III, & Gilbert, R. (2013). 3D Virtual worlds and the metaverse. *ACM Computing Surveys*, 45(3), 1–38. DOI: 10.1145/2480741.2480751

Dwivedi, Y. K. (2022). Metaverse beyond the hype: Multidisciplinary Perspectives on Emerging challenges, opportunities, and Agenda for research, Practice and Policy. *International Journal of Information Management, 66*(66), 102542. Sciencedirect. DOI: 10.1145/2480741.2480751

Fairfield, J. (2005). Vrtual Property. *Boston University Law Review. Boston University. School of Law*, 85, 1047–1102. https://www.bu.edu/law/journals-archive/bulr/volume85n4/FAIRFIELD.pdf

Gadekallu, T. R., Huynh-The, T., Wang, W., Yenduri, G., Ranaweera, P., Pham, Q.-V., Benevides, D., & Liyanage, M. (2022). *Blockchain for the Metaverse: A Review*. https://doi.org//arxiv.2203.09738DOI: 10.48550

Gervais, D. J. (2021). *The future of intellectual property*. Edward Elgar Publishing Limited. DOI: 10.4337/9781800885349

Hildebrandt, M., & Rouvroy, A. (2011). *Law, Human Agency and Autonomic Computing - The Philosophy of Law Meets the Philosophy of Technology*. Routledge.

Kahui, V., Armstrong, C. W., & Aanesen, M. (2024). Comparative analysis of Rights of Nature (RoN) case studies worldwide: Features of emergence and design. *Ecological Economics*, 221, 108193–108193. DOI: 10.1016/j.ecolecon.2024.108193

Kasiyanto, S., & Klinic, M. R. (2022). The Legal Conundrums of the Metaverse. *Journal of Central Banking Law and Institutions*, 1(2), 299–322. DOI: 10.21098/jcli.v1i2.25

Koops, B.-J., Hildebrandt, M., & Jaquet-Chiffelle, D.-O. (2010). Bridging the Accountability Gap: Rights for New Entities in the Information Society? *Minnesota Journal of Law, Science & Technology*, 11(2), 497–561. https://scholarship.law.umn.edu/mjlst/vol11/iss2/4/

Lastowkat, F. G., & Hunter, D. (2004). The Laws of the Virtual Worlds. *California Law Review*, 92(1), 1–72. https://lawcat.berkeley.edu/record/1119331/files/fulltext.pdf. DOI: 10.2307/3481444

Middlemiss, M. (2022, April 27). *E-Residency in the metaverse?* E-Residency. https://www.e-resident.gov.ee/blog/posts/virtual-e-residency-a-future-in-the-metaverse/

Porto, F., & Foà, D. (2023). *DEFINING VIRTUAL WORLDS: MAIN FEATURES AND REGULATORY CHALLENGES*. Centre on Regulation in Europe. https://cerre.eu/wp-content/uploads/2023/07/CERRE-Virtual-Worlds-Issue-Paper-0723.pdf

Salmond, J. W. (1907). *Jurisprudence or the theory of the law*. Stevens and Haynes.

Schmidt, E., & Cohen, J. (2013). *The New Digital Age: Reshaping the Future of People, Nations and Business*. Knopf Doubleday Publishing Group.

Staszkiewicz, P., Horobiowski, J., Szelągowska, A., & Strzelecka, A. M. (2024). Artificial intelligence legal personality and accountability: Auditors' accounts of capabilities and challenges for instrument boundary. *Meditari Accountancy Research*, 32(7), 141–167. DOI: 10.1108/MEDAR-10-2023-2204

Stephenson, N. (1992). *Snow Crash*. Bantam Books.

Stone, C. D. (1972). Should Trees Have Standing—Toward Legal Rights for Natural Objects. *Southern California Law Review*, 45(2), 450–501. https://southerncalifornialawreview.com/wp-content/uploads/2022/03/Christopher-D.-Stone-Should-Trees-Have-Standing_%E2%80%94Toward-Legal-Rights-for-Natural-Objects-45-S.-CAL.-L.-REV.-450-1972.pdf

Chapter 10

# The Influence of AI on Social Interactions and Community Dynamics

**Jasjeet Singh**
*Chandigarh College of Engineering and Technology, Panjab University, Chandigarh, India*

**Sunil K. Singh**
https://orcid.org/0000-0003-4876-7190
*Chandigarh College of Engineering and Technology, Panjab University, Chandigarh, India*

**Sudhakar Kumar**
https://orcid.org/0000-0001-7928-4234
*Chandigarh College of Engineering and Technology, Panjab University, Chandigarh, India*

**Samar Pratap Singh**
https://orcid.org/0009-0005-1606-0731
*Chandigarh College of Engineering and Technology, Panjab University, Chandigarh, India*

**Rakesh Kumar**
*CSE Department, Gautam Buddha University, Greater Noida, India*

**Shavi Bansal**
https://orcid.org/0009-0009-8699-6884
*Insights2Techinfo, India*

**Kwok Tai Chui**
*Hong Kong Metropolitan University, Hong Kong*

## ABSTRACT

*The rapid advancement of Artificial Intelligence (AI) has transformed social interaction, reshaping communication, relationship-building, and community engagement. This chapter examines AI's multifaceted impact on human social dynamics, highlighting both the benefits and challenges posed by AI technologies in modern communication tools, social media, and online platforms. While AI-driven algorithms and automated responses personalize interactions, they also raise concerns about authenticity and emotional connection, making relationships paradoxically impersonal. The chapter explores how AI enhances communication efficiency through real-time translation and AI-assisted moderation, while also addressing ethical dilemmas related to online echo chambers, social behavior influence, and algorithmic bias. By providing a balanced perspective on AI's role in social contexts, the chapter advocates for responsible AI development and emphasizes the need to maintain ethical standards and safeguard human-centered social values in an AI-driven world.*

DOI: 10.4018/979-8-3693-8628-6.ch010

## 1. INTRODUCTION

In the 21st century, Artificial Intelligence (AI) emerged as one of the most transformative technologies, influencing industries ranging from healthcare to finance (Aggarwal, K. et al., 2022). However, one of AI's most profound yet subtle impacts has been on social interaction. As AI technologies become more integrated into everyday life, they are increasingly shaping the way individuals communicate, form relationships, and engage in social communities. From algorithm-driven social media platforms to AI-powered virtual assistants and chatbots, AI has altered both the medium and the nature of human interaction (Singh, S. K. et al., 2022; Devlin, J. et al., 2019). This chapter explores the growing influence of AI on social dynamics in the digital age.

The ways in which we connect with one another, whether through online communities, social media, or personal conversations, are now mediated by algorithms designed to optimize engagement, predict behavior, and even simulate human emotions. While these technologies offer unprecedented convenience and customization, they also pose new challenges to traditional notions of privacy, authenticity, and emotional connection. The implications of AI's involvement in social interaction extend beyond mere convenience (Mengi, G. et al., 2023; Peñalvo, F. J. G. et al., 2022). AI-powered tools are actively shaping the content we consume, the relationships we maintain, and even the decisions we make as individuals and collectives. From personalized news feeds that curate our online experiences to AI-driven emotional support systems designed to provide companionship, the boundaries between human and machine-mediated interaction are increasingly blurred. This chapter begins by tracing the evolution of AI in social contexts, outlining how early AI systems gradually infiltrated social platforms and communication tools. It will then examine the modern applications of AI in social media algorithms, messaging apps, and virtual assistants, analyzing both the positive and negative consequences for interpersonal communication. Key ethical concerns, such as privacy, bias, and emotional manipulation, will also be discussed, highlighting the broader societal implications of these technologies. Finally, the chapter will offer insights into the future of AI in social interaction, reflecting on the potential for both enhanced human connection and new forms of social alienation in an AI-driven world (Kumar, S. et al.,2021).

By understanding the dual role AI plays as both facilitator and disruptor in social relationships, this chapter aims to provide a comprehensive overview of the profound impact AI is having on the way we interact in the digital age, while encouraging thoughtful consideration of the ethical and societal responsibilities that accompany these advancements (Kumar, S. et al., 2022).

Figure 1. Various social media platforms

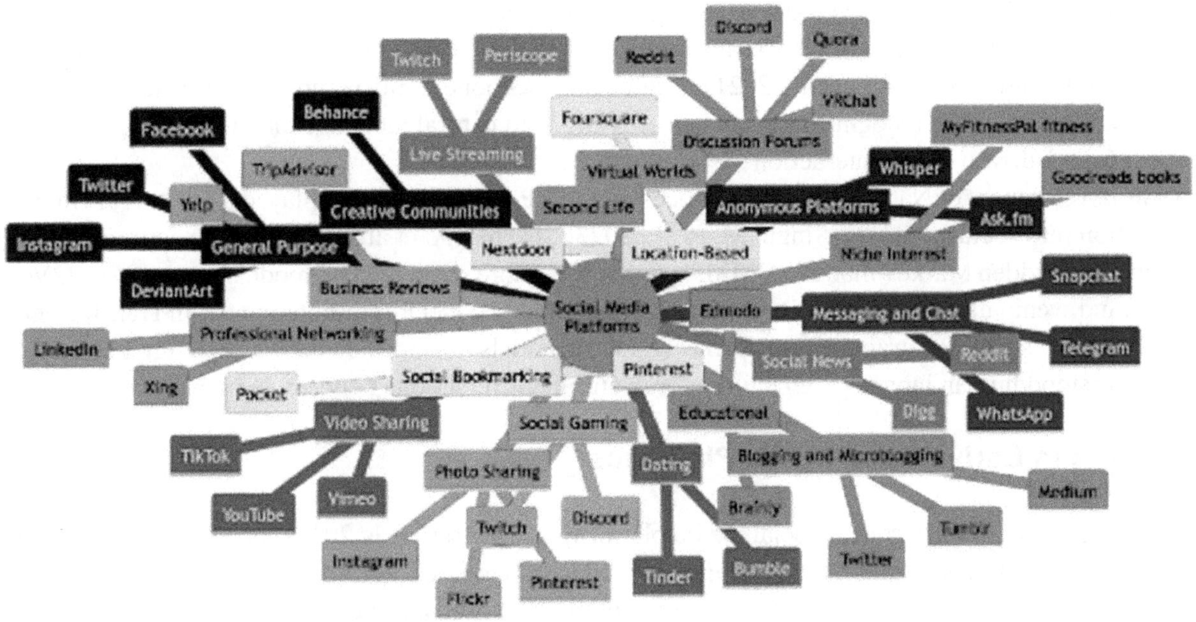


## 2. THE EVOLUTION OF AI IN SOCIAL CONTEXTS

Artificial Intelligence (AI) has evolved dramatically since its inception, playing a transformative role in social interaction. This section delves into the historical development of AI technologies, the early integration of AI in social media platforms, and the transition to AI-driven communication systems. By examining these stages, we can understand how AI algorithms have progressed from simple data-processing tools to complex systems capable of shaping human social behavior at scale.

### Historical Development of AI Technologies

The roots of AI trace back to the mid-20th century, with early attempts to create machines capable of mimicking human cognition. The term "Artificial Intelligence" was first coined in 1956 by John McCarthy during the Dartmouth Conference, where the idea of building machines that could think and learn like humans was first discussed. Early AI efforts were largely symbolic in nature, focusing on rule-based systems and logic programming, which led to the creation of expert systems in the 1970s and 1980s (Peñalvo, F. J. G. et al., 2022). These systems, such as MYCIN and DENDRAL, were designed to make decisions based on predefined sets of rules, but they lacked adaptability (Kumar, A. et al., 2023) and scalability.

The field took a significant leap forward with the development of machine learning algorithms in the 1990s. This era saw the rise of neural networks, specifically backpropagation, which allowed computers to learn from data (Sharma, A. et al., 2023) rather than relying solely on rule-based systems. However, these early networks were limited by computational (Gupta, S. et al., 2023) power and the availability of large datasets (Gupta, S. et al., 2023). In the early 2000s, the advent of deep learning and improvements in hardware (GPUs) enabled the training of larger, more complex models, such as convolutional neural networks (CNNs) (Singh, I. et al., 2022) and recurrent neural networks (Kumar, R. et al., 2024) (RNNs). These architectures (Kumar, S. et al., 2021) became the backbone of many modern AI systems, particularly in areas like image recognition, speech processing, and natural language understanding, which are critical for AI-driven social interaction systems.

The development of Natural Language Processing (NLP) algorithms also played a pivotal role in AI's integration into social contexts (Singh, M. et al., 2023; Sharma, A. et al ., 2023). Early approaches like n-grams and hidden Markov models (HMMs) gave way to more sophisticated models such as Word2Vec, GloVe, and eventually transformers like BERT (Bidirectional Encoder Representations from Transformers) and GPT (Generative Pre-trained Transformers). These models transformed the way machines processed and understood human language, enabling more natural conversations between humans and machines.

## AI's Role in Early Social Media Platforms

AI began to play a key role in social media platforms during the early 2010s, primarily through content recommendation systems. These systems utilized collaborative filtering and content-based filtering algorithms to analyze user behavior and recommend posts, friends, or groups that might interest them. The goal was to increase engagement by presenting users with personalized content tailored to their preferences.

One of the earliest examples is Facebook's News Feed algorithm, which used a combination of EdgeRank (an early machine learning model) and gradient boosting to determine the relevance of posts in a user's feed. EdgeRank was based on three factors:

1. **Affinity:** The strength of the connection between the user and the content creator (e.g., frequency of interactions).
2. **Weight:** The type of interaction (e.g., comments were weighted higher than likes).
3. **Time Decay:** Older content was given less priority.

These AI-driven algorithms made it possible to curate vast amounts of content into individualized social feeds, fundamentally changing how users engaged with social media (Sharma, A. et al., 2023). Instead of seeing posts chronologically, users began to see content that was algorithmically determined to be the most engaging based on their previous behaviors and interactions. As these platforms grew, so did the complexity of their AI systems. The introduction of graph-based algorithms allowed platforms to better understand the relationships between users, content, and topics (Vats, T. et al., 2024). For example, Facebook's Graph Search and Twitter's follow recommendations relied on graph theory to map out complex networks of relationships, enabling more targeted social recommendations.

## Transition to AI-Driven Communication

The shift from basic recommendation systems to AI-driven communication marked a significant evolution in AI's role in social interaction. Advances in machine learning and natural language processing (NLP) allowed platforms to move beyond passive content delivery and into active conversation facilitation (Sharma, A. et al., 2023).

One major advancement in this area was the development of chatbots and virtual assistants. Early chatbots, such as ELIZA (created in the 1960s), were simple rule-based systems that used keyword matching to simulate conversations. However, modern chatbots leverage deep learning and transformers to process and respond to natural language inputs with greater contextual understanding. For example, the introduction of OpenAI's GPT models demonstrated how generative AI could hold more nuanced and human-like conversations. These models use a self-attention mechanism, allowing them to focus on different parts of the input text, making them highly effective at understanding context and generating coherent responses.

Another significant milestone was the integration of AI-driven communication systems in platforms like Google Assistant, Apple's Siri, and Amazon's Alexa (Setia, H. et al., 2024). These systems rely on complex pipelines involving:

- Automatic Speech Recognition (ASR) to convert spoken language into text. (Kumar, S. et al., 2021)
- NLP models to understand user intent and context.
- Dialogue management systems to determine the appropriate response.
- Speech synthesis (TTS) to convert text back into speech for a conversational experience.

Moreover, these systems are constantly learning from user interactions through reinforcement learning algorithms, which optimize responses based on user satisfaction and engagement metrics (Goyal, S. et al., 2024). In social media, AI-driven communication tools like AI moderators and sentiment analysis tools play a key role in shaping conversations. Platforms like YouTube, Facebook, and Reddit use AI systems to automatically detect and moderate inappropriate content, utilizing computer vision and text classification models to flag harmful posts. AI's influence on communication (Mengi, G. et al., 2023) also extends to real-time collaboration (Aggarwal, K. et al., 2022) platforms like Zoom and Microsoft Teams, where AI-enhanced features like real-time transcription, noise cancellation, and meeting analytics improve the overall user experience (Sarin, S. et al., 2024).

*Figure 2. AI Powered transitions systems*

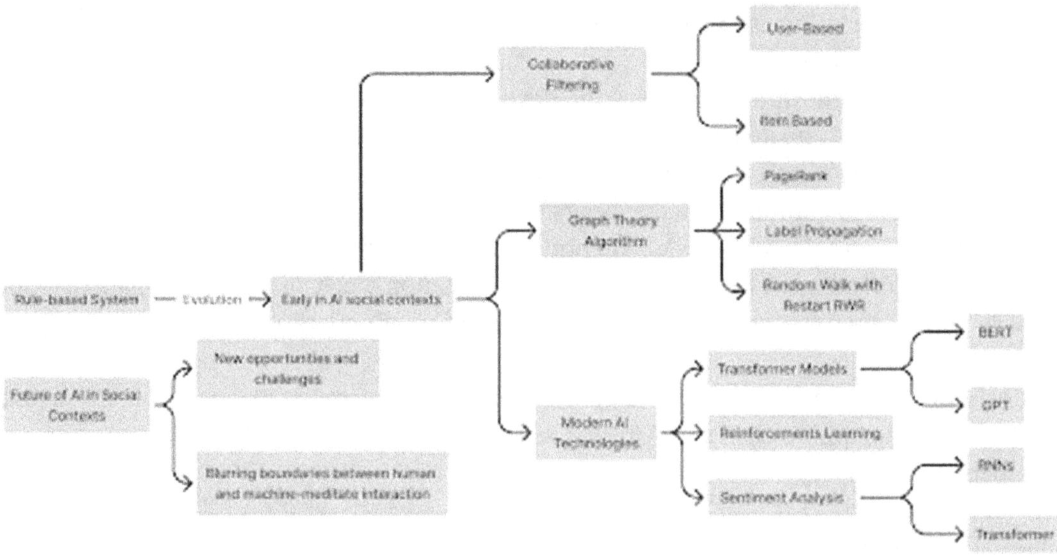


## 3. AI IN MODERN COMMUNICATION TOOLS

AI has dramatically enhanced modern communication tools, particularly in messaging apps, virtual assistants, chatbots, and real-time translations. These AI-driven systems rely on cutting-edge machine learning (ML) and natural language processing (NLP) algorithms to understand user input, generate responses, and facilitate seamless communication across language barriers. This section provides a detailed and technical explanation of how AI functions within these tools, highlighting the core algorithms and models that power them.

## AI in Messaging Apps and Virtual Assistants

Messaging apps and virtual assistants are some of the most ubiquitous examples of AI-enhanced communication tools. These systems use a combination of automatic speech recognition (ASR), natural language understanding (NLU), natural language generation (NLG), and speech synthesis to interpret and respond to user inputs in a natural, conversational manner (Vats, T. et al., 2024).

> "Voice-based communication systems, such as virtual assistants, rely on a series of interconnected components to understand and respond to user requests. The first step involves Automatic Speech Recognition (ASR), which converts spoken language into text. This text is then processed by Natural Language Understanding (NLU) systems to extract the user's intent and identify relevant entities.

Once the system understands the user's request, it generates a suitable response using Natural Language Generation (NLG) (A. Kumar et al ., 2023) . Finally, the generated response is converted into spoken language through Speech Synthesis,"

"ASR algorithms often employ Hidden Markov Models (HMMs) combined with deep learning models like recurrent neural networks (RNNs) and long short-term memory (LSTM) network.. These models capture both the acoustic features and temporal dependencies (Kumar, S. et al., 2023) in speech signals. NLU systems, on the other hand, rely on transformer-based architectures like BERT or GPT (Sharma, A. et al ., 2023), which utilize self-attention mechanisms to understand the relationships between words in a sentence. For example, in virtual assistants, the NLU system identifies the user's intent (e.g., "set an alarm") and extracts key entities (e.g., time). NLG systems leverage probabilistic language models, such as transformers, to generate coherent and contextually appropriate responses. For instance, messaging apps use NLG for smart replies, where AI suggests responses based on the conversation context. Speech Synthesis, the final component, converts generated text into speech using algorithms like WaveNet, which produces highly realistic human-like speech." (Devlin, J. et al., 2019).

## Chatbots and Automated Responses

Chatbots are AI-driven agents that simulate human conversation. They have evolved from basic rule-based systems to sophisticated AI models (Radford, A. et al., 2019) capable of engaging in multi-turn dialogues, answering queries, providing recommendations, or facilitating customer service. There are two primary types of chatbots: rule-based chatbots and AI-based chatbots.

## Rule-Based Chatbots

Rule-based chatbots use pre-defined rules and decision trees to respond to user inputs. These bots are limited in scope, as they can only respond to specific queries for which they have been explicitly programmed. These systems typically rely on pattern matching algorithms, such as those based on finite state machines (FSMs) or regular expressions. Each input pattern triggers a specific response, but the chatbot lacks the flexibility to handle unforeseen queries (Mehrabi, N. et al., 2021).

## AI-Based Chatbots

AI-based chatbots, by contrast, leverage machine learning and NLP to enable more dynamic conversations. They can understand and generate language using large-scale language models.

Key techniques include:

1. Sequence-to-Sequence (Seq2Seq) Models:
    - Seq2Seq models are foundational to modern chatbots. They consist of two parts: an encoder and a decoder. The encoder processes the user's input into a fixed-dimensional representation, while the decoder generates an appropriate response.
    - Originally, RNNs and LSTMs were used for Seq2Seq models. However, the introduction of transformer architectures (e.g., GPT, BERT) has made the models more efficient by capturing relationships between words across long sentences using self-attention mechanisms.
2. Dialogue Management:

- Dialogue management involves tracking the context of the conversation, handling multiple turns, and managing conversation flow. It often uses reinforcement learning to improve the bot's responses based on feedback from user interactions. A chatbot learns to choose the best action (i.e., response) by receiving rewards (positive feedback) or penalties (negative feedback) for each action taken during the dialogue.
- In advanced AI-based systems, such as GPT-3-powered chatbots, context is maintained across multiple conversation turns, allowing the chatbot to handle more complex, natural dialogues (Zuboff, S. et al., 2019).

3. Knowledge-Based Chatbots:

Some chatbots integrate knowledge graphs to provide factual information. These bots query external knowledge (Sharma, A. et al., 2024) bases (e.g., WolframAlpha or Wikipedia) to answer questions beyond their initial training data. These systems rely on graph traversal algorithms such as PageRank or Random Walk to find relevant information.

4. Sentiment Analysis:

Many chatbots use sentiment analysis to gauge the emotional tone of the conversation and tailor their responses accordingly. Sentiment analysis models are typically built on RNNs, CNNs, or transformer architectures (e.g., BERT), and classify text into categories such as positive, negative, or neutral.

### The Role of AI in Real-Time Translations

Real-time translation is one of the most impressive applications of AI in communication, enabling cross-linguistic conversations in messaging apps, video calls, and virtual assistants. AI-powered real-time translation systems leverage advanced NLP techniques to instantly convert spoken or written language from one language to another.

## 4. AI AND SOCIAL MEDIA ALGORITHMS

AI plays a central role in modern social media platforms by driving content personalization, optimizing user engagement, and influencing social behaviors. Through the use of advanced machine learning (ML) algorithms, social media companies can tailor content to individual users, maximize time spent on the platform, and influence social discourse (Acquisti, A. et al., 2015) . However, these technologies also raise concerns about the creation of echo chambers, polarization, and their potential impact on mental health. This section provides a technical, in-depth exploration of the algorithms involved in content personalization, user engagement, and their societal implications.

## Content Personalization and User Engagement

### Content Personalization in Social Media: A Deep Dive

Content personalization has become the cornerstone of modern social media platforms, driving user engagement and retention. By leveraging a combination of machine learning, recommender systems, and reinforcement learning, these platforms tailor content recommendations to individual user preferences.

Matrix factorization, a sophisticated technique, is widely used in recommendation systems. It involves factoring a large user-item interaction matrix into lower-dimensional matrices representing latent factors. These latent factors capture underlying features that influence user preferences. Singular Value Decomposition (SVD) is a common implementation of matrix factorization, breaking down the user-item matrix into separate matrices that describe users and items in terms of their hidden features (Kosinski, M. et al., 2013). YouTube's recommendation algorithm utilizes variations of matrix factorization to suggest relevant videos based on past user behavior.

Deep learning approaches, such as neural collaborative filtering (NCF), have significantly enhanced traditional recommendation methods. These models learn complex non-linear patterns in user behavior and item interactions using multi-layer perceptions (MLPs). Additionally, deep learning models like convolutional neural networks (CNNs) analyze content itself (e.g., images or videos) to understand the features that appeal to users, leading to more sophisticated recommendations. Instagram and TikTok employ deep neural networks (DNNs) to process visual data and rank posts based on user engagement patterns.

Reinforcement learning (RL) plays a pivotal role in real-time content recommendation. Platforms use RL to continuously improve content suggestions by learning from user feedback. In RL, the recommendation system is modeled as an agent that interacts with the environment (the user). The agent's goal is to maximize long-term user engagement, measured by metrics like dwell time or interaction frequency. Deep Q-Networks (DQN), a commonly used algorithm in social media, learns optimal policies for content delivery by exploring different recommendation strategies and updating its action-value function based on rewards (positive feedback from user engagement). Facebook's News Feed utilizes RL to optimize post ranking, ensuring that users see the most engaging content at the top of their feeds (Vinyals, O., et al. 2019).

### Social Media Echo Chambers and Polarization

While content personalization enhances user engagement, it also leads to the unintended consequence of echo chambers—situations where users are primarily exposed to content that aligns with their pre-existing views, reinforcing biases and fostering social polarization. AI-driven algorithms, particularly in social media platforms, inadvertently amplify this phenomenon by optimizing for engagement rather than diversity of perspectives.

1. Filter Bubbles:
    - Filter bubbles occur when algorithms curate content that isolates users from information or viewpoints that differ from their own. These bubbles are created by content recommendation systems designed to maximize engagement by repeatedly showing users content they are likely to interact with, which often results in a narrowed scope of information.

- The algorithmic basis for filter bubbles lies in the user similarity scoring and reinforcement learning feedback loops used in collaborative filtering. For example, when a user engages with content that aligns with their views, the system continually prioritizes similar content, reinforcing the user's pre-existing beliefs and reducing exposure to alternative perspectives.

2. Graph Theory and Community Detection:

Social media platforms rely on graph theory to model relationships between users and content. In these graphs, users are represented as nodes, and edges represent interactions such as friendships, follows, or likes. Algorithms like Louvain modularity and Label Propagation are used to detect communities—groups of users who are closely connected and share similar interests. These communities can exacerbate echo chambers, as algorithms tend to suggest content from within a user's community rather than from outside of it.

For example, on Twitter, users in politically polarized communities are often recommended content that originates from users within the same political circle, increasing ideological homogeneity.

3. Algorithmic Bias in Content Delivery:
   - The use of biased training data—such as historical user interaction data—further exacerbates polarization. For instance, if a user frequently interacts with politically charged content, the system learns to prioritize similar content, reinforcing the bias.
   - Bias regularization techniques are sometimes implemented to address this issue by introducing diversity constraints into the content recommendation algorithms. These constraints encourage the recommendation of content from different viewpoints, albeit at the potential cost of short-term engagement metrics (Craig, A. B. et al., 2013).
4. Sentiment Analysis and Emotional Polarization:
   - Sentiment analysis is often used to analyze the emotional tone of posts and gauge their potential to drive user engagement. Sentiment models, based on RNNs or transformers (e.g., BERT), classify content as positive, negative, or neutral, and social media platforms tend to prioritize emotionally charged content (especially negative or controversial content) due to its higher likelihood of generating engagement.
   - This emphasis on emotionally polarizing content contributes to the amplification of extreme views and the deepening of social divisions (Ball, M. et al., 2022).

*Figure 3. AI powered translation system*

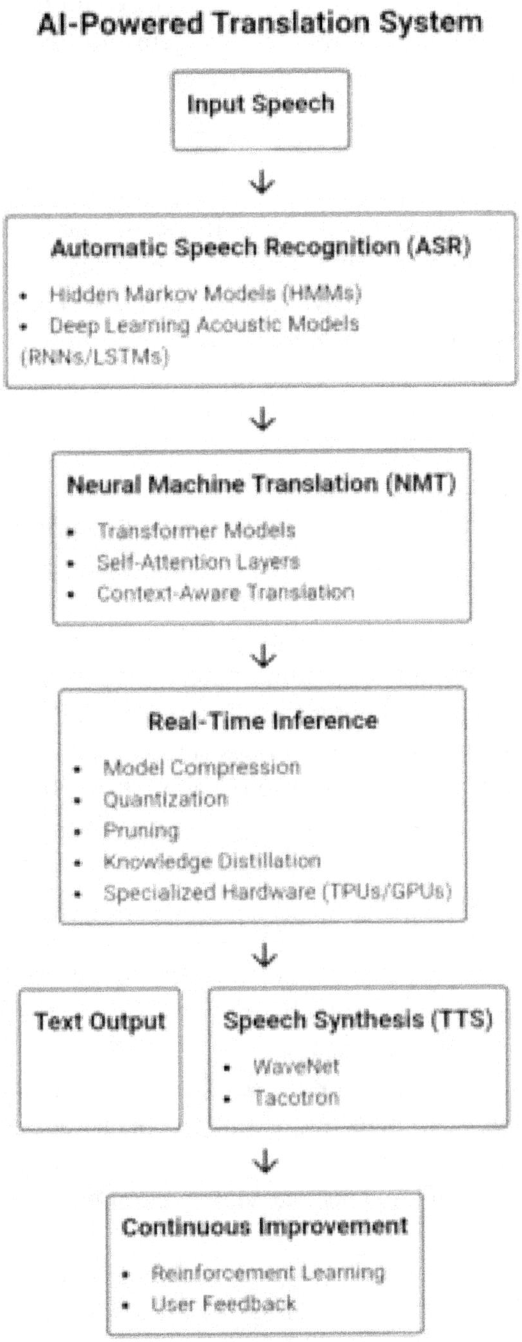

## Impact on Mental Health and Social Behaviors

AI-driven social media algorithms are increasingly recognized for their impact on mental health and social behaviors. The optimization of platforms for engagement often results in addictive behaviors, exposure to harmful content, and negative psychological effects, such as anxiety and depression.

1. Dopamine Feedback Loops:
   - Social media platforms are often designed to exploit dopamine feedback loops—neural mechanisms in the brain that reward behaviors associated with pleasure and gratification. AI systems leverage reinforcement learning to create environments that maximize these rewards, resulting in compulsive behavior patterns such as endless scrolling, frequent checking of notifications, and interaction with viral content.
   - Algorithms monitor user behavior (e.g., time spent on the platform, frequency of interactions) and adjust content delivery to maintain high levels of engagement. The use of multi-armed bandit algorithms allows platforms to explore and exploit content strategies to increase user retention(Gupta, P. et al., 2020).
   - Instagram's feed algorithm, for example, is designed to prioritize content that generates instant gratification (likes, comments, shares), creating a dopamine-driven cycle of interaction.
2. AI-Driven Targeted Content:
   - AI is used to micro-target users with specific ads or posts that exploit vulnerabilities related to mental health. For example, algorithms detect patterns in user behavior that suggest susceptibility to certain types of content, such as posts related to body image or anxiety, and target users with ads for products or services catering to those vulnerabilities.
   - Facebook's advertising algorithms utilize behavioral profiling and psychographic targeting, where machine learning models analyze vast amounts of user data (likes, clicks, searches) to create highly personalized ad campaigns, which can sometimes exacerbate mental health issues by reinforcing negative behaviors.
3. Detection of Harmful Content:
   - To mitigate the negative impact on mental health, social media platforms deploy AI-based content moderation systems to detect harmful or inappropriate content, such as cyberbullying, hate speech, and self-harm posts.
   - These systems use deep learning models, particularly convolutional neural networks (CNNs) for image moderation (e.g., detecting explicit content) and transformers for text analysis (e.g., identifying offensive language). For example, YouTube and Facebook use automated moderation systems to flag content that violate community guidelines (Shoham, Y. et al., 2009).
   - However, the challenge lies in balancing the speed of content moderation with the accuracy (Khade et al., 2012) of detecting nuanced or context-dependent harmful behavior, which often leads to false positives or negatives.
4. Time Spent Metrics and Negative Psychological Effects:
   - Platforms rely heavily on time spent as a key engagement metric, with algorithms optimizing for long session durations. This metric, however, correlates with negative psychological outcomes such as social comparison, anxiety, and depression, as users may spend extended periods consuming content that portray unrealistic standards of beauty, success, or happiness.

- Reinforcement learning algorithms used by platforms like TikTok and Instagram

*Table 1. Impact of AI on Mental Health*

| Category | AI Techniques | Impact |
|---|---|---|
| Dopamine Feedback Loops | • Reinforcement Learning<br>• Multi-armed Bandit Algorithms | • Addic<br>• Comp<br>• Frequ check |
| AI-Driven Targeted Content | • Machine Learning<br>• Behavioral Profiling<br>• Psychographic Targeting | • Explo vulne<br>• Reinf behav<br>• Exac health |
| Detection of Harmful Content | • Convolutional Neural Networks (CNNs)<br>• Transformers<br>• Deep Learning Models | • Mitiga<br>• Redu<br>• Identi conte |
| Time Spent Metrics | • Reinforcement Learning | • Socia<br>• Anxie<br>• Depre<br>• Unrea expos |

## 6. AI'S INFLUENCE ON GROUP DYNAMICS AND COMMUNITIES

Artificial intelligence has become deeply embedded in online communities and collaborative workspaces, shaping group dynamics and influencing collective decision-making processes. AI-powered systems, such as automated moderation tools, virtual assistants, and decision-support algorithms (Singh et al., 2022), are designed to enhance collaboration, enforce rules, and streamline the management of large groups (Joshi et al., 2022). This section provides a detailed technical exploration of AI's influence on group dynamics, focusing on moderation in online communities, its role in collaborative workspaces, and how it shapes collective decision-making.

### AI Moderation in Online Communities

Online communities—whether social media platforms, discussion forums, or collaborative platforms—require robust moderation systems to ensure healthy group dynamics. AI-driven moderation plays a critical role in maintaining order, enforcing guidelines, and fostering respectful communication. By analyzing vast amounts of content in real-time, AI systems can automatically detect and respond to toxic behavior, harmful content, and rule violations.

## AI-Powered Content Moderation: A Deep Dive

AI-powered content moderation has become an essential tool for online platforms to maintain safe and positive community environments (Yen et al., 2021). By leveraging advanced techniques in natural language processing (NLP), deep learning, computer vision, and reinforcement learning, these systems can effectively detect and mitigate harmful content.

Natural language processing (NLP) plays a crucial role in understanding and classifying user-generated text. Models like BERT are employed for text classification tasks, enabling systems to comprehend the context and intent behind the text. Sentiment analysis and toxicity detection (Verma, V. et al., 2023) models further enhance the ability to identify harmful or offensive content. Deep learning and transformer models, such as GPT-3 or RoBERTa, provide more nuanced responses to user behavior. These models can distinguish between productive discussions and escalating conflicts, allowing for more informed moderation decisions. Additionally, sequence modeling enables the detection of patterns of repeated toxic behavior, identifying users who consistently violate community guidelines.

For platforms that share images and videos, computer vision techniques are employed to analyze visual content. Convolutional Neural Networks (CNNs) are commonly used to detect inappropriate visual content, flagging material that contains nudity, violence, or illegal activities (Kumari K., 2021). Algorithms like ResNet and EfficientNet are capable of identifying detailed features in images and videos, enabling accurate detection of policy violations.

Reinforcement learning (RL) offers a dynamic approach to content moderation. By learning from moderator feedback and user behavior, RL systems can optimize moderation strategies over time. The RL framework models content moderation as a Markov Decision Process (MDP), where the AI system receives rewards or penalties based on the quality of its moderation decisions. This allows for continuous improvement in maintaining a positive community atmosphere.

In conclusion, AI-powered content moderation systems have significantly enhanced the ability of online platforms to address harmful content. By combining NLP, deep learning, computer vision, and reinforcement learning, these systems can effectively detect and mitigate offensive language, hate speech, cyberbullying, and inappropriate visual content, fostering safer and more positive online communities (Thanaporn P, 2024).

## AI's Role in Collaborative Workspaces

AI has transformed collaborative workspaces by streamlining project management, enhancing productivity, and facilitating communication. Virtual assistants, smart task managers, and collaboration tools use AI to improve group dynamics, helping teams to work more efficiently and cohesively.

## AI-Powered Collaboration: Boosting Efficiency and Creativity

The rise of AI has fundamentally transformed how teams collaborate. From optimizing workflows to fostering creative co-creation, AI tools offer a range of capabilities to enhance productivity and communication.

### 1. Task Allocation and Streamlined Workflows

AI systems take the guesswork out of task assignment. Optimization algorithms, like genetic algorithms and linear programming, analyze skills, availability, and workload to distribute tasks efficiently across team members. Tools like Asana and Trello leverage machine learning to recommend tasks based on historical data and complexity. Additionally, priority-based scheduling ensures high-importance tasks are completed first, maximizing efficiency.

### 2. AI-Powered Communication for Enhanced Teaming

Communication leaps forward with AI assistants that leverage NLP. Tools like Zoom, Slack, and Microsoft Teams utilize AI to automate tasks like note-taking, summarizing conversations, and setting reminders (Zhang, Z. et al., 2018). Summarization algorithms, powered by transformer models, extract key points and action items from lengthy discussions, boosting communication efficiency. Real-time transcription services convert spoken language into text, making meetings more accessible and searchable.

### 3. Collaborative AI Systems: Unleashing Co-Creation Potential

AI is no longer just a tool, but a co-creator. Google Docs, Figma, and Notion integrate AI co-authors that suggest improvements, correct grammar, and even brainstorm ideas. Reinforcement learning engines analyze user interactions and preferences, suggesting design changes or content improvements during collaborative work sessions. For example, Google Docs offers grammar suggestions powered by AI and auto-complete features leveraging GPT models. By combining task allocation, communication tools, and co-creation capabilities, AI empowers teams to work smarter, not harder, fostering a more collaborative and productive work environment.

## How AI Shapes Collective Decision-Making

AI is revolutionizing group decision-making by providing data-driven insights, modeling complex scenarios, and simulating potential outcomes. By offering unbiased recommendations based on statistical analysis, optimization models, and simulations, AI systems support human decision-makers in making more informed and effective choices.

### 1. Decision Support Systems (DSS)

DSS leverage AI algorithms to analyze historical data, predict trends, and recommend the best course of action. Multi-criteria decision-making (MCDM) methods, like AHP and TOPSIS, combined with AI techniques like fuzzy logic, help evaluate conflicting criteria and handle uncertainty. For example, a DSS might assist a corporation in deciding which markets to enter by analyzing financial performance, consumer behavior, and market trends.

## 2. Collaborative Filtering for Group Preferences

Collaborative filtering, commonly used in recommendation systems, is also applicable to group decision-making. By aggregating individual preferences, these algorithms suggest options that align with the group's collective interests. This is particularly useful when group members have diverse backgrounds and conflicting opinions. For example, movie recommendation systems use group-based collaborative filtering to suggest content that suits the collective preferences of a group of users.

## 3. Game Theory and AI in Collective Decision-Making

Game theory and multi-agent systems (MAS) play a vital role in modeling complex decision-making environments with multiple stakeholders. AI uses Nash equilibrium concepts to predict the outcome of strategic interactions and guide groups towards optimal decisions. Reinforcement learning integrates into game-theoretical frameworks (Vats, T. et al., 2024), allowing AI agents to learn optimal strategies in dynamic, multi-agent settings. For instance, in business negotiations, AI systems can simulate different strategies and predict outcomes, helping teams make informed decisions (Sahoo, S. R., et al., 2019).

## 4. AI-Driven Simulations for Scenario Analysis

AI-powered simulation models, such as Monte Carlo simulations or agent-based modeling (ABM), explore different scenarios and their potential outcomes. These models represent stakeholders and external factors, interacting in a virtual environment to produce outcomes based on various decision-making strategies. This allows groups to visualize how different decisions would play out in practice, leading to more informed choices.

By using AI, groups can make more informed and effective decisions, enhancing collaboration and problem-solving capabilities.

*Figure 4. AI technologies in content moderation and community management*

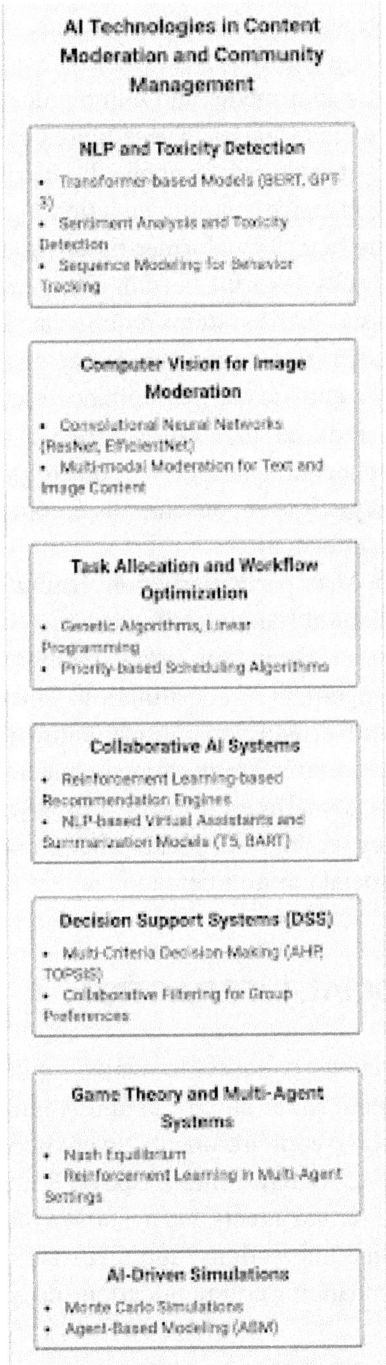

## 7. ETHICAL CONSIDERATIONS OF AI IN SOCIAL INTERACTIONS

As AI becomes increasingly integrated into social interactions, several ethical concerns arise, particularly regarding biases in AI-driven algorithms, privacy, and the potential for emotional manipulation. AI systems, especially those used in social media and communication platforms, are trained on large datasets that often contain implicit societal biases. These biases can lead to discriminatory outcomes, as algorithms may reinforce existing stereotypes or unevenly distribute opportunities, such as content visibility or access to resources. For instance, recommendation algorithms, which use techniques like collaborative filtering or deep learning (e.g., Transformer-based models like BERT), often reflect biased training data, perpetuating inequalities by favoring certain user groups or content.

Privacy is another major ethical issue, as AI systems require vast amounts of personal data to function effectively. Algorithms used for content recommendation, personalized ads, or behavioral prediction rely on user data collected through sophisticated surveillance techniques, such as web tracking and social graph analysis (Sahoo, S. R., et al., 2020) . For example, AI models powered by Graph Neural Networks (GNNs) analyze users' connections and interactions to predict future behavior. This level of data collection, often done without explicit user consent, raises concerns about privacy, data ownership, and the potential misuse of sensitive information.

Emotional manipulation through AI is particularly concerning as advanced algorithms can detect and predict human emotions using Natural Language Processing (NLP), Sentiment Analysis, and Deep Reinforcement Learning. These systems can exploit users' emotions by presenting content designed to evoke specific reactions, such as engagement or consumption. This can lead to unethical practices like targeted emotional manipulation in advertising or political campaigns. For instance, AI systems may deliver emotionally charged content to maximize user engagement, using reinforcement learning techniques to optimize for user reactions, sometimes at the cost of psychological well-being. These issues underscore the need for transparency, ethical AI development, and robust regulatory frameworks to protect individuals in AI-mediated social environments.

## 8. THE FUTURE OF AI IN SOCIAL INTERACTION

The future of AI in social interactions is poised to evolve rapidly with advancements in emerging technologies like the Metaverse (Singh, M. et al., 2022) and Augmented Reality (AR). AI will play a pivotal role in enhancing these immersive environments by enabling more intelligent, responsive, and personalized experiences. For example, AI algorithms based on Reinforcement Learning (RL) and Deep Neural Networks (DNNs) will power virtual agents and avatars in the Metaverse, allowing them to adapt to user behaviors, simulate human-like interactions, and facilitate social engagements. In AR, AI will drive real-time contextual overlays, enhancing communication and collaboration by recognizing objects, environments, and emotions.

In parallel, Predictive Analytics is expected to revolutionize social forecasting, where AI models such as LSTM (Long Short-Term Memory) and Graph Neural Networks (GNNs) analyze massive datasets to predict social trends, behaviors, and even cultural shifts. By mining data from social media, communication platforms, and societal events, AI will provide organizations and governments with powerful tools for forecasting social dynamics, aiding in policy decisions or marketing strategies. However, challenges such as algorithmic transparency, ethical use of predictive models, and ensuring human agency in AI collaborations will remain critical. Human-AI collaboration offers opportunities for enhancing productivity and creativity, but it also necessitates frameworks for ethical oversight, ensuring that AI complements human social interactions rather than undermining them. This future will require balancing the potential for AI to augment social technology with careful attention to privacy, autonomy, and fairness.

## 9. CONCLUSION

The integration of AI into social interactions marks a profound transformation, reshaping the way humans communicate, collaborate, and form relationships. AI-driven algorithms, such as Natural Language Processing (NLP) models and deep learning systems, have revolutionized platforms ranging from social media to virtual assistants, enhancing user engagement, content personalization, and decision-making processes. However, this technological advancement brings with it significant ethical challenges, such as biases in algorithmic decision-making, privacy concerns due to pervasive data collection, and the potential for emotional manipulation through AI-driven content targeting. As AI continues to advance in areas like Predictive Analytics and Augmented Reality (AR), the future promises both remarkable opportunities and complex challenges, particularly around human-AI collaboration. Balancing these opportunities with responsible AI development will require robust frameworks for transparency, fairness, and ethical oversight. Ultimately, the ongoing evolution of AI in social interactions demands that we critically assess its impact on human society while ensuring that technology serves to enhance, rather than diminish, the richness of human connection.

## REFERENCES


Acquisti, A., Brandimarte, L., & Loewenstein, G. (2015). Privacy and Human Behavior in the Age of Information. *Science*, 347(6221), 509–514. DOI: 10.1126/science.aaa1465 PMID: 25635091

Aggarwal, K., Singh, S. K., Chopra, M., Kumar, S., & Colace, F. (2022). Deep learning in robotics for strengthening Industry 4.0: Opportunities, challenges and future directions. In N. Nedjah, A. A. Abd El-Latif, B. B. Gupta, & L. M. Mourelle (Eds.), *Robotics and AI for Cybersecurity and Critical Infrastructure in Smart Cities* (pp. 1–25). Studies in Computational Intelligence (Vol. 1030). Springer. DOI: 10.1007/978-3-030-96737-6_1

Ball, M. (2022). *The Metaverse: And How it Will Revolutionize Everything*. Liveright. DOI: 10.15358/9783800669400

Craig, A. B. (2013). *Understanding Augmented Reality: Concepts and Applications*. Morgan Kaufmann.

Devlin, J., Chang, M. W., Lee, K., & Toutanova, K. (2019). BERT: Pre-training of Deep Bidirectional Transformers for Language Understanding. *Proceedings of NAACL-HLT*, 2019, 4171–4186. DOI: 10.18653/v1/N19-1423

Goyal, S., Kumar, S., Singh, S. K., Sarin, S., Priyanshu, , Gupta, B. B., Arya, V., Alhalabi, W., & Colace, F. (2024). Synergistic application of neuro-fuzzy mechanisms in advanced neural networks for real-time stream data flux mitigation. *Soft Computing*, 28(20), 12425–12437. Advance online publication. DOI: 10.1007/s00500-024-09938-y

Gupta, P., & Reddy, C. K. (2020). Machine Learning for Social Science: Predictive Models for Complex Social Phenomena. *ACM Computing Surveys*, 53(1), 1–34. DOI: 10.1145/3373142

Gupta, S., Agrawal, S., Singh, S. K., & Kumar, S. (2023). A Novel Transfer Learning-Based Model for Ultrasound Breast Cancer Image Classification. In Smys, S., Tavares, J. M. R. S., & Shi, F. (Eds.), *Computational Vision and Bio-Inspired Computing. Advances in Intelligent Systems and Computing* (Vol. 1439). Springer. DOI: 10.1007/978-981-19-9819-5_37

Joshi, S., Koparrati, S., & Singhal, V. (2022). Marketing analytics for analyzing social media and branding efforts of indian telecom operators. [IJCAC]. *International Journal of Cloud Applications and Computing*, 12(1), 1–18. DOI: 10.4018/IJCAC.297092

Khade, G., Kumar, S., & Bhattacharya, S. (2012). Classification of web pages on attractiveness: A supervised learning approach. *2012 4th International Conference on Intelligent Human Computer Interaction (IHCI)*, 1–5. DOI: 10.1109/IHCI.2012.6481867

Khushboo Kumari. (2021) Online social media threat and It's solution, Insights2Techinfo, pp.1, https://insights2techinfo.com/online-social-media-threat-and-its-solution/

Kosinski, M., Stillwell, D., & Graepel, T. (2013). Private traits and attributes are predictable from Kumar, A., Nelson, L., & Kumar, S. (2023). Enhancing haemorrhage detection in head CT scans using deep learning. *2023 3rd International Conference on Smart Generation Computing, Communication and Networking (SMART GENCON)*, 1–6. DOI: 10.1109/SMARTGENCON60755.2023.10442342

Kumar, A., Nelson, L., & Kumar, S. "Enhancing Haemorrhage Detection in Head CT Scans Using Deep Learning," 2023 3rd International Conference on Smart Generation Computing, Communication and Networking (SMART GENCON), Bangalore, India, 2023, pp. 1-6, DOI: 10.1109/SMARTGENCON60755.2023.10442342

Kumar, R., Singh, S. K., Lobiyal, D. K., Kumar, S., & Jawla, S. (2024). Security metrics and authentication-based routing (SMART) protocol for vehicular IoT networks. *SN Computer Science*, 5(2), 236. DOI: 10.1007/s42979-023-02566-7

Kumar, S., Singh, S., Aggarwal, N., & Aggarwal, K. (2021). Evaluation of automatic parallelization algorithms to minimize speculative parallelism overheads: An experiment. *Journal of Discrete Mathematical Sciences and Cryptography*, 24(5), 1517–1528. DOI: 10.1080/09720529.2021.1951435

Kumar, S., Singh, S. K., & Aggarwal, N. (2021). Efficient speculative parallelization architecture for overcoming speculation overheads. SysCom. https://ceur-ws.org/Vol-3080/19.pdf

Kumar, S., Singh, S. K., & Aggarwal, N. (2023). Sustainable data dependency resolution architectural framework to achieve energy efficiency using speculative parallelization. *2023 3rd International Conference on Innovative Sustainable Computational Technologies (CISCT)*, 1–6. DOI: 10.1109/CISCT57197.2023.10351343

Kumar, S., Singh, S. K., Aggarwal, N., Gupta, B. B., Alhalabi, W., & Band, S. S. (2022). An efficient hardware supported and parallelization architecture for intelligent systems to overcome speculative overheads. *International Journal of Intelligent Systems*, 37(12), 11764–11790. DOI: 10.1002/int.23062

Mehrabi, N., Morstatter, F., Saxena, N., Lerman, K., & Galstyan, A. (2021). A Survey on Bias and Fairness in Machine Learning. *ACM Computing Surveys*, 54(6), 1–35. DOI: 10.1145/3457607

Mengi, G., Singh, S. K., Kumar, S., Mahto, D., & Sharma, A. (2023). Automated machine learning (AutoML): The future of computational intelligence. In N. Nedjah, G. Martínez Pérez, & B. B. Gupta (Eds.), *International Conference on Cyber Security, Privacy and Networking (ICSPN 2022)* (pp. 443–458). Lecture Notes in Networks and Systems (Vol. 599). Springer, Cham. https://doi.org/DOI: 10.1007/978-3-031-22018-0_28

Peñalvo, F. J. G., Maan, T., Singh, S. K., Kumar, S., Arya, V., Chui, K. T., & Singh, G. P. (2022). Sustainable Stock Market Prediction Framework Using Machine Learning Models. *International Journal of Software Science and Computational Intelligence*, 14(1), 1–15. DOI: 10.4018/IJSSCI.313593

Radford, A., Wu, J., Child, R., Luan, D., Amodei, D., & Sutskever, I. (2019). Language Models are Unsupervised Multitask Learners. *OpenAI Blog*. https://openai.com/research/language-models

Sahoo, S. R., & Gupta, B. B. (2019). Classification of various attacks and their defence mechanism in online social networks: A survey. *Enterprise Information Systems*, 13(6), 832–864. DOI: 10.1080/17517575.2019.1605542

Sahoo, S. R., & Gupta, B. B. (2020). Classification of spammer and nonspammer content in online social network using genetic algorithm-based feature selection. *Enterprise Information Systems*, 14(5), 710–736. DOI: 10.1080/17517575.2020.1712742

Sarin, S., Singh, S. K., Kumar, S., Goyal, S., Gupta, B. B., Alhalabi, W., & Arya, V. (2024). Unleashing the Power of Multi-Agent Reinforcement Learning for Algorithmic Trading in the Digital Financial Frontier and Enterprise Information Systems. Computers, Materials & Continua/Computers. *Computers, Materials & Continua*, 80(2), 3123–3138. DOI: 10.32604/cmc.2024.051599

Setia, H., Chhabra, A., Singh, S. K., Kumar, S., Sharma, S., Arya, V., Gupta, B. B., & Wu, J. (2024). Securing the road ahead: Machine learning-driven DDoS attack detection in VANET cloud environments. *Cyber Security and Applications*, 2, 100037. DOI: 10.1016/j.csa.2024.100037

Sharma, A., Singh, S. K., Chhabra, A., Kumar, S., Arya, V., & Moslehpour, M. (2023). A Novel Deep Federated Learning-Based Model to Enhance Privacy in Critical Infrastructure Systems. *International Journal of Software Science and Computational Intelligence*, 15(1), 1–23. DOI: 10.4018/IJSSCI.334711

Sharma, A., Singh, S. K., & Kumar, S. (2024). Revolutionizing healthcare systems: Synergistic multimodal ensemble learning & knowledge transfer for lung cancer delineation & taxonomy. *2024 IEEE International Conference on Consumer Electronics (ICCE)*, 1–6. DOI: 10.1109/ICCE59016.2024.10444476

Sharma, A., Singh, S. K., Kumar, S., Chhabra, A., & Gupta, S. (2023). Fuzzy-based clustering of consumers' big data in industrial applications. *2023 IEEE International Conference on Consumer Electronics (ICCE)*, 1–3. DOI: 10.1109/ICCE56470.2023.10043451

Sharma, A., Singh, S. K., Kumar, S., Chhabra, A., & Gupta, S. (2023). Security of Android visionBanking Mobile Apps: Challenges and Opportunities. In: Nedjah, N., Martínez Pérez, G., Gupta, B.B. (eds) International Conference on Cyber Security, Privacy and Networking (ICSPN 2022). ICSPN 2021. Lecture Notes in Networks and Systems, vol 599. Springer, Cham. DOI: 10.1007/978-3-031-22018-0_39

Shoham, Y., & Leyton-Brown, K. (2009). *Multiagent Systems: Algorithmic, Game-Theoretic, and Logical Foundations*. Cambridge University Press.

Singh, I., Singh, S. K., Kumar, S., & Aggarwal, K. (2022). Dropout-VGG Based Convolutional Neural Network for Traffic Sign Categorization. In Saraswat, M., Sharma, H., Balachandran, K., Kim, J. H., & Bansal, J. C. (Eds.), *Congress on Intelligent Systems. Lecture Notes on Data Engineering and Communications Technologies* (Vol. 114). Springer. DOI: 10.1007/978-981-16-9416-5_18

Singh, I., Singh, S. K., Singh, R., & Kumar, S. (2022). Efficient loop unrolling factor prediction algorithm using machine learning models. *2022 3rd International Conference for Emerging Technology (INCET)*, 1–8. DOI: 10.1109/INCET54531.2022.9825092

Singh, M., Singh, S. K., Kumar, S., Madan, U., & Maan, T. (2023). Sustainable framework for metaverse security and privacy: Opportunities and challenges. In N. Nedjah, G. Martínez Pérez, & B. B. Gupta (Eds.), *International Conference on Cyber Security, Privacy and Networking (ICSPN 2022)* (pp. 473–486). Lecture Notes in Networks and Systems (Vol. 599). Springer. DOI: 10.1007/978-3-031-22018-0_30

Thanaporn, P. (2024) Decoding Offensiveness: Exploring Ethical Ideology, Social Competence, and Humanlikeness in Human-AI Chatbot Interaction, Insighrs2Techinfo, pp.1, https://insights2techinfo.com/decoding-offensiveness-exploring-ethical-ideology-social-competence-and-humanlikeness-in-human-ai-chatbot-interaction/

Vats, T., Kumar, S., Singh, S. K., Madan, U., Preet, M., Arya, V., Bansal, R., & Almomani, A. (2024). Navigating the Landscape: Safeguarding Privacy and Security in the Era of Ambient Intelligence within Healthcare Settings. *Cyber Security and Applications*, 2, 100046. Advance online publication. DOI: 10.1016/j.csa.2024.100046

Vats, T., Singh, S. K., Kumar, S., Gupta, B. B., Gill, S. S., Arya, V., & Alhalabi, W. (2024). Explainable context-aware IoT framework using human digital twin for healthcare. *Multimedia Tools and Applications*, 83(22), 62489–62490. DOI: 10.1007/s11042-023-16922-5

Verma, V., Benjwal, A., Chhabra, A., Singh, S. K., Kumar, S., Gupta, B. B., Arya, V., & Chui, K. T. (2023). A novel hybrid model integrating MFCC and acoustic parameters for voice disorder detection. *Scientific Reports*, 13(1), 22719. DOI: 10.1038/s41598-023-49869-6 PMID: 38123627

Vinyals, O., Babuschkin, I., Czarnecki, W. M., Mathieu, M., Dudzik, A., Chung, J., Choi, D. H., Powell, R., Ewalds, T., Georgiev, P., Oh, J., Horgan, D., Kroiss, M., Danihelka, I., Huang, A., Sifre, L., Cai, T., Agapiou, J. P., Jaderberg, M., & Silver, D. (2019). Grandmaster Level in StarCraft II Using Multi-Agent Reinforcement Learning. *Nature*, 575(7782), 350–354. DOI: 10.1038/s41586-019-1724-z PMID: 31666705

Yen, S., Moh, M., & Moh, T. S. (2021). Detecting compromised social network accounts using deep learning for behavior and text analyses. [IJCAC]. *International Journal of Cloud Applications and Computing*, 11(2), 1–13. DOI: 10.4018/IJCAC.2021040106

Zhang, Z., & Gupta, B. B. (2018). Social media security and trustworthiness: Overview and new direction. *Future Generation Computer Systems*, 86, 914–925. DOI: 10.1016/j.future.2016.10.007

Zuboff, S. (2019). *The Age of Surveillance Capitalism: The Fight for a Human Future at the New Frontier of Power*. PublicAffairs.

# Chapter 11
# Enhancing Community Detection With Hybrid Quantum-Inspired Evolutionary Algorithms

**Akshat Gaurav**
https://orcid.org/0000-0002-5796-9424
*International Center for AI and Cyber Security Research and Innovations (CCRI), Asia University, Taichung, Taiwan*

**Achit Katiyar**
*International Center for AI and Cyber Security Research and Innovations (CCRI), Asia University, Taichung, Taiwan*

**Brij B. Gupta**
https://orcid.org/0000-0003-4929-4698
*Asia University, Taiwan*

## ABSTRACT

*The chapter expands upon the concepts of using hybrid QIEAs in enhancing the existing community detection networks. Thus, as communities are becoming more digital the untold need for sophisticated algorithms that can handle and coordinate interactions is becoming critical. In this chapter, the reader will be introduced to the general concepts of quantum computing and an overview of the technique of evolutionary algorithms, which will allow the subsequent detailed elaboration of the interconnection between the two fields. In this chapter, we first introduce the idea of the development and usage of the hybrid QIEAs, focusing on the theoretical methods to integrate the classical and quantum information for solving problems that cannot be approached by the traditional EA.*

DOI: 10.4018/979-8-3693-8628-6.ch011

## 1. INTRODUCTION

In the modern world, such activities have started to take place virtually, and this makes the communities become active and changeable social structures determined by interaction (Sahoo & Gupta, 2020, 2020). It is equally crucial when it comes to interactions taking place in social networks, online gaming, communities, and professional collaboration platforms since poor and ineffective communication can lead to decline of the experience and results achieved by the clients and stakeholders. This normally presents a challenge for traditional algorithms that are used in analysing interaction complexity and size, hence the need to adopt more advanced methods. This chapter focuses on the extent of improving community participation with the help of the development of hybrid quantum-inspired evolutionary algorithms (QIEAs) and realizing that it can turn into the new potential for optimization of the digital environment.

### 1.1 Background and Motivation

Thus, belonging to the communities in the age of information is more crucial than ever. Starting with social networking sites, through gaming forums, and professional social networks these environments enable communication, cooperation, and educational processes (Arowolo et al., 2023; Joshi et al., 2022; Stergiou et al., 2022). However, there have been a lot of challenges when it comes to managing and optimizing this interaction with relations within the community since such relations and communities are highly complex and have very dynamic behaviour. It is for these reasons that conventional methods fail to address these issues, and more complex and flexible solutions are needed. Introducing hybrid quantum-inspired evolutionary algorithms (QIEAs) as a solution. These algorithms signify a combination of quantum computing heuristics and evolutionary algorithms and are recognized as a form of potent new thinking to develop community interactions. Quantum computing, which has superposition and entanglement as its theoretical framework cannot be matched by mining with classical computers (Nielsen & Chuang, 2000; Perez & Coello, 2023). Another type of learning algorithm is evolutionary ones that have its roots in the natural world's selection processes; it provides stable methods for solving given optimization problems through the evolution of solutions during the time (Holland, 1992; Marín et al., 2022).

Hybrid QIEAs use the principles of quantum mechanics as well as evolutionary algorithms, which strengthens the theoretical foundations of the model. Together they can effectively counter or manage the difficulties that are characteristic of this type of community interaction, thus presenting a higher level of optimization (Holland, 1992).

### 1.2 Objectives of the Study

The objective of this research is to identify and establish how hybrid QIEAs can improve interactions in the community on digital platforms. The specific objectives include:

- Explaining the basics of quantum computing and evolutionary algorithms will help in further understanding the Hybrid QIEAs.
- Describing how hybrid QIEAs are formed and put into operation, it outlines the procedures that have to be followed to combine classical and quantum approaches and ensure their proper functioning.

- Presenting actual cases where hybrid QIEAs have been implemented with a step-by-step demonstration of the methods for enhancing the communication patterns of communities.
- Realizing the existing limitations and developing the possibilities for further investigation aimed at raising the effectiveness of the advanced hybrid QIEAs.

## 2. FUNDAMENTALS

This section focuses on the fundamental elements of the methodologies underlying the development and use of hybrid QIEAs. This section provides foundations on how such preliminary concepts in quantum computing and evolutionary algorithms are, and how they can be applied to stand-in interaction in communities.

### 2.1 Quantum Computing Basics

Quantum computing is a new computing model that is different from the classical one and based on the principles of quantum mechanics. The basis of quantum computing is qubits that are different from classical bits in some crucial aspects. A qubit, unlike a classical bit that can only be in one state at a time, 0 or 1, holds both states at once in a superposition. It enables quantum computers to work in parallel and brings exponential advantages to some tasks in the classical system (W. Li, 2024; Nielsen & Chuang, 2000). Figure 1 presents some quantum computing principles.

*Figure 1. Quantum computing principles*

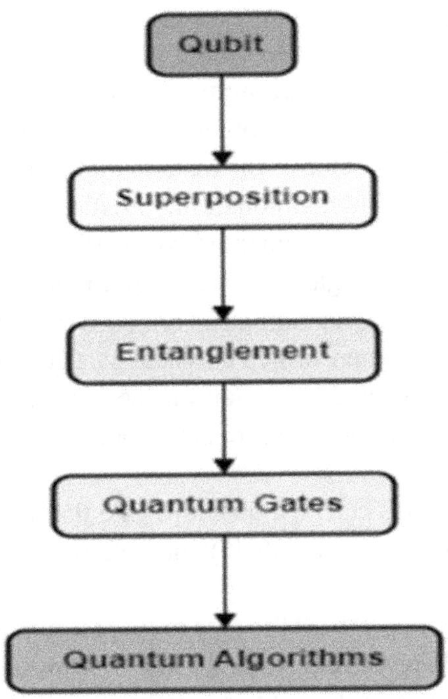

Among all the principles in quantum mechanics and quantum computing, *superposition* is easily one of the most famous and useful. It is an idea that is related to the probability of a quantum system, for example a qubit, being in more than one state simultaneously. This means for a qubit they are capable of being in a state of 0, in a state of 1, or in both at the same time (Nielsen & Chuang, 2000).

In classical computing, an element of information can be either 0 or 1 but it can never be both a 0 and 1 at the same time. But in quantum computers, the qubit in superposition can process several evaluations at the same time, in parallel. There must then be some advantage that can be attributed to quantum computing and it can, therefore, be stated that the strength of quantum computing lies in its ability to generate and test out numerous possibilities at once. For now, it is imperative to remember that when the qubit is in a superposition state, conducting the measurement will yield only 0 or 1 for the qubit but the probabilities of having or measuring the qubit being in state 0 or 1 will depend on the coefficient of superposition (Gan et al., 2024; Nielsen & Chuang, 2000).

For example, a qubit might be in $|\psi\rangle = \alpha|0\rangle + \beta|1\rangle$; here: $|0\rangle$ and $|1\rangle$ are base states, and $\alpha$, $\beta$ are complex probabilities of the qubit being in $|0\rangle$ or $|1\rangle$ state. The state probabilities that the qubit will be spit and found to be in state 0 or state 1 are $|\alpha|^2$ and $|\beta|^2$.

Firstly, because superposition can pack many possible solutions, one of the characteristics is that it provides a certain superiority when it comes to the search among the different solutions, which is one of the advantages that quantum computers can significantly outperform classical computers in certain problems.

Another important idea of quantum computing is *entanglement*; here, two qubits become dependent on one another in such a way that if the state of one qubit is interfered with, the state of the other qubit is also affected regardless of the distance between the two qubits. Based on this property, quantum computers are capable of solving multidimensional problems much faster than classical computers (Preskill, 2018).

A historical detail on the efficiency of quantum algorithms includes Shor's algorithm, which deals with factoring large numbers that are practically impossible to solve by classical computers, and Grover's algorithm for searching an unsorted database. As for the goal, however, it is still partially achieved, with practical applications of quantum computing continuing to be actively implemented. As Grover's database search or Shor's factoring algorithm shows such problems are easily solvable on quantum computers while it is a nightmare for classical computers. One of the matters that should be said is that the opportunities offered by quantum computing are infinite, although the broad uses of such computing are introduced practically all over the world at the present moment (Grover, 1997; Shor, 1994).

**Quantum Gates:** Similar to the logic gates that are used in the classical circuits the quantum gates are the bricks in quantum circuits. But Quantum gates are used on qubits and perform operations with the help of superposition and entanglement which classical gates cannot do (Preskill, 2018).

While performing the calculations and operation on the data, the quantum gates are supposed to transform the state of the qubits. Common quantum gates include:

- **Pauli-X Gate (NOT Gate):** This can be a quantum gate that flips the state of a qubit. If the state of the qubit is $|0\rangle$ it will change the state into $|1\rangle$ and vice versa if the state of the qubit is $|1\rangle$ it will change the state into $|0\rangle$.
- **Hadamard Gate (H Gate):** This makes the gate prepare a superposition state from a bas state as it pulls the state into the right place relative to the site. For instance, it can swap the state of $|0\rangle$ or $|1\rangle$ to state $|\psi\rangle = \frac{1}{\sqrt{2}}(|0\rangle + |1\rangle)$ of the qubit. It entails that it can put a qubit in a state of $|\Psi\rangle$ that is, the qubit is in both states of $|0\rangle$ and $|1\rangle$ at the same time.

- **CNOT Gate (Controlled-NOT Gate):** This gate is operated on two qubits of which one is called the control qubit and the other one is called the target qubit. The CNOT gate sets the target qubit to exactly the opposite of the state of the control qubit when the latter is set to |1⟩; otherwise, the target qubit does not change its state. This gate is very important especially when specification is being made on the generation of entangled states.

The representation of the quantum gates is always in the form of unitary matrices that operate on the state of the qubits. Superposition, entanglement, and interference of states are created by connective several quantum gates in a quantum circuit to gain an extensive quantum algorithm that is more efficient than a normal algorithm (Nielsen & Chuang, 2000).

## 2.2 Evolutionary Algorithms

Evolutionary algorithms (EAs) are optimization methods that mimic the biological evolution process. Similarly, the species in the natural environment are evolved using the selection, crossover, and mutation process and similarly, the evolutionary algorithms are used to solve complex problems. This approach is more helpful when there is a large and comprehensive search space for the solution of the given problem or when the problem space is not very well defined (Holland, 1992). Figure 2 shows the working overflow of the evolutionary algorithms.

*Figure 2. Working overflow of EAs*

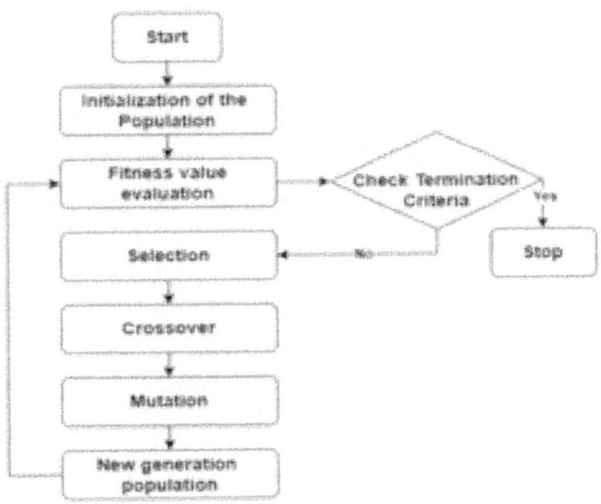


### 2.2.1 An Introduction to Evolutionary Algorithms

Basically, an evolutionary algorithm is an optimization heuristic that aims at solving problems and identifying the best or near-best solutions through the enhancement of a population of possible solutions.

- **Initialization:** It starts with the creation of a population of individuals at random, and each individual will be a possible solution to the problem. These individuals are represented as strings (or chromosomes) that can be binary or numerical and can also be other forms depending on the specific problem.

- **Selection:** At each generation, the population members are ranked according to their fitness, which quantifies the quality of a solution to the given problem. The most suitable individuals are forwarded to the next generation as they are in a position to reproduce; the same way as natural selection promotes the reproduction of the fittest organisms (Holland, 1992).
- **Crossover (Recombination):** Some of the parties are picked and put together to breed new generations. This process is called crossover and implies combining the genetic material (or the solution representation) of two parents to generate one or more offspring. This makes it possible for the algorithm to search for new solutions space by creating new individuals by merging the useful features of other individuals (D. E. (David E. Goldberg, 1989).
- **Mutation:** To increase the genetic variation in the population, certain changes are made randomly in some of the offspring. Mutation changes one or more genes in a chromosome since if this does not happen the population will not diversify and stagnate. This is important in order to allow the algorithm to search for more possible solutions (Mitchell, 1996).
- **Replacement:** The offspring take the place of some or all of the old population, thus forming a new generation of solutions. The process of selection, crossover, mutation, and replacement goes on until a certain criterion is met for instance, a maximum number of generations or once a certain level of fitness has been achieved.
- **Convergence:** In this way, the population gradually approaches the global optimum, and the poor solutions or individuals with poor traits are eliminated and the excellent traits are inherited. In practice, this leads to identifying a rather efficient solution to the problem at hand.

The main elements that define evolutionary algorithms are:

- **Population:** A collection of possibilities of how the problem could be solved (individuals).
- **Fitness Function:** A quantitative assessment of the quality of a solution to the problem's goal/objective.
- **Selection Mechanism:** A way of selecting which of the population of organisms gets to reproduce based on the fitness of the organism.
- **Crossover:** A process by which the genes of parents are mixed to create new generations of offspring.
- **Mutation:** A process that creates variations in the individuals so that genetic variation is not lost in a population.
- **Generations:** Stages of the algorithm in which the new population is produced based on the previous one.

**Applications of Evolutionary Algorithms:** EA are very general and can be used to solve a vast number of problems in different fields. Some common applications include:

- **Optimization Problems:** EAs are usually applied in optimization problems, including engineering design, machine learning model parameter tuning, and other challenging scheduling problems.
- **Artificial Intelligence:** EAs are applied in the growth of AI especially in neuro-evolution and formation of decision-making systems in games and simulations.

- **Robotics:** In the area of robotics, EAs are employed in the design of control policies, the enhancement of the robot's functionality, and the creation of structures that are capable of learning and adapting.
- **Economics and Finance:** EAs are used to improve investment approaches, pricing concepts, and market modelling, while the classical methods are not always effective in handling the complex and changing environment of the financial markets.
- **Bioinformatics:** EAs are employed in bioinformatics for problems like protein structure prediction, genetic sequence comparison, and drug synthesis where space solutions is quite large and comprehensive.

**Genetic Algorithms and Their Applications:** Genetic Algorithms are based on the processes of natural evolution for solving optimization and search problems. They operate by evolving a population of candidate solutions to a given problem, using principles similar to biological evolution. Three basic genetic operations are used in the genetic algorithm and are selection, crossover, and mutation. Over some time, the population evolves and it is expected that every successive generation will try to advance on the solutions provided by the previous generations. The main advantages of GAs are that they are general and can escape local optima easily (D. E. (David E. Goldberg, 1989). Algorithm 1 presents the pseudo-code algorithm of the genetic algorithm.

**Genetic Algorithm Elements:** To understand how GAs work, it's important to know their key components:

- **Population:** In a genetic algorithm a population is a set of possible solutions to the given problem. Every individual is generally represented by a chromosome, which is a list of genes that can be binary variables, integers, or any other data type based on the given problem.
- **Chromosomes and Genes:** It can be considered to be a chromosome that holds the possible solution to the given problem. Each chromosome contains genes and each of the genes is connected with a particular element of the solution. For example, in a binary GA, an individual can be thought of as a string of 0's and 1's for example a bit or gene may or may not influence the solution.
- **Fitness Function**: The fitness function: measures the quality of the solution which is a chromosome in genetics terminology. It assigns a fitness value for each member of the population that attempts to estimate the quality of the solution. In this case, the fitness score helps to assess the quality of the solution and the one that is better holds a higher fitness score.
- **Selection:** From the fitness scores, a selection method is applied to select the parents that will mate and come up with the offspring of the new generation. Common selection methods include:

    1. **Roulette Wheel Selection:** It is a process of selection of individuals at a certain rate like choosing numbers on a wheel of fortune, where some numbers have larger parts than others, so do the people with higher fitness have larger parts on the wheel.
    2. **Tournament Selection:** A group of people is randomly selected and the fittest of them all is selected as a parent.
    3. **Rank-Based Selection:** Selection is not by fitness value but through the orders that individuals are arranged in thus the order they are arranged in.

- **Crossover (Recombination):** Crossover, is the process in which two parents create one or more offspring. This process is an aspect of heredity, one of the fundamental aspects of life that involves the passing on of some characteristics from one generation to the other, in this case from the mother and the father to the offspring. Common crossover techniques include:

  1. **Single-Point Crossover:** One crossover point is chosen for the two parents and genes are exchanged after this crossover point.
  2. **Two-Point Crossover:** Two crossover points are chosen and then all the genes between these two points are interchanged between the two parents.
  3. **Uniform Crossover:** In contrast, no two genes from the parents will be the same in which every single gene has an unpredictable chance of being passed down from one parent to the offspring.

- **Mutation:** Random change in the genetic component, that is situated on the chromosome by changing the DNA sequence of the genes. This helps in the conservation of the genetic diversity in the population and prevent the population from settling on suboptimal solutions. For instance, in a binary GA mutation may be flipping one bit that is from 0 to 1 or from 1 to 0.
- **Replacement:** Crossover and mutation are followed by the replacement of the new generation of offspring on the old population. It then moves on to the new population and hence the subsequent generations of the improved solutions are obtained.
- **Convergence:** Stating the process, the algorithm is to go on with the generations until a condition is met which is called the stopping criteria. This may be after a specific number of generations or a specific level of fitness or when there is no significant improvement in the subsequent generations. At its best, the population has converged to a solution that is precise and optimal in its functioning (D. E. Goldberg & Holland, 1988).

### 2.2.2 Algorithm 1: Pseudocode Algorithm of the Genetic Algorithm

Start:
Randomly initialize the population S(t), (t=0)
Evaluate the fitness value S(t)
While (check the termination criteria = false) do: t=t+1
B(t) = selection of parent individual form S(t)
P(t) = recombination (B(t)); #Crossover the genes of selected parents
P'(t) = mutation (p(t)); #mutate the mated population stochastically
Evaluate the P'(t) using the same evaluation function that was used to evaluate the S; S = best fitness score (S,P'(t)); #Select the best fitness individual from actual fitness
End.

### 2.2.3 Applications of Genetic Algorithms

Due to their capacity to solve problems that cannot be solved by conventional means, genetic algorithms are used in numerous fields. Here are some notable applications:

- **Optimization Problems:** GAs are excellent for problems that have very large and/or unpredictable solution sets such as engineering design, scheduling, and resource allocation.
- **Machine Learning:** GA has been used in feature selection, hyper-parameters tuning, and creation of the artificial neural network structure (Neuro-evolution).
- **Artificial Intelligence:** GAs are used in AI for the formulation of game strategies, formulation of decision-making structures, and system optimization.
- **Robotics:** These are useful in the development and optimization of controllers for robots, the generation of behavior, and increasing the self-regulation of the robotic system.
- **Finance:** In finance, GAs enhance trading strategies, investment strategies/portfolio choice and decision-making, and other risk management strategies amongst others.

## 2.3 Quantum-Inspired Evolutionary Algorithms

Quantum-Inspired Evolutionary Algorithms (QIEAs) are newly developed and efficient methods that utilize the principles of Quantum Computing integrated with Evolutionary Algorithms. Although QIEAs do not require actual quantum computers, they implement quantum mechanics to enhance the features of classical evolutionary algorithms in the context of solving optimization problems. Quantum-Inspired Evolutionary Algorithms are a Metaheuristic that has incorporated the ideas of quantum computing such as Superposition and Entanglement into Evolutionary algorithms. The general concept is based on the use of quantum concepts to improve the effectiveness of evolutionary algorithms in the learning process and the search for the solution space and to prevent such negative phenomena as premature convergence (Han & Kim, 2002; Narayanan & Moore, 1996).

There are important fields of evolutionary algorithms that have been combined with quantum computing: Quantum Evolutionary Algorithms (QEA), Evolutionary-Designed Quantum Algorithms (EDQA), and Quantum-Inspired Evolutionary Algorithms (QIEA).

In this chapter, we will discuss only QIEAs (Zhang, 2011).

Quantum-inspired Evolutionary Algorithms can be categorized as quantum-inspired algorithms which is a subfield of evolutionary computing. In 1996, Narayanan and Moore came up with Quantum-inspired evolutionary algorithms to enhance the rate of evolutionary algorithms by introducing quantum mechanical concepts. Evolutionary algorithms (EAs) are a class of optimization algorithms that mimic the process of evolution aimed at producing better solutions as a result of the processes similar to mutation and crossover. QIEAs enhance these conventional techniques by incorporating quantum considerations; therefore, the algorithm's efficiency in searching and determining the solution space is enhanced. A QIEA that has been designed based on the principles of quantum computing such as qubits and Q-gates possesses the following characteristics;

- Especially the QIEA defines it in such a way that individual belonging to a certain population can be characterized by a vector of qubits. A Q-bit representation is a probability picture of all the states in between the two base states, and all the states have an equal chance of being the actual state (Han & Kim, 2002).
- A QIEA employs a Q-gate to initiate individual focus on better solutions and, therefore, creates the next generation (Han & Kim, 2002).
- Thus, it can be stated that a QIEA is capable of trying to achieve a global solution with some number of particles or with a single particle (Han & Kim, 2002).

Let's understand the very first implementation of quantum-inspired evolutionary algorithms, which is "Original Binary Observation Quantum inspired Evolutionary Algorithms (bQIEAo)". Algorithm 2 shows the pseudocode algorithm of bQIEAo (Zhang, 2011) (Han & Kim, 2002).

The bQIEAo Algorithm in details:

Step 1. Initialization:

- The algorithm begins with setting a time counter t to 0. This countermeasure is the number of iterations or generations that the algorithm has been able to go through.
- **Initialize Q(t):** Q(t) is the quantum state at time t, in this step the quantum state will be initialized with certain probability amplitudes which will be the potential solution to the optimization problem.
- **Make P(t) by observing the states of Q(t):** Thus, P(t) is the classical population obtained from Q(t). This step projects the quantum representation onto the classical bit string, or population, by measuring the quantum bits in Q(t). In other words, this leads to the reduction of the quantum superpositions to definite classical states.
- **Evaluate P(t):** In the presented algorithm, the fitness of each person from the classical population P(t) is assessed based on a pre-defined fitness function. This calculation defines the extent to which each person (or solution) meets the optimization criteria.
- **Store the best solutions among P(t) into B(t) and the best solution b among B(t):** Following the evaluation, the algorithm selects and keeps the most promising solutions from P(t) into another population represented by B(t). Furthermore, the single best solution b is also determined and separately recorded for future use.

Step 2. Main Loop (While Loop):

- This process is to be repeated until a certain condition is met, the termination condition. This condition is usually defined in terms of a maximum number of steps or by a certain criterion that has to be met.
- **t ← t + 1:** Move the time counter to the next time step and go to the next generation.
- **Make P(t) by observing the states of Q(t-1):** In a similar manner to point 3, step 1, the quantum population from the previous iteration, Q(t−1), is used to generate a new classical population P(t). This step aids in the creation of new possible solutions from the quantum states obtained from the preceding generation.
- **Evaluate P(t):** As in point 4, step 1, assess the newly generated classical population P(t) with the help of the fitness function.
- **Update Q(t) using Q-gates:** Quantum gates are applied to the quantum population at time t denoted as Q(t). These gates control the probability amplitudes of the quantum bits that can affect the potential solutions to be searched for in the subsequent iterations. The quantum gates may for instance include rotations that enhance or reduce the probability of certain bits being in a certain state. This step is important in the preservation of diversity to direct the search most efficiently.
- **Store the best solutions among P(t) and B(t-1) into B(t) and the best solution b among B(t):** The best solutions of the population P(t) at the current stage and the previous genera-

tion B(t-1) are preserved in the new best solutions population B(t). The overall best solution also changes b if a better solution is found.

- **If (migration condition):** The algorithm verifies whether there is a migration condition. This condition can be based on certain criteria like the number of generations since the last migration or stagnation of the solution.
- **Migrate b or $b_j^t$ to B(t) globally or locally, respectively:** If the migration condition is met, the best solution b or its modified version $b_j^t$ is introduced into the current population B(t). This migration can be global that is, it can affect all the members of the population, or local that is it can only affect some of the members of the population. Thus, migration enables the introduction of fresh genetic material into the population which reduces the risk of the algorithm sticking in local optima and generating a larger solution space.

Step-3. End of Loop:

The loop goes on until the stopping criterion is fulfilled, and at this point, the algorithm provides the optimum solution found in the search process (Han & Kim, 2002).

### 2.3.1 Algorithim 2: Working Process of bQIEA0

Start:
Randomly initialize the population Q(t), (t=0)
Create P(t) by observing the states of Q(t)
Evaluate the fitness value P(t)
Update the Q(t) population by using quantum rotation gate
Store the best solution s among P(t) and B(t-1) into B(t) and the best solution bs among B(t)
If (migration criteria)
Migrate bs to B(t) globally or locally, respectively
End

**Applications of the QIEAs:** They are particularly helpful when facing problems of optimization, that is when the area of search is large and intricate. Some common applications include:

- **Combinatorial Optimization:** For instance, the traveling salesman problem where the aim is to find the least cost possible route that passes through all the required cities and returns to the original city can be solved well by QIEAs because of their capability in searching (Talbi & Talbi, 2009).
- **Machine Learning:** They have been used in the identification of the appropriate structure of the neural networks and the most suitable hyperparameters of the model hence enhancing the performance of the machine learning models.
- **Engineering Design:** In engineering, QIEAs can be useful when working with the optimization of the design parameters of complex structures, for example, airfoils or structural parts, when other methods might be lost in the vast number of solutions.
- **Finance and Economics:** QIEAs are utilized for instance in finding the best investment portfolios, risk management, and market modeling where the mutual relationship of the variables is quite complicated.

## 3. HYBRID QUANTUM-INSPIRED EVOLUTIONARY ALGORITHMS

HQIEAs combine attributes of quantum computations with classical ones, which form the basis of evolutionary algorithms and help in improving the optimization capabilities of systems. In this section, many aspects consisting of methods of merging classical and quantum models and strategies of creating and operating HQIEAs, their architecture, components, and parameters, will be discussed. Table 1 presents the key components and parameters of HQIEAs.

Key Elements:

- **Quantum Representation:** Where or instead of the conventional bits, quantum bits or qubits are used. A qubit can be in state 0 or state 1 or both at the same time which is known as superposition and this is how several solutions can be encoded.
- **Evolutionary Process:** The genetic operators which are selection, crossover, and mutation will be used but the quantum operators like quantum gate or quantum observation may modify or control these operators.
- **Hybrid Mechanisms:** The quantum population is generally combined with the classical population in which they can exchange their positions most of the time.

*Table 1. Key Components and parameters of HQIEAs*

| Component/Parameter | Description | Impact on HQIEA Performance |
|---|---|---|
| **Quantum Superposition** | Represents multiple solutions simultaneously through quantum states. | Enhances exploration; allows the algorithm to consider many potential solutions at once. |
| **Quantum Entanglement** | Correlates the states of different qubits, linking them for more coordinated evolution. | Improves solution quality; helps maintain population diversity and prevents premature convergence. |
| **Quantum Gates (e.g., Rotation Gates)** | Operations that adjust the probabilities of qubit states. | Fine-tunes search process; guides the evolution toward optimal solutions. |
| **Fitness Function** | Evaluates how well a solution meets the optimization criteria. | Critical for guiding selection; directly influences the effectiveness of the evolutionary process. |
| **Population Size** | The number of individuals (solutions) in the population. | Larger populations increase diversity but require more computational resources. |
| **Mutation Rate** | The frequency at which mutations occur in the population. | Higher rates increase exploration but may disrupt convergence; must be carefully balanced. |
| **Crossover Rate** | The frequency at which solutions are combined to create new offspring. | Balances exploration and exploitation; influence how quickly the algorithm converges. |
| **Termination Criteria** | Conditions under which the algorithm stops, such as reaching a maximum number of generations. | Determines when the algorithm has sufficiently explored the solution space. |

## 3.1 Hybridization Techniques

By 'hybridization' for the described use of HQIEAs is meant the combination of concepts originating from quantum computing with those from classical evolutionary algorithms. This fusion makes use of what the two paradigms can offer to combine them in a way that would produce a stronger framework for the expression of algorithms. In the following section, we shall describe and elaborate on the means of hybridization; we also provide examples of best practices. Techniques, which can be used to mix the best of classical and quantum theories are given below.

- **Quantum-Inspired Initialization:**

The initial population in an HQIEA can be created by employing quantum-inspired techniques. In contrast to the stochastic or ad hoc chosen population, the principles of quantum superposition let the algorithm code several possible solutions at once, endowing the evolution with a more extensive and diverse population to search from the very beginning.

For example, by performing computations using a qubit and assigning 0 and 1 for a population simultaneously, an optimization problem can be solved by the same population from the very beginning which helps in the diversification of the initial solutions as well as the quality of the solutions.

- **Quantum-Guided Mutation and Crossover:**

In classical evolutionary algorithms, mutation and crossover are the initial techniques for searching solution space and for bringing diversity into the population. If quantum operations are used, and such include quantum gates, then these processes are boosted.

I. **Quantum Mutation:** While a classical mutation is usually completed by flipping a bit at random, quantum mutation can include turning the state of a qubit to control the probability density of solutions.
II. **Quantum Crossover:** Entanglement of quantum states of parent solutions can yield some properties of offspring, which are more extensive or more optimal than solutions obtained by classical means.

**Example:** A quantum gate could possibly change the probability of a given trait (bit value) being passed by the next generation of qubits.

- **Hybrid Population Dynamics:**

HQIEAs can include the maintenance and change of multiple quantum and classical populations. The presence of such populations enables the algorithm to complement the strength of one while introducing the other at certain points.

I. **Quantum Population:** Presents solutions in quantum form so that one can search many states at once.
II. **Classical Population:** Delivers a quantifiable, comprehensible set of solutions that can be assessed based on predefined or created classical fitness functions.

**Example:** While a quantum population may explore numerous areas of solutions the classical population applies the rules of the fitness landscape to develop the solutions and make sure the superior solutions are kept.

## 3.2 Algorithm Design and Implementation

Thus, at the time of developing the Hybrid Quantum-Inspired Evolutionary Algorithm, a decision has to be made on such aspects as the individualities of the architecture, its components, and the parameters that control the algorithm's operation. The above aspects are explained as follows:

### 3.2.1 Physical Design of Hybrid QIEAs

The architecture of an HQIEA typically consists of the following key layers.

- **Quantum Layer:**

  I. **Qubit Representation:** This is why solutions are stored in qubits and can work not only on the concept of quantum superposition but also on quantum entanglement. This layer is meant to control the quantum state, gates, as well as measurements that are used in the computation.
  II. **Quantum Gates:** Such matrices of operations as for instance Hadamard or rotation gates are applied to control the probability amplitudes in which the evolution takes place.

- **Classical Evolutionary Layer:**

  I. **Population Initialization:** This layer gives the first classical population from the outcomes obtained from the quantum layer.
  II. **Evolutionary Operations:** The crossover and the mutation functions are carried out on the population and the selection of the individuals is done as per the evolutionary model. These operators can be influenced or steered by the quantum layer's result.
  III. **Fitness Evaluation:** For every solution candidate there is a pre-defined fitness function that quantifies to what extent the solution optimizes the objective.

- **Hybrid Interaction Layer:**

  I. **Feedback Loop:** These quantum and classical layers are coupled together, and they interact with one another; while the quantum layer communicates the result of the fitness test back to the classical layer that, in turn, uses the information in the management of the quantum layer in the next round.
  II. **Migration Mechanism:** This way, such a population transfers solutions from the quantum population to the classical one to avoid that early convergence and vice versa (Han & Kim, 2002). A Comparison of traditional evolutionary algorithms with hybrid quantum-inspired evolutionary algorithms is given in Table 2.

### 3.2.2 Main Sub-Processes and Variables

- **Qubit Initialization:** However, in the case of quantum-layered algorithms, the setting of qubits lays a constructive crux in the exploration capacity of the algorithm. Correct setting of charges ensures that there is a great variety of uniqueness from the results of the search.
- **Quantum Gate Operations:** The types of quantum gates like the Hadamard gate, Pauli-X gate, and the rotation gates, as well as their parameters for the rotation angle, are the primary controllers of the state evolution and the strategies for the search.
- **Population Size and Diversity:** The size of the quantum and classical populations, as well as mechanisms to maintain diversity (e.g., quantum-inspired mutation), are essential to balancing exploration and exploitation.
- **Fitness Function:** In the classical layer, a fitness function is also employed to evaluate the solutions and regulate the process's subsequent development. This must be properly designed to fit the problem being solved in as much as defined by the objectives.
- **Termination Criteria:** Among the most used termination conditions one can mention the maximum number of iterations, the quality of the fitness function, or whether there is no improvement for some number of generations (Han & Kim, 2002).

*Table 2. Comparison of traditional evolutionary algorithms with HQIEAs*

| Feature | Traditional Evolutionary Algorithms | Hybrid Quantum-Inspired Evolutionary Algorithms (HQIEAs) |
|---|---|---|
| Exploration Capability | Limited by classical mechanisms; prone to local optima. | Enhanced by quantum superposition; better global exploration. |
| Population Diversity | Depends on mutation and crossover; can diminish over time. | Maintained through quantum-inspired mutation and entanglement. |
| Scalability | Struggles with large-scale and high-dimensional problems. | More efficient handling of complex, large-scale problems. |
| Convergence Speed | Slower; requires extensive tuning of parameters. | Faster convergence due to quantum-inspired operators. |
| Computational Complexity | Lower, but requires more iterations to reach optimal solutions. | Higher due to quantum operations, but fewer iterations are needed. |
| Adaptability | Less adaptive to dynamic environments. | Highly adaptive; quantum elements allow for continuous adjustment. |
| Use of Quantum Principles | None. | Incorporates quantum principles such as superposition and entanglement. |

## 4. APPLICATIONS AND CASE STUDIES IN ENHANCING COMMUNITY DETECTION

In this section, the specific subject of concern is an investment in the Hybrid Quantum-Inspired Evolutionary Algorithms (HQIEAs) in improving interactivity within the community, especially in such contexts as the digital space. Thus, by applying high-level computational approaches, the various communities can enhance interaction, cooperation, and overall social relations. They will have real examples, methodologies, and metrics that will show how the HQIEAs have been used to enhance more favorable and efficient detection within the community part (Gupta et al., 2014).

Such examples help in establishing real-life contexts as to how HQIEAs have been implemented to increase interaction with the community. Inferring these examples, it becomes clear that these algorithms can be used to solve various social issues illustrating their efficiency.

- **Real-world examples of community detection enhancement**

1. Social Network Analysis:

Quantum-inspired evolutionary algorithms improve the detection of connected user groups in social media and online communities. For instance, these algorithms help identify groups with shared interests on platforms like Twitter and Facebook. Table 3 shows the definition difference between social networks and quantum social networks.

***Application: Quantum social network analysis for community detection***

Community detection within social networks has grown rapidly in various domains. There are some classical approaches like modularity optimization and clustering that struggle with the increasing scale and complexity of modern networks. This could be a limitation. Because of this limitation, researchers have explored some approaches related to quantum computing. There are some strategies like quantum-inspired algorithms as potential solutions for enhancing community detection (Muhuri & Singh, 2024).

*Table 3. Definitions of the social network and quantum social network*

| Social Networks | Quantum Social Networks |
|---|---|
| Social networks are the platforms where individuals the communities share, connect, and communicate. Websites like LinkedIn, Twitter, and Facebook are included in social networks. These networks are very useful for personal as well as professional interactions. Social networks are used to analyze user behavior, trends, and information flow. There is a basic task in social networks, that is community detection. Communities are groups of nodes with strong internal connections. There are some classical social network methods like clustering and graph partitioning. Classical approaches face some challenges with scale and complexity, as the network rapidly grows. | Quantum social networks combine quantum computing with social network analysis. Quantum social networks can explore vast solution spaces more efficiently. It provides potential speed and accuracy improvements in community detection. Hybrid quantum approaches combine quantum principles with classical methods of optimization. These algorithms overcome some limitations of traditional social network analysis techniques. Quantum social networks propose new highlights into interconnected, secure information sharing. This new field of research helps advancements in analyzing large complex networks. |

***Comparison of Quantum-based community detection techniques (Muhuri & Singh, 2024):*** Discussion and comparison of quantum-based community detection algorithms are shown in Table 4.

*Table 4. Comparison of quantum-based community detection techniques*

| Technique | Principle | Strengths | Limitations | Optimal Use case |
|---|---|---|---|---|
| **Quantum-inspired evolutionary algorithms (Yuanyuan & Xiyu, 2018)** | Helps to divide the communities with an approximate optimal value of modularity. | High modularity scores. | Not working properly for overlapping social networks and disjoint graphs. | QIEAs are used for General-purpose community detection with balanced complexity. |
| **Quantum-inspired algorithms for community detection (Cade et al., 2022)** | Improvements in Louvain algorithms. | Modest polynomial speedups over their classical counterparts are achieved. | Works properly only for small datasets. | Quantum-inspired Louvain algorithms are used. |
| **Quantum annealing for community detection in electrical grids (Fernández-Campoamor et al., 2021)** | Partitions of the graphs by using the electrical modularity. | Helpful in getting a high modularity score. | Works properly only for small datasets. | Quantum Annealing. |
| **Discrete time by using quantum walk (Mukai & Hatano, 2020)** | Complex network detection by using Fourier-coin quantum walk. | Time complexity would be the order of $\sqrt{n}$. | Not working properly for overlapping social networks and disjoint graphs. | Quantum Fourier walk. |
| **Quantum particle swarm optimization** (Y. Li et al., 2015) | To take the spectral details of the line graph by using the spectral method. | Works for Overlapping community detection. | Works properly only for small datasets. | QPSO |

***Performance comparison of quantum-based and classical community detection methods (Muhuri & Singh, 2024):***Table 5 presents the performance analysis of the quantum-based and classical community detection techniques.

*Table 5. Performance comparison of quantum-based and classical community detection methods*

| Criteria | Quantum-Based Methods | Classical Methods | Remarks |
|---|---|---|---|
| **Modularity Optimization** | More precise community structures; higher modularity scores. | It is suitable for small to medium size networks but falls short for large-scale data. | Quantum methods excel at identifying well-defined communities in complex networks. |
| **Execution Speed** | Quantum parallelism has the potential for significant speed-up. | Especially for large and dense networks, slower. | It is simple to see how quantum computing can reduce processing time drastically as a range of problems increases. |
| **Scalability** | However, limited by current quantum hardware, whether better scalability in theory. | Provides limited scalability and struggles with very large datasets. | The classical approaches struggle with scale, and the quantum one has potential but hardware evolution is needed. |

continued on following page

*Table 5. Continued*

| Criteria | Quantum-Based Methods | Classical Methods | Remarks |
|---|---|---|---|
| **Accuracy** | Improved finding optimal community partitions. | May miss optimal partitions in complex data with moderate accuracy. | A quantum technique can explore larger solution spaces more efficiently. |
| **Overlapping Communities** | QPSO, like some of the quantum methods, can find overlapping communities. | In some cases, overlapping detection may require advanced algorithms. | But quantum methods are still developing and can be adapted more naturally to complex overlaps. |
| **Error Sensitivity** | The limited current implementation is sensitive to noise and coherence issues. | Stable execution is less prone to environmental noise. | Error is more prone in quantum techniques due to the evolving state of quantum technology. |

2. Complex networks:

Community detection is a fundamental task in understanding complex networks, from the social to the biological and the technological. In practice, traditional algorithms can be limited in their ability to depend on parameters and achieve suboptimal solutions. In response to these challenges, quantum computing-based evolutionary algorithms (QIEAs) emerged, where superposition is exploited to represent and optimize many solutions efficiently. In this study, authors (Yuanyuan & Xiyu, 2018) introduced QIEA-net and iQIEA-net algorithms, which combine quantum-inspired strategies for reducing convergence times and distinguishing community structures with high modularity. Experiments on real networks validate the effectiveness of the techniques and, in some cases, demonstrate superior computational advantages relative to conventional approaches (Yuanyuan & Xiyu, 2018).

***Conceptual Framework:*** In this paper, authors focus on developing this proposed approach to understanding the underlying structure of community detection in complex network problems (and understanding social, biological, and technological networks). Two QIEA-based algorithms (QIEA-net and iQIEA-net) are then introduced by the authors (Yuanyuan & Xiyu, 2018). Without requiring prior knowledge of the number of communities, these algorithms find the community structure such that modularity is optimized (Yuanyuan & Xiyu, 2018).

***Methodology:***

- **QIEA-net:** Community detection in complex networks is an important task and QIEA-net, an innovative algorithm based on the principles of quantum-inspired evolutionary algorithms (QIEAs), is presented. The fundamental unit of representation it uses is each solution can be superposition of the states. The feature used by QIEA-net to explore and search through a relatively smaller population than traditional evolutionary algorithm enables vast search space. In particular, starting from a population of quantum individuals, we initialize and observe binary solutions representing possible community structures. We then evaluate these solutions in terms of quality, using the modularity function which quantifies the validity of the community division. Using the iterated application of quantum gates, the algorithm updates the quantum states to maximize solution quality while maintaining diversity to prevent premature convergence. The authors aimed to maximize modularity and find the most suitable community configuration, a new approach to unsupervised community detection without the need for pre-determined community count parameters. The pseudocode algorithm for QIEA-net is given in Algorithm 3 (Yuanyuan & Xiyu, 2018).

- **iQIEA-net**:
    - An enhancement over QIEA-net with faster convergence.
    - Integrates a **guiding quantum individual** initialized using the result of a classical algorithm (e.g., BGLL) to steer the population evolution effectively.
    - Reduces computation time by ensuring better initial conditions for larger networks (Yuanyuan & Xiyu, 2018).

## 4.1 Algorithm 3: QIEA Net for Community Detection

Input:

- Adjacency matrix representing the network.
- Maximum number of iterations (MaxGen).

Output:

- Highest modularity value found.
- Corresponding community structure.

Procedure:

Initialization:

- Set iteration counter t = 0.
- Initialize the quantum population Q(t) based on the network's size.

Observation and Transformation:

- Observe Q(t) to create a population P(t)
- Transform P(t) into a community structure C(t)

Evaluation:

- Compute the modularity of C(t)
- Store the best solutions from P(t) in the solution set B(t)

Iterative Optimization: while t is less than or equal to MaxGen:

- Increment the iteration counter: t=t+1
- Observe the states of Q(t-1) to create P(t)
- Convert P(t) into C(t)
- Evaluate C(t) with the modularity function
- Update Q(t) using quantum gate operations
- Save the top solutions between B(t-1) and P(t) into B(t)
- Determine the best solution b from B(t)

Output Transformation:

- Assign cluster labels to each vertex according to b
- Return the best modularity value and clustering result

***Experimental results and comparison analysis:***

The algorithms were tested on five well-known networks: Zachary's Karate Club, Dolphins Social Network, American College Football, Polbooks, and Jazz Musicians Collaboration Network. The performance was benchmarked against existing methods like BGLL, FN, MODPSO, and other evolutionary-based algorithms (Yuanyuan & Xiyu, 2018).

Real-world networks have the following features:

1. **Zachary's Karate Club** (34 vertices, 78 edges)
2. **Dolphins Social Network** (62 vertices, 159 edges)
3. **American College Football Network** (115 vertices, 613 edges)
4. **Political Books Network** (105 vertices, 441 edges)
5. **Jazz Musicians Network** (198 vertices, 2742 edges)

The modularity values for different algorithms are shown in the Table 6 (Yuanyuan & Xiyu, 2018).

*Table 6. Modularity values for different-different algorithms*

| Networks | Modularity Metric (Q) | BGLL | FN | MODPSO | QIEA-net | iQIEA-net |
|---|---|---|---|---|---|---|
| Zachary's Karate Club | Max | 0.4188 | 0.3807 | 0.4198 | 0.4198 | 0.4198 |
| | Avg | 0.4188 | 0.3807 | 0.4182 | 0.4198 | 0.4198 |
| Dolphins Social Network | Max | 0.5118 | 0.4897 | 0.5265 | 0.5213 | 0.5213 |
| | Avg | 0.5118 | 0.4897 | 0.5250 | 0.5199 | 0.5211 |
| American College Football Network | Max | 0.6046 | 0.5497 | 0.6046 | 0.5824 | 0.5988 |
| | Avg | 0.6046 | 0.5497 | 0.6015 | 0.5567 | 0.5812 |
| Political Books Network | Max | 0.4986 | 0.5020 | 0.5264 | 0.5214 | 0.5269 |
| | Avg | 0.4986 | 0.5020 | 0.5263 | 0.5209 | 0.5266 |
| Jazz Musicians Network | Max | 0.4433 | 0.4389 | 0.4449 | 0.4451 | 0.4451 |
| | Avg | 0.4420 | 0.4389 | 0.4312 | 0.4442 | 0.4450 |

**Key Findings:**Figure 3 shows the comparison of the maximum modularity values across the algorithms (Yuanyuan & Xiyu, 2018).

- iQIEA-net outperformed most algorithms in modularity metrics across multiple networks.
- Both QIEA-net and iQIEA-net showed better performance than traditional evolutionary and swarm intelligence algorithms.
- The improved convergence speed of iQIEA-net highlights its efficacy in quickly attaining optimal modularity values (Yuanyuan & Xiyu, 2018).

*Figure 3. Maximum modularities across the algorithms*

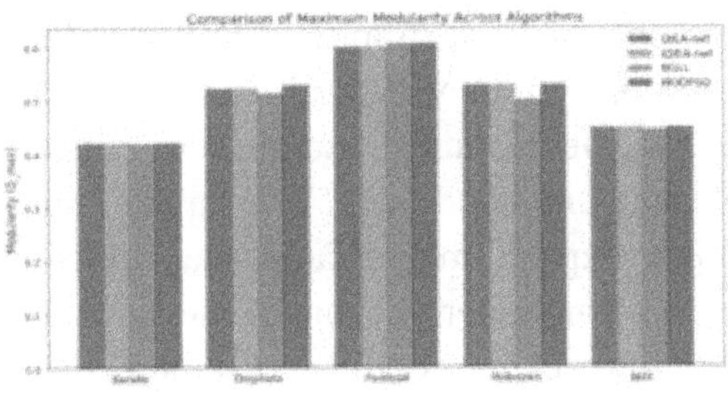


## 5. CHALLENGES AND FUTURE DIRECTIONS

HQIEAs have been conducted to indicate the occurrence of the potential for solving optimization problems, particularly in improving interaction in a community. However, like any other growing technology, there are disadvantages or rather challenges that have to be met to help the particular technology grow. This section offers further information about these problems and, simultaneously, a prospect of further research possibilities.

### 5.1 Technical Challenges

- **Scalability Issues:** However, where the sizes of the problems that have to be addressed increase, the quest for optimality in the efficiency and effectiveness of the HQIEAs becomes an issue. In case there is a need to manage more extensive datasets or more engaging community interaction paradigms the current model of HQIEAs has to be scaled which is a computationally complex process. The results given by components based on quantum computing increase the difficulty of the task more than before and that is why the methods of operation as well as the computations should be searched to decentralize the load in the best way possible to cause more performance.
- **Quantum Noise and Error Control:** Due to the imitation of quantum appearances in non-quantum hardware, errors, and noise are inevitably incurred which adversely affect HQIEAs. Even though several evolutionary algorithm methods exist, they are costly in computational terms eradicating the advantages that HQIEAs offer. The improvements of the quantum debiasing approach that could be used in future research are as follows: There is a necessity to work on the methods that would allow combating the quantum noise and errors not worsening, at the same time, the algorithm's efficiency.

### 5.2 Future Directions

- **Quantum Communications:** As the systems used for quantum computing extend, coupling of HQIEAs with the real quantum processors can be accomplished to improve the methods still more. Some might consider broadening the investigation of this area to ensure the development of the algorithms that employ the classical and quantum computing methodologies to address the computational challenges because the present state of affairs entails the lack of ability to simulate certain quantum processes on classical computers.

- **Concerning the Advancements of Evolutionary Methods:** Thus, the continuum development of HQIEAs is very much still in its infancy. It would indeed be possible to mention other methods that can be used to improve the development and propose other more complex procedures to be used in the application of quantum standards. For example, new crossover and mutation techniques based on the principles of quantum mechanics may allow the evaluation of the solutions to become much faster acting as a parameter to enhance the algorithm.
- **Broadening Applications:** However, successful social interactions with the community involved can be noted while using the HQIEAs Hence, the above can be adapted to other domains such as healthcare, financial, and smart cities among others. Other research could look into how these algorithms could be applied in solving these other optimization problems in these fields; this has the potential to have positive social effects.

## 7. CONCLUSION

The analysis of Hybrid Quantum-Inspired Evolutionary Algorithms (HQIEAs) in this chapter has clearly illustrated their effectiveness in settling various-sided optimization problems mainly in accessing detection in communities. HQIEAs uses quantum rules with the conventional heuristic algorithms hence providing a better way of solving problems that may be a challenge to traditional computing methods.

This is because when HQIEAs are implemented in communities, more effective resource acquisition, communication, and overall decision-making are realized. The results presented in this chapter are evidence of the higher effectiveness of HQIEAs in comparison with other conventional EAS in dynamic and complex problem-solving. Several open challenges can still be identified in the field, some of them among which are scaling, dealing with quantum noise, fairness of the proposed algorithms, and interpretability. These challenges will therefore have to be tackled through a conjugated approach that sees researchers from various fields such as quantum computing, evolutionary computation, ethics, etc.

For future work, the combination of HQIEAs with the quantum computing hardware, further development of the use of the evolutionary techniques, and the expansion of the field of application are very promising. In this regard, as these complex algorithms develop, it is possible to speak about the emergence of new social interactions and communities, as well as the transformation of a significant number of industries and issues in society.

## REFERENCES


Arowolo, M. O., Misra, S., & Ogundokun, R. O. (2023). A machine learning technique for detection of social media fake news. *International Journal on Semantic Web and Information Systems*, 19(1), 1–25. Advance online publication. DOI: 10.4018/IJSWIS.326120

Cade, C., Folkertsma, M., Niesen, I., & Weggemans, J. (2022). *Quantum Algorithms for Community Detection and their Empirical Run-times* (arXiv:2203.06208). arXiv. https://doi.org//arXiv.2203.06208DOI: 10.48550

Fernández-Campoamor, M., O'Meara, C., Cortiana, G., Peric, V., & Bernabé-Moreno, J. (2021). *Community Detection in Electrical Grids Using Quantum Annealing* (arXiv:2112.08300). arXiv. https://doi.org//arXiv.2112.08300DOI: 10.48550

Gan, L., Guo, Y., & Yang, T. (2024). Machine learning for depression detection on web and social media: A systematic review. *International Journal on Semantic Web and Information Systems*, 20(1), 1–28. Advance online publication. DOI: 10.4018/IJSWIS.342126

Goldberg, D. E. (David E. (with Internet Archive). (1989). *Genetic algorithms in search, optimization, and machine learning*. Reading, Mass.: Addison-Wesley Pub. Co. https://archive.org/details/geneticalgorithm0000gold

Goldberg, D. E., & Holland, J. H. (1988). Genetic Algorithms and Machine Learning. *Machine Learning*, 3(2), 95–99. DOI: 10.1023/A:1022602019183

Grover, L. K. (1997). Quantum Mechanics helps in searching for a needle in a haystack. *Physical Review Letters*, 79(2), 325–328. DOI: 10.1103/PhysRevLett.79.325

Gupta, S., Taneja, S., & Kumar, N. (2014). Quantum inspired genetic algorithm for community structure detection in social networks. *GECCO 2014 - Proceedings of the 2014 Genetic and Evolutionary Computation Conference*. DOI: 10.1145/2576768.2598277

Han, K.-H., & Kim, J.-H. (2002). Quantum-inspired evolutionary algorithm for a class of combinatorial optimization. *IEEE Transactions on Evolutionary Computation, 6*(6), 580–593. *IEEE Transactions on Evolutionary Computation*. Advance online publication. DOI: 10.1109/TEVC.2002.804320

Holland, J. H. (1992). *Adaptation in Natural and Artificial Systems: An Introductory Analysis with Applications to Biology, Control, and Artificial Intelligence*. The MIT Press., DOI: 10.7551/mitpress/1090.001.0001

Joshi, S., Koparrati, S., & Singhal, V. (2022). Marketing analytics for analyzing social media and branding efforts of indian telecom operators. *International Journal of Cloud Applications and Computing*, 12(1), 1–18. Advance online publication. DOI: 10.4018/IJCAC.297092

Li, W. (2024). Analyzing the impact of information features on user continuance intent in recommendation systems. *International Journal on Semantic Web and Information Systems*, 20(1), 1–36. Advance online publication. DOI: 10.4018/IJSWIS.353905

Li, Y., Wang, Y., Chen, J., Jiao, L., & Shang, R. (2015). Overlapping community detection through an improved multi-objective quantum-behaved particle swarm optimization. *Journal of Heuristics*, 21(4), 549–575. DOI: 10.1007/s10732-015-9289-y

Marín, E. C., González-Tejero, C. B., García, M. G., & García, F. J. S. (2022). Catholic impact evolution through public twitter data during CoVId-19. *International Journal of Cloud Applications and Computing*, 12(1), 1–17. Advance online publication. DOI: 10.4018/IJCAC.305211

Mitchell, M. (1996). *An Introduction to Genetic Algorithms*. The MIT Press., DOI: 10.7551/mitpress/3927.001.0001

Muhuri, S., & Singh, S. S. (2024). Quantum-Social Network Analysis for Community Detection: A Comprehensive Review. *IEEE Transactions on Computational Social Systems, 11*(5), 6795–6806. *IEEE Transactions on Computational Social Systems*. Advance online publication. DOI: 10.1109/TCSS.2024.3397967

Mukai, K., & Hatano, N. (2020). Discrete-time quantum walk on complex networks for community detection. *Physical Review Research*, 2(2), 023378. DOI: 10.1103/PhysRevResearch.2.023378

Narayanan, A., & Moore, M. (1996). Quantum-inspired genetic algorithms. *Proceedings of IEEE International Conference on Evolutionary Computation*, 61–66. DOI: 10.1109/ICEC.1996.542334

Nielsen, M. A., & Chuang, I. L. (2000). *Quantum Computation and Quantum Information*. Cambridge University Press.

Perez, M., & Coello, D. (2023). Sociocultural factors in times of global crisis. *International Journal of Cloud Applications and Computing*, 13(1), 1–21. Advance online publication. DOI: 10.4018/IJCAC.316868

Preskill, J. (2018). Quantum Computing in the NISQ era and beyond. *Quantum : the Open Journal for Quantum Science*, 2, 79. DOI: 10.22331/q-2018-08-06-79

Sahoo, S. R., & Gupta, B. B. (2020). Classification of spammer and nonspammer content in online social network using genetic algorithm-based feature selection. *Enterprise Information Systems*, 14(5), 710–736. DOI: 10.1080/17517575.2020.1712742

Shor, P. W. (1994). Algorithms for quantum computation: Discrete logarithms and factoring. *Proceedings 35th Annual Symposium on Foundations of Computer Science*, 124–134. DOI: 10.1109/SFCS.1994.365700

Stergiou, C. L., Psannis, K. E., & Gupta, B. B. (2022). InFeMo: Flexible Big Data Management Through a Federated Cloud System. *ACM Transactions on Internet Technology*, 22(2), 1–22. DOI: 10.1145/3426972

Talbi, & Talbi, E.-G. (2009). Metaheuristics: From Design to Implementation. In *Metaheuristics: From Design to Implementation* (Vol. 74). DOI: 10.1002/9780470496916

Yuanyuan, M., & Xiyu, L. (2018). Quantum inspired evolutionary algorithm for community detection in complex networks. *Physics Letters. [Part A]*, 382(34), 2305–2312. DOI: 10.1016/j.physleta.2018.05.044

Zhang, G. (2011). Quantum-inspired evolutionary algorithms: A survey and empirical study. *Journal of Heuristics*, 17(3), 303–351. DOI: 10.1007/s10732-010-9136-0

# Chapter 12
# Protecting Digital Assets in Cloud Environments

**Binastya Anggara Sekti**
https://orcid.org/0000-0001-5489-4888
*Universitas Esa Unggul, Indonesia*

**Mohammad Norman Gaza Laksono**
https://orcid.org/0009-0005-2863-5483
*Universitas Indonesia, Indonesia*

**Mohamad Iqbal Ajie Laksono**
https://orcid.org/0009-0007-7028-1046
*Universitas Esa Unggul, Indonesia*

**Nizirwan Anwar**
https://orcid.org/0000-0003-1189-9093
*Universitas Esa Unggul, Indonesia*

**Agung Mulyo Widodo**
https://orcid.org/0000-0002-9792-7114
*Universitas Esa Unggul, Indonesia*

**Yohanes Bowo Widodo**
https://orcid.org/0000-0001-6135-3350
*Universitas Mohammad Husni Thamrin, Indonesia*

## ABSTRACT

*Cloud computing, which offers unmatched scalability, flexibility, and cost efficiency, has completely changed the way businesses manage their digital assets. But as more and more companies move their vital data and apps to the cloud, protecting these resources has become of utmost importance. The techniques, tools, and best practices required to safeguard digital assets in cloud environments are thoroughly examined in this chapter. It starts with comprehending the different service models and other cloud models. We explore the changing threat landscape, going over both established and new threats, including ransomware, supply chain assaults, advanced persistent threats, insider threats, data breaches, and denial of service attacks. In conclusion, securing digital assets in the cloud is an ongoing journey that demands vigilance, adaptability, and collaboration. By understanding the specific risks associated with cloud computing and implementing tailored best practices, organizations can significantly reduce their exposure to threats and protect their most valuable assets.*

DOI: 10.4018/979-8-3693-8628-6.ch012

# 1. INTRODUCTION

Cloud computing has revolutionized the way organizations store, manage, and access data, offering a flexible and scalable solution without requiring direct management of physical resources. It provides remote access via the Internet, eliminating the need for local servers, platforms, or software installations (Park, Kim, Yun, & Yeom, 2020). As cloud computing evolves, it has transformed various industries, providing them with operational and competitive advantages (Azizi, Zandsalimi, & Li, 2021). The rapid development of Information and Communication Technology (ICT) has played a critical role in this transformation, making cloud computing one of the fastest-growing trends in the IT industry. It significantly affects how software is developed and how hardware resources, such as servers, are utilized, often accelerating the obsolescence of these systems (Poniszewska-Maranda, Matusiak, Kryvinska, & Yasar, 2020).

The key benefits of cloud computing—scalability, cost-efficiency, and accessibility—make it indispensable for businesses of all sizes. A smart dashboard, for example, can contain system models, connectors, optimization algorithms, and simulation engines, all stored in a private cloud for seamless management (Madni, 2021). However, with more digital assets migrating to cloud environments, the need to protect these assets from cyber threats, unauthorized access, and data misuse becomes increasingly critical.

Digital assets—data stored in electronic form—are at the core of modern business operations. The adoption of cloud computing has revolutionized how organizations manage and access these assets, yet they remain vulnerable to security threats, such as data leaks, data loss, and data breaches caused by unauthorized entities (Park et al., 2020). These threats present significant risks to organizations, particularly in industries that handle sensitive information.

In the context of Healthcare 4.0, for instance, online health systems store sensitive personal data that must be protected from cyberattacks. Cryptographic algorithms are applied to ensure secure storage, sharing, and access to medical data hosted by cloud service providers (Mahajan et al., 2023; Fairosebanu & Jebaseeli, 2023). Several cloud architectures, such as Infrastructure as a Service (IaaS), Platform as a Service (PaaS), and Software as a Service (SaaS), play a critical role in cloud adoption, each with unique benefits and challenges (Poniszewska-Maranda et al., 2020).

Cloud computing offers a variety of service models that cater to different needs and levels of management responsibilities. The three most widely used cloud models are Infrastructure as a Service (IaaS), Platform as a Service (PaaS), and Software as a Service (SaaS). Each model represents a different level of abstraction and provides varying degrees of control and flexibility for users.

Infrastructure as a Service (IaaS). IaaS provides the most basic level of cloud services, offering virtualized computing resources over the Internet. With IaaS, organizations rent infrastructure components such as virtual machines (VMs), storage, networks, and servers on a pay-as-you-go basis. In a cloud data center, multiple Virtual Machines (VMs) may run on a Physical Machine (PM) using virtualization technology. The Virtual Machine Placement (VMP) problem is the mapping of virtual machines across multiple physical machines (Azizi et al., 2021). This model allows companies to avoid the cost and complexity of buying and managing their own physical servers and data centers. IaaS is a system in which IT infrastructure is deployed in a data center as a virtual machine (Sanaj & Joe Prathap, 2020).

*Figure 1. Infrastructure as a Service (IaaS)*

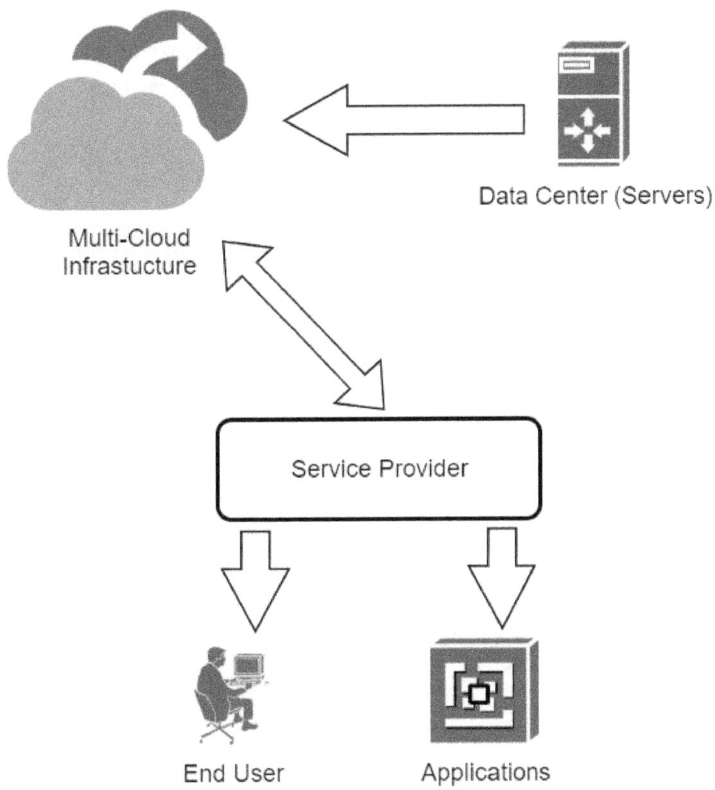


Key Features of IaaS:

- **Scalability:** Resources can be scaled up or down based on demand, making IaaS ideal for handling varying workloads.
- **Flexibility:** Users can configure and manage their infrastructure, choosing the operating systems, storage types, and security settings.
- **Cost Efficiency:** IaaS can significantly reduce capital expenditure (CapEx) since resources are rented rather than owned.

Platform as a Service (PaaS). PaaS provides a platform that allows developers to build, deploy, and manage applications without worrying about the underlying infrastructure (Bharany et al., 2022). In this model, cloud providers deliver a full development and deployment environment that includes operating systems, databases, runtime environments, and development tools.

Key Features of PaaS:

- **Application Development Focus:** PaaS environments are designed to streamline the application development process, allowing developers to focus on writing code without managing servers or storage.

- **Integrated Tools:** PaaS platforms often come with pre-configured environments for specific programming languages, frameworks, or databases, along with tools for version control, testing, and debugging.
- **Managed Infrastructure:** The cloud provider manages infrastructure elements such as scaling, patching, and security updates, allowing developers to concentrate on application logic.

*Figure 2. Platform as a Service (PaaS)*

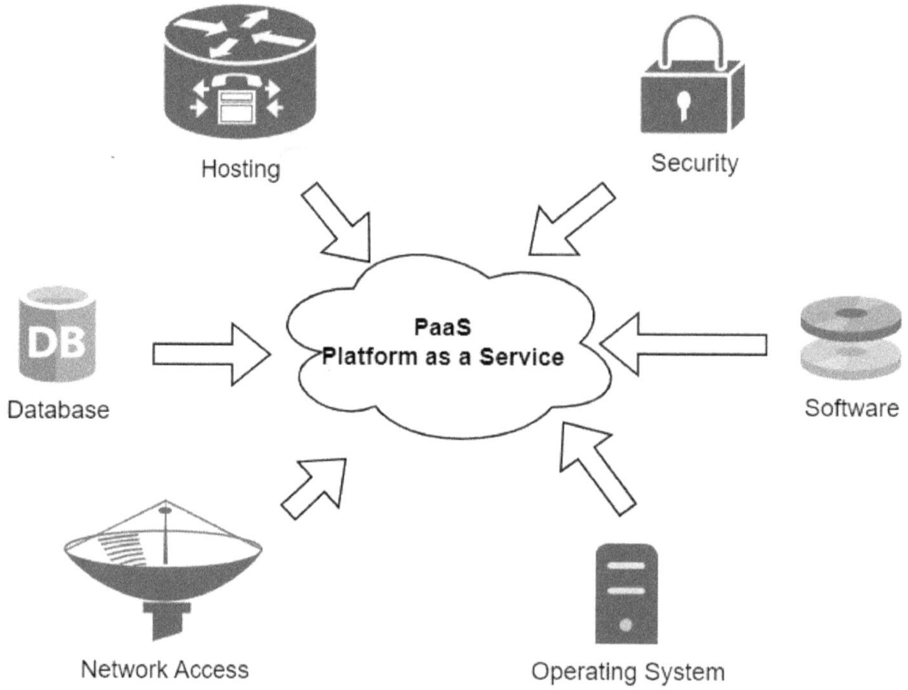


Software as a Service (SaaS). SaaS delivers fully managed software applications over the internet on a subscription basis (Xiao, Sarker, Wright, Sarker, & Mariadoss, 2020). Users can access the software from anywhere using a web browser without installing or maintaining it on their local devices. The cloud provider handles all aspects of application management, including updates, security, and performance. The development of security in the cloud with the implementation of SaaS is carried out by implementing a service architect who can make policy customization (Chang et al., 2022).

*Figure 3. Software as a Service (SaaS)*

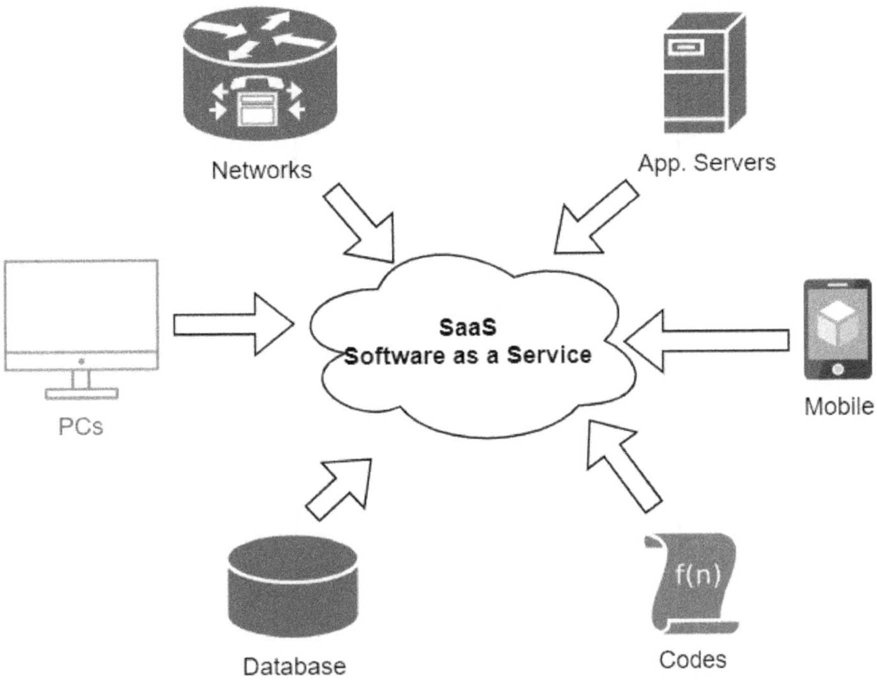


Key Features of SaaS:

- **Ease of Access:** SaaS applications are typically available via a web browser, requiring no installation or maintenance on the user's side.
- **Automatic Updates:** The provider manages software updates and patches, ensuring users always have the latest version of the application.
- **Subscription-Based Model:** SaaS applications are usually billed on a per-user or per-month basis, offering predictable costs.

*Figure 4. Cloud Computing Service ModelC (Poniszewska-Maranda et al., 2020)*

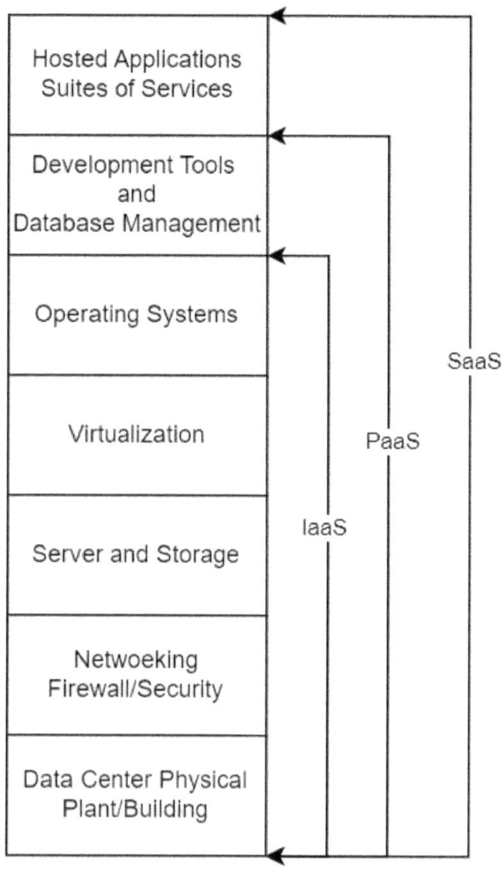


Despite the advantages of cloud computing, significant security concerns remain. Being an online-based system, cloud services are accessible from anywhere, which introduces vulnerabilities if security measures are not properly enforced. Additionally, cloud performance can suffer under high demand, such as during flash crowds—sudden spikes in user traffic, often triggered by viral social media posts. Platforms like Instagram, Facebook, Twitter, and LinkedIn experience these events, which strain cloud resources and degrade performance (Adewojo & Bass, 2023). As cloud usage grows, ensuring that cloud infrastructure can scale to meet these demands while maintaining security becomes essential. Load-balancing algorithms and resource management strategies play a crucial role in maintaining both performance and security in such situations.

This chapter will explore fundamental principles and best practices for protecting digital assets in cloud environments. Specific focus will be given to challenges unique to cloud computing, including multi-tenancy, data sovereignty, and the shared responsibility model between cloud providers and their customers. The chapter will also cover important factors for optimizing cloud security and performance, such as CPU utility, memory management, active thread counts, and network buffers, in addition to load-balancing algorithms that help optimize resource utilization. Currently, there are 3 main clout and

IoT service providers, namely Amazon Web Services (AWS), Google Clor Platform (GCP), and Azzure which use several types of Role-based Access Control (RBAC) (Bhatt et al., 2021).

## 2. UNDERSTANDING DIGITAL ASSETS IN THE CLOUD

### 2.1 Definition of Digital Assets

Digital assets refer to any content or information stored in digital form that holds value for an organization. This includes data, documents, images, videos, intellectual property, software, etc. Other examples of open digital assets, such as urban layouts, buildings, city maps, and vehicles (Madni, 2021). Other digital assets can be in the context of Non-Fungible Tokens (NFT) in the form of videos, texts, animated GIFs, and audio (Nadini et al., 2021). In a cloud environment, digital assets are often stored in virtualized data centers managed by third-party cloud service providers.

*Figure 5. Digital assets (Nadini et al., 2021)*

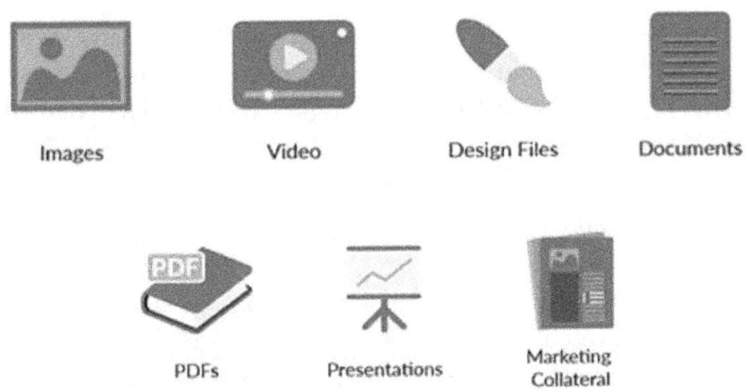


In cloud computing, computing, data communication, and data storage are currently carried out in a distributed manner. With the advent of metaverse applications, where users consume multimedia experiences resulting from real-time combinations of distributed sources, a lot of data will undergo an integration process (Cai, Llorca, Tulino, & Molisch, 2022).

### 2.2 Types of Digital Assets in the Cloud

Based on the type of structure, the data is structured and unstructured data, including customer information, financial records, and operational data.

- **Structured Data:** This includes databases that are organized in tables, rows, and columns, such as SQL databases. Structured data is typically easy to query and analyze, making it suitable for applications that require fast data retrieval and manipulation.

- **Unstructured Data:** This refers to data that doesn't have a predefined structure, such as text files, emails, social media posts, and multimedia content. Cloud storage solutions are often used to store and manage large volumes of unstructured data.
- **Big Data:** Encompasses massive datasets that require specialized cloud-based tools for processing, analysis, and storage. Examples include logs from IoT devices, large-scale e-commerce transactions, and social media analytics. Current advances have occurred in computing, multiphysics solvers, artificial intelligence, big data cybernetics, data processing, and management tools (Rasheed, San, & Kvamsdal, 2020).

Big Data in Cloud Computing:

- o Big Data refers to massive datasets that cannot be easily processed, analyzed, or stored using traditional database systems due to their volume, velocity, and variety. Cloud computing provides the necessary infrastructure to handle Big Data efficiently by offering scalable storage, high-performance computing power, and specialized tools for processing. This includes real-time data analytics, batch processing, and large-scale data storage solutions. The relationship between Big Data and cloud storage is vital, as cloud platforms enable businesses to store vast amounts of data without worrying about the limitations of on-premise infrastructure.
- o Cloud storage services such as AWS S3, Google Cloud Storage, and Azure Blob Storage offer highly scalable, cost-effective solutions for storing raw data, while cloud-based analytics tools such as Google BigQuery, AWS Redshift, and Azure Synapse Analytics allow for efficient processing and analysis. For example, a global e-commerce company may generate terabytes of transaction data, website logs, and customer behavior data every day. Storing this data in cloud-based systems like AWS S3 ensures that it is easily accessible, durable, and secure, while analytics services such as AWS Redshift or Google BigQuery can be used to perform complex queries on the data, revealing valuable insights for decision-making. Cloud-based Big Data solutions also integrate with machine learning and artificial intelligence services, enabling businesses to build predictive models and automate decision processes based on insights from their massive datasets. For instance, Azure Machine Learning integrates with Azure Databricks to process large-scale datasets and generate real-time predictions for industries such as healthcare, finance, and retail.
- o Advances in computing power, multiphysics solvers, AI, and data management tools (Rasheed et al., 2020) have further enhanced the ability to store, process, and analyze Big Data, making cloud computing the backbone of Big Data management across industries.

*Figure 6. Big data*

Figure 6 above explains that:

- Depicting the interaction between Big Data and cloud storage: Show the flow of data from IoT devices, social media platforms, and e-commerce transactions into cloud storage solutions like AWS S3, Google Cloud Storage, and Azure Blob Storage.
- Including cloud-based analytics tools: Illustrate how these data sets are processed by services like AWS Redshift, Google BigQuery, or Azure Synapse Analytics, and linked to real-world use cases such as e-commerce analytics or IoT monitoring.
- Real-world examples: Highlight specific industries or applications (e.g., retail, healthcare, finance) where Big Data is used in the cloud, focusing on how data is stored, processed, and analyzed for insights.

Other forms of data in cloud computing are outlined below.
Documents and Files, which consist of

- Text Documents: Common file formats such as Word documents, PDFs, and spreadsheets are frequently stored in the cloud for easy access and collaboration.
- Presentations and Spreadsheets: These assets are often used in business environments and are stored in the cloud for seamless sharing and editing by multiple users.
- Code Repositories: Software development projects often use cloud-based version control systems like GitHub, where code, documentation, and other related files are stored and managed.

Media Assets, which consists of

- Images and Graphics: Photos, illustrations, and design assets are stored in cloud-based platforms for use in marketing, branding, and other visual content creation.
- Audio Files: Podcasts, music files, and other audio content are often managed and distributed via cloud services to ensure broad accessibility and high availability.
- Video Content: Videos, whether for entertainment, marketing, or training, are stored in cloud environments to benefit from scalable storage and streaming capabilities.

Applications and Software is software and applications that run in the cloud, including Software as a Service (SaaS) platforms, which consists of

- SaaS Applications: Software as a Service (SaaS) applications are hosted in the cloud, allowing users to access software through a web browser without needing to install or maintain it locally.
- Microservices: These are small, modular services that are deployed in the cloud, often as part of a larger application. They can be scaled independently, offering flexibility in resource management.
- APIs: Application Programming Interfaces (APIs) are often deployed in the cloud, providing a way for different software systems to communicate and exchange data.

Intellectual Property is a proprietary algorithms, designs, and business processes that offer competitive advantages, which consists of

- Digital Rights Management (DRM) Files: These include encrypted files and licenses that control the usage of digital media, ensuring that content is accessed and used according to licensing agreements.
- Patents, Trademarks, and Copyrights: Intellectual property documentation is increasingly stored in the cloud to ensure secure, easily accessible, and organized records.

Virtual Assets, which consists of

- Virtual Machines (VMs): These are software-based representations of physical computers, running an operating system and applications. Cloud platforms allow the creation, management, and scaling of VMs on demand.

- Containers: Lightweight, portable, and executable packages that contain software and its dependencies. Containers are often used in cloud environments to ensure consistent performance across different environments.

Analytics and Insights, which consists of

- Business Intelligence (BI) Reports: BI tools generate reports and dashboards that are often stored in the cloud, allowing organizations to make data-driven decisions with real-time insights.
- Machine Learning Models: These are trained models that can be deployed in the cloud to analyze data, predict outcomes, and automate decision-making processes.

Social Media and Web Content, which consists of

- Web Pages and Blogs: These are often hosted in the cloud to ensure high availability, scalability, and performance for users worldwide.
- Social Media Content: Posts, images, videos, and other content shared on social media platforms are stored and managed in cloud environments, providing rapid access and distribution.

User Credentials is an authentication and access management data, including usernames, passwords, and encryption keys.

## 3. CLOUD SECURITY CHALLENGES

As cloud computing continues to grow in popularity, it brings with it a host of security challenges that organizations must address to protect their data and maintain compliance with regulatory standards. These challenges are inherent to the nature of cloud environments, which involve shared infrastructure, complex compliance requirements, and the need for robust data protection measures. In this section, we explore some of the most significant cloud security challenges, including the Shared Responsibility Model, Multi-Tenancy Risks, and Data Sovereignty and Compliance.

### 3.1 The Shared Responsibility Model

One of the most critical aspects of cloud security is the Shared Responsibility Model. This model is to describe security responsibilities between customers and cloud service providers (CSPs). Understanding and correctly implementing this model is essential for minimizing security risks in the cloud.

**CSP Responsibilities:** Cloud service providers are responsible for securing the physical infrastructure that supports the cloud environment. This includes maintaining the security of data centers, servers, networking equipment, and the hypervisor layer in virtualized environments. The CSP is also responsible for ensuring that their cloud services comply with relevant regulatory standards and for managing the security of the underlying cloud platform, such as patching vulnerabilities and protecting against DDoS attacks.

**Customer Responsibilities:** Customers are responsible for securing the data, applications, and workloads they deploy in the cloud. This includes implementing access controls, encrypting sensitive data, and ensuring that their cloud environment is configured securely. Customers must also manage user identities and permissions, regularly monitor their cloud environment for suspicious activity, and maintain compliance with industry regulations specific to their data and operations.

**Consequences of Misunderstanding the Model:** A common pitfall in cloud security is the misinterpretation of the Shared Responsibility Model. Some organizations may assume that their CSP is responsible for all aspects of security, leading to gaps in their security posture. For example, if a customer fails to properly configure access controls or neglects to encrypt sensitive data, this could result in a data breach, even though the CSP has secured the underlying infrastructure. Conversely, CSPs that do not clearly communicate their security responsibilities can contribute to customer confusion and potential security vulnerabilities.

## 3.2 Multi-Tenancy Risks

Multi-tenancy is a core feature of cloud environments, where multiple customers share the same physical infrastructure. While this model offers significant cost savings and resource efficiency, it also introduces unique security risks that must be carefully managed.

**Data Leakage Between Tenants:** In a multi-tenant cloud environment, there is a risk of data leakage between tenants. This can occur if there are misconfigurations in the cloud environment or if there are security vulnerabilities in the underlying infrastructure. For instance, a flaw in the hypervisor could potentially allow one tenant to access the data of another tenant. Although such breaches are rare, the potential impact can be severe, leading to loss of sensitive information and damage to an organization's reputation.

**Isolation Mechanisms:** To mitigate the risks associated with multi-tenancy, CSPs implement strong isolation mechanisms that prevent one tenant's data from being accessed by another. These mechanisms include virtual network isolation, encryption of data at rest and in transit, and strict access controls. However, the effectiveness of these measures depends on both the CSP's security practices and the customer's ability to configure their environment correctly.

**Shared Resources and Performance Impact:** Multi-tenancy can also lead to performance issues, where one tenant's use of resources impacts the performance of another tenant's applications. This is known as the "noisy neighbor" problem. While not strictly a security issue, it can affect the availability and reliability of cloud services, which are critical components of a comprehensive security strategy.

## 3.3 Data Sovereignty and Compliance

Data sovereignty is an increasingly important concern in cloud security, especially as organizations operate in a globalized environment with varying legal requirements for data privacy and protection.

**Legal Implications of Data Storage Locations:** Data sovereignty refers to the principle that data is subject to the laws and regulations of the country in which it is stored or processed. This can create significant challenges for organizations that operate across multiple jurisdictions. For example, a company based in the United States but storing data in the European Union must comply data protection regulations in EU and USA, such as the General Data Protection Regulation (GDPR).

**Challenges of Cross-Border Data Transfers:** Cross-border data transfers add another layer of complexity to compliance efforts. Different countries have different standards for data protection, and some may require that certain types of data remain within national borders. This can make it difficult for organizations to fully leverage the benefits of cloud computing, as they may need to establish multiple cloud environments in different regions or implement additional security measures to ensure compliance with local laws.

**Compliance in Multi-Cloud Environments:** Many organizations adopt a multi-cloud strategy, using services from multiple CSPs to meet their needs. While this approach offers flexibility and reduces the risk of vendor lock-in, it also complicates compliance efforts. Each CSP may have different approaches to data storage, encryption, and regulatory compliance, requiring organizations to carefully manage and monitor their cloud environments to ensure that they remain compliant with all applicable regulations.

**Strategies for Managing Data Sovereignty:** To address data sovereignty challenges, organizations can implement data localization strategies, where sensitive data is stored and processed only in specific regions that meet regulatory requirements. Additionally, organizations can work with CSPs that offer data residency options, allowing customers to choose where their data is stored. Regular audits, compliance checks, and collaboration with legal and compliance teams are also essential for managing data sovereignty risks in the cloud.

In conclusion, cloud security challenges such as the Shared Responsibility Model, Multi-Tenancy Risks, and Data Sovereignty and Compliance are critical considerations for any organization utilizing cloud services. By understanding these challenges and implementing appropriate security measures, organizations can protect their data, maintain compliance, and fully realize the benefits of cloud computing.

## 4. BEST PRACTICES FOR PROTECTING DIGITAL ASSETS

### 4.1 Encryption and Data Protection

Encryption is one of the most effective tools for protecting digital assets in the cloud. It involves converting data into a coded format that can only be accessed or decrypted by those with the correct encryption key. This practice is critical for ensuring data security, both when the data is stored (at rest) and when it is being transmitted (in transit).

**Encryption at Rest:** Encrypting data at rest ensures that information stored on cloud servers remains secure even if unauthorized individuals gain physical or virtual access to the storage systems. This is particularly important for sensitive data such as personal identifiable information (PII), financial records, and intellectual property. Cloud service providers often offer built-in encryption options, but customers should ensure that encryption keys are managed securely and consider using customer-managed keys for added control.

**Encryption in Transit:** Data in transit, which refers to data being transferred between systems, devices, or users, is vulnerable to interception. Encrypting this data using secure protocols like TLS (Transport Layer Security) ensures that even if data is intercepted during transmission, it cannot be read or altered by unauthorized parties. Organizations should enforce the use of encryption for all data transfers, including API communications, remote access connections, and data exchanges with third-party services.

**Key Management:** Effective key management is essential to the success of encryption strategies. Organizations should implement strong key management practices, including using hardware security modules (HSMs) for key storage, rotating encryption keys regularly, and restricting access to keys based on the principle of least privilege. Additionally, organizations should have clear policies for key revocation and backup to ensure keys are available when needed and securely destroyed when no longer required.

## 4.2 Identity and Access Management (IAM)

Identity and Access Management (IAM) is crucial for controlling access to digital assets in the cloud. A robust IAM strategy ensures that only authorized users have access to specific resources; and that their access is appropriate to their role within the organization. Identity and Access Management (IAM) is a cornerstone of cloud security, enabling organizations to control who can access specific resources, what actions they can perform, and under what circumstances. A well-designed IAM strategy ensures that users are granted appropriate levels of access based on their role, and unauthorized access is minimized through rigorous authentication and authorization processes.

*Figure 7. Identity and access management*

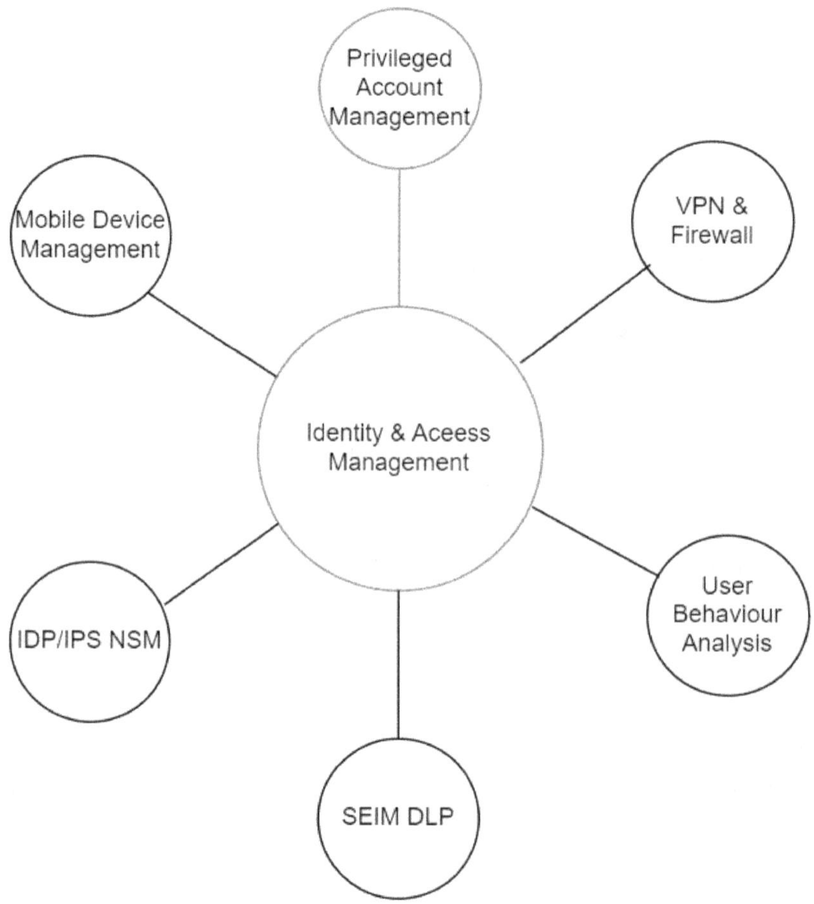


Key Best Practices for IAM:

- **Role-Based Access Control (RBAC):** Implementing RBAC ensures that users have the minimum permissions necessary to perform their duties. For instance, a developer might have access to development servers but not production environments. Cloud platforms like AWS IAM, Azure Active Directory (AAD), and Google Cloud Identity provide robust RBAC systems.

- **Multi-Factor Authentication (MFA):** Adding an extra layer of security beyond passwords, MFA can include SMS-based codes, email verification, or authentication apps such as Google Authenticator. This ensures that even if a password is compromised, unauthorized users will still be unable to access sensitive systems.
- **Least Privilege Principle:** Always assign the least amount of privilege required for a user to complete their task. This minimizes potential damage if an account is compromised.

### 4.2.1 Encryption Best Practices

In addition to IAM, encryption plays a critical role in safeguarding digital assets, both at rest and in transit. Encryption ensures that even if data is intercepted or accessed by unauthorized users, it remains unreadable without the appropriate decryption keys.

- **Encryption at Rest:** Data stored in the cloud should be encrypted using strong encryption standards to protect it from unauthorized access. The widely used AES-256 (Advanced Encryption Standard) is a highly secure method of encryption that is employed by cloud service providers such as AWS, Microsoft Azure, and Google Cloud. AES-256 offers 256-bit key encryption, which is nearly impossible to break using current computational methods.
    - AWS S3: Supports server-side encryption (SSE-S3) with AES-256 by default, ensuring that data stored in S3 buckets is always protected.
    - Azure Storage: Uses Storage Service Encryption (SSE), which also supports AES-256 to secure data at rest.
    - Google Cloud Storage: Employs Google-managed encryption keys (CMEK) or customer-supplied keys, with AES-256 encryption as the default standard.
- **Encryption in Transit:** Data moving between clients, cloud services, or within internal cloud environments must be encrypted to protect against man-in-the-middle (MITM) attacks. For data encryption in transit, TLS (Transport Layer Security) is the most widely used protocol, with versions like TLS 1.2 and TLS 1.3 offering high levels of security.
    - TLS 1.2 and TLS 1.3: Both versions provide strong encryption algorithms and are essential for secure communications. They ensure that data traveling between a user's browser and the cloud server, for example, remains encrypted and secure.
    - SSL/TLS Certificates: These certificates are used by websites and applications to initiate encrypted sessions, ensuring that sensitive information such as login credentials, payment information, and personal data remains secure during transmission.

### 4.2.2 Regular Security Audits and Monitoring

To maintain a strong security posture, organizations must conduct regular audits of their IAM policies, encryption standards, and general cloud configurations. This includes:

- **Penetration Testing:** Simulating attacks on the cloud infrastructure to identify vulnerabilities.

- **Security Information and Event Management (SIEM):** Tools like AWS CloudTrail, Azure Security Center, and Google Cloud Security Command Center (SCC) offer continuous monitoring, logging, and alerting for security events.

By combining IAM, strong encryption practices (e.g., AES-256 and TLS 1.3), and regular security audits, organizations can effectively mitigate the risks associated with storing and managing digital assets in the cloud. These best practices provide a comprehensive security framework for protecting sensitive data and ensuring regulatory compliance.

## 4.3 Regular Security Audits and Penetration Testing

Regular security audits and penetration testing are critical of a security strategy. These practices help organizations identify and address vulnerabilities before they can be exploited by attackers.

**Security Audits:** A security audit involves a comprehensive evaluation of an organization's security policies, procedures, and controls. Audits should assess compliance with internal policies and external regulations, as well as the effectiveness of security measures in place. Regular audits ensure that security practices are not only implemented but also maintained over time. Audits should also include a review of third-party services and cloud service providers to ensure they meet the organization's security requirements.

**Penetration Testing:** Penetration testing, or "pen testing," simulates cyberattacks on an organization's systems to identify vulnerabilities that could be exploited by real attackers. Penetration testing provides a realistic assessment of how well security measures can withstand an attack and helps uncover weaknesses that may not be apparent through regular audits. Organizations should conduct penetration tests regularly, especially after significant changes to their cloud environment, such as deploying new applications or migrating to a different cloud service provider.

**Continuous Monitoring and Vulnerability Management:** In addition to periodic audits and testing, continuous monitoring of cloud environments is necessary to detect and respond to security incidents in real-time. Vulnerability management processes should be established to regularly identify, prioritize, and remediate security vulnerabilities. This includes keeping systems and applications up-to-date with security patches and ensuring that cloud configurations adhere to security best practices.

## 4.4 Incident Response and Disaster Recovery

Despite the best security precautions, security incidents are still very likely. Having a well-defined incident response plan and disaster recovery strategy is crucial for minimizing the impact of such incidents and ensuring business continuity.

**Incident Response Plan:** An incident response plan outlines the steps an organization will take in the event of a security breach or cyberattack. The plan should include procedures for detecting, reporting, containing, and mitigating security incidents, as well as communication protocols for informing stakeholders. Regular training and drills should be conducted to ensure that all relevant personnel are familiar with the plan and can respond effectively in the event of an incident.

**Disaster Recovery Plan:** A disaster recovery plan focuses on restoring critical systems, applications, and data after a major incident, such as a data breach, ransomware attack, or natural disaster. The plan should include strategies for data backup, system restoration, and failover to secondary systems or cloud environments. Regular testing of disaster recovery procedures is essential to ensure that data can be restored quickly and that the organization can resume normal operations with minimal disruption.

**Data Backup and Redundancy:** Regular data backups are a cornerstone of any disaster recovery strategy. Backups should be stored in secure, geographically diverse locations to protect against regional disasters. Organizations should also implement redundancy for critical systems and data, ensuring that if one component fails, another can take over without loss of service.

**Post-Incident Review and Continuous Improvement:** After a security incident or disaster recovery event, a thorough post-incident review should be conducted to identify what went well and where improvements are needed. Lessons learned from each incident should be used to refine and enhance security policies, procedures, and response plans, ensuring that the organization is better prepared for future incidents.

By adhering to these best practices—encryption and data protection, identity and access management, regular security audits and penetration testing, and incident response and disaster recovery—organizations can create a robust security framework that effectively protects their digital assets in the cloud. As the threat landscape continues to evolve, staying proactive and continuously improving security measures will be key to safeguarding sensitive information and maintaining trust in cloud services.

## 5. CASE STUDIES

Cloud service providers such as Amazon Web Services (AWS), Microsoft Azure, and Google Cloud Platform (GCP) are the leading players in the cloud computing industry, offering various services across IaaS, PaaS, and SaaS models. These platforms offer high scalability, robust security features, and compliance options, yet they also come with unique challenges. This section will examine two case studies to illustrate both the vulnerabilities and successes in securing cloud environments.

### 5.1 Case Study 1: Data Breach Due to Misconfigured Cloud Storage

This case study investigates a high-profile data breach that occurred due to misconfigured cloud storage on AWS S3 (Simple Storage Service). The breach exposed sensitive customer information to unauthorized access, raising concerns about the security of cloud-based services.

Platform: AWS S3

- Incident Overview: In this case, a global organization storing customer data in AWS S3 had accidentally set the storage permissions to public access, allowing anyone with the correct URL to download sensitive files. This misconfiguration went unnoticed for several months, during which unauthorized individuals accessed millions of records containing customer names, addresses, and financial details.
- Causes:
    - o Misconfiguration of S3 Bucket Permissions: Instead of configuring the storage for restricted access, permissions were set to “public,” allowing open access to the stored data.
    - o Lack of Proper Monitoring and Alerts: The organization lacked automated alerts for unusual access patterns and failed to conduct regular security audits to check for such vulnerabilities.
- Impact:

- The breach resulted in significant financial losses, legal liabilities, and severe damage to the organization's reputation.
- The company faced compliance violations, particularly regarding GDPR and other privacy regulations, which resulted in hefty fines.

- Lessons Learned:
  - Importance of Default Security Settings: Organizations must ensure that default security configurations, such as restricting public access, are in place from the outset.
  - Implementation of Monitoring Tools: AWS offers services like Amazon GuardDuty and CloudTrail, which can detect and alert administrators of abnormal behavior or unauthorized access attempts in real time.
  - Regular Security Audits: Periodic reviews of cloud configurations and permissions can prevent such breaches. AWS's Identity and Access Management (IAM) should be utilized to enforce stricter policies.

This case demonstrates the critical importance of correctly configuring cloud storage settings and employing robust monitoring tools to mitigate the risk of accidental data exposure.

## 5.2 Case Study 2: Successful Implementation of Cloud Security Best Practices

This case study highlights an organization that effectively adopted cloud security best practices using Microsoft Azure, resulting in enhanced security posture and regulatory compliance.

- Platform: Microsoft Azure
- Implementation Overview: A healthcare provider implemented cloud security best practices while migrating sensitive patient data to Microsoft Azure. The organization was particularly concerned about HIPAA compliance and ensuring that patient data was securely stored and accessed.
- Key Security Practices Implemented:
  - Encryption in Transit and at Rest: The healthcare provider used Azure's Storage Service Encryption (SSE) to encrypt all data stored in its cloud services. Additionally, they employed Transport Layer Security (TLS) to protect data in transit between the cloud and end-users.
  - Multi-Factor Authentication (MFA): The organization implemented Azure Active Directory (AAD) with MFA to ensure that only authorized personnel could access the sensitive data, providing an additional layer of security beyond passwords.
  - Role-Based Access Control (RBAC): By using Azure's RBAC, the organization ensured that users were granted the least amount of privilege necessary to perform their tasks, reducing the risk of accidental data exposure.
  - Regular Penetration Testing: To identify potential vulnerabilities, the organization conducted regular penetration testing using Azure Security Center. This allowed them to proactively identify and mitigate security risks before they could be exploited.
- Impact:
  - The implementation of these best practices allowed the healthcare provider to achieve HIPAA compliance, securing patient data and avoiding potential legal issues.
  - The organization reported an improved security posture, with no significant breaches or security incidents in the two years following the implementation.

- As a result, their customer trust and brand reputation improved, giving them a competitive advantage in the healthcare industry.

- Lessons Learned:
    - End-to-End Encryption: Encrypting data both at rest and in transit is crucial for ensuring sensitive information remains secure.
    - Strong Identity and Access Management (IAM): Implementing MFA and RBAC are essential best practices for limiting access and preventing unauthorized users from compromising cloud environments.
    - Proactive Security Measures: Regular penetration testing and security assessments provide organizations with early warnings of vulnerabilities that may arise over time.

This case study showcases how leveraging Azure's security features and best practices can result in both regulatory compliance and enhanced data protection.

## 5.3 Case Study 3: Google Cloud Platform (GCP) Securing a Global E-commerce Company

This case study focuses on a global e-commerce company that leveraged Google Cloud Platform (GCP) to improve its scalability and security posture in response to increasing cyber threats.

- Platform: Google Cloud Platform (GCP)
- Implementation Overview: As the e-commerce company expanded, it needed a platform that could scale to handle the growing traffic while securing sensitive financial and customer data. GCP was chosen for its robust security features, ease of integration, and support for global-scale operations.
- Key Security Practices Implemented:
    - Zero Trust Security Model: The company adopted GCP's BeyondCorp model, a Zero Trust framework that assumes no user, inside or outside the network, can be trusted by default. All access is verified before granting any permissions.
    - Encryption and Key Management: The company utilized Cloud KMS (Key Management Service) for centralized key management and encryption at rest using Customer-Managed Encryption Keys (CMEK), ensuring that only authorized users could decrypt the data.
    - Automated Security Scans and Logging: Google Cloud's Security Command Center (SCC) was used to continuously scan for vulnerabilities and suspicious activity, providing real-time security insights and alerts.
- Impact:
    - The company successfully scaled its operations without compromising data security, maintaining both high availability and customer trust.
    - By using automated security scans and real-time alerts, the company reduced the time to detect and respond to potential threats, minimizing security risks.
    - GDPR and PCI DSS compliance were achieved due to the stringent security protocols in place.
- Lessons Learned:

- o Zero Trust Architecture: Implementing a Zero Trust security model is critical for organizations that operate on a global scale, ensuring that access is only granted after thorough verification.
- o Centralized Key Management: Using centralized encryption and key management services, like GCP's Cloud KMS, can simplify the process of securing sensitive data.
- o Proactive Security Monitoring: Continuous security monitoring through services like Google's SCC allows for early threat detection and rapid response.

This case study illustrates how GCP's advanced security features and scalability helped a global organization meet the security challenges posed by its expanding e-commerce operations.

## 6. FUTURE TRENDS IN CLOUD SECURITY

As cloud computing continues to evolve, so too will the methods and technologies for securing digital assets. Organizations must stay ahead of these developments to protect their data and maintain a robust security posture in an increasingly complex threat landscape. This section explores emerging trends that are shaping the future of cloud security, including the integration of artificial intelligence, the application of blockchain technology for data integrity, and the growing importance of zero-trust architectures.

### 6.1 Artificial Intelligence in Cloud Security

Artificial Intelligence (AI) is playing an increasingly vital role in enhancing cloud security. The ability of AI to analyze vast amounts of data, identify patterns, and make decisions with minimal human intervention makes it an indispensable tool for modern security strategies.

**AI-Driven Threat Detection:** AI can significantly improve the detection of security threats by continuously monitoring cloud environments and analyzing data in real-time. Machine learning algorithms can identify unusual patterns or behaviors that may indicate a security breach, such as an unauthorized access attempt or an unusual data transfer. AI-driven systems can provide faster and more accurate threat detection than traditional methods, enabling organizations to respond to potential incidents before they cause significant damage.

**Automated Incident Response:** AI can also be used to automate certain aspects of incident response, reducing the time it takes to contain and mitigate security incidents. For example, AI systems can automatically quarantine compromised accounts, block malicious IP addresses, or isolate affected cloud resources, all without requiring immediate human intervention. This level of automation is particularly valuable in large-scale cloud environments where manual intervention may be too slow or impractical.

**Threat Intelligence and Predictive Analytics:** Historical data analysis and threat intelligence activities, AI has the ability to predict potential security threats before they occur. Predictive analytics can help organizations proactively strengthen their defenses against emerging threats and identify vulnerabilities that could be exploited in the future. AI-driven threat intelligence platforms can also correlate data from multiple sources to provide a more comprehensive view of the threat landscape.

**Challenges and Considerations:** While AI offers significant benefits for cloud security, it also presents challenges, such as the potential for adversarial attacks where attackers attempt to deceive AI models. Additionally, the implementation of AI in cloud security requires careful consideration of data privacy, as AI systems often rely on large datasets for training and decision-making. Organizations must ensure that AI-driven security solutions are transparent, explainable, and compliant with relevant regulations.

## 6.2 Blockchain for Data Integrity

Blockchain technology, best known as the foundation for cryptocurrencies, is emerging as a powerful tool for ensuring data integrity in cloud environments. The decentralized and immutable nature of blockchain makes it an ideal solution for securing digital assets and maintaining trust in distributed cloud systems.

**Decentralized Data Management:** Blockchain enables decentralized data management, where data is stored across multiple nodes in a network, rather than in a single centralized location. This decentralization reduces the risk of data tampering or unauthorized access, as altering data on one node would require simultaneous changes on all other nodes in the network. For cloud security, this means greater resilience against data breaches and higher assurance that data remains unaltered.

**Immutable Audit Trails:** One of the key benefits of blockchain is its ability to create immutable audit trails. Every transaction or change made to data in a blockchain is recorded in a secure and unalterable ledger. This provides a transparent and verifiable record of all actions taken within a cloud environment, which is particularly valuable for compliance and forensic investigations. Organizations can use blockchain to track the lifecycle of their data, ensuring that all changes are documented and can be independently verified.

**Smart Contracts and Automated Compliance:** Blockchain can also support the use of smart contracts—self-executing contracts with the terms of the agreement directly written into code. In a cloud security context, smart contracts can automate compliance with security policies and regulatory requirements. For example, a smart contract could automatically enforce encryption policies for sensitive data or ensure that data deletion requests are carried out within a specified timeframe. This automation reduces the risk of human error and ensures consistent adherence to security protocols.

**Challenges and Adoption:** Despite its potential, blockchain adoption in cloud security is still in its early stages, and there are challenges to overcome. These include the scalability of blockchain networks, the complexity of integrating blockchain with existing cloud infrastructures, and the need for standardized protocols. However, as these challenges are addressed, blockchain is likely to become an increasingly important tool for ensuring data integrity and trust in cloud environments.

## 16.6.3 The Growing Importance of Zero-Trust Architectures

Zero-trust architectures are becoming increasingly important as organizations move more of their operations to the cloud. The zero-trust model is based on the principle of "never trust, always verify," where no user or device is trusted by default, regardless of whether they are inside or outside the network perimeter.

**Contextual Access Control:** In a zero-trust architecture, access to cloud resources is granted based on a variety of contextual factors, such as the user's identity, location, device security posture, and the sensitivity of the data being accessed. This ensures that access is only granted to those who meet strict security criteria, reducing the risk of unauthorized access. Continuous verification of these factors is also a key component of zero-trust, meaning that access permissions are regularly re-evaluated and adjusted as necessary.

**Micro-Segmentation:** Zero-trust architectures often involve the use of micro-segmentation, where the cloud environment is divided into smaller, isolated segments. Each segment has its own security controls and policies, limiting the potential impact of a security breach. If an attacker gains access to one segment, micro-segmentation prevents them from easily moving laterally across the network to access other segments. This containment strategy is particularly effective in limiting the scope of an attack and protecting sensitive data.

**Identity as the New Perimeter:** In a zero-trust model, identity becomes the new security perimeter. Traditional security models relied on securing the network perimeter, but in a cloud environment where resources are distributed and accessed remotely, identity is the primary factor determining access. This shifts the focus to strong identity management practices, such as MFA, single sign-on (SSO), and robust identity governance, to ensure that only authenticated and authorized users can access cloud resources.

**Implementation and Best Practices:** Implementing a zero-trust architecture requires a shift in mindset and a rethinking of traditional security approaches. Organizations should begin by identifying and mapping their critical assets and access points, implementing strong identity and access management controls, and deploying continuous monitoring and analytics to detect and respond to threats in real-time. Collaboration between IT, security, and business teams is essential to successfully implement zero-trust and to ensure that security does not hinder business operations.

**Challenges and Future Adoption:** While zero-trust architectures offer significant security benefits, they can be challenging to implement, particularly in large, complex cloud environments. Organizations may face difficulties in gaining visibility into all cloud resources, integrating zero-trust with existing security systems, and managing the continuous verification process. However, as cloud environments become more complex and threats more sophisticated, the adoption of zero-trust architectures is likely to accelerate, becoming a standard approach for cloud security.

## 7. CONCLUSION

Protecting digital assets in cloud environments is a dynamic and ongoing challenge that requires a comprehensive and proactive approach. As organizations increasingly rely on cloud computing for critical operations, the importance of understanding and addressing cloud security cannot be overstated. The cloud offers unparalleled flexibility, scalability, and cost-efficiency, but these benefits come with unique risks that must be carefully managed.

By understanding the unique risks associated with cloud environments—such as the complexities of the Shared Responsibility Model, the potential vulnerabilities in multi-tenant architectures, and the legal intricacies of data sovereignty—organizations can better navigate the cloud security landscape. Awareness is the first step toward effective protection; without a clear understanding of these risks, even the most sophisticated technology solutions may fall short in safeguarding digital assets.

**Implementing Best Practices:** Organizations must adopt and continuously refine best practices tailored to their specific cloud environments. This includes robust identity and access management (IAM) to ensure that only authorized individuals can access sensitive data, consistent monitoring and logging of cloud activities to detect and respond to security incidents, and regular security assessments to identify and mitigate potential vulnerabilities.

Data encryption, both at rest and in transit, should be a standard practice to protect information from unauthorized access. Additionally, organizations should develop comprehensive incident response plans that outline specific actions to take in the event of a security breach.

**Staying Informed and Adapting:** The cloud landscape is constantly evolving, driven by rapid technological advancements and shifting regulatory requirements. As new services, features, and tools become available, they bring both opportunities and challenges. To maintain a robust security posture, organizations must stay informed about the latest developments in cloud security and adapt their strategies accordingly.

This involves not only keeping up with technological trends but also understanding the changing threat landscape. Cyber threats are becoming increasingly sophisticated, with attackers leveraging new techniques to exploit vulnerabilities in cloud environments. Organizations must invest in continuous education and training for their security teams to ensure they are equipped to handle these emerging threats.

**Collaboration and Shared Responsibility:** Cloud security is not a responsibility that can be entirely outsourced to cloud service providers (CSPs). While CSPs play a crucial role in securing the infrastructure, customers must actively manage their own security responsibilities, particularly in areas such as data protection, application security, and compliance. Successful cloud security is a collaborative effort between the CSP and the customer, with clear communication and understanding of each party's role being essential.

**Future-Proofing Cloud Security:** As cloud adoption continues to grow, organizations must also focus on future-proofing their security strategies. This includes adopting a multi-layered defense approach, embracing automation and AI-driven security tools to enhance threat detection and response capabilities, and staying agile to quickly adapt to new security challenges as they arise.

Moreover, organizations should consider the broader impact of their cloud security strategies, such as their alignment with corporate governance, risk management, and sustainability goals. Integrating security into the core business strategy will help organizations build a resilient cloud infrastructure that can withstand evolving threats while supporting long-term growth and innovation.

**Final Thoughts:** In conclusion, securing digital assets in the cloud is an ongoing journey that demands vigilance, adaptability, and collaboration. By understanding the specific risks associated with cloud computing and implementing tailored best practices, organizations can significantly reduce their exposure to threats and protect their most valuable assets. As the cloud landscape continues to evolve, the ability to stay informed, adapt to new challenges, and maintain a strong security posture will be key to ensuring the safety and integrity of digital assets in the cloud.

## REFERENCES


Adewojo, A. A., & Bass, J. M. (2023). A Novel Weight-Assignment Load Balancing Algorithm for Cloud Applications. *SN Computer Science*, 4(3), 1–17. DOI: 10.1007/s42979-023-01702-7

Azizi, S., Zandsalimi, M., & Li, D. (2021). An energy-efficient algorithm for virtual machine placement optimization in cloud data centers. *Automation in Construction*, 122, 103441. https://doi.org/https://doi.org/10.1016/j.autcon.2020.103441

Bharany, S., Kaur, K., Badotra, S., Rani, S., Kavita, , Wozniak, M., Shafi, J., & Ijaz, M. F. (2022, July 02). Kavita, Wozniak, M., … Ijaz, M. F. (2022). Efficient Middleware for the Portability of PaaS Services Consuming Applications among Heterogeneous Clouds. *Sensors (Basel)*, 22(13), 5013. Advance online publication. DOI: 10.3390/s22135013 PMID: 35808508

Bhatt, S., Pham, T. K., Gupta, M., Benson, J., Park, J., & Sandhu, R. (2021). Attribute-Based Access Control for AWS Internet of Things and Secure Industries of the Future. *IEEE Access : Practical Innovations, Open Solutions*, 9, 107200–107223. DOI: 10.1109/ACCESS.2021.3101218

Cai, Y., Llorca, J., Tulino, A. M., & Molisch, A. F. (2022). Compute-and data-intensive networks: The key to the metaverse. In *2022 1st international conference on 6G networking (6GNet)* (pp. 1–8). IEEE.

Chang, V., Golightly, L., Modesti, P., Xu, Q. A., Doan, L. M. T., Hall, K., Boddu, S., & Kobusińska, A. (2022). A Survey on Intrusion Detection Systems for Fog and Cloud Computing. *Future Internet*, 14(3), 89. Advance online publication. DOI: 10.3390/fi14030089

Fairosebanu, A. A., & Jebaseeli, A. C. N. (2023). Data security in cloud environment using cryptographic mechanism. *Bulletin of Electrical Engineering and Informatics*, 12(1), 462–471. DOI: 10.11591/eei.v12i1.4590

Madni, A. M. (2021). Mbse testbed for rapid, cost-effective prototyping and evaluation of system modeling approaches. *Applied Sciences (Basel, Switzerland)*, 11(5), 1–19. DOI: 10.3390/app11052321

Mahajan, H. B., Rashid, A. S., Junnarkar, A. A., Uke, N., Deshpande, S. D., Futane, P. R., Alkhayyat, A., & Alhayani, B. (2023). Integration of Healthcare 4.0 and blockchain into secure cloud-based electronic health records systems. *Applied Nanoscience*, 13(3), 2329–2342. DOI: 10.1007/s13204-021-02164-0 PMID: 35136707

Nadini, M., Alessandretti, L., Di Giacinto, F., Martino, M., Aiello, L. M., & Baronchelli, A. (2021). Mapping the NFT revolution: Market trends, trade networks, and visual features. *Scientific Reports*, 11(1), 1–11. DOI: 10.1038/s41598-021-00053-8 PMID: 34686678

Park, J., Kim, U., Yun, D., & Yeom, K. (2020). Approach for Selecting and Integrating Cloud Services to Construct Hybrid Cloud. *Journal of Grid Computing*, 18(3), 441–469. DOI: 10.1007/s10723-020-09519-x

Poniszewska-Maranda, A., Matusiak, R., Kryvinska, N., & Yasar, A. U. H. (2020). A real-time service system in the cloud. *Journal of Ambient Intelligence and Humanized Computing*, 11(3), 961–977. DOI: 10.1007/s12652-019-01203-7

Rasheed, A., San, O., & Kvamsdal, T. (2020). Digital twin: Values, challenges and enablers from a modeling perspective. *IEEE Access : Practical Innovations, Open Solutions*, 8, 21980–22012. DOI: 10.1109/ACCESS.2020.2970143

Sanaj, M. S., & Joe Prathap, P. M. (2020). Nature inspired chaotic squirrel search algorithm (CSSA) for multi objective task scheduling in an IAAS cloud computing atmosphere. *Engineering Science and Technology, an International Journal*, 23(4), 891–902. https://doi.org/https://doi.org/10.1016/j.jestch.2019.11.002. DOI: 10.1016/j.jestch.2019.11.002

Xiao, X., Sarker, S., Wright, R. T., Sarker, S., & Mariadoss, B. J. (2020). Commitment and replacement of existing saas-delivered applications: A mixed-methods investigation. *Management Information Systems Quarterly*, 44(4), 1811–1858. DOI: 10.25300/MISQ/2020/13216

# Chapter 13
# Learning Reimagined:
## Role of AI in Empowering Classroom Education

**Rushil Chandra**
https://orcid.org/0009-0005-1647-1549
*Gujarat National Law University, Gandhinagar, India*

## ABSTRACT

*Artificial Intelligence (AI) has emerged as a transformative force in the educational sector, offering opportunities for personalized learning, enhanced student engagement, and administrative efficiency. This chapter explores the dual impact of AI on education, highlighting its potential to empower learning while also raising concerns about widening inequality. Through an analysis of technological advancements, ethical challenges, and policy considerations, this chapter examines how AI-driven educational tools can improve student outcomes but may also exacerbate existing disparities. The discussion emphasizes the importance of equitable access to AI technologies, robust governance frameworks, and teacher preparation for AI-powered classrooms. Case studies further illustrate the real-world implications of AI in education, focusing on the balance between innovation and ethics.*

## 1. INTRODUCTION

The integration of Artificial Intelligence (AI) into educational settings marks one of the most transformative developments in contemporary education. From personalized learning systems to AI-powered tutoring and administrative automation, AI has the potential to revolutionize how education is delivered, accessed, and experienced by learners worldwide (Luckin, 2017). With the promise of enhancing the efficiency, equity, and quality of education, AI-driven solutions are being embraced by educational institutions across the globe. However, as with any transformative technology, the adoption of AI in education also raises significant concerns about deepening existing inequalities, data privacy, and the ethical use of AI in learning environments (Williamson & Eynon, 2020).

This chapter seeks to critically explore the role of AI in education, focusing on whether it is primarily a tool for empowering learning or if it risks widening educational disparities. By examining the technological advancements in AI, its potential benefits, the ethical concerns it poses, and the emerging policy frameworks, this chapter aims to provide a balanced assessment of the impact of AI in modern education.

DOI: 10.4018/979-8-3693-8628-6.ch013

The focus will be on how AI can be both a democratizing force that brings personalized learning to all students and a contributor to the digital divide, which leaves marginalized populations behind.

## 2. AI IN EDUCATION: A TECHNOLOGICAL REVOLUTION

Artificial Intelligence has certainly left its footprints on the education sector with an assurance of enabling a new age personalized effective learning. As for AI applications in the education domain, they may range from adaptive learning platforms and AI tutors to automated grading systems and educational chatbots. By personalizing educational content to individual student needs, facilitating real-time feedback and automating time-consuming administrative activities, these tools aim at optimizing the learning process for both students and educators: the latter can then concentrate on more complex dimensions of teaching (Holmes et al., 2019).

By consuming a large amount of student data and predicting learning patterns, AI systems work best in processing such data to develop content that can be the most effective. Therefore, AI is particularly appealing to educational) institutions that wish to improve the way they engage with students and ensure better learning outcomes (Zawacki-Richter et al., 2019). And AI systems have the potential for sleepless, inexhaustible educational solutions which could go a long way to ease teacher shortages and bring education into regions with few resources. AI systems are very useful for that as they take away some of the manual work These AI can allocate more time to teachers which would have historically been spent on tasks like sorting students into groups, therefore freeing up more dedicated… and influences learning opportunities as well (Luckin et al., 2017).

However, while these advances are appreciated in education but the integration of AI faces severe ethical and practical problems. Data privacy, algorithmic bias and the digital divide have been pinpointed as some of the most pressing challenges that must be tackled (Williamson & Eynon 2020). With the increasing penetration of AI into educational practices, there is a growing concern about the transparency and responsibility issues in using these systems for teaching and learning processes concerning automatic decision-making.

## 3. EMPOWERING LEARNING: THE POTENTIAL BENEFITS OF AI IN EDUCATION

AI in the classroom aims to cultivate individual talent through personalized learning experiences; it is referred to as an engaging education-guiding direction. Adaptive learning platforms, which include both those powered by AI (like DreamBox) and others like Knewton, change content as the student completes courses in real-time to accommodate each learner on an individual basis as needed by adapting their personalized educational experiences accordingly (Holmes et al., 2019). This level of customisation facilitates learning at an individual pace, thus enabling students to better learn the topics and get through them before moving on. The idea of personalized learning, that had for a long time been confined to private or elite settings, is now being democratized across the masses with help from AI technologies (Luckin 2017).

One of the biggest benefits of AI in education is that it can enable instant feedback. Whether a student is achieving well in his tests, assignments or essays, your smart AI system will be able to provide feedback within seconds that he can use to understand what went wrong and correct himself. The instant connection thus allows deep learning and keeps students on their toes (Zawacki-Richter et al., 2019). With AI providing support in reducing administrative burdens such as grading, attendance tracking and scheduling, teachers have more time for curriculum development and direct interaction with students which eventually improves the quality of education (Holmes et al., 2019).

In addition to that, we have seen AI technology improving accessibility for students with disabilities. Voice recognition software, AI-enabled language translation and accessibility tools for visually/hearing impaired students support educational inclusion (Williamson & Eynon 2020). It will also contribute to breaking down language limitations, or in other words; while imparting education and learning students can help of support mechanisms like multilingual interfaces through AI-based technologically driven inclusive educational solutions (Luckin, 2017).

Additionally, AI can help fill the gap between places like rural parts of our world where limited resources or teacher shortages impede access to a quality education. AI-powered platforms can augment conventional training models, hence offering students in disadvantaged areas access to an expanded number and higher quality learning resources they may not have access otherwise. This scalability has the potential to democratize education, enable superior learning experiences available for a greater number and range of students globally (Holmes et al., 2019).

Although the promise of AI is great, we should not lose sight of potential risks and social inequities that may arise if AI technologies are unequally distributed or made available to all. Indeed, with widespread adoption of AI in educational technologies, which could even deepen existing disparities on the quality of education if there is no active intervention for ensuring equal access to these tools (Williamson & Eynon 2020).

Figure 1 below is 2024 research in the U.S. wherein adult's opinion on the impact of AI on education in the U.S. is studied gender-wise (YouGov, 2024). The study found that around 37% men respondents perceived that AI would benefit education as opposed to 29% men respondents. However, 44% of men respondents were either not sure about the impact or perceived it to be both positive and negative. On the other hand, only 27% women perceived that AI would benefit education whereas 36% women respondents perceived it to have negative impact while the remaining 37% respondents were either not sure about the impact or perceived it to be both positive and negative.

*Figure 1. Adult's opinion on the effect of AI on education in the U.S., by gender (2024)*

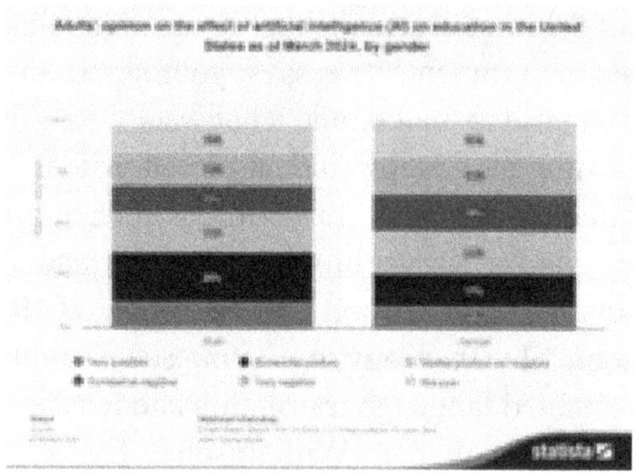

Figure 2 below depicts the value of AI investment deals in education industry in China from the year 2012 to early 2019. The statistics show an increasing trend in AI investment in the education industry (EqualOcean, 2019).

*Figure 2. Value of AI investment deals in education industry in China from 2012 to early 2019.*

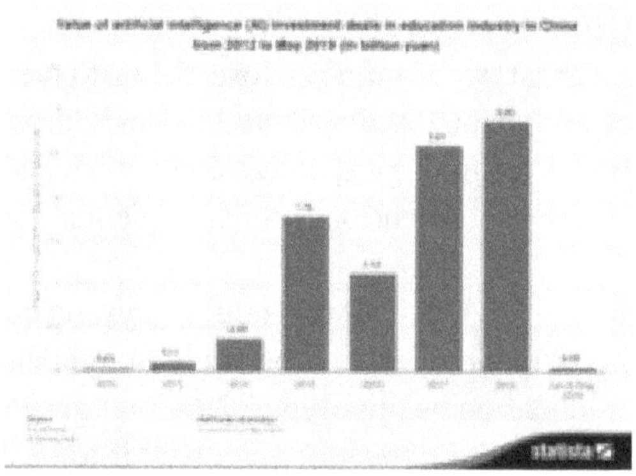

Figure 3 is research undertaken in the year 2018 on the question whether AI applications will aid global education in India or not. 89% of the respondents believed that AI is important for global education (PwC, 2018).

*Figure 3. Share of participants who believe AI applications will aid global education in India*

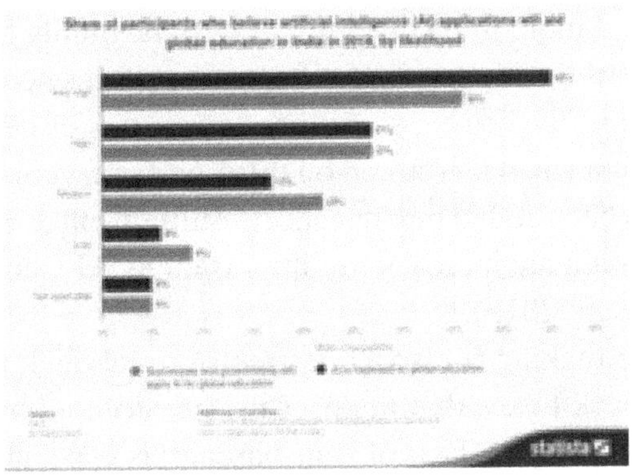

## 4. WIDENING INEQUALITY: THE DARK SIDE OF ARTIFICIAL INTELLIGENCE

While there are high hopes attached to the power of Artificial Intelligence (AI) in education, worries have also increased that it could mirror and intensify inequalities. For example, the so-called digital divide creates unequal opportunities for access to AI-powered educational tools and is particularly felt among different socioeconomic groups (Williamson & Eynon, 2020). AI schools in well-funded districts or countries with more money often already have access to state-of-the-art AI technologies, while underfunded ones — especially those based in the developing world, looking to effectively introduce even basic digital infrastructure struggle. This rift threatens to make a two-tier education system — one in which privileged students receive personalized AI-enriched learning, and another for those who are disadvantaged with resources that have either gone out of date or been inadequate (Zawacki-Richter et al., 2019).

They enable algorithmic bias and reinforcing inequities. If an AI system is fed biased data, then the decisions it makes may compound and exacerbate already present biases in society (Binns, 2018). For example, if AI systems are fed with datasets that contain biases in it then system may end up recommending wrong or inaccurate recommendations to minority/marginalized students. It might have a negative effect on student performance especially, the auto grading tools in AI based student assessments; where biassed algorithms can give unfair decisions (O'Neil, 2016).

And the expense of deploying AI technologies raises a barrier to entry. A significant portion of the AI-powered platforms and tools are expensive, which restricts their access largely to well-funded educational bodies. The financial barrier this presents ensures that students of low socio-economic status (SES) and typically under-represented in top academic institutions are disadvantaged when starting with AI, further widening the educational divide between populations (Selwyn et al., 2019).

In addition, there is a fear that the rise of AI systems in teaching (and learning) could reduce the role human teachers play in under-resourced contexts. With AI taking over more and more tasks, that teachers currently do, there is a real danger of students in low-income or rural regions being educated by machines while their wealthier counterparts continue to have teacher-student interaction thus continuing the stereotypes (Holmes et al., 2019).

## 5. THE ETHICAL CONSIDERATIONS OF AI IN EDUCATION

When AI integrates more and more into education, it will inevitably bring a large number of ethical challenges. Data privacy is one of the biggest issues here. AI systems need data on a scale to work well, and in education that often means harvesting significant quantities of personal student information. In particular, the security of this data when it is stored on third-party servers — or when shared with private companies more broadly — has been called into question (Williamson & Eynon 2020). The safeguarding and appropriate use of student data are increasingly important as AI technology permeates educational innovation (Zawacki-Richter et al., 2019).

Transparency in AI decision making is also a question. A great deal of AI systems, especially those reliant on deep learning, are black boxes that the user neither do not know nor have control over how decisions emerge (Pasquale 2015). Such lack of transparency is especially worrying in the context of education, as student's lives take unforeseen paths due to hidden AI algorithms. For example, an AI system may identify a student as high-risk or suggest remedial support without providing any explanation for its determination. This could pose problems of accountability and unfairness (Binns, 2018).

A further ethical concern surrounds student autonomy. According to Selwyn (2019) as AI systems start deciding on what a student learns and potentially even the career s/he should enter, this carries potential for students' agency pertaining their learning pursuit. If, as students and educators alike, we accept the AI-driven recommendations at face value then it could lead to certain educational pathways being laid out for them without truly appreciating or consenting to this decision. AI systems should not reduce stakes for students, instead it will increase the sense on education by students (Luckin, 2017).

In addition, a major ethical problem that may come with algorithms is algorithmic bias. AI can also create and exacerbate social inequities, providing discriminatory results for some student populations. This is especially troubling in education, where AI systems that are biased could serve to reinforce the disadvantages suffered by already-marginalized groups (O'Neil 2016). We need to advance our ethical frameworks so that AI in education will work fairly and inclusively.

## 6. POLICY AND GOVERNANCE: REGULATING AI IN EDUCATION

The recent adoption of AI in education has prompted the need for policy frameworks and governance structures to ensure responsible use of AAIS. There is also growing political and public support for the regulation of AI technologies to prevent abuse, facilitate justice in access and implementation (Williamson & Eynon 2020).

One major prickly issue is regulating data privacy. AI systems generate massive student data; governments and educational bodies must define the scope of permissible collection, use, storage and sharing South Korea has implemented a national talent programme – what it calls "smart education" — that relies on AI algorithms to optimise placement of Grades 9-12 students... This involves adhering to current data protection laws, such as the General Data Protection Regulation (GDPR) in Europe and developing further protections where needed (Zawacki-Richter et al., 2019). Selwyn (2019) emphasises the need for a greater burden of responsibility on schools and educational institutions to safeguard young people's information, as well as increased accountability with respect to how AI-driven technologies are implemented in ways that comply with stringent privacy criteria.

Secondly, there is an urgent need to regulate AI algorithms so that they are transparent and fair. Finally, governments and educational authorities should develop policies that require the exposition of decisional processes behind AI systems and monitor those in order to remove bias (Pasquale 2015). Given that AI technologies in education are frequently developed and deployed by multinational companies to users across countries, international collaboration is key.

There is also mounting pressure for policies that address equity in AI. Access to AI educational tools should be available for all students regardless of socioeconomic circumstances. This might include public investment in AI infrastructure for under-resourced schools, and subsidies to get more students access to AI-powered learning tools, as well as public-private partnerships that are designed specifically with the intention of ameliorating at least part of today's digital divide (Williamson & Eynon 2020).

## 7. CASE STUDIES: AI IN EDUCATION - SUCCESSES AND CHALLENGES

**Case Study 1. Personalized Learning in Developed Nations:** We see that schools (especially, in example of countries like the US and UK) already adopt AI driven personalized learning platforms allowing students to have individualistic customized experiences. An example of this is the capacity in platforms like DreamBox and Knewton which take account for nuances such as pedagogic learning styles and paces, to create tailored content from what students have memorised (Luckin 2017). These tools appear to have been associated with student level increased engagement and achievement, specifically in mathematics arid reading (Holmes et al., 2019). There was a significant expounding of the advantages, but these have been limited largely to well-endowed institutions that can afford such infrastructure and tackle immediate commitments (Williamson & Eynon, 2020); this flags larger concerns around inequality.

**Case Study 2. The Digital Divide in Developing Countries:** Whereas developing countries encountered tough situations to implement AI tools for education. Meaning adequate basic simple digital infrastructure, using AI-driven learning tools is unfeasible in schools across different regions (Zawacki-Richter et al., 2019). In many cases, AI technology is limited by access to a tiny segment of the population — typically city-slickers or wealthy folk. Due to the substantial discrepancies in infrastructure and AI access, rural or low-income students will find themselves on an uneven playing field (Selwyn, 2019).

**Case Study 3. Special Education AI for Specially Abled Students:** Specially-able students are also benefited by application of AI technologies. Such as AI-based speech-to-text and text translation tools to help make it more accessible for a deaf student in the class (Williamson & Eynon, 2020). For students with visual impairments, AI tools that can convert text to speech and vice versa have been used similarly. If utilised properly these technologies can make educational more inclusive and accessible (Luckin, 2017) but the cost of access is one likely reason increased use has not been seen.

**Case Study 4. Mitigating Bias in AI Systems:** One of the biggest hurdles for any AI-driven education system, however, has been tackling algorithmic bias. In the US, there are issues with a live AI system that is supposed to determine your performance on standardized test and admission (GRE in this case). A number of studies have found that AI systems are more likely to treat students from minority communities tendentiously; these findings reflect broader social biases (O'Neil, 2016). This has led to efforts developing more inclusive AI systems that are better for the diverse student body and work at reducing bias in education outcomes (Binns, 2018).

## 8. AI AND THE FUTURE OF EDUCATION

The future of education is bound to be significantly shaped by the development in this domain as Artificial Intelligence (AI) continues to grow. AI has the ability to transform how students learn, teachers teach, and educational institutions operate. Personalized Learning Experiences: AI in education is the most promising role to check One of the biggest upsides of using AI for Personalized learning experiences. AI systems can be used to analyse the input data of individual students, just as a tutor would do in the classroom with their knowledge about learning styles and prior attainment to propose content that is suitable for each student (Luckin 2017). If This was employed, it could lead to large increases in student engagement and success as learners would always be taught at their zone of proximal development, utilizing the medium which best suits how they learn (Holmes et al., 2019).

In addition to this, AI could automate certain administrative functions freeing up teachers' time which they can spend on teaching and interacting with students. AI can help in reducing the administrative load on teachers by taking care of tasks like grading, scheduling and attendance so that they have more time to devise innovative lessons (Williamson & Eynon, 2020). This has the potential to create a better, more efficient education system and free teachers up for what should be their primary focus: teaching.

Yet, the use of AI in education brings a critical question to this — what will be the future for human educators? Although AI can help with administrative tasks and furnish customized learning opportunities, it is not a substitute for the social-emotional skills, mentoring or advice that human teachers provide (Selwyn 2019). As AI is used more extensively in education, there will be a greater need to re-imagine the role of teachers so that technology not only does things for us but also with and by means of we humans (Luckin 2017).

In addition, the future of AI in education may also involve intelligent tutoring systems. Similar to a human tutor, these systems enable students to receive real-time feedback and support (Zawacki-Richter et al. With continuous improvements to AI-powered tutoring systems, students without access to traditional Tutoring services may be able to get a hold of high-quality educational support for themselves.

The potential of AI certainly extends to assessment practices in education as well. Moreover, traditional methods of assessment (especially things like standardized tests) are simply not efficient in recognizing the total potentiality a student brings to learning. AI systems, however, are able to analyse a number of features related to student performance such as problem-solving skills; creativity and collaboration (Williamson & Eynon 2020). If done right, AI could be used to provide a more comprehensive assessment of student learning than traditional testing methods allow.

## 9. THE PATH FORWARD

As AI evolves and begins to play a more significant role in the context of educational experiences, it is important we consider what challenges as well as opportunities await. In education, we must work together to get AI right. This involves the collaboration of educators, policymakers, technology developers and researchers on how to have transparent AI systems which are fair and inclusive (Binns 2018).

Equally important in the years to come is making sure that AI technologies are available fairly for all. Both the government and educational institutions need to invest in infrastructure such as web capability and IT resources that would facilitate AI-based learning among all students—including those who hail from different economic backgrounds (Holmes et al., 2019). This might involve direct investment in schools that are at risk of falling behind, along with policies designed to incentivize rapid deployment of AI across the educational enterprise.

High-quality policies and governance frameworks are also necessary to guide the application of AI in education. These regulations should emphasize preserving data privacy, mandatory transparency of AI decision-making processes and tackling algorithmic bias (Pasquale 2015). It is possible for policymakers to proactively intervene and guide the use of AI, setting clear expectations around quality standards.

Another focus will be on training educators for the AI classroom. Using AI effectively in teaching is a new skill educators will have to learn. Future teachers will need support in the form of professional development programs focused on how to deploy AI technologies not only into learning and teaching routines, but also with due consideration for — as well as awareness about— many ethical and practical issues associated with their use (Luckin 2017). If we arm teachers with the knowledge and abilities they require, ensure AI ameliorates instead of obliterates teaching.

Lastly, we need to bring students into conversation around AI in education. It is important to empower learners with the ability to understand how AI works and what opportunities it can bring about, as well as an appreciation for where its limitations lie. Through developing digital literacy and teaching critical understanding, we can help turn students away from becoming naively competent in general as users of AI technologies (Selwyn, 2019). This will help students walk their way in a world that is more and more dependent on AI, which at the same time allows them to engage with setting the stage themselves for how education could look like.

## 10. CONCLUSION

In education, AI can be a game-changer — from customizing learning experiences to automating administrative processes and delivering intelligent tutoring systems that advance student performance. While AI in education is potentially revolutionary, there are also huge downsides to consider — the way that it can further inequality and propagate bias; how exactly young people will negotiate their place within these spaces designed (and seemingly required) by adults. Therefore, it is crucial to develop policies and governance frameworks that address how AI should be introduced so as not to perpetuate disparities in student experience. On the one hand educators need to be trained — not only in skills and knowledge that make it possible for them effectively incorporate AI into their practices but also students should understand these technologies, how they work, when can use it. Working collectively, stakeholders can build a system of education in which AI complements learning without losing the important human qualities that are critical to student development.

Moving forward, the challenge of reconciling innovation with ethics in AI-enabled education will be met through cooperation and transparency to ensure that we not only work together for an equitable future where all learners stand to benefit from educational AI. The future of education is deeply linked to AI, and it's our duty to ensure that this future brings with it opportunity, equity and empowerment.

## REFERENCES


Binns, R. (2018). Fairness in machine learning: Lessons from political philosophy. *Proceedings of the 2018 Conference on Fairness, Accountability, and Transparency*, 149-159.

EqualOcean. (June 12, 2019). Value of artificial intelligence (AI) investment deals in education industry in China from 2012 to May 2019 (in billion yuan) [Graph]. In Statista. Retrieved December 09, 2024, from https://www-statista-com.elibrary.siu.edu.in/statistics/1026507/chinese-ai-investment-deals-in-education-industry/

Holmes, W., Bialik, M., & Fadel, C. (2019). *Artificial intelligence in education: Promises and implications for teaching and learning*. Center for Curriculum Redesign.

Luckin, R. (2017). Towards artificial intelligence-based assessment systems. *Nature Human Behaviour*, 1(3), 1–3. DOI: 10.1038/s41562-016-0028

O'Neil, C. (2016). *Weapons of Math Destruction: How Big Data Increases Inequality and Threatens Democracy*. Crown.

Pasquale, F. (2015). *The black box society: The secret algorithms that control money and information*. Harvard University Press. DOI: 10.4159/harvard.9780674736061

PwC. (February 14, 2018). Share of participants who believe artificial intelligence (AI) applications will aid global education in India in 2018, by likelihood [Graph]. In Statista. Retrieved December 09, 2024, from https://www-statista-com.elibrary.siu.edu.in/statistics/823674/india-opinion-on-artificial-intelligence-assisting-global-education-by-likelihood/

Selwyn, N. (2019). Should robots replace teachers? AI and the future of education. *Polity*.

Williamson, B., & Eynon, R. (2020). Artificial intelligence in education: What is it, and why should we care? *Learning, Media and Technology*, 45(2), 102–113.

YouGov. (April 9, 2024). Adults' opinion on the effect of artificial intelligence (AI) on education in the United States as of March 2024, by gender [Graph]. In Statista. Retrieved December 09, 2024, from https://www-statista-com.elibrary.siu.edu.in/statistics/1462497/opinion-ai-effect-education-gender-united-states/

Zawacki-Richter, O., Marín, V. I., Bond, M., & Gouverneur, F. (2019). Systematic review of research on artificial intelligence applications in higher education – where are the educators? *International Journal of Educational Technology in Higher Education*, 16(1), 39. DOI: 10.1186/s41239-019-0171-0

# Chapter 14
# Exploring Ethical and Cultural Considerations in Metaverse-Based Digital Marketing

**Ruchika Rastogi**
https://orcid.org/0000-0001-7144-4387
*Pranveer Singh Institute of Technology, Kanpur, India*

**Mohammad Irfan**
https://orcid.org/0000-0002-4956-1170
*Christ University, Bengaluru, India*

## ABSTRACT

*New opportunities for digital marketing have emerged with the emergence of the metaverse, a virtual setting where users can communicate with one another and other digital beings. This article tries to investigate the cultural and ethical issues of metaverse-based digital marketing. It is crucial to consider the ethical ramifications of these behaviours as marketers increasingly use the metaverse as a platform for connecting with and engaging with consumers. This cover concerns including consent, data security, and privacy. The massive collection of personal information in the metaverse raises questions regarding its use, storage, and security. It becomes crucial to provide openness, responsibility, and user control over their data in order to preserve consumer and marketer confidence. Cultural factors are as crucial for digital marketing that uses the metaverse. The metaverse is a worldwide network with participants from many racial and cultural origins. Marketing professionals must be aware of cultural conventions, beliefs, and sensitivities in order to prevent unintentionally offending people or feeding prejudices. Users may have a terrible user experience and react negatively to cultural appropriation, misrepresentation, and exclusionary practices. Therefore, it is essential for encouraging favourable brand perception and user engagement to include cultural diversity and inclusivity into marketing tactics within the metaverse. This article discusses several ethical and cultural issues that marketers in the metaverse face and suggests solutions. It highlights the requirement for unambiguous moral principles and business norms that are consistent with the principles of user empowerment, privacy, and inclusivity. Additionally, it emphasizes the significance of cultural sensitivity and localization in order to efficiently and politely customize marketing messages to various audiences inside the metaverse. Marketers can design meaningful and genuine user experiences while avoiding potential problems by taking the ethical and cultural aspects*

DOI: 10.4018/979-8-3693-8628-6.ch014

*of metaverse-based digital marketing into account. This work will aid in the creation of ethical and culturally aware marketing techniques within the metaverse, encouraging consumer participation, trust, and beneficial brand-customer connections in this new digital environment.*

## 1. INTRODUCTION

Digital marketing is one of the interactive marketing to retain customers. Companies use websites, emails, search engines, and social media websites for digital marketing. It is generally said that the first step to enter in the digital marketing is to have a beautiful website which should visually appealed to the customers (Ali & Khan, 2023). Talking further about the new things in digital marketing is metaverse marketing. Neal Stephenson first used the word "Metaverse" to refer to a virtual reality setting that was beyond the scope of the internet at the time in his science fiction book Snow Crash from 1992 (Sparkes, 2021). However, with the quick development of technology and the appearance of platforms for virtual and augmented reality, the idea of the Metaverse has grown more and more likely. In essence, the Metaverse is a fully immersive virtual reality world where users can seamlessly and realistically interact with one another and with digital items. Businesses are beginning to look into the Metaverse's possibilities as a marketing tool as it gains acceptance and accessibility. Other people believe it to be a "black hole of consumption" that feeds users' fantasies (Bogost, 2021). However, it is more than just a fad; it is a fundamental shift that has already set the path for the future (Lee, 2021). It is evident that small, medium, and large organizations collaborate to create metaverse ecosystems and simulate the actual world (Caulfield, 2021).

It was the vision of Zukerberg to create a platform where a user can see himself /herself with the people in a place rather than only a spectator (Biocca et al., 2003). It was his vision to facilitate activities like sports, education, and socialization which was beyond the imagination of human beings. It represents a new change in the world of the internet, characterized by many factors like interactivity, simulation, decentralized environment, and persistence reality (Mourtzis et al., 2022). Companies like Snoop Dogs and Paris Hilton use metaverse to show their collection to the customers where they can surf and buy the products.

In digital marketing, ownership is by networks and by the individuals whereas in metaverse, the ownership is by individuals. Digital marketing has a business model of B2B (Business to Business), B2C (Business to Consumers) and D2C (Direct to consumers) but in metaverse its all about D2A (Direct to Avatars).

Despite the abundant data availability of literature on metaverse, this concept will increase immensely with the development of AI, Block technology, Augmented reality and Virtual reality. This paper will focus on certain aspects like a) The role of metaverse in digital business, b) Cultural and ethical aspects of metaverse in digital business, and c) Importance of data analytics in a metaverse business environment.

## 2. LITERATURE REVIEW

The implementation of metaverse is not cost effective as it needs to revamp the procedures and infrastructure too. Installation of software, training, and other changes increases the cost of implementation of metaverse (Khatri, 2022). High-cost implementation comes with benefits too. It provides real time experience to the customers in a 3D environment like some gaming giants provide. For advertisement, metaverse will use smart cities with different marketing trends and customer's perceptions. As per the latest trends, metaverse can disseminate information easily to a large number of customers (Gadalla et al., 2013). Metaverse allows marketers to work on influence marketing which creates awareness of the brand and the customers can enjoy this with their avatars. By this, customers can interact with bloggers, content creators, and influencers which increases the product understanding of the customer. Virtual rooms, conferences, and seminars are the part of metaverse where virtual interaction between marketers and the customers can be done easily (Kraus et al., 2022).

Metaverse is creating milestones in marketing. It can be seen as Facebook has rebranded itself as "Meta". Snapchat has already used various AR applications in social media and customers are enjoying this. Big companies like Gucci and Prada have also used metaverse in designing and knowing the choices of customers through AR and VR. Apple has announced to invest 30 trillion US dollar in metaverse which can bring revolution in metaverse marketing (Dawson, 2022).

Metaverse can help marketers to be highly imaginative where they can offer creative and unique combinations of goods to the customers, which is not possible in physical space. Generally, advertisement is considered to be a part of one-way communication but metaverse makes the advertisement more interactive and lead to much more robust purchase of the goods and services. Adidas has launched virtual wearables and artwork of Lamborghini has created another kind of revenue model with the help of metaverse (Gautam, 2022).

Target market of metaverse is different as they are targeting generation X, generation Y and generation alpha. Their understanding because of gaming is much stronger to use and understand metaverse marketing (BE Staff, 2022). Many innovations are in line and influencing youth to purchase avatars of their choices with different outfits.

However, there are certain drawbacks and challenges which are very novel and different. It creates technical and infrastructural issues to understand the multicultural metaverse. It's also not easy for the companies to adapt and tech customers to use AR and VR headsets and other related accessories (Dolan et al., 2016). Conventional retailing which has already become the part and parcel of the customers, it will be very tough to take the customers on this platform. Initially, lots of efforts are to be put by the marketers to understand the consumption pattern of the customers regarding metaverse. Companies like Apple, and Gucci are actively participating in metaverse as these companies are organising events on this platform and giving opportunities to the customers to purchase in virtual space (Faridani, 2022). It is also very challenging to survive in real time and in a 3D virtual world. Even if companies are able to manage everything initially on metaverse, there may be some scalability issues. It can be said that metaverse has benefits but challenges too which is to be understood by the marketer well advanced.

There is no certainty regarding the behaviour and responses of the customers when they will interact in the metaverse. There could be a possibility of strategic war for the different brands to choose the best metaverse platform. Different platforms should also analyze the skills, capabilities, and interest of the customers to use the metaverse in future for their personal and professional work (Dolan et al., 2016).

## 2.1 Metaverse

In recent years, digital marketing has become an important part of marketing strategies. The advent of social media, e-commerce, and online advertising has changed the way businesses interact with customers and market their products. But Metaverse has the potential to take digital marketing to a new level.

In the Metaverse, businesses can create the best experiences for businesses that engage with customers in ways that digital marketing cannot. For example, in a virtual reality store, customers can browse, interact with, and even try products before purchasing in an authentic, immersive environment. The potential of immersive products go beyond the retail store. In Metaverse, businesses can create interactive and immersive experiences for customers in any industry. For example, virtual reality experiences in the travel industry allow customers to explore destinations and activities before traveling. In the entertainment industry, virtual reality concerts and events can provide fans with an immersive experience. The possibilities are endless. Metaverse is a virtual space closely associated with technologies such as Augmented Reality (AR) and Virtual Reality (VR) (Ali & Khan, 2023). It offers real time opportunities without creating virtual needs. The term took on more meaning when social distancing was ordered during Covid19. Marketers use many digital platforms to promote their products, but thinking about products and services requires innovation.

*Figure 1. Metaverse opportunities*

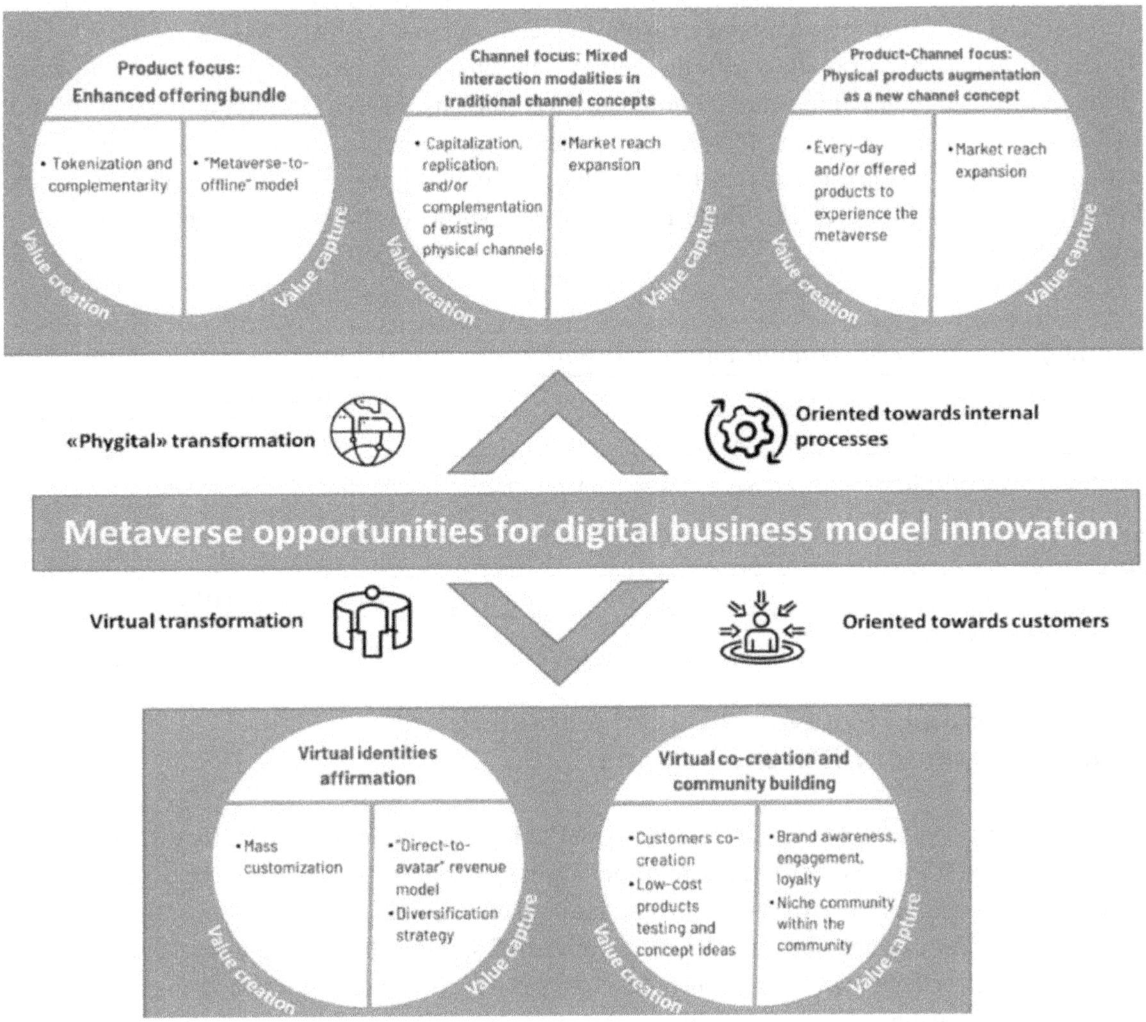


A new virtual world is created by metaverse which creates value around two main concepts i.e., internal process and the customers (Marcon et al., 2022). It is shown in Fig. 2. that internal process consists of product, channel and product-channel process which talks about metaverse to offline model, market reach expansion and new products/services. Its all called "phygital transformation" which allows users to be a part of both physical and digital world.

Instead metaverse create opportunities for customers which focus on direct to avatar models and product testing in pure digital and virtual world.

## 2.2 Digital Marketing

"Digital marketing is the marketing of products or services using digital technologies, mainly on the internet, but also including mobile phones, display advertising, and any other digital medium" (Desai, 2019). Digital marketing is possible with the help of the internet which is a communication platform and through this tool, many things are communicated to the customers (Olsan et al., 2021). With the use of the internet and other technologies, digital marketing has replaced the traditional methods of marketing (Alnsour, 2018). It has given the advantage of reducing the cost and growing the business world widely (Rafiq & Malik, 2018). Table 1 is mentioned below for the difference between digital and metaverse marketing.

*Table 1. Difference between digital and metaverse marketing*

| Digital Marketing | Metaverse Marketing |
|---|---|
| Ownership of digital platform is by networks and firms. | Ownership by the individuals. |
| Transaction is physical and digital | Transaction is digital and virtual |
| Merchandising is Physical and digital | Merchandising is virtual only |
| There is a need of warehouse in digital marketing | There is no need of warehouse in metaverse marketing |
| Business model is B2B, B2C, and D2C | Business model is D2A |

## 2.3 Global Trends in Metaverse-Based Marketing and their Implications for Different Regions

Here are some global trends in metaverse-based marketing and their implications for different regions:

**Trend 1:** Rise of Virtual Advertising and Immersive Experiences: Brands are increasingly using virtual advertising and immersive experiences to engage consumers in the metaverse (Ianenko et al., 2023); (Ramadan, 2023). For example, brands are setting up virtual storefronts, hosting virtual events, and creating interactive experiences that allow consumers to try products and services in a virtual environment.

**Regional Implications:** This trend is likely to be particularly impactful in regions with high levels of internet and smartphone penetration, such as North America, Europe, and East Asia. These regions also have a large number of early adopters of new technologies, which could make them more receptive to metaverse-based marketing (Dwivedi et al., 2022).

**Trend 2:** Growing Importance of Virtual Influencers and User-Generated Content: Virtual influencers and user-generated content are becoming increasingly important in the metaverse (Aria et al., 2023); (Lee et al., 2021). Brands are partnering with virtual influencers to promote their products and services, and they are also encouraging users to create and share their own content about their experiences in the metaverse.

**Regional Implications:** This trend is likely to be particularly impactful in regions with a strong culture of influencer marketing and social media, such as East Asia and Southeast Asia (Dwivedi et al., 2022). These regions also have a young and digitally savvy population, which is more likely to be engaged with virtual influencers and user-generated content.

**Trend 3:** Integration of Blockchain and NFTs: Blockchain technology and non-fungible tokens are being used to create new opportunities for metaverse-based marketing (Aria et al., 2023); (Xu et al., 2022). For example, brands are using NFTs to create unique digital assets that can be sold or traded within the metaverse, and they are also using blockchain to create more secure and transparent marketing campaigns.

**Regional Implications:** This trend is likely to be particularly impactful in regions with a growing interest in blockchain and NFTs, such as North America, Europe, and East Asia. These regions also have a strong regulatory framework for these technologies, which could make it easier for brands to launch metaverse-based marketing campaigns that incorporate blockchain and NFTs (Eyada, 2023).

**Trend 4:** Focus on Accessibility and Inclusivity: As the metaverse continues to evolve, there is a growing focus on making it more accessible and inclusive for everyone. Brands are working to create metaverse experiences that are accessible to people with disabilities, and they are also working to ensure that their metaverse marketing campaigns are inclusive and representative of all consumers (Radanliev et al., 2023).

**Regional Implications:** This trend is likely to be important in all regions, as brands seek to reach a global audience. However, it may be particularly important in regions with a strong commitment to diversity and inclusion, such as North America and Europe.

It is important for brands to consider the regional implications of these trends when developing their metaverse-based marketing strategies. By understanding the unique characteristics of different regions, brands can create more effective and engaging campaigns that resonate with consumers around the world.

Additional Points to Consider:

1. **Cultural Differences:** It is important to be aware of cultural differences when developing metaverse-based marketing campaigns. What works in one region may not work in another. For example, humor and tone should be carefully considered (Eyada, 2023; Lin et al., 2017).
2. **Language Barriers:** Language barriers can also be a challenge for metaverse-based marketing. Brands need to ensure that their campaigns are translated into the local language and that they are using culturally appropriate language (Nguyen & Rudawska, 2022).
3. **Data Privacy:** Data privacy is a major concern for consumers in the metaverse. Brands need to be transparent about how they are collecting and using consumer data, and they need to comply with all applicable data privacy regulations (Wang et al., 2023; Zhao et al., 2022).

By carefully considering these factors, brands can create metaverse-based marketing campaigns that are effective, engaging, and respectful of consumers around the world.

## 3. POTENTIAL OF METAVERSE FOR DIGITAL MARKETING

The virtual reality-based digital world known as the metaverse has received a lot of attention and is expected to completely change how we use technology and the internet (Alpala et al., 2022). Beyond just being entertaining, the metaverse has enormous possibilities for online advertising. For marketers, the metaverse offers a singular opportunity to develop immersive brand experiences that go beyond conventional techniques (Barrera & Shah, 2023). Virtual reality (VR) and augmented reality (AR) technology can be used by marketers to immerse users in captivating virtual worlds. These immersive experiences give customers a memorable and intensely engaging way to connect with goods, services, and brand storylines, strengthening their bond with the brand (Rauschnabel et al.,2022a; Hollensen et al., 2022; Rauschnabel et al., 2019).

In the metaverse, marketers may design interactive, dynamic, and engaging experiences for customers. Brands may create virtual events, gamified experiences, and social interactions that motivate people to engage with their content by utilizing the metaverse's capabilities. This greater level of involvement might result in a stronger emotional bond with the brand, which would boost brand advocacy and loyalty (Miao et al., 2022). Marketers can now offer highly personalized and specific ads to their customers because of the abundance of client information available in the metaverse. In order to more effectively target specific customers with their messages and services, marketers can benefit from understanding user behaviour and preferences within the metaverse. When marketing communications are specifically customized, they are more pertinent and likely to generate purchases (Hollensen et al., 2022).

The metaverse is about to see a transformation in e-commerce. Brands can set up online shops where customers can browse, interact with, and buy things without leaving the virtual space. The metaverse's virtual money and digital assets offer fresh opportunities for monetization and income production. Further enriching the shopping experience, marketers can experiment with virtual try-on experiences that let customers virtually try things before making a purchase (Bloomberg, 2022).

Unfortunately, we're still in the early stages of metaverse marketing, and publicly available case studies with detailed results, especially those focusing on specific cultural adaptations, are rare. However, there are some hypothetical examples inspired by real-world marketing strategies and trends:

## Hypothetical Example: Indian Market

**Brand:** EROS NOW global streaming service launching in India.
Metaverse Adaptation:

- **Virtual Diwali Celebration:** They could create a vibrant virtual space inspired by Diwali, featuring traditional decorations, music, and dance performances. Users could customize their avatars with traditional Indian clothing, participate in virtual fireworks displays, and send virtual gifts to friends and family (Mishra et al., 2011).
- **Bollywood-Themed Games:** Interactive games could be centered around popular Bollywood movies or music, allowing users to test their knowledge, engage with their favorite stars, and win virtual rewards (Jain et al., 2013).
- **Partnerships with Local Artists and Influencers:** Collaborating with Indian artists, musicians, and social media influencers would add authenticity and resonate with the local audience (Kharb, 2023).

## Hypothetical Example: International Market

**Brand:** A global sportswear company TOPTEN10 targeting Gen Z in Japan.
Metaverse Adaptation:

- **Virtual Streetwear Experience:** Partnering with a metaverse platform popular in Japan, they could create a virtual replica of Tokyo's Harajuku district, known for its unique street style. Users could customize their avatars with virtual streetwear, participate in fashion battles, and attend virtual fashion shows featuring local designers (Bredikhina et al., 2020).

- **Anime and Manga Integration:** Incorporating elements from popular anime and manga series into the metaverse experience, such as character skins, virtual items, and storylines, would appeal to the target audience's interests (Zhang, 2023).
- **Japanese Language and Etiquette:** Ensuring the metaverse experience is fully localized in Japanese, including language, cultural references, and social etiquette, would demonstrate respect and enhance user engagement (Shi et al., 2022).

Key Considerations for Real-World Examples:

- **Data Privacy:** Companies need to be mindful of local data privacy regulations, especially in regions with strict data protection laws.
- **Cultural Sensitivity:** Thorough research and consultation with cultural experts are crucial to avoid misrepresenting or appropriating cultural elements.
- **Authenticity:** Partnerships with local creators and influencers can help ensure that metaverse experiences feel authentic and relevant to the target audience.

As the metaverse evolves, we can expect to see more concrete examples of brands successfully adapting to local cultures. Keep an eye on marketing publications and industry reports for case studies that highlight these strategies.

## 3.1 Nike's Model to Operate in Metaverse

Nike has been using Artificial Intelligence, AR/VR as an important feature in digital marketing from last many years. After partnership with Roblox, it moved into metaverse in 2021. Nikeland which is a metaverse space for Nike allow users to experience brand and other event virtually (Futurumresearch, 2022). Users can also play multiple games and win rewards to create their own personal space in Nikeland.

Digital showrooms give a vast shopping experience to purchase virtual items. When Nike moved further into metaverse, it came up with NFT sneaker collection like Cryoto Kicks Dunk Genesis, Space Drip somewhat like its real-world sneakers. It was assumed that when the avatars will purchase these items and will walk in Nikeland, they may try to purchase these goods from the physical shops too. NFT sneaker virtual collection was able to influence many young millennials and Generation Z as every pair of this is giving opportunity to fully customizable the shoes by "skin vials" which can be added in the base sneaker (Forbes, 2022).

Two value captured mechanisms for operating in metaverse of Nike are:

a. Company is able to connect a big population of young millennials who are engaged in virtual shopping of products and services.
b. Second, the company is looking to increase revenue with the help of NFT sneaker collection which can enhance both traditional and metaverse.

## 4. CULTURAL AND ETHICAL ASPECTS OF METAVERSE IN DIGITAL BUSINESS

With the emergence of the metaverse, there is a growing concern about the possibility of inappropriate and immoral use of metaverse data, and privacy concerns are a constant and significant problem (Dwivedi et al., 2021). There are still some questions which are unanswered like the emergence of metaverse as a boundless marketplace and its twining with the physical shopping. Ethical concerns while virtually interacting with brands are always there. Do firms possess adequate computing infrastructure to support service offerings enabled by the metaverse? Furthermore, would such a service be accessible to individuals of all age groups, particularly seniors? To surmount these obstacles, marketers must pledge to mitigate ethical and moral violations in the metaverse by establishing a responsible metaverse government.

The Metaverse facilitates the establishment of virtual communities centered on common interests, ideals, or experiences, surpassing the constraints of geography and physical environment (Wang et al., 2023). It provides a platform for neglected communities to establish connections and engage in unrestricted interactions. In its capacity to foster creative expression, the Metaverse has the potential to engender whole new cultural activities, including virtual concerts, art forms, and festivals that amalgamate components from many civilizations in innovative ways.

The Metaverse sustains its own economic systems, that facilitate the exchange of virtual commodities, services, and real estate. The commodification of cultural products such as digital fashion or virtual performances gives rise to concerns around ownership, appropriation, and equitable remuneration. The facile adoption of cultural symbols or behaviours in virtual settings may give rise to discussions about cultural appropriation and intellectual property rights, particularly when aspects of minority cultures are transformed into commodities. The metaverse opens up intriguing technological possibilities as well as ethical and cultural questions as it develops traction and becomes a significant component of our digital landscape. We can create a responsible and welcoming metaverse that respects different viewpoints and encourages beneficial societal effects by being aware of it.

The metaverse has the ability to close the digital gap and make the internet a more welcoming place for people from all walks of life. The metaverse can develop into a platform that celebrates diversity and encourages inclusivity by emphasizing accessible features, providing for a range of abilities, and guaranteeing equitable access to virtual experiences (Dwivedi, Ismagilova, et al., 2021; Hilken, Keeling, et al., 2022).

### 4.1 Ethical Dilemma on the Metaverse Privacy Violation

The need for ethical data governance is urgent as the metaverse gathers enormous amounts of user data. Data protection, transparency, and consent ought to be prioritized during the development of the metaverse (Dwivedi, Ismagilova, et al., 2021; Fernandez & Hui, 2022). Users should be in charge of their data and be aware of how it is gathered, stored, and used. The metaverse can build trust and protect user data by putting in place strong privacy safeguards (Donthu et al., 2021).

Notwithstanding the platform provider's attempts to guarantee the confidentiality and protection of user data, concerns may emerge regarding the utilization of artificial intelligence to surveil users' personalities or to surreptitiously analyse users' behaviours, or the possibility of unauthorized collection of user data by third parties. In order to prevent consumers from being unaware of the process and rationale behind data mining for profit maximisation, even with their consent, it is advisable to prohibit it. Engaging in privacy infringement or interference with other human rights is morally wrong without the explicit agreement of an individual (Finn & Wright, 2012). Few examples of metaverse with ethical considerations are mentioned below:

Example 1: The "Skill-Based" Virtual Concert

**Brand:** A music streaming service

**Goal:** Drive new subscriptions, appealing to a Gen Z audience interested in both music and gaming.

Metaverse Execution:

1. **Partnership:** They collaborate with a popular metaverse platform frequented by their target demographic (e.g., Roblox, Fortnite).
2. **The Event:** Instead of a passive concert, they create an interactive experience. Users participate in mini-games testing their music knowledge or rhythm skills, earning in-game rewards (virtual merchandise, access to exclusive areas) redeemable with a free trial subscription.
3. **Virtual Influencer Tie-in:** A popular metaverse musician (or a real artist's avatar) could be the "face" of the event, promoting it and engaging with users.

Ethical Considerations:

- **Age-Appropriate Content:** Ensuring the games and overall experience are suitable for the platform's age demographics.
- **Clear Value Exchange:** Users understand the trial period and how to opt-out if they choose. Rewards are attainable, not tied to microtransactions.
- **Data Privacy:** Data collected is limited to what's necessary for the game and clearly communicated. Parental consent mechanisms are in place if needed.

Example 2: The "Sustainable Fashion" Showcase

**Brand:** A clothing company focused on eco-friendly practices

**Goal:** Increase brand awareness among environmentally conscious consumers and drive sales of a new sustainable line.

Metaverse Execution:

1. **Virtual Fashion Show:** Partner with a metaverse platform known for its visually rich environments. The show features avatars modeling the new line, highlighting the materials and production processes.
2. **Interactive Exhibits:** Users can explore virtual exhibits detailing the brand's sustainability efforts, from sourcing to manufacturing.
3. **NFT-Based Rewards:** Attendees receive limited-edition NFTs that grant discounts on the new line or unlock exclusive digital clothing items for their avatars.

Ethical Considerations:

- **Transparency:** The environmental claims made are backed up by verifiable information available to users.
- **NFT Sustainability:** The NFTs are minted on a blockchain known for its low energy consumption, or the environmental impact is offset.

- **Inclusivity:** Avatars of diverse body types and ethnicities are used to promote body positivity and representation.

**Key Takeaway:** These are just starting points. Successful and ethical metaverse marketing requires creativity, a deep understanding of the target audience, and a commitment to responsible practices within the virtual space.

The metaverse presents an exceptional chance to celebrate and preserve many civilizations. Through the creation of virtual places that highlight cultural heritage, traditions, and art forms, people from all over the world are able to learn about and enjoy one another's cultures (Rauschnabel et al., 2019). Mutual respect, understanding, and cultural enrichment can all be fostered by this interchange (Buhalis, 2022). Navigating cultural differences is essential for brands seeking global relevance in the metaverse (Eyada, 2023). Here's how brands can approach this challenge:

Research and Cultural Sensitivity:

- **Target Audience Segmentation:** Go beyond basic demographics. Understand the cultural nuances of your target audience within specific metaverse platforms and virtual regions (Ramadan, 2023).
- **Cultural Consultants:** Engage with cultural experts who can provide insights into local customs, values, and sensitivities. This helps avoid unintentional offense or misinterpretations (Aririguzoh, 2022).
- **Local Partnerships:** Collaborating with local creators, influencers, or organizations within the metaverse can provide valuable cultural context and credibility (Lee & Law, 2023).

Adapting Content and Experiences:

- **Language Localization:** Accurate and culturally appropriate translation is crucial. Consider using multiple languages or partnering with platforms that offer real-time translation features (Lee et al., 2021).
- **Visual Representation:** Avatars, environments, and visual elements should reflect the diversity of the target audience. Avoid stereotypes and ensure representation across ethnicities, body types, and cultural backgrounds (Tiffany et al., 2023).
- **Interactive Elements:** Games, challenges, or interactive experiences should be designed with cultural sensitivity in mind. Consider local holidays, traditions, or cultural references that resonate with the target audience (Häkkilä et al., 2020).

## 5. IMPORTANCE OF DATA ANALYTICS IN A METAVERSE BUSINESS ENVIRONMENT

Large volumes of user data are generated by the metaverse, giving marketers deep insights into user behavior, preferences, and engagement patterns. To better understand their target demographic, to make data-driven decisions, and to optimize their marketing strategies, marketers can use advanced data analytics and AI algorithms. This information can aid marketers in campaign optimization, user experience enhancement, and improved business results (Sharma & Giannakos, 2020).

Businesses must give privacy and data security a priority given the enormous amount of user data collected in the Metaverse (Nevelsteen, 2018; Zackery et al., 2016). Important factors to take into account include putting effective data protection mechanisms in place, following pertinent laws, and getting user consent before collecting any data. Building trust and preserving the reputation of companies doing business in the Metaverse depend on securing users' personal information and ensuring secure transactions (Amazon Web Services, 2015).

## 6. CONCLUSION

The metaverse has transformative marketing consequences, giving new degrees of consumer involvement and a large potential to place companies throughout customer journeys (Dwivedi, et al., 2022; Hollensen et al., 2022). Digital marketing on the Indian subcontinent's Metaverse presents some interesting ethical and cultural challenges. Safeguarding and managing Metaverse user data on the basis of consent requires marketers to adhere to data protection legislation and guidelines. For the sake of authenticity and openness, businesses should clearly label their promotional content in the Metaverse. Honesty is the best defence against lying. Advertisements in the Metaverse must not perpetuate bias or exclusion of any kind. Cultural and social understanding in advertising content is essential. Culture is an important factor to consider for anyone working in Metaverse marketing. The ability to communicate depends on localization. Diversity and inclusion: do not use cultural appropriation in marketing materials for the Metaverse. In the Indian context, digital marketers in the Metaverse must take into account linguistic and cultural diversity. Success is based on cultural factors such as variety and local customs. Marketers in the Metaverse need to be sensitive to regional and national variations in their target audiences. Marketing to a global audience necessitates sensitivity to different cultures. These factors highlight the importance of ethics, cultural sensitivity, and customization in Metaverse marketing to a wide range of Indian and worldwide consumers.

### 6.1 The Future of Metaverse Marketing

- **Personalized and Immersive Experiences:** Imagine attending a virtual concert where the music, visuals, and even the crowd's energy adapt to your preferences, or stepping into a virtual store where AI tailors product recommendations based on your cultural background and style (Eyada, 2023).
- **Seamless Integration with the Physical World:** AR could bridge the gap between the metaverse and reality. Picture scanning a product in a physical store and instantly accessing its virtual counterpart, complete with culturally relevant information and reviews (Márquez & Ziegler, 2020).
- **Decentralized and User-Driven Environments:** As the metaverse becomes more decentralized, brands will need to engage with communities and empower users to co-create experiences. This could involve collaborating with local creators in different regions to develop culturally authentic content (Stokel-Walker, 2022).

Leveraging Technology for Ethical and Culturally Sensitive Campaigns:

- **AI-Powered Cultural Sensitivity Tools:** AI can be trained on vast datasets of cultural norms and sensitivities to help brands avoid gaffes and ensure their metaverse experiences are respectful and appropriate for diverse audiences (Hermann, 2021).
- **VR for Cultural Immersion:** VR can create powerful empathy experiences, allowing users to step into the shoes of someone from a different culture and gain a deeper understanding of their perspectives and values (Peck et al., 2021).
- **AR for Localized Storytelling:** Brands can use AR to overlay culturally relevant stories and information onto physical locations, creating engaging and educational experiences that connect with local communities (Schroeder et al., 2023).

Ethical Considerations Remain Paramount:

- **Data Privacy and Security:** As metaverse experiences become more personalized, brands must prioritize data privacy and security, ensuring transparency and user control over personal information (Nair et al., 2022; Connor & Ross, 2018).
- **Bias in AI and Algorithms:** It's crucial to address potential biases in AI algorithms used for cultural sensitivity analysis or personalization to avoid perpetuating stereotypes or excluding certain groups (Shams et al., 2023).
- **Accessibility and Inclusivity:** Metaverse experiences should be designed to be accessible to users of all abilities and backgrounds, ensuring that cultural sensitivity doesn't come at the expense of inclusivity (Peck et al., 2021).

The metaverse presents exciting opportunities for brands to connect with global audiences in innovative ways. By embracing ethical considerations and leveraging technologies like AI, AR, and VR responsibly, we can create a more inclusive, understanding, and culturally rich metaverse for everyone.

## REFERENCES


Ali, S. A., & Khan, R. (2023). Metaverse Marketing vs Digital Marketing. *Inter-national Journal of Innovative Science and Research Technology*, 8(1), 385–388.

Alnsour, M. (2018). Social Media Effect on Purchase Intention: Jordanian Airline Industry. *Journal of Internet Banking and Commerce*, 23(2), 20–28.

Alpala, L. O., Quiroga-Parra, D. J., Torres, J. C., & Peluffo-Ordóñez, D. H. (2022). Smart factory using virtual reality and online multi-user: Towards a metaverse for experimental frameworks. *Applied Sciences (Basel, Switzerland)*, 12(12), 6258. DOI: 10.3390/app12126258

Amazon Web Services. (2015), Introduction to AWS Security by Design, Retrieved from https://reciprocity.com/resources/what-is-security-by-design/

Aria, R., Archer, N., Khanlari, M., & Shah, B. (2023, March 30). Influential Factors in the Design and Development of a Sustainable Web3/Metaverse and Its Applications. *Future Internet*, 15(4), 131–131. DOI: 10.3390/fi15040131

Aririguzoh, S. A. (2022, March 23). Communication competencies, culture and SDGs: Effective processes to cross-cultural communication. *Humanities & Social Sciences Communications*, 9(1), 96. Advance online publication. DOI: 10.1057/s41599-022-01109-4

Barrera, K. G., & Shah, D. (2023). Marketing in the Metaverse: Conceptual understanding, framework, and research agenda. *Journal of Business Research*, 155, 113420. DOI: 10.1016/j.jbusres.2022.113420

Biocca, F., Harms, C., & Burgoon, J. K. (2003). Toward a more robust theory and measure of social presence: Review and suggested criteria. *Presence (Cambridge, Mass.)*, 12(5), 456–480. DOI: 10.1162/105474603322761270

Bloomberg. (2022). Metaverse's $80 billion etf assets by 2024 virtually a reality. Accessed 23.05.23 (https://www.bloomberg.com/professional/blog/metaverses80-billion-etf-assets-by-2024-virtually-a-reality/)

Bogost, I. 2021. "The Metaverse Is Bad." The Atlantic, October 22, https://www.theatlantic.com/technology/archive/2021/10/facebook-metaverse-name-change/620449/

Buhalis, D., & Karatay, N. (2022). Mixed reality (MR) for generation Z in cultural heritage tourism towards metaverse. In Information and Communication Technologies in Tourism 2022: Proceedings of the ENTER 2022 eTourism Conference, January 11–14, 2022 (pp. 16-27). Springer International Publishing.

Camacho, D., Lara-Cabrera, R., Merelo-Guervós, J. J., Castillo, P. A., Cotta, C., Fernández-Leiva, A. J., de Vega, F. F., & Chávez, F. (2018). From ephemeral computing to deep bioinspired algorithms: New trends and applications. *Future Generation Computer Systems*, 88, 735–746. DOI: 10.1016/j.future.2018.07.056

Caulfield, B. 2021. "What Is the Metaverse?" The Official NVIDIA Blog, August 10, https://blogs.nvidia.com/blog/2021/08/10/what-is-the-metaverse/

David, S. (2023). Metaverse in 2023: A whole new world for brand engagement. Retrieved 2 january 2023, from https://www.exchange4media.com/digital-news/metaverse-in-2023-is-it-going-to-be-a-whole-new-world-124532.html

Dawson, A. (2022). Data-driven Consumer Engagement, Virtual Immersive Shopping Experiences, and Blockchain-based Digital Assets in the Retail Metaverse. *Journal of Self-Governance and Management Economics*, 10(2), 52. DOI: 10.22381/jsme10220224

Dolan, R., Conduit, J., Fahy, J., & Goodman, S. (2016). Social media engagement behaviour: A uses and gratifications perspective. *Journal of Strategic Marketing*, 24(3-4), 261–277. DOI: 10.1080/0965254X.2015.1095222

Donthu, N., Kumar, S., Pattnaik, D., & Lim, W. M. (2021). A bibliometric retrospection of marketing from the lens of psychology: Insights from Psychology & Marketing. *Psychology and Marketing*, 38(5), 834–865. DOI: 10.1002/mar.21472

Dubey, R., Gunasekaran, A., Childe, S. J., Bryde, D. J., Giannakis, M., Foropon, C., Roubaud, D., & Hazen, B. T. (2020). Big data analytics and artificial intelligence pathway to operational performance under the effects of entrepreneurial orientation and environmental dynamism: A study of manufacturing organisations. *International Journal of Production Economics*, 226, 107599. DOI: 10.1016/j.ijpe.2019.107599

Dwivedi, Y K., Hughes, L., Baabdullah, A M., Ribeiro-Navarrete, S., Giannakis, M., Al-Debei, M M., Dennehy, D., Mäntymäki, M., Buhalis, D., Cheung, C M., Conboy, K., Doyle, R., Dubey, R., Dutot, V., Felix, R., Goyal, D., Gustafsson, A., Hinsch, C., Jebabli, I., . . . Wamba, S F. (2022, October 1). Metaverse beyond the hype: Multidisciplinary perspectives on emerging challenges, opportunities, and agenda for research, practice and policy. Elsevier BV, 66, 102542-102542. DOI: 10.1016/j.ijinfomgt.2022.102542

Dwivedi, Y. K., Hughes, L., Baabdullah, A. M., Ribeiro-Navarrete, S., Giannakis, M., Al-Debei, M. M., Dennehy, D., Metri, B., Buhalis, D., Cheung, C. M. K., Conboy, K., Doyle, R., Dubey, R., Dutot, V., Felix, R., Goyal, D. P., Gustafsson, A., Hinsch, C., Jebabli, I., & Wamba, S. F. (2022). Metaverse beyond the hype: Multidisciplinary perspectives on emerging challenges, opportunities, and agenda for research, practice and policy. *International Journal of Information Management*, 66, 102542. DOI: 10.1016/j.ijinfomgt.2022.102542

Dwivedi, Y. K., Hughes, L., Ismagilova, E., Aarts, G., Coombs, C., Crick, T., Duan, Y., Dwivedi, R., Edwards, J., Eirug, A., Galanos, V., Ilavarasan, P. V., Janssen, M., Jones, P., Kar, A. K., Kizgin, H., Kronemann, B., Lal, B., Lucini, B., & Williams, M. D. (2021). Artificial Intelligence (AI): Multidisciplinary perspectives on emerging challenges, opportunities, and agenda for research, practice and policy. *International Journal of Information Management*, 57, 101994. DOI: 10.1016/j.ijinfomgt.2019.08.002

Dwivedi, Y. K., Hughes, L., Kar, A. K., Baabdullah, A. M., Grover, P., Abbas, R., Andreini, D., Abumoghli, I., Barlette, Y., Bunker, D., Chandra Kruse, L., Constantiou, I., Davison, R. M., De', R., Dubey, R., Fenby-Taylor, H., Gupta, B., He, W., Kodama, M., & Wade, M. (2022). Climate change and COP26: Are digital technologies and information management part of the problem or the solution? An editorial reflection and call to action. *International Journal of Information Management*, 63, 102456. DOI: 10.1016/j.ijinfomgt.2021.102456

Dwivedi, Y. K., Ismagilova, E., Hughes, D. L., Carlson, J., Filieri, R., Jacobson, J., Jain, V., Karjaluoto, H., Kefi, H., Krishen, A. S., Kumar, V., Rahman, M. M., Raman, R., Rauschnabel, P. A., Rowley, J., Salo, J., Tran, G. A., & Wang, Y. (2021). Setting the future of digital and social media marketing research: Perspectives and research propositions. *International Journal of Information Management*, 59, 102168. DOI: 10.1016/j.ijinfomgt.2020.102168

Dwivedi, Y. K., Ismagilova, E., Hughes, D. L., Carlson, J., Filieri, R., Jacobson, J., & Wang, Y. (2021). Setting the future of digital and social media marketing research: Perspectives and research propositions. *International Journal of Information Management*, 59, 102168. DOI: 10.1016/j.ijinfomgt.2020.102168

Dwivedi, Y. K., Ismagilova, E., Hughes, D. L., Carlson, J., Filieri, R., Jacobson, J., & Wang, Y. (2021). Setting the future of digital and social media marketing research: Perspectives and research propositions. *International Journal of Information Management*, 59, 102168. DOI: 10.1016/j.ijinfomgt.2020.102168

Exploring the Metaverse: Challenges and Opportunities for India in the 'Next Internet' | ORF (orfonline.org)

Eyada, B. (2023, January 15). Advertising in the Metaverse: Opportunities and Challenges. *Canadian Center of Science and Education*, 15(1), 22–22. DOI: 10.5539/ijms.v15n1p22

Faridani, A. (2022). Council post: why the metaverse is marketing's next big thing. Retrieved 19 August 2022, from https://www.forbes.com/ sites/forbesbusinessdevelopmentcouncil/2021/12/21/why-themetaverse-is-marketings-next-big-thing/?sh=14bca7f

Fernandez, C. B., & Hui, P. (2022, July). Life, the metaverse and everything: An overview of privacy, ethics, and governance in metaverse. In 2022 IEEE 42nd International Conference on Distributed Computing Systems Workshops (ICDCSW) (pp. 272-277). IEEE.

Finn, R. L., & Wright, D. (2012). Unmanned aircraft systems: Surveillance, ethics and privacy in civil applications. *Computer Law & Security Report*, 28(2), 184–194. DOI: 10.1016/j.clsr.2012.01.005

Flavián, C., Ibáñez-Sánchez, S., & Orús, C. (2019). The impact of virtual, augmented and mixed reality technologies on the customer experience. *Journal of Business Research*, 100, 547–560. DOI: 10.1016/j.jbusres.2018.10.050

Forbes (2022), "The Amazing Ways Nike Is Using The Metaverse, Web3 And NFTs", available at: https://www.forbes.com/sites/bernardmarr/2022/06/01/the-amazing-ways-nike-is-using-the-metaverse-web3-and-nfts/

Futurumresearch (2022), "Nike's Metaverse Store Paves a Pathway into the Future", available at: https://futurumresearch.com/research-notes/nikes-metaverse-store-paves-a-pathway-into-the-future/

Gadalla, E., Keeling, K., & Abosag, I. (2013). Metaverseretail service quality: A future framework for retail service quality in the 3D internet. *Journal of Marketing Management*, 29(13-14), 1493–1517. DOI: 10.1080/0267257X.2013.835742

Gautam, V. (2022). 10 Big brands that have dipped their toes into the nft world. Retrieved 26 August 2022, from https://www.indiatimes. com/worth/investment/brands-that-have-entered-nft-world560907.html

Ghose, R., Bantanidis, S., Shah, R. S., Surendran, N., Master, K., & Singhvi, P. (2022), "Metaverse and Money" available at: https://www.citifirst.com.hk/home/upload/citi_research/AZRC7.pdf (accessed 29 August 2022).

Hilken, T., Keeling, D. I., Chylinski, M., de Ruyter, K., Golf Papez, M., Heller, J., Mahr, D., & Alimamy, S. (2022). Disrupting marketing realities: A research agenda for investigating the psychological mechanisms of next-generation experiences with reality-enhancing technologies. *Psychology and Marketing*, 39(8), 1660–1671. DOI: 10.1002/mar.21678

Hoffman, D. L., & Novak, T. P. (2009). Flow online: Lessons learned and future prospects. *Journal of Interactive Marketing*, 23(1), 23–34. DOI: 10.1016/j.intmar.2008.10.003

Hofstetter, R., de Bellis, E., Brandes, L., Clegg, M., Lamberton, C., Reibstein, D., Rohlfsen, F., Schmitt, B., & Zhang, J. Z. (2022). Crypto-marketing: How non-fungible tokens (NFTs) challenge traditional marketing. *Marketing Letters*, 33(4), 705–711. DOI: 10.1007/s11002-022-09639-2

Hollensen, S., Kotler, P., & Opresnik, M. O. (2022). Metaverse—The new marketing universe. *The Journal of Business Strategy*. Advance online publication. DOI: 10.1108/JBS-01-2022-0014

Ianenko, M., Ianenko, M., & Shevchuk, E. (2023, May 22). Innovative Promotion Technologies: Brand Management in the Digital Environment. *Multidisciplinary Digital Publishing Institute*, 1(1), 18–25. DOI: 10.3390/platforms1010003

ISACA. (2014). Generating value from big data analytics [White paper]. Information Systems Audit and Control Association, Retrieved from http://www.isaca.org/Knowledge-Center/ Research/Research-Deliverables/Pages/Generating-Value-From-Big-Data-Analytics.aspx

Kache, F., & Seuring, S. (2017). Challenges and opportunities of digital information at the intersection of Big Data Analytics and supply chain management. *International Journal of Operations & Production Management*, 37(1), 10–36. DOI: 10.1108/IJOPM-02-2015-0078

Khatri, M. (2022). Revamping the marketing world with metaverse–The future of marketing. *International Journal of Computer Applications*, 975(29), 8887. DOI: 10.5120/ijca2022922361

Kim, J. (2021). Advertising in the metaverse: Research agenda. *Journal of Interactive Advertising*, 21(3), 141–144. DOI: 10.1080/15252019.2021.2001273

Kozinets, R. V. (2022). Immersive netnography: A novel method for service experience research in virtual reality, augmented reality and metaverse contexts. *Journal of Service Management*, 34(1), 100–125. DOI: 10.1108/JOSM-12-2021-0481

Lee, A. 2021. "With the Metaverse Hype Cycle at Full Blast, Experts Take the Long View." Digiday, August 4, https://digiday.com/marketing/with-the-metaverse-hype-cycle-at-full-blast-experts-take-the-long-view/

Lee, K. J., & Law, E. (2023, January 1). Towards a More Inclusive Metaverse via Designing Tools That Support Collaborative Virtual World Building by Users With and Without Disabilities. Cornell University. https://doi.org//arxiv.2305.04368DOI: 10.48550

Lee, L., Braud, T., Zhou, P., Wang, L., Xu, D., Wang, L., Kumar, A., Bermejo, C., & Hui, P. (2021, January 1). All One Needs to Know about Metaverse: A Complete Survey on Technological Singularity, Virtual Ecosystem, and Research Agenda. Cornell University. https://doi.org//arxiv.2110.05352 Xu, H., Li, Z., Li, Z., Zhang, X., Shi, G., & Zhang, L. (2022, January 1). Metaverse Native Communication: A Blockchain and Spectrum Prospective. Cornell University. https://doi.org//arxiv.2203.08355DOI: 10.48550

Lin, H., Swarna, H., & Bruning, P F. (2017, September 1). Taking a global view on brand post popularity: Six social media brand post practices for global markets. Elsevier BV, 60(5), 621-633. DOI: 10.1016/j.bushor.2017.05.006

Malhotra, V. (2022). How the metaverse will change digital marketing. Retrieved 13 september 2022,from https://timesofindia.indiatimes.com/blogs/voices/how-the-metaverse-will-change-digital-marketing/

Marcon, É., Le Dain, M. A., & Frank, A. G. (2022). Designing business models for Industry 4.0 technologies provision: Changes in business dimensions through digital transformation. *Technological Forecasting and Social Change*, 185, 122078. DOI: 10.1016/j.techfore.2022.122078

McKinsey & Company. (2022a). Value creation in the metaverse. https:// www.mckinsey.com/business -functions/growth-marketing-and-sales/ our-insights/value-creation-in-the-metaverse

McKinsey & Company. (2022b). Marketing in the metaverse: An opportunity for innovation and experimentation. Accessed on 5th September 2022. https://www.mckinsey.com/business-functions/growth-marketing-and-sales/our-insights/marketing-in-the-metaversean-opportunity-for-innovation-and-experimentationMalhotra, 2022

Miao, F., Kozlenkova, I. V., Wang, H., Xie, T., & Palmatier, R. W. (2022). An emerging theory of avatar marketing. *Journal of Marketing*, 86(1), 67–90. DOI: 10.1177/0022242921996646

Michopoulou, E., & Buhalis, D. (2013). Information provision for challenging markets: The case of the accessibility requiring market in the context of tourism. *Information & Management*, 50(5), 229–239. DOI: 10.1016/j.im.2013.04.001

Mourtzis, D., Panopoulos, N., Angelopoulos, J., Wang, B., & Wang, L. (2022). Human centric platforms for personalized value creation in metaverse. *Journal of Manufacturing Systems*, 65, 653–659. DOI: 10.1016/j.jmsy.2022.11.004

Naaz, F. (2023).India Metaverse platform Bharatmeta receives global recognition at VivaTech in Paris. Retieved 16 June 2023, from https://www.livemint.com/news/india/indias-metaverse-platform-bharatmeta -receives-global-recognition-at-vivatech-in-paris-11686902824568.html

Nevelsteen, K. J. (2018). Virtual world, defined from a technological perspective and applied to video games, mixed reality, and the Metaverse. *Computer Animation and Virtual Worlds*, 29(1), e1752. DOI: 10.1002/cav.1752

Nguyen, T. H. N., & Rudawska, E. (2022, September 15). Integrated Cultural Theories on Mobile Marketing Acceptance: Literature Review. *Kozminski University*, 30(3), 112–135. DOI: 10.7206/cemj.2658-0845.84

Olson, E. M., Olson, K. M., Czaplewski, A. J., & Key, T. M. (2021). Business strategy and the management of digital marketing. *Business Horizons*, 64(2), 285–293. DOI: 10.1016/j.bushor.2020.12.004

Pandey, N., Nayal, P., & Rathore, A. S. (2020). Digital marketing for B2B organizations: Structured literature review and future research directions. *Journal of Business and Industrial Marketing*, 35(7), 1191–1204. DOI: 10.1108/JBIM-06-2019-0283

Radanliev, P., Roure, P. D. D., Novitzky, D. P., & Sluganovic, D. I. (2023, January 1). Accessibility and Inclusiveness of New Information and Communication Technologies for Disabled Users and Content Creators in the Metaverse. Cornell University. https://doi.org/DOI: 10.48550/arXiv.2308

Rafiq, M., & Malik, A. (2018). Impact of Social Media on Purchasing Decision of Consumerwith Special Reference to Lahore, Pakistan. *Journal of Social Sciences*, 4(2), 268–2733.

Ramadan, Z. (2023, March 17). Marketing in the metaverse era: toward an integrative channel approach. Springer Science+Business Media, 27(3), 1905-1918. DOI: 10.1007/s10055-023-00783-2

Rauschnabel, P. A., Babin, B. J., tom Dieck, M. C., Krey, N., & Jung, T. (2022). What is augmented reality marketing? Its definition, complexity, and future. *Journal of Business Research*, 142, 1140–1150. DOI: 10.1016/j.jbusres.2021.12.084

Rauschnabel, P. A., Felix, R., & Hinsch, C. (2019). Augmented reality marketing: How mobile AR-apps can improve brands through inspiration. *Journal of Retailing and Consumer Services*, 49, 43–53. DOI: 10.1016/j.jretconser.2019.03.004

Rogers, C. E., Witt, A. W., Solomon, A. D., & Venkatasubramanian, K. K. (2015, September). An approach for user identification for head-mounted displays. In *Proceedings of the 2015 ACM International Symposium on Wearable Computers* (pp. 143-146). DOI: 10.1145/2802083.2808391

Schneegass, S., Oualil, Y., & Bulling, A. (2016, May). SkullConduct: Biometric user identification on eyewear computers using bone conduction through the skull. In *Proceedings of the 2016 CHI Conference on Human Factors in Computing Systems* (pp. 1379-1384). DOI: 10.1145/2858036.2858152

Sengupta, D. (2021). Nike Acquired This Company That Makes Virtual Sneakers and NFTs for the Metaverse. Retrieved from https://beebom.com/nikeacquired-company-makes-virtual-sneakers-nfts-metaverse/. Accessed April 12, 2022.

Sharma, K., & Giannakos, M. (2020). Multimodal data capabilities for learning: What can multimodal data tell us about learning? *British Journal of Educational Technology*, 51(5), 1450–1484. DOI: 10.1111/bjet.12993

Sheehan, D. (2022). CitizenM announce opening a hotel in the Metaverse. https://www. hospitalityandcateringnews.com/2022/04/citizenm-announce-opening-a-hotel-inthe-metaverse/

Snider, M., & Molina, B. (2021). Everyone wants to own the metaverse including Facebook and Microsoft. But what exactly is it? USA Today Tech. https://eu. usatoday. com/story/tech/2021/11/10/metaverse-what-is-it-explained-facebook-microsoft-meta-vr/6337635001/(nd).

"Someone just paid $450,000 to be Snoop Dogg's neighbor in the metaverse. Here's how you can live by a celebrity too | Fortune." https://fortune.com/2022/02/02/how-to-buy-metaverse real-estate-snoop-dogg-celebrity-neighbor/

Sparkes, M. (2021). What is a metaverse.

Staff, B. E. (2022). Metaverse is emerging not only for GenX or Millennials: Report. ET BrandEquity., Retrieved August 19, 2022, from.

Stephenson, N. (2003). *Snow crash: A novel. Spectra*. Bantam Books.

Sung, E. C., Bae, S., Han, D. I. D., & Kwon, O. (2021). Consumer engagement via interactive artificial intelligence and mixed reality. *International Journal of Information Management*, 60, 102382. DOI: 10.1016/j.ijinfomgt.2021.102382

Swilley, E. (2015). Moving Virtual Retail into Reality: Examining Metaverse and Augmented Reality in the Online Shopping Experience. Looking Forward, Looking Back. *Drawing on the Past to Shape the Future of Marketing*, 675–677, 675–677. Advance online publication. DOI: 10.1007/978-3-319-24184-5_163

Uricchio, W. (2011). The algorithmic turn: Photosynth, augmented reality and the changing implications of the image. *Visual Studies*, 26(1), 25–35. DOI: 10.1080/1472586X.2011.548486

Visser, A., & Molin, M. (2022). Where should I buy my sofa?: A qualitative study on Swedish digital natives in the omni-channel furniture retailing environment.

Wajire, P. (2022). Exploring the Metaverse: Challenges and Opportunities for India in the 'Next Internet. Retieved 23 August 2023, from https://www.orfonline.org/research/exploring-the-metaverse/

Wang, H., Ning, H., Lin, Y., Wang, W., Dhelim, S., Farha, F., Ding, J., & Daneshmand, M. (2023). A survey on the metaverse: The state-of-the-art, technologies, applications, and challenges. *IEEE Internet of Things Journal*, 10(16), 14671–14688. DOI: 10.1109/JIOT.2023.3278329

Wang, X., Su, Z., & Miao, Y. (2023, September 1). Social Metaverse: Challenges and Solutions. *IEEE Internet of Things Magazine*, 6(3), 144–150. DOI: 10.1109/IOTM.001.2200266

Zackery, A., Shariatpanahi, P., Zolfagharzadeh, M. M., & Pourezzat, A. A. (2016). Toward a simulated replica of futures: Classification and possible trajectories of simulation in futures studies. *Futures*, 81, 40–53. DOI: 10.1016/j.futures.2015.11.002

Zhao, R., Zhang, Y., Zhu, Y., Lan, R., & Hua, Z. (2022, January 1). Metaverse: Security and Privacy Concerns. Cornell University. https://doi.org//arxiv.2203.03854DOI: 10.48550

# Chapter 15
# Transforming User Experience in the Metaverse Through Emotional Intelligence and Affective Computing

**Manvi Saini**
https://orcid.org/0009-0001-0739-9275
*Chandigarh College of Engineering and Technology, Panjab University, Chandigarh, India*

**Aditi Bansal**
https://orcid.org/0009-0008-0870-7832
*Chandigarh College of Engineering and Technology, Panjab University, Chandigarh, India*

**Sudhakar Kumar**
https://orcid.org/0000-0001-7928-4234
*Chandigarh College of Engineering and Technology, Panjab University, Chandigarh, India*

**Chunjia Han**
*University of London, UK*

**Sunil K. Singh**
https://orcid.org/0000-0003-4876-7190
*Chandigarh College of Engineering and Technology, Panjab University, Chandigarh, India*

**Brij B. Gupta**
https://orcid.org/0000-0003-4929-4698
*Asia University, Taiwan & University of Economics and Human Science, Warsaw, Poland*

**Konstantinos Psannis**
https://orcid.org/0000-0003-0020-6394
*University of Macedonia, Greece*

## ABSTRACT

*Affective Computing in the Metaverse marks a crucial step in integrating emotional engagement into user experiences. Recognizing and responding to users' emotions is key to fostering meaningful interactions in immersive virtual environments. This chapter explores the impact of emotion theory on human-computer interaction (HCI), examining how emotions influence user personality, interests, and cognitive development in virtual spaces. Technological advancements like emotion detection, multi-modal recognition, and emotion synthesis are highlighted for their role in enhancing emotional awareness. A framework for ethical decision-making stresses the importance of user consent and feedback, ensuring emotional engagement is respectful of individual rights. The focus is on developing emotionally intelligent systems that deepen connections and offer richer experiences. By combining theoretical insights with practical applications, this chapter lays the groundwork for creating more empathetic and user-centered digital*

DOI: 10.4018/979-8-3693-8628-6.ch015

*environments in the Metaverse.*

## 1. INTRODUCTION

Affective computing is rapidly emerging within the digital world, especially when digging deeper into immersive environments just like the Metaverse. The intersection of affective computing and the Metaverse holds the ability to reshape how we interact with digital structures, fostering emotional connections and improving user reviews in ways previously unimagined. As users navigate digital areas, the capacity of structures to apprehend and reply to emotional states becomes important for developing environments that are personalized, and true.The introduction sets the foundation for understanding how emotional engagement is essential in shaping virtual interactions.

### 1.1 Definition of Affective Computing

Affective computing (Wu et al., 2015) is the area of studying, designing and developing software and hardware systems that can recognize, interpret, process, and simulate human effects. Rosalind Picard referenced it in 1997 — Emotional Intelligence + Computation Technology = Affect Computing. Affective computing is being done to study and make devices and programmed systems that can identify, interpret, process, and simulate human effects (emotions) and also understand how technology((Kumar, Shankar, Behl, et al., 2023)) can take advantage of this sensing; it is the way computing (Sudhakar Kumar, 2017) in technology needs to work to be able to detect emotional cues from users through facial expression recognition, speech or other signal modalities like brainwaves act etc.

### 1.2 Overview of Metaverse

The Metaverse (M. Singh et al., 2021) is regularly described as the evolution of the internet, presenting an immersive, continual, and shared digital surroundings in which users can have interaction with virtual gadgets and digital space across time. The Metaverse represents a mixing of digital and physical truth, in which the online and offline lifestyles are blurred. The Metaverse is a massive, interconnected network (S. K. Singh et al., 2022) of three-D digital worlds and environments that customers can find out and interact with the usage of numerous technologies together with virtual reality (VR)(Gupta, Gaurav, Albeshri, & Alsalman, 2023), Augmented reality (AR), and combined reality (MR). It is a collective digital shared area created by means of the convergence of reality and digital reality, unlike conventional video games or social media (Aggarwal et al., 2022) platforms, the Metaverse is characterised by using:

- Immersion: Customers experience fully enveloped in a virtual environment, with senses along with sight, sound, or even touch being stimulated to imitate actual reports.
- Patience: The Metaverse exists continuously, even if users are offline. adjustments made in the virtual global continue to be while customers return.
- Interactivity: Customers can have interaction with the surroundings and other members in actual-time, making the virtual revel in surprisingly dynamic.
- Consumer-Generated Content Material: The Metaverse empowers customers to create, personal, and proportion virtual property, such as avatars, environments, and digital items.

The scope of the Metaverse extends beyond leisure and gaming. It has the capacity to convert diverse domains, consisting of social interplay, trade, schooling, healthcare, or even governance.

## 1.3 Importance of Emotional Engagement in Virtual Interactions

Emotional engagement plays a vital role in enhancing user experiences within the metaverse, a virtual space where complete immersion is crucial. Unlike the conventional way humans interact with computers, the metaverse offers more instantaneous and constantly evolving experiences, leading to more intense emotional responses. When people develop strong emotional connections to the digital spaces, avatars, and communities they interact with, they are more likely to feel a deep sense of presence and immersion. This strong bond between users and the brand encourages active participation, shapes choices, and enhances overall contentment. Whether it's through compelling storytelling, social interactions, or decision-making processes, emotions play a vital role in shaping the user's experience and cultivating a deep sense of connection within the virtual world.

The demand for intelligence (Mengi et al., 2023) thinking in the virtual world is increasing. Business efficiency, the technology (S. Gupta et al., 2021) that allows machines to perceive and respond to human emotions, has great potential to create virtual environments that adapt to users' needs. By analyzing emotions through facial expressions, speech, or movement, the Metaverse can provide creative experiences for those looking for competition by making users feel anxious or positive. Avatars (Fokides, 2020) and virtual environments that understand and respond to user emotions can provide realism and authenticity, thus improving the overall experience in the virtual world. Emotional collaboration can also increase user satisfaction and retention during the transition. Users who feel emotionally connected to virtual environments and avatars are more likely to return and invest in digital ecosystems. Users are expected to become more active participants through social networking, virtual shopping, or participation in virtual communities. This not only supports the development of society, but also supports the business in the transition because the desire to connect to digital assets increases their perceived value. In today's digital revolution, emotional engagement is essential for the Metaverse to create meaningful, long-lasting experiences for its users.

The key contributions are as follows:

1. Discussion of advanced technologies like emotion detection systems, multi (Naveen Aggarwal, n.d.) modal recognition, and emotion synthesis to enhance emotional awareness in the Metaverse.
2. Emphasis on ethical considerations, including user consent and feedback, to ensure emotional engagement respects individual rights.
3. Focus on developing emotionally intelligent systems that foster deeper connections and meaningful user experiences within virtual spaces.
4. Contribution to integrating theoretical knowledge with practical applications to advance emotionally responsive environments in the Metaverse.

The rest of this chapter is structured as follows: Section 2 discusses the theoretical foundations of affective computing and its connection to emotional psychology and human-computer interaction. Section 3 provides an overview of the current state of affective computing in the metaverse, including existing tools, case studies, and the challenges faced in enhancing emotional engagement. In Section 4, various techniques for recognizing emotions and designing emotionally responsive virtual environments are explored. Section 5 delves into the principles of emotional design, focusing on how avatars and digital personas contribute to user experience and empathy. Ethical considerations surrounding privacy, manipulation (Calo, 2013), and accessibility in affective computing are addressed in Section 6. The future scope of affective computing in virtual interactions is presented in Section 7 before concluding the chapter in Section 8. Finally, Section 9 summarizes the chapter.

## 2. THEORETICAL FOUNDATIONS

The theoretical foundations of affective computing is essential for exploring its applications inside the Metaverse. This segment delves into the psychology of feelings, the connection among human-laptop interplay (HCI) and emotional responses, and the technology that facilitate affective computing. By analyzing these foundational ideas, we are able to better admire how emotional engagement can be integrated into digital environments, leading to richer and greater meaningful interactions between users and era.

### 2.1 The Psychology of Emotions

Good psychology is essential to understanding how affecting computing works, especially in a virtual environment like the Metaverse. Emotions (Weiss, 2000) are complex, multifaceted responses that arise from external stimuli and internal states, they influence knowledge, behaviour, and decision-making that are important in creating user experiences. Understanding emotions from a psychological perspective is essential to building systems that can capture, interpret, and respond to users' emotions in the Metaverse. Many psychological models (Wang et al., 2022), such as the James-Lange theory (which considers the body's most physiological responses) and cognitive appraisal (which proposes a measure of the mental deterioration of events), provide a framework (Peñalvo et al., 2022) for thinking about what happens in a virtual environment. This knowledge is essential to creating a virtual environment that elicits the desired response and creates an effective and engaging user experience.In metadata, emotions are not only experienced in person, but also shared and spread across social contexts, making them contagious and important to understand. By integrating psychology into the workings of thinking, machine learning can create machines that think and work better, interact better, and own people.

## 2.2 Human-Computer Interaction (HCI) and Emotion

*Figure 1. Emotional engagement in metaverse*

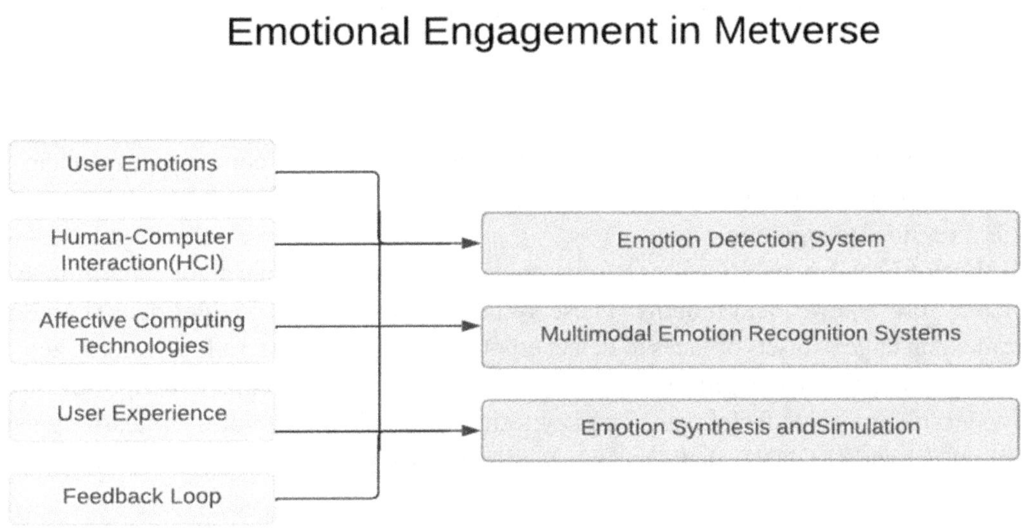


Fig.1. illustrates the human-computer interaction in the metaverse. Human-Computer Interaction (HCI) (Picard, 1999) is the study of the way human beings interact with digital interactions and how feelings play a great role in shaping those interactions. Human-computer interplay specialises in usability (Lim et al., 2022), functionality, and performance, but as digital experiences end up greater suitable, the concept of the interplay impact is becoming an increasing number of essentials, emotions affect how users see, sense, and engage with era, which in turn affects delight, motivation, and the overall user enjoy.

The boundary between the physical and digital worlds blurs, making emotional responses even more prominent in the Metaverse. Users emotionally connect with virtual objects and spaces in these environments. Users expect emotional experiences that mirror real-world interactions in the design of virtual worlds. By using technology to sense and respond to emotional states, it can create more personalised and adaptive experiences. For example, systems that recognize frustration or excitement can adjust difficulty levels or give feedback.

In the Metaverse, emotion and HCI intersect. Digital avatars are extensions of the user's identity, and their ability to convey emotional cues through facial expressions, body language, or voice affects the quality of social interactions. To ensure that virtual interactions feel authentic and emotionally satisfying, the research in emotion must focus on designing interfaces that allow for rich emotional expression. The Metaverse is able to create more engaging, human-centered experiences that cater to users' emotional and cognitive needs.

## 2.3 Affective Computing Technologies

Affective computing technologies are designed to detect, interpret, and simulate human emotions, enhancing user engagement in virtual environments such as the Metaverse. These systems use a combination of machine learning algorithms, computer vision techniques, and physiological sensors to enable real-time emotional analysis and adaptive behavior in virtual spaces.

### 2.3.1 Emotion Detection Systems

Emotion detection systems are fundamental components of affective computing, focusing on interpreting a user's emotional state based on various data inputs:

Facial Expression Recognition:

**How It Works**: Facial recognition uses computer vision and deep learning algorithms to analyze facial features like eyebrows, eyes, and mouths. These systems typically use convolutional neural networks (CNNs) trained on large datasets of faces to detect emotions like happiness, sadness, anger, and surprise.

**Technology Used**: Facial recognition typically uses an RGB camera to capture images and uses neural networks to learn large-scale facial data. The key to its success is the use of deep learning techniques such as neural networks (CNNs) that can extract features from images and identify relevant patterns that influence thinking.

Voice-based Emotion Recognition:

**How It Works**: The process involves using speech recognition techniques to analyze audio data. It determines the emotional state by examining characteristics such as tone, volume, pitch, and speech pattern. For example, speaking loudly and quickly can indicate happiness, while speaking softly and slowly can indicate anger or sadness.

**Technology Used**: Voice-based emotion recognition uses techniques from signal processing and machine learning, such as Hidden Markov Models (HMMs) (Sharma et al., 2023)or deep learning models like Long Short-Term Memory Networks (LSTMs). These algorithms are trained on large datasets of audio recordings labeled with emotions, allowing systems to identify patterns in speech related to different emotional states.

Sensor-based Emotion Recognition:

**How It Works**: These systems use the body's own sensors to monitor signals such as heart rate, skin conductance, and pupil dilation. For example, a stressed user may see increased heart rate or changes in skin tone, while a happy user may see changes in pupils.

**Technology Used**: Sensors such as electrocardiogram (ECG) sensors, electrodermal activity (EDA) sensors, and infrared cameras are often used in conjunction with machine learning algorithms. These algorithms analyze data from the sensors to detect changes in the body that may be related to an emotional state.

### 2.3.2 Multimodal Emotion Recognition Systems

Multimodal emotion recognition enhances emotion detection by integrating data from multiple sources, providing a more comprehensive understanding of user emotions:

**How It Works:** Multimodal systems use data from facial expressions, voice patterns, and text inputs to create a more detailed emotional profile. For instance, combining facial expression analysis, voice tone, and sentiment analysis (Singh et al., 2022) from text data allows systems to make more accurate predictions about complex emotions like nostalgia or surprise.

**Technology Used**: These systems often use cross-modal data fusion techniques, such as deep learning models like deep belief networks (DBNs) or recurrent neural networks (RNNs) (Buchanan, 2001), which can process and integrate data from different modalities (e.g., audio, video, text) in real time. Machine learning models use algorithms such as conditional random fields (CRFs) or support vector machines (SVMs) to correlate data across modalities.

**Real-Time Synchronization**: These systems are designed to update in real-time, allowing virtual environments to dynamically adapt based on the user's emotional state. For example, if a user shows signs of excitement, the virtual environment could change lighting, music, or scene elements to reflect that emotion, enhancing user engagement and immersion.

### 2.3.3 Emotion Synthesis and Simulation

Affective computing also involves the ability to generate emotions and behaviors in virtual environments, making interactions in the Metaverse more dynamic and engaging:

Emotionally Sensitive Avatars:

**How It Works**: Emotionally sensitive avatars are programmed to express emotions in response to set conditions or user input. For example, an avatar may smile when a user completes a task or frown when the user shows frustration. These avatars use rule-based systems or deep learning models to trigger expressions based on user input or context.

**Technology Used**: Emotionally sensitive avatars are often powered by artificial intelligence and machine learning models, which analyze user interactions and emotional cues. For instance, natural language processing and computer vision algorithms can be combined to create avatars that respond to user input with appropriate emotional expressions.

Emotionally Adaptive Virtual Environments:

**How It Works**: These virtual environments adapt based on users' emotional states. For example, lighting, background music, and scene elements can be changed to match a user's emotional condition. If a user feels stressed, the environment might shift to a calmer atmosphere, while a positive emotional state might lead to a vibrant and upbeat environment.

**Technology Used**: Emotionally adaptive environments use artificial intelligence and machine learning algorithms, often based on techniques like genetic algorithms or reinforcement learning. These algorithms can predict environmental changes that correlate with emotional states, ensuring that the virtual environment supports user engagement and emotional immersion.The Fig.2. illustrates a framework for emotion detection and synthesis, comprising Emotion Detection Systems, Multimodal Emotion Recognition Systems with integration layers and real-time adaptation modules, and Emotion Synthesis and Simulation. It focuses on the integration of detection, processing, and simulation in emotion-centric systems.

*Figure 2. Affective computing systems*

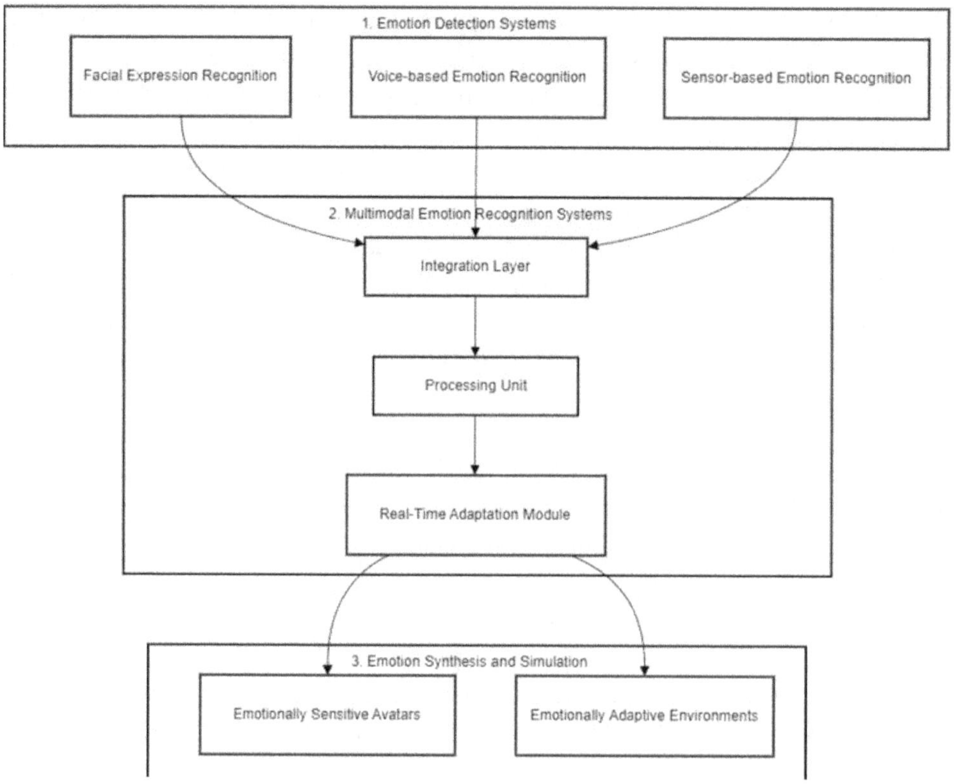


## 2.3.4 AI in Affective Computing

Machine learning (ML) and artificial intelligence (AI) are at the heart of affective computing, allowing machines to learn and improve their cognitive abilities over time.

**Emotion Classification Models:** Deep learning (Thakur et al., 2022) models such as convolutional neural networks (CNN) (Karthika & Jegatha Deborah, 2021) and neural networks (RNN) are trained on large emotion datasets (images of faces, audio recordings, etc.) to separate imagination from reality. This model can detect (A. Gupta et al., 2023) subtle changes in customer behaviour over time.

**Predictive Emotional Modeling:** AI (A. Gupta et al., 2022) can predict a user's future emotions based on their past interactions. This is useful in a personalized virtual environment where the system can predict what the user is thinking and adjust accordingly. For example, if the user often gets stressed during a virtual meeting, the system can provide instructions to calm down or adjust the environment to reduce stress.

Affective computing (Raji & Buolamwini, 2022) technologies are remodeling the manner emotions are integrated into virtual studies, specially within the Metaverse. From emotion detection via sensors and NLP to synthesizing emotions in avatars and virtual worlds, those technologies decorate emotional engagement, making interactions extra immersive and sensible. As these structures continue to evolve, the capacity for deeper emotional connections in the Metaverse will amplify, paving the way for new kinds of conversation and emotional understanding in virtual spaces. Table 1 discusses the comparison between the various frameworks like GDPR,HIPAA,CCPA etc.

*Table 1. Comparison between different ethical frameworks*

| Framework | Data Protection Measures | Consent Requirements | User Rights |
|---|---|---|---|
| **GDPR** | Strong data encryption; right to access and delete data | Explicit consent required for data processing | Right to data portability; right to be forgotten |
| **Proposed Framework for Affective Computing** | Contextual data protection; real-time monitoring | Continuous consent; ability to withdraw consent anytime | Right to emotional data access; right to opt-out of emotional tracking |
| **HIPAA (Health Insurance Portability and Accountability Act)** | Data anonymization for health-related data | Implied consent for treatment; explicit for sharing data | Right to view health records; right to amend health information |
| **California Consumer Privacy Act (CCPA)** | Data minimization; right to request information on data usage | Opt-out consent model | Right to know about personal data collection; right to delete personal data |

## 3. CURRENT STATE OF AFFECTIVE COMPUTING IN THE METAVERSE

The mixing of affective computing into the Metaverse is a region of development that promises to enhance emotional engagement in digital environments. By means of exploring the affective computing within the Metaverse, some insights into how those technologies are shaping the future of virtual interactions are provided.

### 3.1 Existing Applications and Tools

Affective computing plays a key role in improving emotional communication (Pitale & Bhumgara, 2019) by integrating technologies that recognize, interpret, and respond to human (Ennouamani & Mahani, 2017) emotions. Some famous apps and tools that are used to create greater awareness include:

#### 3.1.1.Emotion Detection Software

- Affectiva: This software uses advanced facial recognition (Gupta, Gaurav, Chui, & Arya, 2024) recognition technology to measure emotions based on facial expressions. It is widely used in education and training to change content and presentation based on the user's mood. Affectiva reports an accuracy rate of over 90%, making it reliable for applications that require instant feedback (Affectiva, 2022).
- Realeyes: Realeyes analyzes facial expressions to gain insight into the viewer's emotional response. Its applications range from business environments to educational settings, where it helps adjust the learning experience based on student feedback (Realeyes, 2022).

### 3.1.2. Adaptive Learning Systems

- Smart Sparrow: This learning tool measures student engagement through a variety of metrics, including emotional responses, to personalize learning content (Gee, 2003). Research shows that using Smart Sparrow can improve retention and improve learning by up to 25% (Smart Sparrow, 2021).
- Knewton: Knewton uses algorithms that adapt the learning process to the individual needs of students, including emotional engagement. This personalized approach is associated with better motivation and performance, with some studies showing users' test scores increased by 15% (Knewton, 2020).

### 3.1.3.Virtual Reality Environments

- ENGAGE: It is a social VR platform designed for education and training, allowing users to create experiences where they can express their emotions through avatars. The platform integrates tools for teachers to measure student feedback and adjust teaching accordingly, resulting in a 30% increase in student engagement during virtual classrooms (ENGAGE, 2022).
- AltspaceVR: This social VR environment encourages interaction between users through shared experiences. AltspaceVR allows users to interact with avatars that express emotions, support non-verbal communication, and encourage connection between users, which is essential for collaboration (AltspaceVR, 2021).

### 3.1.4.Social Learning Platforms

- Edmodo: An educational platform widely used for social communication to improve relationships with peers. Edmodo's thought-provoking tools greatly enhance the classroom experience by encouraging students to share thoughts and ideas. Research shows that 78% of Edmodo users report good relationships with their peers, leading to collaboration and motivation (Hew & Cheung, 2013).
- Flipgrid: This interactive video platform encourages students to share their thoughts through video responses. The ability to communicate via video instead of text fosters deeper emotional connection and has been shown to increase student engagement by 45% (Flipgrid, 2021).

### 3.1.5.Gamification Elements

- Kahoot! Kahoot! increases collaboration by encouraging thinking through competition and collaboration; 90% of users say they feel more engaged when using the platform (Kahoot!, 2022).
- Classcraft: Classcraft gamifies science education by allowing students to earn rewards based on thinking and social interaction. The platform reports that 85% of teachers see a connection between students who participate in the game environment (Classcraft, 2022).

These applications demonstrate the transformative potential of affective computing in the Metaverse, enhancing emotional engagement and fostering meaningful interactions in educational settings. The successful integration of these tools not only improves user experience but also promotes a deeper understanding of emotional dynamics in virtual environments.

## 3.2 Case Studies of Emotional Engagement

Several case studies illustrating how affective computing enhances emotional engagement in virtual environments are given below. These examples demonstrate many applications of emotional technologies within the Metaverse, highlighting their potential to improve user experience and foster meaningful interactions.

### 3.2.1 CUNY Affective and Responsive Virtual Environment (CARVE) Hub

CARVE Hub is the largest platform for integrating interventions into the learning environment, especially the virtual classroom. This new system uses emotion-detection technology to engage students by analyzing facial expressions. CARVE uses a face-to-face classification model to provide teachers with instant feedback and allow them to adjust lessons to student needs. Research shows that this response not only increases engagement, but also fosters a sense of connection among students. Specifically, one study found that student engagement increased by 25% and satisfaction increased by 30% when using CARVE Hub compared to traditional online courses. Avatars used in CARVE express emotions through emoticons, facilitating nonverbal communication and increasing the authenticity of virtual interactions (D'Mello and Graesser, 2015).

### 3.2.2 Minecraft as a Constructivist Learning Environment

Minecraft is an effective learning environment that encourages collaborative learning and imagination among students. In a collaborative environment, students engage in activities that require teamwork, problem-solving, and deep thinking. Each session includes content, guided games, and discussions that encourage thinking and trust among participants. Research shows that students build strong relationships when they work together on challenges like surviving a zombie apocalypse. In one study, 85% of participants said they had better relationships with their peers after completing a collaborative project, and 90% said the experience improved their educational outcomes. This case study highlights the importance of collaboration in learning and demonstrates how digital environments can contribute (Blikstein, 2013).

### 3.2.3 Digital Fabrication and Maker Education

Digital production activities in educational design provide educational experiences that support thinking. A study conducted on children (4-5 years old) showed that helping an owl prepare a healthy plate of food, encouraging creativity and communication collaboration, are good explanations. Using Fab Lab resources, children can experience excitement, curiosity and challenge in a supportive environment. Approximately 75% of participants expressed pleasure in the activity, and 80% expressed curiosity about their work. The combination of making, cooking and crafts encourages imagination connection and enhances the transformation of educational culture. This literature emphasizes the importance of emotional awareness and management in collaboration and highlights the role of disclosure in emotional development (Resnick et al., 2009).

### 3.2.4 Facilitating Learning in Fab Labs

Fab Lab facilitators play a key role in enhancing students' learning experiences through digital design. One study examined how technical professionals encouraged participation in inappropriate problem-solving environments. By observing student interactions and interviews, researchers identified the need for teaching strategies that encouraged emotional and social engagement. Caregiver support in solving problems and encouraging collaboration is important for developing a sense of community and unity. Specifically, 65% of students said they felt more confident in their problem-solving skills after receiving guidance from a mentor, and 70% reported a good sense of their learning community. These data highlight the importance of education needed to create a positive attitude toward learning where students feel valued and motivated to participate (Hew & Cheung, 2013).

### 3.2.5 Emotional Engagement through Social Networking in Education

The integration of social networks into education fosters solidarity through social support and advocacy. Platforms like Edmodo and Facebook Groups allow students to share their thoughts, share experiences, and build mutual understanding. Research shows that this type of thinking has a positive impact on student motivation and engagement in the learning environment. One study found that 78% of students who used these platforms reported feeling more connected to their peers, and 82% reported feeling motivated to participate in discussions. By providing a space for open communication, these systems foster a community of students interested in contributing to the successes and challenges of their peers. These data demonstrate the potential of social communication to improve learning outcomes and facilitate discussion of educational technology (Egger et al., 2019).

*Table 2. Different case studies and their findings*

| Case Study | Description | Key Findings | Quantitative Data |
|---|---|---|---|
| **CUNY Affective and Responsive Virtual Environment (CARVE) Hub** | Integrates affective computing to enhance student engagement in VR classrooms. | Immediate feedback improves teaching effectiveness. | 25% increase in student engagement; 30% improvement in satisfaction scores. |
| **Minecraft as a Constructivist Learning Environment** | Uses collaborative quests in Minecraft to foster teamwork and emotional connections among students. | Emotional bonds enhance learning outcomes. | 85% felt more connected; 90% stated emotional experiences improved learning. |
| **Digital Fabrication and Maker Education** | Engages young children in narrative-driven digital fabrication projects to inspire creativity. | Promotes excitement and curiosity in hands-on learning. | 75% felt excited; 80% expressed curiosity about projects. |
| **Facilitating Learning in Fab Labs** | Explores the role of facilitators in enhancing student engagement in digital fabrication settings. | Facilitators boost confidence and sense of community. | 65% felt more confident; 70% indicated a greater sense of belonging. |
| **Emotional Engagement through Social Networking in Education** | Utilizes platforms like Edmodo to foster peer interactions and emotional connections. | Enhances motivation and collaboration among students. | 78% felt more connected; 82% reported increased motivation to participate. |

Table 2 illustrates the significant impact of affective computing on emotional engagement in virtual environments. Technologies like the CARVE Hub and Minecraft enhance collaboration, creativity, and learning outcomes by detecting and responding to users' emotions. The findings highlight that emotional connections are crucial for effective education in the Metaverse, leading to increased engagement, motivation, and satisfaction. As the Metaverse evolves, the integration of affective computing will shape future educational experiences, making them both intellectually stimulating and emotionally resonant.

### 3.3 Challenges and Limitations

Despite the early use of affective computing in the Metaverse, there are a number of challenges and limitations that need to be addressed:

1. Privacy and Ethical Issues: The collection and analysis of emotional data raises significant privacy issues. Users may feel uncomfortable with a machine monitoring their emotional state, which can raise ethical issues around consent and data use. Proper documentation is essential for users to feel safe and understand how their information is being used.
2. Technical Limitations: Existing opinion research tools can be difficult to get right, especially among diverse groups of people who share different opinions. Misinterpretation of sensory information can lead to inappropriate responses from the system, potentially increasing rather than reducing user stress.
3. Integration Challenges: Integrating related tools with existing learning technologies can be difficult. Developers face challenges in ensuring integration and functionality compatibility, which can limit widespread use of these innovations.
4. Cultural differences: There can be huge differences in thinking across different cultures, which affects the performance of the cognitive algorithm. There is a risk that the system may not correctly interpret the views of users with different ethnic backgrounds, resulting in a lack of engagement.
5. User Resistance: Some users may object to systems that monitor their emotional state, believing them to be intrusive or inappropriate. Building trust and demonstrating the benefits of these tools is key to overcoming this issue.
6. Resource Intensity: Implementing brainstorming will require significant resources(Bisht & Vampugani, 2022), such as technology or staff training. Schools may face financial constraints that limit their ability to use this technology.
7. Limited Research on Long-Term Impact: Although preliminary research shows benefits of meditation over meditation, there is no long-term research examining the long-term effects of technology on academic outcomes and happiness.

Solving these problems is important for the success of the integration of communication barriers, ensuring that technology is not only practical, but also fair and leading.

## 4. ENHANCING EMOTIONAL ENGAGEMENT

Enhancing emotional engagement inside the Metaverse is a key goal of affective computing, as it ends in richer, more significant interactions between users and virtual(Singh, Malhotra, & Sharma, 2022) environments. By focusing on those factors, stories that resonate with users to an emotional degree can be created, making deeper connections and engagement in the digital areas.

### 4.1 Techniques for Emotion Recognition

Emotional (Buolamwini & Gebru, 2018) awareness is the foundation of thinking in the mind, allowing the body to interpret and respond to the user's emotional state. Many strategies have been developed to increase the accuracy and efficiency of cognitive experiences in virtual environments, especially in the Metaverse.

#### 4.1.1 Facial Expression Analysis

Facial expression is an important indicator of emotional state. Facial recognition technology includes:

1. **Feature detection and extraction:** Uses computer vision algorithms to detect and identify specific facial features (such as eyebrows, mouth lines, and eye shapes). The process involves:
   - **Landmark Detection:** Algorithms detect important points on the face, such as the corners of the eyes and the corners of the mouth, and determine their location and movement.
   - **Action Units (AU):** According to the Facial Action Coding System (FACS), AUs classify facial actions associated with certain emotions (e.g., raising eyebrows in surprise).

**Machine learning classification** (Amiryousefi et al., 2023)**:** The extracted features are fed into a machine learning model (such as a support vector machine, decision tree, or neural network) and trained by representing the face in a datasheet. This model classifies emotions as a diagnosis.

**Real-time processing:** Advanced facial recognition can display emotions in real time, allowing the virtual character to instantly reflect the user's instructions and improve the editing experience.

2. Voice Emotion Recognition

Speech recognition is an important part of thought computing that focuses on analyzing sounds to interpret thoughts. Acoustic feature extraction is a simple tool that analyzes speech signals to identify features such as tone, pitch, volume, and speech rate. Commonly used features include Mel Frequency Cepstral Coefficients (MFCCs) that capture the quality of speech, and quality features such as intonation, rhythm, and stress, all of which provide information about the speaker's perspective. Additionally, Emotional Analysis in speech uses natural language processing (NLP) to analyze speech content by combining acoustic and linguistic content to understand the emotional state of the speaker.

Situational understanding takes this analysis even further; advanced models allow virtual characters to change and respond appropriately by taking into account issues such as previous discussion topics or urgency for better interpretation in thought, increasing user engagement.

3. Physiological Signal Analysis

Physiological signals are useful for understanding emotions because they often involve unconscious responses to stimuli. Technologies for detecting these signals often include biometric(Gupta, Gaurav, & Arya, 2024) sensors in wearable devices such as smartwatches or fitness trackers, which track things like heart rate variability (HRV), skin and body temperature behavior. These indicators can reveal emotional responses such as anxiety or happiness. Signal processing is applied to the raw physiological data to extract important points, such as changes in HRV, where low changes often indicate stress, or electrodermal activity (EDA), which tracks skin arousal as a sign of stress. By combining physical data with other models such as facial and voice analysis, the system can better understand the user's emotional state and create a more responsive and real-time virtual experience.

4. Contextual and Environmental Factors

Understanding the context of interactions is crucial for accurate emotion recognition. Techniques involve:

- Context-Aware systems: These systems include contextual information such as user history, social interactions, and the environment. For example, users may react differently in a cooperative gaming scenario than in a competitive gaming(Singh & Rawat, 2024) scenario.
- User feedback loop: Provide feedback to users to improve the user experience to ensure the system can adapt to individual differences in opinion and culture.
- Dynamic environment response: By understanding the situation and the user's mood, the virtual environment can adjust its features (such as lighting, sound) to create a pleasant experience.

## 4.2 Designing Emotionally Responsive Environments

Creating an emotional environment in the Metaverse by creating virtual environments that adapt to a user's emotional state(Lim et al., 2022), encouraging deep connection and understanding. These spaces are designed to respond immediately to the user's emotional cues, creating personal experiences that resonate on a deeper, more emotional level. By integrating intelligence into the fabric of the virtual world, the environment becomes more intuitive, empowering, and engaging, resulting in similarly meaningful experiences.

The descriptions and interactions in these areas can also be designed to suit the needs of the users. The intensity of the story can be changed according to the user's level of interest or stress, providing more information and a pleasant feeling. The AI-powered (Francesco Colace, n.d.) characters in this virtual world can also react, adjusting their behavior and dialogue to suit the user's preferences. If you are feeling stressed or confused, virtual friends can provide support or guidance and help you maintain a positive mindset. In situations such as games, the difficulty level of the task or challenge can be changed to prevent stress or anxiety, allowing users to immerse themselves in the experience without stress.

Instant feedback plays a key role in controlling emotions in the mind. Using biometric sensors or wearable devices, the system can continuously monitor body parameters such as heart rate and skin tone to detect changes in mood. Signs will now alert the environment to update to ensure that the environment is in line with the user's emotional state. Facial and voice recognition can detect changes in mood, allowing virtual characters or assistants to respond to suggestions in real time, creating a harmonious and conscious relationship.

## 5. USER EXPERIENCE AND EMOTIONAL DESIGN

*Figure 3. Comprehensive framework for understanding Design Principles*

Figure 3. outlines a comprehensive framework for understanding and implementing emotional design principles in virtual environments. It focuses on the importance of identifying user emotions through various research methods, including user surveys, interviews, and emotion detection technologies.

### 5.1 Principles of Emotional Design in Virtual Spaces

Designing in a virtual environment involves creating experiences that encourage user feedback. The main goal is to improve the overall user experience by encouraging deep interaction and satisfaction. Here are the key principles:

### 5.1.1. Identify User Emotions

Understanding user emotions is crucial. This can be achieved through:

- User Research: Employ methods like surveys, interviews, and focus groups to gather qualitative data on user expectations and emotional needs (De la Torre & Cohn, n.d.).
- Emotion Detection: Use biometric sensors (like heart rate monitors) or AI-based sentiment analysis of text and speech to assess users' emotional states.

### 5.1.2. Select Design Principles

Once emotions are identified, designers can apply specific principles:
Visual Aesthetics (Vats et al., 2023):

- Color Theory: Colors have psychological implications; for example, blue often conveys trust and calmness, while red can evoke excitement or urgency.
- Typography and Layout: Font choices and arrangements can affect readability and emotional perception. A clean, modern design often feels more inviting.

Narrative Structuring:

- Dynamic Storytelling: Implement branching narratives where users' choices lead to different story outcomes. This technique enhances emotional investment, making users feel more connected to the virtual world.
- Character Development: Creating relatable characters within narratives fosters empathy, encouraging users to engage emotionally with the storyline.

### 5.1.3. Implement Dynamic Visual Elements

Dynamic elements keep the experience fresh and engaging:

- Animations and Transitions: Clean transitions and animations could make studies sense greater fluidity, helping customers experience greater on top of things and much less annoyed at some stage in interactions.
- Real-time Environmental Modifications: Alter the surroundings based totally on consumer actions or emotional states. as an instance, lighting might dim in response to consumer misery, creating a chilled impact.

### 5.1.4. Feedback Mechanisms

Incorporating feedback loops is essential for emotional design:

- Haptic Feedback: Devices like VR gloves or vests can offer tactile responses, improving the interactions and making emotional experiences more real.

- Auditory Feedback: Sounds should correspond to actions—soft tones for success and deeper sounds for failure—to reinforce emotional reactions.

### 5.1.5. Personalization Algorithms

Utilizing machine learning and AI:

- Tailored Experiences: By analyzing user behavior, algorithms can adapt experiences to match individual preferences and emotional responses. For instance, if a user enjoys adventure, they might be guided toward more action-oriented experiences.

## 5.2 Role of Avatars and Digital Personas

Avatars and digital personas are essential components of a person dealing in digital environments, acting as extensions of users' identities and facilitating interaction. Their layout and capability significantly have an impact on emotional engagement.

### 5.2.1. Identity Representation via Digital Avatars

Digital avatars serve as a reflection of a user's identity within virtual spaces, offering a means to embody personal traits and preferences in a custom form. The ability to modify avatars to closely match a user's physical (Provence & Forcehimes, 2024) characteristics fosters a deep emotional connection. Users can mix and match components to create personalized digital representations. As game engines like Unreal Engine and Unity offer robust frameworks for implementing asset packs, users can easily tailor their avatar to reflect their personal style, enhancing their emotional engagement in the virtual world.

### 5.2.2. Social Interaction Frameworks

Avatars play a pivotal role in facilitating social interactions inside digital environments by way of mimicking human behaviors, which includes both verbal and non-verbal conversation. The combination of motion-sensing technology, consisting of Kinect or jump movement, permits actual-time tracking of person gestures and actions, translating them into the avatar's actions to complement social engagement. This allows for extra herbal and fluid conversation, corresponding to real-global interactions. Moreover, avatars can express feelings through facial expressions and body language using superior 3-D modeling strategies like blend shapes and rigging. Those elements allow avatars to visually replicate emotions, including layers of emotional intensity to social exchanges, making digital verbal exchange greater intuitive and immersive.

### 5.2·3. Empathy Algorithms

Empathy algorithms in virtual environments aim to enhance user experience by enabling avatars to adapt to the emotional state of the user, promoting a more empathetic interaction. Avatars equipped with machine learning models trained on emotional datasets can dynamically change behavior based on biometric data or sentiment analysis. For instance, if a user shows signs of frustration or fatigue, the avatar could provide encouragement, offer helpful hints, or adjust the environment to ease the user's experience. This kind of adaptive response fosters emotional engagement, as users feel their emotions are being recognized and validated by their digital companions. Incorporating such systems makes avatars not only interactive but emotionally responsive, strengthening the bond between users and their virtual environments.

### 5.2.4. Immersive Interaction Models

Creating immersive interactions is fundamental to enhancing emotional engagement in virtual spaces, and avatars play a central role in this by integrating high-quality graphics and realistic physics. Using advanced rendering techniques such as ray tracing can significantly enhance the visual quality of avatars, creating lifelike lighting, shadows, and reflections, which deepen the emotional connection users feel toward their digital personas. Additionally, implementing realistic physics using engines like Unity with NVIDIA PhysX or Havok ensures that avatar movements and interactions with the environment feel natural and believable. This realism in both visuals and physics helps users become more immersed in the virtual world, enhancing both the emotional and experiential aspects of their interactions.

## 5.3 Building Empathy through Design

Designing for empathy involves creating virtual environments that emotionally resonate with users, fostering understanding and connection. This approach treats empathy (Qi et al., 2023) as an active engagement with others' experiences, emphasising its importance in a digital world where meaningful interactions may be diminished by technology. Empathetic design also cultivates supportive environments that enhance mental well-being and reduce feelings of isolation. By aligning technology with human emotions and social dynamics, users are more likely to navigate virtual spaces in a meaningful way. This leads to richer interactions and a stronger sense of community, ultimately enhancing individual experiences and promoting emotional and social thriving.

### 5.3.1. User-Centered Design Approach

A user-centered design approach is fundamental to cultivating empathy in virtual environments (Dhar Dwivedi et al., 2012). By emphasizing the emotional and practical needs of users throughout the design process, developers can create immersive experiences that resonate on a profound emotional level. Employing iterative prototyping and Agile methodologies facilitates the continuous development and evaluation of designs with real users, ensuring that feedback is effectively integrated at each stage. This adaptive process results in products that are not only functionally efficient but also finely attuned to the emotional landscape of users. Understanding and addressing users' emotional requirements empowers designers to create environments that foster deeper connections and enhanced understanding among users (Hwang & Chien, 2022).

*Figure 4. Iterative Process of creating a prototype*

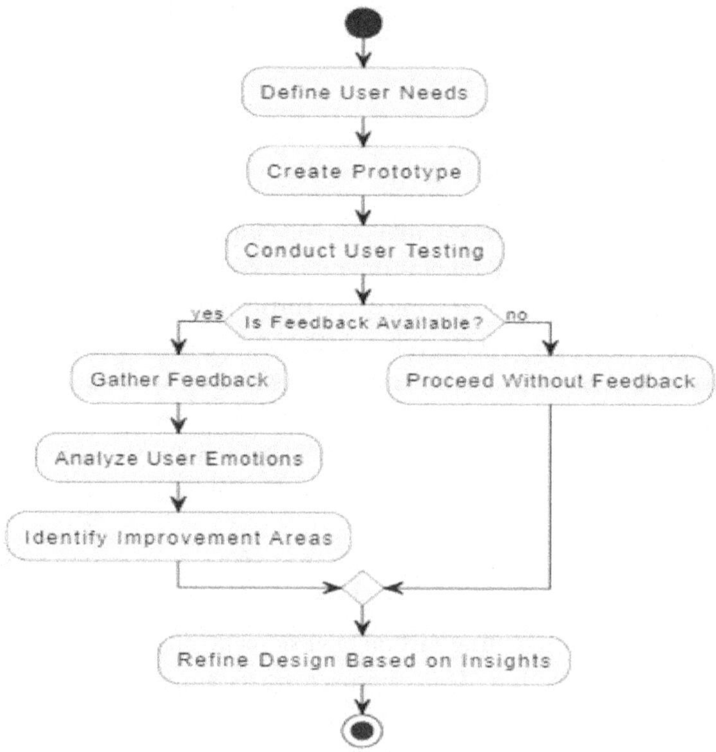


Fig.4 illustrates the iterative process of creating a prototype, showcasing the key stages involved in user-centred design. It begins with user research, where designers gather insights about users' emotional and practical needs through various methods. This is followed by brainstorming to generate diverse design concepts.

Low-fidelity prototypes are created for initial testing and user feedback. This feedback informs the refinement stages, enhancing the prototypes (Vats et al., 2023) based on user experiences. Ultimately, the process leads to high-fidelity prototypes that closely resemble the final product, allowing for comprehensive testing before launch. This adaptive approach ensures the final design not only meets functional requirements but also resonates deeply with users, fostering connection and understanding (Buchanan, 2001).

### 5.3.2. Inclusive and Accessible Design

Empathy in design is necessary for the creation of digital environments which are inclusive and accessible to all customers, no matter their abilities. The implementation of complete accessibility features—consisting of screen readers, customizable manage schemes, and opportunity input strategies—is critical for accommodating people with disabilities. By means of improving accessibility, designers cultivate a deeper emotional connection between customers and the digital environment, facilitating a broader spectrum of participation. ARIA (accessible wealthy net packages) standards offers a strong framework for ensuring that digital digital (Shneiderman & Plaisant, 2010) content is navigable and comprehensible for diverse audiences. This dedication to inclusivity not simplest enriches the overall user level in however additionally fosters a sense of belonging and engagement inside the digital area, ultimately contributing to an extra equitable and enriching interplay for all users.

### 5.3.3. Emotional Interfaces

The development of emotional interfaces is important for enhancing empathy within virtual environments. By creating adaptive user interfaces that dynamically respond to users' emotional states, developers can deliver more engaging and supportive experiences. For example, if a user shows signs of confusion, the interface can automatically simplify or clarify the available options, alleviating frustration and promoting a sense of understanding. To enable this adaptive behaviour, implementing AI algorithms that analyse user interactions in real-time is essential. Leveraging frameworks such as TensorFlow for behavioural analysis allows for the dynamic adjustment of UI elements, creating a responsive environment that effectively recognizes and addresses users' emotional needs. This approach is depicted in the Fig.5 shown below. It not only improves user interactions but also supports emotional well-being within the virtual space .

*Figure 5. Flowchart of behavioral analysis*

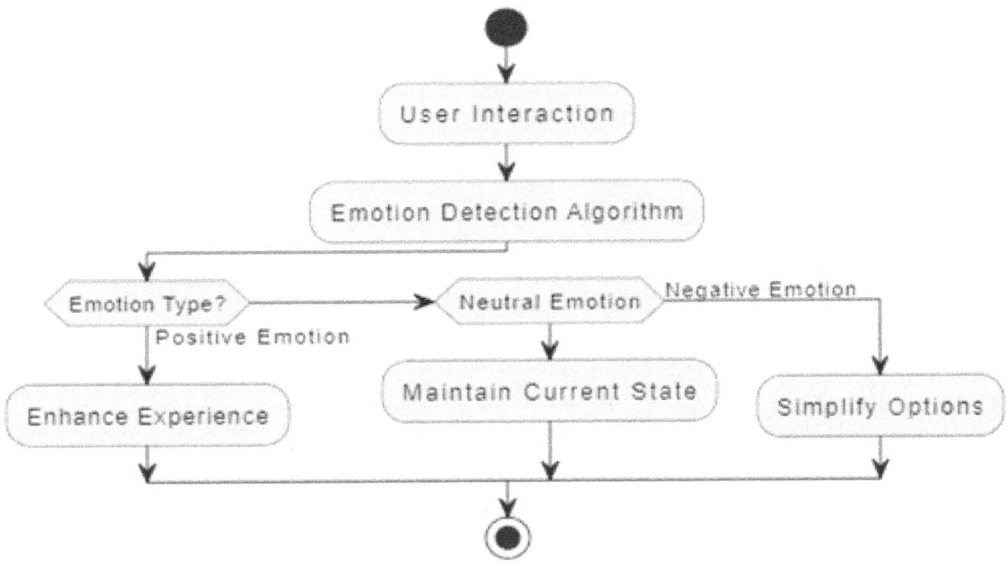


### 5.3.4. Community and Social Connection

Establishing a sense of community within virtual environments is essential for enhancing empathy among users. By designing collaborative (Acquisti et al., 2015) spaces that enable participants to engage in joint activities and discussions, developers can foster emotional connections through shared experiences. Features such as collaborative projects, discussion forums, and social events contribute to a dynamic community atmosphere, allowing users to connect in meaningful ways. The effective implementation of real-time communication tools, such as WebSocket, is crucial for facilitating seamless interactions in multiplayer environments. By promoting community engagement, designers can create a supportive network that nurtures empathy and connection, ultimately enriching the overall virtual experience.

## 6. ETHICAL CONSIDERATIONS

The integration of affective computing and logic in a collaborative virtual environment like the Metaverse presents unique challenges. These issues arise particularly in the context of privacy, emotional intelligence, and participation. Addressing these ethical issues is critical to ensuring that technology works for respectful, safe, and inclusive users.

*Figure 6. Process of ethical decision-making*

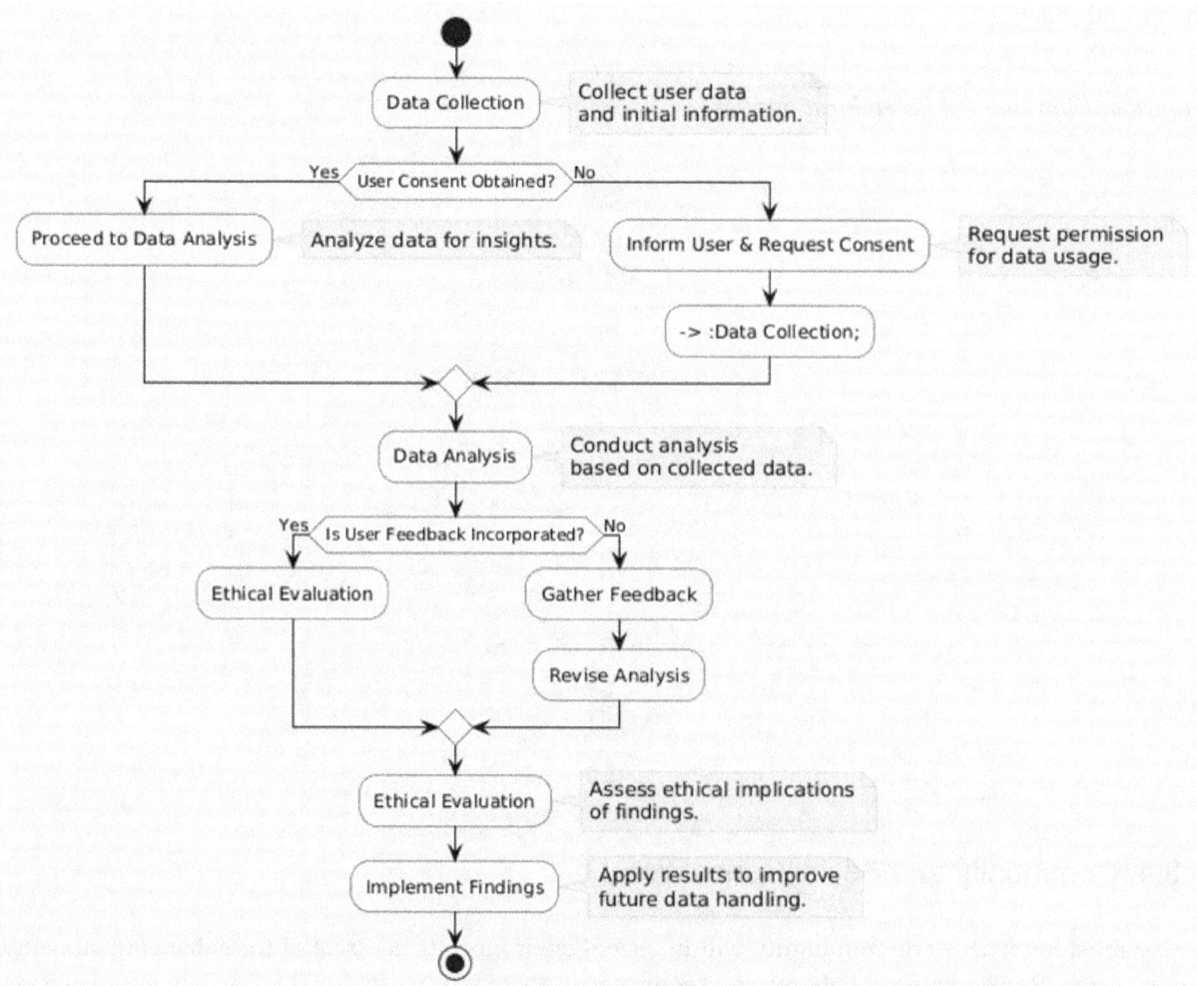

Fig.6 above outlines this process, starting with Data Collection, where user data and initial information are gathered. It emphasizes the importance of obtaining User Consent, which serves as a gateway to Data Analysis. The analysis phase assesses insights from the collected data, followed by evaluating whether User Feedback is incorporated. This feedback loop is vital for refining analyses and ensuring alignment with user expectations. The final steps include Ethical Evaluation, where potential implications of the findings are scrutinized, and the Implementation of Findings, which applies results to improve future data handling practices.

## 6.1 Privacy and Data Security (Anureet Chhabra, n.d.) in Emotion Tracking

The ability to track, interpret, and respond to user sentiment raises serious privacy concerns (Buolamwini & Gebru, 2018). Emotional tracking relies on sensitive data, including facial expressions, vocal patterns, and body signals such as heart rate and skin activity. whilst this record is useful for producing insights from virtual statistics, it may additionally lead to critical dangers if not controlled properly. customers must be confident that their private facts are collected, stored, and used securely and are blanketed from unauthorized get right of entry to or misuse.The consequences of data breaches or misuse of such data can be serious and can lead to exploitation, abuse and discrimination. Therefore, strong data protection is essential to protect users' information. While existing systems such as the General Data Protection Regulation (GDPR) provide a framework for protecting user data, additional specific standards will be needed to think about technology.

## 6.2 Manipulation vs. Enhancement of User Emotions

One of the most important social challenges in computing is the potential for rational thinking. While the main goal is to improve the user experience by creating an intuitive environment, there is a balance between development and management. Systems that adapt to the user's mood can use psychological factors to drive certain behaviors, from stimulating emotions such as fear or happiness to long-term engagement with content or increased spending in the virtual environment. For example, in the Metaverse business (S. K. Singh et al., 2024) and games companies can use emotional intelligence to control users from making decisions or engaging in behaviors that could lead to drug addiction. This raises serious concerns about user freedom and ability to use. Therefore, ethics (Picard, 1999) must be established to ensure that opinions are used to improve the user's health (Vajrobol, V. et al., 2024)) and overall experience rather than as a means of exercising power.

## 6.3 Inclusivity and Accessibility in Affective Computing

Affective computing technologies in the Metaverse have to prioritize inclusivity and accessibility. Emotion recognition structures often face challenges deciphering feelings across various racial, gender, age, and cultural agencies. Bias in facial and speech recognition can cause the exclusion of people with darker pores and skin tones, facial capabilities, or unique linguistic backgrounds. To counter this, builders want to apply diverse training datasets that reflect a wide range of customers, making sure structures correctly apprehend emotions throughout all demographics. Also, affective (Nguyen et al., 2021) systems should accommodate users with disabilities, such as speech impairments or facial paralysis, by incorporating alternative input methods like gesture recognition or physiological signals (e.g., heart rate). Ensuring affordability and technical accessibility is also crucial to avoid excluding users from virtual (Shneiderman et al., 2016) experiences.Ethical framework that supports data diversity, algorithmic integrity, and user-centered design (Kumar & Singh, 2021) should guide development. By ensuring fairness and transparency across the business value chain, developers can create systems that enhance strategic thinking while reducing equity risk.

## 7. FUTURE SCOPE

The integration of emotional intelligence into the Metaverse will be driven by many new technologies that help with mental representations, understanding, and virtual spaces. AI and machine learning will improve facial and speech recognition, while multimodal systems will provide physiological data to help with mood swings. Platforms like OpenFace, Affectiva, Beyond Verbal, and Vocalis Health will lead the way, while Realeyes and EmoReact will power many of the emerging trends. Immersive technologies like Oculus, HTC Vive, and Microsoft HoloLens will integrate AI into VR/AR environments, adapting the avatar and surrounding environment based on the user's emotional state and enabling innovation in feedback through platforms like TeslaSuit and SenseGlove. Emotionally responsive avatars, powered by tools like Ready Player Me and the Avatar SDK, will continue to evolve to recognize and respond to emotions, while AI-powered virtual assistants like Replika will provide motivation and experience. Social VR platforms like AltspaceVR, Rec Room will leverage real-time mood swings alongside cognitive abilities to enhance social interaction and improve relationships over the next 2-3 years. Privacy solutions like TrustArc and BigID will protect emotional data to ensure secure and inclusive communication, while Microsoft and Google's AI ethics group will emphasize unfairness by creating an inclusive system.

## 8. CONCLUSION

The integration of affective computing into the Metaverse is a significant step for virtual knowledge. Designers will use technologies such as cognitive and multisensory experiences to create an environment that changes instantly according to the user's mood, ultimately leading to user enjoyment and deepening connections. This not only enhances the personal experience, but also contributes to the health of relationships within the virtual community, paving the way for a kinder, gentler network.

All of these technologies face ethical issues such as biases in emotional intelligence, privacy concerns, access difficulties, etc., and these issues need to be resolved so that the use of interventions is inclusive and meets the needs of diverse user groups. Through ethical and constructive collaboration between developers, researchers, and stakeholders, this will be a valuable resource where thinking intelligence can be developed, improving user experience and connectivity.

## REFERENCES


Acquisti, A., Brandimarte, L., & Loewenstein, G. (2015). Privacy and human behavior in the age of information. *Science*, 347(6221), 509–512. DOI: 10.1126/science.aaa1465 PMID: 25635091

Aggarwal, K., & Colace, F. (2024). Deep learning in robotics for strengthening Industry 4.0: Opportunities, challenges, and future directions. In *Robotics and AI for Cybersecurity and Critical Infrastructure in Smart Cities* (Vol. 1030, pp. 1–19). Springer.

Aggarwal, K., Singh, S. K., Chopra, M., & Kumar, S. (2022). Role of social media in the COVID-19 pandemic: A literature review. In B. B. Gupta, D. Peraković, A. A. Abd El-Latif, & D. Gupta (Eds.), Advanced computer science applications (pp. [1-19]). IGI Global. https://doi.org/DOI: 10.4018/978-1-7998-8413-2.ch004

Amiryousefi, M., Amirian, Z., & Ansari, A. (2023). Relationship between classroom environment, teacher behavior, cognitive and emotional engagement, and state motivation. *Journal of English Language Teaching and Learning, Volume, Page Range.*https://doi.org/[DOI]

Bisht, J., & Vampugani, V. S. (2022). Load and cost-aware min-min workflow scheduling algorithm for heterogeneous resources in fog, cloud, and edge scenarios. [IJCAC]. *International Journal of Cloud Applications and Computing*, 12(1), 1–20. DOI: 10.4018/IJCAC.2022010105

Blikstein, P. (2013). Digital fabrication and 'making' in education: The democratization of invention. In Büching, C., & Walter-Herrmann, J. (Eds.), *FabLabs: Of machines, makers and inventors* (pp. 203–220). Transcript Publishers., DOI: 10.14361/transcript.9783839423820.203

Buchanan, R. (2001). Design research and the new learning. *Design Issues*, 17(4), 3–23. DOI: 10.1162/07479360152681056

Buolamwini, J., & Gebru, T. (2018). Gender shades: Intersectional accuracy disparities in commercial gender classification. In *Proceedings of the Conference on Fairness, Accountability, and Transparency* (pp. 77-91). PMLR.



Buolamwini, J., & Gebru, T. (2018). Gender shades: Intersectional accuracy disparities in commercial gender classification. In *Proceedings of the Conference on Fairness, Accountability, and Transparency* (pp. 77-91). PMLR.



Calo, R. (2013). Digital market manipulation. *The George Washington Law Review*, 82, 995–1051.

De la Torre, F., & Cohn, J. F. (Year). Facial expression analysis. In *Visual Analysis of Humans* (pp. 377–409). Springer.

Dhar Dwivedi, S. K., Upadhyay, S., & Tripathi, A. K. (2012). A working framework for the user-centered design approach and a survey of the available methods. *International Journal of Scientific and Research Publications, 2*(4), 1-5. ISSN 2250-3153.

Dubey, H., & Chhabra, A. (2022). Cyber security model to secure data transmission using cloud cryptography. *Cyber Security Insights Magazine*, 2, 9–12.

Egger, M., Ley, M., & Hanke, S. (2019). Emotion recognition from physiological signal analysis: A review. *Electronic Notes in Theoretical Computer Science*, 343, 35–55. DOI: 10.1016/j.entcs.2019.04.009

Ennouamani, S., & Mahani, Z. (2017). An overview of adaptive e-learning systems. In *Proceedings of the 2017 Eighth International Conference on Intelligent Computing and Information Systems (ICICIS)* (pp. 1-6). IEEE. https://doi.org/DOI: 10.1109/INTELCIS.2017.8260060

Fokides, E. (2020). My avatar and I: A study on avatars, personality traits, self-attributes, and their perceived importance. *Journal of Ambient Intelligence and Humanized Computing*, 12(1), 359–373. DOI: 10.1007/s12652-020-01977-1

García Peñalvo, F. J., Maan, T., Singh, S. K., Kumar, S., Arya, V., Chui, K. T., & Singh, G. P. (2022). Sustainable stock market prediction framework using machine learning models. *International Journal of Software Science and Computational Intelligence*, 14(11), 1–15. DOI: 10.4018/IJSSCI.313593

Gee, J. P. (2003). What video games have to teach us about learning and literacy. *Technology, Pedagogy and Education*, 1(1), 20–29. DOI: 10.1145/950566.950595

Gupta, A., & Kumar, S. (2017). Cloud computing & fog computing: A solution for high-performance computing. In *Proceedings of the 2017 4th International Conference on Computing for Sustainable Global Development (INDIACom-2017)*. New Delhi, India.

Gupta, A., Singh, S. K., & Chopra, M. (2023). Impact of artificial intelligence and the Internet of Things in modern times and hereafter: An investigative analysis. In *Advanced Computer Science Applications* (pp. 157–173). Apple Academic Press. DOI: 10.1201/9781003369066-14

Gupta, A., Singh, S. K., Chopra, M., & Gill, S. S. (2022). An inquisitive prospect on the shift toward online media, before, during, and after the COVID-19 pandemic: A technological analysis. In *Advances in Data Computing, Communication and Security: Proceedings of I3CS2021* (pp. 229–238). Springer Nature Singapore. DOI: 10.1007/978-981-16-8403-6_20

Gupta, B. B., Gaurav, A., Albeshri, A. A., & Alsalman, D. (2023). New paradigms of sustainable entrepreneurship in metaverse: A micro-level perspective. *The International Entrepreneurship and Management Journal*, 19(3), 1449–1465. DOI: 10.1007/s11365-023-00875-0

Gupta, B. B., Gaurav, A., & Arya, V. (2024). Fuzzy logic and biometric-based lightweight cryptographic authentication for metaverse security. *Applied Soft Computing*, 164, 111973. DOI: 10.1016/j.asoc.2024.111973

Gupta, B. B., Gaurav, A., Chui, K. T., & Arya, V. (2024, January). Deep learning-based facial emotion detection in the metaverse. In *2024 IEEE International Conference on Consumer Electronics (ICCE)* (pp. 1-6). IEEE. DOI: 10.1109/ICCE59016.2024.10444217

Gupta, S., Chhabra, A., Agrawal, S., & Singh, S. K. (2021). A comprehensive comparative study of machine learning classifiers for spam filtering. In *International Conference on Cyber Security, Privacy and Networking* (pp. 257-268). Springer International Publishing.

Hew, K. F., & Cheung, W. S. (2013). Use of Web 2.0 technologies in K-12 and higher education: The search for evidence-based practice. *Educational Research Review*, 9, 47–64. DOI: 10.1016/j.edurev.2012.08.001

Hwang, G.-J., & Chien, S.-Y. (2022). Definition, roles, and potential research issues of the metaverse in education: An artificial intelligence perspective. *Computers and Education: Artificial Intelligence*, 3, 100082. DOI: 10.1016/j.caeai.2022.100082

Karthika, R., & Jegatha Deborah, L. (2021). Enhanced learning experiences based on regulatory fit theory using affective state detection. [IJSWIS]. *International Journal on Semantic Web and Information Systems*, 17(4), 37–55. DOI: 10.4018/IJSWIS.2021100103

Kumar, A., Shankar, A., Behl, A., Gupta, B. B., & Mavuri, S. (2023). Lights, camera, metaverse!: Eliciting intention to use industrial metaverse, organizational agility, and firm performance. [JGIM]. *Journal of Global Information Management*, 31(8), 1–20. DOI: 10.4018/JGIM.333169

Kumar, S., & Aggarwal, N. (2023). Speculative parallelism on multicore chip architecture strengthen green computing concept: A survey. In Advanced computer science applications (1st ed., pp. 1–14). Apple Academic Press., 10.978-1-00-336906-6. DOI: 10.1201/9781003369066-2

Kumar, S., & Singh, S. K. (2021). Brain-computer interaction (BCI): A way to interact with brain waves. *Insights2Techinfo,* 1-1.

Lim, Y., Ng, K.-W., Naveen, P., & Haw, S.-C. (2022). Emotion recognition by facial expression and voice: Review and analysis. *Journal of Informatics and Web Engineering*, 1(2), 45–54. DOI: 10.33093/jiwe.2022.1.2.4

Mengi, G., Singh, S. K., Kumar, S., Mahto, D., & Sharma, A. (2023). Automated machine learning (AutoML): The future of computational intelligence. In Nedjah, N., Martínez Pérez, G., & Gupta, B. B. (Eds.), *International Conference on Cyber Security, Privacy and Networking (ICSPN 2022)* (Vol. 599, pp. 401-414). Springer. https://doi.org/DOI: 10.1007/978-3-031-22018-0_28

Nguyen, S. H., Sun, Q., & Williams, D. (2021). How do we make the virtual world a better place? Social discrimination in online gaming, sense of community, and well-being. *Telematics and Informatics*, 63, 101747. DOI: 10.1016/j.tele.2021.101747

Picard, R. W. (2000). *Affective computing*. MIT Press. DOI: 10.7551/mitpress/1140.003.0008

Pitale, A., & Bhumgara, A. (2019). Human-computer interaction strategies—Designing the user interface. In *Proceedings of the 2019 International Conference on Smart Technologies* (pp. 1-5). IEEE. https://doi.org/DOI: 10.1109/ICST.2019.8747675

Provence, S., & Forcehimes, A. A. (2024). Algorithms for empathy: Using machine learning to categorize common empathetic traits across professional and peer-based conversations. *Cureus*, 16(4), e57719. DOI: 10.7759/cureus.57719 PMID: 38711721

Qi, J., Tang, H., & Zhu, Z. (2023). Exploring an affective and responsive virtual environment to improve remote learning. *Virtual Worlds*, 2(1), 53–74. DOI: 10.3390/virtualworlds2010004

Raji, I. D., & Buolamwini, J. (2022). Actionable auditing revisited: Investigating the impact of publicly naming biased performance results of commercial AI products. *Communications of the ACM*, 65(12), 68–77. DOI: 10.1145/3569496

Resnick, M., Maloney, J., Monroy-Hernández, A., Rusk, N., Eastmond, E., Brennan, K., Millner, A., Rosenbaum, E., Silver, J., Silverman, B., & Kafai, Y. (2009). Scratch: Programming for all. *Communications of the ACM*, 52(11), 60–67. DOI: 10.1145/1592761.1592779

Sharma, A., Singh, S. K., Badwal, E., Kumar, S., Gupta, B. B., Arya, V., . . . Santaniello, D. (2023, January). Fuzzy based clustering of consumers' big data in industrial applications. In *2023 IEEE International Conference on Consumer Electronics (ICCE)* (pp. 01-03). IEEE. http://doi.org/DOI: 10.1109/ICCE56470.2023.10043451

Shneiderman, B., & Plaisant, C. (2010). *Designing the user interface: Strategies for effective human-computer interaction* (5th ed.). Addison-Wesley.

Shneiderman, B., Plaisant, C., Cohen, M., Jacobs, S., Elmqvist, N., & Diakopoulos, N. (2016). *Designing the user interface: Strategies for effective human-computer interaction* (6th ed.). Pearson Education.

Singh, G., Malhotra, M., & Sharma, A. (2022). An adaptive mechanism for virtual machine migration in the cloud environment. [IJCAC]. *International Journal of Cloud Applications and Computing*, 12(1), 1–10. DOI: 10.4018/IJCAC.311504

Singh, G., & Rawat, Y. (2024). Advancements in metaverse gaming technologies. Insights2Techinfo, 1. https://insights2techinfo.com/advancements-in-metaverse-gaming-technologies/

Singh, I., Singh, S. K., Singh, R., & Kumar, S. (2022). Efficient loop unrolling factor prediction algorithm using machine learning models. In 2022 3rd International Conference for Emerging Technology (INCET) (pp. 1-8). IEEE. https://doi.org/DOI: 10.1109/INCET54531.2022.9825092

Singh, M., Singh, S. K., Kumar, S., Madan, U., & Maan, T. (2021, September). Sustainable framework for metaverse security and privacy: Opportunities and challenges. In *International Conference on Cyber Security, Privacy and Networking* (pp. 329-340). Cham: Springer International Publishing.

Singh, S. K., Gupta, S., Kumar, S., Gupta, B. B., Alhalabi, W., Arya, V., & Zhang, J. (2024). A novel cumulative indicator score using indicator averaging for optimizing local business websites of enterprise systems. *Enterprise Information Systems*, 18(2), 2301658. DOI: 10.1080/17517575.2023.2301658

Singh, S. K., Sharma, S. K., Singla, D., & Gill, S. S. (2022). Evolving requirements and application of SDN and IoT in the context of industry 4.0, blockchain and artificial intelligence. *Software Defined Networks: Architecture and Applications,* 427-496.

Thakur, N., Singh, S. K., Gupta, A., Jain, K., Jain, R., Peraković, D., Nedjah, N., & Rafsanjani, M. K. (2022). A novel CNN, bidirectional long-short term memory, and gated recurrent unit-based hybrid approach for human activity recognition. [IJSSCI]. *International Journal of Software Science and Computational Intelligence*, 14(1), 1–19. DOI: 10.4018/IJSSCI.311445

Vajrobol, V. (2024). Metaverse in healthcare domain. Insights2Techinfo, 1. https://insights2techinfo.com/metaverse-in-healthcare-domain/

Vats, T., & Kumar, S. Next-generation towards construction of cyber-physical systems and digital twins. *Insights2Techinfo,* 1-1.

Vats, T., Singh, S. K., Kumar, S., Gupta, B. B., Gill, S. S., Arya, V., & Alhalabi, W. (2023). Explainable context-aware IoT framework using human digital twin for healthcare. *Multimedia Tools and Applications*, 83(22), 1–25. DOI: 10.1007/s11042-023-16922-5

Wang, Y., Song, W., Tao, W., Liotta, A., Yang, D., Li, X., Gao, S., Sun, Y., Ge, W., Zhang, W., & Zhang, W. (2022). A systematic review on affective computing: Emotion models, databases, and recent advances. *Information Fusion*, 83–84, 19–52. DOI: 10.1016/j.inffus.2022.03.009

Weiss, R. P. (2000). Emotion and learning. *Training & Development*, 54(2), 34–38.

Wu, C.-H., Huang, Y.-M., & Hwang, J.-P. (2015). Review of affective computing in education/learning: Trends and challenges. *British Journal of Educational Technology*, 47(6), 1304–1323. DOI: 10.1111/bjet.12324

# Chapter 16
# Creating and Sustaining Virtual Communities in the Metaverse:
## Concept and Case Study

**Vitri Tundjungsari**
*Esa Unggul University, Indonesia*

## ABSTRACT

*The metaverse is characterized by its ability to create shared spaces that are persistent, synchronous, and interactive, so users can experience a sense of presence and connection that rivals, and often enhances, real-world interactions. Within the metaverse, the boundaries between the digital and physical blur, opening up new opportunities for creativity, collaboration, and commerce. In this chapter, we discuss the character of Metaverse, strategy, tools, and compare Metaverse with community in real-life and social media platform. We also examine a case study of the metaverse social interaction and connection, i.e. Decentraland, Roblox, and Meta Horizon. At the end of this book chapter, we conclude that research in Metaverse is essential because the metaverse is a rapidly evolving digital frontier that has the potential to transform various aspects of society, technology, and economics. We also discuss some considerations for future research in Metaverse, such as: long-term sustainability, potential technologies and social trends that may shape the future of Metaverse.*

## 1. INTRODUCTION

The concept of the Metaverse has rapidly transitioned from a speculative vision to a tangible reality, capturing the imagination of technologists, entrepreneurs, and users alike. The Metaverse has been defined in various studies. Chakraborty (2024) defines Metaverse as a collective virtual space that integrates aspects of physical and digital realities, offering seamless immersive experiences beyond traditional virtual reality. While Bhasin et al. (2024) mention that Metaverse is a digital domain where individuals interact in real-time using avatars, creating a new dimension for social, economic, and entertainment

DOI: 10.4018/979-8-3693-8628-6.ch016

activities. Sharma and Mahindru (2024) state that metaverse transcends the boundaries of the physical and digital worlds, aiming to change how we interact with technology and each other.

Metaverse is an ecosystem built on the convergence of advanced technologies such as virtual reality (VR), augmented reality (AR), blockchain, and artificial intelligence (AI). These technologies collectively enable the creation of virtual environments where users, represented by their digital avatars, can engage in activities ranging from socializing and gaming to learning and working (Anter et al., 2022; Amos, 2022; Ning et al., 2021; Kohli et al., 2021).

As the metaverse rapidly evolves into a significant part of our digital lives, the importance of building communities within these virtual spaces cannot be overstated. The metaverse is not merely a collection of virtual environments; it represents a new paradigm of social interaction, where people from all corners of the globe can connect, collaborate, and create in ways that were previously unimaginable (Daradkeh, 2023; Zhai et al., 2023; Hwang, 2023).

Research in Metaverse is essential because the metaverse is a rapidly evolving digital frontier that has the potential to transform various aspects of society, technology, and economics. Here are key reasons why research into the metaverse is crucial:

1. The metaverse integrates multiple advanced technologies
2. The metaverse offers new business models and virtual economies
3. The metaverse has Social and cultural implications (Interaction and Communities, Identity and Representation) as well as Environmental Impact and Economic Sustainability, metaverse provide Education and Virtual Learning Environments,
4. The metaverse has Decentralized Governance and provide User Empowerment, Inclusivity and Accessibility.

This book chapter consists of four sections. Section one introduces the background and motivation of this book chapter. Section two discusses concept and characteristics of Metaverse as a recent and innovative alternative for digital lives. In section two, we also compare The Metaverse, physical/real, and social media platform in terms of social interaction and experience, personalization and identity, social structures and dynamics, limitations. In an increasingly digital age, the metaverse offers a platform where people can experience a sense of belonging and connection. Unlike traditional social media, where interactions are often fleeting and superficial, the metaverse allows for more immersive and meaningful engagements. Building communities in the metaverse can help combat the isolation and fragmentation that often accompany digital life, providing a space where people can form lasting relationships and support networks.

In section three we present case studies of three leading Metaverse platform, i.e.: Decentraland, Roblox, and Meta Horizon. In this section we explore more detailed metaverse platform in order to provide valuable insights into how the platform and its technology could support community interaction, engagement and governance. In section three, we also compare those three Metaverse platforms (Decentraland, Roblox, Meta Horizon) in terms of: community engagement, growth metrics, economic sustainability, technological foundations, governance, and limitations. Finally in section four we conclude and suggest future research relate to technology, sustainability, and social trends that may shape the future of Metaverse community.

## 2. COMMUNITY IN THE METAVERSE

As we have discussed briefly in section one, the Metaverse is an important and promising research field, we will explore more detailed characteristics of the Metaverse, as follows:

1. The Metaverse offer technological challenges and immersive experiences (Zhao and Huang, 2021; Evans, 2020):
    - Technological Advancements: The metaverse integrates multiple advanced technologies, including virtual reality (VR), augmented reality (AR), artificial intelligence (AI), blockchain, and decentralized systems. Research is needed to explore how these technologies can work together seamlessly, ensuring scalability, interoperability, and user experience.
    - Research and Technical Challenges: The metaverse presents significant technical challenges, such as optimizing VR/AR environments, improving real-time rendering, and addressing latency issues. Research can help overcome these hurdles and push the boundaries of immersive experiences.
2. The Metaverse provide economic opportunities and virtual economies (Wong, 2021; Smith, 2022):
    - New Business Models: The metaverse introduces unique economic ecosystems, including virtual real estate, NFTs, and decentralized finance (DeFi). Research helps identify sustainable business models, assess their viability, and explore new opportunities for creators, businesses, and investors.
    - Virtual Economies: In-depth study is required to understand the dynamics of virtual economies, including currency systems, digital ownership, and marketplace structures. Research can guide the development of fair, transparent, and resilient virtual economic systems.
3. The Metaverse deliver social and cultural implications (Parker and Johnson, 2021; Davis, 2020):
    - Social Interaction and Communities: Research is necessary to explore how human interaction changes in virtual environments. The metaverse will redefine how people communicate, collaborate, and build communities. Understanding these dynamics is critical for designing inclusive and engaging virtual spaces.
    - Identity and Representation: The metaverse allows users to experiment with virtual identities through avatars and other means of representation. Research is needed to understand the psychological, social, and ethical implications of this flexibility in identity.
4. The Metaverse provide education and virtual learning environments (Thomas, 2021; Williams and Harris, 2020). It has potential to transform education by offering immersive, interactive learning environments. Research is needed to explore how virtual worlds can enhance learning outcomes, provide access to global education, and improve knowledge retention. It also provides virtual workplace. Research into the productivity, challenges, and benefits of working in the metaverse can inform the development of effective virtual work solutions.
5. The Metaverse comprises decentralized governance and user empowerment (Hall, 2021; Patel, 2021) by providing privacy and security. Research is essential to ensure that personal information, virtual assets, and intellectual property are protected in these vast, interconnected digital spaces. As the metaverse grows, it will require governance systems to manage virtual interactions, digital ownership, and behavior. Research into decentralized governance, legal frameworks, and regulatory approaches will be key to creating a safe and fair metaverse.

6. The Metaverse employs inclusivity and accessibility (Rees, 2020; Evans, 2021) by ensuring equal access and bridging digital divides. Research is required to make the metaverse accessible to people with different abilities, economic backgrounds, and geographic locations. This includes studying ways to provide affordable access to VR/AR technology and designing inclusive user experiences for all.
7. The Metaverse affects environmental impact and sustainability (Green, 2021; Johnson, 2022): As the metaverse grows, it will require massive computational resources, leading to environmental concerns. Research is needed to explore sustainable solutions for powering virtual worlds, reducing energy consumption, and minimizing the environmental impact of blockchain and virtual infrastructure.

The concept of community in the metaverse presents a unique blend of characteristics from both physical and social media communities, offering a novel environment for interaction. While physical communities are grounded in shared spaces and experiences, and social media communities are defined by digital interactions across distances, the metaverse combines elements of both, creating immersive, interactive spaces that transcend traditional boundaries. This synthesis of environments allows for new forms of social engagement and community building, which are distinct from both physical and social media communities.

We compare Metaverse, Real life, and social media in terms of: (1) technological foundations; (2) community engagement; (3) governance; (4) growth metrics; (5) economic sustainability; (6) user demographics; (7) technical challenges; (8) user retention; and (9) limitation. The comparison is gathered and resumed from various researches, i.e.: Smith (2022), Zhao and Huang (2021), Davis and Thomas (2020), Wright (2023), Johnson (2021), Rees (2019), Evans (2020), Parker (2021), Gordon and Haris (2019), Yang and Wu (2022), West (2021), Hall (2021), and Patel (2022). Table 1 shows the comparison of Metaverse, real life/physical, and social media; as mentioned above.

*Table 1. Comparison of metaverse, real life, and social media*

| Features | Decentraland | Roblox | Meta Horizon |
|---|---|---|---|
| **Technological Foundations** | Blockchain-based (Ethereum, IPFS), browser-based access, decentralized infrastructure | Proprietary game engine (Roblox Studio), cross-platform (PC, mobile, console), centralized infrastructure | VR-first, relies on Meta's Oculus hardware, centralized infrastructure |
| **Community Engagement** | Ownership-driven engagement, decentralized economy, NFT-based virtual spaces and events | User-created games, developer monetization via Robux, strong social interactions in user-generated experiences | VR-based social engagement, real-time interactions, collaborative spaces, less developed creator economy |
| **Governance** | Decentralized governance through DAO, user voting on policies, transparency through blockchain | Centralized governance by Roblox Corporation, limited user influence, developer-focused feedback | Centralized governance by Meta, corporate oversight, strict content moderation |

continued on following page

*Table 1. Continued*

| Features | Decentraland | Roblox | Meta Horizon |
|---|---|---|---|
| **Growth Metrics** | - Grew significantly in 2020-2022 due to increased interest in NFTs and virtual real estate.<br>- Active users fluctuate due to market volatility and NFT speculation.<br>- Steady growth of virtual land ownership and event participation | - Continuous exponential growth with over 200 million monthly active users as of 2023.<br>- Over 40 million user-generated experiences.<br>- Huge growth driven by global popularity, especially during the pandemic | - Growing user base but slower adoption compared to Roblox.<br>- Primarily targeted at VR users.<br>- Meta aims to increase Horizon's adoption as part of their push into the metaverse, but current numbers lag behind other platforms |
| **Economic Sustainability** | - Powered by a decentralized economy based on Ethereum, with virtual land and NFTs driving most of its economic activity.<br>- Users buy and sell virtual land and assets as NFTs, using MANA tokens for transactions.<br>- Long-term sustainability depends on the growth of the NFT market and adoption of decentralized platforms | - Highly sustainable through its robust developer economy.<br>- Roblox's virtual currency, Robux, drives in-game purchases and revenue generation.<br>- Developers can monetize their games, making Roblox one of the most lucrative platforms for creators | - Currently lacks a strong creator economy compared to Roblox and Decentraland.<br>- Horizon's economy is still in development, focusing more on social engagement than economic transactions.<br>- Meta is working to introduce monetization tools, but this will take time to reach full scale |
| **User Demographics** | - Primarily appeals to crypto enthusiasts, NFT collectors, and digital artists.<br>- Attracts users interested in virtual real estate, decentralized governance, and blockchain technology.<br>- Smaller, niche user base compared to Roblox | - Appeals to a wide range of users, but especially younger demographics (ages 9-16).<br>- Roblox's user base includes millions of children and teenagers worldwide.<br>- Strong global reach with significant engagement across age groups, though mainly popular among younger users | - Focused on users with VR headsets, particularly tech-savvy individuals and gamers interested in immersive social experiences.<br>- More mature user base compared to Roblox, targeting adults and professionals<br>- Demographic is limited by VR hardware accessibility, resulting in a narrower audience compared to Roblox and Decentraland |
| **Technical Challenges** | - Blockchain Scalability: As Decentraland grows, scalability issues on the Ethereum blockchain, such as slow transaction speeds and high gas fees, can affect user experience<br>- Decentralized Hosting: Content hosted on IPFS may experience slower loading times and issues with consistency, impacting performance for some users | - Server Overload: Roblox has experienced server issues during peak usage times, leading to downtime and instability in user experience<br>- Cross-Platform Optimization: Ensuring a seamless experience across different devices (PC, mobile, console) can lead to varying performance, especially in complex games<br>- Complex Game Logic: Some developers face difficulties with Roblox's Lua scripting, leading to technical limitations in game development | - VR Optimization: Meta Horizon must overcome the high computational demands of rendering complex virtual environments in real-time for VR, which can lead to performance issues on less powerful VR hardware<br>- Latency: As a VR-focused platform, reducing latency is critical to avoid motion sickness and ensure a smooth experience, especially in social interactions<br>- Limited Developer Support: Meta Horizon's developer tools are not as robust as other platforms, posing challenges to creating complex user-generated content. |

continued on following page

*Table 1. Continued*

| Features | Decentraland | Roblox | Meta Horizon |
|---|---|---|---|
| **User Retention** | - Niche Audience: Retention is higher among crypto-enthusiasts and NFT collectors but struggles to retain casual users unfamiliar with blockchain technology<br>- Event-Driven Retention: Virtual events and unique NFT drops keep users engaged, though retention fluctuates with market trends | - Highly Engaged User Base: Roblox boasts strong user retention, particularly among younger audiences, driven by a continuous stream of user-generated games and social interaction<br>- Frequent Updates: Regular platform updates and events contribute to high engagement, keeping users coming back for new experiences | - Limited Retention: Due to the current requirement for VR hardware and the early-stage development of social experiences, user retention is lower than other platforms<br>- Engagement through Social Spaces: Meta Horizon retains users by promoting social interaction and collaboration in virtual environments, but faces challenges in expanding beyond its VR-focused audience |
| **Limitation** | - Hardware Dependency: Requires powerful computers for optimal experience, limiting accessibility for users without high-performance hardware<br>- Crypto Volatility: As it relies heavily on blockchain and NFTs, its user base is affected by fluctuations in cryptocurrency markets.<br>- Learning Curve: Creating content requires familiarity with blockchain and decentralized technologies, which can deter casual users. | - Age Restrictions: Primarily appeals to younger users, limiting its appeal to older demographics<br>- Content Moderation: Difficulty managing inappropriate content due to the sheer volume of user-generated games, leading to concerns over safety for younger players<br>- Monetization Pressure: Some developers face challenges with monetizing their games, creating a competitive environment that can discourage smaller creators. | - VR Hardware Requirement: Requires VR headsets like Oculus, limiting access to users with VR equipment and contributing to slow adoption.<br>- Lack of Robust Creator Tools: While immersive, the platform lacks the extensive creator tools that other metaverse platforms offer, reducing its appeal to content creators.<br>- Limited Interoperability: Currently lacks cross-platform integration, limiting its potential to attract a broader audience. |

Figures 1 and 2 show how communities interact in physical/real life, while Figure 3 shows how Metaverse works.

Figure 1. Workspace in a real community

*Figure 2. Meeting in a real community*

*Figure 3. Avatar in the Metaverse*

## 3. CASE STUDY

When writing about platforms to build the metaverse, it is essential to cover the various ecosystems that provide the tools, technologies, and frameworks necessary to create immersive virtual environments and communities. We choose three platforms of Metaverse, i.e.: Decentraland, Roblox, amd Meta Horizon.

We will discuss overview of key platforms that are currently being used to build the metaverse (Gupta, 2024):

1. Decentraland

Decentraland is one of the most prominent and well-established platforms within the metaverse, offering a decentralized virtual world where users can create, explore, and trade virtual assets. Built on the Ethereum blockchain, Decentraland combines the concepts of virtual reality, digital ownership, and decentralized governance to create an immersive and user-driven environment.

*Figure 4. Decentraland*

The following is detailed overview of Decentraland (Franceschet, 2023; Gupta, 2024):

1. Overview and History

Decentraland was officially launched to the public in February 2020, after several years of development and testing. The project was initiated in 2015 by Esteban Ordano and Ariel Meilich, who envisioned a decentralized world where users could truly own and control their digital assets. Decentraland is built on the Ethereum blockchain, which enables the use of smart contracts to manage ownership, transactions, and governance within the platform.

2. Core Components
   - LAND: LAND is the basic unit of ownership in Decentraland. Each LAND is a non-fungible token (NFT) represented by a unique parcel on the Decentraland map. LAND parcels measure 16x16 meters in virtual space, and owners can develop these parcels into anything from art galleries and virtual shops to interactive games and social hubs.
   - MANA: MANA is the native cryptocurrency of Decentraland, used for transactions within the platform. Users can buy, sell, and trade LAND, virtual goods, and services using MANA. It is also used in Decentraland's governance system.
   - Marketplace: The Decentraland Marketplace is where users can buy and sell LAND, estates (which are multiple connected parcels of LAND), wearables, and other digital assets. The marketplace operates using MANA, and transactions are secured by the Ethereum blockchain.
3. Creation and Development
   - Builder Tool: Decentraland offers a drag-and-drop Builder tool that allows users to create and customize their virtual environments without needing advanced programming skills. This tool provides a wide range of pre-made assets and customization options, making it accessible for creators of all skill levels.
   - SDK (Software Development Kit): For more advanced users, Decentraland provides a Software Development Kit (SDK) that allows developers to create complex interactive experiences using JavaScript and TypeScript. The SDK gives developers full control over the behavior of objects, animations, and user interactions within their virtual spaces.
4. Social Interaction and Community Building
   - Avatars: Users in Decentraland are represented by customizable avatars. These avatars can be personalized with a variety of wearables, which are also tradable NFTs. Avatars enable users to interact with each other, attend events, and explore different virtual spaces.
   - Events and Experiences: Decentraland hosts a wide range of events, from virtual concerts and art exhibitions to educational seminars and gaming tournaments. These events are often organized by the community or by individual creators, fostering a vibrant and dynamic social environment.
   - Community and DAO: Decentraland is governed by a Decentralized Autonomous Organization (DAO), which allows the community to have a say in the platform's development and policies. MANA holders can vote on proposals related to platform upgrades, content moderation, and economic policies, making Decentraland a truly user-driven ecosystem.
5. Economic Ecosystem

- Virtual Commerce: Decentraland has a thriving virtual economy where users can buy and sell digital assets, including LAND, wearables, and other collectibles. The marketplace for these assets is decentralized, allowing users to trade directly with each other.
- Monetization Opportunities: Creators in Decentraland can monetize their virtual spaces by charging entry fees, hosting sponsored events, or selling digital goods. The platform provides various avenues for users to generate income from their creativity and innovation.
- Interoperability with Other Platforms: Decentraland supports interoperability with other blockchain-based platforms and ecosystems. For instance, users can import NFTs from other platforms and use them within Decentraland, enhancing the platform's utility and value.

6. Technical Architecture
   - Ethereum Blockchain: Decentraland's core architecture is built on the Ethereum blockchain, which ensures transparency, security, and decentralization. All transactions, ownership records, and governance activities are recorded on the blockchain, providing a trustless environment where users have full control over their assets.
   - Smart Contracts: Smart contracts play a critical role in managing the functionality of Decentraland. These self-executing contracts govern everything from the ownership of LAND to the distribution of MANA tokens and the implementation of governance decisions.
   - IPFS (InterPlanetary File System): Decentraland uses IPFS for decentralized file storage. This ensures that the content created within the platform is distributed across a network of nodes, making it more resilient and censorship-resistant.
7. Governance and Decentralization
   - DAO Governance: The Decentraland DAO empowers users to participate in the decision-making process. Proposals can be submitted by any MANA holder, and voting is proportional to the amount of MANA staked. The DAO has control over key elements of the platform, including the content moderation policies, marketplace fees, and the development of new features.
   - Community-Driven Development: The decentralized nature of Decentraland allows the community to shape the platform's future. Users can propose and fund new projects, features, and content, ensuring that the platform evolves in line with the community's needs and interests.
8. Security and Privacy
   - Ownership and Security: In Decentraland, users have true ownership of their digital assets, secured by the Ethereum blockchain. This means that assets cannot be censored, altered, or taken away by any central authority, providing a high level of security and trust.
   - Anonymity and Privacy: While Decentraland allows for anonymous participation, it also provides tools for users to control their personal data and interactions. Users can choose how they present themselves and with whom they interact, maintaining control over their privacy in the virtual world.
9. Future Developments and Challenges
   - Scalability: As Decentraland grows, scalability becomes a key challenge. The platform is exploring various solutions, including layer-2 scaling options, to ensure that it can handle an increasing number of users and transactions without compromising performance.

- Interoperability: Decentraland continues to explore ways to enhance interoperability with other metaverse platforms and blockchain ecosystems. This could involve cross-platform avatar support, shared digital assets, and collaborative virtual environments.
- Adoption and Growth: The success of Decentraland will depend on its ability to attract a broader user base and maintain a vibrant, engaged community. Ongoing efforts to improve user experience, expand content offerings, and foster innovation will be critical to its long-term growth.

2. Roblox

Roblox is a pioneering platform in the world of user-generated content and virtual environments, playing a significant role in shaping the concept of the metaverse. With its accessible game development tools, extensive social features, and vast user base, Roblox has become a cornerstone of interactive digital experiences.

*Figure 5. Roblox*

We present more detailed exploration of Roblox (Blackwood, 2023; Christopher, Coutinho, 2023):

1. Overview and History
    - Founding and Launch: Roblox was founded in 2004 by David Baszucki and Erik Cassel, and officially launched in 2006. Originally conceived as a platform for educational physics simulations, Roblox quickly expanded into a comprehensive environment where users could create and play games, leading to its reputation as a platform for user-generated content.
    - Growth and Development: Over the years, Roblox has seen tremendous growth, particularly among younger audiences. By 2023, Roblox had more than 200 million monthly active users and millions of user-created games, making it one of the most popular gaming platforms globally.
2. Core Components
    - Roblox Studio: Roblox Studio is the platform's development environment, allowing users to create games and experiences without needing extensive programming knowledge. It provides a range of tools for building 3D worlds, scripting interactions using Lua, and testing creations in real-time.
    - User-Generated Content: At the heart of Roblox is its user-generated content ecosystem. Users can create anything from simple games to complex simulations, and these creations are accessible to the entire Roblox community. The platform encourages creativity and innovation by providing tools that are powerful yet easy to use.
    - Robux: Robux is the virtual currency used within Roblox. It allows users to purchase in-game items, avatar accessories, and premium content. Developers can earn Robux through in-game purchases, which can be exchanged for real-world currency, creating a monetization pathway for creators.
3. Creation and Development
    - Game Development: Roblox's ease of use has democratized game development, enabling anyone to create a game, regardless of their technical background. The platform supports a wide range of game genres, from adventure and role-playing games to simulations and educational experiences.
    - Scripting with Lua: Roblox uses Lua as its scripting language, which allows developers to control game mechanics, create interactive elements, and build complex systems within their games. Lua's simplicity makes it accessible for beginners while still being powerful enough for advanced users.
    - Asset Creation: Roblox Studio allows creators to design and import custom 3D models, textures, animations, and audio assets. The platform's marketplace also provides a vast library of user-created assets that can be used to enhance games.
4. Social Interaction and Community
    - Avatars and Customization: Roblox features highly customizable avatars that represent users within the platform. Players can personalize their avatars with clothing, accessories, and animations, many of which are available for purchase using Robux.
    - Social Features: Roblox is designed to be a social platform, with features that include chat, friend lists, groups, and in-game messaging. These features facilitate interaction among players, fostering a sense of community and collaboration.

- Events and Experiences: Roblox hosts virtual events, such as concerts, product launches, and educational sessions, where users can participate in real-time. These events often attract millions of attendees and provide unique experiences that blend entertainment with social interaction.

5. Economic Ecosystem
    - Monetization: Roblox offers various monetization opportunities for creators. Developers can earn Robux through in-game purchases, premium access to games, and sales of virtual items. The Developer Exchange (DevEx) program allows developers to convert their Robux earnings into real-world currency.
    - Marketplace: The Roblox Marketplace is a vibrant ecosystem where users can buy and sell virtual items, such as clothing, accessories, and game assets. The marketplace is user-driven, allowing creators to monetize their work and offering players a wide array of customization options.
    - Premium Membership: Roblox offers a premium membership called Roblox Premium, which provides benefits such as a monthly Robux allowance, discounts on purchases, and access to exclusive items. Premium members also receive a higher percentage of earnings from the sale of their creations.
6. Educational and Professional Development
    - Learning and Skill Development: Roblox is increasingly recognized as a tool for education. It provides a hands-on way to learn game design, programming, and digital storytelling. Many educational institutions use Roblox to teach students about coding, problem-solving, and teamwork.
    - Professional Opportunities: The success of Roblox has led to the emergence of a professional development community, where individuals can pursue careers as game developers, designers, and content creators. Some developers have built successful businesses around their Roblox creations.
7. Safety and Moderation
    - Content Moderation: Roblox has a comprehensive content moderation system to ensure that the platform remains safe for users, particularly younger players. All user-generated content is subject to review, and the platform uses automated systems alongside human moderators to detect and remove inappropriate content.
    - Parental Controls: Roblox offers robust parental controls, allowing parents to manage their children's interactions, restrict access to certain games, and monitor their activity. The platform's commitment to safety has helped maintain its reputation as a child-friendly environment.
8. Technical Architecture
    - Cloud-Based Infrastructure: Roblox operates on a cloud-based infrastructure, which supports the platform's scalability and reliability. This architecture allows for seamless updates, real-time game hosting, and cross-platform play, ensuring a consistent experience for users on different devices.
    - Cross-Platform Play: Roblox is available on multiple platforms, including PC, Mac, iOS, Android, and Xbox. This cross-platform accessibility allows players to interact and collaborate regardless of the device they are using.

- Rendering and Physics Engine: Roblox's proprietary rendering and physics engines are optimized for performance across various devices. The engines ensure that games run smoothly, even on lower-end hardware, while providing realistic physics and graphics.

9. Governance and Community Engagement
    - Developer Community: Roblox has a vibrant developer community, supported by forums, events, and online resources. The platform regularly hosts developer conferences (RDC) and offers mentoring programs to help creators improve their skills and grow their games.
    - User Feedback and Updates: Roblox actively engages with its community through feedback loops, allowing users to suggest features and report issues. The platform frequently updates its tools and features based on community input, ensuring that it evolves in line with user needs.
10. Challenges and Future Directions
    - Scalability: As Roblox continues to grow, managing scalability becomes increasingly important. The platform is investing in infrastructure and technology to handle the growing number of users, games, and experiences.
    - Content Quality and Diversity: With millions of games available, ensuring high-quality content and diversity of experiences is a challenge. Roblox is working on algorithms and curation tools to help users discover the best and most relevant content.
    - Metaverse Vision: Roblox is positioning itself as a key player in the metaverse, focusing on expanding its virtual economy, enhancing social interactions, and enabling more immersive experiences. The platform's future developments will likely involve deeper integration with emerging technologies such as virtual reality (VR) and augmented reality (AR).

3. Meta's Horizon Worlds

Meta Horizon (formerly Facebook Horizon) was developed by Meta (previously Facebook) to provide a fully immersive VR experience, primarily accessible through the **Oculus VR headsets**. The platform is centered around building social connections and experiences within virtual worlds. It reflects Meta's broader vision of the metaverse, focusing on social interaction, creativity, and collaboration in real-time.

Meta Horizon allows users to create and explore social experiences in virtual reality. Meta's Horizon Worlds has many features, i.e.:

1. VR Creation Tools: Horizon Worlds offers intuitive tools for creating 3D environments, games, and interactive experiences directly within VR.
2. Social Spaces: The platform emphasizes social interaction, allowing users to meet, collaborate, and play in shared virtual spaces.
3. Community Guidelines: Meta provides robust community management features to ensure safe and inclusive environments.
4. Use Cases: Ideal for building VR communities, hosting virtual events, and creating immersive social experiences.
5. Immersive Social Experience: Meta Horizon allows users to meet, interact, and collaborate in virtual worlds using customizable avatars. These avatars can mimic real-life gestures and expressions thanks to VR hardware, providing an engaging and lifelike experience. It also has 3D spatial audio enhances communication by simulating how sound behaves in the real world, improving the sense of presence and immersion.

6. Has Horizon Worlds and Workrooms. Horizon Worlds is the main social VR platform within Meta Horizon, allowing users to create and explore different virtual worlds. Users can design their worlds using intuitive creation tools, play games, host events, and socialize in real-time. The user-generated content aspect allows for creativity and community-driven experiences. Horizon Workrooms: A VR workspace tool that supports virtual meetings, collaboration, and productivity. Workrooms integrate VR-based collaboration with non-VR users via video conferencing, making it suitable for hybrid work scenarios. Features include virtual whiteboards, hand-tracking, and shared virtual spaces for team collaboration.
7. Customizable Avatars. Users in Meta Horizon can create avatars that represent their virtual identity. These avatars can be personalized with different clothing, facial features, and accessories, making social interactions more engaging.
8. Creation Tools use World Building. It offers a user-friendly, no-code creation tool that allows users to build interactive 3D worlds and experiences. This empowers users to not only participate in existing environments but also to craft their own virtual experiences.
9. Virtual Economy (in development). Meta is working on introducing monetization features, allowing creators to sell virtual goods and services within Horizon Worlds. Although still in development, this would enable a virtual economy similar to what Roblox offers, where users can earn real money through their creations.
10. Social Features. Meta Horizon focuses on fostering social connections by hosting virtual events, meetups, and collaborative experiences. Whether it's a virtual concert, art exhibition, or casual gathering, the platform offers various avenues for users to connect.
11. Safety and Moderation. Meta Horizon places significant emphasis on user safety. Personal boundaries are enforced to prevent avatars from getting too close to each other, ensuring a comfortable space for users. There are also reporting tools for users to flag inappropriate behavior, helping maintain a safe environment. Meta employs both human and AI-based moderation to review reports and enforce platform guidelines, striving for a secure, inclusive virtual space.

Table 2 below presents the comparison of those three Metaverse platforms which we have discussed before.

*Table 2. Features comparison of three Metaverse platforms (Decentraland, Roblox, and Meta Horizon)*

| Features | Decentraland | Roblox | Meta Horizon |
|---|---|---|---|
| **Technological Foundations** | Blockchain-based (Ethereum, IPFS), browser-based access, decentralized infrastructure | Proprietary game engine (Roblox Studio), cross-platform (PC, mobile, console), centralized infrastructure | VR-first, relies on Meta's Oculus hardware, centralized infrastructure |
| **Community Engagement** | Ownership-driven engagement, decentralized economy, NFT-based virtual spaces and events | User-created games, developer monetization via Robux, strong social interactions in user-generated experiences | VR-based social engagement, real-time interactions, collaborative spaces, less developed creator economy |
| **Governance** | Decentralized governance through DAO, user voting on policies, transparency through blockchain | Centralized governance by Roblox Corporation, limited user influence, developer-focused feedback | Centralized governance by Meta, corporate oversight, strict content moderation |

continued on following page

*Table 2. Continued*

| Features | Decentraland | Roblox | Meta Horizon |
|---|---|---|---|
| **Growth Metrics** | - Grew significantly in 2020-2022 due to increased interest in NFTs and virtual real estate.<br>- Active users fluctuate due to market volatility and NFT speculation.<br>- Steady growth of virtual land ownership and event participation | - Continuous exponential growth with over **200 million monthly active users** as of 2023.<br>- Over **40 million user-generated experiences**.<br>- Huge growth driven by global popularity, especially during the pandemic | - Growing user base but slower adoption compared to Roblox<br>- Primarily targeted at VR users<br>- Meta aims to increase Horizon's adoption as part of their push into the metaverse, but current numbers lag behind other platforms |
| Economic Sustainability | - Powered by a **decentralized economy** based on Ethereum, with virtual land and NFTs driving most of its economic activity<br>- Users buy and sell virtual land and assets as NFTs, using MANA tokens for transactions.<br>- Long-term sustainability depends on the growth of the NFT market and adoption of decentralized platforms | - **Highly sustainable** through its robust developer economy.<br>- Roblox's virtual currency, **Robux**, drives in-game purchases and revenue generation.<br>- Developers can monetize their games, making Roblox one of the most lucrative platforms for creators | - Currently lacks a strong creator economy compared to Roblox and Decentraland.<br>- Horizon's economy is still in development, focusing more on social engagement than economic transactions.<br>- Meta is working to introduce monetization tools, but this will take time to reach full scale |
| User Demographics | - Primarily appeals to **crypto enthusiasts,** NFT collectors, and digital artists.<br>- Attracts users interested in virtual real estate, decentralized governance, and blockchain technology.<br>- Smaller, niche user base compared to Roblox | - Appeals to a wide range of users, but especially **younger demographics** (ages 9-16).<br>- Roblox's user base includes millions of children and teenagers worldwide.<br>- Strong global reach with significant engagement across age groups, though mainly popular among younger users | - Focused on users with **VR headsets,** particularly tech-savvy individuals and gamers interested in immersive social experiences.<br>- More mature user base compared to Roblox, targeting adults and professionals<br>- Demographic is limited by VR hardware accessibility, resulting in a narrower audience compared to Roblox and Decentraland . |
| Technical Challenges | - **Blockchain Scalability**: As Decentraland grows, scalability issues on the Ethereum blockchain, such as slow transaction speeds and high gas fees, can affect user experience<br>- **Decentralized Hosting**: Content hosted on IPFS may experience slower loading times and issues with consistency, impacting performance for some users | - **Server Overload**: Roblox has experienced server issues during peak usage times, leading to downtime and instability in user experience<br>- **Cross-Platform Optimization**: Ensuring a seamless experience across different devices (PC, mobile, console) can lead to varying performance, especially in complex games<br>- **Complex Game Logic**: Some developers face difficulties with Roblox's Lua scripting, leading to technical limitations in game development | - **VR Optimization**: Meta Horizon must overcome the high computational demands of rendering complex virtual environments in real-time for VR, which can lead to performance issues on less powerful VR hardware<br>- **Latency**: As a VR-focused platform, reducing latency is critical to avoid motion sickness and ensure a smooth experience, especially in social interactions<br>- **Limited Developer Support**: Meta Horizon's developer tools are not as robust as other platforms, posing challenges to creating complex user-generated content. |

continued on following page

*Table 2. Continued*

| Features | Decentraland | Roblox | Meta Horizon |
|---|---|---|---|
| User Retention | - **Niche Audience**: Retention is higher among crypto-enthusiasts and NFT collectors but struggles to retain casual users unfamiliar with blockchain technology<br>- **Event-Driven Retention**: Virtual events and unique NFT drops keep users engaged, though retention fluctuates with market trends | - **Highly Engaged User Base**: Roblox boasts strong user retention, particularly among younger audiences, driven by a continuous stream of user-generated games and social interaction<br>- **Frequent Updates**: Regular platform updates and events contribute to high engagement, keeping users coming back for new experiences | - **Limited Retention**: Due to the current requirement for VR hardware and the early-stage development of social experiences, user retention is lower than other platforms<br>- **Engagement through Social Spaces**: Meta Horizon retains users by promoting social interaction and collaboration in virtual environments, but faces challenges in expanding beyond its VR-focused audience |
| Limitation | - **Hardware Dependency**: Requires powerful computers for optimal experience, limiting accessibility for users without high-performance hardware<br>- **Crypto Volatility**: As it relies heavily on blockchain and NFTs, its user base is affected by fluctuations in cryptocurrency markets<br>- **Learning Curve**: Creating content requires familiarity with blockchain and decentralized technologies, which can deter casual users | - **Age Restrictions**: Primarily appeals to younger users, limiting its appeal to older demographics<br>- **Content Moderation**: Difficulty managing inappropriate content due to the sheer volume of user-generated games, leading to concerns over safety for younger players<br>- **Monetization Pressure**: Some developers face challenges with monetizing their games, creating a competitive environment that can discourage smaller creators | - **VR Hardware Requirement**: Requires VR headsets like Oculus, limiting access to users with VR equipment and contributing to slow adoption<br>- **Lack of Robust Creator Tools**: While immersive, the platform lacks the extensive creator tools that other metaverse platforms offer, reducing its appeal to content creators<br>- **Limited Interoperability**: Currently lacks cross-platform integration, limiting its potential to attract a broader audience |

## 4. CONCLUSION AND FURTHER RESEARCH

Building a community in the metaverse presents unique challenges that differ significantly from those in traditional online or physical communities. These challenges arise from the complex interplay of technology, social dynamics, governance, and user experience within virtual environments. Below are some of the key challenges to building and sustaining a community in the metaverse (Khaldy et al., 2024; Yang et al., 2024):

1. Technological Barriers
   - Hardware and Accessibility: The metaverse often requires access to advanced hardware, such as VR headsets, powerful computers, or high-speed internet. These requirements can limit the accessibility of the metaverse to a broader audience, particularly in regions with limited technological infrastructure. Ensuring that communities can be inclusive and accessible to users with varying levels of technology is a significant challenge.
   - Interoperability: The metaverse is composed of various platforms and virtual worlds, many of which operate in silos. Creating a seamless experience where users can move between different metaverse environments, taking their identities, assets, and experiences with them, is a complex challenge. Interoperability is essential for fostering larger, interconnected communities but requires standardization and collaboration among platforms.

- Scalability: As communities grow, the underlying technology must scale to support increased user activity without compromising performance. This includes handling more simultaneous users, managing larger virtual spaces, and ensuring low latency for real-time interactions. Achieving scalability while maintaining a high-quality user experience is a continuous challenge.

2. Social Dynamics and Community Building
   - User Engagement: Keeping users engaged over the long term is a challenge in the metaverse, where users have endless options for entertainment and interaction. Communities must provide ongoing value, whether through events, content, or social interactions, to retain and grow their membership.
   - Social Fragmentation: The metaverse's vast and diverse landscape can lead to social fragmentation, where communities become isolated or niche, limiting broader interaction and collaboration. Balancing the creation of specialized communities with opportunities for cross-community interaction is important for a vibrant metaverse.
   - Identity and Representation: In the metaverse, users create and interact through avatars, which can lead to challenges around identity and representation. Issues such as anonymity, authenticity, and the pressure to conform to certain visual or social norms can impact community dynamics. Ensuring that users feel safe and represented while navigating these complexities is crucial for healthy community building.
3. Governance and Moderation
   - Decentralized Governance: Many metaverse platforms advocate for decentralized governance, where community members have a say in decision-making processes. While this empowers users, it also presents challenges in achieving consensus, managing conflicts, and ensuring fair representation. Balancing decentralization with effective governance structures is essential for sustainable community growth.
   - Content Moderation: Maintaining a safe and welcoming environment requires effective content moderation to address issues such as harassment, hate speech, and inappropriate content. In a decentralized and user-driven environment like the metaverse, moderating vast amounts of content and user interactions is a daunting task. Automated tools, human moderators, and community-driven reporting systems all play a role, but finding the right balance is challenging.
   - Legal and Ethical Considerations: The global and virtual nature of the metaverse complicates the application of legal frameworks and ethical standards. Different jurisdictions have varying laws on privacy, intellectual property, and user rights, making it difficult to enforce consistent rules across the metaverse. Communities must navigate these legal and ethical challenges while ensuring compliance and protecting users' rights.
4. Economic and Monetization Challenges
   - Sustainability of Virtual Economies: Virtual economies in the metaverse, driven by virtual goods, services, and digital currencies, face challenges related to inflation, value stability, and equitable distribution of wealth. Ensuring that virtual economies are sustainable and beneficial to all community members requires careful planning and management.
   - Monetization Models: Communities often rely on monetization strategies, such as membership fees, virtual goods sales, or event tickets, to sustain themselves. However, finding a bal-

ance between monetization and user experience can be difficult. Over-commercialization can alienate users, while under-monetization can limit a community's growth and sustainability.

- Digital Ownership and Property Rights: Ensuring true ownership of digital assets within the metaverse is a challenge, particularly when it comes to intellectual property and copyright issues. Users need confidence that their creations and purchases are secure, transferable, and legally recognized, which requires robust blockchain solutions and legal frameworks.

5. Cultural and Ethical Challenges
    - Cultural Sensitivity: The metaverse brings together users from diverse cultural backgrounds, each with their own values, norms, and behaviors. Building inclusive communities that respect and celebrate this diversity while avoiding cultural appropriation, discrimination, or misunderstandings is challenging.
    - Digital Well-Being: The immersive nature of the metaverse can lead to concerns about digital addiction, social isolation, and mental health. Communities must be mindful of promoting healthy digital habits and providing support for members who may be struggling with the effects of prolonged virtual engagement.
    - Misinformation and Trust: Just as in the broader internet, the metaverse is susceptible to the spread of misinformation, scams, and false identities. Building trust within communities requires mechanisms to verify information, protect against fraud, and educate users about the risks of the digital environment.
6. User Experience and Design
    - Immersive Experience Design: Creating truly immersive and engaging experiences in the metaverse requires advanced design skills that blend aesthetics, functionality, and interactivity. Ensuring that these experiences are intuitive and accessible to a wide range of users, including those with disabilities, is a significant challenge.
    - Onboarding New Users: The complexity of the metaverse can be daunting for new users. Effective onboarding processes that guide users through account setup, avatar creation, and community engagement are essential for lowering barriers to entry and helping users feel comfortable in the virtual world.
    - Consistency Across Platforms: As users interact with multiple metaverse platforms, maintaining a consistent experience—whether in terms of user interface, avatar functionality, or social norms—can be challenging. Inconsistencies can disrupt the user experience and make it harder to build cohesive communities across different virtual environments.

Finally, as a remark of this book chapter, building a community in the metaverse is a multifaceted endeavour that requires addressing a range of technological, social, economic, and ethical challenges. As the metaverse continues to evolve, those who can successfully navigate these challenges will be well-positioned to create thriving, engaged, and resilient communities. By focusing on inclusivity, sustainability, governance, and user experience, community builders can contribute to the development of a metaverse that is rich in diversity, innovation, and connection.

## REFERENCES


Al Khaldy, M. A., Al-Qerem, A., Aldweesh, A., & Alauthman, M. (2024, September 01). Mohammad, Al, Khaldy., Ahmad, Al–Qerem., Amjad, Aldweesh., Mohammad, Alauthman. (2024). A general framework for metaverse based on parallel computing and HPC. *Indonesian Journal of Electrical Engineering and Computer Science*, 35(3), 1895. Advance online publication. DOI: 10.11591/ijeecs.v35.i3.pp1895-1905

Blackwood, G. (2023). *Roblox and Meta Verch.* M/C Journal., DOI: 10.5204/mcj.2958

Cheryl, Bhasin., Hritik, Dilawari., Prasath, K, Yuvaa., Shiv, Shankar, Kumar, Yadav. (2024). The Metaverse. Advances in marketing, customer relationship management, and e-services book series, DOI: 10.4018/979-8-3693-2754-8.ch022

Davis, K., & Thomas, P. (2020). Identity and Self-Representation in Virtual Worlds: An Analysis of Avatar Use in the Metaverse. *Digital Society Journal*, 11(4), 220–238.

Decentraland official site https://decentraland.org/

Evans, B. (2020). The Role of Authenticity in Face-to-Face Social Interactions. *Human Behavior and Society*, 18(3), 145–160.

Gordon, A., & Harris, P. (2019). The Limitations of Geographical Boundaries in Physical Communities. *Regional Social Dynamics Review*, 13(1), 50–65.

Hall, J. (2020). The Role of Algorithms in Shaping Social Media Communities. *Journal of Medical Technology*, 19(3), 92–105.

Johnson, D. (2021). Technological Barriers to Accessibility in the Metaverse. *Journal of Emerging Technologies*, 14(1), 33–47.

Liu, Y. Yi, Xu., Hui, Pan. (2024). Metaverse Identity: Core Principles and Critical Challenges. doi: / arxiv.2406.08029DOI: 10.48550

Mandeep, G. (2024). *Comparative Analysis of Metaverse Platforms: Sandbox, MANA (Decentraland), and Bloktopia*. Deleted Journal., DOI: 10.36676/sjmbt.v2.i2.29

Massimo, F. (2023). Decentraland: The Alleged Decentralization of Blockchain Applications. *Communications of the ACM*, 66(6), 45–47. Advance online publication. DOI: 10.1145/3563942

Meta Horizon official site https://horizon.meta.com/

Mohammad, Aljanabi., Sahar, Yousif, Mohammed. (2023). Metaverse: open possibilities. Iraqi journal for computer science and mathematics, DOI: 10.52866/ijcsm.2023.02.03.007

Mohammad, Daradkeh. (2023). Unveiling the Path to Knowledge Sharing and Innovation in Metaverse Virtual Communities. Advances in computational intelligence and robotics book series, DOI: 10.4018/978-1-6684-9151-5.ch018

Oindrila, Chakraborty. (2024). Introduction to Metaverse. Advances in e-business research series, DOI: 10.4018/979-8-3693-2422-6.ch002

Parker, L. (2021). Traditional Social Structures and Group Dynamics in Physical Communities. *Cultural Interaction Quarterly*, 10(4), 78–92.

Patel, R. (2022). Online Harassment and Misinformation in Social Media Communities. *Journal of Digital Ethics*, 14(2), 201–220.

P.B., Sharma., Bhavuk, Mahindru. (2024). Exploring the Metaverse. Advances in e-business research series, DOI: 10.4018/979-8-3693-2422-6.ch014

Prasad, Kulkarni., Alok, Gaddi., Ramona, Birău., Virgil, Popescu., Virupakshi, Hiremath., K., Shivashankar., Sharan, Kumar, Shetty., Shivanand, Kagawade. (2024). A Sustainable Approach on Metaverse in Education. Advances in environmental engineering and green technologies book series, DOI: 10.4018/979-8-3693-2845-3.ch011

Rees, M. (2019). Social Bonds and Emotional Connection in Physical Communities. *Community Interaction Studies*, 7(2), 82–95.

Roblox official site www.roblox.com

Saverio, Iacono. (2023). How to Prepare High-Level Massive Online Open Courses for the Metaverse: Tools and Needs. DOI: 10.3390/engproc2023038002

Se, H. (2023, May 15). Hwang. (2023). Creating Communities for Burn Survivors Using Metaverse Platform. *Journal of Burn Care & Research; Official Publication of the American Burn Association*, 44(Supplement_2), S103. Advance online publication. DOI: 10.1093/jbcr/irad045.141

Sergei, Ivanovich, Rodzin., Viktoriia, Viktorovna, Bova. (2024). The Metaverse as one of the foundations of future education. DOI: 10.31483/r-112497

Shrushti, S. (2024). *Zade., Sakshi, S., Atrik., Aarti, P., Pimpalkar*. Metaverse & NFT Blockchain., DOI: 10.59256/indjcst.20240302005

Smith, J. (2022). Immersive Virtual Worlds and Social Presence in the Metaverse. *Journal of Virtual Interaction*, 15(2), 101–120.

West, C. (2021). Curating Identity: Social Media and Self-Presentation in the Digital Age. *Journal of Social Media Studies*, 12(1), 120–135.

Wright, M. (2023). Decentralized Governance in the Metaverse: A Case Study of DAOs. *Blockchain and Society Review*, 12(1), 98–112.

Yang, S., & Wu, Q. (2022). The Impact of Asynchronous Communication on Social Media Engagement. *Digital Communication Research*, 8(2), 33–47.

Zhai, X.-S., Chu, X.-Y., Chen, M., Shen, J., & Lou, F.-L.Xue-song. (2023, December). Zhai., Xiaoyan, Chu., Min, Tsuei, Chen., Jun, Shen. (2023). Can Edu-Metaverse Reshape Virtual Teaching Community (VTC) to Promote Educational Equity? An Exploratory Study. *IEEE Transactions on Learning Technologies*, 16(6), 1130–1140. Advance online publication. DOI: 10.1109/TLT.2023.3276876

Zhao, L., & Huang, R. (2021). Metaverse Platforms and Their Impact on User Engagement. *Virtual Reality Research Review*, 9(3), 55–70.

# Chapter 17
# A Review of Understanding the Social Engineering in the Context of Cybersecurity

**Arijit Bardhan Roy**
https://orcid.org/0000-0002-5246-5825
*SRM Institute of Science and Technology, India*

## ABSTRACT

*Social engineering represents a critical threat vector within the domain of cybersecurity, leveraging human psychology rather than technical vulnerabilities to breach systems. This paper aims to explore the multifaceted nature of social engineering, dissecting its various forms, including phishing, pretexting, baiting, and tailgating, among others. By examining case studies and statistical data, we reveal the pervasive and adaptive nature of these attacks, which exploit human trust, curiosity, and fear. Furthermore, we assess the psychological principles underpinning social engineering, such as authority, reciprocity, and social proof, to understand why individuals and organizations fall victim to these schemes. The paper also evaluates the effectiveness of current preventive measures, including employee training, awareness programs, and technological defenses, highlighting areas where improvements are needed.*

## INTRODUCTION

In the realm of cybersecurity, social engineering stands out as a pervasive and often underestimated threat. Unlike traditional cyber-attacks that rely on technical vulnerabilities, social engineering exploits human psychology to gain unauthorized access to systems and sensitive information. This journal aims to explore the various facets of social engineering, its methodologies, and the measures that can be adopted to mitigate such threats.

In the constantly evolving landscape of cybersecurity, technical defences such as firewalls, encryption, and intrusion detection systems are often at the forefront of protective measures. However, an equally significant threat targets the human element of security: social engineering. Social engineering leverages psychological manipulation to deceive individuals into divulging confidential information or performing actions that compromise security. Unlike conventional cyberattacks that exploit technical

DOI: 10.4018/979-8-3693-8628-6.ch017

vulnerabilities, social engineering exploits human psychology and behaviours, making it a particularly insidious tool for cybercriminals.

Social engineering encompasses a variety of tactics, including phishing, pretexting, baiting, and tailgating, each designed to exploit trust, curiosity, fear, or other psychological triggers. For example, phishing attacks frequently involve deceptive emails or messages that appear legitimate, coaxing recipients to click on malicious links or provide sensitive data. The prevalence and success of phishing as a social engineering tactic are underscored by numerous studies and reports [1-10].

Understanding social engineering is critical for developing robust cybersecurity strategies. Recognizing the psychological underpinnings of these attacks and educating individuals on how to identify and respond to social engineering attempts can significantly bolster defences. As cybersecurity threats continue to evolve, integrating social engineering awareness and prevention into the broader security framework is essential for protecting sensitive information and maintaining organizational integrity.

## Defining Social Engineering

Social engineering, in the context of cybersecurity, refers to a range of malicious activities accomplished through human interactions. It involves manipulating individuals into performing actions or divulging confidential information. The success of social engineering attacks hinges on the attacker's ability to deceive and influence their target, leveraging trust, curiosity, fear, or urgency.

## Common Social Engineering Techniques

Figure 1. shows the different types of common social engineering techniques.

*Figure 1. Types of common social engineering techniques.*

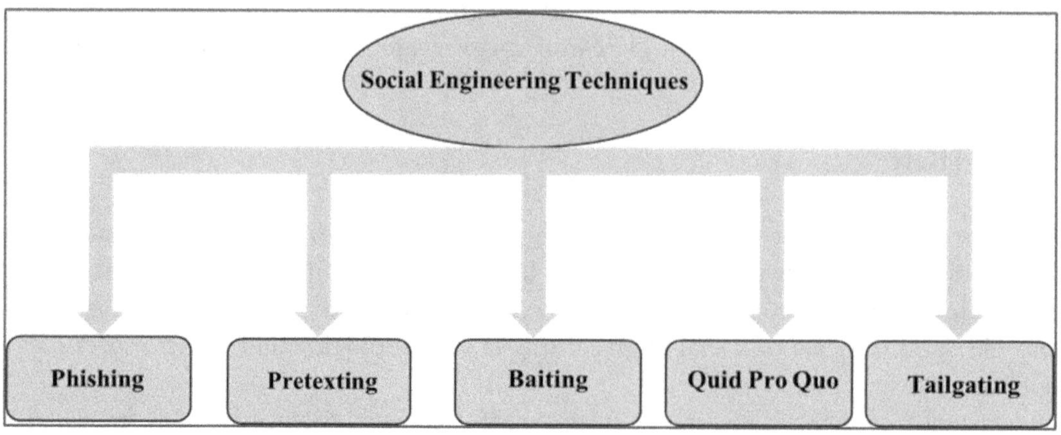

## 1. Phishing

Phishing is one of the most prevalent and insidious forms of cybercrime, targeting individuals and organizations through deceptive communications designed to steal sensitive information. It involves masquerading as a trustworthy entity in electronic communications to trick recipients into divulging personal information, such as passwords, credit card numbers, and other confidential data. Despite significant advancements in cybersecurity, phishing remains a persistent threat due to its ability to exploit human psychology and the ever-evolving tactics used by cybercriminals.

The term “phishing” is a play on the word “fishing,” where attackers lure victims with bait, hoping they will “bite” by responding to the malicious message. This bait often comes in the form of emails, instant messages, or social media posts that appear to be from reputable sources such as banks, government agencies, or well-known companies. These messages typically contain urgent language or enticing offers, prompting recipients to click on a link or download an attachment.

One of the most common types of phishing is email phishing. In a typical email phishing attack, the attacker sends a fraudulent email that appears to come from a legitimate source. The email might contain a link to a fake website that mimics a legitimate one, where victims are prompted to enter their login credentials. Once the attacker has this information, they can access the victim's accounts, steal money, or commit identity theft.

Spear phishing is a more targeted form of phishing, where the attacker customizes the attack to a specific individual or organization. By using information gleaned from social media or other sources, the attacker crafts a highly personalized message that increases the likelihood of success. For example, an attacker might research a company's organizational structure and send an email that appears to be from a senior executive to an employee, requesting sensitive information.

The impact of phishing attacks can be severe, leading to financial losses, identity theft, and data breaches. According to the FBI's Internet Crime Complaint Center (IC3), phishing was the most common type of cybercrime in 2020, with reported losses exceeding $1.8 billion (FBI, 2020). The COVID-19 pandemic exacerbated the situation, as cybercriminals exploited the increased reliance on digital communication and remote work. [11].

## 2. Pretexting

Pretexting is a sophisticated social engineering technique used by cybercriminals to obtain sensitive information under false pretences. Unlike phishing, which typically involves mass deception through emails or messages, pretexting involves creating a fabricated scenario or pretext to engage a specific target in revealing confidential data.

In a typical pretexting scenario, the attacker assumes the identity of a trusted figure or organization, such as a bank employee, IT support technician, or law enforcement officer. By meticulously crafting a believable story, the attacker persuades the victim to divulge information that would normally be kept secure. This might include personal identification numbers, social security numbers, account details, or other private information.

For example, an attacker might call an individual pretending to be from their bank's fraud department, claiming there has been suspicious activity on their account. Under this guise, the attacker asks the victim to verify their account information or provide their password, ostensibly to secure the account. Once the attacker has this information, they can exploit it for financial gain or further fraudulent activities.

Pretexting is particularly dangerous because it relies on building trust and exploiting the victim's natural inclination to help and cooperate with perceived authority figures. To protect against pretexting, individuals and organizations should be cautious about sharing personal information and verify the identity of anyone requesting sensitive data through independent means [12-15] .

## 3. Baiting

Baiting is a sophisticated form of social engineering attack that preys on human curiosity, greed, and trust to manipulate victims into compromising their own security. Unlike phishing or pretexting, which typically involve deceptive communications, baiting introduces physical or digital enticements designed to lure victims into performing actions that can lead to the installation of malware or the disclosure of sensitive information.

One of the most classic forms of baiting involves the use of physical media, such as USB drives. An attacker might leave a malware-infected USB drive in a public place where it is likely to be found, such as a parking lot, office lobby, or conference room. The drive might be labelled with something intriguing, like “Confidential” or “Salary Information,” to entice the finder to plug it into their computer. Once connected, the malware on the USB drive is automatically executed, potentially giving the attacker access to the victim’s system and network.

Digital baiting is also common and can be even more effective. This method often involves offering something that seems too good to pass up, such as free software downloads, exclusive content, or irresistible deals. For instance, an attacker might create a fake website that promises a free download of popular software. The victim, driven by the desire to obtain the software without paying, downloads what appears to be the legitimate software but is, in fact, malware.

Baiting can also be executed through online advertisements, peer-to-peer networks, and social media platforms. Cybercriminals might use these channels to distribute malicious links or files disguised as popular movies, music, or other types of digital media. When victims download and open these files, they unwittingly install malware that can steal personal information, track keystrokes, or give attackers remote control over their computers.

To defend against baiting attacks, individuals and organizations must adopt a combination of vigilance, education, and technical safeguards. Regular cybersecurity training can help raise awareness about the dangers of baiting and teach employees to recognize and avoid potential threats. For example, employees should be trained never to insert unknown USB drives into their computers and to be cautious of downloading software or files from unverified sources.

Technical defences are also crucial. Implementing robust antivirus and anti-malware software can help detect and block malicious files before they can cause harm. Network security measures, such as firewalls and intrusion detection systems, can further protect against unauthorized access and malware infections. Additionally, organizations should consider disabling the auto-run feature for USB drives and other removable media to prevent automatic execution of malware.

## 4. Quid Pro Quo

In the context of cybersecurity, “Quid Pro Quo” refers to a type of social engineering attack that leverages the expectation of reciprocity to manipulate victims into divulging sensitive information or performing actions that compromise security. Unlike other social engineering techniques, which may rely on fear or curiosity, quid pro quo exploits the natural human inclination to return favours or adhere to perceived social contracts.

The term “quid pro quo” is Latin for “something for something,” highlighting the mutual exchange nature of this tactic. Attackers typically offer a service or benefit in exchange for the target’s compliance, which often involves providing sensitive information or access.

One common scenario involves attackers posing as IT support personnel. They contact employees of a targeted organization, helping with a purported technical issue. In exchange for this “help,” they request login credentials or other access details. Because the victim believes they are receiving legitimate support, they are more likely to comply.

Another example is offering free software or services that require the victim to enter their login information. The attacker promises a benefit, such as a software upgrade or troubleshooting, and in return, the victim unknowingly provides credentials that can be exploited for further attacks.

A historical example of quid pro quo in action is the attack on a major U.S. hospital system. Attackers posed as technical support staff and called various hospital employees, claiming they needed to update software on the employees' computers. In exchange for the supposed update, the attackers asked for the employees' login information. Many employees complied, resulting in a significant breach that compromised patient records and other sensitive information .

Quid pro quo attacks can also occur in more subtle ways. For instance, an attacker might send a survey offering a gift card upon completion. To claim the reward, the victim might have to provide personal information or even install software that turns out to be malicious. This method exploits the victim’s desire for a reward, making them overlook potential risks.

Defending against quid pro quo attacks requires a combination of vigilance, education, and technical safeguards. Organizations should conduct regular training sessions to raise awareness about social engineering tactics and stress the importance of verifying the identity of anyone requesting sensitive information. Employees should be encouraged to report suspicious interactions and consult their IT departments before providing any information or access.

Technical defences include implementing strong authentication protocols and monitoring for unusual access patterns. Multi-factor authentication (MFA) can add an additional layer of security, making it harder for attackers to exploit stolen credentials. Regular audits and updates to security policies can also help identify and mitigate potential vulnerabilities.

Moreover, a culture of scepticism and verification should be promoted within organizations. Employees should be trained to verify the authenticity of offers or requests, especially if they involve providing sensitive information or access. This might include contacting the purported requester through official channels to confirm their identity and the legitimacy of their request.

In summary, quid pro quo is a potent social engineering technique that preys on the expectation of reciprocity. By offering a service or benefit, attackers manipulate victims into compromising their security. Combating this threat requires a multifaceted approach that includes employee education, strong technical defences, and a culture of verification and scepticism. As cyber threats continue to evolve, understanding and defending against quid pro quo attacks is essential for maintaining robust cybersecurity [16-19].

## 5. Tailgating (or Piggybacking)

Tailgating is a physical security breach where an unauthorized person follows an authorized individual into a restricted area, often without the latter’s knowledge.

## Psychological Principles Behind Social Engineering

Social engineering is a sophisticated manipulation technique that exploits the psychological tendencies and behaviours of individuals to breach security protocols and gain unauthorized access to systems, information, or physical locations. While technological defences against cyber threats continue to advance, the human element remains a significant vulnerability. Understanding the psychological principles behind social engineering can help organizations and individuals develop more effective countermeasures. This comprehensive analysis explores various psychological principles and tactics used in social engineering attacks, supported by research and expert insights.

### 1. Reciprocity

The principle of reciprocity is a fundamental social rule that dictates the obligation to return a favour when one is received. This principle is deeply ingrained in human behaviour and is exploited by social engineers to manipulate their targets.

Mechanism

Social engineers often provide a seemingly genuine service or offer help to create a sense of obligation. For example, an attacker might pose as a helpful IT support technician, resolving a fake issue for the target. Once the target feels indebted, they are more likely to comply with requests for sensitive information or access.

Research

Cialdini (2001) describes reciprocity as one of the six key principles of persuasion, highlighting how it can compel individuals to act against their better judgment. Studies show that even small favours can create a powerful sense of obligation.

Here's a simple table that summarizes the key elements of **Cialdini's Reciprocity Principle (2001):**

*Table 1. Key elements of Cialdini's Reciprocity Principle (2001)*

| Element | Description | Example |
|---|---|---|
| Unsolicited Favors | People feel obligated to return favors, even if unsolicited. | Free samples in stores leading to future purchases. |
| Concessions/Compromise | Making a concession leads others to feel obligated to reciprocate by conceding as well. | "Door-in-the-face" technique: asking for a large favor first, then a smaller one. |
| Social Norms | Reciprocity is a universal social norm that exists across different cultures. | A colleague buys lunch, so you feel inclined to buy lunch next time. |

## 2. Commitment and Consistency

People have a strong desire to appear consistent in their actions and decisions. Once they commit to something, they are likely to follow through to maintain their self-image.

Mechanism

Social engineers exploit this by getting targets to make small commitments that gradually escalate. For instance, an attacker might first ask for harmless information, then use this initial compliance to justify requesting more sensitive data.

Research

The principle of commitment and consistency is extensively discussed by Cialdini . Research by Freedman and Fraser (1966) demonstrated that individuals who agreed to small initial requests were significantly more likely to comply with larger subsequent requests.

## 3. Social Proof

Social proof refers to the tendency of individuals to look to others for cues on how to behave, especially in uncertain situations. When people are unsure, they often follow the actions of others to determine appropriate behaviour.

Mechanism

Social engineers use social proof by creating scenarios where the target believes that others are complying with the request. This can be achieved through fake testimonials, endorsements, or the illusion that many people are participating in an activity.

Research

Cialdini (2001) notes that social proof is particularly effective in situations of uncertainty or similarity. Bandura (1977) also discusses how observational learning influences behaviour, emphasizing the role of social proof in shaping actions.

## 4. Authority

People tend to obey authority figures, often without questioning their legitimacy. This tendency is rooted in societal norms and the perceived legitimacy of authority.

Mechanism

Attackers often impersonate authority figures such as managers, IT personnel, or law enforcement officials to gain compliance. The target's respect for authority leads them to follow instructions without verifying the authenticity of the request.

Research

Milgram's (1963) obedience experiments illustrate the powerful influence of authority on behaviour. His findings show that individuals are likely to follow orders from perceived authority figures, even when those orders conflict with their personal morals.

Here is a block diagram representing Milgram's (1963) obedience experiments. The flow of authority, obedience, and distress between the experimenter, participant, and learner is visually represented to illustrate the structure of the study.

## 5. Liking

People are more likely to be influenced by individuals they like or find attractive. Factors such as physical attractiveness, similarity, compliments, and familiarity can all increase likability.

Mechanism

Social engineers often establish rapport and build a friendly relationship with the target. By appearing likable and trustworthy, they lower the target's defenses and increase the likelihood of compliance.

Research

Cialdini (2001) highlights liking as a key principle of influence, noting that individuals are more likely to say yes to requests from people they like. Research by Berscheid and Walster (1974) supports this, showing that physical attractiveness and similarity significantly impact likability and influence.

## 6. Scarcity

Scarcity is a powerful motivator; people tend to perceive items or opportunities as more valuable when they are scarce or limited in availability.

Mechanism

Attackers create a sense of urgency by implying that a resource or opportunity is scarce. This pressure can lead targets to act quickly without thoroughly considering the legitimacy of the request.

Research

Worchel, Lee, and Adewole (1975) demonstrated that participants rated cookies as more desirable when they were scarce. Cialdini (2001) also discusses how the scarcity principle can drive people to make irrational decisions under perceived pressure.

## 7. Urgency

Creating a sense of urgency compels individuals to act quickly, often bypassing rational decision-making processes. This is frequently combined with other principles, such as authority or scarcity, to heighten the impact.

Mechanism

Social engineers often craft messages that demand immediate action, such as urgent security updates or immediate account verification. The sense of urgency prevents targets from taking the time to verify the request's authenticity.

Research

Studies on decision-making under time pressure, such as those by Zakay (1993), show that urgency can significantly impair judgment and lead to hasty decisions. This makes targets more susceptible to social engineering attacks.

## 8. Familiarity and Trust

People are more likely to comply with requests from individuals or organizations they are familiar with and trust. Familiarity breeds comfort and reduces suspicion.

Mechanism

Attackers often impersonate known contacts or reputable organizations. They may use information from social media or other sources to establish familiarity and gain the target's trust.

Research

Research by Langer, Blank, and Chanowitz (1978) shows that people are more likely to comply with requests when the context or the requester appears familiar. This familiarity creates a sense of security, making targets more vulnerable to manipulation.

## 9. Fear and Threats

Inducing fear or presenting a threat can override rational thinking and compel individuals to act defensively. Fear-based tactics are particularly effective in creating immediate compliance.

Mechanism

Attackers may use scare tactics, such as threatening legal action, financial penalties, or security breaches, to pressure targets into providing information or taking specific actions.

Research

Janis and Feshbach (1953) found that fear-arousing communications can significantly influence behaviour. However, the effectiveness of fear tactics depends on the perceived severity of the threat and the individual's belief in their ability to mitigate it (Witte, 1992).

### 10. Cognitive Overload

Cognitive overload occurs when individuals are presented with more information or tasks than they can process, leading to impaired decision-making. Social engineers exploit this by overwhelming targets with complex or confusing scenarios.

Mechanism

Attackers may present targets with excessive information, technical jargon, or multiple simultaneous requests. This overload can cause the target to comply with the attacker's demands to simplify the situation.

Research

Sweller (1988) introduced the concept of cognitive load theory, explaining how excessive information can hinder learning and decision-making. Subsequent research supports the idea that cognitive overload can lead to increased susceptibility to manipulation (Paas, Renkl, & Sweller, 2003). [20-23]

## Case Studies and Real-World Examples

### Case Study 1: The Target Data Breach

In 2013, Target Corporation experienced one of the largest data breaches in history, affecting over 40 million customers. The breach was facilitated by social engineering tactics targeting a third-party HVAC contractor. Attackers used phishing emails to obtain network credentials, which were then used to infiltrate Target's systems.

This case highlights the effectiveness of combining psychological principles such as trust, authority, and urgency. The attackers impersonated trusted entities and created a sense of legitimacy and urgency to bypass security measures.

However, here's a summary of some **relevant statistics** and **table data** for the **2013 Target data breach**:

*Table 2. Relevant statistics of data breach*

| Data | Details |
|---|---|
| Date of Breach | November-December 2013 |
| Number of Payment Cards Affected | 40 million |
| Number of Customer Records Affected | 70 million |
| Type of Data Stolen | Credit card information, customer contact details |
| Detection | Discovered by Target in December 2013 |
| Attack Vector | Compromised third-party vendor credentials |
| Financial Impact | Over $290 million in total costs by 2017 |
| Settlement Costs | $18.5 million multi-state settlement (2017) |

### Case Study 2: The RSA SecurID Breach

In 2011, RSA, a cybersecurity company, suffered a significant breach when attackers used a phishing email to compromise the company's SecurID two-factor authentication system. The email contained an Excel file titled "2011 Recruitment Plan," which exploited curiosity and trust. Once the file was opened, malware infected the system, leading to the theft of sensitive data.

This case demonstrates how leveraging familiarity (the recruitment plan) and curiosity can lead to successful social engineering attacks, even against highly secure organizations. To mitigate the risk of social engineering attacks, organizations and individuals must adopt a multi-faceted approach that combines awareness, training, and technological defences.

## EDUCATION AND TRAINING

Conduct regular training sessions to educate employees about common social engineering tactics and how to recognize them. Also need to use simulated phishing and social engineering attacks to test and improve employees' responses. Then establish and enforce clear policies for handling sensitive information and verifying requests.

### Technical Defences

### Multi-Factor Authentication (MFA)

Implement MFA to add an additional layer of security. In today's rapidly evolving digital landscape, where cyber threats loom large, safeguarding sensitive information has become more crucial than ever. Multi-Factor Authentication (MFA) stands out as one of the most effective strategies for enhancing security across various platforms, systems, and applications. This detailed exploration delves into the essence of MFA, its mechanisms, advantages, challenges, and its evolving role in ensuring cybersecurity.

*Figure 2. Multi-Factor Authentication (MFA) system*

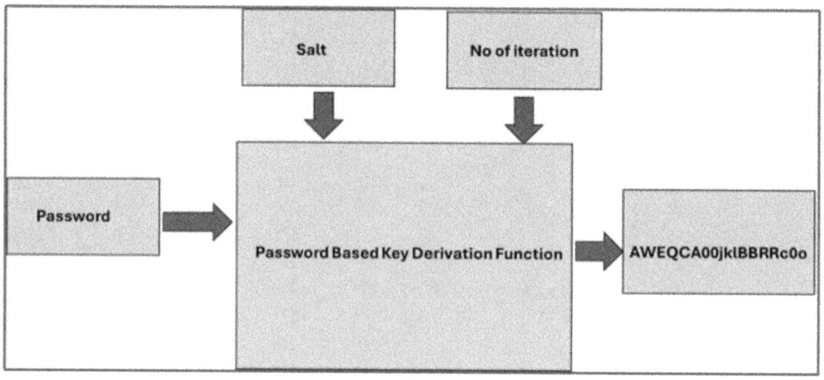


At its core, Multi-Factor Authentication (MFA) is a security protocol that requires users to verify their identity using multiple methods before they are granted access to a system, application, or network. Traditionally, access control has relied on single-factor authentication, typically a username and password. However, with the rise in sophisticated cyber-attacks, the need for more robust security measures has become apparent shown by fig.2. MFA introduces additional layers of security by requiring not just one, but multiple forms of verification. These methods are typically categorized into three main factors:

a. **Something You Know (Knowledge Factor):** This is the most common form of authentication, including passwords, PINs, or security questions. The user provides a piece of information that only they should know.
    a. **Something You Have (Possession Factor):** This involves a physical device or object that the user possesses, such as a smartphone, hardware token, or a smart card. For instance, a one-time passcode (OTP) sent to a user's phone serves as a possession factor.
    b. **Something You Are (Inherence Factor):** This factor involves biometric verification, such as fingerprint scanning, facial recognition, or voice recognition. It is based on the unique physical attributes of the user.

By requiring two or more of these factors, MFA significantly reduces the likelihood of unauthorized access, even if one factor (like a password) is compromised.

The concept of Multi-Factor Authentication is not entirely new; it has evolved over decades as technology and threats have advanced. Initially, two-factor authentication (2FA) was the standard, primarily combining a password (knowledge) with a physical token (possession). However, as cyber-attacks became more sophisticated, the need for additional factors became evident, leading to the broader adoption of MFA.

MFA's evolution has also been influenced by advancements in mobile technology and biometrics. Smartphones, now ubiquitous, have made it easier for users to receive OTPs or use biometric authentication on the go. Similarly, improvements in biometric technology have made inherence factors more reliable and accessible.

## How MFA Works

The process of Multi-Factor Authentication typically unfolds as follows:

*Figure 3. Working principle of Multi-Factor Authentication (MFA) system*

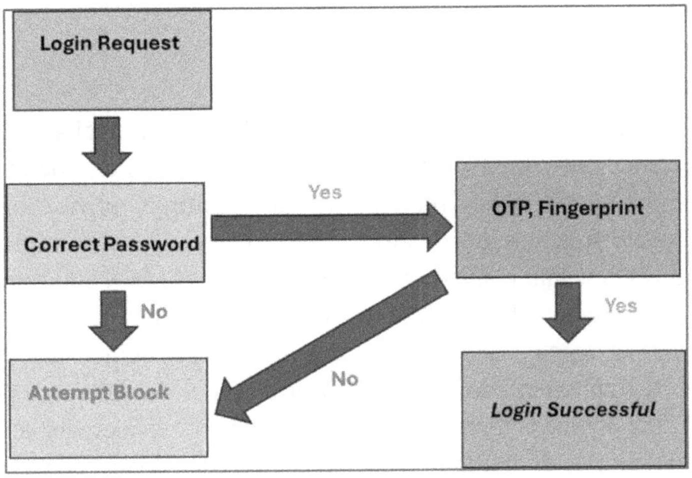


The user attempts to log in by entering their username and password (something they know). This is the first layer of authentication. Upon successfully entering the correct credentials, the system prompts the user to provide additional verification. This could be an OTP sent to their registered phone number, a push notification on an authentication app, or a biometric scan. The user provides the second form of authentication. For instance, they may enter the OTP received on their phone or use a fingerprint scanner. Once the second factor is verified, the user is granted access to the system. If any of the factors fail, access is denied, thus protecting the system from unauthorized entry.

## Benefits of MFA

The adoption of Multi-Factor Authentication offers numerous benefits, making it a critical component of modern cybersecurity strategies:

a. **Enhanced Security:** By requiring multiple forms of verification, MFA makes it exponentially more difficult for attackers to gain unauthorized access. Even if one factor is compromised, the additional layers provide a safety net.
b. **Protection Against Credential Theft:** With the increasing prevalence of phishing attacks and data breaches, passwords are often compromised. MFA mitigates this risk by adding layers beyond just passwords.
c. **Regulatory Compliance:** Many industries are subject to stringent regulatory requirements regarding data protection. Implementing MFA can help organizations comply with these regulations, such as the General Data Protection Regulation (GDPR) or the Health Insurance Portability and Accountability Act (HIPAA).

d. **User-Friendly Experience:** While adding extra layers of security might seem cumbersome, many modern MFA solutions are designed with user convenience in mind. Features like push notifications or biometric authentication offer quick and seamless verification.
e. **Reduction in Fraud:** MFA is particularly effective in reducing fraud, especially in financial transactions. For instance, many banks require MFA for online banking transactions, ensuring that only the authorized user can approve transactions.

## Challenges and Limitations of MFA

While Multi-Factor Authentication offers robust security, it is not without its challenges and limitations: Striking the right balance between security and user convenience can be challenging. Users may find MFA cumbersome, especially if they must go through multiple verification steps each time they log in. But Implementing MFA across an organization can be costly and complex, especially for large enterprises with diverse systems and platforms. The integration of MFA solutions with legacy systems may require significant resources. While MFA enhances security, it is not foolproof. Sophisticated attackers may still find ways to bypass MFA, such as through social engineering, phishing, or exploiting vulnerabilities in the MFA implementation. The MFA often relies on the user's possession of a device, such as a smartphone. If the device is lost, stolen, or unavailable, it can create access challenges for the user the use of biometric data as an authentication factor raises privacy concerns. Unlike passwords, biometric data is immutable; if compromised, it cannot be changed. This makes the secure storage and handling of biometric data critical.

## The Role of MFA in Modern Cybersecurity

As cyber threats continue to evolve, the role of Multi-Factor Authentication in cybersecurity becomes increasingly vital. MFA is now considered a best practice for securing access to sensitive systems and data. Many organizations are moving towards a "Zero Trust" security model, where MFA plays a central role in ensuring that only verified users gain access to resources, regardless of their location or network.

MFA is also becoming integral to identity and access management (IAM) frameworks, helping organizations manage and secure user identities across various platforms and applications. In cloud environments, where traditional network-based security measures may be insufficient, MFA provides an additional layer of protection.

## Future Trends in MFA

The future of Multi-Factor Authentication is likely to be shaped by several emerging trends:

a. **Adaptive Authentication:** Also known as risk-based authentication, adaptive MFA analyses various factors, such as the user's location, device, and behaviour, to determine the level of risk and adjust the authentication process accordingly. For example, a user logging in from a trusted device at a usual location might face fewer authentication steps than someone attempting to log in from an unfamiliar location.

b. **Password less Authentication:** As the weaknesses of passwords become more apparent, there is a growing trend towards password less authentication methods, where MFA is implemented without relying on passwords at all. For instance, biometric authentication combined with device possession can provide a secure and user-friendly login experience.
c. **Integration with AI and Machine Learning:** AI and machine learning are being integrated into MFA solutions to enhance security further. These technologies can analyse patterns, detect anomalies, and provide real-time risk assessments, enabling more dynamic and context-aware authentication processes.
d. **Increased Adoption of Biometrics:** With continuous improvements in biometric technology, we can expect to see broader adoption of biometric authentication methods. Innovations like facial recognition, iris scanning, and behavioural biometrics (e.g., typing patterns) will become more prevalent in MFA implementations.
e. **Regulatory Mandates:** As cyber threats intensify, regulatory bodies may impose stricter requirements for MFA across various industries. This could drive wider adoption of MFA as a standard security measure.[24-27]

## Email Filters: Use Advanced Email Filtering Solutions to Detect and Block Phishing Attempts.

Email filters are an essential tool in managing the deluge of messages that inundate inboxes daily. These automated systems help categorize, prioritize, and sometimes eliminate emails based on predefined criteria, making them indispensable for both personal and professional communication. In this detailed exploration, we'll delve into what email filters are, how they work, their various types, advantages, limitations, and the evolving role they play in email management and cybersecurity.

### Understanding Email Filters

Email filters are automated processes that categorize or manage incoming and outgoing emails based on a set of rules defined by the user or the email service provider. These filters can sort emails into folders, mark them as read, forward them to another address, or delete them entirely, among other actions. The primary purpose of email filters is to help users manage their inbox more efficiently, ensuring that important emails are easily accessible and that unwanted messages do not clutter the inbox.

### How Email Filters Work

Email filters operate by scanning the content and metadata of incoming or outgoing emails and then applying a set of rules to determine the appropriate action. These rules are typically based on various criteria, such as:

Filters can identify emails from specific senders and apply actions based on the sender's email address or domain. For instance, emails from a particular colleague can be automatically routed to a specific folder. Filters can scan the subject line or the body of an email for specific keywords or phrases. If an email contains these terms, it can trigger a particular action, such as moving the email to a designated folder or marking it as important. Emails with attachments can be filtered based on the file type, size, or the mere presence of an attachment. For example, an email filter can be set to automatically move all emails with .pdf attachments to a folder labelled "Documents." Filters can act on emails based on when they were received. This can be useful for sorting emails by time-sensitive content or organizing emails received during a specific period. Email filters often include rules for identifying and filtering out spam or junk mail. These rules can be based on various factors, including the reputation of the sender's domain, the presence of certain keywords, or patterns that are commonly associated with spam.

*Figure 4. Working principle of Email Filters.*

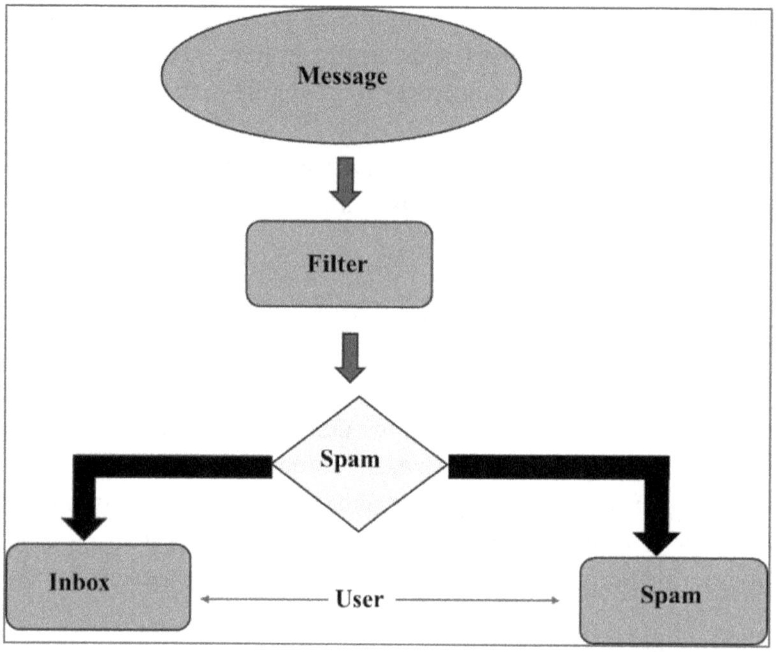


## Types of Email Filters

There are several types of email filters, each serving a specific purpose. Understanding these types can help users configure their email systems more effectively.

Spam Filters:

Spam filters are perhaps the most widely used type of email filter. They are designed to identify and isolate unsolicited, irrelevant, or harmful emails that are often sent in bulk to many recipients. Spam filters use a combination of techniques, including blacklists, heuristics, and machine learning algorithms, to distinguish between legitimate emails and spam. These filters often place suspected spam in a separate folder, where users can review and delete them if necessary.

Content Filters:

Content filters analyse the content of emails, including the subject line and body, to determine if the message meets specific criteria. For example, a content filter might be configured to flag emails containing explicit language, block emails with sensitive information, or categorize emails with specific keywords into different folders.

Attachment Filters:

These filters focus on emails that contain attachments. They can be used to block emails with certain types of files (e.g., .exe files, which may contain malware), move emails with large attachments to a specific folder, or prevent the delivery of attachments that exceed a certain size limit.

Blacklist and Whitelist Filters:

Blacklist filters block emails from specific senders or domains, while whitelist filters ensure that emails from trusted sources are always delivered to the inbox. These filters are useful for both preventing unwanted emails and ensuring that important communications are not mistakenly marked as spam.

Automated Sorting Filters:

These filters help users organize their inboxes by automatically sorting incoming emails into different folders based on predefined rules. For example, a user might set up filters to move all emails from their manager to a "Work" folder or to categorize newsletters into a "Subscriptions" folder.

Priority Filters:

Priority filters help users focus on the most important emails by marking them as high priority or moving them to the top of the inbox. These filters often use criteria such as the sender's identity, keywords indicating urgency, or the user's past interaction patterns.

## Advantages of Email Filters

Email filters offer numerous benefits, making them a valuable tool for managing email communication:

a. **Enhanced Productivity:**

By automating the sorting and categorization of emails, filters allow users to focus on important tasks without being constantly interrupted by incoming messages. This helps reduce the time spent managing emails and improves overall productivity.

b. **Improved Organization:**

Filters help keep the inbox organized by automatically sorting emails into relevant folders. This ensures that users can quickly find the emails they need without having to sift through a cluttered inbox.

c. **Reduced Spam and Unwanted Emails:**

Spam filters play a crucial role in protecting users from unwanted and potentially harmful emails. By isolating spam, these filters help prevent phishing attacks, malware infections, and other security threats.

d. **Customizability:**

Email filters can be highly customized to meet individual needs. Users can create filters that match their specific email management preferences, ensuring that their inboxes are tailored to their workflows.

e. **Enhanced Security:**

In addition to filtering spam, email filters can be configured to block emails with suspicious attachments or content, adding an extra layer of security to the user's email account.

## Challenges and Limitations of Email Filters

While email filters offer many advantages, they are not without their challenges and limitations:

a. **False Positives and Negatives:**

One of the most significant challenges with email filters is the possibility of false positives (legitimate emails being marked as spam) and false negatives (spam emails making it to the inbox). This can lead to important emails being missed or unwanted emails cluttering the inbox.

b. **Complexity in Configuration:**

Setting up email filters, especially for complex sorting and categorization rules, can be time-consuming and require a certain level of technical expertise. Users may need to experiment with different settings to find the configuration that works best for them.

c. **Over-Reliance on Filters:**

Relying too heavily on email filters can lead to complacency, where users may overlook important emails or fail to regularly check their spam or junk folders. This can result in missed opportunities or delayed responses.

d. **Limited Effectiveness Against Sophisticated Threats:**

While spam filters are effective against common types of spam, they may struggle to detect more sophisticated phishing attacks or targeted emails that do not fit typical spam patterns. Advanced threats often require additional security measures, such as email encryption or user training.

e. **Potential for Filter Misconfiguration:**

If filters are not configured correctly, they can cause important emails to be misdirected or lost. For example, an overly aggressive spam filter might block legitimate business communications, leading to misunderstandings or missed deadlines.

## The Role of Email Filters in Modern Communication

In today's digital age, email remains a primary mode of communication for both personal and professional purposes. With the sheer volume of emails that individuals and organizations receive daily, email filters have become indispensable tools for managing and securing inboxes.

For businesses, email filters play a critical role in protecting against cyber threats, maintaining communication efficiency, and ensuring regulatory compliance. Many organizations implement enterprise-level email filtering solutions that integrate with their overall cybersecurity framework, providing protection against phishing, malware, and data breaches.

For individual users, email filters help maintain a clean and organized inbox, reducing the stress associated with managing large volumes of emails. They also provide a first line of defence against unwanted and potentially harmful messages. Table.4 shows the recent advancement about email filter data.

*Table 3. Summary table of Email Filter Data*

| Aspect | Data |
|---|---|
| Predicted Email Users | 4.48 billion |
| Average Emails per Office Worker | 121 emails/day |
| Email Checking Frequency | 91% of consumers check email daily |
| Email Marketing ROI | $42 for every $1 spent |
| Mobile Email Readership | 42% of all emails read on mobile |

## Future Trends in Email Filtering

The future of email filtering is likely to be shaped by several emerging trends and technologies:

a. **Artificial Intelligence and Machine Learning:**

AI and machine learning are becoming increasingly integrated into email filtering systems. These technologies enable filters to learn from user behaviour, adapt to new threats, and provide more accurate filtering with fewer false positives and negatives.

b. **Integration with Email Encryption:**

As concerns about data privacy and security grow, there is a trend towards integrating email filters with encryption technologies. This combination enhances security by ensuring that only authorized recipients can access the content of filtered emails.

c. **Cloud-Based Filtering Solutions:**

With the shift towards cloud computing, many organizations are adopting cloud-based email filtering solutions. These systems offer scalability, ease of management, and the ability to integrate with other cloud-based services.

d. **Contextual Filtering:**

Future email filters may become more context-aware, considering factors such as the user's location, device, and current activity to provide more relevant filtering. For example, an email filter might prioritize work-related emails during business hours and personal emails in the evening.

e. **Enhanced User Control:**

There is a growing demand for email filters that offer more user control and transparency. Users want to understand why certain emails are filtered in a particular way and to have the ability to easily adjust the filtering rules as needed.

## Network Monitoring: Continuously Monitor Networks for Unusual Activity That Could Indicate A Breach

In the increasingly connected digital world, the performance, security, and reliability of computer networks are critical to the success of any organization. Network monitoring is a vital process that allows businesses, institutions, and individuals to ensure that their networks are functioning optimally and securely. This detailed exploration covers the fundamentals of network monitoring, its importance, the tools and techniques used, the challenges faced, and the future trends shaping this crucial aspect of IT management.

### Understanding Network Monitoring

Network monitoring involves the continuous observation of a computer network to identify performance issues, security threats, and potential outages. This process includes tracking various network components such as routers, switches, firewalls, servers, and endpoints, as well as the data traffic that flows through them. The primary goal of network monitoring is to ensure that the network operates smoothly, efficiently, and securely, while minimizing downtime and maximizing performance.

Network monitoring systems (NMS) are designed to automatically detect, diagnose, and alert administrators to problems in real-time. These systems collect data from network devices and use it to create reports, generate alerts, and provide insights into the network's overall health.

## Why Network Monitoring is Important

The importance of network monitoring cannot be overstated, as it plays a critical role in maintaining the stability and security of IT infrastructure. Here are some key reasons why network monitoring is essential:

a. **Proactive Problem Identification:**

Network monitoring enables IT teams to identify and resolve issues before they escalate into major problems. By continuously tracking network performance, administrators can detect anomalies, such as unusual spikes in traffic or latency, and address them proactively. This reduces the likelihood of network outages and ensures that potential issues are mitigated before they impact users or business operations.

b. **Minimizing Downtime:**

Downtime can be costly for businesses, leading to lost productivity, revenue, and customer trust. Network monitoring helps minimize downtime by providing real-time alerts when issues arise, allowing for quick resolution. In some cases, automated responses can be configured to take corrective actions immediately, further reducing downtime.

c. **Ensuring Network Security:**

With the rise of cyber threats, network security has become a top priority for organizations. Network monitoring plays a crucial role in detecting and preventing security breaches. By continuously monitoring network traffic and device activity, administrators can identify suspicious behaviour, such as unauthorized access attempts or data exfiltration, and take action to mitigate the threat.

d. **Optimizing Network Performance:**

Network monitoring provides valuable insights into network performance, including bandwidth usage, latency, and packet loss. By analysing this data, IT teams can optimize network configurations, improve resource allocation, and ensure that critical applications receive the bandwidth they need to perform effectively.

e. **Compliance and Auditing:**

Many industries are subject to regulatory requirements that mandate the monitoring and reporting of network activity. Network monitoring helps organizations comply with these regulations by providing detailed logs and reports that can be used for auditing purposes. This is particularly important in industries such as healthcare, finance, and government, where data privacy and security are paramount.

f. **Capacity Planning:**

As organizations grow, their network needs evolve. Network monitoring provides insights into current usage patterns, helping IT teams plan for future capacity requirements. By understanding how network resources are being utilized, organizations can make informed decisions about upgrades, expansions, and investments in new technology.

## Key Components of Network Monitoring

Network monitoring involves several key components, each playing a specific role in ensuring the network's health and performance. These components include:

a. **Network Devices:**

The devices within a network, such as routers, switches, firewalls, servers, and endpoints, are the primary focus of network monitoring. Monitoring these devices involves tracking their status, performance metrics, and traffic patterns to ensure they are functioning correctly and efficiently.

b. **Traffic Analysis:**

Traffic analysis involves monitoring the data packets that flow through the network. This includes tracking bandwidth usage, identifying bottlenecks, and detecting abnormal traffic patterns that could indicate a security threat or performance issue.

c. **Logs and Event Monitoring:**

Network devices generate logs and events that provide detailed information about their activity. Network monitoring systems collect and analyse these logs to identify issues such as failed login attempts, configuration changes, or hardware errors.

d. **Performance Metrics:**

Performance metrics, such as latency, jitter, packet loss, and throughput, are critical indicators of network health. Network monitoring tools track these metrics in real-time, allowing administrators to quickly identify and address performance issues.

e. **Alerts and Notifications:**

When network monitoring systems detect issues, they generate alerts and notifications to inform administrators. These alerts can be configured based on severity levels, ensuring that critical issues are prioritized and addressed promptly.

f. **Reporting and Visualization:**

Network monitoring systems often include reporting and visualization tools that provide administrators with a clear overview of network performance. Dashboards, charts, and graphs help visualize data, making it easier to identify trends, patterns, and potential issues.

## Tools and Techniques in Network Monitoring

Several tools and techniques are employed in network monitoring to ensure comprehensive coverage and effective management of network infrastructure. These include:

SNMP is a widely used protocol for monitoring and managing network devices. It allows network monitoring systems to collect data from devices, such as routers and switches, and provides a standardized way to track performance metrics, configuration changes, and device status.

NetFlow and sFlow are other protocols used for traffic analysis. They provide detailed information about network traffic, including source and destination addresses, packet sizes, and flow duration. This information is valuable for understanding traffic patterns, detecting anomalies, and optimizing bandwidth usage.

Another important protocol named Packet sniffing involves capturing and analysing network packets to understand the data flow within a network. Tools like Wireshark are commonly used for packet sniffing, allowing administrators to troubleshoot issues, identify security threats, and monitor network performance at a granular level.

At last NPM tools focus on tracking the performance of network devices and traffic. These tools provide real-time monitoring of key performance metrics, generate alerts for potential issues, and offer insights into network health through reports and dashboards. Examples of NPM tools include SolarWinds Network Performance Monitor and PRTG Network Monitor.

## Challenges in Network Monitoring

Despite its importance, network monitoring comes with several challenges that can complicate the task of maintaining network health and security:

a. **Complexity of Modern Networks:**

Modern networks are increasingly complex, often spanning multiple locations, cloud environments, and devices. This complexity makes it challenging to monitor all network components effectively and can lead to blind spots where issues go undetected.

b. **Volume of Data:**

Network monitoring generates vast amounts of data, including logs, metrics, and traffic information. Managing and analysing this data to identify meaningful insights can be overwhelming, especially for large organizations with extensive networks.

c. **Integration with Existing Systems:**

Integrating network monitoring tools with existing IT infrastructure and management systems can be challenging. Compatibility issues, data silos, and the need for custom configurations can complicate the implementation of comprehensive monitoring solutions.

d. **Real-Time Monitoring:**

Real-time monitoring is essential for quickly detecting and responding to issues, but it requires significant processing power and efficient data handling. Delays in data collection or analysis can result in missed alerts and delayed responses to critical issues.

e. **Security Concerns:**

Network monitoring systems themselves can become targets for cyberattacks. If compromised, these systems could be used to gather sensitive information, disrupt network operations, or hide malicious activities. Ensuring the security of network monitoring tools is therefore a critical concern.

f. **Cost and Resource Requirements:**

Implementing and maintaining network monitoring solutions can be costly, especially for small and medium-sized businesses. The need for specialized hardware, software, and skilled personnel can strain budgets and resources.

g. **False Positives and Negatives:**

Network monitoring tools may generate false positives (alerts for non-issues) or false negatives (failure to alert for real issues). These inaccuracies can lead to unnecessary troubleshooting efforts or missed opportunities to address critical problems.

## Best Practices for Effective Network Monitoring

To overcome the challenges and maximize the effectiveness of network monitoring, organizations should follow several best practices:

a. **Define Clear Objectives:**

Start by defining clear objectives for network monitoring. Determine what aspects of the network need to be monitored, what metrics are most important, and what goals the monitoring should achieve (e.g., minimizing downtime, improving security, optimizing performance).

b. **Choose the Right Tools:**

- **Network Performance Monitoring Tools**: Tools like SolarWinds, PRTG, and Nagios can provide real-time network performance data.
- **Security Information and Event Management (SIEM)**: Tools like Splunk or ArcSight are crucial for logging and security event monitoring.

- **Packet Sniffers and Traffic Analysers**: Tools like Wireshark help analyze traffic for anomalies.

## MITIGATING SOCIAL ENGINEERING ATTACKS

### a. Education and Training

Social engineering attacks are manipulative tactics employed by malicious actors to deceive individuals into divulging sensitive information or performing actions that compromise security. These attacks exploit human psychology rather than technical vulnerabilities, making them particularly challenging to defend against. To combat these threats effectively, comprehensive education and training programs are essential. These initiatives empower individuals to recognize, resist, and respond appropriately to social engineering tactics.

#### i. Understanding Social Engineering

Social engineering refers to the psychological manipulation of people to perform actions or divulge confidential information. Phishing, pretexting, baiting, tailgating, and quid pro quo are among the most frequently used social engineering tactics. Attackers often target employees, customers, or individuals with access to sensitive information, making it crucial for everyone, from entry-level staff to top executives, to be aware of these threats.

#### ii. Importance of Education and Training

Education programs aim to increase awareness about the nature of social engineering attacks, how they are carried out, and the potential consequences. Training equips individuals with the knowledge and skills needed to identify and avoid falling victim to these attacks, thereby reducing organizational and personal risk. Continuous education fosters a culture of security within organizations, where security awareness becomes a part of everyday operations.

#### iii. Components of Effective Training Programs

The training should cover various types of social engineering attacks, real-world examples, and the psychology behind these tactics. Interactive scenarios, such as simulated phishing attacks, help learners practice recognizing and responding to threats in a safe environment. As social engineering techniques evolve, training programs must be regularly updated to reflect the latest threats and best practices. Training should be tailored to the specific roles within an organization, addressing the unique risks faced by different departments.

### iv. Techniques for Enhancing Training Effectiveness

Incorporating game-like elements can make training more engaging and memorable. Participants can engage in role-playing exercises to simulate social engineering scenarios, enhancing their ability to recognize and respond to attacks. Regular assessments help gauge the effectiveness of the training and identify areas for improvement. Providing feedback helps reinforce learning. Involving organizational leaders in training sessions emphasizes the importance of the initiative and encourages widespread participation.

### v. Response and Recovery

Employees should be trained on the importance of reporting suspicious activities and the procedures for doing so. Post-Incident Training: If a social engineering attack occurs, conducting post-incident training can help prevent similar incidents in the future by addressing any identified weaknesses.

### vi. Long-Term Strategies

Social engineering training should not be a one-time event but rather a continuous process to keep up with evolving threats. Security teams should work with HR, legal, and other departments to ensure a holistic approach to mitigating social engineering risks. Empower employees to question and verify unusual requests, even if they come from senior management, to prevent manipulation.

## b. Security Policies

Social engineering attacks are sophisticated threats that exploit human psychology rather than technical vulnerabilities. Attackers use manipulation techniques to trick individuals into divulging sensitive information or performing actions that compromise security. To effectively mitigate these threats, organizations must implement robust security policies that establish clear guidelines, procedures, and practices aimed at reducing the risk of social engineering attacks.

Enforcement and Compliance

- **Policy Enforcement** Establish mechanisms to enforce compliance with security policies. This may include disciplinary actions for violations and rewards for adherence to best practices. Conduct regular audits and assessments to ensure that security policies are being followed and are effective in mitigating social engineering risks. Security policies should be reviewed and updated regularly to address new threats and changes in the organizational environment. Involve key stakeholders in the review process to ensure comprehensive coverage.
- **Incident Response Plans**:

The primary goal of an IRP for social engineering attacks is to provide a clear and systematic approach to managing and mitigating the impact of such incidents. It ensures that the organization can quickly identify an attack, contain the damage, and restore normal operations while learning from the incident to prevent recurrence.

This plan applies to all types of social engineering attacks, including phishing, pretexting, baiting, and other manipulation tactics. It covers the roles and responsibilities of employees, incident response teams, and management throughout the incident lifecycle.

## KEY COMPONENTS OF AN INCIDENT RESPONSE PLAN

### a. Preparation

Regular training programs should be conducted to ensure that all employees are aware of social engineering threats and understand their role in preventing them. This preparation phase also includes simulations and drills to test the effectiveness of the response plan. Ensure that the incident response team has access to necessary tools, such as monitoring systems, communication platforms, and forensic tools, to effectively manage incidents. Documenting procedures for using these tools is essential. Maintain an updated contact list for key personnel involved in incident response, including IT staff, legal advisors, communication teams, and external partners like cybersecurity consultants.

### b. Identification

Implement systems to detect social engineering attempts, such as email filtering, anomaly detection, and user behaviour analytics. Employees should be trained to recognize suspicious activities and report them immediately. Upon detection, conduct an initial assessment to determine the nature and scope of the attack. This includes identifying the type of social engineering tactic used, the systems or data affected, and the potential impact on the organization. Classify the incident based on severity (e.g., low, medium, high) to prioritize response efforts and allocate resources appropriately.

### c. Containment

Once an attack is identified, take immediate steps to contain the damage. This might involve isolating affected systems, disabling compromised accounts, or shutting down malicious communication channels. So its need to Implement temporary measures to limit the spread of the attack and prevent further damage. For example, resetting passwords or blocking suspicious IP addresses. After that Develop and deploy longer-term containment strategies, such as patching vulnerabilities or strengthening access controls, to prevent the attacker from regaining access.

### d. Eradication

Root Cause Analysis Identify the root cause of the incident, such as a specific vulnerability or human error, and take steps to eliminate it. This might involve updating software, changing security policies, or reinforcing employee training. If the attack involved malware, ensure that it is completely removed from all affected systems. Conduct thorough scans and inspections to confirm eradication. Post-eradication, enhance security measures to address any weaknesses exposed by the attack. This might include improving email filtering, enhancing authentication methods, or revising security protocols.

### e. Recovery

Restore affected systems to their normal state, ensuring that any compromised data is recovered, and that the system is fully operational. Validate the integrity of backups before restoring them. Closely monitor systems for any signs of residual threats or further attempts by the attacker. Increased vigilance is essential during the recovery phase to prevent follow-up attacks. Inform all relevant stakeholders, including employees, customers, and partners, about the incident and the steps taken to resolve it. Transparency helps maintain trust and manage reputation.

### f. Post-Incident Review

Conduct a thorough post-incident review to understand what happened, how the incident was handled, and what could be improved. Documenting lessons learned is crucial for refining the incident response plan and enhancing overall security. Based on the findings of the post-incident review, update security policies, training programs, and incident response procedures. Ensure that all changes are communicated to relevant personnel. Continuously monitor for potential threats and improve the incident response plan as needed. Regular reviews and updates ensure that the organization remains resilient against evolving social engineering tactics.

### g. Roles and Responsibilities

Incident Response Team (IRT) should be a dedicated group of professionals with clear roles in the incident response process. This team typically includes IT security experts, legal advisors, PR/communications specialists, and senior management. All employees should be aware of their responsibilities in detecting and reporting potential social engineering attacks. They should know the proper channels for reporting and be familiar with basic response procedures. Senior management should be involved in decision-making during critical phases of the response, particularly when it comes to public communication and resource allocation.

### h. Legal and Regulatory Considerations

Ensure that the incident response plan aligns with relevant legal and regulatory obligations, such as data breach notification laws. Non-compliance can lead to significant legal and financial penalties. Maintain thorough documentation of the incident, response actions, and communications. This is important for legal purposes and future audits.

### i. Communication and Coordination

Establish clear lines of communication within the organization to ensure that everyone is informed and coordinated during an incident. Use secure channels to prevent eavesdropping by attackers. Due to this need to have a communication plan for informing external stakeholders, such as customers, partners, and regulatory bodies. Messaging should be clear, concise, and consistent to maintain trust and comply with legal requirements. [28-33]

## CONCLUSION

Social engineering represents a significant challenge in the field of cybersecurity, as it exploits the human element, which is often the weakest link in the security chain. By understanding the techniques used by attackers and the psychological principles they exploit, organizations can develop more effective defences. Continuous education, robust security policies, and advanced authentication methods are key components in mitigating the risk of social engineering attacks. As cyber threats continue to evolve, maintaining vigilance and adapting to new tactics is essential in safeguarding sensitive information and maintaining organizational integrity. In conclusion, the review of social engineering in the context of cybersecurity highlights the growing sophistication of attacks and the necessity of implementing robust countermeasures. Multi-Factor Authentication (MFA) emerges as a critical defence, adding an extra layer of security by requiring multiple forms of verification, making it harder for attackers to gain unauthorized access even if credentials are compromised. Email filters also play a significant role in mitigating phishing attempts, one of the most prevalent forms of social engineering, by identifying and blocking malicious content before it reaches the user. Additionally, continuous network monitoring ensures real-time detection of abnormal behaviour or unauthorized access, enabling quick responses to potential breaches. Together, these techniques form an essential part of a comprehensive cybersecurity strategy that addresses the evolving threats posed by social engineering. By incorporating MFA, email filters, and network monitoring, organizations can significantly reduce their vulnerability to manipulation-based attacks.

## REFERENCES


Aldawood, H., & Skinner, G. (2019). Reviewing Cyber Security Social Engineering Training and Awareness Programs—Pitfalls and Ongoing Issues. *Future Internet*, 11(3), 73. DOI: 10.3390/fi11030073

Bandura, A. (1977). *Social learning theory. Englewood Cliffs.* Prentice-Hall.

Berscheid, E., & Walster, E. (1974). Physical Attractiveness. *Advances in Experimental Social Psychology*, 7, 157–215. DOI: 10.1016/S0065-2601(08)60037-4

Cialdini, R. B. (2001). *Influence: Science and Practice.* Allyn & Bacon.

Conti, M., Gangwal, A., & Ruj, S. (2018). On the Economic Significance of Ransomware Campaigns: A Data-driven Analysis and Research Roadmap. *Journal of Computer Virology and Hacking Techniques*, 14(3), 177–195. DOI: 10.1007/s11416-018-0310-3

Cost of a Data Breach Report. Retrieved from IBM Security, https://www.ibm.com/security/digital-assets/cost-data-breach-report/1Cost%20of%20a%20Data%20Breach%20Report%202020.pdf, 2020.

*Data Breach Investigations Report*, Verizon, https://www.verizon.com/business/resources/reports/dbir/, 2021.

Data Breach Investigations Report, Verizon Enterprise, https://www.verizon.com/about/news/verizon-2021-data-breach-investigations-report, 2021.

*Data Breach Investigations Report*, Verizon,2021.

Freedman, J. L., & Fraser, S. C. (1966). Compliance without pressure: The foot-in-the-door technique. *Journal of Personality and Social Psychology*, 4(2), 195–202. DOI: 10.1037/h0023552 PMID: 5969145

Georgi, T., Roumen, T., Ognian, N., Slavcho, M., & Galya, P. Cyber security: Threats and Challenges, *International Conference Automatics and Informatics (ICAI)*, 2020.

Hadnagy, C. (2010). *Social Engineering: The Science of Human Hacking*. Wiley.

Hadnagy, C, "*The Science of Human Hacking*", 978-1-119-43375-0, 2018.

Hadnagy, C, *Social Engineering: The Science of Human Hacking*. 978-1-119-43375-0, 2018.

How Employees are Making Businesses Vulnerable from Within. Retrieved from Kaspersky, https://www.kaspersky.com/blog/the-human-factor-in-it-security/, 2020.

Internet, S. T. R. Retrieved from Symantec, https://www.broadcom.com, 2019.

*Internet Crime Report 2020,*https://www.fbi.gov/news/press-releases/fbi-releases-the-internet-crime-complaint-center-2020-internet-crime-report-including-covid-19-scam-statistics, 2020.

Janis, I. L., & Feshbach, S. (1953). Effects of fear-arousing communications. *Journal of Abnormal and Social Psychology*, 48(1), 78–92. DOI: 10.1037/h0060732 PMID: 13022199

Langer, E. J., Blank, A., & Chanowitz, B. (1978). The mindlessness of ostensibly thoughtful action: The role of "placebic" information in interpersonal interaction. *Journal of Personality and Social Psychology*, 36(6), 635–642. DOI: 10.1037/0022-3514.36.6.635

Lee, S., & Lee, D. (2020). Social Engineering Attacks: Recent Advances and Countermeasures. *Computers & Security*, 90, 101700. DOI: 10.1016/j.cose.2019.101700

Milgram, S. (1963). Behavioral study of obedience. *Journal of Abnormal and Social Psychology*, 67(4), 371–378. DOI: 10.1037/h0040525 PMID: 14049516

Mitnick, K. D., & Simon, W. L, "*The Art of Deception: Controlling the Human Element of Security*", 978-0-471-23712-9, 2011.

Paas, F., Renkl, A., & Sweller, J. (2003). Cognitive load theory and instructional design: Recent developments. *Educational Psychologist*, 38(1), 1–4. DOI: 10.1207/S15326985EP3801_1

Phishing and Other Social Engineering Attacks. https://www.cisa.gov/news-events/news/avoiding-social-engineering-and-phishing-attacks, 2021.

Regan, D. T. (1971). Effects of a Favor and liking on compliance. *Journal of Experimental Social Psychology*, 7(6), 627–639. DOI: 10.1016/0022-1031(71)90025-4

Roumani, Y. (2022). Detection time of data breaches. *Computers & Security*, 112, 102508. DOI: 10.1016/j.cose.2021.102508

State of the Phish Report. Retrieved from Proofpoint, https://go.proofpoint.com/state-of-the-phish-report.html, 2021.

Sweller, J. (1988). Cognitive load during problem solving: Effects on learning. *Cognitive Science*, 12(2), 257–285. DOI: 10.1207/s15516709cog1202_4

Witte, K. (1992). Putting the fear back into fear appeals: The extended parallel process model. *Communication Monographs*, 59(4), 329–349. DOI: 10.1080/03637759209376276

Worchel, S., Lee, J., & Adewole, A. (1975). Effects of supply and demand on ratings of object value. *Journal of Personality and Social Psychology*, 32(5), 906–914. DOI: 10.1037/0022-3514.32.5.906

Zakay, D. (1993). The impact of time perception processes on decision making under time stress. In Svenson, O., & Maule, A. J. (Eds.), *Time pressure and stress in human judgment and decision making* (pp. 59–72). DOI: 10.1007/978-1-4757-6846-6_4

# Chapter 18
# Unmasking Virtual Crimes: Investigating and Proving Evidence in the Metaverse

**Ramy El-Kady**
https://orcid.org/0000-0003-2208-7576
*Police Academy, Egypt*

## ABSTRACT

*This chapter is a crucial exploration of Metaverse technology, a modern leading topic in the global arena. Anticipated to be the dominant form of internet development, the Metaverse is propelling humanity into new technological frontiers. However, the absence of legislation to address various infractions in the Metaverse is not just a pressing issue but an urgent one that requires immediate attention. This chapter aims to fill this gap by elucidating methods for gathering digital evidence in the Metaverse. It concludes the emergence of the Metaverse led to the urgent need for collaborative global initiatives to revise international agreements on cybercrime. The collaboration is crucial in combating the global nature of Metaverse-related crimes. We can effectively address these challenges through collective action, underscoring the necessity for unified efforts in this arena. Alternatively, it suggests the possibility of creating a new international convention that governs the obligations of Metaverse service providers and mandates their cooperation in combating criminal activities.*

## INTRODUCTION

The Metaverse, a transformative force of the twenty-first century, is not just a new tool but a paradigm shift poised to revolutionize human life according to its new social dynamics and community Interaction, which will change the life of humans into a new virtual life. This new technology, introduced by Meta, elevates the individual from a passive user of technology, such as the Internet, to an active participant and contributor to its evolution. Virtual reality tools enable users to transcend the Internet, creating a virtual community where they can live and interact with others, thereby redefining the human experience. The transformative potential of the Metaverse is not just thrilling but also heralds a new era of human

DOI: 10.4018/979-8-3693-8628-6.ch018

interaction and development, fostering a sense of community and connection that we can all anticipate with eagerness and enthusiasm.

The metaverse is the integration of physical and virtual environments experienced via computers. This integration is facilitated by powerful immersive technologies like virtual reality, augmented reality, and mixed reality. These are not just gadgets, but the building blocks of a three-dimensional virtual realm that advocates characterize as the future version of the Internet. This three-dimensional virtual realm is conceptualized as a lasting, communal environment where digital representations of ourselves, known as avatars, transition effortlessly between different experiences, carrying our identities and financial resources along, fostering a sense of community and shared experiences.

Concepts of an alternate digital realm where individuals can encounter existence in manners similar to and unattainable in the physical world are not novel. They existed before the advent of the internet. However, in recent decades, the idea of a combined physical and digital world has become more concrete due to technical progress. This includes the widespread use of mobile phones, the proliferation of high-speed internet, and the popularity of games like Pokémon Go. These developments have made the metaverse appear less implausible (Tucci, 2024).

The current landscape is ablaze with the global interest in Metaverse technology. From Japan to the United States, South Korea to Singapore, and Indonesia, several countries are actively adopting and experimenting with this technology, underscoring its relevance and potential impact on a global scale. This widespread adoption is not just a trend but a global movement shaping the future of human interaction and development. Other countries are formulating strategies to expand the use of this technology, such as Dubai's strategy for Metaverse in the UAE.

Third countries are enhancing their experiences with this technology, like Egypt, which launched the first Metaverse hackathon. This event, which includes a series of competitions and interactive activities, is implemented in a hybrid system that combines online events and interactive activities to enhance the use of various technologies that contribute to building and developing the 'Metaverse' world in a way that supports the construction of many applications and technological solutions, as well as Creating the first Egyptian city in the virtual world called 'Metatot.'

The Metaverse, a technological marvel, is a revolution in human life and a potential economic powerhouse. The positive economic indicators show the global shift towards embracing this technology. International estimates suggest that the Metaverse market, valued at $39 billion in 2021, is set to rise to $47 billion in 2022 and further to $56.6 billion in 2023, eventually reaching a staggering $679 billion by 2030 (IDSC, 2022). These positive economic indicators instill confidence in the potential of the Metaverse to significantly impact the global economy, offering a promising outlook for the future. Figure1). Other experts expected Metaverse to contribute to generating commercial and economic opportunities amounting to $13 trillion by 2030 (Citi, 2022). This promising economic outlook underscores the significant impact of the Metaverse on the global economy (El-Kady, 2023), making it a topic of great interest and intrigue.

*Figure 1. Projected market growth of the metaverse (2021-2030)*

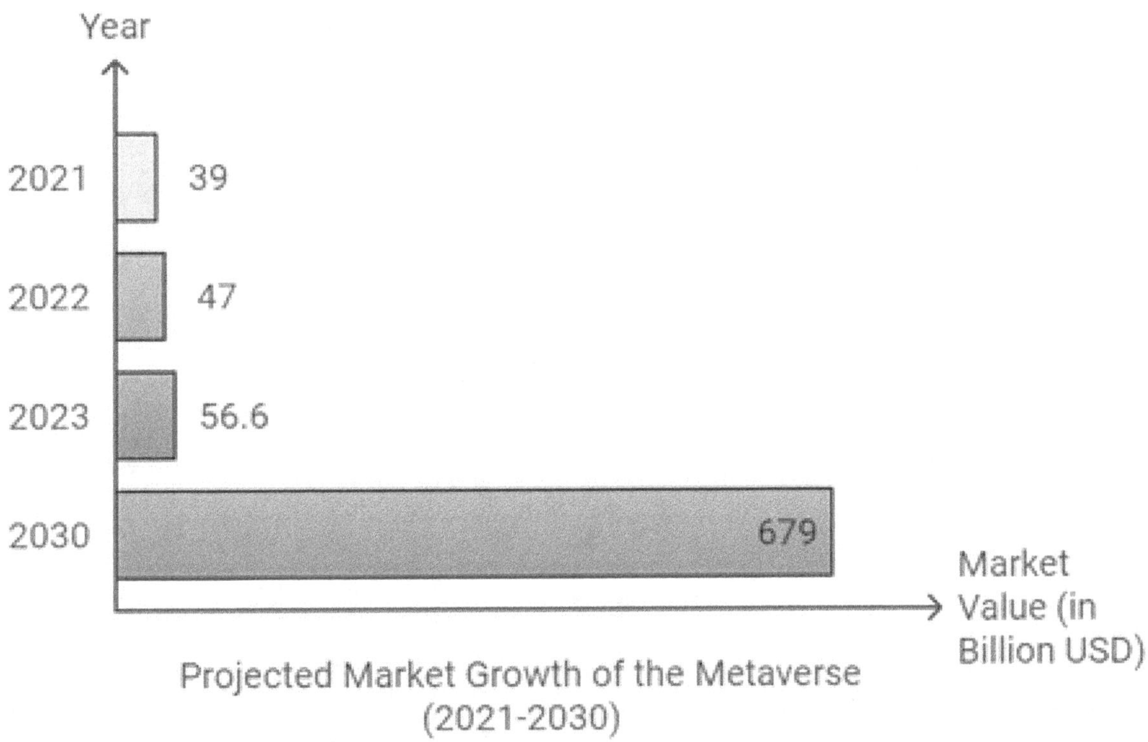


While the potential of Metaverse technology is promising, it is essential to acknowledge that it has risks. There are concerns about the emergence of new criminal activities in VR environments. Some argue that the Metaverse could provide a new platform for existing Internet crimes, potentially leading to a quantitative increase in criminal activity (Elshenraki, 2024). However, the consensus is that developing entirely new forms of criminality is unlikely. This awareness is crucial as we navigate the future of this transformative technology. By understanding the potential risks, we can better prepare for the challenges and ensure the responsible and ethical use of the Metaverse.

Other concerns have emerged about the appearance of some types of virtual crimes created by this technology. Then, questions have become about how to prove this new type of virtual crime and collect and extract the evidence obtained about it. In light of the Metaverse technology, which opens the way to enter a virtual world of 3D using virtual reality (VR) and augmented reality (AR) tools, as well as the risks of privacy violations for users in light of the novelty of this technology and it is still under development (Abdel Majeed, 2023:76), with the expectation that the potential threat of crime in the world of Metaverse will be a concern in human reality; Given its remarkable similarity to the real world, the real world can be influenced by events that take place in the virtual world (Seo et al., 2023). (see Figure 2)

*Figure 2. The Metaverse: A Comprehensive Overview*

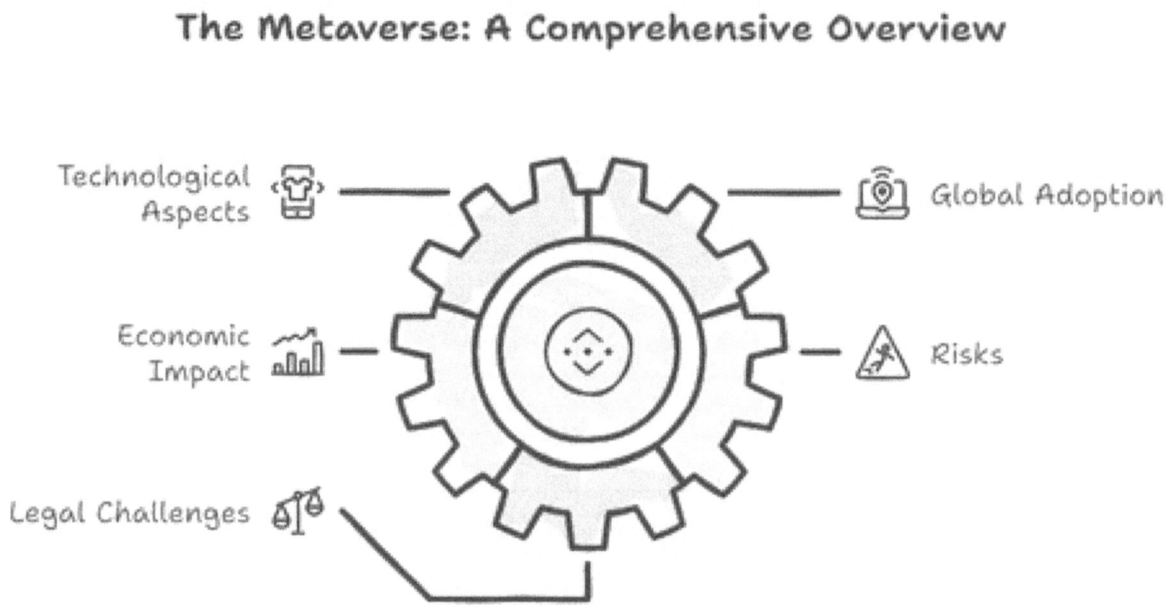


The study focuses on the Metaverse, which is expected to shine during the coming period as the most prominent image of the development of the Internet, which will move humanity to new technological dimensions (Marshall, 2023) despite the existence of legal provisions governing the confrontation of crimes in cyberspace. However, these rules are perceived as incapable of confronting modern criminal phenomena across Metaverse, which are based on non-traditional alphabets and different elements regarding people, facts, and spatial and temporal limits (Jibril, 2023).

The importance of this study is also evident in light of the absence of laws that exist to combat all forms of violations that occur in the world of Metaverse (El-Kady, 2023). There is no doubt that the current criminal laws are idle in the face of successive technological developments that cannot be dealt with criminally, except through existing criminal provisions due to the principle of criminal legality, which means only the legislation can define a crime and prescribe a penalty (Bu, 2019), not to mention that all criminal proceedings to confront all forms of violations that occur in the world of the Metaverse must be by law due to the same principle (procedural legitimacy), Metaverse is seen as taking the world to different and unconventional horizons that will undoubtedly raise unlimited problems from the perspective of criminal law (El-Kady, 2023).

It also highlights the importance of researching digital evidence in this new virtual world in light of the latest means used in accessing it, which are virtual or augmented reality tools, mobile phones, and gaming platforms, where this technology uses devices and tools for perception, sensation, and recall, such as Glasses, gloves, jackets, sensors, and sensors combine Internet of Things (IoT), VR, AR, and 3D technology.

Therefore, this issue is expected to become more critical with the expected developments of the Metaverse, when the users can engage in any activity and handle anything they need from one place. When the Metaverse reaches the ideal state, it can be applied to anything, becoming the new hypothetical conception of human life. Although no cases related to Metaverse have yet been brought before the courts, this technology, including its digital forensics, is expected to be problematic. This is in light of the rapid technological changes in which the world is moving towards total dependence on Metaverse and fast steps to the stage of virtual life.

The importance of the topic is apparent when we examine examples of incidents within virtual environments, such as the online gaming community, which has increased in numbers, and the types of games and cybercrimes that can also occur in gaming environments. Modern criminals have demonstrated abilities to compromise information systems that provide this form of entertainment. During this time, the advent of the multi-user dungeons (MUD) enabled players to interact in a social setting, using text-based messages in a process known as ''mudding.'' Some believe mudding created the foundation for MMORPGs, for what is now known as social networking, and for the social engineering that frequently occurs within these environments and is fundamental to the commission of cybercrimes. For example, Everquest and World of Warcraft MMORPGs are frequently targeted by cybercriminals who attack players' character profiles and then sell the information to other players for money or in-game items, which is expected to increase in the Metaverse. This highlights the urgency of addressing these emerging issues.

Nevertheless, this technical advancement raises severe worries about the potential for engaging in various criminal acts (Zhou et al., 2024; Dwivedi et al., 2023; Kim et al., 2023). The issues arise from the intrinsic weaknesses of metaverse technologies and the lack of a robust regulatory structure. In January 2024, the UK police initiated an investigation into their inaugural instance of a virtual reality assault targeting a minor when the minor's avatar was subjected to non-consensual sexual assault (Camber, 2024). This is not the inaugural instance of sexual assault occurring within the metaverse. There are concerns, as well as emerging evidence, that the phenomenon known as "gamergate" culture, which involves the harassment of women in online gaming environments, may persist in the metaverse and cannot be effectively resolved by technological remedies alone (Zhou et al., 2024).

Furthermore, money laundering can also be facilitated through digital assets, like virtual real estate and wearables provided by metaverse platforms (Annison, 2022). Moreover, the absence of educational consciousness among platform users creates suitable conditions for various fraudulent schemes, including Ponzi schemes, rug pulls, and deceitful giveaway scams (Zhou et al., 2024; Wu et al., 2023). Additional problems arise from the challenges of confirming the age of youngsters online, particularly about grooming and minor abuse. Various metaverse enterprises have reacted to these emerging issues in distinct ways but have gradually handled them in general (Bibri & Allam, 2022).

Additionally, law enforcement agencies could face many challenges in combating cybercrimes in the metaverse, such as Anonymity. Many individuals use pseudonyms, which poses a challenge in determining their true identities. Moreover, the worldwide scope of the metaverse complicates determining legal jurisdiction and enforcement, and collecting digital evidence necessitates using specific equipment and expertise in virtual settings. Furthermore, potential privacy issues could impede data collection without obtaining user consent.

On the other side, Interpol indicates that the most prominent challenges that may face the use of metaverse technology in law enforcement are technology and infrastructure requirements; to leverage the metaverse effectively, it is necessary to invest heavily in technology and infrastructure, which includes advanced virtual reality equipment, strong network capabilities, and employee training. Data privacy and ethical concerns to protecting personal information and ensuring the ethical use of data in the metaverse are significant concerns, especially when virtual environments intersect with personal data in the real world. Legal and jurisdictional ambiguity: The legal framework for actions taken in virtual environments remains unclear, and this ambiguity extends to judicial matters. Cybersecurity Threats: Increased reliance on virtual systems may expose law enforcement agencies to new cybersecurity threats, including data breaches and virtual impersonation.

Furthermore, future expectations for using metaverse technology in law enforcement are crystallized as integration with artificial intelligence to create more dynamic and responsive training scenarios and to aid in predictive policing within the virtual world. Moreover, expanded virtual operations: Law enforcement agencies can expand the scope of their operations within the metaverse, which may lead to more diverse use cases.

On the other hand, metaverse raises several legal problems in criminal law, most notably the lack of criminal provisions related to this technology and offending behaviors committed through it. In addition, traditional criminal adaptations are inadequate for crimes committed through Metaverse technology, particularly crimes of assault on persons, as well as for the time and place conditions in Metaverse crimes. Metaverse has created a new concept of the crime scene, in that the conduct of a single actor may have an effect in several places at a single moment, unlike the temporal dimension of the act, which varies from state to state due to the timing between states, with the consequence that the legal description of the act differs (Jibril, 2023), the changing and volatile nature of this new virtual space will undoubtedly affect the reliability of digital evidence of new crimes within it, which will certainly reflect on how digital evidence is collected and extracted in this virtual world.

The study mainly aims to study digital forensics in Metaverse and branches from this goal a set of sub-goals, most notably Shedding light on Metaverse technology, its dimensions, characteristics, and risks of its use. It will investigate the criminal patterns that can arise in Metaverse technology and ways to counter them. It will also highlight ways to collect and extract digital evidence using Metaverse technology.

The study hypothesizes that the evolution toward Web3 creates an environment that may have severe implications for crimes in the metaverse and severely diminishes law enforcement's ability to apprehend suspects who commit them. This affects the process of collecting digital evidence of crimes in the Metaverse, which is expected to face difficulty, given the novelty of this technology and the development and integration of its elements. Law enforcement agencies expect to face other problems due to the metaverse's 3D nature, which affects data collection from different sources, such as user devices, service providers' servers, and the Metaverse platform. This data needs to be analyzed massively, and new tools are designed and utilized to collect data from these modern devices and platforms (Maathuis et al., 2023; Europol, 2022:20).

In addition, presenting the evidence gathered from the crime scene in Metaverse in 3D form given to the courts may cause some information or alter its content when presented in a 2D paper form. Add to that the international interest in this new technology, which may tempt criminal elements to exploit it to commit various criminal activities for profit (Europol, 2022:13). This will place the burden on investigators and criminal justice agencies to confront these crimes as a priority and collect evidence of them.

## LITERATURE REVIEW

Research indicates that the metaverse influences social dynamics and community cohesion by generating fresh possibilities for significant involvement, altering socio-spatial relationships, and providing substitutes for physical social interactions. The metaverse, a digital realm facilitated by innovative technologies like virtual reality (VR) and augmented reality (AR), is revolutionizing human interaction and community formation. This meta-synthesis examines the influence of the metaverse on social dynamics and community interaction, drawing on up-to-date research. The metaverse profoundly influences social dynamics and community involvement by augmenting social connectedness, promoting inclusiveness, and generating new socio-technological groupings. Although technology can facilitate significant and productive exchanges, it also presents hazards such as social division, disparity, and limitations on privacy.

The ongoing evolution of the metaverse is expected to revolutionize social structures by incorporating real-world activities into a virtual environment, redefining the dynamics of human interaction and community formation. The metaverse facilitates enhanced social connectedness by enabling users to engage in realistic virtual environments replicating real-world social interactions, promoting immediate presence and active involvement. By reinstating "we-mode" processes, the Metaverse can facilitate more meaningful and constructive interactions in online communities (Riva et al., 2023).

The Metaverse can revolutionize our work, learning, and leisure activities, generating novel prospects for societal and economic advancement (A et al., 2023). A Metaverse is a virtual social environment that exhibits multi-technology convergence, social interaction, and hyper-spatial-temporality (Wang et al., 2023).

This technology offers possibilities for more immediate and tangible engagements, which may diminish conventional societal obstacles such as race, gender, and physical impairment, fostering inclusiveness. The metaverse's capacity to establish a lifelike society characterized by more immediate and tangible connections has the potential to undermine notions of race, gender, and physical impairment (Duan et al., 2021).

Virtual and augmented reality technologies that form the foundation of the metaverse can stimulate neurobiological and cognitive processes comparable to those experienced in real-world settings (Riva et al., 2023). This can potentially foster more significant and productive interactions within online communities. Anticipated with the metaverse are novel socio-spatial interactions and the emergence of new socio-technological collectives, combining tangible and digital encounters. The metaverse presents a novel form of organization for physical and virtual socio-spatial interactions, leading to socio-technological groups inside and through their utilization (Hamurcu, 2022).

The absence of physical co-presence in digital communities in the metaverse may result in intensified radicalism and reduced accuracy, contributing to social polarization and disparities in social capital allocation (Riva et al., 2023). Worries exist around the dominance of a single platform, the protection of user privacy, and the possibility of addiction, all of which may have adverse effects on social interactions. The metaverse can tackle global issues but also creates hazards such as establishing platform monopolies and infringing user privacy (Wu & Li, 2023; A et al., 2023). Metaverse seeks to establish a completely immersive, fully spatiotemporal, and self-sustaining virtual communal environment for humans to engage in recreational activities, work, and socialize (Wang et al., 2022).

The metaverse is revolutionizing social frameworks by reducing physical obstacles and establishing a hyper-spatial-temporal virtual realm where users can engage in social interactions, professional activities, and recreational pursuits without being limited by time and physical distance (Wu & Li, 2023; Wang et al., 2022). A metaverse is a virtual universe that offers alternate social experiences in many domains, extending beyond the confines of the actual world (BÜYÜKBAYKAL & Sönmezer, 2022).

Some scholars show that the metaverse is an intermediary between real and virtual experiences. It enables users to convert real-world activities into a virtual environment, facilitating a seamless integration of physical and digital interactions (Hamurcu, 2022). The metaverse enhances various societal applications and is an exceptionally competitive instrument for governments, corporations, universities, and media (Crespo-Pereira et al., 2023).

Several studies propose that deterring crimes in the metaverse requires the establishment of global legal frameworks, the implementation of precise punitive legislation, classifying offenses, and the development of a dedicated metaverse criminal justice system. The metaverse, an ever-changing virtual realm, poses distinct obstacles to preventing criminal activities. As consumers progressively participate in virtual realms, guaranteeing their security is paramount. This synthesis examines approaches and suggestions from recent research on crime prevention in the metaverse. Adopting a comprehensive strategy encompassing international cooperation, tailored legislative structures, uniform industry standards, and technical safeguards is necessary to prevent crimes in the metaverse effectively. Through the integration of these solutions, stakeholders can establish a virtual environment that is more secure for all users.

Many believe creating a global legal structure is essential for fostering cooperation between countries, expediting criminal investigations, and upholding democratic governance in the metaverse. An internationally recognized legal system that encourages cooperation between states can enhance the investigation of crimes and uphold democratic governance in the metaverse (Qin et al., 2022). Nations are urged to develop their criminal systems specifically for the Metaverse, and the global community should prioritize this issue (Bovenzi, 2023).

Some scholars believe that distinct laws, like a "metaverse criminal law," are necessary to deal with crimes unique to the metaverse. This would require the incorporation of cybercrime legislation into a unified legal structure. Implementing a comprehensive "metaverse criminal law system" that incorporates general rules and specific regulations can effectively deter illegal activities within the metaverse (Lee, 2022). Some argue that distinct punitive policies should be developed for particular offenses, such as avatar sex crimes, as current legislation may not sufficiently address these types of acts. One approach to deter crimes in the metaverse involves implementing distinct punitive measures and developing strategies to obstruct criminal activities effectively (Lee, 2022).

Others see that establishing robust and uniform industry standards is crucial to mitigating a range of financial crimes, including frauds, code exploits, and money laundering, within the metaverse. To mitigate crimes in the metaverse, it is essential to classify them and establish appropriate procedures and governance (Lin et al., 2023). Another sees that implementing technological solutions, such as restrictions on avatar-to-avatar interactions within a specific range, might effectively mitigate the incidence of avatar-related sexual offenses (Lee, 2022). Some argue that Criminal law should be prominent in preventing and repressing crimes in the metaverse. However, it needs to be backed by specific laws that recognize the distinct characteristics of virtual crimes (Lee, 2022).

Some scholars perceive that to mitigate criminal activities in the metaverse, it is of utmost importance to categorize financial security risks, ascertain existing anti-crime strategies, and investigate the potential in behavioral mining and regulation (Wu et al., 2022). Another researcher observes that engaging in discussions regarding legislation that satisfies the industry and users is imperative to deter criminal activities in the metaverse. Additionally, gathering input from pertinent industries, users, and expert groups is crucial (Lee & Min, 2022).

Others see that a Metaverse Model Criminal Code will provide regulations and offenses relevant to electronic jurisdictions, deterring criminal activities within the metaverse (Kostenko et al., 2023). Another researcher believes that Metaverses have limited potential for the emergence of entirely new types of criminal activities, and the field of criminology encounters difficulties in studying abnormal behavior in virtual realms. Others see that it is evident that the development of effective health promotion initiatives in the metaverse necessitates many studies and investments (Petrigna & Musumeci, 2022).

In summary, Crime Prevention in the Metaverse depends on several factors, such as the global legal frameworks with a tailored legislative structure and punitive legislation, establishing the Metaverse Criminal Justice system with a classification of offenses, and empowering international cooperation and uniform Industry standards with a technical safeguard (see: Figure 3)

*Figure 3. Comprehensive Crime Prevention in the Metaverse*

## METHODOLOGY

The study's methodology is the analytical descriptive approach, which deals with the technology of the Metaverse in all its aspects and dimensions. It addresses the metaverse's definitions, key features, fundamental elements, mechanism, essence, advantages, and dangers. It uses the comparative method by reviewing comparative experiments on this subject worldwide.

A descriptive analytical approach is a comprehensive method that describes scientific phenomena and problems, solves problems and questions within the scientific research department, and analyzes the collected data using the descriptive analytical approach to extract appropriate explanations and results. The descriptive analytical approach allows us to compare different phenomena and collect data on their differences and similarities. This fundamental characteristic distinguishes the analytical descriptive approach from other scientific methods and dramatically enhances its applications in scientific research.

## The Chapter Plan

The detailed plan of the chapter has three main parts: The first provides a detailed introduction to the Metaverse by describing the metaverse's definitions, key features, fundamental elements, mechanism, essence, advantages, and dangers of Metaverse technology in criminal terms. It also briefs the metaverse's social dynamics and community interaction and explains its complexities in the context of criminal law. The second part describes metacrimes and their definitions and classifications. The third part describes the procedures for collecting digital evidence in the Metaverse.

## PART ONE: INTRODUCTION TO METAVERSE

### Definition of Metaverse

The Metaverse is a concept that scholars have defined in various ways, including an information network and developed Internet model, a vast and interconnected network of virtual spaces, and a digital platform that meets the physical and virtual worlds. It can be defined as a parallel 3D digital virtual world that allows users to log in with specific tools and use an animated avatar (avatar) to perform various activities without moving from their place. The metaverse is often described as a hypothetical iteration of the internet as a universal virtual world that presents an immersive experience that feels 'real,' usually through a headset. Its recent definition can blur the lines between the physical and virtual worlds to create a single blended, extended, or mixed reality (Gupta & Pal, 2023).

As a result, the metaverse is now primarily focused on virtual reality (VR) but is increasingly being defined in terms of augmented reality (AR) or extended or mixed reality (XR). The term "Metaverse" refers to the metaphysical world, which consists of two parts: "meta" (meaning beyond) and "Verse" (meaning beyond the world). The term was first used in Neil Stephenson's 1992 science fiction novel Snow Crash, in which humans, as avatars, interact with each other and software in a virtual 3D space similar to the real world (Innocente et al., 2024; Khalifa, 2022:8). (see Figure 4)

The Metaverse is a shared virtual environment that merges digitally augmented physical reality with physically extended virtual reality. Virtual reality (VR) includes a broad spectrum of digital experiences, including gaming, social networking, virtual commerce, and education. With users' growing involvement in these environments, comprehending the social dynamics in promoting favorable community interactions becomes crucial (El-Kady, 2024).

*Figure 4. Definition of the Metaverse*

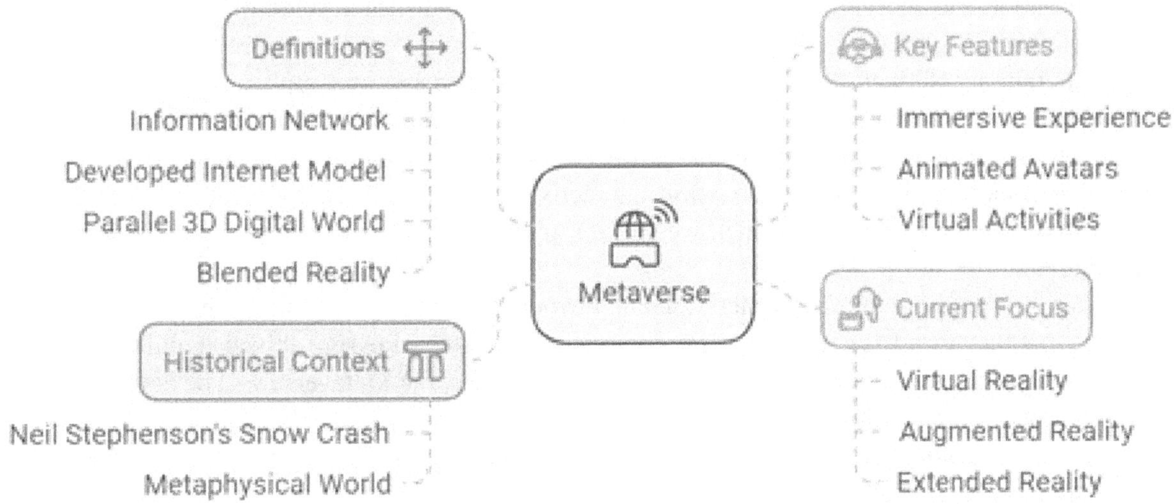


## Key Features of the Metaverse

Some characteristics of the Metaverse technique include creating a third world for the user between two worlds: the tangible material world, the natural life that humans live in, and the virtual world created by modern technology, cyberspace. This virtual world transfers the individual from just a user of the Internet to a part of it and a participant in it, where users who turn into avatars participate in the same experience in the same place and at the same time as in the real world.

The Metaverse may significantly develop human life and behavior, bridging the gap between natural and digital worlds to reveal a third, virtual, parallel world that takes elements from reality and imagination, the Internet, intelligent technologies, things, and other characteristics. Through Metaverse, individuals can create a virtual life across different areas of the Internet, allowing them to meet, work, teach, and entertain within it while providing an experience that will enable them to watch remotely through smart devices and enter this world in the form of an animated image representing the person (avatar) in the 3D world through virtual metaverse techniques (Abdel Sadik, 2022: 404).

The Metaverse is an advanced form of the Internet that allows users to enter and practice an integrated virtual life, allowing them to carry out activities and operations they used to undertake in their everyday physical lives. It relies on cryptographic technology based on electronic technology on Internet platforms, allowing users to carry out their activities via the Internet using specific tools that help them enter the virtual world. However, the absence of legal regulation in the Metaverse exposes users to fraud and raises problems with extracting and collecting evidence in this new digital environment with complex technologies.

Metaverse technology relies on two essential elements: the Internet and virtual and augmented reality tools. The connection of the Metaverse with the Internet has led to the Metaverse environment becoming part of a global village on the Internet, governed by a virtual reality not subject to traditional concepts that set geographical and political borders. Metaverse technology relies on technical tools, such as virtual reality glasses and augmented reality, and wearing jackets and gloves equipped with sensors. These intelligent technologies act as mediators between users in the Metaverse world, conveying a feeling of physical sensation and allowing users to feel sensory and physical stimuli through jackets and gloves.

The Metaverse is based on a new technological strategy that relies on the unprecedented development of third-generation web (web-3.0) applications, which allow websites and applications to deal with information in a human-like manner through machine learning techniques and big data. Users will be able to interact with tools, equipment, and data in a way that reshapes social media, allowing users to move, enter, and interact within the metaverse world interactively in a digital environment that simulates the natural or physical environment in which we live through the use of Avatar characters for interaction and interaction.

With fast internet from the fifth generation and beyond, technology will change in its dealings with the user so that they turn from a mere user or viewer into an integral part of this virtual life. Instead of entering cyberspace through computer screens and smartphones, the Metaverse will be entered through virtual reality glasses currently used in video games, which will be redesigned to become an alternative to smartphones and integrated with augmented reality technologies, displaying all information about anything your eye sees in objective reality. (see Figure 5)

*Figure 5. Key Components of the Metaverse*

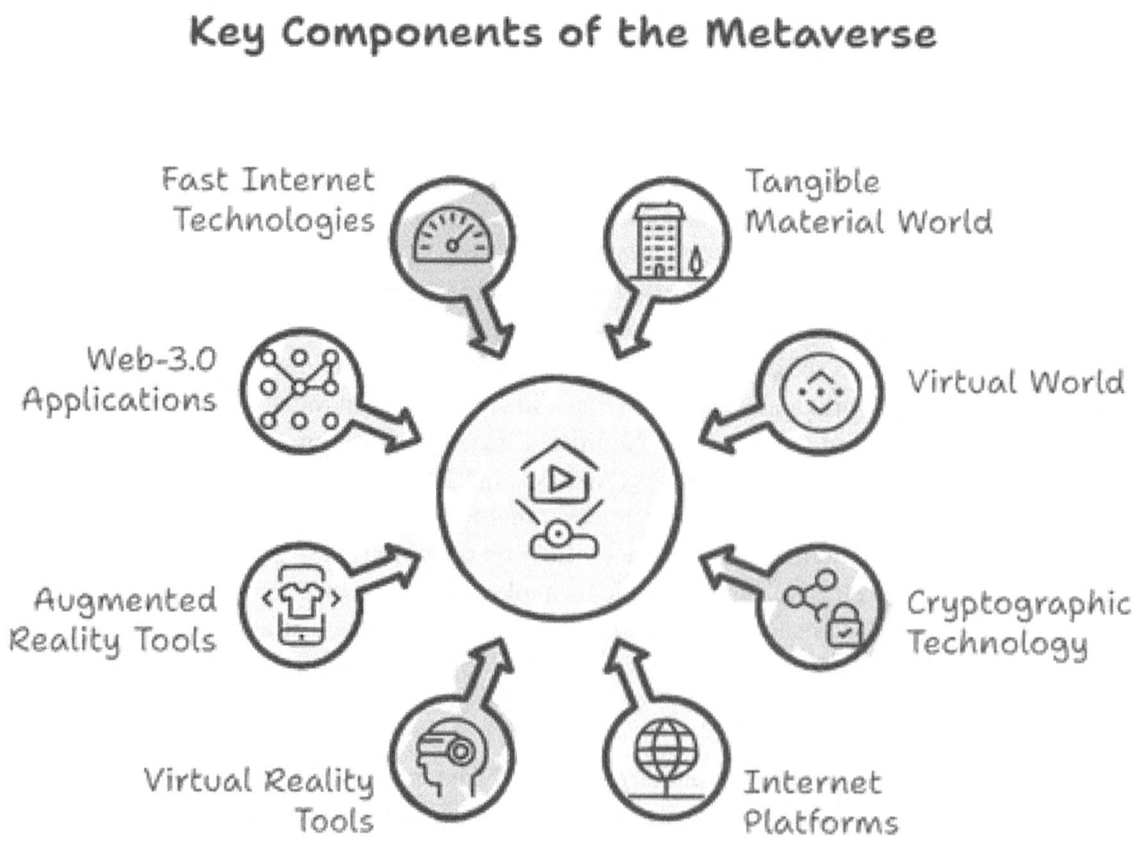

## The Fundamental Elements of the Metaverse

The metaverse consists of several essential elements that essentially constitute this new virtual world, as follows: -

1- **Metaverse platforms:** Virtual platforms are an essential component of metaverse technology, as they are considered the space through which users receive and practice virtual activities, such as working, learning, playing, shopping, etc. Several virtual platforms, such as The Sandbox, Decentraland, Roblox, and Nakamoto, have appeared recently. Experts believe these platforms will represent the new development of social networking sites. In light of this, many major technology companies worldwide have begun building their virtual worlds, such as Meta and others.

2- **Non-Fungible Tokens (NFT):** Non-Fungible Tokens (NFT) are digital assets with certain identifying information stored and documented via Blockchain technology. NFTs can be avatars, costumes, and items in video games, homes, virtual lands, or other places.

These digital codes are considered a significant component of the metaverse, as they represent the essential elements that users rely on in their immersive experiences. The avatars representing users, lands, real estate, clothing, and other elements present within virtual worlds are considered non-transferable codes for replacement. Digital avatars, widely used within the metaverse to represent users, are the best-selling NFT category, achieving sales of more than $16 billion in 2021, representing 46% of the non-fungible token market's sales volume.

3- **Digital currencies:** Digital currencies have a significant role within the metaverse, as they are considered the money through which all financial transactions are completed. Each metaverse world contains a specific currency that is used within it. For example, SAND is the currency of The Sandbox world, and MANA is the currency of Decentraland. Holders of these currencies can pay for any service or product within these worlds. Each metaverse currency has a specific value, which can change occasionally, just like other digital currencies. Metaverse currencies recorded a remarkable rise during the last period, coinciding with the world's technology giants racing to break into this world and pumping billions of investments into it (El-Kady, 2024).

4- **Virtual and augmented reality: The metaverse relies on various technologies**. This is to enable users to interact virtually in its environments. Virtual reality (VR) and augmented reality (AR) technology are considered among the most critical technologies on which the metaverse relies. These two technologies provide immersive experiences for users in 3D virtual environments through their hardware and software, which make the user feel as if he is inside the real world. For example, metaverse platforms that take advantage of virtual reality technology provide users with an immersive experience through which the most significant number of senses are simulated to deceive the human mind and immerse themselves in the virtual environment. This is done by using headphones, touch gloves, etc. In light of this, experts view virtual and augmented reality technologies as an integral part of the metaverse technology.

5- **Blockchain:** Blockchain is a giant database through which transactions and data are recorded and documented in a decentralized manner, ensuring security, speed, and efficiency for users. This technology is considered one of the most critical technologies based on the metaverse. All platforms rely primarily on Blockchain To store data securely and immutably. This technology also plays an essential role in documenting non-fungible tokens within the metaverse. Experts expect that the future metaverse will consist of open, interconnected, and decentralized virtual worlds, each with a local functional economy based on blockchain.

**6- Artificial Intelligence:** Artificial intelligence refers to a non-human model that can solve complex tasks and perform cognitive functions such as learning, problem-solving, reasoning, perception, etc. Many major technology companies have begun to benefit from artificial intelligence's enormous capabilities, building their virtual worlds and making and designing NFTs through artificial intelligence. For example, the CEO of Meta, Mark Zuckerberg, announced using artificial intelligence experts to develop a tool known as Builder Bot, which allows users in a virtual world to change their surroundings using voice commands. On a related note, artificial intelligence can create avatars for users that closely resemble them, which makes the metaverse experience more realistic. This technology also relies heavily on designing many other digital assets and symbols within the metaverse worlds. Therefore, AI technology has recently become a significant component of the metaverse. (see Figure 6)

*Figure 6. Metaverse Components*

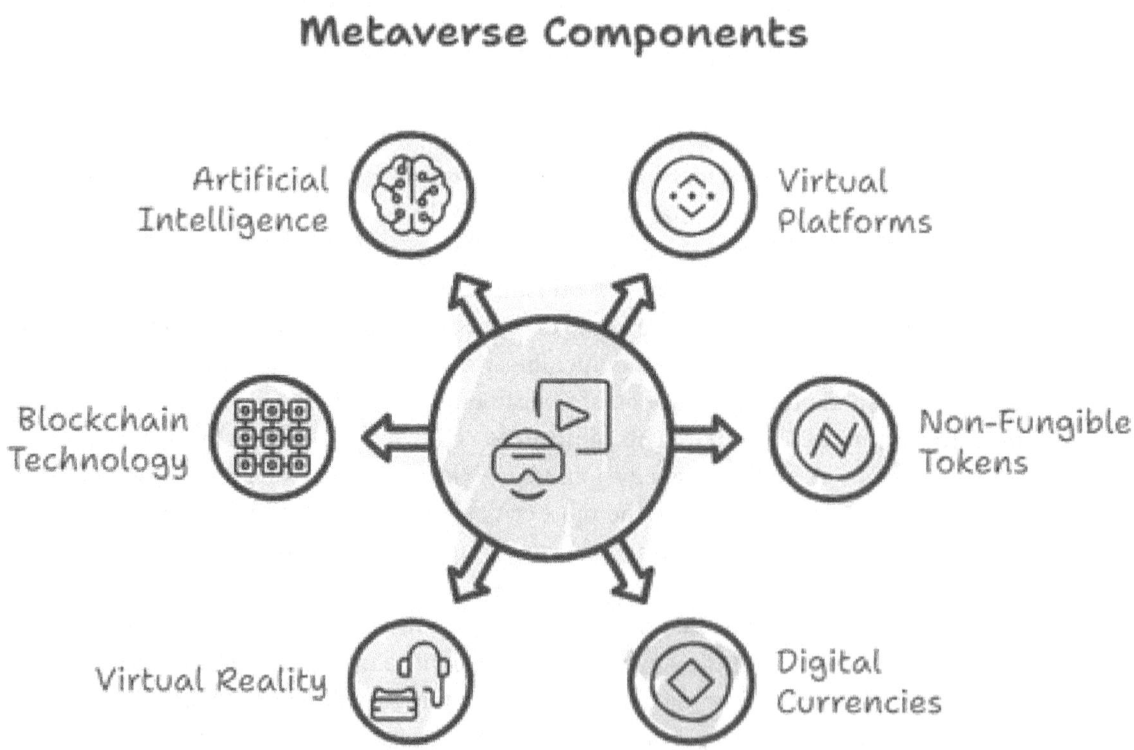

## Mechanism of the Metaverse

So that the reader can visualize the questions raised, it is worth noting the nature of the metaverse technology, which is based on a new technological strategy based on the unprecedented development in applications of the third generation of things web-3.0, which will allow websites and applications to deal with information in a way that mimics humans, through machine learning techniques and big data. The data will be linked to transaction protocols in a decentralized manner based on blockchain technologies and crypto-currencies. Users will be able to interact with tools, equipment, and data in a way that will reshape social media. This allows its users to move, enter, and interactively interact within the metaverse technology in a digital environment that simulates the natural or physical environment we live in through the users' use of symbolic characters, "Avatar," to interact and interact.

It is like turning the Internet into a community that surrounds the person with a three-dimensional feature. Then, the user enters this world in his virtual avatar using virtual reality technologies. Such as glasses, jackets, and gloves, to find himself inside a group of endless interconnected virtual worlds. He can also meet a large number of people in their avatars as well, and deal with them. So that the user of the metaverse is part of the virtual world, It is possible shortly for the user to become a participant and maker of this world if he is provided with the requirements of a suit, glasses, headset, and gloves, and with fast Internet from the fifth generation and beyond, technology will change in its dealings with the user, transforming him from a mere user or viewer into an integral part of this virtual life.

Instead of entering cyberspace through computer screens and smartphone devices, as is the current situation on the Internet, it will be accessed through virtual reality glasses, which are currently used in video games, but instead of using them as a means of entertainment, they will be redesigned to become An alternative to smartphones; It becomes connected to the Internet, and augmented reality technologies will be integrated with it, which displays all information about anything you see in objective reality. Thus, virtual reality technology, dominated by digital designs, is combined with augmented reality, which is dominated by reality, creating a mixed world that is the Metaverse. (see Figure 7)

*Figure 7. User Interaction cycle in the Metaverse*

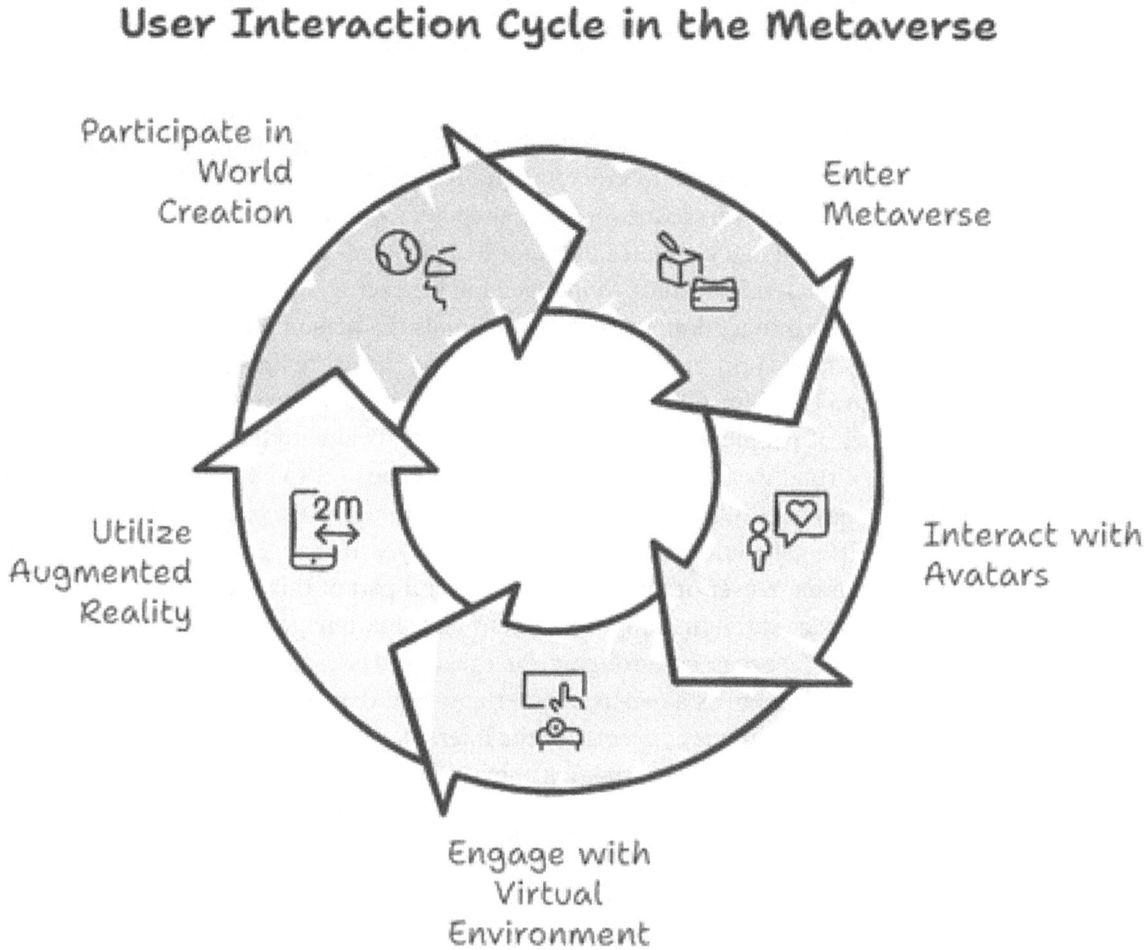


## Metaverse in the Balance Cuff

Although there are great expectations regarding metaverse technology in light of the various advantages expected for its use, there are some concerns regarding its use, as follows: -

**1- Advantages of metaverse:** Supporters of metaverse technology point out that it brings many advantages to its users in various economic, social, scientific, cultural, and political fields, as metaverse technology will constitute a new reality that will completely change the nature of the world in terms of communication, social, behavioral and economic aspects. The most prominent advantages of metaverse technology are - For example, but not limited to: -
A- Transforming the Internet into a three-dimensional world that provides interactive living and sharing of events instead of being limited to viewing them only through electronic devices.

B- Giving individuals the ability to move anywhere around the world freely and at any time.
C- Removing geographical barriers between people.
D- The possibility of finding and getting to know people with the same interests and ideas.
E- Developing social media and interactive communication technologies.
F- Creating many economic fields and business opportunities. The market value of the metaverse is expected to reach $5 trillion by 2030, which confirms the importance of investing in it.
G- Providing new forms of marketing and advertising on social media platforms.
H- Developing the online education and learning system, developing the medical and health system, and achieving the sustainable development goals of countries.

**2- The dangers of the Metaverse:** Despite the many advantages claimed by metaverse supporters, the reality of the metaverse could be more apparent. One of the reports issued by Kaspersky Information Security indicated that electronic risks could accompany new phenomena such as Metaverse. Virtual reality headsets can be subjected to attacks aimed at manipulating content, and virtual assets acquired in Metaverse can even be stolen, which poses a threat to entire virtual economies, in addition to concerns related to privacy violations, through extensive data collection operations related to users' actions and aspects of Their behavior and preferences, which can be exploited for identity theft or to impose censorship. Among the most prominent risks of using metaverse technology are the following:

**A-It is easy to commit crimes through it**. A person enters the metaverse secretively and interacts with programmable avatars and other people in a three-dimensional virtual space, such as sexual crimes, immoral practices, intentionally disturbing others, insulting and defaming, violating public morals, outraging modesty, public indecent acts, outraging a woman's modesty in private, incitement to immorality and prostitution, sexual exploitation of children, eavesdropping, breach of family values, and theft, fraud, and other money crimes. It is a means of committing cybercrimes; some believe many crimes may be committed through the metaverse.

**B- The emergence of a new type of cybercrime linked to the nature of metaverse**: Some expect the risks of cybercrime to increase with the presence of metaverse technology, as this new world - which is still under development - does not have advanced security levels; Which may make it a wide area for committing many illegal activities, such as impersonation, fraud, virtual theft, vandalism of virtual works and art collectibles, money laundering, counterfeiting virtual currencies, exploitation of children in prostitution, trafficking in illegal goods and drugs, etc.

**C- There are concerns related to cybersecurity**: A study by Kaspersky Information Security showed that most employees in Egypt (78%) believe that metaverse technology represents the future of the Internet and will revolutionize all sectors. A small number of them (13.5%) doubted this shift, saying it is just a trend and will end soon. (52.5%) their companies have already developed projects related to metaverse technologies or specific plans for such projects (26%). However, this shift will be accompanied by new cybersecurity challenges (El-Kady, 2023).

In conclusion, the metaverse, a new technology, presents numerous challenges and concerns, including privacy, data protection, and security. Companies implementing this technology face criticism for their potential to collect biometric data, making individuals vulnerable to cybercrimes. Governments must prepare a robust network infrastructure and financial and technical capabilities to ensure a sound regulatory environment. Data privacy, security, and integrity concerns are significant, as companies like Meta's virtual reality headsets collect sensitive data, such as location, physical features, and audio recordings, which can target users with personalized ads. Cyberattacks can cause bodily harm, and attackers can influence users' activities.

The metaverse may lead to addiction and the end of direct communication between individuals. There is no final vision for the metaverse, and no frameworks, ethics, or controls have been defined. The metaverse will enable the purchase of virtual property in the form of NFTs, but challenges arise in granting ownership rights to creators and verifying ownership in the metaverse. Content creators may need help to protect their intellectual property due to the difficulty of tracking instances of copyright infringement in the virtual realm.

From a criminal perspective, the dangers of the metaverse include the ease of committing crimes through it, as users log into the metaverse in a secret encrypted way and interact with programmable avatars and other people in a virtual three-dimensional space. Some believe that many crimes may be committed through the metaverse, such as sexual crimes, immoral practices, deliberately disturbing others, insulting and defamation, violating public morals, outrageous modesty, public indecency, breaching the modesty of a woman in private, incitement to immorality and prostitution, sexual exploitation of children, eavesdropping, breach of family values, theft, fraud, and other money crimes (Al-Marri, 2020).

The metaverse lacks advanced security levels, which may make it a vast arena for committing many illegal activities such as identity impersonation, fraud, virtual theft, vandalism of virtual works and art collections, money laundering, counterfeiting virtual currencies, exploitation of children in prostitution, trafficking in illegal goods and drugs, etc. Some reports indicate the possibility of sexual crimes occurring in the metaverse, such as the crime of virtual Rape and Sexual Harassment. A research study on the countermeasures of Avatar sex crimes reveals that such offenses in the metaverse result in significant psychological trauma and consequential harm to users, rendering them equivalent to real-world offenses (Lee, 2022).

Europol sees these kinds of virtual experiences pose serious questions about the applicability of current legislation. The crude delineation between physical and virtual will become increasingly problematic as technology becomes more sophisticated. As virtual experiences become more embodied and natural, it will be essential to have a clear idea of what is considered criminal behavior in the metaverse and to have matching laws to provide the means to prosecute these transgressions. The Metaverse has the potential to become a central space for digital money laundering. Illegal money laundering criminal groups can purchase and sell virtual assets on metaverses due to the anonymity of avatar creation and the potential misuse of Metaverse currency, the Metaverse Coin.

Terrorists will exploit new technological options to facilitate their activities, such as propaganda, recruitment, and training in the metaverse. With more immersive technology and related generated data, it becomes easier for terrorists to target vulnerable people and tailor their messages to their biases, enabling them to target their propaganda and recruit people more effectively (Khalifa, 2024). The absence of oversight in this new world raises the expected cybersecurity risk due to the need for more organized controls. Monitoring a vast number of users at one time will be difficult, but it is almost impossible, especially since no organized controls have been established to operate it yet. This concludes that the Metaverse may be one of the causes of the increasing risk and spread of cybercrime in our world today to a greater extent than what currently exists.

Some questions arise about the extent to which crimes can occur within the Metaverse, as the law is directed only at external material behavior in actual society and does not consider intentions or psychological feelings that do not appear in reality. The law may not govern what a person does in the virtual world as long as it does not cause harm to others or does not represent behavior that constitutes a crime according to the provisions of the law.

Others argue that virtual worlds can be regarded as separate societies for which the effects of deviant behavior can be analyzed by criminology, leading to severe conceptual and methodical problems. The answer to the last question is essential in criminal law, as these rules will evolve with the development of the Metaverse and its ramifications in all aspects of life. Jurisprudence suggests that some may call for granting avatars limited legal personality.

The digital virtual metaverse environment is a virtual world with no spatial boundaries, and research focuses on the means and tools used to carry out crimes through electronic devices and international electronic networks. Digital evidence in the metaverse is divided into physical evidence from virtual and augmented reality tools and digital evidence from the virtual Metaverse world and smartphone applications. (see Figure 8)

*Figure 8. Balancing the benefits and risks of metaverse technology*

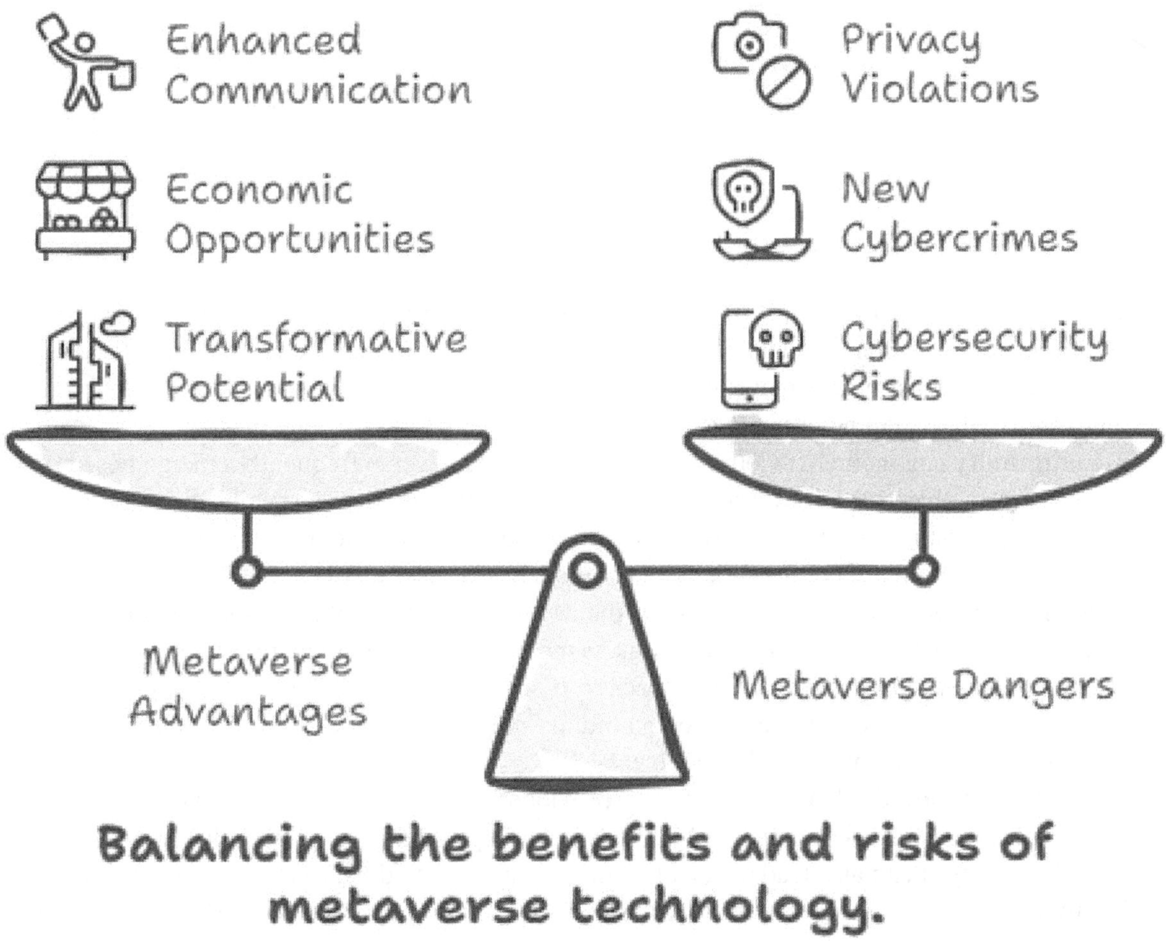

## Social Dynamics and Community Interaction in the Metaverse

The Metaverse is a novel domain in digital interaction, featuring virtual settings that enable social dynamics and community involvement in unparalleled ways. This paper investigates these virtual spaces' complex interactions and behaviors, analyzing how users engage, establish communities, and negotiate social norms. By examining several facets of community interaction in the Metaverse, our objective is to reveal the fundamental mechanisms that regulate social conduct in these immersive settings (see Figure 9).

*Figure 9. Social Dynamics in the Metaverse*

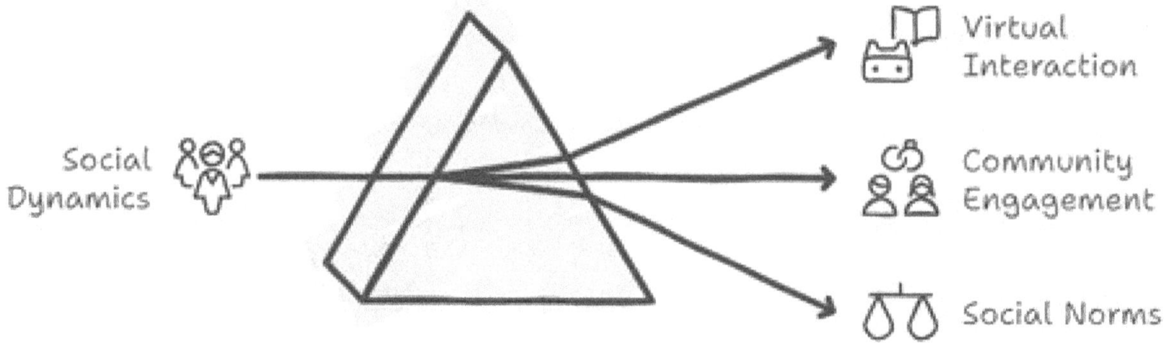


**1- Virtual Interaction:** User engagement in the Metaverse is complex, encompassing synchronous and asynchronous communication approaches. Avatars function as virtual manifestations of users, enabling a distinct form of self-representation. The capacity to personalize avatars promotes uniqueness while shaping users' perceptions and behaviors toward each other.

**2-Community engagement:** Communities inside the Metaverse frequently emerge based on the same interests, objectives, or experiences. These virtual communities can exhibit either transience or persistence as their members collaborate, attend events, or interact socially. The sense of affiliation that emerges from these communities is a potent driver of user involvement.

3- **Social Norms:** Like any social setting, the Metaverse has established social conventions and etiquette. To ensure peaceful interactions, users must diligently negotiate these implicit guidelines. A comprehensive grasp of the cultural backdrop of various virtual environments is essential, as activities considered acceptable in one community may be disapproved of in another.

4- Complexities of Community Engagement

**A- Anonymity and Identity:** The anonymity provided by the Metaverse can have both advantageous and disadvantageous consequences. Although technology enables users to delve into many facets of their identity, it can also lead to harmful conduct and targeted harassment. Achieving a balance between anonymity and accountability poses a considerable problem for community management.

**B- The Digital Divide:** Equitable access to the Metaverse needs to be more consistent, and technology differences can create a digital gap. This division might impede community engagement since individuals with restricted access may feel marginalized from social activities. Rectifying these disparities is crucial for cultivating inclusive communities.

In conclusion, The Metaverse is fundamentally transforming the terrain of social interaction, presenting novel prospects for community involvement and cooperation. By comprehending social dynamics, we can traverse these virtual spaces more effectively and foster constructive connections. Continual study and discussion will be crucial in tackling the obstacles and fully utilizing the potential of these digital communities as the Metaverse progresses (El-Kady, 2023). (see Figure 10)

*Figure 10. Social Interaction in the Metaverse*

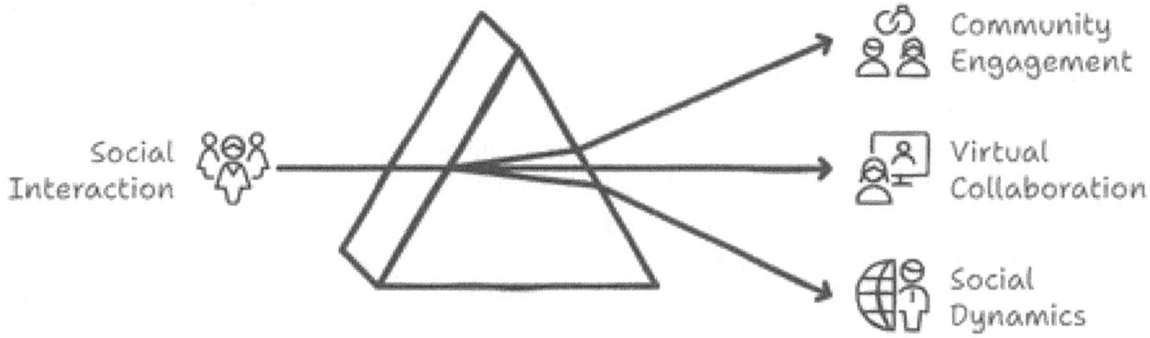


## Metaverse and Complexities of Criminal Law

Metaverse technology raises several legal complexities in the context of criminal law. The most prominent of these is the absence of criminal texts related to this technology and the violative behaviors committed through it, in addition to the inadequacy of traditional criminal adaptations for crimes committed through metaverse technology, especially crimes of assault on persons and circumstances of time and place in metaverse crimes.

The metaverse has created a new concept of the crime scene, as one actor's behavior may impact several places simultaneously. In addition to the time dimension of the act, which varies from country to country due to the timings between countries, this results in a difference in the legal description of the act. There is no doubt that the changing and volatile nature of this new virtual space will affect the reliability of the digital evidence obtained about the new crimes occurring within it, which will be reflected - without a doubt - in the methods of collecting and extracting digital evidence in this virtual world.

## Metaverse and the Principle of Legality

A fundamental principle governs criminal law, the legality of crimes and punishments, which is the known principle that "*There is no crime and no punishment except by a text or based on the law,*" as stated in various constitutions. It is the main principle in criminal law. Thus, the question arises about how texts relating to information technology crimes, information crimes, cybercrimes, or information network crimes apply to metaverse crimes. The law texts on combating cybercrimes or information technology crimes will apply to metaverse crimes, given that metaverse technology represents the new generation of the Internet. Therefore, the crimes occurring within the metaverse are nothing but new crimes to which the legal texts criminalizing cybercrimes apply. Which constitutes an integrated legal umbrella to deal with this range of crimes, such as the crimes contained in the Law on Combating Information Technology Crimes, the Personal Data Protection Law, the Electronic Signature Law, the Communications Regulatory Law, and the Civil Status Law, which guarantees the protection of personal data.

Some may see that - in the absence of a law regulating the use of metaverse technology - there are some crimes in metaverse technology to which the existing legal rules cannot be applied because they are not compatible with the nature of this technology, such as crimes of assault on people, insults, defamation, and virtual rape, and hence the absence of a legal framework. The organization of this technique would exhaust the criminal judge, who finds himself faced with general rules that do not help him achieve the desired justice and proper legal application of these crimes, in addition to the impermissibility of analogy in criminalization and punishment articles, and thus the judge's obligation to rule the acquittal of the perpetrators due to the absence of the criminal text. Implementation of the principle of legality of penal crimes will lead to impunity for perpetrators (Jibril, 2023). The general legal framework contained in the Penal Code can apply to these crimes, given their assault on interests worthy of legal protection that the criminal legislator seeks to criminalize acts under the provisions of the Penal Code (El-Kady, 2023).

## Can Some Behaviors in the Metaverse Be Described as Crimes?

Some have raised an important question about the extent to which crimes can occur within the world of the Metaverse from a logical legal standpoint, which states that the metaverse is an imaginary virtual world and that the criminal law is directed only to external physical behavior in real society, and the consequences. Moreover, the law does not take into account intentions. It does not apply to what is happening inside a person's secrets or dreams and wishes, just as the law has nothing to do with a person's psychological feelings that do not appear in reality and take on an external appearance, or his fears or delusions that do not appear in reality (Jibril, 2023).

Therefore, it can be said as a conclusion that the law may not govern what a person does in the virtual world as long as he does not cause harm to others or does not represent behavior that constitutes a crime according to the provisions of the law. Then, the previous opinion ends with subjecting metaverse technology to the rule of law. Then, it is permissible to punish behavior that occurs via metaverse technology as long as it constitutes criminal behavior according to the law. The previous opinion is based on the nature of criminal law as a tool for controlling individuals' social behavior. Criminal law does not hold the individual accountable for his internal, non-material intentions. Instead, it holds him accountable for his external material actions that constitute a violation of the rule of law and an assault on the legal interest worthy of protection by the legislator (El-kady, 2023).

## The Incompatibility of the Legal Adaptations of Metaverse Crimes With the Traditional Rules of Criminal Law

Some believe that the adaptations of some metaverse crimes are incompatible with the traditional rules of criminal law and the texts of criminal law, which were designed to be applied according to specific material standards in the tangible physical reality and cannot be applied with the relevant metaverse technology of virtual nature (Jibril, 2023).

**A- In terms of the structure of the crime (the physical and moral element):** Some crimes require harm to the body or soul as determined by the law in a way that is inconsistent with the nature of the virtual metaverse, as in crimes of murder, violence, physical abuse, and rape, where violence occurs against natural bodies and not virtual symbols such as avatars. In the metaverse technology, the previous opinion believes that the material element of the crimes committed through the metaverse technology is surrounded by difficulties related to its elements (behavior, result, causal relationship), which necessitates the necessity of legislative intervention to criminalize those acts committed through the metaverse technology (Ali & Khalifa, 2023).

**B- In terms of place:** On the other hand, some add the inadequacy of legal adaptations to the circumstances of time and place via metaverse technology. The crimes that occur via metaverse technology, which are virtual, cross the boundaries of time and space, and thus, there can be unlimited and unknown arenas in virtual space. To protect the metaverse, it is the scene where the crimes take place. Failure to accurately determine the crime scene committed through metaverse technology results in legal problems in determining the spatial jurisdiction rules that govern accountability for these crimes, as the elements and elements of the crime are distributed among multiple locations. The problem specific to metaverse technology is that the tools of this technology have led to the occurrence of crimes characterized by uniformity of time and multiple places of occurrence. Thus, this technology created a new concept for the virtual crime scene in which the behavior of a single individual creates multiple effects in several places at one moment (Jibril, 2023).

**C - In terms of time:** On the other hand, committing metaverse crimes in the virtual environment of the metaverse, in which times may differ between countries, may lead to a difference in the legal conditions of the crimes, given the difference in the time of committing the crime from one country to another, so the crime is committed in one country during the day due to the difference in time. Committing it in another country at night may lead to a difference in its legal status due to the availability of the night condition as an aggravating circumstance in some crimes, which may also impact the evidentiary evidence of the crime (Jibril, 2023).

**4- Is it possible to say that the avatar is granted legal personality?** From the previous question arises another question about the extent to which people in the world of the metaverse, especially the avatar, enjoy legal personality. The answer to this question is that the law grants legal personality to natural humans and not to other inanimate objects and animals and does not address the person's symbol. Alternatively, his image or anything that represents him as his image or the symbol that indicates him in the metaverse technology.

Therefore, the natural person remains criminally responsible for his actions through the metaverse technology. However, the avatar, the holographic symbol that represents the natural person in the metaverse technology, his actions, and the transgressions that occur against him are not considered unless Issued by a natural person or issued against him. The preceding indicates that crimes the avatar commits may not constitute a crime at all, such as the crime of rape, which is only conceivable to occur on a female and to be committed on her natural body, and not its symbol through metaverse technology, and likewise the crime of murder, which only occurs on a living human being (Jibril, 2023).

The answer to the last question is critical in criminal law. These rules are expected to develop with the development of metaverse technology and the expansion of its use in all aspects of life, which may be reflected in the rules of criminal law in the future. In light of the previous indicators, the researcher expects to find that Jurists in the future may call for granting the avatar, the human avatar within the metaverse, a limited legal personality. (see Figure 11)

Finally, we should suggest a model for addressing the legal complexities of metaverse technology in criminal Law by updating the existing laws, creating new laws handling metaverse crimes on a case-by-case basis, and empowering international cooperation. (see Figure 12)

*Figure 11. Identification of Legal Complexities*

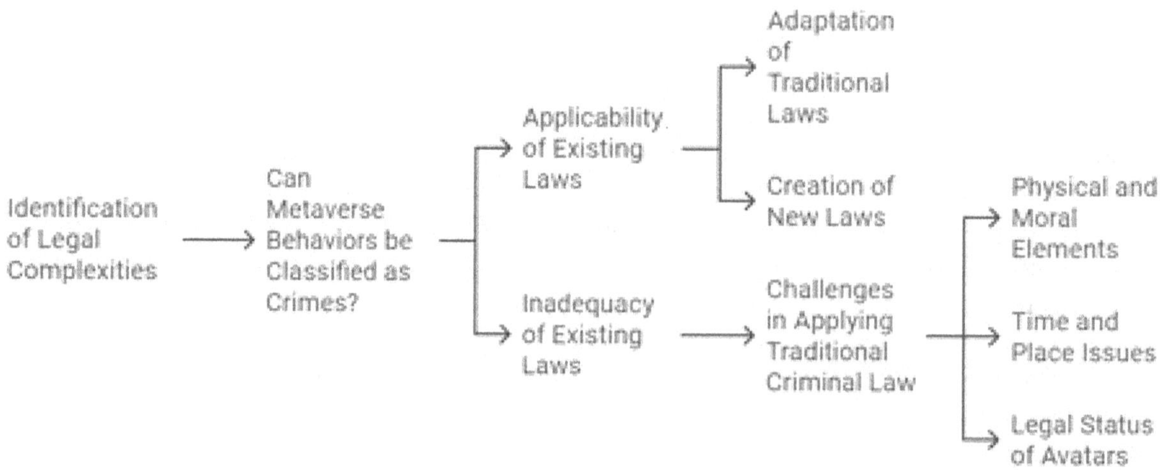

*Figure 12. Addressing the legal complexities of the metaverse technology in criminal law*

## PART TWO: METACRIMES

### Definition of Metacrimes

Metacrimes or metaverse crimes refer to criminal activities within immersive three-dimensional Internet environments, the metaverse. This concept is closely connected to the emergence and appearance of the metaverse, as it offers unique characteristics and a close organic connection to cybercrime (Zhou et al., 2024; Seo et al., 2023; Ritterbusch & Teichmann, 2023). INTERPOL has established a crime classification based on specific methods of operation, which divides metacrime into ten overarching categories, including cybercrime, financial crimes, property crimes, sexual offenses and assault, identity crimes, terrorism, intellectual property crimes, crimes against children, acts aimed at instilling fear or emotional distress, and crimes against public safety (INTERPOL, 2024).

Some scholars view metaverse crimes as an evolution of cybercrime, revealing many unprecedented criminal opportunities. The results extend far beyond the limits observed historically and in traditional cyber contexts, heralding a new era of digital criminality. With the increasing use of the metaverse and the number of participants, some criminal and terrorist elements may exploit this unique technology to commit criminal activities in its context (Gómez-Quintero et al., 2024).

Metacrime or Metaverse crimes are a growing concern for law enforcement. They are expected to become a significant problem as the new world becomes part of our daily lives. Law enforcement agencies must anticipate potential challenges by listing potential threats and identifying gaps, including those in legal frameworks that criminalize them.

There is an urgent need to determine whether individual and collective activities and behaviors constitute harm or crimes in the metaverse. Effective police and law enforcement responses depend on clear legislation and explicit laws. Interpol International has published reports on current and potential criminal activities in the metaverse, including NFT fraud, cyber-physical attacks, impersonation by stealing digital identities, theft of 3D properties and virtual assets, child grooming, stalking, and virtual sexual harassment. As the popularity of the metaverse increases, the list of crimes will expand, and police agencies will be challenged to address these emerging criminal activities.

In summary, this study acknowledges the intricacy of defining and quantifying metacrime and embraces the more comprehensive conceptualization proposed by Seo et al. (2023). A significant research gap arises about the epistemic connection between metacrime and cybercrime, raising whether metacrime is merely a repackaged version of an old phenomenon (Marshall & Tompsett, 2024). Analyzing the congruities and disparities between the two forms of digital criminality will not only enhance our comprehension of the degree to which the metaverse and its complex technologies enable novel criminal possibilities but also expose the varying need to formulate tailored and focused regulatory measures for reducing and preventing metacrime (Zhou et al., 2024).

## Exploring the Nexus between Metacrimes and Cybercrimes

Some scholars showed that meta-crimes are a novel category of criminal activities occurring in the metaverse and identified five shared characteristics between these two crime types: crime classification, continuous evolution, hyper-spatial-temporality(global reach), anonymity, and governance challenges (Zhou et al., 2024). So, meta crimes should be a development of Cybercrimes. They argue that metacrime, as a characteristic of evolution in cyberspace, maintains fundamental resemblances to cybercrime and reveals several unparalleled criminal possibilities. The findings transcend the limitations in physical and traditional cyber environments, signaling a new age of digital criminal activity (Zhou et al., 2024).

### 1. History of Cybercrime Terminology

Cybercrime has been a subject of extensive research and understanding, with various terms used to describe illegal actions in cyberspace. The term "cybercrime" has been the prevailing phrase since 1995 and has gained widespread validation in academic and practical spheres. However, a lack of universally accepted definitions and classifications of cybercrime leads to various interpretations among academics, practitioners, and policymakers. A well-recognized definition defines cybercrime as "crimes that occur within cyberspace." This broad scope may overlook the complexities and unique characteristics of cybercrimes. However, it offers a flexible framework for accommodating the wide range of criminal activities caused by the unpredictable advancement of technology (Zhou et al., 2024).

Various typologies and taxonomies have been documented for categorizing cybercrimes, with the binary classification structure being the most commonly used. This structure divides cybercrimes into two categories: cyber-dependent and cyber-enabled crimes. Cyber-dependent crimes, such as hacking, ransomware, and cyber warfare, depend primarily on digital technologies. In contrast, cyber-enabled crimes, such as crimes against machines, the use of machines, and crimes in machines, are accelerated by the emergence of digital technologies (Phillips et al., 2022). (see Figure 13)

Figure 13. History of cybercrime

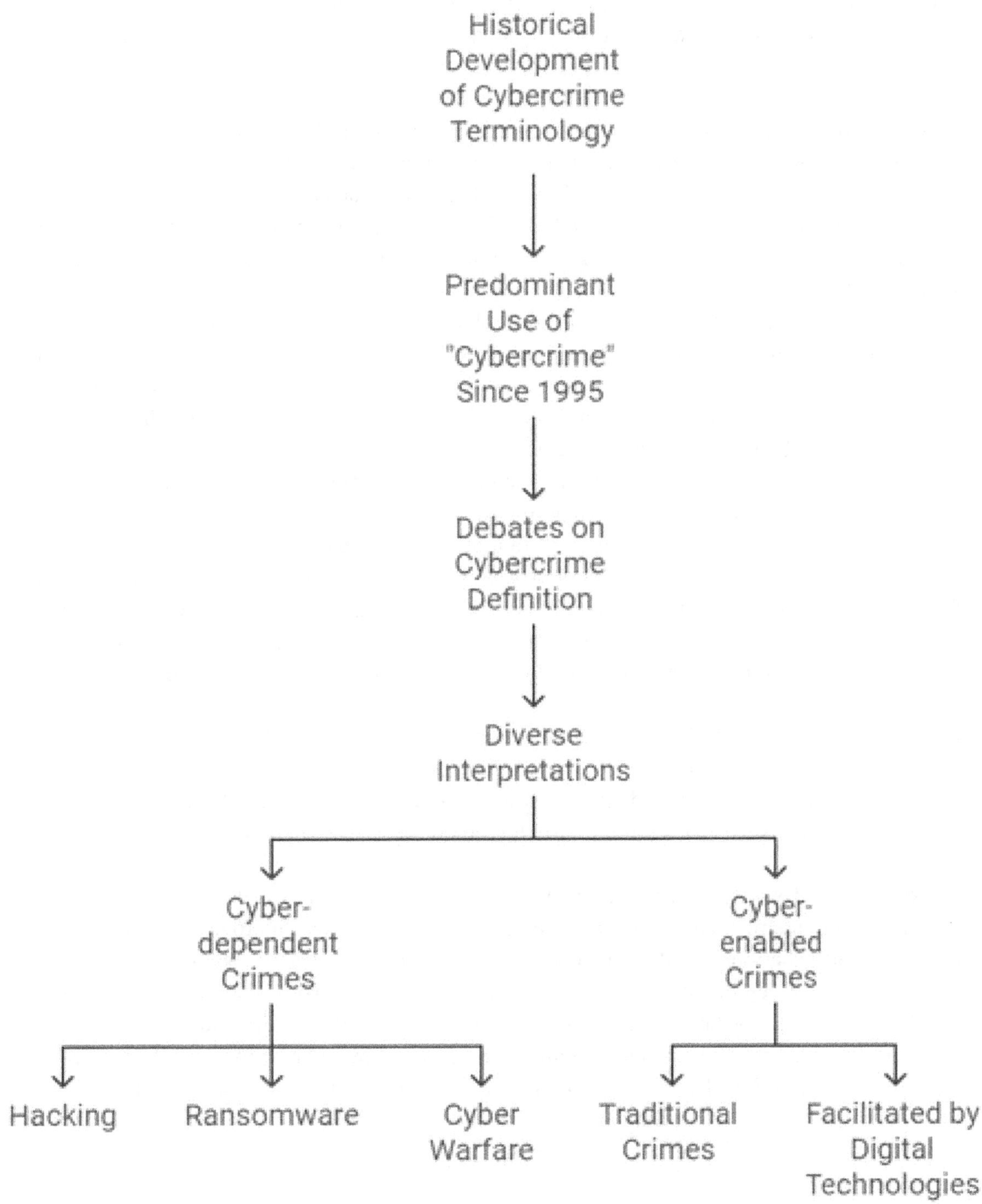

## 2. Key Features of Cybercrimes

Current academic research has identified at least four essential features of cybercrimes: development driven by technology, hyper-spatial-temporality (global reach), anonymity, and regulatory issues (Zhou et al., 2024).

**A- Development driven by technology:** Cybercrime is a complex phenomenon that has evolved in parallel with technological advancements. The introduction of information and communication technologies (ICTs) has led to increased criminal activities such as hacking, ransomware, botnets, and distributed denial of services (DDoS). This has also led to the conversion of offline crimes into their online equivalents, including cyber fraud, cyberbullying, online harassment, and online stalking (Marshall & Tompsett, 2024).

**B- Hyper-spatial-temporality:** Cybercrime lacks the spatial and temporal convergence between victims and perpetrators, which is invalid in cyberspace. It does not possess a discernible spatial structure and an innate "temporal sequence and order." This paradigm shift allows motivated criminals to easily target victims over long distances and time frames, highlighting the hyper-spatial-temporality of cybercrime (Zhou et al., 2024).

**C- Anonymity:** Information and Communication Technologies (ICTs) provide cybercriminals with additional levels of anonymity and pseudonymity, setting them apart from traditional criminal activities. Cybercrime capitalizes on a substantial level of "anonymity and plasticity" by creating online identities, which serve as precursors to a broad spectrum of cybercrimes, including cyber fraud, cyberbullying, cyberstalking, online money laundering, hacking, data breaches, online illicit markets, and online hate crimes. The illusion of anonymity and fake identities enable cybercriminals to avoid legal investigations and provide significant legal and regulatory obstacles.

The ongoing advancement of technology, cyberspace's intrinsic global nature, and its widespread anonymity present substantial obstacles to controlling and administrating cybercrime. The rapid rate of technological progress often exceeds the expediency of laws, reducing the deterrent impact of legal structures and the effectiveness of prompt law enforcement measures (Zhou et al., 2024).

**D- Regulatory issues:** The transnational nature of cybercrime requires international collaboration in law enforcement endeavors, but the lack of a complete international legal framework and conflicting jurisdictions greatly hinder the desire and procedures for cross-border cooperation in investigating, prosecuting, and punishing cyber criminals. Extensive anonymity adds complexity to ethical concerns for law enforcement, always posing challenges in finding a middle ground between safeguarding privacy and enabling the exchange of information with technology firms and other public bodies. Based on these facts, it is natural to infer that the ongoing development of cybercrime, enabled by technical advancements, may create growing challenges for criminal control and administration (Zhou et al., 2024).

## 3. A Comparative Analysis of Metacrime and Cybercrime

Metacrime and cybercrime are two distinct domains with similarities in crime categorization, ongoing development, hyper-spatial-temporality, anonymity, and governance challenges. The categorizations of aberrant and unlawful behaviors within the metaverse closely resemble those recognized in cybercrimes. However, the metaverse functions as selectable and displaceable platforms that motivated criminals may consider while making illicit decisions (Zhou et al., 2024; Phillips et al., 2022; Gómez-Quintero et al., 2024). (see Figure 14)

*Figure 14. Shared Characteristics of Metacrime and Cybercrime*

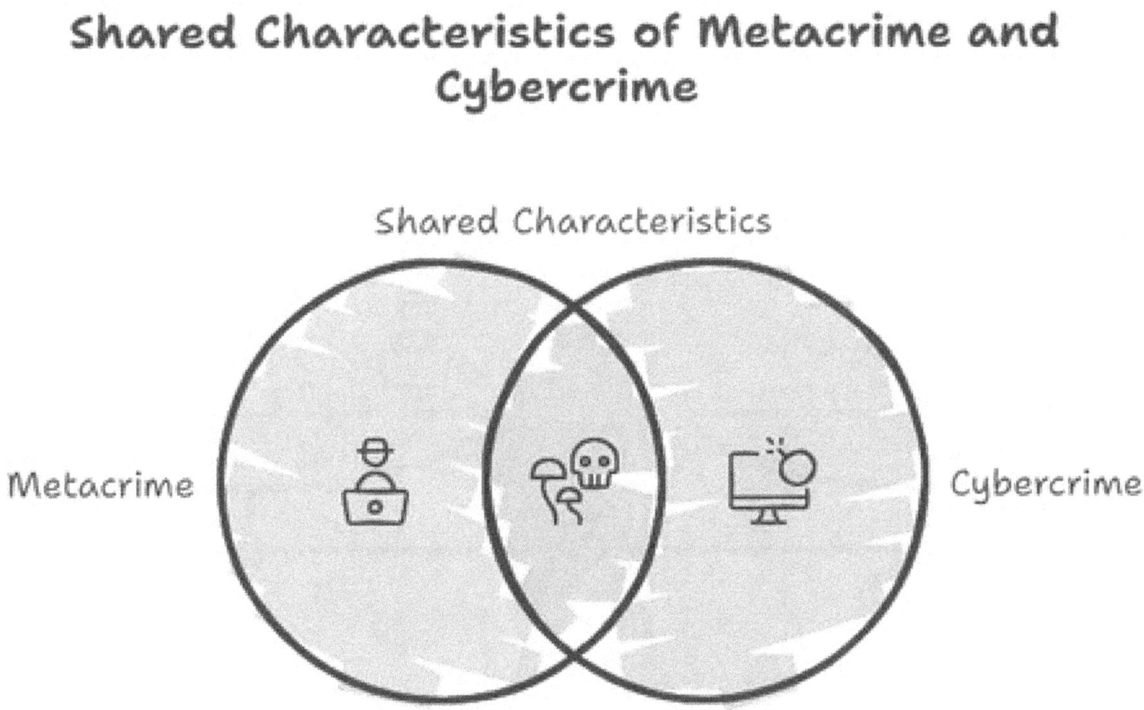


Analogous to cybercrime, metacrime is inherently dynamic, developing alongside the ongoing technical progress and incorporation of immersion-based technology. With its foundation in a wide array of technologies such as ICTs, cloud computing, artificial intelligence (AI), computer vision, blockchain, robotics/Internet of Things (IoTs), user engagement, and extended reality, the metaverse fosters an ideal setting for the emergence of new cybercrimes (Lee et al., 2022). The emergence of each fundamental technology reveals numerous technical and societal weaknesses that motivate criminals to exploit easily. Their combined effect and the introduction of new technologies consistently create an increasing number of criminal possibilities within the metaverse (Zhou et al., 2024; Dwivedi et al., 2023).

The metaverse replicates the hyper-spatial-temporality intrinsic to cyberspace and reduces the distinction between actual and virtual domains through holographic structures and simulations. The metaverse enables users to participate in transnational interactions using various modalities such as avatars, digital cameras, and head-mounted displays (HMDs) (Wang et al., 2022). The emergence of digital twins, virtual replicas of physical objects, reduces the disparity and blurs the parameters between real and virtual environments. This hyper-spatial-temporal characteristic, enabled by holographic simulation, transforms and adds complexity to location-based criminal activity (Zhou et al., 2024; Lee et al., 2022). (see Figure 15)

*Figure 15. Comparing metacrime and cybercrime aspects*

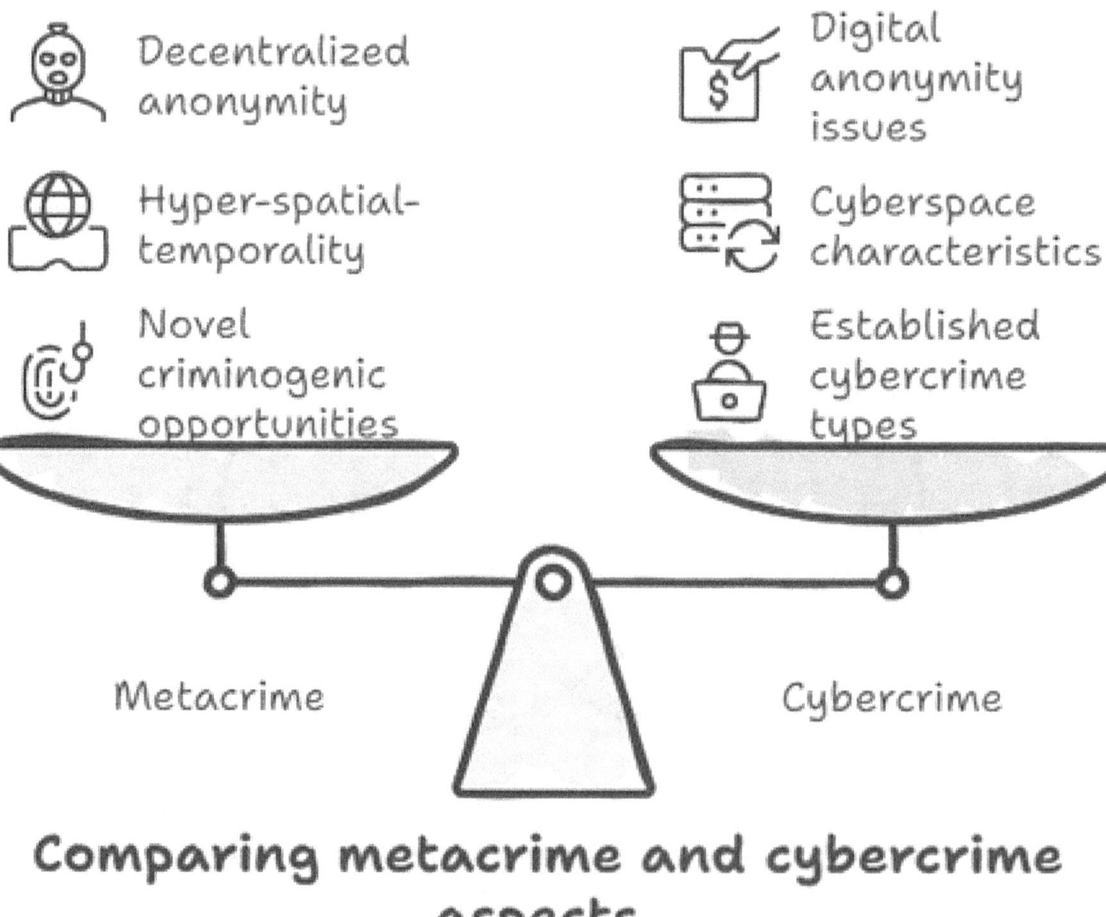


The continuing problem of anonymity is present in the metaverse and might be exacerbated by the extensive use of decentralized financial transaction platforms, such as cryptocurrency. The metaverse presents a comprehensive range of issues related to anonymity, including privacy concerns, the use of customized avatars, pseudonyms, the malleability of identity, and the establishment of Bitcoin as the primary means of payment. Robust research has extensively recorded the use of cryptocurrencies in enabling illegal activities, such as money laundering, hacking, fraud, terrorism, and geopolitical conflicts, owing to their anonymity and the challenges in tracking transactions (Dwivedi et al., 2023; Gómez-Quintero et al., 2024).

Government issues in both cybercrime and metacrime include contemporary legal frameworks, jurisdictional discrepancies, the necessity of international cooperation, digital forensic proficiency and capabilities, privacy issues, and a deficiency in public awareness. The metaverse's distinctive characteristics, such as holographic simulation and the extensive use of avatars, give rise to specific legal and regulatory challenges. An ongoing debate persists over whether and how terrestrial legal concepts should be applied to avatars and digital twins (Zhou et al., 2024). (see Figure 16)

*Figure 16.* **Metacrime and Cybercrime**

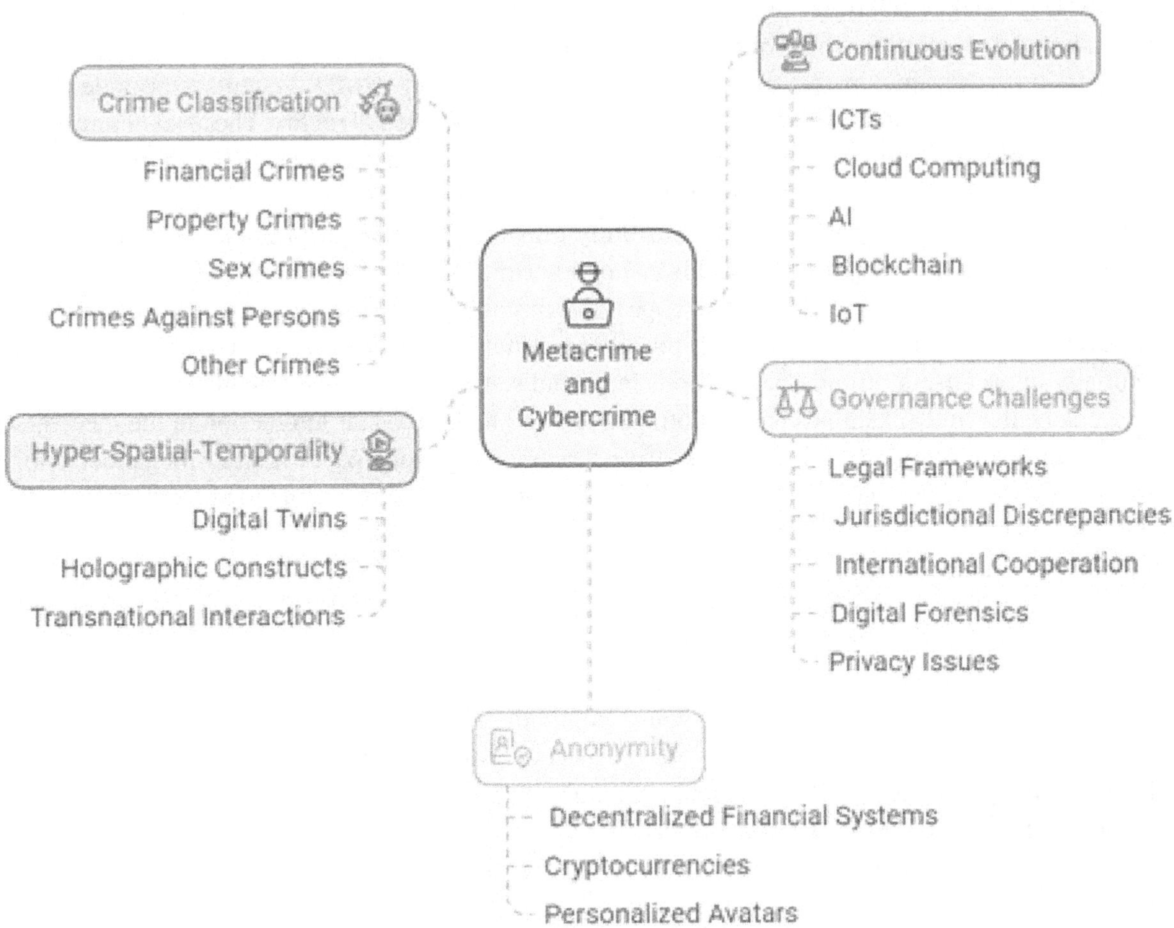

## Uniqueness of Metacrime

Some scholars show that metacrime is unique, unlike cybercrime; the metaverse presents novel criminogenic possibilities, including virtual-to-physical and immersive virtual reality attacks. These attacks exploit immersive online environments, head-mounted displays (HMDs), and haptic technologies, enabling criminals to cause significant physical harm to various targets. Virtual-to-physical attacks exploit digitally generated models or VR sensors to cause physical damage on-site, while immersive virtual reality attacks alter the technical settings of HMDs (Gómez-Quintero et al., 2024). These attacks can result in physical injuries and more intense psychological suffering, such as ocular dryness, visual vertigo, motion sickness, and neurological pain. The psychological consequences of these attacks can be more invasive due to the intentional and coercive superimposition of harmful material within immersive online settings (Zhou et al., 2024).

On the other hand, Metacrime victimization in the metaverse is characterized by a heightened sense of immersion and credibility, which bridges the sensory gap between cyberspace and the actual world. This immersion is measured by the ability of Head-Mounted Display (HMD) systems to provide a comprehensive, extensive, contextually immersive, and vivid representation of reality. The level of immersion results in a heightened feeling of presence when individuals see virtual surroundings as physical settings rather than artificial structures created by HMDs.

This heightened sense of presence and plausibility illusions can lead to more significant psychological, financial, and physical harm than traditional cybercrime. The distinction between immersive and non-immersive avatars may introduce a new aspect to criminological etiology in the metaverse through human-avatar interaction. The Proteus theory posits that digital avatars' visual characteristics and qualities substantially impact users' attitudes and actions in virtual settings (Zhou et al., 2024).

Conversely, the study examines harm neutralization and human-avatar interaction in the metaverse. Neutralization theory suggests individuals use five strategies to rationalize deviant or illegal behaviors, including denying guilt, injury, victimhood, criticizing supporters, and appealing to higher loyalties. The flexibility of avatar identities and self-representation can impact individuals' dependence on neutralizing strategies (Zhou et al., 2024).

Last, metacrime presents new ethical and regulatory challenges, such as the potential for widespread abuse of biometric data and the growing vulnerability of people. The interoperability and decentralized characteristics of the metaverse offer concentrated possibilities and motivations for malicious intent to manipulate biometric data. The presence of young populations in the metaverse increases susceptibility and vulnerability to victim-focused crimes. Regulation of avatars in the metaverse presents new difficulties, including lacking specific laws and procedures for violent actions. The absence of statutory, regulatory, and industrial codes against metacrime will place victims in legally, psychophysically, and socioeconomically vulnerable situations, undermining democratic legitimacy (Zhou et al., 2024). (see Figure 17)

*Figure 17. Uniqueness of metacrime*

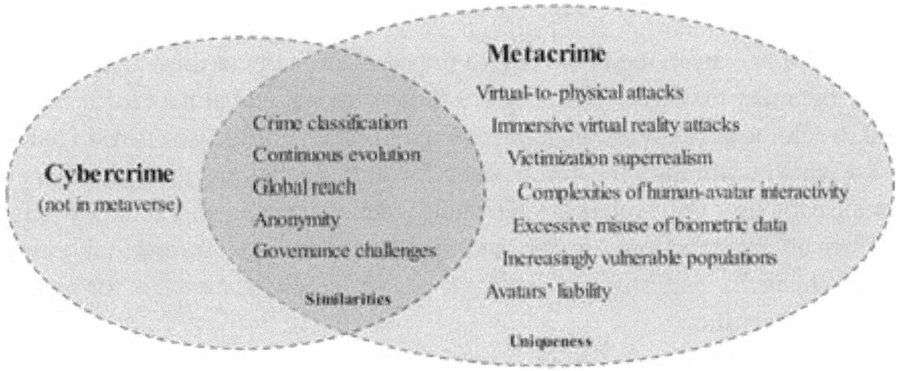


## Classification of Metaverse Crimes

In fact, as part of the work of Interpol to combat crime and update and harmonize classifications of crime and the current harms resulting from them, Interpol was keen to develop a chart that shows a classification of some emerging crimes and potential harms in the metaverse. Some metacrimes can extend into the real world. The World Economic Forum has stressed that damage in the metaverse can be local or culturally specific, just as in the physical world. At the same time, the metaverse will add spatial damages such as gestures, postures, and digital assets, which will require a customized approach. Given the newness of the metaverse technology and its failure to reach the final stages of operation, developing a vision for the crimes expected to occur depends on the idea of hypotheses and expected scenarios.

It is essential to understand and realize properly that the metaverse is a digital platform or a complex virtual environment and that these scenarios' Hypotheses about potential crimes can evolve rapidly. There are also many other ways criminal actors or elements can engage in different forms of crime within the metaverse, including existing, emerging, and entirely new types. The crimes expected to be committed in the metaverse world are many and varied, given the unique nature of this new technology. The most prominent crimes expected to be committed through this technology may be digital identity crimes, financial crimes, intellectual property rights crimes, digital sexual assault crimes, crimes against children, cybercrimes, acts of intimidation and emotional disturbance, crimes of terrorism, and crimes against public safety.

## Types of Metaverse Crimes

According to the above, many images of metaverse crimes exist, but we will highlight the most prominent ones.

**A- Hacking and digital identity theft:** Criminals can gain unauthorized access to a user's account and digital assets through hacking or identity theft. They can also steal, reproduce, and sell others' identities, including digital fingerprints. Once stolen, fake avatars can be used to commit Crimes.

Additionally, tokenization risks include fraudulent token issuance, token theft, and fraudulent exploitation of the token gateway system.

Some link the use of avatars in the metaverse to impersonation operations. Users have an avatar that represents them in the metaverse world, usually in a three-dimensional human form. Users customize it uniquely, from skin color to accessories, in detail when registering for the first time in the metaverse, and they get to know each other through the avatar when forming a relationship. with others or conducting transactions Because the user only enters simple data; Such as ID, age, and gender when registering in the metaverse. Since all avatar actions are exposed to all users in the metaverse, unique characteristics, such as appearance, behavior patterns, and gestures, can be identified by users for malicious purposes only through simple observation.

In addition, the user's personal information is readily displayed to other users on the metaverse, where the unique profile picture pattern and personal information can be used for impersonation or social engineering attacks, such as phishing and persistent threats to obtain financial gain. Social engineering attacks are more challenging to identify than in reality because the metaverse has no restrictions on changes to the avatar's form. Incidents of digital theft are not something that should be expected. In 2012, a digital theft incident occurred in the Netherlands in an electronic game, where several teenagers stole a digital amulet from another teenager in the "Run Scape" game. The case was presented to the Dutch Supreme Court, which considered the matter a crime. Ordinary theft because that amulet has real value in terms of the time and effort spent to obtain it, and the teenagers who stole the amulet were convicted.

**B- Deepfake:** Criminals use deepfake technology to impersonate other users and commit various illegal activities. They can undermine the integrity of information and graphic materials by publishing false data about organizations and individuals and spreading propaganda and fake news. Criminal elements may also threaten victims by creating Fake sexual exploitation material to defame them.

**C- Violation of digital privacy:** Criminals may violate users' online privacy by tracking their movement, activities, interests, and personal information. This private data can be used for cyberbullying or harassment.

**D- Phishing:** Criminals may steal another user's login credentials, personal information, or virtual assets through phishing. SMS phishing can also occur through the unauthorized collection of personal data such as voices and phone numbers.

**E- Money laundering:** Criminals may purchase digital assets such as NFTs or virtual currencies from the proceeds of crime and sell them for clean assets in the metaverse environment, which limits the ability to trace the original source of funds in this new environment. Some point out that the metaverse could be a central space or area of communication between money launderers. Criminal groups can launder illicit money and carry out purchases and sales of virtual assets on the Metaverse by uploading virtual content to the Metaverse market, then purchasing through fake companies or companies of suspicious ownership with the currency used only within the Metaverse, or the so-called Metaverse Coin, which are expected to be misused in illegal money laundering operations in the future; This is because the user creates avatars anonymously, and metaverse currency can be purchased with real money and exchanged for real money. For example, criminals can buy metaverse currencies through multiple accounts obtained from shareholders or mixed companies and sell fake virtual objects placed in advance.

**F- Digital fraud:** Criminals can deceive and inflate the prices of digital assets or create fake virtual markets to defraud other users by selling products that do not exist. They may also introduce malware into the metaverse to steal virtual assets. Some examples include impersonation scams, investment scams, romance scams, tech support scams, fake metaverse scams, NFT scams, gift scams, payment scams, job scams, and intelligent contract scams. Non-fungible tokens (NFTs) are a form of blockchain-based evidence of ownership, but they are also susceptible to fraudulent activities and theft of assets. NFTs can be sold multiple times using smart contracts or on different blockchains, and sellers do not need to own the item to sell it as an NFT. Significant marketplaces may claim ownership authenticity, but this is not feasible due to the many NFTs available. Up to 80% of NFTs generated using OpenSea's minting tool are considered fraudulent. Despite numerous NFTs provided by unidentified companies, it is challenging for genuine producers to prove their ownership rights. Law enforcement organizations must stay updated on NFT advancements and potential exploitations to prevent these issues.

**G- Avatar Theft and Theft of Virtual Property and Assets:** Criminals may anonymously steal virtual assets or property for financial gain, resulting in significant financial losses in the real world. This stark reality underscores the urgent need to address virtual theft. They may also steal cultural property to imitate, resell, or undervalue. Virtual theft violates others' virtual property by stealing virtual objects in the digital world. Some point out that there are cases in which virtual theft has been punished as a criminal act in actual courts.

Avatar and virtual property theft in the metaverse can occur through various methods, including account takeover, phishing scams, social engineering, and cyberpiracy. Account takeover involves unauthorized access to a user's account through weak passwords, phishing attempts, or data breaches. Phishing scams involve deceiving users into divulging login information through counterfeit websites or messages. Social engineering involves criminals deceiving users into divulging personal information or login credentials by assuming the identity of trusted entities. Malicious software, including viruses, can illicitly acquire login credentials or confidential data from users' devices. However, users can protect themselves from these threats with the proper knowledge and awareness. Cybercriminals exploit weaknesses in the metaverse platform to illicitly access virtual assets, including digital currencies, NFTs, and virtual real estate.

Scams and fraud involve deceiving users into transferring virtual assets to criminals through fraudulent schemes. Smart contract exploits on blockchain technology can also be leveraged to acquire virtual assets illicitly. However, with the proper knowledge and awareness, users can protect themselves. Strategies for mitigation include multi-factor authentication (MFA), periodic updates of software and platforms, and, most importantly, user education about potential dangers associated with phishing and social engineering. By understanding these risks and being equipped with the proper knowledge, users can take proactive steps to safeguard their virtual assets. Monitoring and reporting systems to detect and track suspicious actions are crucial in this fight against virtual theft. Law enforcement agencies must be knowledgeable about these dangers and collaborate closely with metaverse platform providers to develop successful solutions.

**H- Damage to digital property:** Criminals may disrupt virtual events, target specific users for blackmail, or cause chaos by damaging virtual property and engaging in virtual vandalism. They can also destroy cultural assets such as art objects for personal, political, or ideological motives.

**I- Intellectual Property Rights Crimes:** These crimes conceivably include copyright infringement and counterfeiting, whereby criminals may copy or sell copyrighted NFT works that commit pattern and trademark infringement in the virtual marketplace. Copyrighting counterfeit images, videos, written products, and materials can be a money laundering tactic and also disrupt the virtual economy.

**J- Digital sexual assault crimes:** These crimes are conceivable to include acts of assault, abuse, harassment, exploitation, and indecent exposure. Criminals may engage in virtual interactions with other users to commit assaults or crimes of a non-consensual and illicit sexual nature towards their avatars. This can range from instances of harassment to the creation and distribution of sexually explicit content.

Some reports indicate the possibility of sexual crimes occurring in the metaverse, such as the hypothetical crime of rape and sexual harassment. One of the English women claimed that other people's avatars raped her avatar and that she was exposed to severe psychological damage and trouble as a result of the rape incident that she experienced while she was in the metaverse. She demanded that these avatars be punished for the crime of rape they committed, where the facts of the incident are summarized in That the lady, once she entered the world of the metaverse.

Within a minute of entering, she was subjected to verbal and sexual harassment by four avatars through their avatars. They were not satisfied with the verbal or sexual harassment, but they went further, and her avatar was raped, although the crime of rape was unlike any other. It is difficult to imagine crimes of honor occurring in the metaverse environment, given that they assume direct, non-consensual sexual intercourse between a male and a female, which is inconceivable in the metaverse environment (Jibril, 2023).

Several studies propose that successful strategies for preventing virtual sex crimes in online contexts include implementing avatar distance restrictions, enacting punishment legislation, targeting certain offenders and groups, and utilizing intelligent chatbots for suspect profiling. Instances of virtual sex crimes, encompassing acts of harassment and sexual violence, are ever more widespread across digital platforms such as social networking, interactive gaming, and virtual reality (VR). Implementing efficient strategies to deter these offenses guarantees individuals' security and psychological welfare. This synthesis examines many tactics and technologies suggested to reduce virtual sex crimes. To effectively prevent virtual sex crimes, a comprehensive approach is necessary. This includes the establishment of targeted regulatory frameworks, using sophisticated technology tools such as chatbots to identify offenders, and integrating educational and support networks inside virtual environments. The cooperation among metaverse operators, academics, and government is crucial to establishing a secure and protected online environment.

Some scholars recognize the need for explicit legal measures to tackle avatar sex crimes in the metaverse, as existing laws are inadequate. It is advisable to establish restrictions prohibiting avatars from interacting with others beyond a specific distance and introduce new legislation to penalize such offenses. Propose a technique to restrict avatars from interacting with other avatars beyond a specific distance and implement distinct regulations for punishing avatar-related sexual offenses (Lee, 2022).

Some perceive that explicit legal measures are required to address avatar sex crimes in the metaverse, as current laws are insufficient. It is recommended that regulations be implemented that forbid avatars from engaging with others beyond a specified distance and that new laws be enacted to punish such violations. They are suggesting a method to limit avatars from engaging with other avatars beyond a designated distance and enforcing specific rules to penalize sexual offenses involving avatars. C3-Sex is an intelligent chatbot that uses Natural Language Processing to analyze suspects' interest in online child sexual abuse. It can assist in identifying those who are apathetic, intrigued, or perverted in their behavior (Rodriguez et al., 2020).

Some perceive that there is an increasing amount of information that investigates methods to avoid sexual violence in virtual reality (VR) and uses this technology to act constructively. Virtual reality (VR) technologies can be created to educate users, provide bystander interventions, and alter biases and perceptions using embodiment. Additionally, these tools can facilitate the process of recovery for individuals who have experienced sexual abuse within virtual reality environments. Virtual reality (VR) forensic nursing avatars can evaluate the adverse effects of VR and collaborate with private and government entities to shape legislation and policies. This technique can advance health and safety strategies in virtual settings (Porta et al., 2023). (see Figure 18)

*Figure 18.* **Metaverse Crimes**

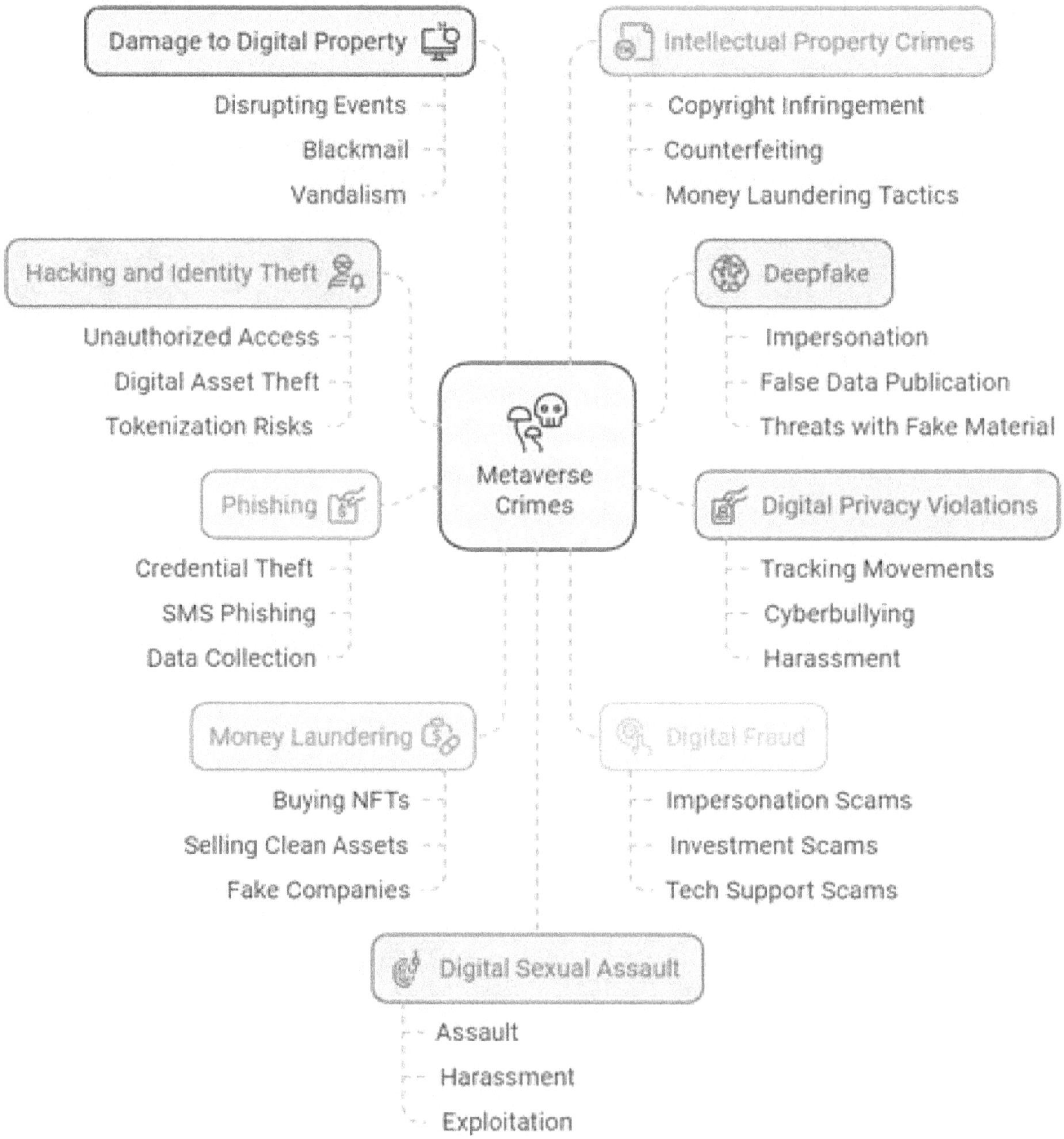

## PART THREE: EXAMINING DIGITAL EVIDENCE IN THE METAVERSE AND INVESTIGATIVE PROCEDURES

Forensic evidence refers to how facts are linked to individuals' conviction or innocence during criminal trials. It is a set of clues through which facts about the crime can be established and the ability to attribute it to a specific offender. Digital evidence is recognized by law to convince the judge of the truth of the incident, and it is obtained from the crime scene. Several legislations have developed a definition of digital evidence, such as the Egyptian legislation, which defines digital evidence as "*any electronic information that has evidentiary value or power that is stored, transmitted, extracted or taken from computers or information networks and the like, it can be collected and analyzed using special technological devices, programs, or applications*." Digital evidence in the metaverse is characterized by several characteristics, including the need for specialized scientific and technical knowledge, its technical nature, its intangible electronic form, its high-speed dynamic, its ability to be retrieved after erasing, repaired after being destroyed, and shown after concealment, and its ability to record the individual's movements, behaviors, and personal matters about them (El-Kady, 2023).

The importance of digital evidence in the metaverse is rooted in the widespread use of technology in various aspects of life and the spread of electrical and technological devices and the Internet. With the widespread use of new technologies, such as IoT, dark web networks, high-level encryption, virtual currencies, and Metaverse technology, the importance of digital evidence in the criminal field is expected to increase. This will require law enforcement agencies to make radical changes in collecting evidence and mechanisms of international cooperation in criminal matters.

The changing moral nature of digital evidence is characterized by its changing moral nature, as the information stored on computers or cloud storage is not always secure and can be easily accessed by criminal justice personnel. As the importance of digital evidence in the metaverse increases, law enforcement agencies need to adapt their methods and mechanisms to ensure the protection and accuracy of this new type of forensic evidence (El-Kady, 2023). (see Figure 19)

*Figure 19. Digital Evidence in the Metaverse*

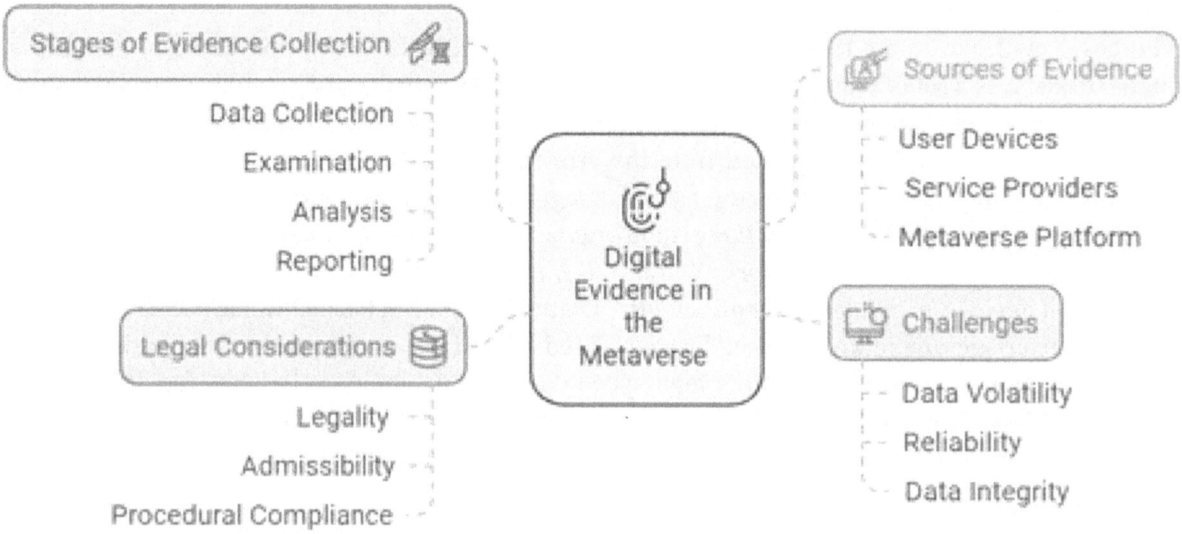


## Investigational Challenges of Metacrimes

The investigation of metacrimes as virtual crimes poses distinct obstacles, which include:

- **Anonymity**: Many individuals use pseudonyms, which makes it challenging to determine their true identities. Legal professionals must start discussing the implications of pseudonymity and anonymity in virtual spaces, which complicate the attribution of crimes to individuals.
- **Jurisdiction**: The worldwide scope of the metaverse adds complexity to determining legal jurisdiction and enforcement. Determining the jurisdiction of crimes committed across multiple virtual platforms is difficult, particularly when they span international borders. International cooperation is needed to establish legal regulations to organize the jurisdiction of these crimes.
- **Evidence Collection:** Collecting digital evidence necessitates using specific equipment and expertise in virtual settings.
- **User Consent:** Potential privacy issues could impede data collection without obtaining user consent. (see Figure 20)

*Figure 20. Challenges in Investigating Virtual Crimes*

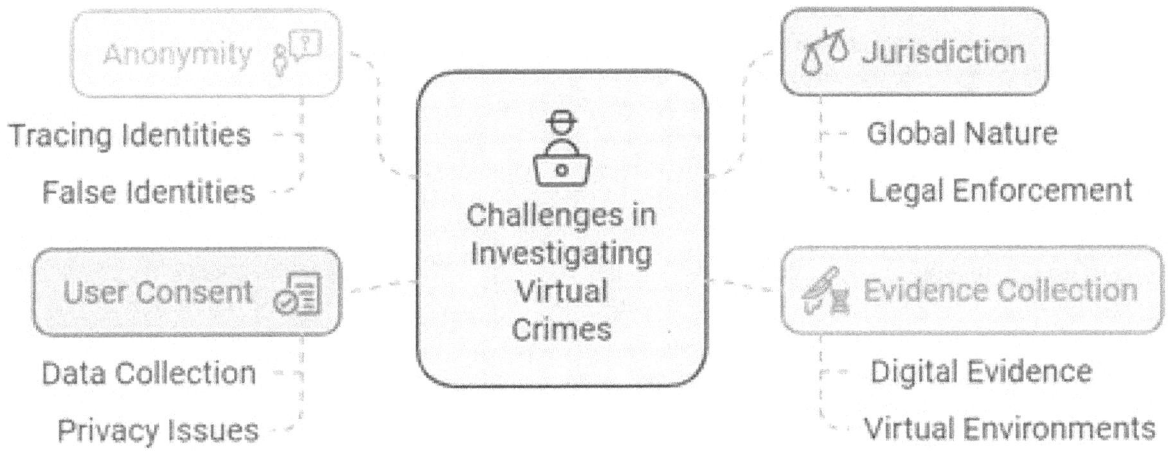


## Proving Evidence in the Metaverse

The successful establishment of evidence in the metaverse necessitates investigators carefully considering various crucial elements.

- **Digital Footprints:** Each activity performed within the metaverse creates a digital footprint. Analyzing logs, transaction histories, and user interactions enables investigators to construct a chronological sequence of events. This information can be crucial in identifying culprits and verifying witness testimonies.
- **Blockchain Technology:** Blockchain technology facilitates transactions in several virtual worlds. The unchangeable nature of this decentralized ledger facilitates the tracking of fraudulent transactions and the establishment of ownership of digital assets.
- **Forensic Analysis:** Digital forensics is crucial in investigating virtual crimes. Specialized software can retrieve erased data, examine virtual environments, and collect evidence from user devices. Professional competence in technological and legal norms is necessary for this procedure.
- **Collaboration with Platforms:** Collaboration with platforms is vital for law enforcement organizations to facilitate access to essential data and resources within the metaverse. Establishing partnerships can expedite responses to crises and improve the overall efficacy of investigations (see Figure 21).

Ultimately, the metaverse offers novel prospects and substantial obstacles in virtual criminal activities. In tandem with technology's ongoing progress, our methodologies for examining and substantiating evidence in digital environments must also evolve. Adopting inventive approaches and promoting stakeholder cooperation is imperative to achieve a safer and more secure metaverse for all users.

*Figure 21.* **Proving Evidence in the Metaverse**

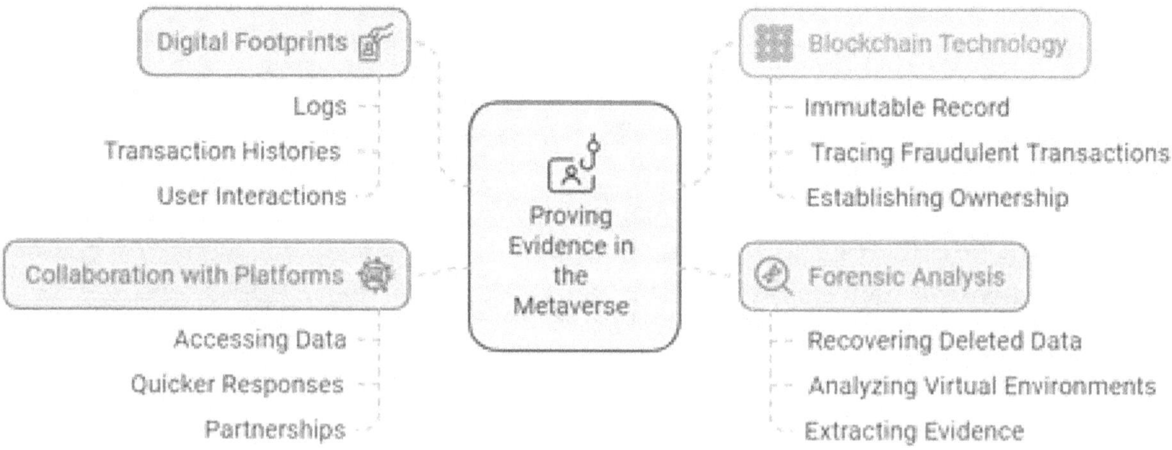


## EXAMINING THE VALIDITY AND ADMISSIBILITY OF DIGITAL EVIDENCE IN FRONT OF A CRIMINAL JUDGE

### Investigating the Digital Evidence in the Metaverse

Investigating the digital evidence in the Metaverse is divided into three stages: data collection, examining and retrieving evidence, data analysis, and preparing reports to present to the court. The first stage involves collecting data on the occurrence of crime in the Metaverse, which requires identifying sources that appear to have evidence, such as physical devices, information systems, or services. Researchers must obtain evidence from these sources and ensure it is in a format that can be easily copied while preserving the original state as an image and the integrity of the data.

Metaverse data may include evidence of traditional crimes in the real world due to the mutual influence between them and the Metaverse. Real-world data is a guide when investigating a case in the Metaverse, so investigators must analyze all evidence from both worlds in some cases. The evidence of Metaverse crimes is divided according to the location of the crime according to four hypotheses:

It is a crime that occurs in the Metaverse, and all evidence is inherently within the Metaverse. A crime that occurs in the Metaverse, and some evidence is outside the Metaverse. A crime that happened in the real world, some of which is evidence from the Metaverse. The crime occurred through the Metaverse and the real world, and the evidence is from both.

The procedures for collecting digital evidence in the Metaverse are particular and linked to the unique nature of this world. The methods include three sources or constituent domains of the Metaverse: user devices, service providers' servers, and the Metaverse platform itself. The user domain contains everything that users in the real world can do, including avatars they control in the Metaverse. The connection layer represents users' connection to the Metaverse and all communication actions, and the interaction layer represents users' interactions in the Metaverse.

External service providers have resorted to providing data related to managing user data, such as financial services and payment services if the service involved in the incident uses its resources. Investigators must request relevant data from the service provider's infrastructure, and the data collection procedure may only be possible when the service provider is legally obligated to provide the data.

The Metaverse platform domain encompasses all functions related to the system or administrator, including the management and data layers. The management layer implements the system that maintains the Metaverse and requires Artificial Intelligence (AI) technology to manage problems that are too significant for humans to handle automatically. In the data layer, technologies such as Blockchain, Edge Computing, and cloud concepts are needed to ensure the integrity and stability of data up to the zettabyte level and beyond in the Metaverse.

The Metaverse contains a volume of data that must be communicated with the user. Data on objects executed in the virtual space and the contents created by the user must be stored and managed in real-time. Due to time and money constraints, long distances, and the possibility of legal problems between countries, investigators should collect data generated by the Metaverse platform through the data management system.

Law enforcement agencies must work on all three levels to obtain evidence about crimes committed in the Metaverse context when collecting data on Metaverse crimes. Examining and retrieving digital proof in the Metaverse involves extracting and evaluating crime-related data elements from the collected raw data set. The collected data may be in a form that cannot transmit meaningful information due to coding or compression, and it also includes neutralizing those that hinder the interpretation of the data.

In the data collection stage, investigators gather different types of data according to the considerations of each domain (the user, service providers, and the Metaverse platform). The method differs for user-domain data, as the data source's operating system and file system interpret the collected data. The data type, directory structure, and file format for service provider domain data can vary depending on the service framework technical stack and local storage provided. Research is required to interpret compressed or encrypted data to protect it or increase storage efficiency. The analysis stage involves analyzing data and evidence extracted from each of the three domains that investigators in the Metaverse work on. Collecting data leads to conclusions about the case, and approval is made during this stage. Prioritization, order of data analysis, and obtained outputs depend on the investigator's intuition and experience. Evidence gathered from different sources in the Metaverse may have meaning in itself. However, new meanings can be created through correlation analyses between it and other outputs obtained from other Metaverse domains (user domain, service domain).

The reporting phase Indicates how to present and explain the conclusion that results from the analysis phase. There is concern about how the evidence in 3D form gathered from the crime scene in Metaverse will be presented to the courts when the 3D data is presented in a 2D paper form, which may raise concerns about losing some information or altering its content. As the meaning of the information can become ambiguous depending on the angle and distance the VR/AR glasses are exposed to, it is necessary to study the methodology and special considerations related to 3D data before it is recognized as evidence in court.

Those in charge of criminal investigations of Metaverse crimes face several challenges, including the reliability of the evidence obtained from Metaverse and the amount and quality of the primary data collected. Within the domain of the Metaverse platform, big and distributed data from Metaverse must be collected selectively, considering time and cost efficiency. Data collection procedures may be opaque, so when presenting evidence in Court, it is necessary to prove the suitability of selective data collection on the Metaverse platform and discuss the reliability of results in the Metaverse world when data is collected selectively using technologies such as machine learning and artificial intelligence (El-Kady, 2024).

Additionally, because the data generated in the Metaverse is more volatile than the data recorded in the real world, and it is impossible to record all of the data that occurs in the Metaverse, it is not easy to develop a technology to monitor tens of thousands of terabytes of data generated in chunks. Suppose Metaverse does not operate a separate logging system or forensic data center for incident responses. In that case, the computing resources of the Metaverse model must be used to investigate incidents or problems. In addition to these challenges, the analysis technology must be fully developed to collect or analyze data from the input or output device while protecting users' privacy in the Metaverse and the extent to which investigators can access information and evidence recorded on screens on the user's head.

Digital evidence is a crucial tool in criminal investigations, and its legality depends on the legitimate means of obtaining it, the implementation of procedures according to the law, and the access to it through free will without any assault on the will of the accused or others. The legality of these procedures must also align with societal moral principles. For instance, the Belgian Court of Cassation ruled that the description of an illegal act is not limited to the act that the law expressly prohibits but includes all acts that contradict fundamental rules of criminal procedures or legal principles.

An American court ruled that law enforcement agencies can collect information about a crime by sharing information with their friends on social networking sites without violating the Fourth Amendment. This decision highlights the importance of maintaining privacy when sharing information with friends, as the more significant the circle of friends, the greater the likelihood that the accused's correspondence will be seen by someone they are not expected to see. The accused's legitimate expectations of maintaining privacy end when publishing his correspondence to his friends, as they are free to use this information however they like, including sharing it with state agencies.

The criminal judiciary in some countries sets rules or standards to assess the acceptability of digital evidence, ensure its reliability, and examine the extent to which it can be relied upon in judicial procedures. The most important rules for determining the admissibility of digital evidence before criminal courts include the need for the court to be sure of the integrity and authenticity of the digital evidence, not to be subjected to any attempt to tamper with it, and the responsibility of the accusing authority to prove that the evidence was initially obtained by a legitimate means.

Those in charge of collecting digital evidence from the crime scene must take necessary measures to preserve its integrity, from its creation to its submission before the court. This includes maintaining the continuity of evidence on the physical devices containing the data (when it was received or captured) and the data stored on the devices.

The investigating authority must present to the court the procedures for preserving the integrity of the digital evidence, indicate the mechanism used to protect the evidence, document its chronological history, and ensure that it has not undergone any change or tampering. The court favors the idea of reliability and trustworthiness of the digital evidence. In conclusion, for digital evidence to be accepted by criminal courts, the evidence collection procedures must be carried out in a manner that guarantees the legal validity of the collection procedures, the preservation of the integrity of the evidence, the non-change of its form, and the continuity of its condition throughout the entire period separating its seizure from its use in the trial.

## Future Developments in Detecting Metacrimes

As societies face increasingly complex cyber dangers, digital crimes, and data integrity concerns, emerging technologies like AI-driven forensics and quantum computing are poised to have crucial roles in ensuring the long-term viability of legal systems.

### 1. Artificial Intelligence-Powered Forensics

Advanced artificial intelligence (AI) forensics has the potential to revolutionize the methods of gathering, examining, and utilizing evidence in judicial processes. AI algorithms can efficiently analyze extensive datasets, such as social media posts, emails, or digital files, to detect patterns or anomalies pertinent to investigations. This helps guarantee that crucial evidence is not disregarded because of its significant quantity. By analyzing behavioral patterns, predictive forensics trains artificial intelligence (AI) to anticipate probable criminal actions. This technology enables preemptive intervention before crimes are committed. Its uses extend to fields including fraud prevention, cybersecurity, and terrorism. Artificial intelligence (AI) can also mitigate human biases in forensic analysis inside legal processes. By utilizing machine learning models for the objective analysis of evidence, legal systems have the potential to enhance their impartiality. The emergence of blockchain technology has enabled the domesticating and verification of digital evidence, guaranteeing its immutability. Subsequently, artificial intelligence would guarantee the integrity and appropriate utilization of this evidence validated by blockchain technology (El-kady, 2024).

### 2. Quantum Computing (QC)

The introduction of quantum computing has the potential to significantly impact legal frameworks, specifically in cybersecurity, intellectual property, and data protection. Quantum computers could undermine existing encryption protocols fundamental to contemporary cybersecurity. As this becomes feasible, legal frameworks must adjust to ensure that data protection rules remain current with advancements in quantum technology. The development of quantum-resistant encryption standards will be necessary. The application of quantum computing can potentially enhance data verification and integrity. Implementing quantum-based techniques in legal systems could enhance the authentication and security of evidence, guaranteeing its integrity and preventing tampering. Quantum computing, through its exceptional processing capabilities, has the potential to augment the effectiveness and expandability of blockchain networks. Smart contracts would profit from this by facilitating more intricate and secure contractual connections, particularly automated ones, revolutionizing legal agreements.

As artificial intelligence and quantum computing progress, legal systems will need to adapt:

In light of AI systems' ability to analyze extensive datasets in real-time and the possibility of quantum computing compromising encryption, strengthening data privacy legislation to safeguard personal information in the emerging technological environment is imperative. The capacity of quantum computing to decrypt encryption and the predictive skills of artificial intelligence could potentially give rise to novel manifestations of cybercrime. Comprehensive legal frameworks should be established to address quantum-enhanced hacking or AI-driven fraud, and after that, legislation should be revised as necessary. The increasing prevalence of autonomous AI systems may intensify legal concerns around accountability, namely determining the party responsible for AI-directed decisions or actions. E

Establishing accountability, particularly in cases of AI mistakes, would necessitate implementing new legislation. Legal frameworks must be modified to incorporate AI-driven forensics and quantum-verified data to maintain the admissibility and verifiability of digital evidence. Blockchain technology has the potential to function as a fundamental support system for preserving the integrity of this data.

## AI-Driven Crime Detection Tools and Blockchain-Based Digital Forensics

The convergence of artificial intelligence (AI) and blockchain in the current dynamic technological environment has created novel opportunities for criminal detection and digital forensics. This study analyzes two novel methodologies to offer valuable perspectives on their potential to improve law enforcement and investigative procedures. Artificial intelligence (AI)-powered crime detection systems and blockchain-based digital forensics provide distinct prospects and obstacles in law enforcement and crime prevention. While artificial intelligence (AI) provides robust capabilities for data analysis and criminal behavior prediction, blockchain technology offers a secure and transparent framework for dealing with digital evidence. With ongoing technological progress, incorporating these applications has the potential to enhance the efficiency and fairness of crime detection and investigation methods. It is crucial for stakeholders to carefully consider the ethical and practical consequences of emerging technologies to optimize their advantages while reducing possible hazards (El-Kady, 2024).

## AI-Driven Crime Detection Tools

Artificial intelligence (AI)-powered crime detection systems use machine learning algorithms and data analytics to spot patterns, forecast criminal behavior, and support law enforcement agencies in generating well-informed recommendations. These programs can analyze vast quantities of data from many sources, such as social media, surveillance footage, and past crime reports, to identify irregularities and possible dangers. Artificial intelligence systems can examine crime data to predict the locations and timing of imminent crimes, enabling law enforcement to spend resources more efficiently.

AI-powered face recognition systems can identify suspects in real-time by comparing photos captured by surveillance cameras with databases containing information on known criminals. Natural Language Processing (NLP) refers to the ability of artificial intelligence (AI) to rapidly process and analyze extensive amounts of textual data, such as police reports and social media posts, to extract pertinent information and detect developing patterns (Dunsin et al., 2024).

The efficiency of AI technologies lies in their ability to handle data at a speed and scale that greatly surpasses human skills, facilitating faster reactions to possible threats. Machine learning models have the potential to enhance their accuracy over time, resulting in more precise predictions and a decrease in false positives in crime detection. Law enforcement may strategically allocate a workforce by predicting crime hotspots and averting crimes before they occur. Artificial intelligence systems have the potential to unintentionally sustain biases in the training data, resulting in the unjust targeting of particular communities. Monitoring and data gathering raises substantial privacy concerns, which require meticulous examination of ethical ramifications. AI methodologies' efficacy significantly depends on the quality and comprehensiveness of the data utilized for training (El-Kady, 2024).

## Blockchain-Based Digital Forensics

Blockchain technology's decentralized and unchangeable ledger can potentially transform digital forensics significantly. By securely and openly storing and authenticating data, blockchain technology can effectively preserve the integrity of evidence and optimize investigative procedures. Data integrity refers to the mechanism of blockchain technology that guarantees the preservation of the authenticity of digital evidence by preventing any modification or deletion of recorded data. Blockchain technology's inherent transparency enables a very transparent and verifiable chain of custody, a critical aspect of legal processes. Automated contracts can optimize the secure exchange of information among parties engaged in an inquiry, hence improving collaboration (Ragu & Ramamoorthy, 2023).

Blockchain technology's decentralized structure renders it impervious to manipulation and cyber threats, guaranteeing the protection of confidential information. Every transaction recorded on a blockchain is readily available to the public, promoting confidence among all parties involved in the investigative procedure. Blockchain technology can optimize the data collection, storage, and sharing procedures, minimizing investigation delays. The growth in data volume can make it difficult for blockchain systems to handle and optimize performance. The regulatory landscape surrounding blockchain technology and its applications in forensics is now undergoing changes, which may give rise to anticipated challenges in terms of compliance. Implementing blockchain technologies necessitates specific expertise and resources, which may not be easily accessible to all law enforcement organizations (El-Kady, 2024).

## The Authoritativeness of the Digital Evidence in Proof

The reliability of digital evidence in criminal courts is crucial, as demonstrated by an American court's appeal regarding the security gaps in operating systems and programs that could threaten the integrity of digital information. The court ruled that computer-generated information, such as log file records, provides details of the activities of the computer, network, and other devices that could be vulnerable if the system generating the information did not contain strong security controls.

The American judiciary relied on five primary conditions for accepting digital evidence: it must be related to the incident to be proven, original, reliable, not tampered with or altered, best presented as an original copy, and not auditory testimony. This approval is due to a case between Lorrinace and Markel American Insurance, an important judicial precedent.

Chat rooms and recordings are stored and transmitted regarding the admissibility of evidence extracted from electronic devices. Digital evidence in criminal proof can be considered authoritative, as it contains numerous pictures, videos, email messages, conversation records, and system data. However, the question arose whether this new digital evidence enjoys the same legal authority as traditional evidence in proving crime despite its moral nature. Legislators have answered this question in anti-information technology legislation by giving it the legal authority prescribed for traditional physical evidence over digital evidence of an intangible nature in criminal evidence. Egyptian legislators have decided that evidence derived or extracted from devices, equipment, media, electronic supports, information systems, computer programs, or any means of information technology has the value and authority of physical forensic evidence in criminal evidence when it meets the technical conditions stipulated in the executive regulations of this law. The Saudi judiciary also took this approach, as the General Authority of the Supreme Court in the Kingdom of Saudi Arabia issued Decision No. 34 of 4/24/1439 AH regarding digital evidence and its validity, which stipulates that digital evidence is a valid argument in proof when it is free from symptoms and varies in strength and weakness according to the incident, its circumstances, and the evidence it contains.

## International Cooperation for Collecting Digital Evidence

International cooperation is crucial in combating digital evidence and Metaverse crimes due to their transnational nature, which often involves the Internet and digital evidence. These crimes are outside the legal jurisdiction of law enforcement agencies, requiring legal rules for cooperation between countries. The unstable nature of digital evidence necessitates quick responses from investigation authorities and strengthening mechanisms for international collaboration on a large scale.

The United Nations Office on Drugs and Crime (UNODC) believes that more than traditional means of formal international cooperation is required to respond promptly to the requirements of obtaining ephemeral and changing digital evidence in multiple locations. Most countries (over 70%) respond to these requests using the formal mutual legal assistance request mechanism, which usually takes about 150 days. This may exceed the data retention period by the service provider or during which the perpetrators can destroy digital evidence.

The unique nature of Metaverse crimes requires rapid investigations characterized by unprecedented experience and cooperation, necessitating law enforcement agencies to cooperate quickly and effectively across national borders. Cloud computing poses an increasing challenge to international cooperation as computer services are increasingly moved to geographically distributed servers and data centers, making it challenging to locate digital evidence.

The principle of territoriality of the criminal rule limits the scope of criminal laws' applicability to the state's territory, resulting in procedural difficulties in confronting these crimes. Most bilateral, regional, and international agreements include provisions requiring mutual judicial assistance to speed up and improve the effectiveness of prosecuting offenders and collecting digital evidence.

International cooperation in combating Metaverse crimes should not be limited to international security cooperation in information exchange and international judicial cooperation in the field of judicial delegation and extradition of criminals. Instead, it requires international cooperation in training security and judicial cadres to detect and investigate Metaverse crimes. The international community has been interested in activating international cooperation in combating cybercrime through various solutions, including the Budapest Agreement, the European Union's framework decision, legislative activities, and capacity-building activities supported by regional international organizations.

## The Role of INTERPOL in Dealing with Digital Evidence

INTERPOL is a global organization that enhances international police cooperation among its 195 member countries by providing field support services, specialized assistance in forensic evidence, and guidance on setting up and maintaining state-of-the-art laboratories. The organization also develops training programs focused on unified curricula and solutions in digital forensics in collaboration with law enforcement agencies, the private sector, and university circles.

INTERPOL combats cybercrimes by preparing publications dealing with digital evidence, such as Global Guidelines for Digital Forensic Laboratories and Guidelines for First Insights in Digital Forensics. These guidelines advise the search, seizure, identification, and treatment of digital evidence, ensuring its integrity for admissibility in judicial proceedings.

INTERPOL organizes several forums related to dealing with digital evidence, such as the INTERPOL Digital Forensics Expert Group Meeting (annual meeting), which is open to specialists and managers from law enforcement agencies, government agencies, digital forensics companies, and university institutions. The study reviewed the issue of digital forensic evidence in the Metaverse era through two parts, focusing on the nature of Metaverse technology and procedures for collecting and extracting evidence obtained from crimes committed within it (El-Kady, 2024).

## Uses of Metaverse Technology in Law Enforcement

In parallel, the importance of using metaverse technology in law enforcement is highlighted in light of successive developments in this technology and its effects on information security. This will require the development of cybersecurity strategies to adapt to address the threats and vulnerabilities arising from the expansion of this technology.

Interpol has paid attention to metaverse technology in light of the emerging risks and challenges that successive technological developments pose. In October 2022, it created a "metaverse expert team" within the organization to provide recommendations and guidance to combat the potential misuse of the metaverse by criminal parties. Effectively, Interpol is using the metaverse as a law enforcement tool.

In addition, Interpol launched a virtual version of its headquarters in Lyon, France, within the metaverse technology, allowing registered users to explore it without any geographical or physical restrictions. Interpol indicates that as metaverse technologies develop, officers concerned with member countries can interact with their counterparts through their photos, symbolism, and participation in meetings and training courses on police capabilities.

On a parallel level, in January 2024, Interpol issued an official report (white book/white paper) on (The Metaverse from a Law Enforcement Perspective "Use Cases, Crime, Forensics, Investigation and Governance"). These efforts made by Interpol indicate its endeavor to provide guidance for the global law enforcement community and coordinate an effective response to keep this virtual world safe and secure in light of the threats and damage expected to arise from metaverse technology.

## Areas of Use of Metaverse Technology in Police Work

Interpol believes that metaverse technology can be used to serve justice and law enforcement agencies. The future vision is to adapt this technology to serve justice and law enforcement, given that metaverse technology is transforming the law enforcement landscape by providing innovative tools for augmented reality, virtual reality, and extended reality. These advanced virtual reality solutions use spatial awareness and awareness to create an immersive workspace for law enforcement through a 3D user interface. These tools leverage humans' natural spatial reasoning and memory abilities, providing investigators with a unique way to address complex cognitive challenges. This revolutionary approach is poised to reshape how law enforcement agencies approach complex cases, bringing a new perspective and increased clarity to investigations.

The most prominent security areas in which metaverse technology can be used are Developing police training, enhancing police cooperation by holding virtual meetings, Supporting the crime scene analysis system, providing technical support to law enforcement agencies, providing public services, and receiving reports and complaints, Planning for security crises and disasters, command and control in the theater of operations using metaverses and drones.

Finally, Advocates argue that in the foreseeable future, the Metaverse will become an integral aspect of daily life, as people will use online 3D virtual environments for work, education, social interaction, entertainment, and even vital services such as banking and healthcare, much as how people now use smartphones to access the digital realm. Naturally, the ambitious vision for the future of the Metaverse, propelled mainly by major technology companies, relies on several technological breakthroughs in areas such as augmented reality, virtual reality, mixed reality (MR), edge computing, artificial intelligence (AI), 5G, blockchain, Non-Fungible Tokens (NFTs), and other decentralized applications. This Future development will affect the increasing growth of metacrime types, emphasizing the need for global collaboration in combating metaverse crimes and the development of international treaties specific to virtual environments.

## CONCLUSION

The study indicates that the emergence of Metaverse technology as a virtual world parallel to the real world has led to speculation that it could be misused for cybercrime and violating user privacy. Legal texts regulating the use of this technology and confronting new forms of cybercrime committed during it are absent. The metaverse presents numerous challenges and concerns, including privacy, data protection, and security. The metaverse offers novel prospects and substantial obstacles to virtual criminal activities. In tandem with technology's ongoing progress, our methodologies for examining and substantiating evidence in digital environments must also evolve.

Adopting inventive approaches and promoting stakeholder cooperation is imperative to achieve a safer and more secure metaverse for all users. The unique nature of Metaverse crimes requires rapid investigations characterized by unprecedented experience and collaboration, necessitating law enforcement agencies to cooperate quickly and effectively across national borders. Interpol had an essential initiative to empower international cooperation efforts to combat metacrimes and avoid related challenges.

The integration of AI-driven forensics and quantum computing is significantly influencing the future of judicial systems, guaranteeing their resilience in the face of ever-changing technical challenges. This transition necessitates the proactive formulation of legislation incorporating developing technologies to guarantee security, equity, and responsibility. There is an urgent need for global collaboration in combating Metaverse crimes, and the development of international treaties specific to virtual environments would

The study recommends updating legislative frameworks to make them more suitable for application in the virtual environment provided by metaverse technology, including collecting and processing data through virtual reality systems. International efforts are needed to amend international conventions on cybercrime, particularly the Budapest Convention, or develop a new global agreement that regulates the responsibility of Metaverse service providers and obliges them to comply with cooperation in combating crimes, following up on infringements and violations, exchanging evidence and information related to these cases, and identifying applicable laws and controls based on them.

The author calls on the Arab Parliament to update the provisions of the 2010 Arab Convention on Combating Information Technology Crimes to ensure that new forms of cybercrime, Metaverse crimes, are confronted. Strengthening international judicial and security cooperation and facilitating the exchange of information between countries is necessary to reduce the types of Metaverse crimes, especially in countries where servers operate this new technology. Building an international network of law enforcement experts to exchange experiences will help develop knowledge faster and more efficiently.

## REFERENCES


A, J., Khanum, A., A, S., S, A., Latheef, A., & S, D. (2023). METAVERSE. *International Journal of Innovative Research in Information Security*. https://doi.org/.DOI: 10.26562/ijiris.2023.v0903.29

Abdel Majeed, O. (2023, September). Metaverse Technology in The Criminal Justice System: "Reality and Hope," (Muskat: Sultan Qaboos University). *Journal of Sultan Qaboos University for Legal Studies*, 2(1), 75–106.

Abdel Sadik, A. (2022, January). What impact does the Metaverse have on the human future in the digital age? Future Horizons Magazine. *Information and Decision Support Center of the Egyptian Council of Ministers*, (2), 401–408.

Al-Marri, B. (2022). Social Media Crimes (Cairo: Dar Al-Ahram for Legal Publications).

Ali, A., & Khalifa, M. (2023). Critical Analysis of The Legal Elements of Crimes Committed in the Metaverse in Light of The Egyptian Criminal Law. *International Journal of Doctrine. Judiciary and Legislation*, 4(2), 737–757.

Annison, T. (2022). The Future of Financial Crime in the Metaverse. Fighting Crypto-crime in Web3. 0. *Elliptic Metaverse Report 2022*.

Bibri, S. E., & Allam, Z. (2022). The Metaverse as a virtual form of data-driven smart urbanism: On post-pandemic governance through the prism of the logic of surveillance capitalism. *Smart Cities, 5*(2).

Bovenzi, G. (2023). MetaCrimes: Criminal accountability for conducts in the Metaverse. *Companion Proceedings of the ACM Web Conference 2023*. https://doi.org/DOI: 10.1145/3543873.3587535

Bu, Q. (2019). Reassess the Law and Ethics of Heritable Genome Editing Interventions: Lessons for China and the World. *Issues in Law & Medicine*, 34(2), 115–145. PMID: 33950602

BÜYÜKBAYKAL, A., & Sönmezer, Z. (2022). The Relationship Between Metaverse and Social Life. *Uluslararası Kültürel ve Sosyal Araştırmalar Dergisi (UKSAD)*. https://doi.org/.DOI: 10.46442/int-jcss.1099798

Camber, R. (2024). British police probe VIRTUAL rape in metaverse: Young girl's digital persona is sexually attacked by a gang of adult men in immersive video game'-sparking the first investigation of its kind and questions about the extent current laws apply in the online world. *Daily Mail*.

Citi, G. P. S. (2022). Metaverse and Money, Decrypting the Future. *Citi ICG.(2022-03-03)[2022-10-08]*. https://icg. citi. com/icghome/what-we-think/citigps/insights/metaverse-and-money_20220330

Crespo-Pereira, V., Sánchez-Amboage, E., & Membiela-Pollán, M. (2023). Facing the challenges of metaverse: A systematic literature review from Social Sciences and Marketing and Communication. *El Profesional de la Información*, e320102. Advance online publication. DOI: 10.3145/epi.2023.ene.02

Duan, H., Li, J., Fan, S., Lin, Z., Wu, X., & Cai, W. (2021). Metaverse for Social Good: A University Campus Prototype. *Proceedings of the 29th ACM International Conference on Multimedia*. https://doi.org/DOI: 10.1145/3474085.3479238

Dunsin, D., Ghanem, M. C., Ouazzane, K., & Vassilev, V. (2024). A comprehensive analysis of the role of artificial intelligence and machine learning in modern digital forensics and incident response. *Forensic Science International Digital Investigation*, 48, 301675. DOI: 10.1016/j.fsidi.2023.301675

Dwivedi, Y. K., Kshetri, N., Hughes, L., Rana, N. P., Baabdullah, A. M., Kar, A. K., Koohang, A., Ribeiro-Navarrete, S., Belei, N., Balakrishnan, J., Basu, S., Behl, A., Davies, G. H., Dutot, V., Dwivedi, R., Evans, L., Felix, R., Foster-Fletcher, R., Giannakis, M., & Yan, M. (2023). Exploring the darkverse: A multi-perspective analysis of the negative societal impacts of the metaverse. *Information Systems Frontiers*, 25(5), 2071–2114. DOI: 10.1007/s10796-023-10400-x PMID: 37361890

El-Kady, R. (2023). Handling E-evidence in Egyptian and Comparative Legislation: A Comparative Analytical Study. *Arab Journal of Forensic Sciences & Forensic Medicine*, 6(1), 37–68. DOI: 10.26735/WGZY6322

El-Kady, R. (2024). Artificial Intelligence and Criminal Law. In Tavares, M., Azevedo, G., Vale, J., Marques, R., & Bastos, M. (Eds.), *Artificial Intelligence Approaches to Sustainable Accounting* (pp. 34–52). IGI Global., DOI: 10.4018/979-8-3693-0847-9.ch003

El-Kady, R. (2024). Investigating Forensic Evidence in Metaverse: A Comparative Analytical Study. In Elshenraki, H. (Ed.), *Forecasting Cyber Crimes in the Age of the Metaverse* (pp. 227–258). IGI Global., DOI: 10.4018/979-8-3693-0220-0.ch012

El-Kady, R. (2024). Navigating the Legal Maze: Electric Self-Driving Cars and the Complexities of Criminal Law. In Shaik, M. (Ed.), *Solving Fundamental Challenges of Electric Vehicles* (pp. 215–247). IGI Global., DOI: 10.4018/979-8-3693-4314-2.ch009

Elshenraki, H. (2024). Forecasting Cyber Crime in the Metaverse Era: Future Criminal Methods - Readiness Requirements. In Elshenraki, H. (Ed.), *Forecasting Cyber Crimes in the Age of the Metaverse* (pp. 1–23). IGI Global., DOI: 10.4018/979-8-3693-0220-0.ch001

Europol (2022), Policing in the metaverse: what law enforcement needs to know, an observatory report from the Europol Innovation Lab, Publications Office of the European Union, Luxembourg.

Falchuk, B., Loeb, S., & Neff, R. (2018). The social metaverse: The battle for privacy. *IEEE Technology and Society Magazine*, 37(2), 52–61. DOI: 10.1109/MTS.2018.2826060

Gómez-Quintero, J., Johnson, S. D., Borrion, H., & Lundrigan, S. (2024). A scoping study of crime facilitated by the metaverse. *Futures*, 157, 103338. DOI: 10.1016/j.futures.2024.103338

Gupta, R., & Pal, S. K. (2023). Concept of Metaverse. In *Introduction to Metaverse: Technology Landscape, Applications, and Challenges* (pp. 1–21). Springer Nature Singapore. DOI: 10.1007/978-981-99-7397-2_1

Hamurcu, A. (2022). The metaverse, online communities, and (real) urban space. *Urbani Izziv*, 33(2), 73–81. Advance online publication. DOI: 10.5379/urbani-izziv-en-2022-33-02-01

Huq, N., Reyes, R., Lin, P., & Swimmer, M. (2022). *Cybersecurity threats against the Internet of Experiences*. Trend Micro Research.

Innocente, C., Nonis, F., Ruggieri, R., Ulrich, L., & Vezzetti, E. (2024). A Metaverse Platform for Preserving and Promoting Intangible Cultural Heritage. *Applied Sciences (Basel, Switzerland)*, 14(8), 3426. DOI: 10.3390/app14083426

INTERPOL. (2024). *Metaverse: A law enforcement perspective*. INTERPOL. https://www.interpol.int/content/download/20828/file/Metaverse%20-%20a%20law%20enforcement%20perspective.pdf. Accessed 4 Feb 2024.

Jibril, M. (2023). The Legal Challenges of Metaverse Technology from the Criminal Point of View (Cairo: Dar Al-Ahram for Legal Publications).

Khalifa, E. (2022). The Metaverse of the Future of Human Urbanization in a Post-Internet World (Abu Dhabi: The Future Center for Research and Advanced Studies), Dirasat Series, Issue 17, November 2022.

Khalifa, E. (2024). Potential Threats: Extremism and Terrorism in the Metaverse. In Elshenraki, H. (Ed.), *Forecasting Cyber Crimes in the Age of the Metaverse* (pp. 171–181). IGI Global., DOI: 10.4018/979-8-3693-0220-0.ch009

Kim, D., Oh, S., & Shon, T. (2023). Digital forensic approaches for metaverse ecosystems. *Forensic Science International Digital Investigation*, 46, 301608. DOI: 10.1016/j.fsidi.2023.301608

Kostenko, O., Zhuravlov, D., Dniprov, O., & Korotiuk, O. (2023). METAVERSE: MODEL CRIMINAL CODE. *Baltic Journal of Economic Studies*. https://doi.org/.DOI: 10.30525/2256-0742/2023-9-4-134-147

Lee, D. (2022). A Study on the Countermeasures of Avatar Sex Crime. *Forum of Public Safety and Culture*. https://doi.org/.DOI: 10.52902/kjsc.2022.19.155

Lee, J., & Min, H. (2022). *Review of legal protection measures against security threats related to Metaverse*. Korean Association of Public Safety and Criminal Justice., DOI: 10.21181/KJPC.2022.31.3.321

Lee, L. H. (2021). All one needs to know about metaverse: A complete survey on technological singularity, virtual ecosystem, and research agenda. *arXiv preprint arXiv:2110.05352.*

Lee, W. (2022). *A Study on the Role of Criminal Law in Metaverse*. Institute for Legal Studies Chonnam National University., DOI: 10.38133/cnulawreview.2022.42.3.177

Lin, K., Wu, J., Lin, D., & Zheng, Z. (2023). A Survey on Metaverse: Applications, Crimes and Governance. *2023 IEEE International Conference on Metaverse Computing, Networking and Applications (MetaCom)*, 541–549. https://doi.org/DOI: 10.1109/MetaCom57706.2023.00097

Maathuis, C., Kerkhof, I., Godschalk, R., & Passier, H. (2023). Design Lessons from Building Deep Learning Disinformation Generation and Detection Solutions. *European Conference on Cyber Warfare and Security*, 285-293. DOI: 10.34190/eccws.22.1.1071

Marshall, A. M., & Tompsett, B. C. (2023). The metaverse—Not a new frontier for crime. *WIREs Forensic Science*, 1505. Advance online publication. DOI: 10.1002/wfs2.1505

Petrigna, L., & Musumeci, G. (2022). The Metaverse: A New Challenge for the Healthcare System: A Scoping Review. *Journal of Functional Morphology and Kinesiology*, 7(3), 63. Advance online publication. DOI: 10.3390/jfmk7030063 PMID: 36135421

Phillips, K., Davidson, J. C., Farr, R. R., Burkhardt, C., Caneppele, S., & Aiken, M. P. (2022). Conceptualizing cybercrime: Definitions, typologies and taxonomies. *Forensic Science*, 2(2), 379–398. DOI: 10.3390/forensicsci2020028

Porta, C., Frerich, E., Hoffman, S., Bauer, S., Jain, V., & Bradley, C. (2023). Sexual Violence in Virtual Reality: A Scoping Review. *Journal of Forensic Nursing*. Advance online publication. DOI: 10.1097/JFN.0000000000000466 PMID: 38093420

Qin, H., Wang, Y., & Hui, P. (2022). Identity, Crimes, and Law Enforcement in the Metaverse. *ArXiv*, abs/2210.06134. https://doi.org//arXiv.2210.06134.DOI: 10.48550

Ragu, G., & Ramamoorthy, S. (2023). A blockchain-based cloud forensics architecture for privacy leakage prediction with cloud. *Healthcare Analytics*, 4, 100220. DOI: 10.1016/j.health.2023.100220

Ritterbusch, G. D., & Teichmann, M. R. (2023). Defining the metaverse: A systematic literature review. *IEEE Access : Practical Innovations, Open Solutions*, 11, 12368–12377. DOI: 10.1109/ACCESS.2023.3241809

Riva, G., Wiederhold, B., & Mantovani, F. (2023). Searching for the Metaverse: Neuroscience of Physical and Digital Communities. *Cyberpsychology, Behavior, and Social Networking*. Advance online publication. DOI: 10.1089/cyber.2023.0040 PMID: 37057986

Rodriguez, J., Durán, S., Díaz-López, D., Pastor-Galindo, J., & Mármol, F. (2020). C3-Sex: A Conversational Agent to Detect Online Sex Offenders. *Electronics (Basel)*, 9(11), 1779. Advance online publication. DOI: 10.3390/electronics9111779

Seo, S., Seok, B., & Lee, C. (2023). Digital forensic investigation framework for the metaverse. *The Journal of Supercomputing*, 79(9), 9467–9485. DOI: 10.1007/s11227-023-05045-1

Singh, C. (2024). Artificial intelligence and deep learning: Considerations for financial institutions for compliance with the regulatory burden in the United Kingdom. *Journal of Financial Crime*, 31(2), 259–266. DOI: 10.1108/JFC-01-2023-0011

*The Information and Decision Support Center of the Egyptian Council of Ministers*. (2022). World Trends - Metaverse World.

Tucci, L. (2024, March 22). *What is the metaverse? An explanation and in-depth guide*. WhatIs. https://www.techtarget.com/whatis/feature/The-metaverse-explained-Everything-you-need-to-know

United States v. Meregildo, No. 11 Cr. 576 WHP, 2012 WL 3264501, at *2 S.D.N.Y. Aug. 10, 2012.

Wang, H., Ning, H., Lin, Y., Wang, W., Dhelim, S., Farha, F., Ding, J., & Daneshmand, M. (2023). A Survey on the Metaverse: The State-of-the-Art, Technologies, Applications, and Challenges. *IEEE Internet of Things Journal*, 10(16), 14671–14688. DOI: 10.1109/JIOT.2023.3278329

Wang, Y., Su, Z., Zhang, N., Liu, D., Xing, R., Luan, T., & Shen, X. (2022). A Survey on Metaverse: Fundamentals, Security, and Privacy. *IEEE Communications Surveys and Tutorials*, 25(1), 319–352. DOI: 10.1109/COMST.2022.3202047

Wu, C., & Li, Y. (2023). The Metaverse: Exploring the Convergence of Technologies and Social Dynamics. *2023 IEEE 43rd International Conference on Distributed Computing Systems Workshops (ICDCSW)*, 121-126. https://doi.org/DOI: 10.1109/ICDCSW60045.2023.00019

Wu, J., Lin, K., Lin, D., Zheng, Z., Huang, H., & Zheng, Z. (2022). Financial Crimes in Web3-Empowered Metaverse: Taxonomy, Countermeasures, and Opportunities. *IEEE Open Journal of the Computer Society*, 4, 37–49. DOI: 10.1109/OJCS.2023.3245801

Zhou, Y., Tiwari, M., Bernot, A., & Lin, K. (2024). Metacrime and Cybercrime: Exploring the Convergence and Divergence in Digital Criminality. *Asian Journal of Criminology*, 19(3), 1–21. DOI: 10.1007/s11417-024-09436-y

# Compilation of References


Abd El-Latif, A. A., Tawalbeh, L., Mohanty, M., Gupta, B., & Psannis, K. E. (Eds.). (2025). *Digital forensics and cyber crime investigation: Recent advances and future directions* (1st ed.). CRC Press.

Abdel Majeed, O. (2023, September). Metaverse Technology in The Criminal Justice System: "Reality and Hope," (Muskat: Sultan Qaboos University). *Journal of Sultan Qaboos University for Legal Studies*, 2(1), 75–106.

Abdel Sadik, A. (2022, January). What impact does the Metaverse have on the human future in the digital age? Future Horizons Magazine. *Information and Decision Support Center of the Egyptian Council of Ministers*, (2), 401–408.

Abidin, A. Z., & Rachma, I. (2018). Etnografi Virtual Sebagai Teknik Pengumpulan Data Dan Metode Penelitian. *The Journal of Society & Media*, 2(2), 130–145. https://journal.unesa.ac.id/index.php/jsm/index. DOI: 10.26740/jsm.v2n2.p130-145

Acquisti, A., Brandimarte, L., & Loewenstein, G. (2015). Privacy and Human Behavior in the Age of Information. *Science*, 347(6221), 509–514. DOI: 10.1126/science.aaa1465 PMID: 25635091

Adel, M. (2023). The Role of Metaverse to Create an Interactive Experience for Tourists. *Journal of Association of Arab Universities for Tourism and Hospitality*, 24(1), 242–269. DOI: 10.21608/ja-auth.2023.216690.1473

Adewojo, A. A., & Bass, J. M. (2023). A Novel Weight-Assignment Load Balancing Algorithm for Cloud Applications. *SN Computer Science*, 4(3), 1–17. DOI: 10.1007/s42979-023-01702-7

Adomaitis, L., Grinbaum, A., & Lenzi, D. (2022). Identification and specification of potential ethical issues and impacts and analysis of ethical issues Analysis of ethical issues D2.2 Identification and specification of potential ethical issues and impacts and analysis of ethical issues. *TechEthos D2.2, 101006249*. DOI: 10.31009/InDret.2024.i2.03

Agarwal, A., & Alathur, S. (2023). Metaverse Revolution and the Digital Transformation: Intersectional Analysis of Industry 5.0. *Transforming Government*, 17(4), 688–707. DOI: 10.1108/TG-03-2023-0036

Aggarwal, K., Singh, S. K., Chopra, M., & Kumar, S. (2022). Role of social media in the COVID-19 pandemic: A literature review. In B. B. Gupta, D. Peraković, A. A. Abd El-Latif, & D. Gupta (Eds.), Advanced computer science applications (pp. [1-19]). IGI Global. https://doi.org/DOI: 10.4018/978-1-7998-8413-2.ch004

Aggarwal, T., Kumar, S., Singh, S. K., Gupta, B. B., Nedjah, N., & Castiglione, A. (2024). Zero Knowledge Proofs and Their Applications in Cryptography: Advancements, Challenges, and Future Aspects. In *Innovations in Modern Cryptography* (pp. 55–74). IGI Global Scientific Publishing. DOI: 10.4018/979-8-3693-5330-1.ch003

Aggarwal, K., Singh, S. K., Chopra, M., Kumar, S., & Colace, F. (2022). Deep Learning in Robotics for Strengthening Industry 4.0.: Opportunities, Challenges and Future Directions. In Nedjah, N., Abd El-Latif, A. A., Gupta, B. B., & Mourelle, L. M. (Eds.), *Robotics and AI for Cybersecurity and Critical Infrastructure in Smart Cities* (pp. 1–19). Springer International Publishing., DOI: 10.1007/978-3-030-96737-6_1

Akin, I., & Akın, M. (2024). Valuation, Accounting Principles, and Classification of Assets in the Metaverse. *Journal of Metaverse*, 4(1), 43–53. DOI: 10.57019/jmv.1412352

Al Khaldy, M. A., Al-Qerem, A., Aldweesh, A., & Alauthman, M. (2024, September 01). Mohammad, Al, Khaldy., Ahmad, Al–Qerem., Amjad, Aldweesh., Mohammad, Alauthman. (2024). A general framework for metaverse based on parallel computing and HPC. *Indonesian Journal of Electrical Engineering and Computer Science*, 35(3), 1895. Advance online publication. DOI: 10.11591/ijeecs.v35.i3.pp1895-1905

Alamsyah, A., Bratawisnu, M. K., & Sanjani, P. H. (2018). Finding Pattern in Dynamic Network Analysis. *2018 6th International Conference on Information and Communication Technology (ICoICT)*, 141–146. DOI: 10.1109/ICoICT.2018.8528779

Aldawood, H., & Skinner, G. (2019). Reviewing Cyber Security Social Engineering Training and Awareness Programs—Pitfalls and Ongoing Issues. *Future Internet*, 11(3), 73. DOI: 10.3390/fi11030073

Alhakimi, H. (2023). Development of the Metaverse and Learning. *Ijolii*, 1(01), 17–21. DOI: 10.20961/ijolii.v1i01.918

Ali, A., & Khalifa, M. (2023). Critical Analysis of The Legal Elements of Crimes Committed in the Metaverse in Light of The Egyptian Criminal Law. *International Journal of Doctrine. Judiciary and Legislation*, 4(2), 737–757.

Ali, S. A., & Khan, R. (2023). Metaverse Marketing vs Digital Marketing. *Inter-national Journal of Innovative Science and Research Technology*, 8(1), 385–388.

Al-kfairy, M. (2024). *Unveiling the Metaverse: A Survey of User Experience, Social Dynamics, and Technological Interoperability*. DOI: 10.20944/preprints202402.0785.v1

Allam, Z., Sharifi, A., Bibri, S. E., Jones, D., & Krogstie, J. (2022). The Metaverse as a Virtual Form of Smart Cities: Opportunities and Challenges for Environmental, Economic, and Social Sustainability in Urban Futures. *Smart Cities*, 5(3), 771–801. DOI: 10.3390/smartcities5030040

Al-Marri, B. (2022). Social Media Crimes (Cairo: Dar Al-Ahram for Legal Publications).

Alnsour, M. (2018). Social Media Effect on Purchase Intention: Jordanian Airline Industry. *Journal of Internet Banking and Commerce*, 23(2), 20–28.

Alpala, L. O., Quiroga-Parra, D. J., Torres, J. C., & Peluffo-Ordóñez, D. H. (2022). Smart factory using virtual reality and online multi-user: Towards a metaverse for experimental frameworks. *Applied Sciences (Basel, Switzerland)*, 12(12), 6258. DOI: 10.3390/app12126258

Amazon Web Services. (2015), Introduction to AWS Security by Design, Retrieved from https://reciprocity.com/resources/what-is-security-by-design/

Amiryousefi, M., Amirian, Z., & Ansari, A. (2023). Relationship between classroom environment, teacher behavior, cognitive and emotional engagement, and state motivation. *Journal of English Language Teaching and Learning, Volume, Page Range.*https://doi.org/[DOI]

Annison, T. (2022). The Future of Financial Crime in the Metaverse. Fighting Crypto-crime in Web3. 0. *Elliptic Metaverse Report 2022*.

Ao, M., Dong, M., Chu, B., Zeng, X., & Li, C. (2019). Revealing the User Behavior Pattern Using HN-CORS RTK Location Big Data. *IEEE Access : Practical Innovations, Open Solutions*, 7, 30302–30312. DOI: 10.1109/ACCESS.2019.2902577

Aria, R., Archer, N., Khanlari, M., & Shah, B. (2023, March 30). Influential Factors in the Design and Development of a Sustainable Web3/Metaverse and Its Applications. *Future Internet*, 15(4), 131–131. DOI: 10.3390/fi15040131

Aririguzoh, S. A. (2022, March 23). Communication competencies, culture and SDGs: Effective processes to cross-cultural communication. *Humanities & Social Sciences Communications*, 9(1), 96. Advance online publication. DOI: 10.1057/s41599-022-01109-4

Arowolo, M. O., Misra, S., & Ogundokun, R. O. (2023). A machine learning technique for detection of social media fake news. *International Journal on Semantic Web and Information Systems*, 19(1), 1–25. Advance online publication. DOI: 10.4018/IJSWIS.326120

Askarizad, R., & Safari, H. (2020). The influence of social interactions on the behavioral patterns of the people in urban spaces (case study: The pedestrian zone of Rasht Municipality Square, Iran). *Cities (London, England)*, 101, 102687. https://doi.org/https://doi.org/10.1016/j.cities.2020.102687. DOI: 10.1016/j.cities.2020.102687

Atzori, M. (2017). Blockchain Technology and Decentralized Governance: Is The State Still Necessary? *Journal of Governance and Regulation*, 6(1), 45–62. Advance online publication. DOI: 10.22495/jgr_v6_i1_p5

*Axie Infinity Monthly players*. [Dataset]. https://prioridata.com/data/axie-infinity-users/#:~:text=Axie%20Infinity%20Key%20Stats,Axies%20to%20play%20and%20earn

Azizi, S., Zandsalimi, M., & Li, D. (2021). An energy-efficient algorithm for virtual machine placement optimization in cloud data centers. *Automation in Construction*, 122, 103441. https://doi.org/https://doi.org/10.1016/j.autcon.2020.103441

Bahuguna, A. (2022). Intellectual Property and Metaverse. [IJSR]. *International Journal of Science and Research (Raipur, India)*, 11(9), 371–374. DOI: 10.21275/SR22905165231

Bainbridge, W. S. (2012). *The Warcraft civilization: Social science in a virtual world.* MIT Press.

Balkin, J. M. (2017, August 27). *The Three Laws of Robotics in the Age of Big Data*. Papers.*ssrn*.com. https://papers.ssrn.com/sol3/papers.cfm?abstract_id=2890965

Ball, M. (2022). *The Metaverse: And How it Will Revolutionize Everything*. Liveright. DOI: 10.15358/9783800669400

Banaeian Far, S., & Imani Rad, A. (2024). All Things will be Dominated/Controlled by Humans' Imaginations in the Next Generation of Internet of Brains. *Wireless Personal Communications*, 137(2), 795–811. DOI: 10.1007/s11277-024-11053-y

Bandura, A. (1986). Social foundations of thought and action. *Englewood Cliffs, NJ, 1986*(23-28), 2.

Bandura, A. (1977). *Social learning theory. Englewood Cliffs*. Prentice-Hall.

Bardzell, J., Pace, T., & Terrell, J. (2010). Virtual fashion and avatar design: A survey of consumers and designers. *Proceedings of the 6th Nordic Conference on Human-Computer Interaction: Extending Boundaries*, 599–602. DOI: 10.1145/1868914.1868983

Barrera, K. G., & Shah, D. (2023). Marketing in the Metaverse: Conceptual understanding, framework, and research agenda. *Journal of Business Research*, 155, 113420. DOI: 10.1016/j.jbusres.2022.113420

Berscheid, E., & Walster, E. (1974). Physical Attractiveness. *Advances in Experimental Social Psychology*, 7, 157–215. DOI: 10.1016/S0065-2601(08)60037-4

Bharany, S., Kaur, K., Badotra, S., Rani, S., Kavita, , Wozniak, M., Shafi, J., & Ijaz, M. F. (2022, July 02). Kavita, Wozniak, M., … Ijaz, M. F. (2022). Efficient Middleware for the Portability of PaaS Services Consuming Applications among Heterogeneous Clouds. *Sensors (Basel)*, 22(13), 5013. Advance online publication. DOI: 10.3390/s22135013 PMID: 35808508

Bhattacharya, P., Saraswat, D., Savaliya, D., Sanghavi, S., Verma, A., Sakariya, V., Tanwar, S., Sharma, R., Răboaca, M. S., & Manea, D. L. (2023). Towards Future Internet: The Metaverse Perspective for Diverse Industrial Applications. *Mathematics*, 11(4), 941. DOI: 10.3390/math11040941

Bhatt, S., Pham, T. K., Gupta, M., Benson, J., Park, J., & Sandhu, R. (2021). Attribute-Based Access Control for AWS Internet of Things and Secure Industries of the Future. *IEEE Access : Practical Innovations, Open Solutions*, 9, 107200–107223. DOI: 10.1109/ACCESS.2021.3101218

Bibri, S. E., & Allam, Z. (2022). The Metaverse as a virtual form of data-driven smart urbanism: On post-pandemic governance through the prism of the logic of surveillance capitalism. *Smart Cities, 5*(2).

Binns, R. (2018). Fairness in machine learning: Lessons from political philosophy. *Proceedings of the 2018 Conference on Fairness, Accountability, and Transparency*, 149-159.

Biocca, F., Harms, C., & Burgoon, J. K. (2003). Toward a more robust theory and measure of social presence: Review and suggested criteria. *Presence (Cambridge, Mass.)*, 12(5), 456–480. DOI: 10.1162/105474603322761270

Bisht, J., & Vampugani, V. S. (2022). Load and cost-aware min-min workflow scheduling algorithm for heterogeneous resources in fog, cloud, and edge scenarios. [IJCAC]. *International Journal of Cloud Applications and Computing*, 12(1), 1–20. DOI: 10.4018/IJCAC.2022010105

Blackwell, L., Ellison, N. B., Elliott-Deflo, N., & Schwartz, R. (2019). Harassment in Social Virtual Reality. *Proceedings of the Acm on Human-Computer Interaction, 3*(CSCW), 1–25. DOI: 10.1145/3359202

Blackwood, G. (2023). *Roblox and Meta Verch*. M/C Journal., DOI: 10.5204/mcj.2958

Blascovich, J., Loomis, J., Beall, A. C., Swinth, K. R., Hoyt, C. L., & Bailenson, J. N. (2002). Immersive virtual environment technology as a methodological tool for social psychology. *Psychological Inquiry*, 13(2), 103–124. DOI: 10.1207/S15327965PLI1302_01

Blikstein, P. (2013). Digital fabrication and 'making' in education: The democratization of invention. In Büching, C., & Walter-Herrmann, J. (Eds.), *FabLabs: Of machines, makers and inventors* (pp. 203–220). Transcript Publishers., DOI: 10.14361/transcript.9783839423820.203

Bloomberg. (2022). Metaverse's $80 billion etf assets by 2024 virtually a reality. Accessed 23.05.23 (https://www.bloomberg.com/professional/blog/metaverses80-billion-etf-assets-by-2024-virtually-a-reality/)

Bode, M., & Kristensen, D. B. (2016). The digital doppelgänger within: A study on self-tracking and the quantified self movement. In Canniford, R., & Bajde, D. (Eds.), *Assembling Consumption* (pp. 119–135). Routledge.

Boellstorff, T. (2015). *Coming of Age in Second Life: An Anthropologist Explores the Virtually Human*. Princeton University Press., DOI: 10.1515/9781400874101

Bogost, I. 2021. "The Metaverse Is Bad." The Atlantic, October 22, https://www.theatlantic.com/technology/archive/2021/10/facebook-metaverse-name-change/620449/

Bonfert, M., Reinschluessel, A. V., Putze, S., Lai, Y., Alexandrovsky, D., Malaka, R., & Döring, T. (2023). Seeing the faces is so important—Experiences from online team meetings on commercial virtual reality platforms. *Frontiers in Virtual Reality*, 3, 945791. Advance online publication. DOI: 10.3389/frvir.2022.945791

Bourgeois, R., & Jésus, F. (2004, January). Participatory Prospective Analysis: Exploring and anticipating Challenges with Stakehoders. *CAPSA Monograph*, 46, 112.

Bovenzi, G. (2023). MetaCrimes: Criminal accountability for conducts in the Metaverse. *Companion Proceedings of the ACM Web Conference 2023*. https://doi.org/DOI: 10.1145/3543873.3587535

Buchanan, R. (2001). Design research and the new learning. *Design Issues*, 17(4), 3–23. DOI: 10.1162/07479360152681056

Buhalis, D., & Karatay, N. (2022). Mixed reality (MR) for generation Z in cultural heritage tourism towards metaverse. In Information and Communication Technologies in Tourism 2022: Proceedings of the ENTER 2022 eTourism Conference, January 11–14, 2022 (pp. 16-27). Springer International Publishing.

Buolamwini, J., & Gebru, T. (2018). Gender shades: Intersectional accuracy disparities in commercial gender classification. In *Proceedings of the Conference on Fairness, Accountability, and Transparency* (pp. 77-91). PMLR.

Bu, Q. (2019). Reassess the Law and Ethics of Heritable Genome Editing Interventions: Lessons for China and the World. *Issues in Law & Medicine*, 34(2), 115–145. PMID: 33950602

BÜYÜKBAYKAL, A., & Sönmezer, Z. (2022). The Relationship Between Metaverse and Social Life. *Uluslararası Kültürel ve Sosyal Araştırmalar Dergisi (UKSAD).* https://doi.org/.DOI: 10.46442/int-jcss.1099798

Cai, Y., Llorca, J., Tulino, A. M., & Molisch, A. F. (2022). Compute-and data-intensive networks: The key to the metaverse. In *2022 1st international conference on 6G networking (6GNet)* (pp. 1–8). IEEE.

Cai, H. (2020). Sex difference and smoking predisposition in patients with COVID-19. *The Lancet. Respiratory Medicine*, 8(4), e20. DOI: 10.1016/S2213-2600(20)30117-X PMID: 32171067

Çalışkan, G., & Maya, İ. (2024). Opinions and Expectations of Instructors on Metaverse Applications in Higher Education. *Journal of Educational Technology and Online Learning*, 7(2), 273–285. DOI: 10.31681/jetol.1439812

Calo, R. (2013). Digital market manipulation. *The George Washington Law Review*, 82, 995–1051.

Camacho, D., Lara-Cabrera, R., Merelo-Guervós, J. J., Castillo, P. A., Cotta, C., Fernández-Leiva, A. J., de Vega, F. F., & Chávez, F. (2018). From ephemeral computing to deep bioinspired algorithms: New trends and applications. *Future Generation Computer Systems*, 88, 735–746. DOI: 10.1016/j.future.2018.07.056

Camacho, D., Panizo-LLedot, A., Bello-Orgaz, G., Gonzalez-Pardo, A., & Cambria, E. (2020). The four dimensions of social network analysis: An overview of research methods, applications, and software tools. *Information Fusion*, 63, 88–120. DOI: 10.1016/j.inffus.2020.05.009

Camber, R. (2024). British police probe VIRTUAL rape in metaverse: Young girl's digital persona is sexually attacked by a gang of adult men in immersive video game'-sparking the first investigation of its kind and questions about the extent current laws apply in the online world. *Daily Mail.*

Castaldo, A. R. (2022). Anti-Money Laundering Strategies and The Metaverse: New Dangers and Opportunities. *Iura & Legal Systems*, IX(11), 94–97.

Castronova, E. (2006). On the Research Value of Large Games: Natural Experiments in Norrath and Camelot. *Games and Culture*, 1(2), 163–186. DOI: 10.1177/1555412006286686

Caulfield, B. 2021. "What Is the Metaverse?" The Official NVIDIA Blog, August 10, https://blogs.nvidia .com/blog/2021/08/10/what-is-the-metaverse/

Celik, F. (2023). *The Effect of Metaverse on L2 Vocabulary Learning, Retention, Student Engagement, Presence, and Community Feeling*. DOI: 10.21203/rs.3.rs-3763892/v1

Cerezo, R., Sánchez-Santillán, M., Paule-Ruiz, M. P., & Núñez, J. C. (2016). Students' LMS interaction patterns and their relationship with achievement: A case study in higher education. *Computers & Education*, 96, 42–54. https://doi.org/https://doi.org/10.1016/j.compedu.2016.02.006. DOI: 10.1016/j.compedu.2016.02.006

Chang, V., Golightly, L., Modesti, P., Xu, Q. A., Doan, L. M. T., Hall, K., Boddu, S., & Kobusińska, A. (2022). A Survey on Intrusion Detection Systems for Fog and Cloud Computing. *Future Internet*, 14(3), 89. Advance online publication. DOI: 10.3390/fi14030089

Chawki, M., Basu, S., & Choi, K. S. (2024). Redefining Boundaries in the Metaverse: Navigating the Challenges of Virtual Harm and User Safety. *Laws*, 13(3), 1–23. DOI: 10.3390/laws13030033

Cheng, S. (2023). Metaverse. In Cheng, S. (Ed.), *Metaverse: Concept, Content and Context* (pp. 1–23). Springer Nature Switzerland., DOI: 10.1007/978-3-031-24359-2_1

Chen, W., Zhang, J., & Yu, Z. (2023). A Bibliometric Analysis of the Use of the Metaverse in Education Over Three Decades. *International Journal of Information and Communication Technology Education*, 19(1), 1–16. DOI: 10.4018/IJICTE.322101

Chen, Y. (2023). MEC Network Resource Allocation Strategy Based on Improved PSO in 5G Communication Network. [IJSWIS]. *International Journal on Semantic Web and Information Systems*, 19(1), 1–17. DOI: 10.4018/IJSWIS.328526

Cheong, B. C. (2022). Avatars in the metaverse: Potential legal issues and remedies. *International Cybersecurity Law Review*, 3(2), 467–494. Advance online publication. DOI: 10.1365/s43439-022-00056-9

Cheryl, Bhasin., Hritik, Dilawari., Prasath, K, Yuvaa., Shiv, Shankar, Kumar, Yadav. (2024). The Metaverse. Advances in marketing, customer relationship management, and e-services book series, DOI: 10.4018/979-8-3693-2754-8.ch022

Chesterman, S. (2021). *We, the Robots?* Cambridge University Press., DOI: 10.1017/9781009047081

Chhabra, A., Singh, S. K., Sharma, A., Kumar, S., Gupta, B. B., Arya, V., & Chui, K. T. (2024). Sustainable and intelligent time-series models for epidemic disease forecasting and analysis. *Sustainable Technology and Entrepreneurship*, 3(2), 100064. Advance online publication. DOI: 10.1016/j.stae.2023.100064

Chiu, C. M., Hsu, M. H., & Wang, E. T. (2006). Understanding knowledge sharing in virtual communities: An integration of social capital and social cognitive theories. *Decision Support Systems*, 42(3), 1872–1888. DOI: 10.1016/j.dss.2006.04.001

Cialdini, R. B. (2001). *Influence: Science and Practice*. Allyn & Bacon.

Citi, G. P. S. (2022). Metaverse and Money, Decrypting the Future. *Citi ICG.(2022-03-03)[2022-10-08].* https://icg. citi. com/icghome/what-we-think/citigps/insights/metaverse-and-money_20220330

Conti, M., Gangwal, A., & Ruj, S. (2018). On the Economic Significance of Ransomware Campaigns: A Data-driven Analysis and Research Roadmap. *Journal of Computer Virology and Hacking Techniques*, 14(3), 177–195. DOI: 10.1007/s11416-018-0310-3

Cooper, J., & Fazio, R. H. (1986). The formation and persistence of attitudes that support intergroup conflict. In Worchel, S., & Austin, W. (Eds.), *Psychology of intergroup relations* (pp. 183–195). Nelson-Hall.

Cost of a Data Breach Report. Retrieved from IBM Security, https://www.ibm.com/security/digital-assets/cost-data-breach-report/1Cost%20of%20a%20Data%20Breach%20Report%202020.pdf, 2020.

Craig, A. B. (2013). *Understanding Augmented Reality: Concepts and Applications*. Morgan Kaufmann.

Crespo-Pereira, V., Sánchez-Amboage, E., & Membiela-Pollán, M. (2023). Facing the challenges of metaverse: A systematic literature review from Social Sciences and Marketing and Communication. *El Profesional de la Información*, e320102. Advance online publication. DOI: 10.3145/epi.2023.ene.02

Cross, R., & Prusak, L. (2002). The people who make organizations go–or stop. *Networks in the Knowledge Economy*, 80(6), 248–260. PMID: 12048992

Cruz, M., & Oliveira, A. (2024a). Unravelling Virtual Realities—Gamers' Perceptions of the Metaverse. *Electronics (Basel)*, 13(13), 2491. DOI: 10.3390/electronics13132491

Cruz, M., & Oliveira, A. (2024b). Where Are We Now?—Exploring the Metaverse Representations to Find Digital Twins. *Electronics (Basel)*, 13(10), 1984. DOI: 10.3390/electronics13101984

Cruz, M., Oliveira, A., & Pinheiro, A. (2023). Meeting Ourselves or Other Sides of Us?—Meta-Analysis of the Metaverse. *Informatics (MDPI)*, 10(2), 47. DOI: 10.3390/informatics10020047

Curtis, S. J., Trewin, A., McCormack, L. M., Were, K., McDermott, K., & Walsh, N. (2023). Building a safety culture for infection prevention and control adherence at Howard Springs: A workplace survey. *Infection, Disease & Health*, 28(1), 47–53. DOI: 10.1016/j.idh.2022.07.004 PMID: 36127286

Damayanti, A., Hidayat, R., & Afdhal, A. (2023). Building Sociological Imagination Through Social Media. *The Journal of Society & Media*, 7(2), 425–445. DOI: 10.26740/jsm.v7n2.p425-445

Data Breach Investigations Report, Verizon Enterprise, https://www.verizon.com/about/news/verizon-2021-data-breach-investigations-report, 2021.

*Data Breach Investigations Report*, Verizon, https://www.verizon.com/business/resources/reports/dbir/, 2021.

*Data Breach Investigations Report*, Verizon,2021.

David Codish, E. R., & Ravid, G. (2019). User behavior pattern detection in unstructured processes – a learning management system case study. *Interactive Learning Environments*, 27(5–6), 699–725. DOI: 10.1080/10494820.2019.1610456

David, S. (2023). Metaverse in 2023: A whole new world for brand engagement. Retrieved 2 january 2023, from https://www.exchange4media.com/digital-news/metaverse-in-2023-is-it-going-to-be-a-whole-new-world-124532.html

Davis, K., & Thomas, P. (2020). Identity and Self-Representation in Virtual Worlds: An Analysis of Avatar Use in the Metaverse. *Digital Society Journal*, 11(4), 220–238.

Dawson, A. (2022). Data-driven Consumer Engagement, Virtual Immersive Shopping Experiences, and Blockchain-based Digital Assets in the Retail Metaverse. *Journal of Self-Governance and Management Economics*, 10(2), 52. DOI: 10.22381/jsme10220224

De Cruz, M. M., Oliveira, A., Pinheiro, A., La Cruz, M. M. D., Oliveira, A., & Pinheiro, A. (2022). Flowing Through Virtual Animated Worlds – Perceptions of the Metaverse. *Euro-Asia Conference on Frontiers of Computer Science and Information Technology (FCSIT)*, 241–245. DOI: 10.1109/FCSIT57414.2022.00057

De la Torre, F., & Cohn, J. F. (Year). Facial expression analysis. In *Visual Analysis of Humans* (pp. 377–409). Springer.

Decentraland official site https://decentraland.org/

Devlin, J., Chang, M. W., Lee, K., & Toutanova, K. (2019). BERT: Pre-training of Deep Bidirectional Transformers for Language Understanding. *Proceedings of NAACL-HLT*, 2019, 4171–4186. DOI: 10.18653/v1/N19-1423

Dhar Dwivedi, S. K., Upadhyay, S., & Tripathi, A. K. (2012). A working framework for the user-centered design approach and a survey of the available methods. *International Journal of Scientific and Research Publications, 2*(4), 1-5. ISSN 2250-3153.

Dharmarajan, K., & Dorairangaswamy, M. (2017). Web User Navigation Pattern Behavior Prediction Using Nearest Neighbor Interchange from Weblog Data. *International Journal of Pure and Applied Mathematics*, 116(21), 761–775.

Díaz, J. E. M., Saldaña, C. A. D., Ávila, C. A. R., Márquez Díaz, J. E., Domínguez Saldaña, C. A., & Rodríguez Ávila, C. A. (2020). Virtual World as a Resource for Hybrid Education. *International Journal of Emerging Technologies in Learning*, 15(15), 94–109. DOI: 10.3991/ijet.v15i15.13025

*Digital fashion purchase interest in the U.S.2021*. Statista. Retrieved October 18, 2024, from https://www.statista.com/statistics/1311669/digital-fashion-asset-buying-interest/

Dionisio, J. D. N., Burns, W. G.III, & Gilbert, R. (2013). 3D Virtual worlds and the metaverse. *ACM Computing Surveys*, 45(3), 1–38. DOI: 10.1145/2480741.2480751

Djamba, Y. K., & Neuman, W. L. (2002). Social Research Methods: Qualitative and Quantitative Approaches. In *Teaching Sociology* (Vol. 30, Issue 3). DOI: 10.2307/3211488

Dolan, R., Conduit, J., Fahy, J., & Goodman, S. (2016). Social media engagement behaviour: A uses and gratifications perspective. *Journal of Strategic Marketing*, 24(3-4), 261–277. DOI: 10.1080/0965254X.2015.1095222

Donthu, N., Kumar, S., Pattnaik, D., & Lim, W. M. (2021). A bibliometric retrospection of marketing from the lens of psychology: Insights from Psychology & Marketing. *Psychology and Marketing*, 38(5), 834–865. DOI: 10.1002/mar.21472

Duan, H., Li, J., Fan, S., Lin, Z., Wu, X., & Cai, W. (2021). Metaverse for Social Good: A University Campus Prototype. *Proceedings of the 29th ACM International Conference on Multimedia*. https://doi.org/DOI: 10.1145/3474085.3479238

Dubey, H., & Chhabra, A. (2022). Cyber security model to secure data transmission using cloud cryptography. *Cyber Security Insights Magazine*, 2, 9–12.

Dubey, R., Gunasekaran, A., Childe, S. J., Bryde, D. J., Giannakis, M., Foropon, C., Roubaud, D., & Hazen, B. T. (2020). Big data analytics and artificial intelligence pathway to operational performance under the effects of entrepreneurial orientation and environmental dynamism: A study of manufacturing organisations. *International Journal of Production Economics*, 226, 107599. DOI: 10.1016/j.ijpe.2019.107599

Duguleană, A. R., Tănăsescu, C. R., & Duguleană, M. (2024). Emerging Trends in Play-to-Earn (P2E) Games. *Journal of Theoretical and Applied Electronic Commerce Research*, 19(1), 486–506. DOI: 10.3390/jtaer19010026

Dunsin, D., Ghanem, M. C., Ouazzane, K., & Vassilev, V. (2024). A comprehensive analysis of the role of artificial intelligence and machine learning in modern digital forensics and incident response. *Forensic Science International Digital Investigation*, 48, 301675. DOI: 10.1016/j.fsidi.2023.301675

Du, Y., Grace, T. D., Jagannath, K., & Salen-Tekinbas, K. (2021). Connected play in virtual worlds: Communication and control mechanisms in virtual worlds for children and adolescents. *Multimodal Technologies and Interaction*, 5(5), 27. DOI: 10.3390/mti5050027

Du, Y., Yin, H., Wang, C., & Li, C. (2020). Visual analysis of customer switching behavior pattern mining for takeout service. *Journal of Computer Languages*, 57, 100946. https://doi.org/https://doi.org/10.1016/j.cola.2020.100946. DOI: 10.1016/j.cola.2020.100946

Dwivedi, Y. K., Hughes, L., Baabdullah, A. M., Ribeiro-Navarrete, S., Giannakis, M., Al-Debei, M. M., Dennehy, D., Metri, B., Buhalis, D., Cheung, C. M. K., Conboy, K., Doyle, R., Dubey, R., Dutot, V., Felix, R., Goyal, D. P., Gustafsson, A., Hinsch, C., Jebabli, I., & Wamba, S. F. (2022). Metaverse beyond the hype: Multidisciplinary perspectives on emerging challenges, opportunities, and agenda for research, practice and policy. *International Journal of Information Management*, 66, 102542. DOI: 10.1016/j.ijinfomgt.2022.102542

Dwivedi, Y. K., Hughes, L., Ismagilova, E., Aarts, G., Coombs, C., Crick, T., Duan, Y., Dwivedi, R., Edwards, J., Eirug, A., Galanos, V., Ilavarasan, P. V., Janssen, M., Jones, P., Kar, A. K., Kizgin, H., Kronemann, B., Lal, B., Lucini, B., & Williams, M. D. (2021). Artificial Intelligence (AI): Multidisciplinary perspectives on emerging challenges, opportunities, and agenda for research, practice and policy. *International Journal of Information Management*, 57, 101994. DOI: 10.1016/j.ijinfomgt.2019.08.002

Dwivedi, Y. K., Hughes, L., Kar, A. K., Baabdullah, A. M., Grover, P., Abbas, R., Andreini, D., Abumoghli, I., Barlette, Y., Bunker, D., Chandra Kruse, L., Constantiou, I., Davison, R. M., De', R., Dubey, R., Fenby-Taylor, H., Gupta, B., He, W., Kodama, M., & Wade, M. (2022). Climate change and COP26: Are digital technologies and information management part of the problem or the solution? An editorial reflection and call to action. *International Journal of Information Management*, 63, 102456. DOI: 10.1016/j.ijinfomgt.2021.102456

Dwivedi, Y. K., Ismagilova, E., Hughes, D. L., Carlson, J., Filieri, R., Jacobson, J., Jain, V., Karjaluoto, H., Kefi, H., Krishen, A. S., Kumar, V., Rahman, M. M., Raman, R., Rauschnabel, P. A., Rowley, J., Salo, J., Tran, G. A., & Wang, Y. (2021). Setting the future of digital and social media marketing research: Perspectives and research propositions. *International Journal of Information Management*, 59, 102168. DOI: 10.1016/j.ijinfomgt.2020.102168

Dwivedi, Y. K., Kshetri, N., Hughes, L., Rana, N. P., Baabdullah, A. M., Kar, A. K., Koohang, A., Ribeiro-Navarrete, S., Belei, N., Balakrishnan, J., Basu, S., Behl, A., Davies, G. H., Dutot, V., Dwivedi, R., Evans, L., Felix, R., Foster-Fletcher, R., Giannakis, M., & Yan, M. (2023). Exploring the Darkverse: A Multi-Perspective Analysis of the Negative Societal Impacts of the Metaverse. *Information Systems Frontiers*, 25(5), 2071–2114. DOI: 10.1007/s10796-023-10400-x PMID: 37361890

Egger, M., Ley, M., & Hanke, S. (2019). Emotion recognition from physiological signal analysis: A review. *Electronic Notes in Theoretical Computer Science*, 343, 35–55. DOI: 10.1016/j.entcs.2019.04.009

Ehatisham-ul-Haq. M., Awais Azam, M., Naeem, U., Amin, Y., & Loo, J. (2018). Continuous authentication of smartphone users based on activity pattern recognition using passive mobile sensing. *Journal of Network and Computer Applications, 109*, 24–35. https://doi.org/https://doi.org/10.1016/j.jnca.2018.02.020

El-Ansary, A. (2002). Behavioral Pattern Analysis: towards a new representation of systems requirements based on actions and events. *Proceedings of the 2002 ACM Symposium on Applied Computing*, 984–991. DOI: 10.1145/508791.508983

Elizondo-García, M. E. (2023). *Breaking Boundaries*. Ascilite Publications., DOI: 10.14742/apubs.2023.526

El-Kady, R. (2023). Handling E-evidence in Egyptian and Comparative Legislation: A Comparative Analytical Study. *Arab Journal of Forensic Sciences & Forensic Medicine*, 6(1), 37–68. DOI: 10.26735/WGZY6322

El-Kady, R. (2024). Artificial Intelligence and Criminal Law. In Tavares, M., Azevedo, G., Vale, J., Marques, R., & Bastos, M. (Eds.), *Artificial Intelligence Approaches to Sustainable Accounting* (pp. 34–52). IGI Global., DOI: 10.4018/979-8-3693-0847-9.ch003

El-Kady, R. (2024). Investigating Forensic Evidence in Metaverse: A Comparative Analytical Study. In Elshenraki, H. (Ed.), *Forecasting Cyber Crimes in the Age of the Metaverse* (pp. 227–258). IGI Global., DOI: 10.4018/979-8-3693-0220-0.ch012

El-Kady, R. (2024). Navigating the Legal Maze: Electric Self-Driving Cars and the Complexities of Criminal Law. In Shaik, M. (Ed.), *Solving Fundamental Challenges of Electric Vehicles* (pp. 215–247). IGI Global., DOI: 10.4018/979-8-3693-4314-2.ch009

Elsadig, M., Alohali, M. A., Ibrahim, A. O., & Abulfaraj, A. W. (2024). Roles of Blockchain in the Metaverse: Concepts, Taxonomy, Recent Advances, Enabling Technologies, and Open Research Issues. *IEEE Access : Practical Innovations, Open Solutions*, 12, 38410–38435. DOI: 10.1109/ACCESS.2024.3367014

El-Shagi, M., & Von Schweinitz, G. (2016). The Diablo 3 Economy: An Agent Based Approach. *Computational Economics*, 47(2), 193–217. DOI: 10.1007/s10614-014-9480-5

Ennouamani, S., & Mahani, Z. (2017). An overview of adaptive e-learning systems. In *Proceedings of the 2017 Eighth International Conference on Intelligent Computing and Information Systems (ICICIS)* (pp. 1-6). IEEE. https://doi.org/DOI: 10.1109/INTELCIS.2017.8260060

EqualOcean. (June 12, 2019). Value of artificial intelligence (AI) investment deals in education industry in China from 2012 to May 2019 (in billion yuan) [Graph]. In Statista. Retrieved December 09, 2024, from https://www-statista-com.elibrary.siu.edu.in/statistics/1026507/chinese-ai-investment-deals-in-education-industry/

Europol (2022), Policing in the metaverse: what law enforcement needs to know, an observatory report from the Europol Innovation Lab, Publications Office of the European Union, Luxembourg.

Evans, B. (2020). The Role of Authenticity in Face-to-Face Social Interactions. *Human Behavior and Society*, 18(3), 145–160.

Evison, L. (2016). Virtual Economics: Design and Analysis, written by Vili Lehdonvirta and Edward Castronova. *Asiascape: Digital Asia*, 3(1–2), 103–105. DOI: 10.1163/22142312-12340052

Exploring the Metaverse: Challenges and Opportunities for India in the 'Next Internet' | ORF (orfonline.org)

Eyada, B. (2023, January 15). Advertising in the Metaverse: Opportunities and Challenges. *Canadian Center of Science and Education*, 15(1), 22–22. DOI: 10.5539/ijms.v15n1p22

Fadliansyah, H. D. (2022). *Imagining the Metaverse Worlds: The Perspectives of Meta and Indonesians*. Lub.lu.se. https://lup.lub.lu.se/student-papers/search/publication/9079505

Fairfield, J. (2005). Vrtual Property. *Boston University Law Review. Boston University. School of Law*, 85, 1047–1102. https://www.bu.edu/law/journals-archive/bulr/volume85n4/FAIRFIELD.pdf

Fairfield, J. A. T. (2005). Virtual Property. *Boston University Law Review. Boston University. School of Law*, 85, 1047.

Fairosebanu, A. A., & Jebaseeli, A. C. N. (2023). Data security in cloud environment using cryptographic mechanism. *Bulletin of Electrical Engineering and Informatics*, 12(1), 462–471. DOI: 10.11591/eei.v12i1.4590

Faison, T. (1998). *Interaction Patterns for Communicating Processes 1 Abstract 2 Introduction 3 Interaction Dynamics and the Patterns Movement*. 1–35.

Falah, Z. (2023). Exploring the Influence of Virtual Reality on Interpersonal Communication: A Novel Study in Communication Science. *Journal of Social Science (Joss)*, 2(8), 654–660. DOI: 10.57185/joss.v2i8.99

Falchuk, B., Loeb, S., & Neff, R. (2018). The social metaverse: The battle for privacy. *IEEE Technology and Society Magazine*, 37(2), 52–61. DOI: 10.1109/MTS.2018.2826060

Fan, C., Jiang, Y., & Mostafavi, A. (2020). Emergent Social Cohesion for Coping With Community Disruptions in Disasters. *Journal of the Royal Society, Interface*, 17(164), 20190778. DOI: 10.1098/rsif.2019.0778 PMID: 32126194

Faridani, A. (2022). Council post: why the metaverse is marketing's next big thing. Retrieved 19 August 2022, from https://www.forbes.com/ sites/forbesbusinessdevelopmentcouncil/2021/12/21/why-themetaverse-is-marketings-next-big-thing/?sh=14bca7f

Farooq, M. S., Ishaq, K., Shoaib, M., Khelifi, A., & Atal, Z. (2023). The Potential of Metaverse Fundamentals, Technologies, and Applications: A Systematic Literature Review. *IEEE Access : Practical Innovations, Open Solutions*, 11, 138472–138487. DOI: 10.1109/ACCESS.2023.3338627

Fatahi, S., Shabanali-Fami, F., & Moradi, H. (2018). An empirical study of using sequential behavior pattern mining approach to predict learning styles. *Education and Information Technologies*, 23(4), 1427–1445. DOI: 10.1007/s10639-017-9667-1

Fernandez, C. B., & Hui, P. (2022, July). Life, the metaverse and everything: An overview of privacy, ethics, and governance in metaverse. In 2022 IEEE 42nd International Conference on Distributed Computing Systems Workshops (ICDCSW) (pp. 272-277). IEEE.

Finn, R. L., & Wright, D. (2012). Unmanned aircraft systems: Surveillance, ethics and privacy in civil applications. *Computer Law & Security Report*, 28(2), 184–194. DOI: 10.1016/j.clsr.2012.01.005

Flavián, C., Ibáñez-Sánchez, S., & Orús, C. (2019). The impact of virtual, augmented and mixed reality technologies on the customer experience. *Journal of Business Research*, 100, 547–560. DOI: 10.1016/j.jbusres.2018.10.050

Fokides, E. (2020). My avatar and I: A study on avatars, personality traits, self-attributes, and their perceived importance. *Journal of Ambient Intelligence and Humanized Computing*, 12(1), 359–373. DOI: 10.1007/s12652-020-01977-1

Forbes (2022), "The Amazing Ways Nike Is Using The Metaverse, Web3 And NFTs", available at: https://www.forbes.com/sites/bernardmarr/2022/06/01/the-amazing-ways-nike-is-using-the-metaverse-web3-and-nfts/

Freedman, J. L., & Fraser, S. C. (1966). Compliance without pressure: The foot-in-the-door technique. *Journal of Personality and Social Psychology*, 4(2), 195–202. DOI: 10.1037/h0023552 PMID: 5969145

Fu, C., Zheng, G., Huang, C., Yu, Y., & Dong, J. (2023). Multiplex Heterogeneous Graph Neural Network with Behavior Pattern Modeling. *Proceedings of the 29th ACM SIGKDD Conference on Knowledge Discovery and Data Mining*, 482–494. DOI: 10.1145/3580305.3599441

Futurumresearch (2022), "Nike's Metaverse Store Paves a Pathway into the Future", available at: https://futurumresearch.com/research-notes/nikes-metaverse-store-paves-a-pathway-into-the-future/

Gabbiadini, A., Mari, S., Volpato, C., & Monaci, M. G. (2014). Identification Processes in Online Groups. *Journal of Media Psychology*, 26(3), 141–152. DOI: 10.1027/1864-1105/a000119

Gadalla, E., Keeling, K., & Abosag, I. (2013). Metaverseretail service quality: A future framework for retail service quality in the 3D internet. *Journal of Marketing Management*, 29(13-14), 1493–1517. DOI: 10.1080/0267257X.2013.835742

Gan, L., Guo, Y., & Yang, T. (2024). Machine learning for depression detection on web and social media: A systematic review. *International Journal on Semantic Web and Information Systems*, 20(1), 1–28. Advance online publication. DOI: 10.4018/IJSWIS.342126

Gautam, V. (2022). 10 Big brands that have dipped their toes into the nft world. Retrieved 26 August 2022, from https://www.indiatimes. com/worth/investment/brands-that-have-entered-nft-world560907.html

Gee, J. P. (2003). What video games have to teach us about learning and literacy. *Technology, Pedagogy and Education*, 1(1), 20–29. DOI: 10.1145/950566.950595

Georgi, T., Roumen, T., Ognian, N., Slavcho, M., & Galya, P. Cyber security: Threats and Challenges, *International Conference Automatics and Informatics (ICAI)*, 2020.

Gervais, D. J. (2021). *The future of intellectual property*. Edward Elgar Publishing Limited. DOI: 10.4337/9781800885349

Ghose, R., Bantanidis, S., Shah, R. S., Surendran, N., Master, K., & Singhvi, P. (2022), "Metaverse and Money" available at: https://www.citifirst.com.hk/home/upload/citi_research/AZRC7.pdf (accessed 29 August 2022).

Giddens, A., Duneier, M., Appelbaum, R., & Carr, B. (2009). *Introduction to sociology*. WW Norton & Company.

Gilbert, R., & Forney, A. (2013). The distributed self: Virtual worlds and the future of human identity. In *The immersive internet: Reflections on the entangling of the virtual with society, politics and the economy* (pp. 23–36). Palgrave Macmillan UK. DOI: 10.1057/9781137283023_3

Gita Krishna Murti, K., Sri Darma, G., Putu Mahyuni, L., & Ngurah Eddy Supriyadinata Gorda, A. (2023). Immersive Experience in the Metaverse: Implications for Tourism and Business. *International Journal of Applied Business Research*, 2023(2), 187–207. DOI: 10.35313/ijabr.v5i02.329

Godon, M., Feki, M. A., Roelands, M., & Trappeniers, L. (2011). The First Interaction Design Pattern Library for Internet of Things User Created Applications. In Jacko, J. A. (Ed.), *Human-Computer Interaction. Design and Development Approaches* (pp. 229–237). Springer Berlin Heidelberg. DOI: 10.1007/978-3-642-21602-2_26

Gokulapriya, R., & Ganesh Kumar, R. (2019). Research aligned analysis on web access behavioral pattern mining for user identification. *International Journal of Engineering and Advanced Technology*, 8(6), 5062–5067. DOI: 10.35940/ijeat.F9552.088619

Goldberg, D. E. (David E. (with Internet Archive). (1989). *Genetic algorithms in search, optimization, and machine learning*. Reading, Mass.: Addison-Wesley Pub. Co. https://archive.org/details/geneticalgorithm0000gold

Goldberg, D. E., & Holland, J. H. (1988). Genetic Algorithms and Machine Learning. *Machine Learning*, 3(2), 95–99. DOI: 10.1023/A:1022602019183

Goldberg, M., & Schär, F. (2023). Metaverse governance: An empirical analysis of voting within Decentralized Autonomous Organizations. *Journal of Business Research*, 160, 113764. DOI: 10.1016/j.jbusres.2023.113764

Gómez-Quintero, J., Johnson, S. D., Borrion, H., & Lundrigan, S. (2024). A scoping study of crime facilitated by the metaverse. *Futures*, 157, 103338. DOI: 10.1016/j.futures.2024.103338

González-Briones, A., Prieto, J., De La Prieta, F., Demazeau, Y., & Corchado, J. M. (2021). Virtual agent organizations for user behaviour pattern extraction in energy optimization processes: A new perspective. *Neurocomputing*, 452, 374–385. https://doi.org/https://doi.org/10.1016/j.neucom.2020.05.117. DOI: 10.1016/j.neucom.2020.05.117

Gordon, A., & Harris, P. (2019). The Limitations of Geographical Boundaries in Physical Communities. *Regional Social Dynamics Review*, 13(1), 50–65.

Goyal, S., Kumar, S., Singh, S. K., Sarin, S., Priyanshu, , Gupta, B. B., Arya, V., Alhalabi, W., & Colace, F. (2024). Synergistic application of neuro-fuzzy mechanisms in advanced neural networks for real-time stream data flux mitigation. *Soft Computing*, 28(20), 12425–12437. Advance online publication. DOI: 10.1007/s00500-024-09938-y

Goyal, S., Singh, S. K., Kumar, S., Sarin, S., Gupta, B. B., Arya, V., & Chui, K. T. (2024). Hyperdimensional Consumer Pattern Analysis with Quantum Neural Architectures using Non-Hermitian Operators. *Proceedings of the 5th International Conference on Information Management & Machine Intelligence*, 1–5. DOI: 10.1145/3647444.3652458

Greenberg, S., Boring, S., Vermeulen, J., & Dostal, J. (2014). Dark patterns in proxemic interactions: a critical perspective. *Proceedings of the 2014 Conference on Designing Interactive Systems*, 523–532. DOI: 10.1145/2598510.2598541

Grover, L. K. (1997). Quantum Mechanics helps in searching for a needle in a haystack. *Physical Review Letters*, 79(2), 325–328. DOI: 10.1103/PhysRevLett.79.325

Gui, E. M., & MacGill, I. (2018). Typology of future clean energy communities: An exploratory structure, opportunities, and challenges. *Energy Research & Social Science*, 35, 94–107. https://doi.org/https://doi .org/10.1016/j.erss.2017.10.019. DOI: 10.1016/j.erss.2017.10.019

Guo, Y., & Barnes, S. (2009). Virtual item purchase behavior in virtual worlds: An exploratory investigation. *Electronic Commerce Research*, 9(1–2), 77–96. DOI: 10.1007/s10660-009-9032-6

Gupta, S., Taneja, S., & Kumar, N. (2014). Quantum inspired genetic algorithm for community structure detection in social networks. *GECCO 2014 - Proceedings of the 2014 Genetic and Evolutionary Computation Conference*. DOI: 10.1145/2576768.2598277

Gupta, A., Khan, H. U., Nazir, S., Shafiq, M., & Shabaz, M. (2023). Metaverse Security: Issues, Challenges and a Viable ZTA Model. *Electronics (Basel)*, 12(2), 391. DOI: 10.3390/electronics12020391

Gupta, A., & Kumar, S. (2017). Cloud computing & fog computing: A solution for high-performance computing. In *Proceedings of the 2017 4th International Conference on Computing for Sustainable Global Development (INDIACom-2017)*. New Delhi, India.

Gupta, A., Singh, S. K., & Chopra, M. (2023). Impact of artificial intelligence and the Internet of Things in modern times and hereafter: An investigative analysis. In *Advanced Computer Science Applications* (pp. 157–173). Apple Academic Press. DOI: 10.1201/9781003369066-14

Gupta, A., Singh, S. K., Chopra, M., & Gill, S. S. (2022). An inquisitive prospect on the shift toward online media, before, during, and after the COVID-19 pandemic: A technological analysis. In *Advances in Data Computing, Communication and Security: Proceedings of I3CS2021* (pp. 229–238). Springer Nature Singapore. DOI: 10.1007/978-981-16-8403-6_20

Gupta, B. B., Gaurav, A., Albeshri, A. A., & Alsalman, D. (2023). New paradigms of sustainable entrepreneurship in metaverse: A micro-level perspective. *The International Entrepreneurship and Management Journal*, 19(3), 1449–1465. DOI: 10.1007/s11365-023-00875-0

Gupta, B. B., Gaurav, A., & Arya, V. (2024). Fuzzy logic and biometric-based lightweight cryptographic authentication for metaverse security. *Applied Soft Computing*, 164, 111973. DOI: 10.1016/j.asoc.2024.111973

Gupta, B. B., Gaurav, A., Chui, K. T., & Arya, V. (2024, January). Deep learning-based facial emotion detection in the metaverse. In *2024 IEEE International Conference on Consumer Electronics (ICCE)* (pp. 1-6). IEEE. DOI: 10.1109/ICCE59016.2024.10444217

Gupta, P., & Reddy, C. K. (2020). Machine Learning for Social Science: Predictive Models for Complex Social Phenomena. *ACM Computing Surveys*, 53(1), 1–34. DOI: 10.1145/3373142

Gupta, R., & Pal, S. K. (2023). Concept of Metaverse. In *Introduction to Metaverse: Technology Landscape, Applications, and Challenges* (pp. 1–21). Springer Nature Singapore. DOI: 10.1007/978-981-99-7397-2_1

Gupta, S., Agrawal, S., Singh, S. K., & Kumar, S. (2023). A Novel Transfer Learning-Based Model for Ultrasound Breast Cancer Image Classification. In Smys, S., Tavares, J. M. R. S., & Shi, F. (Eds.), *Computational Vision and Bio-Inspired Computing. Advances in Intelligent Systems and Computing* (Vol. 1439). Springer. DOI: 10.1007/978-981-19-9819-5_37

Gupta, S., Chhabra, A., Agrawal, S., & Singh, S. K. (2021). A comprehensive comparative study of machine learning classifiers for spam filtering. In *International Conference on Cyber Security, Privacy and Networking* (pp. 257-268). Springer International Publishing.

Gupta, S., Maple, C., Crispo, B., Raja, K., Yautsiukhin, A., & Martinelli, F. (2023). A survey of human-computer interaction (HCI) & natural habits-based behavioural biometric modalities for user recognition schemes. *Pattern Recognition*, 139, 109453. https://doi.org/https://doi.org/10.1016/j.patcog.2023.109453. DOI: 10.1016/j.patcog.2023.109453

Habiba, M., Islam, M. R., & Ali, A. B. M. S. (2018). A component based unified architecture for utility service in cloud. *Future Generation Computer Systems*, 87, 725–742. https://doi.org/https://doi.org/10.1016/j.future.2017.10.017. DOI: 10.1016/j.future.2017.10.017

Hadi, R., Melumad, S., & Park, E. S. (2023). The Metaverse: A New Digital Frontier for Consumer Behavior. *Journal of Consumer Psychology*, 34(1), 142–166. DOI: 10.1002/jcpy.1356

Hadnagy, C, "*The Science of Human Hacking*", 978-1-119-43375-0, 2018.

Hadnagy, C, *Social Engineering: The Science of Human Hacking*. 978-1-119-43375-0, 2018.

Hadnagy, C. (2010). *Social Engineering: The Science of Human Hacking*. Wiley.

Hall, J. (2020). The Role of Algorithms in Shaping Social Media Communities. *Journal of Medical Technology*, 19(3), 92–105.

Hamurcu, A. (2022). The metaverse, online communities, and (real) urban space. *Urbani Izziv*, 33(2), 73–81. Advance online publication. DOI: 10.5379/urbani-izziv-en-2022-33-02-01

Han, D., Huang, Y., Liu, J., Liao, K., & Lin, K. (2024). LSAB: User Behavioral Pattern Modeling in Sequential Recommendation by Learning Self-Attention Bias. *ACM Transactions on Knowledge Discovery from Data*, 18(3), 1–20. Advance online publication. DOI: 10.1145/3632625

Han, J., Heo, J., & You, E. (2021, October). Analysis of metaverse platform as a new play culture: Focusing on roblox and zepeto. In *Proceedings of the 2nd International Conference on Human-centered Artificial Intelligence (Computing4Human 2021). CEUR Workshop Proceedings, Da Nang, Vietnam (Oct 2021).*

Han, K.-H., & Kim, J.-H. (2002). Quantum-inspired evolutionary algorithm for a class of combinatorial optimization. *IEEE Transactions on Evolutionary Computation, 6*(6), 580–593. *IEEE Transactions on Evolutionary Computation*. Advance online publication. DOI: 10.1109/TEVC.2002.804320

Han, M., Wang, X.-M., & Kuai, S.-G. (2022). Social Rather Than Physical Crowding Reduces the Required Interpersonal Distance in Virtual Environments. *PsyCh Journal*, 12(1), 34–43. DOI: 10.1002/pchj.595 PMID: 36129003

Hauer, T. (2017). Technological determinism and new media. *International Journal of English Literature and Social Sciences*, 2(2), 239174.

Haynes, D. (2024). Ethics of information and the metaverse. *Communication, Technologies et Développement, 14*(December 2023), 0–6. DOI: 10.4000/ctd.9497

Hennig-Thurau, T., Aliman, D. N., Herting, A. M., Cziehso, G. P., Linder, M., & Kübler, R. V. (2023). Social interactions in the metaverse: Framework, initial evidence, and research roadmap. *Journal of the Academy of Marketing Science*, 51(4), 889–913. DOI: 10.1007/s11747-022-00908-0

Hew, K. F., & Cheung, W. S. (2013). Use of Web 2.0 technologies in K-12 and higher education: The search for evidence-based practice. *Educational Research Review*, 9, 47–64. DOI: 10.1016/j.edurev.2012.08.001

Hildebrandt, M., & Rouvroy, A. (2011). *Law, Human Agency and Autonomic Computing - The Philosophy of Law Meets the Philosophy of Technology*. Routledge.

Hilken, T., Keeling, D. I., Chylinski, M., de Ruyter, K., Golf Papez, M., Heller, J., Mahr, D., & Alimamy, S. (2022). Disrupting marketing realities: A research agenda for investigating the psychological mechanisms of next-generation experiences with reality-enhancing technologies. *Psychology and Marketing*, 39(8), 1660–1671. DOI: 10.1002/mar.21678

Hine, E. (2023). Content Moderation in the Metaverse Could Be a New Frontier to Attack Freedom of Expression. *Philosophy & Technology*, 36(3), 1–11. DOI: 10.1007/s13347-023-00645-4

Hoffman, D. L., & Novak, T. P. (2009). Flow online: Lessons learned and future prospects. *Journal of Interactive Marketing*, 23(1), 23–34. DOI: 10.1016/j.intmar.2008.10.003

Hofstetter, R., de Bellis, E., Brandes, L., Clegg, M., Lamberton, C., Reibstein, D., Rohlfsen, F., Schmitt, B., & Zhang, J. Z. (2022). Crypto-marketing: How non-fungible tokens (NFTs) challenge traditional marketing. *Marketing Letters*, 33(4), 705–711. DOI: 10.1007/s11002-022-09639-2

Holland, J. H. (1992). *Adaptation in Natural and Artificial Systems: An Introductory Analysis with Applications to Biology, Control, and Artificial Intelligence*. The MIT Press., DOI: 10.7551/mitpress/1090.001.0001

Hollensen, S., Kotler, P., & Opresnik, M. O. (2022). Metaverse—The new marketing universe. *The Journal of Business Strategy*. Advance online publication. DOI: 10.1108/JBS-01-2022-0014

Holmes, W., Bialik, M., & Fadel, C. (2019). *Artificial intelligence in education: Promises and implications for teaching and learning*. Center for Curriculum Redesign.

How Employees are Making Businesses Vulnerable from Within. Retrieved from Kaspersky, https://www.kaspersky.com/blog/the-human-factor-in-it-security/, 2020.

Huang, L., & Xia, Z. (2009). User Character and Communication Pattern Detecting on Social Network Site. *2009 International Conference on Engineering Computation*, 261–264. DOI: 10.1109/ICEC.2009.70

Huang, Y., Li, Y. J., & Cai, Z. (2023). Security and Privacy in Metaverse: A Comprehensive Survey. *Big Data Mining and Analytics*, 6(2), 234–247. DOI: 10.26599/BDMA.2022.9020047

Huq, N., Reyes, R., Lin, P., & Swimmer, M. (2022). *Cybersecurity threats against the Internet of Experiences*. Trend Micro Research.

Hussain, Z., Khan, A., & Ali, A. (2023). The Impact of User-Generated Content, Social Interactions and virtual Economies on Metaverse Environments. *Journal of Sustainable Economics*, 1(2), 34–44. DOI: 10.32734/jse.v1i2.13798

Hutson, J. H. (2022). Social Virtual Reality: Neurodivergence and Inclusivity in the Metaverse. *Societies (Basel, Switzerland)*, 12(4), 102. DOI: 10.3390/soc12040102

Hwang, G.-J., & Chien, S.-Y. (2022). Definition, roles, and potential research issues of the metaverse in education: An artificial intelligence perspective. *Computers and Education: Artificial Intelligence*, 3, 100082. DOI: 10.1016/j.caeai.2022.100082

Ianenko, M., Ianenko, M., & Shevchuk, E. (2023, May 22). Innovative Promotion Technologies: Brand Management in the Digital Environment. *Multidisciplinary Digital Publishing Institute*, 1(1), 18–25. DOI: 10.3390/platforms1010003

Innocente, C., Nonis, F., Ruggieri, R., Ulrich, L., & Vezzetti, E. (2024). A Metaverse Platform for Preserving and Promoting Intangible Cultural Heritage. *Applied Sciences (Basel, Switzerland)*, 14(8), 3426. DOI: 10.3390/app14083426

*Internet Crime Report 2020,*https://www.fbi.gov/news/press-releases/fbi-releases-the-internet-crime-complaint-center-2020-internet-crime-report-including-covid-19-scam-statistics, 2020.

Internet, S. T. R. Retrieved from Symantec, https://www.broadcom.com, 2019.

INTERPOL. (2024). *Metaverse: A law enforcement perspective*. INTERPOL. https://www.interpol.int/content/download/20828/file/Metaverse%20-%20a%20law%20enforcement%20perspective.pdf. Accessed 4 Feb 2024.

ISACA. (2014). Generating value from big data analytics [White paper]. Information Systems Audit and Control Association, Retrieved from http://www.isaca.org/Knowledge-Center/ Research/Research-Deliverables/Pages/Generating-Value-From-Big-Data-Analytics.aspx

Jain, D. K., Eyre, Y. G.-M., Akshi, K., Gupta, B. B., & Ketan, K. (2023). *Knowledge-based Data Processing for Multilingual Natural Language Analysis*. ACM Transactions on Asian and Low-Resource Language Information Processing., DOI: 10.1145/3583686

Janis, I. L., & Feshbach, S. (1953). Effects of fear-arousing communications. *Journal of Abnormal and Social Psychology*, 48(1), 78–92. DOI: 10.1037/h0060732 PMID: 13022199

Jauhiainen, J. S., Krohn, C., & Junnila, J. (2022). Metaverse and Sustainability: Systematic Review of Scientific Publications Until 2022 and Beyond. *Sustainability (Basel)*, 15(1), 346. DOI: 10.3390/su15010346

Jeong, A. (2005). A Guide to Analyzing Message–Response Sequences and Group Interaction Patterns in Computer-mediated Communication. *Distance Education*, 26(3), 367–383. DOI: 10.1080/01587910500291470

Jeong, M., & Kim, S. (2023). What makes' aespa', the first metaverse girl group in the K-pop universe, succeed in the global entertainment industry? Jiang, Y., & Jiang, J. C. (2014). Diffusion in social networks: A multiagent perspective. *IEEE Transactions on Systems, Man, and Cybernetics. Systems*, 45(2), 198–213.

Jibril, M. (2023). The Legal Challenges of Metaverse Technology from the Criminal Point of View (Cairo: Dar Al-Ahram for Legal Publications).

Jim, J. R., Hosain, M. T., Mridha, M. F., Kabir, M. M., & Shin, J. (2023). Toward Trustworthy Metaverse: Advancements and Challenges. *IEEE Access : Practical Innovations, Open Solutions*, 11, 118318–118347. DOI: 10.1109/ACCESS.2023.3326258

Johann Füller Katja Hutter, J. H., & Matzler, K. (2014). User Roles and Contributions in Innovation-Contest Communities. *Journal of Management Information Systems*, 31(1), 273–308. DOI: 10.2753/MIS0742-1222310111

Johnson, D. (2021). Technological Barriers to Accessibility in the Metaverse. *Journal of Emerging Technologies*, 14(1), 33–47.

Jorritsma, W., Cnossen, F., Dierckx, R. A., Oudkerk, M., & van Ooijen, P. M. A. (2016). Pattern mining of user interaction logs for a post-deployment usability evaluation of a radiology PACS client. *International Journal of Medical Informatics*, 85(1), 36–42. https://doi.org/https://doi.org/10.1016/j.ijmedinf.2015.10.007. DOI: 10.1016/j.ijmedinf.2015.10.007 PMID: 26574241

Joshi, S., Koparrati, S., & Singhal, V. (2022). Marketing analytics for analyzing social media and branding efforts of indian telecom operators. [IJCAC]. *International Journal of Cloud Applications and Computing*, 12(1), 1–18. DOI: 10.4018/IJCAC.297092

Joy, A., Zhu, Y., Peña, C., & Brouard, M. (2022). Digital Future of Luxury Brands: Metaverse, Digital Fashion, and Non-fungible Tokens. *Strategic Change*, 31(3), 337–343. DOI: 10.1002/jsc.2502

Jufri, M., & Awali, N. (2015). FAKTOR-FAKTOR YANG BERHUBUNGAN DENGAN EFEKTIVITAS AREA KAWASAN TANPA ROKOK DI PONDOK PESANTREN NURUL FALAH KAWATUNA KOTA PALU Healthy Tadulako Journal (Muh. Jufri & Nazliani : 33-42) Di Indonesia daerah yang telah menerapkan kawasan tanpa rokok ini ada. *Jurnal Kesehatan Tadulako*, 1(2), 1–78.

Juhaňák, L., Zounek, J., & Rohlíková, L. (2019). Using process mining to analyze students' quiz-taking behavior patterns in a learning management system. *Computers in Human Behavior*, 92, 496–506. https://doi.org/https://doi.org/10.1016/j.chb.2017.12.015. DOI: 10.1016/j.chb.2017.12.015

Kache, F., & Seuring, S. (2017). Challenges and opportunities of digital information at the intersection of Big Data Analytics and supply chain management. *International Journal of Operations & Production Management*, 37(1), 10–36. DOI: 10.1108/IJOPM-02-2015-0078

Kaddoura, S., & Al Husseiny, F. (2023). The Rising Trend of Metaverse in Education: Challenges, Opportunities, and Ethical Considerations. *PeerJ. Computer Science*, 9, e1252. DOI: 10.7717/peerj-cs.1252 PMID: 37346578

Kahui, V., Armstrong, C. W., & Aanesen, M. (2024). Comparative analysis of Rights of Nature (RoN) case studies worldwide: Features of emergence and design. *Ecological Economics*, 221, 108193–108193. DOI: 10.1016/j.ecolecon.2024.108193

Kakade, M. S., Anupama, K. R., Nayak, S., & Garang, S. (2024). Custom Network Protocol Stack for Communication Between Nodes in a Cloudlet System. [IJCAC]. *International Journal of Cloud Applications and Computing*, 14(1), 1–24. DOI: 10.4018/IJCAC.339891

Kalınkara, Y., & Özdemir, O. (2023). Anatomy in the Metaverse: Exploring Student Technology Acceptance Through the UTAUT2 Model. *Anatomical Sciences Education*, 17(2), 319–336. DOI: 10.1002/ase.2353 PMID: 37942914

Kalyvaki, M. (2023). Navigating the Metaverse Business and Legal Challenges: Intellectual Property, Privacy, and Jurisdiction. *Journal of Metaverse*, 3(1), 87–92. DOI: 10.57019/jmv.1238344

Karthika, R., & Jegatha Deborah, L. (2021). Enhanced learning experiences based on regulatory fit theory using affective state detection. [IJSWIS]. *International Journal on Semantic Web and Information Systems*, 17(4), 37–55. DOI: 10.4018/IJSWIS.2021100103

Kasiyanto, S., & Kilinc, M. R. (2022). Legal Conundrums of the Metaverse. *Journal of Central Banking Law and Institutions*, 1(2), 299–322. DOI: 10.21098/jcli.v1i2.25

Khade, G., Kumar, S., & Bhattacharya, S. (2012). Classification of web pages on attractiveness: A supervised learning approach. *2012 4th International Conference on Intelligent Human Computer Interaction (IHCI)*, 1–5. DOI: 10.1109/IHCI.2012.6481867

Khalifa, E. (2022). The Metaverse of the Future of Human Urbanization in a Post-Internet World (Abu Dhabi: The Future Center for Research and Advanced Studies), Dirasat Series, Issue 17, November 2022.

Khan, I., Flores, A. F., & Subhani, A. (2021). It's Just a Game: A Quantitative Study on the Effects of Social Interactions Inside MMORPGs and Its Impact on Loneliness, Depression, and Social Anxiety. *Journal of Administrative and Business Studies*, 7(3). Advance online publication. DOI: 10.20474/jabs-7.3.4

Khan, M. F., Lu, L., Afzal, H., & Nasir, J. A. (2023). PredictionMiner: Mining the latest individual behavioral rules for personalized contextual pattern predictions. *Soft Computing*. Advance online publication. DOI: 10.1007/s00500-023-08572-4

Khatri, M. (2022). Revamping the marketing world with metaverse–The future of marketing. *International Journal of Computer Applications*, 975(29), 8887. DOI: 10.5120/ijca2022922361

Khushboo Kumari. (2021) Online social media threat and It's solution, Insights2Techinfo, pp.1, https://insights2techinfo.com/online-social-media-threat-and-its-solution/

Kiaer, J. (2024). *Conversing in the Metaverse: The Embodied Future of Online Communication*. Bloomsbury Academic. DOI: 10.5040/9781350338548

Kiene, C. (2020). *Challenges and Adaptations to Technological Change in Online Communities* (Doctoral dissertation).

Kim, D., Oh, S., & Shon, T. (2023). Digital forensic approaches for metaverse ecosystems. *Forensic Science International Digital Investigation*, 46, 301608. DOI: 10.1016/j.fsidi.2023.301608

Kim, H., & Kim, M. (2023). Presence and Effectiveness of Online Learning Using a Metaverse Platform: Gather.town. *International Journal of Information and Education Technology (IJIET)*, 13(4), 690–695. DOI: 10.18178/ijiet.2023.13.4.1854

Kim, J. (2021). Advertising in the metaverse: Research agenda. *Journal of Interactive Advertising*, 21(3), 141–144. DOI: 10.1080/15252019.2021.2001273

Kim, M., Oh, J., Son, S., Park, Y., Kim, J., & Park, Y. (2023). Secure and Privacy-Preserving Authentication Scheme Using Decentralized Identifier in Metaverse Environment. *Electronics (Basel)*, 12(19), 4073. DOI: 10.3390/electronics12194073

Köles, B., & Nagy, P. (2012). Who Is Portrayed in Second Life: Dr. Jekyll or Mr. Hyde? The Extent of Congruence Between Real Life and Virtual Identity. *Journal of Virtual Worlds Research*, 5(1). Advance online publication. DOI: 10.4101/jvwr.v5i1.2150

Koops, B.-J., Hildebrandt, M., & Jaquet-Chiffelle, D.-O. (2010). Bridging the Accountability Gap: Rights for New Entities in the Information Society? *Minnesota Journal of Law, Science & Technology*, 11(2), 497–561. https://scholarship.law.umn.edu/mjlst/vol11/iss2/4/

Koreng, R., & Krömker, H. (2021). User Interface Pattern for AR in Industrial Applications. *Information (Basel)*, 12(6), 251. Advance online publication. DOI: 10.3390/info12060251

Kossova, T., Kossova, E., & Sheluntcova, M. (2018). Anti-smoking policy in Russia: Relevant factors and program planning. *Evaluation and Program Planning, 69*(March 2017), 43–52. DOI: 10.1016/j.evalprogplan.2018.04.006

Kostenko, O., Zhuravlov, D., Dniprov, O., & Korotiuk, O. (2023). METAVERSE: MODEL CRIMINAL CODE. *Baltic Journal of Economic Studies*. https://doi.org/.DOI: 10.30525/2256-0742/2023-9-4-134-147

Kozinets, R. V. (2022). Immersive netnography: A novel method for service experience research in virtual reality, augmented reality and metaverse contexts. *Journal of Service Management*, 34(1), 100–125. DOI: 10.1108/JOSM-12-2021-0481

Kraus, S., Jones, P., Kailer, N., Weinmann, A., Chaparro-Banegas, N., & Roig-Tierno, N. (2021). Digital Transformation: An Overview of the Current State of the Art of Research. *SAGE Open*, 11(3), 21582440211047576. DOI: 10.1177/21582440211047576

Kshetri, N. (2017). Will blockchain emerge as a tool to break the poverty chain in the Global South? *Third World Quarterly*, 38(8), 1710–1732. DOI: 10.1080/01436597.2017.1298438

Kuflik, T., Boger, Z., & Zancanaro, M. (2012). Analysis and Prediction of Museum Visitors' Behavioral Pattern Types. In A. Krüger & T. Kuflik (Eds.), *Ubiquitous Display Environments* (pp. 161–176). Springer Berlin Heidelberg. DOI: 10.1007/978-3-642-27663-7_10

Kumar, S., & Aggarwal, N. (2023). Speculative parallelism on multicore chip architecture strengthen green computing concept: A survey. In Advanced computer science applications (1st ed., pp. 1–14). Apple Academic Press., 10.978-1-00-336906-6. DOI: 10.1201/9781003369066-2

Kumar, S., & Singh, S. K. (2021). Brain-computer interaction (BCI): A way to interact with brain waves. *Insights2Techinfo,* 1-1.

Kumar, S., Singh, S. K., & Aggarwal, N. (2021). Efficient speculative parallelization architecture for overcoming speculation overheads. SysCom. https://ceur-ws.org/Vol-3080/19.pdf

Kumar, S., Singh, S. K., & Aggarwal, N. (2023). Sustainable Data Dependency Resolution Architectural Framework to Achieve Energy Efficiency Using Speculative Parallelization. *2023 3rd International Conference on Innovative Sustainable Computational Technologies (CISCT)*, 1–6. DOI: 10.1109/CISCT57197.2023.10351343

Kumar, A., Shankar, A., Behl, A., Gupta, B. B., & Mavuri, S. (2023). Lights, camera, metaverse!: Eliciting intention to use industrial metaverse, organizational agility, and firm performance. [JGIM]. *Journal of Global Information Management*, 31(8), 1–20. DOI: 10.4018/JGIM.333169

Kumar, R., Singh, S. K., Lobiyal, D. K., Kumar, S., & Jawla, S. (2024). Security metrics and authentication-based routing (SMART) protocol for vehicular IoT networks. *SN Computer Science*, 5(2), 236. DOI: 10.1007/s42979-023-02566-7

Kumar, S., Singh, S. K., Aggarwal, N., Gupta, B. B., Alhalabi, W., & Band, S. S. (2022). An efficient hardware supported and parallelization architecture for intelligent systems to overcome speculative overheads. *International Journal of Intelligent Systems*, 37(12), 11764–11790. DOI: 10.1002/int.23062

Kumar, S., Singh, S. K., Ayushi, , Chilkoti, V., Arya, V., Chui, K. T., & Gupta, B. B. (2024). Metaversal 6G: Deciphering Complex Requirements and Multivariate KPIs in High-Performance Computing. *Procedia Computer Science*, 238, 914–919. DOI: 10.1016/j.procs.2024.06.112

Kumar, S., Singh, S. K., Gupta, B. B., Psannis, K., & Wu, J. (2024). Homomorphic Encryption in Smart City Applications for Balancing Privacy and Utility. In *Innovations in Modern Cryptography* (pp. 245–274). IGI Global Scientific Publishing., DOI: 10.4018/979-8-3693-5330-1.ch010

Kumar, S., Singh, S., Aggarwal, N., & Aggarwal, K. (2021). Evaluation of automatic parallelization algorithms to minimize speculative parallelism overheads: An experiment. *Journal of Discrete Mathematical Sciences and Cryptography*, 24(5), 1517–1528. DOI: 10.1080/09720529.2021.1951435

Kuo Siong Tan, G. (2024). Playing for keeps: Digital labor and blockchain precarity in play-to-earn gaming. *Geoforum*, 151, 104009. DOI: 10.1016/j.geoforum.2024.104009

Kurt, İ. (2023). Agents of Socialization Keep in Touch With Socio-Virtualization. *London Journal of Social Sciences*, 5(5), 1–9. DOI: 10.31039/ljss.2023.5.90

Ku, Y., Park, L. H., Shin, S., & Kwon, T. (2019). Draw It As Shown: Behavioral Pattern Lock for Mobile User Authentication. *IEEE Access : Practical Innovations, Open Solutions*, 7, 69363–69378. DOI: 10.1109/ACCESS.2019.2918647

Kwak, H., Blackburn, J., & Han, S. (2015). *Exploring Cyberbullying and Other Toxic Behavior in Team Competition Online Games*. 3739–3748. DOI: 10.1145/2702123.2702529

Kwon, H. J., El Azzaoui, A., & Park, J. H. (2022). Metaq: A quantum approach for secure and optimized metaverse environment. *Hum.-. Cent. Comput. Inf. Sci*, 12, 42.

Langer, E. J., Blank, A., & Chanowitz, B. (1978). The mindlessness of ostensibly thoughtful action: The role of "placebic" information in interpersonal interaction. *Journal of Personality and Social Psychology*, 36(6), 635–642. DOI: 10.1037/0022-3514.36.6.635

Lastowkat, F. G., & Hunter, D. (2004). The Laws of the Virtual Worlds. *California Law Review*, 92(1), 1–72. https://lawcat.berkeley.edu/record/1119331/files/fulltext.pdf. DOI: 10.2307/3481444

Latour, B. (2005). An introduction to actor-network-theory. *Reassembling the social.*

Latour, B. (2007). *Reassembling the social: An introduction to actor-network-theory.* Oup Oxford.

Lee, A. 2021. "With the Metaverse Hype Cycle at Full Blast, Experts Take the Long View." Digiday, August 4, https://digiday.com/marketing/with-the-metaverse-hype-cycle-at-full-blast-experts-take-the-long-view/

Lee, D. (2022). A Study on the Countermeasures of Avatar Sex Crime. *Forum of Public Safety and Culture*. https://doi.org/.DOI: 10.52902/kjsc.2022.19.155

Lee, L. H. (2021). All one needs to know about metaverse: A complete survey on technological singularity, virtual ecosystem, and research agenda. *arXiv preprint arXiv:2110.05352.*

Lee, J.-E. R., & Park, S. G. (2011). "Whose Second Life Is This?" How Avatar-Based Racial Cues Shape Ethno-Racial Minorities' Perception of Virtual Worlds. *Cyberpsychology, Behavior, and Social Networking*, 14(11), 637–642. DOI: 10.1089/cyber.2010.0501 PMID: 21486164

Lee, J., & Min, H. (2022). *Review of legal protection measures against security threats related to Metaverse*. Korean Association of Public Safety and Criminal Justice., DOI: 10.21181/KJPC.2022.31.3.321

Lee, S., & Lee, D. (2020). Social Engineering Attacks: Recent Advances and Countermeasures. *Computers & Security*, 90, 101700. DOI: 10.1016/j.cose.2019.101700

Lee, U.-K., & Kim, H.-K. (2022). UTAUT in Metaverse: An "Ifland" Case. *Journal of Theoretical and Applied Electronic Commerce Research*, 17(2), 613–635. DOI: 10.3390/jtaer17020032

Lee, W. (2022). *A Study on the Role of Criminal Law in Metaverse*. Institute for Legal Studies Chonnam National University., DOI: 10.38133/cnulawreview.2022.42.3.177

Lee, Z. W. Y., Cheung, C. M. K., Chan, T. K. H., & Lee, Y. (2020). Understanding Massively Multiplayer Online Role-playing Game Addiction: A Hedonic Management Perspective. *Information Systems Journal*, 31(1), 33–61. DOI: 10.1111/isj.12292

Lessig, L. (2009). *Code: And Other Laws of Cyberspace*. ReadHowYouWant.com.

Lian, B. (2019). Tanggung Jawab Tridharma Perguruan Tinggi Menjawab Kebutuhan Masyarakat. *Jurnal Cakrawala Ilmiah*, 100–106.

Liang, G., Xin, J., Wang, Q., Ni, X., Guo, X., & Chen, P. (2023). Research on Metaverse Security and Forensics. *Computers, Materials & Continua*, 77(1), 799–825. DOI: 10.32604/cmc.2023.038403

Li, I., & Kim, J. (2023). How Russian Teenagers Are Engaged in the Metaverse Games. *Journal of Digital Art Engineering and Multimedia*, 10(1), 71–79. DOI: 10.29056/jdaem.2023.03.07

Lim, Y., Ng, K.-W., Naveen, P., & Haw, S.-C. (2022). Emotion recognition by facial expression and voice: Review and analysis. *Journal of Informatics and Web Engineering*, 1(2), 45–54. DOI: 10.33093/jiwe.2022.1.2.4

Lin, H., Swarna, H., & Bruning, P F. (2017, September 1). Taking a global view on brand post popularity: Six social media brand post practices for global markets. Elsevier BV, 60(5), 621-633. DOI: 10.1016/j.bushor.2017.05.006

Lin, K., Wu, J., Lin, D., & Zheng, Z. (2023). A Survey on Metaverse: Applications, Crimes and Governance. *2023 IEEE International Conference on Metaverse Computing, Networking and Applications (MetaCom)*, 541–549. https://doi.org/DOI: 10.1109/MetaCom57706.2023.00097

Lippman, S. A., Leslie, H. H., Neilands, T. B., Twine, R., Grignon, J., MacPhail, C., Morris, J., Rebombo, D., Sesane, M., El Ayadi, A. M., Pettifor, A., Kahn, K., Ayadi, A. M. E., Pettifor, A., & Kahn, K. (2018). Context Matters: Community Social Cohesion and Health Behaviors in Two South African Areas. *Health & Place*, 50, 98–104. DOI: 10.1016/j.healthplace.2017.12.009 PMID: 29414427

Liu, Z., Wang, Y., Dontcheva, M., Hoffman, M., Walker, S., & Wilson, A. (2017). Patterns and Sequences: Interactive Exploration of Clickstreams to Understand Common Visitor Paths. *IEEE Transactions on Visualization and Computer Graphics*, 23(1), 321–330. DOI: 10.1109/TVCG.2016.2598797 PMID: 27875148

Li, W. (2024). Analyzing the impact of information features on user continuance intent in recommendation systems. *International Journal on Semantic Web and Information Systems*, 20(1), 1–36. Advance online publication. DOI: 10.4018/IJSWIS.353905

Li, X., Han, D., He, J., Liao, L., & Wang, M. (2019). Next and Next New POI Recommendation via Latent Behavior Pattern Inference. *ACM Transactions on Information Systems*, 37(4), 1–28. Advance online publication. DOI: 10.1145/3354187

Li, Y.-J., Cheung, M. K., Shen, X.-L., & Lee, M. K. O. (2022). Promoting Collaborative Learning in Virtual Worlds: The Power of "We.". *Information Technology & People*, 36(6), 2563–2586. DOI: 10.1108/ITP-11-2021-0870

Li, Y., Wang, Y., Chen, J., Jiao, L., & Shang, R. (2015). Overlapping community detection through an improved multi-objective quantum-behaved particle swarm optimization. *Journal of Heuristics*, 21(4), 549–575. DOI: 10.1007/s10732-015-9289-y

Luckin, R. (2017). Towards artificial intelligence-based assessment systems. *Nature Human Behaviour*, 1(3), 1–3. DOI: 10.1038/s41562-016-0028

Maathuis, C., Kerkhof, I., Godschalk, R., & Passier, H. (2023). Design Lessons from Building Deep Learning Disinformation Generation and Detection Solutions. *European Conference on Cyber Warfare and Security*, 285-293. DOI: 10.34190/eccws.22.1.1071

Madni, A. M. (2021). Mbse testbed for rapid, cost-effective prototyping and evaluation of system modeling approaches. *Applied Sciences (Basel, Switzerland)*, 11(5), 1–19. DOI: 10.3390/app11052321

Mahajan, H. B., Rashid, A. S., Junnarkar, A. A., Uke, N., Deshpande, S. D., Futane, P. R., Alkhayyat, A., & Alhayani, B. (2023). Integration of Healthcare 4.0 and blockchain into secure cloud-based electronic health records systems. *Applied Nanoscience*, 13(3), 2329–2342. DOI: 10.1007/s13204-021-02164-0 PMID: 35136707

Maier, F., & Weinberger, M. (2024). Metaverse Meets Smart Cities—Applications, Benefits, and Challenges. *Future Internet*, 16(4), 126. DOI: 10.3390/fi16040126

Malhotra, V. (2022). How the metaverse will change digital marketing. Retrieved 13 september 2022,from https://timesofindia.indiatimes.com/blogs/voices/how-the-metaverse-will-change-digital-marketing/

Mandeep, G. (2024). *Comparative Analysis of Metaverse Platforms: Sandbox, MANA (Decentraland), and Bloktopia*. Deleted Journal., DOI: 10.36676/sjmbt.v2.i2.29

Mao, Q., Wang, W., You, F., Zhao, R., & Li, Z. (2022). User behavior pattern mining and reuse across similar Android apps. *Journal of Systems and Software*, 183, 111085. https://doi.org/https://doi.org/10.1016/j.jss.2021.111085. DOI: 10.1016/j.jss.2021.111085

Marcon, É., Le Dain, M. A., & Frank, A. G. (2022). Designing business models for Industry 4.0 technologies provision: Changes in business dimensions through digital transformation. *Technological Forecasting and Social Change*, 185, 122078. DOI: 10.1016/j.techfore.2022.122078

Marín, E. C., González-Tejero, C. B., García, M. G., & García, F. J. S. (2022). Catholic impact evolution through public twitter data during CoVId-19. *International Journal of Cloud Applications and Computing*, 12(1), 1–17. Advance online publication. DOI: 10.4018/IJCAC.305211

Marshall, A. M., & Tompsett, B. C. (2023). The metaverse—Not a new frontier for crime. *WIREs Forensic Science*, 1505. Advance online publication. DOI: 10.1002/wfs2.1505

Märtin, C., Herdin, C., Engel, J., & Kampfer, F. (2019). A Structured Approach for Designing Adaptive Interactive Systems by Unifying Situation-Analytics with Model- and Pattern-Based User Interface Development. In Holzinger, A., Silva, H. P., & Helfert, M. (Eds.), *Computer-Human Interaction Research and Applications* (pp. 45–65). Springer International Publishing. DOI: 10.1007/978-3-030-32965-5_3

Märtin, C., Rashid, S., & Herdin, C. (2016). Designing Responsive Interactive Applications by Emotion-Tracking and Pattern-Based Dynamic User Interface Adaptation. In Kurosu, M. (Ed.), *Human-Computer Interaction. Novel User Experiences* (pp. 28–36). Springer International Publishing. DOI: 10.1007/978-3-319-39513-5_3

Massimo, F. (2023). Decentraland: The Alleged Decentralization of Blockchain Applications. *Communications of the ACM*, 66(6), 45–47. Advance online publication. DOI: 10.1145/3563942

Ma, W., Sartipi, K., & Bender, D. (2016). Knowledge-Driven User Behavior Pattern Discovery for System Security Enhancement. *International Journal of Software Engineering and Knowledge Engineering*, 26(03), 379–404. DOI: 10.1142/S0218194016500169

McKenna, B., & Chughtai, H. (2020). Resistance and Sexuality in Virtual Worlds: An LGBT Perspective. *Computers in Human Behavior*, 105, 106199. DOI: 10.1016/j.chb.2019.106199

McKinsey & Company. (2022a). Value creation in the metaverse. https:// www.mckinsey.com/business -functions/growth-marketing-and-sales/ our-insights/value-creation-in-the-metaverse

McKinsey & Company. (2022b). Marketing in the metaverse: An opportunity for innovation and experimentation. Accessed on 5th September 2022. https://www.mckinsey.com/business-functions/ growth-marketing-and-sales/our-insights/marketing-in-the-metaversean-opportunity-for-innovation-and-experimentationMalhotra, 2022

McPherson, M., Smith-Lovin, L., & Cook, J. M. (2001). Birds of a feather: Homophily in social networks. *Annual Review of Sociology*, 27(1), 415–444. DOI: 10.1146/annurev.soc.27.1.415

Mehrabi, N., Morstatter, F., Saxena, N., Lerman, K., & Galstyan, A. (2021). A Survey on Bias and Fairness in Machine Learning. *ACM Computing Surveys*, 54(6), 1–35. DOI: 10.1145/3457607

Mengi, G., Singh, S.K., Kumar, S., Mahto, D., & Sharma, A. (2023). Automated Machine Learning (AutoML): The Future of Computational Intelligence. In International Conference on Cyber Security, Privacy and Networking (ICSPN 2022). ICSPN 2021. Lecture Notes in Networks and Systems (vol. 599). Springer. https://doi.org/10.1007/978-3-031-22018-0_28

Mengi, G., Singh, S. K., Kumar, S., Mahto, D., & Sharma, A. (2023). Automated Machine Learning (AutoML): The Future of Computational Intelligence. In Nedjah, N., Martínez Pérez, G., & Gupta, B. B. (Eds.), *International Conference on Cyber Security, Privacy and Networking (ICSPN 2022)* (Vol. 599, pp. 309–317). Springer International Publishing. DOI: 10.1007/978-3-031-22018-0_28

Menshikova, G., Tikhomandritskaya, O. A., Savel'eva, O. A., & Popova, T. V. (2018). Gender Differences in Interactions With Avatars of Diverse Ethnic Appearances. *Psychology in Russia : State of the Art*, 11(4), 211–222. DOI: 10.11621/pir.2018.0414

Meta Horizon official site https://horizon.meta.com/

Miao, F., Kozlenkova, I. V., Wang, H., Xie, T., & Palmatier, R. W. (2022). An emerging theory of avatar marketing. *Journal of Marketing*, 86(1), 67–90. DOI: 10.1177/0022242921996646

Michopoulou, E., & Buhalis, D. (2013). Information provision for challenging markets: The case of the accessibility requiring market in the context of tourism. *Information & Management*, 50(5), 229–239. DOI: 10.1016/j.im.2013.04.001

Middlemiss, M. (2022, April 27). *E-Residency in the metaverse?* E-Residency. https://www.e-resident .gov.ee/blog/posts/virtual-e-residency-a-future-in-the-metaverse/

Milgram, S. (1963). Behavioral study of obedience. *Journal of Abnormal and Social Psychology*, 67(4), 371–378. DOI: 10.1037/h0040525 PMID: 14049516

Mistretta, S. (2022). The Metaverse—An Alternative Education Space. *Ai Computer Science and Robotics Technology*, 2022, 1–23. DOI: 10.5772/acrt.05

Mitchell, M. (1996). *An Introduction to Genetic Algorithms*. The MIT Press., DOI: 10.7551/mitpress/3927.001.0001

Mitnick, K. D., & Simon, W. L, "*The Art of Deception: Controlling the Human Element of Security*", 978-0-471-23712-9, 2011.

Mitra, S. (2023). Metaverse: A Potential Virtual-Physical Ecosystem for Innovative Blended Education and Training. *Journal of Metaverse*, 3(1), 1. Advance online publication. DOI: 10.57019/jmv.1168056

Moghaieb, H. S. (2020). Estimating local administrators' participation in planning: Case of "Egypt vision 2030.". *Review of Economics and Political Science*, 4(3), 197–223. DOI: 10.1108/REPS-11-2018-0016

Mohamed, M. G., & Saunier, N. (2015). Behavior Analysis Using a Multilevel Motion Pattern Learning Framework. *Transportation Research Record: Journal of the Transportation Research Board*, 2528(1), 116–127. DOI: 10.3141/2528-13

Mohammad, Aljanabi., Sahar, Yousif, Mohammed. (2023). Metaverse: open possibilities. Iraqi journal for computer science and mathematics, DOI: 10.52866/ijcsm.2023.02.03.007

Mohammad, Daradkeh. (2023). Unveiling the Path to Knowledge Sharing and Innovation in Metaverse Virtual Communities. Advances in computational intelligence and robotics book series, DOI: 10.4018/978-1-6684-9151-5.ch018

Molyneux, L., Vasudevan, K., de Zúñiga, H. G., & Zúñiga, H. G. (2015). Gaming Social Capital: Exploring Civic Value in Multiplayer Video Games. *Journal of Computer-Mediated Communication*, 20(4), 381–399. DOI: 10.1111/jcc4.12123

*Monthly NFT Trade Volume (USD)*. [Dataset]. https://dune.com/queries/2344153/3838186

Mourtzis, D., Panopoulos, N., Angelopoulos, J., Wang, B., & Wang, L. (2022). Human centric platforms for personalized value creation in metaverse. *Journal of Manufacturing Systems*, 65, 653–659. DOI: 10.1016/j.jmsy.2022.11.004

Muhammad Sohail Jafar, R., Ahmad, W., & Chen, Y. (2024). Metaverse in Human Behavior: The Role of Telepresence and Flow Experience on Consumers' Shopping Behavior in the Metaverse. *SAGE Open*, 14(2), 21582440241261256. DOI: 10.1177/21582440241261256

Muhuri, S., & Singh, S. S. (2024). Quantum-Social Network Analysis for Community Detection: A Comprehensive Review. *IEEE Transactions on Computational Social Systems, 11*(5), 6795–6806. *IEEE Transactions on Computational Social Systems*. Advance online publication. DOI: 10.1109/TCSS.2024.3397967

Mukai, K., & Hatano, N. (2020). Discrete-time quantum walk on complex networks for community detection. *Physical Review Research*, 2(2), 023378. DOI: 10.1103/PhysRevResearch.2.023378

Murala, D. K. (2024). METAEDUCATION: State-of-the-Art Methodology for Empowering Feature Education. *IEEE Access : Practical Innovations, Open Solutions*, 12, 57992–58020. DOI: 10.1109/ACCESS.2024.3391903

Muza, O., & Debnath, R. (2021). Disruptive innovation for inclusive renewable policy in sub-Saharan Africa: A social shaping of technology analysis of appliance uptake in Rwanda. *Renewable Energy*, 168, 896–912. https://doi.org/https://doi.org/10.1016/j.renene.2020.12.091. DOI: 10.1016/j.renene.2020.12.091 PMID: 33942003

Mystakidis, S. (2022). Metaverse. *Encyclopedia*, 2(1), 486–497. DOI: 10.3390/encyclopedia2010031

Naaz, F. (2023).India Metaverse platform Bharatmeta receives global recognition at VivaTech in Paris. Retieved 16 June 2023, from https://www.livemint.com/news/india/indias-metaverse-platform-bharatmeta-receives-global-recognition-at-vivatech-in-paris-11686902824568.html

Nadini, M., Alessandretti, L., Di Giacinto, F., Martino, M., Aiello, L. M., & Baronchelli, A. (2021). Mapping the NFT revolution: Market trends, trade networks, and visual features. *Scientific Reports*, 11(1), 1–11. DOI: 10.1038/s41598-021-00053-8 PMID: 34686678

Naeem, M., Ozuem, W., Howell, K., & Ranfagni, S. (2023). A Step-by-Step Process of Thematic Analysis to Develop a Conceptual Model in Qualitative Research. *International Journal of Qualitative Methods*, 22, 16094069231205789. DOI: 10.1177/16094069231205789

Nakamoto, S. *A Peer-to-Peer Electronic Cash System*.

Narayanan, A., & Moore, M. (1996). Quantum-inspired genetic algorithms. *Proceedings of IEEE International Conference on Evolutionary Computation*, 61–66. DOI: 10.1109/ICEC.1996.542334

Nelson, Leema & Kumar, Sudhakar. (2023). *Enhancing Haemorrhage Detection in Head CT Scans Using Deep Learning. 1-6.*.DOI: 10.1109/SMARTGENCON60755.2023.10442342

Nesterova, M., Dielini, M., Shynkaruk, L., & Yatsenko, O. (2020). Trust as a Cognitive Base of Social Cohesion in the University Communities. *International Journal of Cognitive Research in Science Engineering and Education*, 8(1), 15–23. DOI: 10.5937/IJCRSEE2001015N

Nevelsteen, K. J. (2018). Virtual world, defined from a technological perspective and applied to video games, mixed reality, and the Metaverse. *Computer Animation and Virtual Worlds*, 29(1), e1752. DOI: 10.1002/cav.1752

Ng, D. T. K., & Kit Ng, D. T. (2022). What Is the Metaverse? Definitions, Technologies and the Community of Inquiry. *Australasian Journal of Educational Technology*, 38(4), 190–205. DOI: 10.14742/ajet.7945

Nguyen, B.-H. T., Dang, T.-Q., Nguyen, L.-T., & Tran, T.-T. T. (2024). Are We Ready for Education in Metaverse? PLS-SEM Analysis. *Edelweiss Applied Science and Technology*, 8(2), 73–83. DOI: 10.55214/25768484.v8i2.693

Nguyen, D., & Beijnon, B. (2024). The data subject and the myth of the 'black box'data communication and critical data literacy as a resistant practice to platform exploitation. *Information Communication and Society*, 27(2), 333–349. DOI: 10.1080/1369118X.2023.2205504

Nguyen, S. H., Sun, Q., & Williams, D. (2021). How do we make the virtual world a better place? Social discrimination in online gaming, sense of community, and well-being. *Telematics and Informatics*, 63, 101747. DOI: 10.1016/j.tele.2021.101747

Nguyen, T. H. N., & Rudawska, E. (2022, September 15). Integrated Cultural Theories on Mobile Marketing Acceptance: Literature Review. *Kozminski University*, 30(3), 112–135. DOI: 10.7206/cemj.2658-0845.84

Nie, B. (2022). Pattern Mining of Smart Home User Behavior in The Context of The Internet of Things: based on Sensor Networks. *2022 3rd International Conference on Smart Electronics and Communication (ICOSEC)*, 398–401. DOI: 10.1109/ICOSEC54921.2022.9952128

Nielsen, M. A., & Chuang, I. L. (2000). *Quantum Computation and Quantum Information*. Cambridge University Press.

Nugrahawati, E. N., Dwarawati, D., Rizal, A. R. S., & Syamsoul Rizal, A. R. (2019). *Muru'ah and Self-Presentation Through Virtual Display of Affection in UNISBA Female Students*. DOI: 10.2991/sores-18.2019.65

O'Neil, C. (2016). *Weapons of Math Destruction: How Big Data Increases Inequality and Threatens Democracy*. Crown.

Oh, C. S., Bailenson, J. N., & Welch, G. (2018). A Systematic Review of Social Presence: Definition, Antecedents, and Implications. *Frontiers in Robotics and AI*, 5, 114. Advance online publication. DOI: 10.3389/frobt.2018.00114 PMID: 33500993

Oindrila, Chakraborty. (2024). Introduction to Metaverse. Advances in e-business research series, DOI: 10.4018/979-8-3693-2422-6.ch002

Oliveira, A., & Cruz, M. (2023). Virtually Connected in a Multiverse of Madness?—Perceptions of Gaming, Animation, and Metaverse. *Applied Sciences (Basel, Switzerland)*, 13(15), 8573. DOI: 10.3390/app13158573

Olson, E. M., Olson, K. M., Czaplewski, A. J., & Key, T. M. (2021). Business strategy and the management of digital marketing. *Business Horizons*, 64(2), 285–293. DOI: 10.1016/j.bushor.2020.12.004

Onosu, O. G. (2021). The Impact of Cultural Immersion Experience on Identity Transformation Process. *International Journal of Environmental Research and Public Health*, 18(5), 2680. DOI: 10.3390/ijerph18052680 PMID: 33799969

Othman, A. (2024). Accessible Metaverse: A Theoretical Framework for Accessibility and Inclusion in the Metaverse. *Multimodal Technologies and Interaction*, 8(3), 21. DOI: 10.3390/mti8030021

P.B., Sharma., Bhavuk, Mahindru. (2024). Exploring the Metaverse. Advances in e-business research series, DOI: 10.4018/979-8-3693-2422-6.ch014

Paas, F., Renkl, A., & Sweller, J. (2003). Cognitive load theory and instructional design: Recent developments. *Educational Psychologist*, 38(1), 1–4. DOI: 10.1207/S15326985EP3801_1

Pandey, N., Nayal, P., & Rathore, A. S. (2020). Digital marketing for B2B organizations: Structured literature review and future research directions. *Journal of Business and Industrial Marketing*, 35(7), 1191–1204. DOI: 10.1108/JBIM-06-2019-0283

Parker, C., Yoo, S., Lee, Y., Fredericks, J., Dey, A., Cho, Y., & Billinghurst, M. (2023). *Towards an Inclusive and Accessible Metaverse*. DOI: 10.1145/3544549.3573811

Parker, L. (2021). Traditional Social Structures and Group Dynamics in Physical Communities. *Cultural Interaction Quarterly*, 10(4), 78–92.

Park, J. H., & Ahn, H. K. (2023). Development of the Capital City of Taebong Kingdom Metaverse and King Gungye Artifical Intelligence Digital Human. In Jung, T., tom Dieck, M. C., & Correia Loureiro, S. M. (Eds.), *Extended Reality and Metaverse* (pp. 217–227). Springer International Publishing. DOI: 10.1007/978-3-031-25390-4_19

Park, J., & Kim, S.-C. (2022). How Do People With Physical Disabilities Want to Construct Virtual Identities With Avatars? *Frontiers in Psychology*, 13, 994786. Advance online publication. DOI: 10.3389/fpsyg.2022.994786 PMID: 36176810

Park, J., Kim, U., Yun, D., & Yeom, K. (2020). Approach for Selecting and Integrating Cloud Services to Construct Hybrid Cloud. *Journal of Grid Computing*, 18(3), 441–469. DOI: 10.1007/s10723-020-09519-x

Park, S. M., & Kim, Y. G. (2022). A metaverse: Taxonomy, components, applications, and open challenges. *IEEE Access : Practical Innovations, Open Solutions*, 10, 4209–4251. DOI: 10.1109/ACCESS.2021.3140175

Park, Y., Ko, E., & Do, B. (2023). The Perceived Value of Digital Fashion Product and Purchase Intention: The Mediating Role of the Flow Experience In metaverse Platforms. *Asia Pacific Journal of Marketing and Logistics*, 35(11), 2645–2665. DOI: 10.1108/APJML-11-2022-0945

Pasquale, F. (2015). *The black box society: The secret algorithms that control money and information*. Harvard University Press. DOI: 10.4159/harvard.9780674736061

Patel, R. (2022). Online Harassment and Misinformation in Social Media Communities. *Journal of Digital Ethics*, 14(2), 201–220.

Patwardhan, A. (2017). Three-Dimensional, Kinematic, Human Behavioral Pattern-Based Features for Multimodal Emotion Recognition. *Multimodal Technologies and Interaction*, 1(3), 19. Advance online publication. DOI: 10.3390/mti1030019

Peña-Acuña, B., & Rubio-Alcalá, F. D. (2024). Ethical approach to the use of immersive technologies. Advance about digitalisation of multilingual programs in the EHEA. *Frontiers in Virtual Reality*, 5(July), 1–10. DOI: 10.3389/frvir.2024.1357595

Peñalvo, F. J. G., Maan, T., Singh, S. K., Kumar, S., Arya, V., Chui, K. T., & Singh, G. P. (2022). Sustainable Stock Market Prediction Framework Using Machine Learning Models. *International Journal of Software Science and Computational Intelligence*, 14(1), 1–15. DOI: 10.4018/IJSSCI.313593

Pendidikan, K. Kebudayaan, R. dan T. (2018). *Data Pokok Pendidikan Direktorat Jenderal Pendidikan Anak Usia Dini, Pendidikan Dasar dan Pendidikan Menengah*. Kementerian Pendidikan, Kebudayaan, Riset Dan Teknologi. https://dapo.kemdikbud.go.id/pd

Peng, Y., & Yu, K. (2016). User behavior analysis of automobile websites based on distributed computing and sequential pattern mining. *2016 IEEE International Conference on Network Infrastructure and Digital Content (IC-NIDC)*, 84–88. DOI: 10.1109/ICNIDC.2016.7974540

Perez, M., & Coello, D. (2023). Sociocultural factors in times of global crisis. *International Journal of Cloud Applications and Computing*, 13(1), 1–21. Advance online publication. DOI: 10.4018/IJCAC.316868

Petrigna, L., & Musumeci, G. (2022). The Metaverse: A New Challenge for the Healthcare System: A Scoping Review. *Journal of Functional Morphology and Kinesiology*, 7(3), 63. Advance online publication. DOI: 10.3390/jfmk7030063 PMID: 36135421

Phillips, K., Davidson, J. C., Farr, R. R., Burkhardt, C., Caneppele, S., & Aiken, M. P. (2022). Conceptualizing cybercrime: Definitions, typologies and taxonomies. *Forensic Science*, 2(2), 379–398. DOI: 10.3390/forensicsci2020028

Phishing and Other Social Engineering Attacks. https://www.cisa.gov/news-events/news/avoiding-social-engineering-and-phishing-attacks, 2021.

Picard, R. W. (2000). *Affective computing*. MIT Press. DOI: 10.7551/mitpress/1140.003.0008

Pietro, R., & Cresci, S. (2021). *Metaverse: Security and Privacy Issues*. DOI: 10.1109/TPSISA52974.2021.00032

Pitale, A., & Bhumgara, A. (2019). Human-computer interaction strategies—Designing the user interface. In *Proceedings of the 2019 International Conference on Smart Technologies* (pp. 1-5). IEEE. https://doi.org/DOI: 10.1109/ICST.2019.8747675

Pollmann, K., & Ziegler, D. (2021). A Pattern Approach to Comprehensible and Pleasant Human–Robot Interaction. *Multimodal Technologies and Interaction*, 5(9), 49. Advance online publication. DOI: 10.3390/mti5090049

Poniszewska-Maranda, A., Matusiak, R., Kryvinska, N., & Yasar, A. U. H. (2020). A real-time service system in the cloud. *Journal of Ambient Intelligence and Humanized Computing*, 11(3), 961–977. DOI: 10.1007/s12652-019-01203-7

Porta, C., Frerich, E., Hoffman, S., Bauer, S., Jain, V., & Bradley, C. (2023). Sexual Violence in Virtual Reality: A Scoping Review. *Journal of Forensic Nursing*. Advance online publication. DOI: 10.1097/JFN.0000000000000466 PMID: 38093420

Porto, F., & Foà, D. (2023). *DEFINING VIRTUAL WORLDS: MAIN FEATURES AND REGULATORY CHALLENGES*. Centre on Regulation in Europe. https://cerre.eu/wp-content/uploads/2023/07/CERRE-Virtual-Worlds-Issue-Paper-0723.pdf

Praetorius, A. S., & Görlich, D. (2020). How Avatars Influence User Behavior: A Review on the Proteus Effect in Virtual Environments and Video Games. *Proceedings of the 15th International Conference on the Foundations of Digital Games*, 1–9. DOI: 10.1145/3402942.3403019

Prasad, Kulkarni., Alok, Gaddi., Ramona, Birău., Virgil, Popescu., Virupakshi, Hiremath., K., Shivashankar., Sharan, Kumar, Shetty., Shivanand, Kagawade. (2024). A Sustainable Approach on Metaverse in Education. Advances in environmental engineering and green technologies book series, DOI: 10.4018/979-8-3693-2845-3.ch011

Prasolova-Førland, E., & Divitini, M. (2003). *Collaborative Virtual Environments for Supporting Learning Communities*. DOI: 10.1145/958160.958170

Preskill, J. (2018). Quantum Computing in the NISQ era and beyond. *Quantum : the Open Journal for Quantum Science*, 2, 79. DOI: 10.22331/q-2018-08-06-79

Provence, S., & Forcehimes, A. A. (2024). Algorithms for empathy: Using machine learning to categorize common empathetic traits across professional and peer-based conversations. *Cureus*, 16(4), e57719. DOI: 10.7759/cureus.57719 PMID: 38711721

PwC. (February 14, 2018). Share of participants who believe artificial intelligence (AI) applications will aid global education in India in 2018, by likelihood [Graph]. In Statista. Retrieved December 09, 2024, from https://www-statista-com.elibrary.siu.edu.in/statistics/823674/india-opinion-on-artificial-intelligence-assisting-global-education-by-likelihood/

Qi, J., Tang, H., & Zhu, Z. (2023). Exploring an affective and responsive virtual environment to improve remote learning. *Virtual Worlds*, 2(1), 53–74. DOI: 10.3390/virtualworlds2010004

Qin, C., Li, Q., Du, M., Yan, W., Tao, L., Wang, Y., Liu, M., & Liu, J. (2022). Neighborhood Social Cohesion Is Associated With the Willingness Toward the Booster Dose of COVID-19 Vaccines Among the Chinese Older Population. *Human Vaccines & Immunotherapeutics*, 18(6), 2140530. Advance online publication. DOI: 10.1080/21645515.2022.2140530 PMID: 36375815

Radanliev, P., Roure, P. D. D., Novitzky, D. P., & Sluganovic, D. I. (2023, January 1). Accessibility and Inclusiveness of New Information and Communication Technologies for Disabled Users and Content Creators in the Metaverse. Cornell University. https://doi.org/DOI: 10.48550/arXiv.2308

Radford, A., Wu, J., Child, R., Luan, D., Amodei, D., & Sutskever, I. (2019). Language Models are Unsupervised Multitask Learners. *OpenAI Blog*. https://openai.com/research/language-models

Rafiq, M., & Malik, A. (2018). Impact of Social Media on Purchasing Decision of Consumerwith Special Reference to Lahore, Pakistan. *Journal of Social Sciences*, 4(2), 268–2733.

Ragu, G., & Ramamoorthy, S. (2023). A blockchain-based cloud forensics architecture for privacy leakage prediction with cloud. *Healthcare Analytics*, 4, 100220. DOI: 10.1016/j.health.2023.100220

Rahaman, M., Lin, C.-Y., Pappachan, P., Gupta, B. B., & Hsu, C.-H. (2024). Privacy-Centric AI and IoT Solutions for Smart Rural Farm Monitoring and Control. *Sensors (Basel)*, 24(13), 13. Advance online publication. DOI: 10.3390/s24134157 PMID: 39000936

Rahaman, M., Pappachan, P., Orozco, S. M., Bansal, S., & Arya, V. (2024). AI Safety and Security. In *Challenges in Large Language Model Development and AI Ethics* (pp. 354–383). IGI Global. DOI: 10.4018/979-8-3693-3860-5.ch011

Rahman, M., Attaufiq, M. M., & Setiyowati, E. (2023). Impact of Metaverse in Educational Environment. *Jurnal Obsesi Jurnal Pendidikan Anak Usia Dini*, 7(6), 7715–7720. DOI: 10.31004/obsesi.v7i6.5820

Raji, I. D., & Buolamwini, J. (2022). Actionable auditing revisited: Investigating the impact of publicly naming biased performance results of commercial AI products. *Communications of the ACM*, 65(12), 68–77. DOI: 10.1145/3569496

Ramadan, Z. (2023, March 17). Marketing in the metaverse era: toward an integrative channel approach. Springer Science+Business Media, 27(3), 1905-1918. DOI: 10.1007/s10055-023-00783-2

Ramadan, O. R. S., Afifi, M. Y. I., & Yahya, A. (2024). A Distributed Cloud Architecture Based on General De Bruijn Overlay Network. *International Journal of Cloud Applications and Computing*, 14(1), 1–19. DOI: 10.4018/IJCAC.339892

Rasheed, A., San, O., & Kvamsdal, T. (2020). Digital twin: Values, challenges and enablers from a modeling perspective. *IEEE Access : Practical Innovations, Open Solutions*, 8, 21980–22012. DOI: 10.1109/ACCESS.2020.2970143

Rauschnabel, P. A., Babin, B. J., tom Dieck, M. C., Krey, N., & Jung, T. (2022). What is augmented reality marketing? Its definition, complexity, and future. *Journal of Business Research*, 142, 1140–1150. DOI: 10.1016/j.jbusres.2021.12.084

Rauschnabel, P. A., Felix, R., & Hinsch, C. (2019). Augmented reality marketing: How mobile AR-apps can improve brands through inspiration. *Journal of Retailing and Consumer Services*, 49, 43–53. DOI: 10.1016/j.jretconser.2019.03.004

Rauschnabel, P. A., Felix, R., Hinsch, C., Shahab, H., & Alt, F. (2022). What is XR? Towards a Framework for Augmented and Virtual Reality. *Computers in Human Behavior*, 133, 107289. DOI: 10.1016/j.chb.2022.107289

Rees, M. (2019). Social Bonds and Emotional Connection in Physical Communities. *Community Interaction Studies*, 7(2), 82–95.

Regan, D. T. (1971). Effects of a Favor and liking on compliance. *Journal of Experimental Social Psychology*, 7(6), 627–639. DOI: 10.1016/0022-1031(71)90025-4

Reis, R., Escudeiro, N., & Escudeiro, N. (2012). Comparing Social Virtual Worlds for Educational Purposes. *Education*, 1(1), 21–26. DOI: 10.5923/j.edu.20110101.04

Resnick, M., Maloney, J., Monroy-Hernández, A., Rusk, N., Eastmond, E., Brennan, K., Millner, A., Rosenbaum, E., Silver, J., Silverman, B., & Kafai, Y. (2009). Scratch: Programming for all. *Communications of the ACM*, 52(11), 60–67. DOI: 10.1145/1592761.1592779

Ritterbusch, G. D., & Teichmann, M. (2023). Defining the Metaverse: A Systematic Literature Review. *IEEE Access : Practical Innovations, Open Solutions*, 11, 12368–12377. DOI: 10.1109/ACCESS.2023.3241809

Ritzer, G., & Stepnisky, J. (2020). *Classical sociological theory*. Sage publications.

Riva, G., Wiederhold, B., & Mantovani, F. (2023). Searching for the Metaverse: Neuroscience of Physical and Digital Communities. *Cyberpsychology, Behavior, and Social Networking*. Advance online publication. DOI: 10.1089/cyber.2023.0040 PMID: 37057986

Robaeyst, B., Baccarne, B., De Meulenaere, J., & Mechant, P. (2022). Online Neighborhood Networks: The Relationship Between Online Communication Practices and Neighborhood Dynamics. *Media and Communication*, 10(2), 108–118. DOI: 10.17645/mac.v10i2.5129

Roblox official site www.roblox.com

Rodriguez, J., Durán, S., Díaz-López, D., Pastor-Galindo, J., & Mármol, F. (2020). C3-Sex: A Conversational Agent to Detect Online Sex Offenders. *Electronics (Basel)*, 9(11), 1779. Advance online publication. DOI: 10.3390/electronics9111779

Rogers, C. E., Witt, A. W., Solomon, A. D., & Venkatasubramanian, K. K. (2015, September). An approach for user identification for head-mounted displays. In *Proceedings of the 2015 ACM International Symposium on Wearable Computers* (pp. 143-146). DOI: 10.1145/2802083.2808391

Rossi, S., Ferland, F., & Tapus, A. (2017). User profiling and behavioral adaptation for HRI: A survey. *Pattern Recognition Letters*, 99, 3–12. https://doi.org/https://doi.org/10.1016/j.patrec.2017.06.002. DOI: 10.1016/j.patrec.2017.06.002

Roumani, Y. (2022). Detection time of data breaches. *Computers & Security*, 112, 102508. DOI: 10.1016/j.cose.2021.102508

Sahin, D. (2023). *Understanding English Language Teachers' Digital Literacies and Their Willingness to Change*. Focus on Elt Journal., DOI: 10.14744/felt.2023.5.2.3

Sahoo, S. R., & Gupta, B. B. (2019). Classification of various attacks and their defence mechanism in online social networks: A survey. *Enterprise Information Systems*, 13(6), 832–864. DOI: 10.1080/17517575.2019.1605542

Sahoo, S. R., & Gupta, B. B. (2020). Classification of spammer and nonspammer content in online social network using genetic algorithm-based feature selection. *Enterprise Information Systems*, 14(5), 710–736. DOI: 10.1080/17517575.2020.1712742

Said, G. R. E., & El Said, G. R. (2023). Metaverse-Based Learning Opportunities and Challenges: A Phenomenological Metaverse Human–Computer Interaction Study. *Electronics (Basel)*, 12(6), 1379. DOI: 10.3390/electronics12061379

Saini, G., Zain, M., Noronha, M., Bonin, R. P., & Lomanowska, A. M. (2024). Virtually Simulated Interpersonal Touch Negatively Affects Perceived Closeness and Social Affiliation to an Avatar Partner. *Scientific Reports*, 14(1), 1347. Advance online publication. DOI: 10.1038/s41598-024-51773-6 PMID: 38228629

Salmond, J. W. (1907). *Jurisprudence or the theory of the law*. Stevens and Haynes.

Sanaj, M. S., & Joe Prathap, P. M. (2020). Nature inspired chaotic squirrel search algorithm (CSSA) for multi objective task scheduling in an IAAS cloud computing atmosphere. *Engineering Science and Technology, an International Journal*, 23(4), 891–902. https://doi.org/https://doi.org/10.1016/j.jestch.2019.11.002. DOI: 10.1016/j.jestch.2019.11.002

Sánchez-Adame, L. M., Monroy-Rodríguez, G., Mendoza, S., Decouchant, D., & Mateos-Papis, A. P. (2023). Framework for Ethically Designed Microtransactions in the Metaverse. *IEEE Access : Practical Innovations, Open Solutions*, 11, 140687–140700. DOI: 10.1109/ACCESS.2023.3341057

Santosa, H. P., Yudono, A., Sutikno, F. R., Adhitama, M. S., Tolle, H., & Zuliana, E. (2023). *Development of a Public Engagement Scenario in Metaverse Toward Maintaining the Sustainability of Valuable Historic Buildings in the Kayutangan Area.*, DOI: 10.2991/978-94-6463-140-1_26

Saphira, H. V. (2024). Metaverse: A Paradigm Shift in STEM Education for Science Learning Beyond the Review. *E3s Web of Conferences, 482*, 4004. DOI: 10.1051/e3sconf/202448204004

Sarin, S., Singh, S. K., Kumar, S., Goyal, S., Gupta, B. B., Arya, V., & Chui, K. T. (2023). Forging Faces: 13th IEEE International Conference on Consumer Electronics - Berlin, ICCE-Berlin 2023. *IEEE International Conference on Consumer Electronics - Berlin, ICCE-Berlin.* DOI: 10.1109/ICCE-Berlin58801.2023.10649659

Sarin, S., Singh, S. K., Kumar, S., Goyal, S., Gupta, B. B., Alhalabi, W., & Arya, V. (2024). Unleashing the Power of Multi-Agent Reinforcement Learning for Algorithmic Trading in the Digital Financial Frontier and Enterprise Information Systems. *Computers, Materials & Continua*, 80(2), 3123–3138. DOI: 10.32604/cmc.2024.051599

Sarin, S., Singh, S. K., Kumar, S., Goyal, S., Gupta, B. B., Arya, V., & Chui, K. T. (2024a). SEIR-driven semantic integration framework: Internet of Things-enhanced epidemiological surveillance in COVID-19 outbreaks using recurrent neural networks. *IET Cyber-Physical Systems*, 9(2), 135–149. DOI: 10.1049/cps2.12091

Saverio, Iacono. (2023). How to Prepare High-Level Massive Online Open Courses for the Metaverse: Tools and Needs. DOI: 10.3390/engproc2023038002

Sawyer, S. M., Azzopardi, P. S., Wickremarathne, D., & Patton, G. C. (2018). The age of adolescence. *The Lancet. Child & Adolescent Health*, 2(3), 223–228. DOI: 10.1016/S2352-4642(18)30022-1 PMID: 30169257

Sbeyti, H. (2016). [MOUBE]. *Mobile User Authentication Based On User Behavioral Pattern*, 10, 120–139.

Schmidt, E., & Cohen, J. (2013). *The New Digital Age: Reshaping the Future of People, Nations and Business*. Knopf Doubleday Publishing Group.

Schneegass, S., Oualil, Y., & Bulling, A. (2016, May). SkullConduct: Biometric user identification on eyewear computers using bone conduction through the skull. In *Proceedings of the 2016 CHI Conference on Human Factors in Computing Systems* (pp. 1379-1384). DOI: 10.1145/2858036.2858152

Schöbel, S., & Leimeister, J. M. (2023). Metaverse Platform Ecosystems. *Electronic Markets*, 33(1), 12. Advance online publication. DOI: 10.1007/s12525-023-00623-w

Se, H. (2023, May 15). Hwang. (2023). Creating Communities for Burn Survivors Using Metaverse Platform. *Journal of Burn Care & Research; Official Publication of the American Burn Association*, 44(Supplement_2), S103. Advance online publication. DOI: 10.1093/jbcr/irad045.141

Selwyn, N. (2019). Should robots replace teachers? AI and the future of education. *Polity*.

Sengupta, D. (2021). Nike Acquired This Company That Makes Virtual Sneakers and NFTs for the Metaverse. Retrieved from https://beebom.com/nikeacquired-company-makes-virtual-sneakers-nfts-metaverse/. Accessed April 12, 2022.

Seo, J., Ko, H., & Park, S. (2024). Space Authentication in the Metaverse: A Blockchain-Based User-Centric Approach. *IEEE Access : Practical Innovations, Open Solutions*, 12, 18703–18713. DOI: 10.1109/ACCESS.2024.3357938

Seo, S., Seok, B., & Lee, C. (2023). Digital forensic investigation framework for the metaverse. *The Journal of Supercomputing*, 79(9), 9467–9485. DOI: 10.1007/s11227-023-05045-1

Sergei, Ivanovich, Rodzin., Viktoriia, Viktorovna, Bova. (2024). The Metaverse as one of the foundations of future education. DOI: 10.31483/r-112497

Setia, H., Chhabra, A., Singh, S. K., Kumar, S., Sharma, S., Arya, V., Gupta, B. B., & Wu, J. (2024). Securing the road ahead: Machine learning-driven DDoS attack detection in VANET cloud environments. *Cyber Security and Applications*, 2, 100037. DOI: 10.1016/j.csa.2024.100037

Sharma, A., Singh, S. K., Kumar, S., Chhabra, A., & Gupta, S. (2023). Security of Android visionBanking Mobile Apps: Challenges and Opportunities. In: Nedjah, N., Martínez Pérez, G., Gupta, B.B. (eds) International Conference on Cyber Security, Privacy and Networking (ICSPN 2022). ICSPN 2021. Lecture Notes in Networks and Systems, vol 599. Springer, Cham. DOI: 10.1007/978-3-031-22018-0_39

Sharma, A., Singh, S. K., Chhabra, A., Kumar, S., Arya, V., & Moslehpour, M. (2023). A Novel Deep Federated Learning-Based Model to Enhance Privacy in Critical Infrastructure Systems. *International Journal of Software Science and Computational Intelligence*, 15(1), 1–23. DOI: 10.4018/IJSSCI.334711

Sharma, A., Singh, S. K., Kumar, S., Chhabra, A., & Gupta, S. (2023). Fuzzy-based clustering of consumers' big data in industrial applications. *2023 IEEE International Conference on Consumer Electronics (ICCE)*, 1–3. DOI: 10.1109/ICCE56470.2023.10043451

Sharma, A., Singh, S. K., Kumar, S., Preet, M., Gupta, B. B., Arya, V., & Chui, K. T. (2024). Revolutionizing Healthcare Systems: Synergistic Multimodal Ensemble Learning & Knowledge Transfer for Lung Cancer Delineation & Taxonomy. *2024 IEEE International Conference on Consumer Electronics (ICCE)*, 1–6. DOI: 10.1109/ICCE59016.2024.10444476

Sharma, K., & Giannakos, M. (2020). Multimodal data capabilities for learning: What can multimodal data tell us about learning? *British Journal of Educational Technology*, 51(5), 1450–1484. DOI: 10.1111/bjet.12993

Sheehan, D. (2022). CitizenM announce opening a hotel in the Metaverse. https://www. hospitalityandcateringnews.com/2022/04/citizenm-announce-opening-a-hotel-inthe-metaverse/

Shen, C., Chen, Y., Guan, X., & Maxion, R. A. (2020). Pattern-Growth Based Mining Mouse-Interaction Behavior for an Active User Authentication System. *IEEE Transactions on Dependable and Secure Computing*, 17(2), 335–349. DOI: 10.1109/TDSC.2017.2771295

Shinder, L., & Cross, M. (2008). The Evolution of Cybercrime. In Shinder, L., & Cross, M. (Eds.), *Scene of the Cybercrime* (2nd ed., pp. 41–75). Syngress., DOI: 10.1016/B978-1-59749-276-8.00002-9

Shiu, J. M., Dallas, M. P., & Lin, P. H. (2024). Collaboration and social capital in meta-organisations: Bonding or bridging? *Technology Analysis and Strategic Management*, •••, 1–13. DOI: 10.1080/09537325.2024.2330549

Shneiderman, B., & Plaisant, C. (2010). *Designing the user interface: Strategies for effective human-computer interaction* (5th ed.). Addison-Wesley.

Shoham, Y., & Leyton-Brown, K. (2009). *Multiagent Systems: Algorithmic, Game-Theoretic, and Logical Foundations*. Cambridge University Press.

Shor, P. W. (1994). Algorithms for quantum computation: Discrete logarithms and factoring. *Proceedings 35th Annual Symposium on Foundations of Computer Science*, 124–134. DOI: 10.1109/SFCS.1994.365700

Short, J., Williams, E., & Christie, B. (1976). The social psychology of telecommunications.

Shrushti, S. (2024). *Zade., Sakshi, S., Atrik., Aarti, P., Pimpalkar*. Metaverse & NFT Blockchain., DOI: 10.59256/indjcst.20240302005

Sims, A. (2019). Blockchain and Decentralised Autonomous Organisations (DAOs): The Evolution of Companies? SSRN *Electronic Journal*. DOI: 10.2139/ssrn.3524674

Singh, G., & Rawat, Y. (2024). Advancements in metaverse gaming technologies. Insights2Techinfo, 1. https://insights2techinfo.com/advancements-in-metaverse-gaming-technologies/

Singh, I., Singh, S. K., Singh, R., & Kumar, S. (2022). Efficient Loop Unrolling Factor Prediction Algorithm using Machine Learning Models. *2022 3rd International Conference for Emerging Technology (INCET)*, 1–8. DOI: 10.1109/INCET54531.2022.9825092

Singh, S. K., Sharma, S. K., Singla, D., & Gill, S. S. (2022). Evolving requirements and application of SDN and IoT in the context of industry 4.0, blockchain and artificial intelligence. *Software Defined Networks: Architecture and Applications,* 427-496.

Singh, C. (2024). Artificial intelligence and deep learning: Considerations for financial institutions for compliance with the regulatory burden in the United Kingdom. *Journal of Financial Crime*, 31(2), 259–266. DOI: 10.1108/JFC-01-2023-0011

Singh, G., Malhotra, M., & Sharma, A. (2022). An adaptive mechanism for virtual machine migration in the cloud environment. [IJCAC]. *International Journal of Cloud Applications and Computing*, 12(1), 1–10. DOI: 10.4018/IJCAC.311504

Singh, I., Singh, S. K., Kumar, S., & Aggarwal, K. (2022). Dropout-VGG Based Convolutional Neural Network for Traffic Sign Categorization. In Saraswat, M., Sharma, H., Balachandran, K., Kim, J. H., & Bansal, J. C. (Eds.), *Congress on Intelligent Systems. Lecture Notes on Data Engineering and Communications Technologies* (Vol. 114). Springer. DOI: 10.1007/978-981-16-9416-5_18

Singh, M., Singh, S. K., Kumar, S., Madan, U., & Maan, T. (2021, September). Sustainable framework for metaverse security and privacy: Opportunities and challenges. In *International Conference on Cyber Security, Privacy and Networking* (pp. 329-340). Cham: Springer International Publishing.

Singh, M., Singh, S. K., Kumar, S., Madan, U., & Maan, T. (2023). Sustainable Framework for Metaverse Security and Privacy: Opportunities and Challenges. In Nedjah, N., Martínez Pérez, G., & Gupta, B. B. (Eds.), *International Conference on Cyber Security, Privacy and Networking (ICSPN 2022)* (Vol. 599, pp. 329–340). Springer International Publishing. DOI: 10.1007/978-3-031-22018-0_30

Singh, N., Singh, S. K., Kumar, S., Rawat, Y., Arya, V., Bansal, R., & Chui, K. T. (2024). Next Gen Security With Quantum-Safe Cryptography. In Gupta, B. B., Kalra, D., & Almomani, A. (Eds.), (pp. 131–164). Advances in Information Security, Privacy, and Ethics. IGI Global., DOI: 10.4018/979-8-3693-5330-1.ch006

Singh, S. K., Gupta, S., Kumar, S., Gupta, B. B., Alhalabi, W., Arya, V., & Zhang, J. (2024). A novel cumulative indicator score using indicator averaging for optimizing local business websites of enterprise systems. *Enterprise Information Systems*, 18(2), 2301658. DOI: 10.1080/17517575.2023.2301658

Slater, M., Gonzalez-Liencres, C., Haggard, P., Vinkers, W., Gregory-Clarke, R., Jelley, S., Watson, Z., Breen, G., Schwarz, R., Steptoe, W., Szostak, D., Halan, S., Fox, D., & Silver, J. (2020). The Ethics of Realism in Virtual and Augmented Reality. *Frontiers in Virtual Reality*, 1, 1. Advance online publication. DOI: 10.3389/frvir.2020.00001

Smith, J. (2022). Immersive Virtual Worlds and Social Presence in the Metaverse. *Journal of Virtual Interaction*, 15(2), 101–120.

Snider, M., & Molina, B. (2021). Everyone wants to own the metaverse including Facebook and Microsoft. But what exactly is it? USA Today Tech. https://eu. usatoday. com/story/tech/2021/11/10/metaverse-what-is-it-explained-facebook-microsoft-meta-vr/6337635001/(nd).

Song, C., Shin, S.-Y., & Shin, K.-S. (2023). Exploring the Key Characteristics and Theoretical Framework for Research on the Metaverse. *Applied Sciences (Basel, Switzerland)*, 13(13), 7628. DOI: 10.3390/app13137628

Sparkes, M. (2021). What is a metaverse.

Staff, B. E. (2022). Metaverse is emerging not only for GenX or Millennials: Report. ET BrandEquity., Retrieved August 19, 2022, from.

Staszkiewicz, P., Horobiowski, J., Szelągowska, A., & Strzelecka, A. M. (2024). Artificial intelligence legal personality and accountability: Auditors' accounts of capabilities and challenges for instrument boundary. *Meditari Accountancy Research*, 32(7), 141–167. DOI: 10.1108/MEDAR-10-2023-2204

State of the Phish Report. Retrieved from Proofpoint, https://go.proofpoint.com/state-of-the-phish-report.html, 2021.

Stephenson, N. (1992). *Snow Crash*. Bantam Books.

Stephenson, N. (2003). *Snow crash: A novel. Spectra*. Bantam Books.

Stergiou, C. L., Psannis, K. E., & Gupta, B. B. (2022). InFeMo: Flexible Big Data Management Through a Federated Cloud System. *ACM Transactions on Internet Technology*, 22(2), 1–22. DOI: 10.1145/3426972

Stingl, V., & Geraldi, J. (2021). A research agenda for studying project decision-behaviour through the lenses of simple heuristics. *Technological Forecasting and Social Change*, 162, 120367. https://doi.org/https://doi.org/10.1016/j.techfore.2020.120367. DOI: 10.1016/j.techfore.2020.120367

Stone, C. D. (1972). Should Trees Have Standing—Toward Legal Rights for Natural Objects. *Southern California Law Review*, 45(2), 450–501. https://southerncalifornialawreview.com/wp-content/uploads/2022/03/Christopher-D.-Stone-Should-Trees-Have-Standing_%E2%80%94Toward-Legal-Rights-for-Natural-Objects-45-S.-CAL.-L.-REV.-450-1972.pdf

Sugaya, N., Shirasaka, T., Takahashi, K., & Kanda, H. (2019). Bio-Psychosocial Factors of Children and Adolescents With Internet Gaming Disorder: A Systematic Review. *BioPsychoSocial Medicine*, 13(1), 3. Advance online publication. DOI: 10.1186/s13030-019-0144-5 PMID: 30809270

Sumon, R. I., Uddin, S. M. I., Akter, S., Mozumder, M. A. I., Khan, M. O., & Kim, H.-C. (2024). Natural Language Processing Influence on Digital Socialization and Linguistic Interactions in the Integration of the Metaverse in Regular Social Life. *Electronics (Basel)*, 13(7), 1331. DOI: 10.3390/electronics13071331

Sung, E. C., Bae, S., Han, D. I. D., & Kwon, O. (2021). Consumer engagement via interactive artificial intelligence and mixed reality. *International Journal of Information Management*, 60, 102382. DOI: 10.1016/j.ijinfomgt.2021.102382

Sunil, S. K. (2021). *Linux Yourself: Concept and Programming*. Routledge & CRC Press. https://www.routledge.com/Linux-Yourself-Concept-and-Programming/KSingh/p/book/9781032037073

Sun, L., Wang, P., Liu, P., & Nie, Z. (2023). Image Processing Method of a Visual Communication System Based on Convolutional Neural Network. [IJSWIS]. *International Journal on Semantic Web and Information Systems*, 19(1), 1–19. DOI: 10.4018/IJSWIS.333063

Swan, M. (2015). *Blockchain: Blueprint for a New Economy*. O'Reilly Media, Inc.

Sweller, J. (1988). Cognitive load during problem solving: Effects on learning. *Cognitive Science*, 12(2), 257–285. DOI: 10.1207/s15516709cog1202_4

Swilley, E. (2015). Moving Virtual Retail into Reality: Examining Metaverse and Augmented Reality in the Online Shopping Experience. Looking Forward, Looking Back. *Drawing on the Past to Shape the Future of Marketing*, 675–677, 675–677. Advance online publication. DOI: 10.1007/978-3-319-24184-5_163

Szita, K. (2022). A Virtual Safe Space? *Journal of Digital Social Research*, 4(3), 34–55. DOI: 10.33621/jdsr.v4i3.91

Tajfel, H. (1978). *Differentiation between social groups. Studies in the social psychology of intergroup relations*. Academic Press.

Tajfel, H., & Turner, J. (1979). An integrative theory of intergroup conflict. In Williams, J. A., & Worchel, S. (Eds.), *The social psychology of intergroup relations* (pp. 33–47). Wadsworth.

Talbi, & Talbi, E.-G. (2009). Metaheuristics: From Design to Implementation. In *Metaheuristics: From Design to Implementation* (Vol. 74). DOI: 10.1002/9780470496916

Tamang, D. B. (2024). Fostering Social Cohesion in Ethnolinguistic Communities Through Mother Tongue-Based Initiatives in Nepal. *Forum for Linguistic Studies*, 6(1). Advance online publication. DOI: 10.59400/fls.v6i1.2092

Tang, B., Wang, N., Li, J., & Shen, Z. (2024). A Multi-task Learning Framework with Features Based on Behavioral Pattern Conversation. In Zaslavsky, A., Ning, Z., Kalogeraki, V., Georgakopoulos, D., & Chrysanthis, P. K. (Eds.), *Mobile and Ubiquitous Systems: Computing, Networking and Services* (pp. 256–267). Springer Nature Switzerland. DOI: 10.1007/978-3-031-63992-0_17

Thakur, N., Singh, S. K., Gupta, A., Jain, K., Jain, R., Peraković, D., Nedjah, N., & Rafsanjani, M. K. (2022). A novel CNN, bidirectional long-short term memory, and gated recurrent unit-based hybrid approach for human activity recognition. [IJSSCI]. *International Journal of Software Science and Computational Intelligence*, 14(1), 1–19. DOI: 10.4018/IJSSCI.311445

Thanaporn, P. (2024) Decoding Offensiveness: Exploring Ethical Ideology, Social Competence, and Humanlikeness in Human-AI Chatbot Interaction, Insighrs2Techinfo, pp.1, https://insights2techinfo.com/decoding-offensiveness-exploring-ethical-ideology-social-competence-and-humanlikeness-in-human-ai-chatbot-interaction/

*The Information and Decision Support Center of the Egyptian Council of Ministers*. (2022). World Trends - Metaverse World.

Thornhill-Miller, B., Camarda, A., Mercier, M., Burkhardt, J.-M., Morisseau, T., Bourgeois-Bougrine, S., Vinchon, F., El Hayek, S., Augereau-Landais, M., Mourey, F., Feybesse, C., Sundquist, D., & Lubart, T. (2023). Creativity, Critical Thinking, Communication, and Collaboration: Assessment, Certification, and Promotion of 21st Century Skills for the Future of Work and Education. *Journal of Intelligence*, 11(3), 54. DOI: 10.3390/jintelligence11030054 PMID: 36976147

Tingting, W. (2020).. . *Research on User Access Pattern Mining Based on Web Log.*, 6(8), 135–148.

Trinidad, D. R., Gilpin, E. A., & Pierce, J. P. (2005). Compliance and support for smoke-free school policies. *Health Education Research*, 20(4), 466–475. DOI: 10.1093/her/cyg143 PMID: 15572436

Truong, V. T., Le, L. B., & Niyato, D. (2023). Blockchain Meets Metaverse and Digital Asset Management: A Comprehensive Survey. *IEEE Access : Practical Innovations, Open Solutions*, 11, 26258–26288. DOI: 10.1109/ACCESS.2023.3257029

Tucci, L. (2024, March 22). *What is the metaverse? An explanation and in-depth guide*. WhatIs. https://www.techtarget.com/whatis/feature/The-metaverse-explained-Everything-you-need-to-know

Tukur, M., Schneider, J., Househ, M., Dokoro, A. H., Ismail, U. I., Dawaki, M., & Agus, M. (2023). The metaverse digital environments: A scoping review of the challenges, privacy and security issues. *Frontiers in Big Data*, 6, 1301812. DOI: 10.3389/fdata.2023.1301812 PMID: 38074486

Tuli, E. A., Lee, J. M., & Kim, D. S. (2024). Integration of Quantum Technologies into Metaverse: Applications, Potentials, and Challenges. *IEEE Access : Practical Innovations, Open Solutions*, 12, 29995–30019. DOI: 10.1109/ACCESS.2024.3366527

Tural, A., & Koçak, N. (2023). Awareness Levels of Social Studies Pre-Service Teachers Regarding Metaverse Use. *Advanced Education*, 11(23), 69–86. DOI: 10.20535/2410-8286.284683

Turner, J. C. (1999). Some current issues in research on social identity and self-categorization theories. In Ellemers, N., Spears, R., & Dossje, B. (Eds.), *Social identity: Context, commitment, content* (pp. 6–34). Blackwell.

Ud Din, I., Awan, K. A., Almogren, A., & Rodrigues, J. J. (2023). Integration of IoT and blockchain for decentralized management and ownership in the Metaverse. *International Journal of Communication Systems*, 36(18), e5612. DOI: 10.1002/dac.5612

Ul Islam, J., & Rahman, Z. (2017). The impact of online brand community characteristics on customer engagement: An application of Stimulus-Organism-Response paradigm. *Telematics and Informatics*, 34(4), 96–109. https://doi.org/https://doi.org/10.1016/j.tele.2017.01.004. DOI: 10.1016/j.tele.2017.01.004

United States v. Meregildo, No. 11 Cr. 576 WHP, 2012 WL 3264501, at *2 S.D.N.Y. Aug. 10, 2012.

Upadhyay, U., Kumar, A., Sharma, G., Gupta, B. B., Alhalabi, W., Arya, V., & Chui, K. T. (2023). Cyberbullying in the Metaverse. *Journal of Global Information Management*, 31(1), 1–25. DOI: 10.4018/JGIM.325793

Uricchio, W. (2011). The algorithmic turn: Photosynth, augmented reality and the changing implications of the image. *Visual Studies*, 26(1), 25–35. DOI: 10.1080/1472586X.2011.548486

Vaingankar, J. A., van Dam, R. M., Samari, E., Chang, S., Seow, E., Chua, Y. C., Luo, N., Verma, S., & Subramaniam, M. (2022). Social Media–Driven Routes to Positive Mental Health Among Youth: Qualitative Enquiry and Concept Mapping Study. *JMIR Pediatrics and Parenting*, 5(1), e32758. DOI: 10.2196/32758 PMID: 35254285

Vajrobol, V. (2024). Metaverse in healthcare domain. Insights2Techinfo, 1. https://insights2techinfo.com/metaverse-in-healthcare-domain/

Vats, T. (2024). OPTUNA—Driven Soft Computing Approach for Early Diagnosis of Diabetes Mellitus Using ANN. In *Proceedings of the 12th International Conference on Soft Computing for Problem Solving. SocProS 2023. Lecture Notes in Networks and Systems* (vol. 995). Springer. https://doi.org/10.1007/978-981-97-3292-0_25

Vats, T., & Kumar, S. Next-generation towards construction of cyber-physical systems and digital twins. *Insights2Techinfo,* 1-1.

Vats, T., Kumar, S., Singh, S. K., Madan, U., Preet, M., Arya, V., Bansal, R., & Almomani, A. (2024). Navigating the landscape: Safeguarding privacy and security in the era of ambient intelligence within healthcare settings. *Cyber Security and Applications*, 2, 100046. DOI: 10.1016/j.csa.2024.100046

Vats, T., Singh, S. K., Kumar, S., Gupta, B. B., Gill, S. S., Arya, V., & Alhalabi, W. (2024). Explainable context-aware IoT framework using human digital twin for healthcare. *Multimedia Tools and Applications*, 83(22), 62489–62490. DOI: 10.1007/s11042-023-16922-5

Vellingiri, J., Kaliraj, S., Satheeshkumar, S., & Parthiban, T. (2015). A novel approach for user navigation pattern discovery and analysis for web usage mining. *Journal of Computational Science*, 11(2), 372–382. DOI: 10.3844/jcssp.2015.372.382

Verma, V., Benjwal, A., Chhabra, A., Singh, S. K., Kumar, S., Gupta, B. B., Arya, V., & Chui, K. T. (2023). A novel hybrid model integrating MFCC and acoustic parameters for voice disorder detection. *Scientific Reports*, 13(1), 22719. DOI: 10.1038/s41598-023-49869-6 PMID: 38123627

Vinyals, O., Babuschkin, I., Czarnecki, W. M., Mathieu, M., Dudzik, A., Chung, J., Choi, D. H., Powell, R., Ewalds, T., Georgiev, P., Oh, J., Horgan, D., Kroiss, M., Danihelka, I., Huang, A., Sifre, L., Cai, T., Agapiou, J. P., Jaderberg, M., & Silver, D. (2019). Grandmaster Level in StarCraft II Using Multi-Agent Reinforcement Learning. *Nature*, 575(7782), 350–354. DOI: 10.1038/s41586-019-1724-z PMID: 31666705

Visser, A., & Molin, M. (2022). Where should I buy my sofa?: A qualitative study on Swedish digital natives in the omni-channel furniture retailing environment.

Wadley, G., Carter, M., & Gibbs, M. (2014). Voice in Virtual Worlds: The Design, Use, and Influence of Voice Chat in Online Play. *Human-Computer Interaction*, 30(3–4), 336–365. DOI: 10.1080/07370024.2014.987346

Wajire, P. (2022). Exploring the Metaverse: Challenges and Opportunities for India in the 'Next Internet. Retieved 23 August 2023, from https://www.orfonline.org/research/exploring-the-metaverse/

Wang, N., Zhang, Q., Yang, L., & Chen, M. (2016). *A Novel E-Commerce Recommendation System Model based on the Pattern Recognition and User Behavior Preference Analysis. 138*(Isi), 105–110. DOI: 10.14257/astl.2016.138.23

Wang, Y., Zhou, S., & Yan, M. (2023). *Social Metaverse: Challenges and Solutions.* https://doi.org//arxiv.2301.10221DOI: 10.48550

Wang, H., Ning, H., Lin, Y., Wang, W., Dhelim, S., Farha, F., Ding, J., & Daneshmand, M. (2023). A survey on the metaverse: The state-of-the-art, technologies, applications, and challenges. *IEEE Internet of Things Journal*, 10(16), 14671–14688. DOI: 10.1109/JIOT.2023.3278329

Wang, S., & Wang, W. (2023). A review of the application of digital identity in the Metaverse. *Security and Safety*, 2, 2023009. DOI: 10.1051/sands/2023009

Wang, X., Su, Z., & Miao, Y. (2023, September 1). Social Metaverse: Challenges and Solutions. *IEEE Internet of Things Magazine*, 6(3), 144–150. DOI: 10.1109/IOTM.001.2200266

Wang, Y., Song, W., Tao, W., Liotta, A., Yang, D., Li, X., Gao, S., Sun, Y., Ge, W., Zhang, W., & Zhang, W. (2022). A systematic review on affective computing: Emotion models, databases, and recent advances. *Information Fusion*, 83–84, 19–52. DOI: 10.1016/j.inffus.2022.03.009

Wang, Y., Su, Z., Zhang, N., Xing, R., Liu, D., Luan, T. H., Shen, X., Zhou, S., Zhang, N., Liu, D., Xing, R., Luan, T. H., Shen, X., Su, Z., Zhang, N., Xing, R., Liu, D., Luan, T. H., Shen, X., & Shen, X. (2022). A Survey on Metaverse: Fundamentals, Security, and Privacy. *IEEE Communications Surveys and Tutorials*, 25(1), 319–352. DOI: 10.1109/COMST.2022.3202047

Weiss, R. P. (2000). Emotion and learning. *Training & Development*, 54(2), 34–38.

Welton-Mitchell, C., James, L., Khanal, S. N., & James, A. S. (2018). An Integrated Approach to Mental Health and Disaster Preparedness: A Cluster Comparison With Earthquake Affected Communities in Nepal. *BMC Psychiatry*, 18(1), 296. Advance online publication. DOI: 10.1186/s12888-018-1863-z PMID: 30223822

Wentzlaff, I., & Specker, M. (2006). Pattern-based development of user-friendly web applications. *Workshop Proceedings of the Sixth International Conference on Web Engineering*, 2–es. DOI: 10.1145/1149993.1149996

West, C. (2021). Curating Identity: Social Media and Self-Presentation in the Digital Age. *Journal of Social Media Studies*, 12(1), 120–135.

Widodo, A. M., Wisnujati, A., Asianto, A. M., Aryani, D. M., Rahaman, M., Arya, V., & Pappachan, P. (2024). Understanding the Metaverse. In *Metaverse Security Paradigms* (pp. 1–38). IGI Global. DOI: 10.4018/979-8-3693-3824-7.ch001

Williamson, B., & Eynon, R. (2020). Artificial intelligence in education: What is it, and why should we care? *Learning, Media and Technology*, 45(2), 102–113.

Witte, K. (1992). Putting the fear back into fear appeals: The extended parallel process model. *Communication Monographs*, 59(4), 329–349. DOI: 10.1080/03637759209376276

Worchel, S., Lee, J., & Adewole, A. (1975). Effects of supply and demand on ratings of object value. *Journal of Personality and Social Psychology*, 32(5), 906–914. DOI: 10.1037/0022-3514.32.5.906

Wright, M. (2023). Decentralized Governance in the Metaverse: A Case Study of DAOs. *Blockchain and Society Review*, 12(1), 98–112.

Wu, C., & Li, Y. (2023). The Metaverse: Exploring the Convergence of Technologies and Social Dynamics. *2023 IEEE 43rd International Conference on Distributed Computing Systems Workshops (ICDCSW)*, 121-126. https://doi.org/DOI: 10.1109/ICDCSW60045.2023.00019

Wu, C.-H., Huang, Y.-M., & Hwang, J.-P. (2015). Review of affective computing in education/learning: Trends and challenges. *British Journal of Educational Technology*, 47(6), 1304–1323. DOI: 10.1111/bjet.12324

Wu, J., Lin, K., Lin, D., Zheng, Z., Huang, H., & Zheng, Z. (2022). Financial Crimes in Web3-Empowered Metaverse: Taxonomy, Countermeasures, and Opportunities. *IEEE Open Journal of the Computer Society*, 4, 37–49. DOI: 10.1109/OJCS.2023.3245801

Wu, Y., Outley, C., & Matarrita-Cascante, D. (2019). Cultural Immersion Camps and Development of Ethnic Identity in Asian American Youth. *Journal of Youth Development*, 14(2), 166–182. DOI: 10.5195/jyd.2019.708

Xi Liu Chaogui Kang, L. G., & Liu, Y. (2016). Incorporating spatial interaction patterns in classifying and understanding urban land use. *International Journal of Geographical Information Science*, 30(2), 334–350. DOI: 10.1080/13658816.2015.1086923

Xiao, X., Sarker, S., Wright, R. T., Sarker, S., & Mariadoss, B. J. (2020). Commitment and replacement of existing saas-delivered applications: A mixed-methods investigation. *Management Information Systems Quarterly*, 44(4), 1811–1858. DOI: 10.25300/MISQ/2020/13216

Xu, C., Zhong, R., Lí, C., & Yan, X.XU. (2023). From Fiction to Reality: Harnessing the Power of Imaginative Narratives to Shape the Future of the Metaverse. *Journal of Metaverse*, 3(2), 108–120. DOI: 10.57019/jmv.1277525

Xu, J., Papagelis, K., Dunham, J., Gonçalves, J., LaLone, N., Chamberlain, A., Lykourentzou, I., Vinella, F. L., & Schwartz, D. J. (2022). Metaverse: The Vision for the Future. *CHI Conference on Human Factors in Computing Systems*. DOI: 10.1145/3491101.3516399

Xun, Y., Zheng, X., Lee, M., & Yang, F. (2023). The Influence of Technology Affordance on Addictive Use In MMOGs: From the Perspective Of virtual-Domain Perfectionism. *Internet Research*. Advance online publication. DOI: 10.1108/INTR-08-2022-0646

Yang, Q., Zhao, Y., Huang, H., Xiong, Z., Kang, J., & Zheng, Z. (2022). Fusing Blockchain and AI With Metaverse: A Survey. *IEEE Open Journal of the Computer Society*, 3, 122–136. DOI: 10.1109/OJCS.2022.3188249

Yang, R., Li, L., Gan, W., Chen, Z., & Qi, Z. (2023). The Human-Centric Metaverse: A Survey. *ACM Web Conference 2023 - Companion of the World Wide Web Conference, WWW 2023*, 1296–1306. DOI: 10.1145/3543873.3587593

Yang, S., Kim, H., Song, M., Lee, S., & Jang, J. (2024). The Double-Edged Influence of Self-Expansion in the Metaverse: A Two-Wave Panel Assessment of Identity Perception, Self-Esteem, and Life Satisfaction. *Cyberpsychology, Behavior, and Social Networking*, 27(1), 37–46. DOI: 10.1089/cyber.2022.0400 PMID: 38197839

Yang, S., & Wu, Q. (2022). The Impact of Asynchronous Communication on Social Media Engagement. *Digital Communication Research*, 8(2), 33–47.

Yang, Z. (2022). FCM Clustering on Interaction Pattern Analysis of Chinese Language Learner Behavior. *Computational Intelligence and Neuroscience*, 2022, 1–8. Advance online publication. DOI: 10.1155/2022/8256646 PMID: 35720927

Yee, N. (2006). Motivations for Play in Online Games. *Cyberpsychology & Behavior*, 9(6), 772–775. DOI: 10.1089/cpb.2006.9.772 PMID: 17201605

Yen, S., Moh, M., & Moh, T. S. (2021). Detecting compromised social network accounts using deep learning for behavior and text analyses. [IJCAC]. *International Journal of Cloud Applications and Computing*, 11(2), 1–13. DOI: 10.4018/IJCAC.2021040106

Yılmaz, G., & Peña, J. (2012). The Influence of Social Categories and Interpersonal Behaviors on Future Intentions and Attitudes to Form Subgroups in Virtual Teams. *Communication Research*, 41(3), 333–352. DOI: 10.1177/0093650212443696

YouGov. (April 9, 2024). Adults' opinion on the effect of artificial intelligence (AI) on education in the United States as of March 2024, by gender [Graph]. In Statista. Retrieved December 09, 2024, from https://www-statista-com.elibrary.siu.edu.in/statistics/1462497/opinion-ai-effect-education-gender-united-states/

Yuan, S.-T. D., & Hsu, S.-T. (2017). Enhancing service system design: An entity interaction pattern approach. *Information Systems Frontiers*, 19(3), 481–507. DOI: 10.1007/s10796-015-9604-z

Yuanyuan, M., & Xiyu, L. (2018). Quantum inspired evolutionary algorithm for community detection in complex networks. *Physics Letters. [Part A]*, 382(34), 2305–2312. DOI: 10.1016/j.physleta.2018.05.044

Yu, K., He, L., Yu, P. S., Zhang, W., & Liu, Y. (2019). Coupled Tensor Decomposition for User Clustering in Mobile Internet Traffic Interaction Pattern. *IEEE Access : Practical Innovations, Open Solutions*, 7, 18113–18124. DOI: 10.1109/ACCESS.2019.2894267

Zackery, A., Shariatpanahi, P., Zolfagharzadeh, M. M., & Pourezzat, A. A. (2016). Toward a simulated replica of futures: Classification and possible trajectories of simulation in futures studies. *Futures*, 81, 40–53. DOI: 10.1016/j.futures.2015.11.002

Zakaria, N., Amelinckx, A., & Wilemon, D. (2004). Working together apart? Building a knowledge-sharing culture for global virtual teams. *Creativity and Innovation Management*, 13(1), 15–29. DOI: 10.1111/j.1467-8691.2004.00290.x

Zakay, D. (1993). The impact of time perception processes on decision making under time stress. In Svenson, O., & Maule, A. J. (Eds.), *Time pressure and stress in human judgment and decision making* (pp. 59–72). DOI: 10.1007/978-1-4757-6846-6_4

Zallio, M., & Clarkson, P. J. (2022). Designing the metaverse: A study on inclusion, diversity, equity, accessibility and safety for digital immersive environments. *Telematics and Informatics*, 75(September), 101909. DOI: 10.1016/j.tele.2022.101909

Zawacki-Richter, O., Marín, V. I., Bond, M., & Gouverneur, F. (2019). Systematic review of research on artificial intelligence applications in higher education – where are the educators? *International Journal of Educational Technology in Higher Education*, 16(1), 39. DOI: 10.1186/s41239-019-0171-0

Zhai, X.-S., Chu, X.-Y., Chen, M., Shen, J., & Lou, F.-L.Xue-song. (2023, December). Zhai., Xiaoyan, Chu., Min, Tsuei, Chen., Jun, Shen. (2023). Can Edu-Metaverse Reshape Virtual Teaching Community (VTC) to Promote Educational Equity? An Exploratory Study. *IEEE Transactions on Learning Technologies*, 16(6), 1130–1140. Advance online publication. DOI: 10.1109/TLT.2023.3276876

Zhang, W. (2020). *Social Interaction Research on Mobile Games: A Case Study of Peace Elite*. DOI: 10.2991/assehr.k.200331.036

Zhang, G. (2011). Quantum-inspired evolutionary algorithms: A survey and empirical study. *Journal of Heuristics*, 17(3), 303–351. DOI: 10.1007/s10732-010-9136-0

Zhang, T., Shen, J., Yang, H., Vijayakumar, P., Gupta, B. B., & Arya, V. (2024). Sustainable Authentication and Key Agreement Protocol Using Chaotic Maps for Industry 5.0. *IEEE Transactions on Consumer Electronics*, 70(1), 1580–1589. DOI: 10.1109/TCE.2023.3339818

Zhang, W., Zhou, W., & Luo, J. (2019). Mining And Application of User Behavior Pattern Based on Operation And Maintenance Data. *2019 IFIP/IEEE Symposium on Integrated Network and Service Management (IM)*, 614–618.

Zhang, X., Chen, Y., Hu, L., & Wang, Y. (2022). The Metaverse in Education: Definition, Framework, Features, Potential Applications, Challenges, and Future Research Topics. *Frontiers in Psychology*, 13, 1016300. Advance online publication. DOI: 10.3389/fpsyg.2022.1016300 PMID: 36304866

Zhang, Z., & Gupta, B. B. (2018). Social media security and trustworthiness: Overview and new direction. *Future Generation Computer Systems*, 86, 914–925. DOI: 10.1016/j.future.2016.10.007

Zhang, Z., Sun, R., Wang, X., & Zhao, C. (2019). A Situational Analytic Method for User Behavior Pattern in Multimedia Social Networks. *IEEE Transactions on Big Data*, 5(4), 520–528. DOI: 10.1109/TBDATA.2017.2657623

Zhao, L., & Huang, R. (2021). Metaverse Platforms and Their Impact on User Engagement. *Virtual Reality Research Review*, 9(3), 55–70.

Zheng, Y. (2023). *The Potential of Metaverse in Speaking Skills of English Education*. DOI: 10.4108/eai.8-9-2023.2340056

Zhong, L., Xu, Z., Morrison, A. M., Li, Y., & Zhu, M. (2023). Metaverse Customer Journeys in Tourism: Building Viable Virtual Worlds. *Tourism Review*, 79(8), 1409–1426. DOI: 10.1108/TR-07-2023-0492

Zhou, Y., Tiwari, M., Bernot, A., & Lin, K. (2024). Metacrime and Cybercrime: Exploring the Convergence and Divergence in Digital Criminality. *Asian Journal of Criminology*, 19(3), 1–21. DOI: 10.1007/s11417-024-09436-y

Zhuk, A. (2024). Ethical implications of AI in the Metaverse. *AI and Ethics*, 0123456789. Advance online publication. DOI: 10.1007/s43681-024-00450-5

Zimmermann, D., Wehler, A., & Kaspar, K. (2023). Self-representation through avatars in digital environments. *Current Psychology (New Brunswick, N.J.)*, 42(25), 21775–21789. DOI: 10.1007/s12144-022-03232-6

Zuboff, S. (2019). *The Age of Surveillance Capitalism: The Fight for a Human Future at the New Frontier of Power*. PublicAffairs.

# About the Contributors

**Brij B. Gupta** is working as Director of International Center for AI and Cyber Security Research and Innovations, and Distinguished Professor with the Department of Computer Science and Information Engineering (CSIE), Asia University, Taiwan. In more than 18 years of his professional experience, he published over 500 papers in journals/conferences including 35 books and 12 Patents with over 25,000 citations. He has received numerous national and international awards including Canadian Commonwealth Scholarship (2009), Faculty Research Fellowship Award (2017), MeitY, GoI, IEEE GCCE outstanding and WIE paper awards and Best Faculty Award (2018 & 2019), NIT KKR, respectively. Prof. Gupta was selected for Clarivate Web of Science Highly Cited Researchers in Computer Science (top 0.1% researchers in the world) consecutively in 2022 and 2023. Also, he was also selected in Stanford University's ranking of the world's top 2% scientists consecutively in 2020, 2021, 2022 and 2023. He is also a visiting/adjunct professor with several universities worldwide. He is also an IEEE Senior Member (2017) and also selected as 2021 Distinguished Lecturer in IEEE CTSoc. Dr Gupta is also serving as Member-in-Large, Board of Governors, IEEE Consumer Technology Society (2022-2024). Prof Gupta is also leading IJSWIS, IJSSCI, STE and IJCAC as Editor-in-Chief. Moreover, he is also serving as lead-editor of a Book Series with CRC and IET press. He also served as TPC members in more than 150 international conferences also serving as Associate/Guest Editor of various journals and transactions. His research interests include information security, Cyber physical systems, cloud computing, blockchain technologies, intrusion detection, AI, social media and networking.

* * *

**Arijit Bardhan Roy** has received his Bachelor of Technology in Electronics and Communication Engineering from West Bengal University of Technology, Kolkata in 2008 and Master of Technology in Electrical Engineering from Tripura University (A Central University), Tripura during the year 2011. He achieved his doctorate from Indian Institute of Engineering Science and Technology, Shibpur in 2018. Presently, he is working as an Assistant Professor in the Dept. of Electronics and Communication Engineering, SRM Institute of Science &Technology, kattankulathur, India. Dr. Roy has eleven years of teaching and research experience in different reputed universities. His current research interest include design and fabrication of flexible Silicon solar cells, heterojunction solar cells and differentnt areas of bio-inspired nanostructures and cyber security. Till today he has published 15 international journal papers with eight published and one granted patent.

**Kwok Tai Chui** received the B.Eng. degree in electronic and communication engineering - Business Intelligence Minor and Ph.D. degree from City University of Hong Kong. He had industry experience as Senior Data Scientist in Internet of Things (IoT) company. He joined the Department of Technology,

School of Science and Technology, at The Open University of Hong Kong as Research Assistant Professor. He was the recipient of 2nd Prize Award (Postgraduate Category) of 2014 IEEE Region 10 Student Paper Contest. Also, he received Best Paper Award in IEEE The International Conference on Consumer Electronics-China, in both 2014 and 2015. He has more than 45 research publications including edited books, book chapters, journal papers, and conference papers. His research interests include computational intelligence, data science, energy monitoring and management, intelligent transportation, smart metering, healthcare, machine learning algorithms and optimization.

**Ramy El-Kady** is a full criminal law professor at the Police Academy and holds the position of department chair of criminal law. He was rewarded with the State Encouragement Award in Legal and Economic Sciences, Citizenship and Human Rights Branch, on the topic of "the right of persons cooperating with justice for protection in international conventions and national legislation. He graduated from the Police College in 1999. He obtained a postgraduate diploma in criminal sciences and public law, which is equivalent to a master's degree in criminal law, in 2003. He received a PhD in criminal law from the Faculty of Law, Cairo University, on the topic of (Mediation as an Alternative to a Criminal Case: A Comparative Study. He currently teaches criminal law subjects to college students. He supervised numerous studies submitted for doctoral degrees and higher diplomas and authored a host of research in the criminal law field. He has previously judged multiple research papers in a number of refereed regional scientific journals. He published a host of research in refereed and indexed periodicals and took part in a number of international and local conferences and symposia.

**Sudhakar Kumar** is working on the post of Assistant Professor(CSE) in Chandigarh College of Engineering and Technology, Sector 26, Chandigarh (under Chandigarh UT Administration). He has pursued his Ph.D. degree in High Performance Computing(Algorithm) and Compiler optimization from Panjab University, Chandigarh, India. He has done his Master in Technology(M. Tech.) degree from Indian Institute of Technology(IIT), Guwahati. His area of specializations are High Performance Computing(HPC), Compiler Optimization, Machine Learning(ML), Artificial Intelligence(AI) and Human Computer Interaction(HCI). He has published more than 40 research papers in different Journals, Conferences, Book Chapters and 2 Design Patents.

**Anushree S Panikkassery** is currently working as Assistant Professor at Christ (Deemed to be University), Bangalore. She holds her Doctoral Degree in Economics from Central University of Tamil Nadu, Thiruvarur. She is an alumnus of University of Hyderabad where she completed her Masters in Economics. Her Research Interest lies in the area of Development economics and Health Economics.

**Princy Pappachan** is a Postdoctoral Researcher at the College of Education, National Chengchi University, Taiwan. She previously served as an Assistant Professor at Asia University, Taiwan, under the Ministry of Education's 'Bilingual Nation by 2030' initiative. She holds a Ph.D. in Applied Linguistics and an M.Phil. in Cognitive Science from the University of Hyderabad, India. Her research interests include Multilingual Education, English Language Teaching, Cognitive Science, Generative AI, and Management Studies, focusing on technology integration in education and organizations. She has delivered keynotes at MIMSE 2023, moderated at the International Conference on EMI and AI, and conducted workshops on technology in education. Her technical skills include R programming, SmartPLS, AVISPA (HLPSL), and

Python. She is also an editor and serves on the Editorial Review Board of IJTEPD and is the Managing Editor of the European Journal of Advanced Computing and Management.

**Prakash Purshewar** is currently working as a Language Resource Person at the Anuvadini Foundation, AICTE, Ministry of Education, New Delhi, where he focuses on research in the intersection of language and technology. He previously served as a Language Resource Person and Translator at the Bharatiya Bhasha Samiti, Ministry of Education, New Delhi, contributing to language-related projects and initiatives. He holds a Doctorate (Ph.D.) in Applied Linguistics from the University of Hyderabad, India, where he also completed his Master of Philosophy (M.Phil.) and Master of Arts (M.A.) in Applied Linguistics. He has presented his research at national and international conferences and has published scholarly papers in UGC-approved journals in India, reflecting his commitment to advancing the field of applied linguistics.

**Mosiur Rahman**, a Research Assistant at the International Center for AI and Cyber Security Research and Innovations (CCRI) at Asia University, Taiwan, holds a PhD in Computer Science and Information Engineering and master's degrees in Business Management and Computer Science and Engineering. With prior roles as a Research Assistant in AI and an Assistant Professor in Computer Science, he has extensive experience in academia. Dr. Rahman has been actively involved in international conferences, serving in significant roles, and is a part-time lecturer in Humanities and Social Science. His research interests include AI, Neural Networks, and Security, and he is a dedicated peer reviewer for over 50 journals, showcasing his commitment to research and academic excellence.

**Ruchika** is an Associate Professor with the Department of Business Administration in PSIT, Kanpur. She has a wide experience of more than 18 years in the field of teaching and published papers in many national/international journals. She holds doctorate degree in the field of management from AKTU (State University), Lucknow.

**Karun Sanjaya** is an Assistant Professor at Symbiosis Law School, Nagpur and a Research Scholar at VIT School of Law, Vellore Institute of Technology, Chennai, India. He specialises in the area of Intellectual Property Laws. He is a recipient of many awards, including the prestigious Justice V.R. Krishna Iyer Memorial Merit Awards in the years 2019 and 2022. He has published over sixty research items and is a keen researcher in diverse areas of law, including intellectual property law.

**Rushil Chandra** is currently pursuing his Ph.D. from Gujarat National Law University and also working in the capacity of Assistant Professor at the School of Law, Dr. Vishwanath Karad MIT World Peace University, Pune. He has a work experience of about 3 years in Acamedia and 1 year in the industry. He has a keen interest in research and philosophy especially related to the legal aspects of Artificial Intelligence and its implications on the society.

**Kavya Sanjaya** is a post-doctoral fellow at the School of Economics, University of Hyderabad. She completed her Ph.D. in Economics from the University of Hyderabad, where she focused on "GI Tagging of Agricultural Products in India: An Economic Analysis of Three Crops". With a strong passion in teaching and research, Kavya has worked as an Assistant Professor at NSS Hindu College, Changanacherry, Kerala where she taught undergraduate and postgraduate courses, including microeconomics, public finance, and mathematical economics. She has also contributed as a Research Associate in an ICSSR-funded project, gaining valuable experience in data analysis and fieldwork. Her research portfolio includes diverse topics such as consumer preferences for GI-tagged agricultural commodities, human hair trade, surrogacy, and governance issues. She is proficient in data analysis tools like Stata and has extensive expertise in conducting primary surveys and fieldwork. Kavya is passionate about advancing research in agricultural and cultural economics while bridging academic knowledge with practical applications. Her professional goal is to contribute to sustainable economic practices and policymaking, particularly in the areas of GI-tagged products and rural development.

**Binastya Anggara Sekti** has been a Lecturer at the faculty of Computer Science, at Esa Unggul University, Jakarta since 2016 and is active in the Artificial Intelligence and Information Security Study Group. He is a graduate of Informatics Engineering from the Bandung Institute of Technology and achieved a Master's Degree from Trisakti University, Jakarta. Before as a Lecture, he was an IT practitioner at several companies in Jakarta for more than 25 years. Some of the projects that have been completed are building Data Centers at Internet Service Providers (LinkNet) and cable TV Providers (Firstmedia). He also finished many projects in Multipolar Technology and Caltex Pacific Indonesia (CPI).

**Soumya Srivastava** is an Assistant Professor at Symbiosis Law School, Nagpur, Symbiosis International (Deemed University), Pune, India.

**Vitri Tundjungsari**, S.T., M.Sc., M.M. is an Associate Professor in the Faculty of Computer Science, Esa Unggul University, Jakarta, Indonesia. Currently, she serves as the Dean of Faculty of Computer Science in Esa Unggul University. She received her Doctoral Degree in Computer Science from Gadjah Mada University, Yogyakarta, Indonesia in 2012. She has research interest in Software Engineering, Data Science, and Social Informatics.

**Agung Mulyo Widodo** received a PhD in Computer Science and Information Engineering, Asia University, Taiwan, in 2022, and currently works as a lecturer and researcher at the Faculty of Computer Science, Esa Unggul University, Jakarta, Indonesia. He has worked as a research assistant to his advising professor while a PostDoc Research Fellow at the Artificial Intelligence and Information Security Laboratory, Department of Computer Science and Information Engineering (CSIE), Asia University, Taiwan. Previous projects were with Caltex Pacific Indonesia (CPI), Siemens-Telecommunications, Nokia-Siemens-Networks (NSN). Currently, his research focuses on wireless communications technologies including NOMA, OMA, NB-IoT, backscatter systems, cognitive radio, smart antennas, artificial intelligence, and information security.

# Index

## A



## B



## C



## D

## E



## F



## G



## H



## I



## J



## L



## M

## N



## P



## Q



## R



## S



## T

www.ingramcontent.com/pod-product-compliance
Lightning Source LLC
LaVergne TN
LVHW081249011026
849162LV00006BA/1245